# Business Book of Lists

# Business Book of Lists

compiled by the Brooklyn Public Library
Business Library Staff

VISIBLE INK PRESS

DETROIT   CHICAGO   WASHINGTON, D.C.   LONDON

# Business Book of Lists

compiled by the Brooklyn Public Library
Business Library staff

Copyright © 1991 by Visible Ink Press

No part of this book may be reproduced in any form without permission in writing from the publisher, except by a reviewer who wishes to quote brief passages in connection with a review written for inclusion in a magazine or newspaper.

Published by Visible Ink Press,
a division of Gale Research Inc.
835 Penobscot Building
Detroit, MI 48226-4094

Visible Ink Press is a trademark of Gale Research Inc.

ISBN 0-8103-9410-3

Art Director: *Arthur Chartow*
Design Supervisor: *Cynthia Baldwin*
Interior Design: *Arthur Chartow, Bernadette Gornie, Mary Krzewinski*
Cover Design: *Bernadette Gornie*

Printed in the United States of America
All rights reserved

10   9   8   7   6   5   4   3   2   1

First Edition

Introduction .................................... xi

## CONTENTS

The thirteen chapters in *Business Book of Lists* are arranged to bring related lists together for comparison and context. To the left we provide examples of the types of topics covered in each chapter, and the order you'll find them in; inside you'll find even more than we could list here!

**BUSINESS CLASS** .............................. 1

*Including lists about:*
- corporations
- acquisitions and mergers
- divestiture
- buyouts
- industry
- small business
- growth companies
- research and development
- law firms
- minority business enterprises
- occupations
- business schools and colleges
- executives
- business services
- service industries
- employment
- labor productivity
- management
- occupational health and safety
- pension plans
- insurance
- security and investigative services
- location of industry
- industrial parks
- factories
- industrial equipment industry
- office buildings
- office equipment industry
- workstations
- business forms
- convention facilities
- business travel
- clock and watch industry

**GETTING SOMEWHERE** ...................... 97

*Including lists about:*
- transportation
- mass transit
- railroads
- roads
- motor vehicles
- trucking industry
- automobile industry
- automobile insurance
- bus lines
- tire industry
- aerospace
- helicopter industry
- airlines
- air freight
- airports
- ports

**RESOURCES** .................................... **139**
*Including lists about:*
- energy industries
- public utilities
- coal industry
- petroleum industry
- pipeline companies
- gas industry
- electric utilities
- rubber industry
- cement industry
- forest products industry
- paper container industry
- containers
- packaging
- mining industry
- metal industry
- gold mines and mining
- silver mines and mining

**GO TECH** ...................................... **171**
*Including lists about:*
- high technology industries
- communication industries
- telecommunications
- telephone companies
- cellular radio service
- facsimile machines
- electronic industries
- printed circuit boards industry
- semiconductor industry
- computer industry
- computer software industry
- on-line data processing
- information systems
- information privacy
- robotics
- instrument industry
- biotechnology
- medical supplies
- drug trade
- chemical industries
- fertilizer industry
- nuclear engineering schools
- hazardous waste
- pollution control industries
- environmental engineering schools

**MASS APPEAL** .................................. **209**
*Including lists about:*
- mass media
- publishers and publishing
- periodicals
- newspaper publishers and publishing
- book industries
- printing industry
- broadcasting industry
- radio
- television
- cable television
- advertising

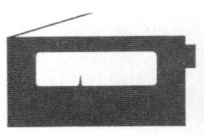

## TO MARKET .................................... 261

*Including lists about:*

- market research
- telemarketing
- direct response advertising
- mail order business
- catalogs
- catalog showrooms
- wholesale trade
- warehouse clubs
- outlet stores
- teleshopping
- shopping
- retail trade
- shopping centers
- stores
- vending machines

## GIMME SHELTER .............................. 295

*Including lists about:*

- cities & towns, suburbs, metropolitan areas
- counties
- states
- moving and storage
- housing
- real estate business
- mortgages
- homeowners' insurance
- construction industry
- engineering schools
- contractors
- building materials industry
- prefabricated building industry
- mobile home industry
- apartment rental
- condominiums

## FEATHERING THE NEST ....................... 333

*Including lists about:*

- furnaces
- water heaters
- air conditioning industry
- household products
- hardware industry
- paint industry
- drapery
- floor coverings
- furniture industry
- home electronics
- housewares
- household linens
- household appliances
- tableware
- glassware
- cleaning products industry

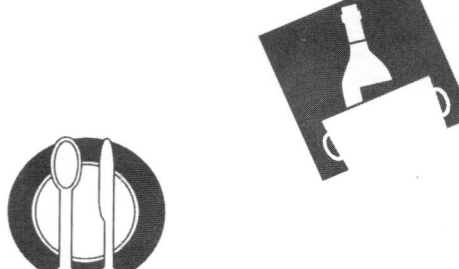

**REFRESHMENT STAND** .......................... **347**
   *Including lists about:*
   farms
   crops
   grain
   meat industry
   seafood
   food industry and
      trade
   grocery trade
   food service
   restaurants
   snacks
   beverage industry
   bottled water
   coffee industry
   tea industry
   soft drink industry
   brewing industry
   wine industry
   liquor industry

**PERSONAL IMAGERY** ............................ **397**
   *Including lists about:*
   textile industry
   fashion designers
   clothing trade
   leather goods
   shoe industry
   jewelry industry
   personal care
      products
   soap industry
   mouthwashes
   perfumes
   razors
   cosmetics industry
   hair care products

**LIFE LESSONS** ................................. **411**
   *Including lists about:*
   diapers
   school districts
   libraries
   colleges and
      universities
   defense industry
   life, property &
      casualty,
      disability
      insurance
   disabled persons
   health care industry
   prescriptions
   home pregnancy
      tests
   vitamins
   analgesics
   sleep aids
   sore throat, cold,
      cough remedies
   healthcare facilities
   nursing
   nursing homes
   charitable bequests
   foundations and
      nonprofit
      institutions
   environmental
      associations

**DIVERSIONS** .................................... **447**
*Including lists about:*

leisure
greeting card industry
photographic industry
toy industry
games
amusement parks
boats and boating
tourist trade
hotels and motels
gambling
souvenirs
collectors and collecting
golf
sporting goods industry
exercise equipment
musical instrument industry
entertainment
entertainers
concerts
recording industry
motion pictures
videotape recorder industry
videocassettes
lotteries

**MONEY MATTERS** .............................. **467**
*Including lists about:*

national economies
gross domestic product
import-export trade
international savings
income
accounting
financial institutions
banks and banking
savings and loan associations
credit unions
credit risk
automated teller machines
credit cards
investments
investment management firms
bonds
stocks
over-the-counter markets
brokers
dividends
employee stock ownership plans
billionaires and millionaires

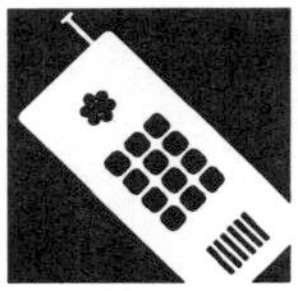

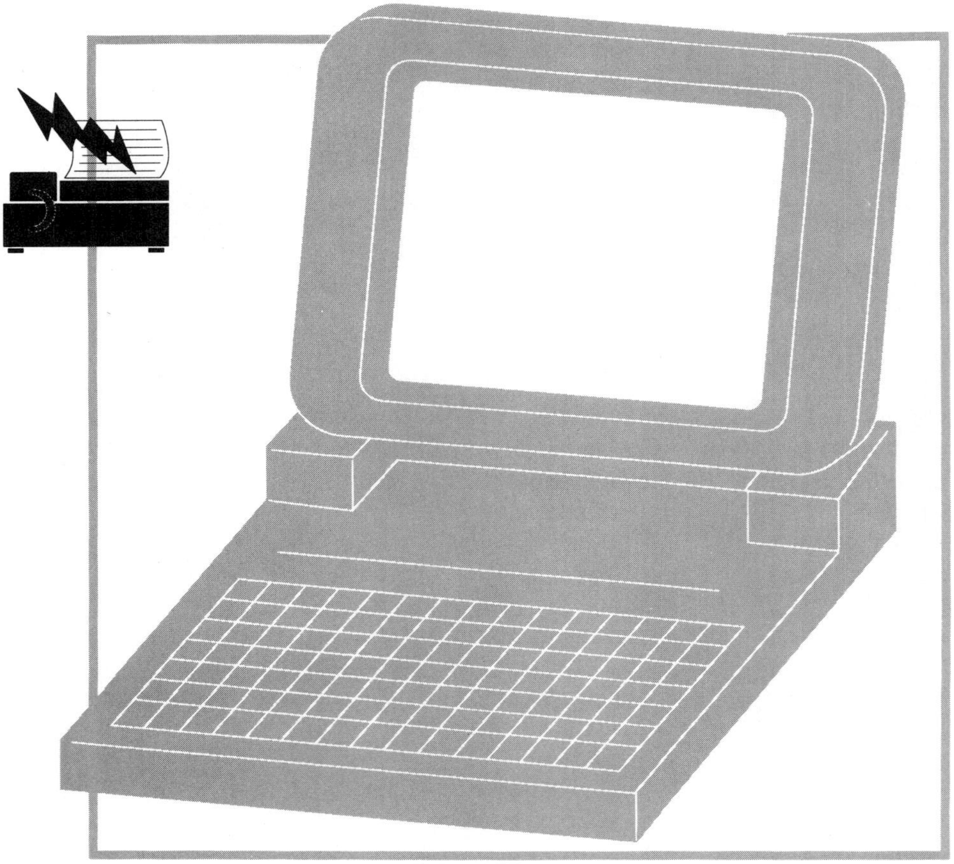

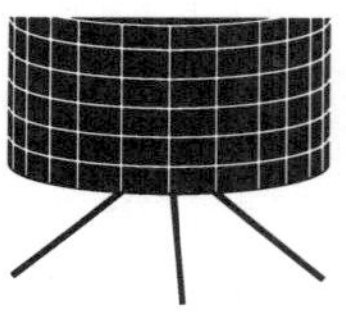

# INTRODUCTION

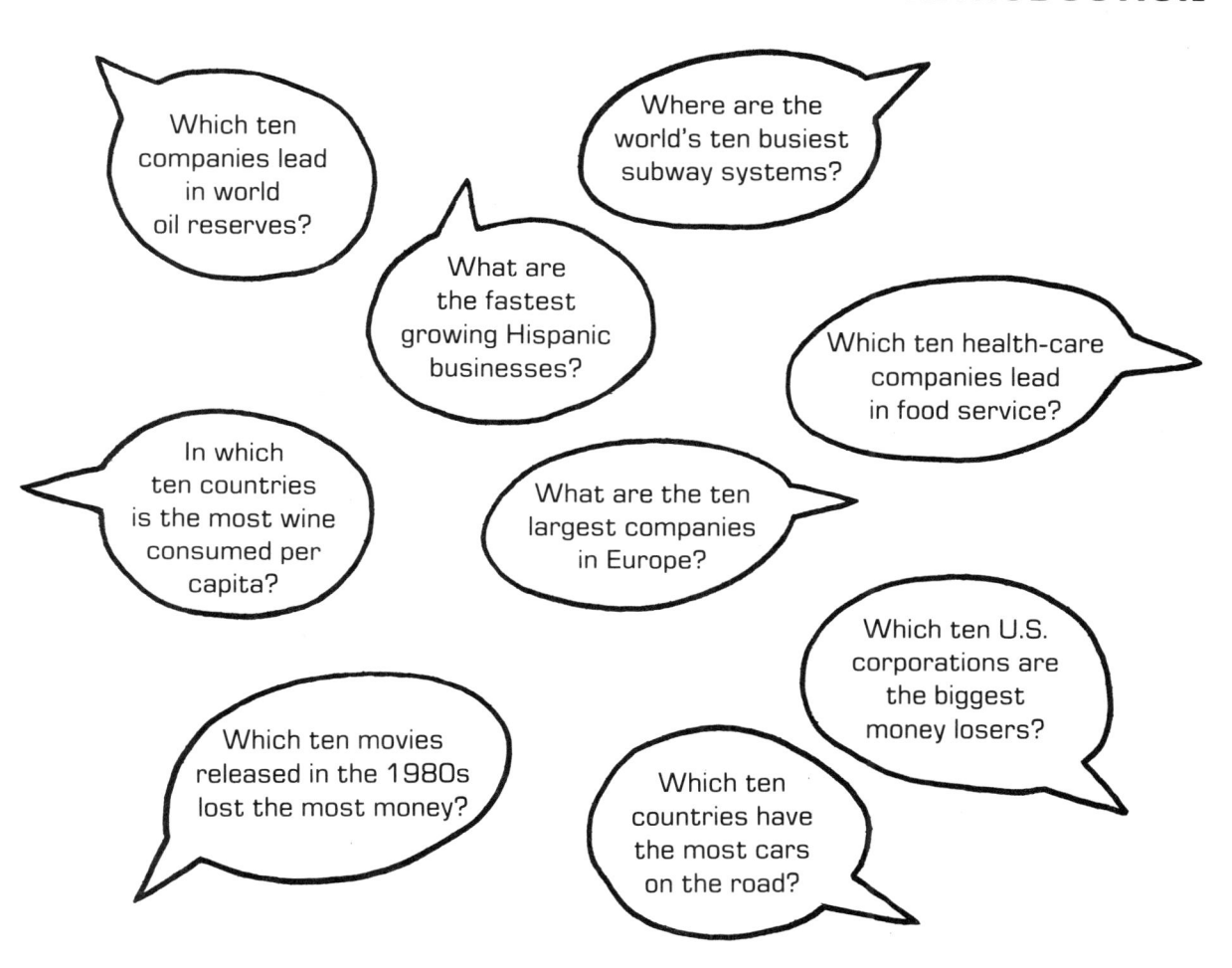

- Which ten companies lead in world oil reserves?
- Where are the world's ten busiest subway systems?
- What are the fastest growing Hispanic businesses?
- Which ten health-care companies lead in food service?
- In which ten countries is the most wine consumed per capita?
- What are the ten largest companies in Europe?
- Which ten U.S. corporations are the biggest money losers?
- Which ten movies released in the 1980s lost the most money?
- Which ten countries have the most cars on the road?

The staff of the Business Library of the Brooklyn Public Library answers over 175,000 reference questions each year, many of them, like these, requests for ranking information. In response, we have culled thousands of items from periodicals, newspapers, financial services, directories, statistical annuals, and other printed material. The "top ten" from more than 2000 of these rankings appears in The *Business Book of Lists*.

"What were the ten most costly insured hurricanes?"

"Who leads Far East countries in hoarding gold?"

"What are the top ten prescription drugs?"

"What are the ten most hazardous industries?"

"In which ten cities are the highest percentage of tax audits conducted?"

"Which ten corporations consume the most packaging materials?"

"Which ten magazines are most popular among college students?"

"Which overseas industry areas attract the most U.S. buyers?"

"In which ten cities do the highest proportion of shoppers live?"

The Business Library subscribes to some eighteen hundred periodicals and eighteen newspapers. Every morning a team of librarians combs through the day's new arrivals looking for lists. Other librarians check through new editions of statistical annuals and directories as they arrive. In fact, every member of the staff is constantly looking for business lists when reading any publication. For *Business Book of Lists* we have selected the lists that are most in public demand.

*Where are the world's top ten international design firms located?*

*For which ten cars is the occupant death rate lowest? Highest?*

*Which ten countries export the most lead crystal to the United States?*

*Which ten countries buy the most agricultural commodities from the United States?*

*What are the ten largest retail outlets for souvenirs and novelties?*

*Which ten countries are tops in exports?*

*Which states spend the least on textbooks per pupil?*

*Which mouthwashes made the top ten in market share?*

*What are the most actively traded shares on stock exchanges from Amsterdam to Manila, Mexico to Zurich?*

The imminently browseable lists in this book have been arranged by thirteen broad subject chapters in an effort to group related topics together. If you're looking for information about a specific business question, check the table of contents, which details the topics covered in each chapter. Otherwise, just start anywhere, and let the facts speak for themselves.

Joan M. Canning
Business Librarian
Brooklyn Public Library
Business Library

Part of the Brooklyn Public Library, the Business Library began operation in 1943 to serve Brooklyn's business and legal community.

Now holding the nation's premiere business collection, the Library provides a vital information resource not only for metropolitan New York City and New York State, but for callers from around the country. The Business Library fields questions from corporate researchers, the media, students, other librarians, and the general public. Of particular interest are the Library's holdings on topics related to small business and entrepreneurship.

# Business Class

**World's largest industrial corporations**

1. General Motors Corp., with $121,085.4 million
2. Ford Motor Co., $92,445.6
3. Exxon Corp., $79,557.0
4. Royal Dutch/Shell Group, $78,381.1
5. IBM, $59,681.0
6. Toyota Motor, $50,789.9
7. General Electric Co., $49,414.0
8. Mobil, $48,198.0
9. British Petroleum, $46,174.0
10. IRI, $45,521.5

*Where'd you hear that?*
Fortune, Fortune International 500. Based on 1988 sales, in millions of dollars.

**World's largest public companies**

1. Nippon Telegraph and Telephone, Japan, with $164,537 million
2. Industrial Bank of Japan, $71,239
3. IBM, U.S., $65,977
4. Sumitomo Bank, Japan, $65,738
5. Dai-Ichi Kangyo Bank, Japan, $64,932
6. Fuji Bank, Japan, $63,364
7. Mitsubishi Bank, Japan, $57,815
8. Exxon Corp., U.S., $56,197
9. Royal Dutch/Shell, Netherlands/U.K., $54,896
10. Toyota Motor, Japan, $52,572

*Where'd you hear that?*
Wall Street Journal. Based on market value, in millions, as of June 30, 1989.

# BUSINESS CLASS

## Companies with the highest sales

1. Mitsui & Co., with $117.0 billion
2. General Motors Corp., $110.0
3. C. Itoh & Co. Ltd., $108.5
4. Sumitomo, $103.6
5. Marubeni, $96.1
6. Mitsubishi, $93.3
7. Ford Motor Co., $92.5
8. Exxon Corp., $87.3
9. Royal Dutch/Shell, $78.4
10. Nissho Iwai, $72.9

*Where'd you hear that?*
Business Week, The Global 1000. Based on sales in billions of U.S. dollars.

## Companies with the highest profits

1. IBM, with $5.49 billion
2. Ford Motor Co., $5.30
3. Exxon Corp., $5.26
4. Royal Dutch/Shell, $5.23
5. General Motors Corp., $4.63
6. General Electric Co., $3.39
7. British Telecom, $2.41
7. Dow Chemical Co., $2.41
9. AT & T, $2.27
10. Du Pont Co., $2.19

*Where'd you hear that?*
Business Week, The Global 1000. Based on profits, in billions of U.S. dollars.

## World's most valuable corporations

1. Nippon Telegraph & Telephone (Japan), with $163.86 billion
2. Industrial Bank of Japan, $71.59
3. Sumitomo Bank (Japan), $69.59
4. Fuji Bank (Japan), $67.08
5. Dai-Ichi Kangyo Bank Ltd. (Japan), $66.09
6. IBM (U.S.), $64.65
7. Mitsubishi Bank (Japan), $59.27
8. Exxon Corp. (U.S.), $54.92
9. Tokyo Electric Power (Japan), $54.46
10. Royal Dutch/Shell Group (Netherlands/Britain), $54.36

*Where'd you hear that?*
Business Week, The Global 1000. Based on market value in billions of U.S. dollars (share price on May 31, 1989 x number of shares outstanding, converted to dollars at May month-end exchange rates).

## Asia's largest quoted companies in profits

1. Toyota Motor Corp., with $4,862,582 thousand
2. Matsushita Electric Industrial Co. Ltd., $4,218,701
3. Hitachi Ltd., $3,913,187
4. Tokyo Electric Power Co. Inc., $2,193,737
5. Toshiba Corp., $1,871,147
6. KEPCO-Korea Electric Power Corp., $1,632,164
7. Nissan Motor Co. Ltd., $1,600,151
8. Nippon Steel Corp., $1,399,068
9. Honda Motor Co. Ltd., $1,371,227
10. Sony Corp., $1,318,853

*Where'd you hear that?*
Asia's 7500 Largest Companies, Dun & Bradstreet. Based on profit, in thousands of U.S. dollars.

## Asia's largest quoted companies in profit margins

1. Glenealy Plantations (M) Bhd, with 98.0%
2. Philippine Telecommunications Investments Corp, 95.0%
3. Marisol Commercial Inc., 94.0%
4. Kuala Lumpur Tin Fields Bhd, 89.0%
5. Liu Chong Hing Investment Ltd., 84.0%
5. Overseas Union Securities Ltd., 84.0%
5. PT Regnis Indonesia, 84.0%
5. Philippine Geotheraml Inc., 84.0%
9. Riverview Rubber Estates Bhd, 81.0%
10. Mercury Group of Companies Inc., 78.0%

*Where'd you hear that?*
Asia's 7500 Largest Companies, Dun & Bradstreet. Based on profit as a percentage of sales.

## Largest publicly-traded, non-financial corporations in Hong Kong

1. Swire Pacific, with $3,219 million
2. Dairy Farm International, $2,255
3. Cathay Pacific Airways, $1,936
4. Jardine Matheson Holdings Ltd., $1,900
5. Hutchinson Whampoa, $1,654
6. Hong Kong Telecommunications, $1,518
7. China Light & Power, $1,251
8. Sun Hung Kai Props, $578

*Where'd you hear that?*
Financial World, FW International 1000. Based on sales, in millions of dollars.

## Asia's largest quoted companies in sales

1. Mitsui & Co. Ltd., with $133,669,498 thousand
2. C. Itoh & Co. Ltd., $127,205,108
3. Mitsubishi Corp., $124,651,912
4. Sumitomo Corp., $118,260,566
5. Marubeni Corp., $116,958,183
6. Nissho Iwai Corp., $91,215,633
7. Toyota Motor Corp., $57,496,398
8. Hitachi Ltd., $51,007,307
9. Toyo Menka Kaisha Ltd., $46,050,805
10. Matsushita Electric Industrial Co. Ltd., $43,858,566

*Where'd you hear that?*
Asia's 7500 Largest Companies, Dun & Bradstreet. Based on sales, in thousands of U.S. dollars.

## Most valuable corporations in Hong Kong

1. Hong Kong Telecommunications, with $7,005 million
2. Hongkong & Shanghai Banking Corp., $4,362
3. Hutchison-Whampoa, $3,855
4. Swire Pacific, $3,716
5. Cathay Pacific Airways, $3,371
6. Hongkong Land Co., $3,010
7. Cheung Kong Holdings, $2,544
8. Hang Seng Bank, $2,505
9. China Light & Power, $2,347
10. Sun Hung Kai Properties, $2,129

**BUSINESS CLASS**

# BUSINESS CLASS

11. Wharf Holdings, $2,038
12. Hongkong Electric Holdings, $1,752

*Where'd you hear that?*
Business Week, The Global 1000. Based on market value in millions of U.S. dollars (share price on May 31, 1989 x number of shares outstanding, converted to dollars at May month-end exchange rates).

## Largest corporations in Indonesia

1. Teijin Indonesia Fibre, with Rp. 223,141 million
2. Unilever Indonesia, Rp. 202,573 million
3. Barkie & Brothers, Rp. 163,626 million
4. Semen Cibinong, Rp. 119,054 million
5. Jakarta International Hotel, Rp. 98,509 million
6. Supreme Cable Manufacturing, Rp. 92,455 million
7. Bayer Indonesia, Rp. 76,852 million
8. Goodyear Indonesia, Rp. 76,535 million
9. BAT Indonesia, Rp. 73,314 million
10. Multi Bintang Indonesia, Rp. 67,879 million

*Where'd you hear that?*
Asian Finance, Asia's Big 500. Based on total assets, in millions of rupiah.

## Largest publicly-traded, non-financial corporations in Japan

1. Mitsui, with $121,281 million
2. C. Itoh & Co. Ltd., $115,495
3. Mitsubishi, $113,151
4. Sumitomo, $107,247
5. Marubeni, $106,204

6. Nissho Iwai, $82,821
7. Toyota Motor, $58,029
8. Hitachi Ltd., $46,309
9. NTT, $42,265
10. Toyo Menka, $41,809

*Where'd you hear that?*
Financial World, FW International 1000. Based on sales, in millions of dollars.

## Japan's largest corporations

1. Nippon Telegraph & Telephone, with 10,953,927 million yen
2. Tokyo Electric Power, 10,252,579 million yen
3. Mitsubishi Corp., 7,721,681 million yen
4. Nomura Securities, 6,230,222 million yen
5. Orient Finance, 5,510,239 million yen
6. Toyota Motor Corp., 5,450,375 million yen
7. Kansai Electric Power, 5,395,363 million yen
8. Daiwa Securities, 5,147,642 million yen
9. Mitsui & Co., 4,854,882 million yen
10. Nissan Motor Co., 4,741,663 million yen

*Where'd you hear that?*
Asian Finance, Asia's Big 500. Based on assets, as of year ending March 31, 1989, in millions of yen.

## Largest companies in Japan

1. Mitsui & Co. Ltd., with $133,669,498 thousand
2. C. Itoh & Co. Ltd., $127,205,108
3. Mitsubishi Corp., $124,651,912

# BUSINESS CLASS

4. Sumitomo Corp., $118,260,566
5. Marubeni Corp., $116,958,183
6. Nissho Iwai Corp., $91,215,633
7. Toyota Motor Corp., $57,496,398
8. Hitachi Ltd., $51,007,307
9. Toyo Menka Kaisha Ltd., $46,050,805
10. Matsushita Electric Industrial Co. Ltd., $43,858,566

*Where'd you hear that?*
Asia's 7500 Largest Companies, Dun & Bradstreet. Based on sales, in thousands of U.S. dollars.

## Largest corporations in Japan

1. Mitsui & Co. Ltd., with $130,667 million
2. Sumitomo Corp., $115,570
3. C. Itoh & Co. Ltd., $112,327
4. Mitsubishi Corp., $104,198
5. Marubeni Corp., $99,475
6. Nissho Iwai Corp., $81,371
7. Toyota Motor Corp., $53,818
8. Hitachi Ltd., $49,897
9. Nippon Telegraph & Telephone Corp., $45,531
10. Matsushita Electric Industrial Co., $42,880

*Where'd you hear that?*
Forbes, Forbes Foreign Rankings. Based on 1988 revenues, in millions of U.S. dollars (converted from local currency at May 31, 1989 exchange rates). Ranks only publicly-traded, private-sector (non-government-owned) companies.

## Most valuable corporations in Japan

1. Nippon Telegraph & Telephone, with $163,862 million
2. Industrial Bank of Japan, $71,587
3. Sumitomo Bank, $69,591
4. Fuji Bank, $67,077
5. Dai-Ichi Kangyo Bank Ltd., $66,086
6. Mitsubishi Bank, $59,274
7. Tokyo Electric Power, $54,458
8. Toyota Motor, $54,166
9. Sanwa Bank, $49,289
10. Nomura Securities, $44,442

*Where'd you hear that?*
Business Week, The Global 1000. Based on market value in millions of U.S. dollars (share price on May 31, 1989 x number of shares outstanding, converted to dollars at May month-end exchange rates).

## Largest companies in South Korea

1. Samsung Co. Ltd., with $9,957,753 thousand
2. Hyundai Corp., $8,219,105
3. Daewoo Corp., $6,914,121
4. KEPCO-Korea Electric Power Corp., $6,463,743
5. Hyundai Motor Co. Ltd., $4,987,056
6. Samsung Electronics Co. Ltd., $4,427,270
7. GoldStar Co. Ltd., $4,130,518
8. Lucky-GoldStar International Co., $3,955,827
9. Yukong Ltd., $3,459,556
10. Sunkyong Ltd., $2,538,265

# BUSINESS CLASS

*Where'd you hear that?*
Asia's 7500 Largest Companies, Dun & Bradstreet. Based on sales, in thousands of U.S. dollars.

### Largest corporations in South Korea

1. Pohang Iron & Steel Co., with 5,562,519 million won
2. Daewoo Corp., 2,553,277
3. Sam Sung Electronics Co., 2,461,986
4. Hyundai Motor Co. Ltd., 2,447,279
5. GoldStar Co. Ltd., 2,228,571
6. Korean Airlines, 2,126,348
7. Hyundai Engineering & Construction Co., 2,111,014
8. Yukong Ltd., 1,383,970
9. Kia Motors Corp., 1,376,000
10. Daelim Industrial Co., 1,260,503

*Where'd you hear that?*
Asian Finance, Asia's Big 500. Based on total assets, in millions of won.

### Largest corporations in South Korea

1. Hyundai Corp., with $7,686 million
2. Hyundai Motor Co., $4,664
3. Bank of Seoul, $4,437
4. GoldStar Co. Ltd., $3,875
5. Hyundai Engineering & Construction Co., $2,848

*Where'd you hear that?*
Forbes, Forbes Foreign Rankings. Based on 1988 revenues, in millions of U.S. dollars (converted from local currency at May 31, 1989 exchange rates). Ranks only publicly-traded, private-sector (non-government-owned) companies.

### Largest companies in Malaysia

1. Sime Darby Bhd., with $1,242,509 thousand
2. Malaysian Airline System Bhd., $595,540
3. Perlis Plantations Bhd., $586,529
4. Shell Refining Co. (Fom.) Bhd., $400,553
5. Esso Malaysia Bhd., $359,548
6. Federal Flour Mills Bhd., $357,450
7. U.M.V. Corp. Bhd., $356,818
8. Tan Chong Motor Holdings Bhd., $337,707
9. Magnum Corp. Bhd., $264,116
10. Rothmans of Pall Mall (M) Bhd., $260,718

*Where'd you hear that?*
Asia's 7500 Largest Companies, Dun & Bradstreet. Based on sales, in thousands of U.S. dollars.

### Largest corporations in Malaysia

1. Sime Darby Bhd., with M$4,562,800 thousand
2. Malayan United Industries, M$4,033,275
3. Malaysian Airline System Bhd., M$3,775,709
4. Malaysian International Shipping Corp., M$3,444,174
5. Multi-Purpose Holdings, M$2,401,563
6. Harrisons Malaysian Plantations, M$2,033,281
7. Kumpulan Guthrie Bhd., M$1,967,266
8. Consolidated Plantations Bhd., M$1,234,685
9. Genting Bhd., M$1,206,657

10. Perlis Plantations Bhd., M$1,205,393

*Where'd you hear that?*
Asian Finance, Asia's Big 500. Based on total assets, in thousands of Malaysian dollars.

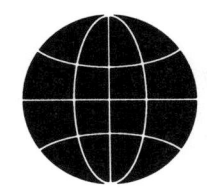

## Largest companies in the Philippines

1. San Miguel Corp., with $970,463 thousand
2. Philippines Associated Smelting & Refining Corp., $384,028
3. Philippine Long Distance Telephone Co., $363,796
4. Atlas Consolidated Mining & Development Corp., $227,403
5. Benguet Corp., $198,876
6. Texas Instruments (Philippines) Inc., $171,749
7. A.G.P. Industrial Corp., $161,594
8. RFM Corp., $130,125
9. A.F. Merchants Inc., $125,637
10. Paper Industries Corp. of the Philippines, $120,681

*Where'd you hear that?*
Asia's 7500 Largest Companies, Dun & Bradstreet. Based on sales, in thousands of U.S. dollars.

## Largest publicly-traded, non-financial corporations in Singapore

1. Singapore Airlines, with $2,347 million
2. Sime Darby, $1,516
3. Neptune Orient Lines, $630
4. Fraser & Neave Ltd., $597

*Where'd you hear that?*
Financial World, FW International 1000. Based on sales, in millions of dollars.

## Largest companies in Singapore

1. Singapore Airlines Ltd., with $2,208,505 thousand
2. Neptune Orient Lines Ltd., $632,051
3. Fraser & Neave Ltd., $516,289
4. Singapore Press Holdings Ltd., $472,616
5. Keppel Corp. Ltd., $400,235
6. Inchcape Bhd., $388,014
7. Malayan Breweries Ltd., $322,694
8. Intraco Ltd., $290,436
9. Times Publishing Bhd., $274,072
10. Haw Par Brothers International Ltd., $234,459

*Where'd you hear that?*
Asia's 7500 Largest Companies, Dun & Bradstreet. Based on sales, in thousands of U.S. dollars.

## Most valuable corporations in Singapore and Malaysia

1. Singapore Airlines, with $4,306 million
2. OCBC Overseas Chinese Bank, $2,858
3. Development Bank of Singapore, $2,048
4. Sime Darby (Malaysia), $1,937

*Where'd you hear that?*
Business Week, The Global 1000. Based on market value in millions of U.S. dollars (share price on May 31, 1989 x number of shares outstanding, converted to dollars at May month-end exchange rates).

# BUSINESS CLASS

# BUSINESS CLASS

**Largest companies in Taiwan**

1. Nan Ya Plastic Corp., with $1,870,192 thousand
2. China Steel Corp., $1,645,035
3. Formosa Plastics Corp., $1,074,308
4. Tatung Co. Ltd., $1,043,258
5. Formosa Chemicals & Fibre Corp., $795,103
6. Far Eastern Textiles Ltd., $780,128
7. Yue Loong Motor Co. Ltd., $590,135
8. Sampo Corp., $466,749
9. Chung Shing Textile Co. Ltd., $418,559
10. Taiwan Cement Corp., $408,552

*Where'd you hear that?*
Asia's 7500 Largest Companies, Dun & Bradstreet. Based on sales, in thousands of U.S. dollars.

**Largest corporations in Taiwan**

1. China Steel Corp., with NT$134,423,111 thousand
2. Nan Ya Plastics Corp., NT$42,898,920
3. Evergreen Marine Corp., NT$38,634,319
4. Far Eastern Textiles, NT$34,427,408
5. Ta Tung Co., NT$34,216,087
6. Formosa Plastics Corp., NT$30,587,877
7. Chung Shing Textile Co. Ltd., NT$20,647,069
8. Asia Cement Corp., NT$19,493,190
9. Hualon Corp., NT$18,700,600
10. Yue Loong Motor Co., NT$16,328,557

*Where'd you hear that?*
Asian Finance, Asia's Big 500. Based on total assets, in thousands of Taiwanese dollars.

**Largest companies in Thailand**

1. Thai Oil Co. Ltd., with $856,636 thousand
2. Seagate Technology (Thailand) Ltd., $470,110
3. Saha-Union Corp. Ltd., $304,083
4. Bangkok Produce Merchandising Co. Ltd., $217,895
5. Siam City Cement Co. Ltd., $185,490
6. Sura Mahathip Co. Ltd., $163,654
7. Unifoods (Thailand) Co. Ltd., $162,274
8. Serm Suk Co. Ltd., $154,589
9. The Thai Plastic & Chemical Co. Ltd., $149,716
10. Teck Bee Hang Co. Ltd., $135,099

*Where'd you hear that?*
Asia's 7500 Largest Companies, Dun & Bradstreet. Based on sales, in thousands of U.S. dollars.

**Largest corporations in Thailand**

1. Siam Cement Co., with 14,195,217 thousand baht
2. Siam Motors Co., 6,113,027
3. Siam City Cement Co., 5,765,463
4. Esso Standard Thailand, 4,950,499
5. United Flour Mill, 4,619,357
6. Mah Boonkrong Drying & Silo, 4,000,588
7. Saha-Union Corp., 3,801,670

8. Thai Central Chemicals Co., 3,440,304
9. Padaeng Industry Co., 3,407,696
10. Toyota Motors (Thailand), 2,984,991

*Where'd you hear that?*
Asian Finance, Asia's Big 500. Based on total assets, in thousands of Thailand baht.

## Largest private companies in India

1. Tata (automobiles, steel), with 66,280.6 million rupees
2. BK-AV Birla (textiles, aluminum), 25,659.0
3. Bajaj (two-wheelers, sugar), 12,094.4
4. Modi (tires, synthetic yarn), 11,904.3
5. Ambani (petrochemicals, synthetic yarns), 10,584.0
6. Thapar (paper, engineering), 10,299.6
7. GP-CK Birla (automobiles, paper), 8,988.0
8. Chhabria (tires, consumer electronics), 8,958.5
9. Maliya (alcohol, pharmaceuticals), 8,504.7
10. Arvind Mafatial (petrochemicals, textiles), 8,482.3

*Where'd you hear that?*
Financial Times. Based on 1987-88 sales, in millions of rupees.

## Largest publicly-traded, non-financial corporations in New Zealand

1. Fletcher Challenge, with $6,859 million
2. Brierley Investments, $3,686
3. Lion Nathan Group, $1,633
4. Carter Holt Harvey, $846
5. Elders Resources NZFP, $769
6. Magnum Corp., $744
7. Waitaki International, $623

*Where'd you hear that?*
Financial World, FW International 1000. Based on sales, in millions of dollars.

## Largest Publicly Traded, non-financial Corporations in Australia

1. Elders IXL Ltd., with $13,884 million
2. Coles Myer Ltd., $11,013
3. Broken Hill Proprietary Co., $8,243
4. News Corp., $6,195
5. Bond Corp. Holdings, $6,027
6. Industrial Equity, $5,869
7. CRA, Ltd., $4,178
8. Pacific Dunlop, $3,529
9. TNT, $3,071
10. Pioneer Intl., $3,042

*Where'd you hear that?*
Financial World, FW International 1000. Based on sales, in millions of dollars.

## Largest corporations in Australia

1. Coles Myer Ltd., with $9,410 million
2. Elders IXL Ltd., $7,626
3. Westpac Banking, $7,089
4. Broken Hill Proprietary Co., $7,085
5. ANZ Banking, $6,089
6. National Austrialia, $5,597
7. News Corp., $4,388
8. CRA Ltd., $4,167
9. Bond Corp., $3,046
10. CSR Group, $2,806

**BUSINESS CLASS**

# BUSINESS CLASS

*Where'd you hear that?*
Forbes, Forbes Foreign Rankings. Based on 1988 revenues, in millions of U.S. dollars (converted from local currency at May 31, 1989 exchange rates). Ranks only publicly-traded, private-sector (non-government-owned) companies.

## Most valuable corporations in Australia

1. Broken Hill Proprietary Co., with $8,824 million
2. Westpac Banking, $3,930
3. BTR Nylex, $3,913
4. National Australia Bank, $3,900
5. CRA, Ltd., $3,827
6. Elders IXL Ltd., $3,479
7. ANZ Group Holdings, $3,203
8. Coles Myer Ltd., $3,198
9. Western Mining, $3,170
10. News, $2,883

*Where'd you hear that?*
Business Week, The Global 1000. Based on market value in millions of U.S. dollars (share price on May 31, 1989 x number of shares outstanding, converted to dollars at May month-end exchange rates).

## Largest corporations in South Africa

1. South African Breweries, with $4,011 million
2. Tradegro, $2,950

*Where'd you hear that?*
Forbes, Forbes Foreign Rankings. Based on 1988 revenues, in millions of U.S. dollars (converted from local currency at May 31, 1989 exchange rates). Ranks only publicly-traded, private-sector (non-government-owned) companies.

## Most valuable corporations in South Africa

1. De Beers, with $7,323 million
2. Consolidated Gold Fields PLC, $4,085
3. Anglo American, $3,965
4. Driefontein Consolidated, $1,812

*Where'd you hear that?*
Business Week, The Global 1000. Based on market value in millions of U.S. dollars (share price on May 31, 1989 x number of shares outstanding, converted to dollars at May month-end exchange rates).

## Largest South African corporations by assets

1. Barlows, with 13,955.8 million rand
2. Remgro, 7,696.8
3. C. G. Smith, 5,715.1
4. Sasol, 5,363.9
5. SA Brews, 5,246.5
6. Amic, 5,093.0
7. CGS Food, 3,804.1
8. Prem Grp., 3,359.2
9. Safren, 3,160.2
10. Malbak, 2,891.0

*Where'd you hear that?*
Financial Mail, Special Survey of Top Companies. Based on assets, in millions of rands.

## Largest corporations in Israel

1. Bank Hapoalim BM, with $5,043 million
2. Bank Leumi le-Israel, $4,266

## BUSINESS CLASS

*Where'd you hear that?*
Forbes, Forbes Foreign Rankings. Based on 1988 revenues, in millions of U.S. dollars (converted from local currency at May 31, 1989 exchange rates). Ranks only publicly-traded, private-sector (non-government-owned) companies.

### Europe's largest companies

1. Royal Dutch/Shell, with $54442.3 million
2. British Petroleum, $24451.9
3. British Telecom, $23478.3
4. Unilever PLC/NV, $17429.9
5. Nestle, $16131.5
6. Generali Group, $15926.6
7. Glaxo Holdings, $15701.9
8. BAT Industries PLC, $15337.5
9. Daimler Benz, $14869.0
10. Siemens, $14494.5

*Where'd you hear that?*
Financial Times, FT Top 500. Based on market capitalization, taken as an average for June, 1989, in millions of U.S. dollars.

### Europe's biggest private employers

1. Siemens, with 353,000
2. Daimler Benz, 338,749
3. BAT Industries PLC, 310,779
4. Philips, 310,258
5. Fiat SpA, 277,353
6. Volkswagen, 252,066
7. British Telecom, 242,723
8. CGE, 204,100
9. Nestle, 197,722
10. ABB Asea Brown Boveri, 169,459

*Where'd you hear that?*
Financial Times, FT Top 500. Based on number of employees.

### Europe's largest companies

1. NV Kon Nederlandse Petroleum Maatschappij, with 68.332.795.108 ECU
2. British Petroleum, 38.086.987.224
3. Fiat SPA, 29.597.744.000
4. Unilever NV, 26.561.999.129
5. BAT Industries PLC, 25.937.411.676
6. Unilever PLC, 25.148.401.872
7. NV Philips' Gloeilampenfabrieken, 24.040.450.431
8. Nestle SA, 22.900.488.005
9. Volkswagen Aktiengesellschaft, 21.376.782.307
10. Renault (Regie Nationale Des Usines), 21.002.031.270

*Where'd you hear that?*
Dun's Europa, Dun & Bradstreet. Based on sales in European Currency Units.

### Europe's largest companies

1. Royal Dutch/Shell, with $68327.600 million
2. IRI, $41322.800
3. British Petroleum, $40251.600
4. Daimler Benz, $37148.700
5. Fiat SpA, $30899.700
6. Siemens, $30011.300
7. Volkswagen, $29933.800
8. Unilever PLC/NV, $26577.600
9. Deutsche Bundespost, $26538.100
10. Philips, $25167.800

# BUSINESS CLASS

*Where'd you hear that?*
Financial Times, FT Top 500. Based on 1989 turnover, in millions of U.S. dollars.

## Europe's largest nonfinancial corporations

1. Royal Dutch Shell, Netherlands/UK, with 66,230 million ECU
2. British Petroleum, UK, 39,016
3. Fiat SpA, Italy, 38,428
4. Daimler Benz, Germany, 35,430
5. Eni, Italy, 28,716
6. Siemens, Germany, 28,622
7. Volkswagen, Germany, 28,549
8. Unilever, Netherlands/UK, 26,488
9. German PTT, Germany, 25,310
10. Philips, Netherlands, 23,974

*Where'd you hear that?*
Eurobusiness, Europe's Top 500 Companies. Based on 1988 sales, in millions of European Currency Units.

## Europe's largest miscellaneous manufacturing companies

1. Kloeckner & Co. Aktiengesellschaft, with 4,616,671,438 ECU
2. Koninklijke Emballage Industrie Van Leer BV, 1,161,428,674
3. BIC (Societe), 855,237,140
4. Unikeller Holding AG, 753,912,096
5. Lyon Alemand Louyot (Comptoir), 644,950,155
6. Valois (Compagnie Financiere Du), 548,524,478
7. Adidas Sportschuhfabriken Adi Dassler Stiftung & Co. KG, 521,377,702
8. Salomon Sa, 361,973,590
9. Engelhard (Compagnie Des Metaux Precieux), 331,589,580
10. Filterwerk Mann & Hummel Gesellschaft Mit Beschraenkter Haftung, 326,613,537

*Where'd you hear that?*
Dun's Europa, Dun & Bradstreet. Based on sales, in European Currency Units.

## Largest publicly-traded, non-financial corporations in Finland

1. Kesko Group, with $6,119 million
2. Nokia Group, $5,110
3. Kymmene Corp., $2,430
4. Enso-Gutzeit, $2,295
5. Rauma-Repola, $2,276
6. Valmet, $1,995
7. United Paper Mills, $1,476
8. Kone, $1,429
9. Wartsila, $1,396
10. Partek, $1,376

*Where'd you hear that?*
Financial World, FW International 1000. Based on sales, in millions of dollars.

## Most valuable corporations in Finland

1. Union Bank of Finland, with $3,191 million
2. Kansallis-Osake-Pankki, $2,501
3. Kymmene Corp., $1,925
4. Pohjola, $1,899
5. Nokia, $1,761

# BUSINESS CLASS

*Where'd you hear that?*
Business Week, The Global 1000. Based on market value in millions of U.S. dollars (share price on May 31, 1989 x number of shares outstanding, converted to dollars at May month-end exchange rates).

## Yugoslavia's largest organizations of associated labor

1. INA, with, 10,961,214 million dinars
2. Naftagas, 8,496,637
3. Energoinvest, 5,374,243
4. RNK Zenica, 5,024,713
5. RTB BOR, 4,471,007
6. Zavodi Crvena Zastava, 4,343,228
7. Poljoprivredni Kombinat Beograd, 3,832,295
8. Exportdrvo, 3,832,165
9. Mercator-KIT, 3,644,447
10. SIPAD, 3,403,968

*Where'd you hear that?*
Ekonomska Politika, 200 Largest. Based on 1988 total revenue, in millions of dinars.

## Largest Publicly Traded, non-financial Corporations in Austria

1. OMV, with $3,220
2. Verbund, $1,095
3. Steyr-Daimler-Puch, $1,037
4. Constantia Industriehold, $895
5. Leykam-Murztaler Papier, $539

*Where'd you hear that?*
Financial World, FW International 1000. Based on sales, in millions of dollars.

## Largest corporations in Austria

1. Creditanstalt, with $3,023 million
2. OMV AG, $2,812

*Where'd you hear that?*
Forbes, Forbes Foreign Rankings. Based on 1988 revenues, in millions of U.S. dollars (converted from local currency at May 31, 1989 exchange rates). Ranks only publicly-traded, private-sector (non-government-owned) companies.

## Largest companies in Western Europe

1. Royal Dutch/Shell, The Hauge/London, with 137465 million Deutschmarks
2. IRI, Rome, 79988
3. British Petroleum, London, 79212
4. Daimler-Benz, Stuttgart, 73495
5. Fiat SpA, Turin, 59805
6. Siemens, Munich, 59374
7. Volkswagen, Wolfsburg, 59221
8. BAT Industries PLC, London 55148
9. Unilever, Rotterdam/London, 55052
10. Deutsche Bundespost, Bonn, 52504

*Where'd you hear that?*
Major Companies in Western Europe, Commerzbank. Based on 1988 sales, in millions of Deutschemarks.

## Largest publicly-traded, non-financial corporations in Belgium

1. Petrofina, with $9,282 million
2. Solvay, $6,452
3. Delhaize Freres-Le Lion, $5,381
4. Arbed, $4,794

# BUSINESS CLASS

5. GB-Inno-BM, $4,361
6. Intercom, $3,111
7. EBES, $2,244
8. Wagons-Lits, $2,041
9. Bekaert Group, $1,163
10. CMB, $977

*Where'd you hear that?*
Financial World, FW International 1000. Based on sales, in millions of dollars.

## Largest corporations in Belgium

1. Petrofina SA, with $13,245 million
2. Solvay Group, $6,894
3. Generale Bank Group, $6,660
4. Delhaize 'Le Lion', $5,739
5. Bank Bruxelles Lambert, $4,359
6. GB-Inno-BM, $3,802
7. Kredietbank NV, $3,559
8. INTERCOM, $3,314

*Where'd you hear that?*
Forbes, Forbes Foreign Rankings. Based on 1988 revenues, in million of U.S. dollars (converted from local currency at May 31, 1989 exchange rates. Ranks only publicly-traded, private-sector (non-government-owned) companies.

## Most valuable corporations in Belgium

1. Petrofina, with $6,904 million
2. Generale de Belgique, $4,594
3. Tractebel, $3,387
4. Solvay, $3,018
5. Intercom, $2,636
6. EBES, $2,035
7. Royale Belge, $2,020
8. Groupe Bruxelles Lambert, $1,975

9. Electrafina, $1,902
10. General de Banque, $1,847

*Where'd you hear that?*
Business Week, The Global 1000. Based on market value in millions of U.S. dollars (share price on May 31, 1989 x number of shares outstanding, converted to dollars at May month-end exchange rates).

## Largest publicly-traded, non-financial corporations in Denmark

1. East Asiatic Co., with $2,439 million
2. Carlsberg, $1,406
3. J. Lauritzen Hldgs., $1,186
4. FLS Inds., $1,110
5. Korn-Og Foderstofkomp, $930
6. Danisco, $922
7. ISS-International Service System, $910
8. Superfos, $886
9. Novo-Nordisk, $724
10. Sophus Berendsen, $580

*Where'd you hear that?*
Financial World, FW International 1000. Based on sales, in millions of dollars.

## Largest corporations in Denmark

1. East Asiatic Co., with $2,632 million

*Where'd you hear that?*
Forbes, Forbes Foreign Rankings. Based on 1988 revenues, in millions of U.S. dollars (converted from local currency at May 31, 1989 exchange rates). Ranks only publicly-traded, private-sector (non-government-owned) companies.

14

## Largest publicly-traded, non-financial corporations in France

1. Peugeot, with $21,777 million
2. Cie Generale d'Electricite, $20,199
3. Elf-Aquitaine, $19,883
4. Cie Generale des Eaux, $13,446
5. Total Francaise des Petroles, $13,098
6. Rhone-Poulenc, $10,310
7. Carrefour, $10,231
8. Saint-Gobain, $9,295
9. Michelin, $8,177
10. Pechiney, $8,097

*Where'd you hear that?*
Financial World, FW International 1000. Based on sales, in millions of dollars.

## Largest corporations in France

1. Peugeot Groupe SA, with $23,166 million
2. Generale d'Electricite, $21,488
3. Elf Aquitaine Group, $21,152
4. Credit Lyonnais, $20,005
5. Banque Nationale de Paris, $18,333
6. Generale des Eaux, $14,303
7. TOTAL-Francaise Petroles, $13,933
8. Societe Generale, $13,675
9. Paribas Group, $12,582
10. Rhone-Poulenc Group, $10,968

*Where'd you hear that?*
Forbes, Forbes Foreign Rankings. Based on 1988 revenues, in millions of U.S. dollars (converted from local currency at May 31, 1989 exchange rates). Ranks only publicly-traded, private-sector (non-government-owned) companies.

## Most valuable corporations in France

1. Elf Aquitaine, with $8,177 million
2. LVMH Moet Hennessy Louis Vuitton, $7,294
3. Peugeot, $6,156
4. Groupe BSN, $5,441
5. Compagnie de Saint-Gobain, $5,197
6. Compagnie du Midi, $5,184
7. Cie Financiere de Suez, $5,177
8. Cie Generale d'Electricite, $4,774
9. Compagnie Generale des Eaux, $4,756
10. Paribas, $4,265

*Where'd you hear that?*
Business Week, The Global 1000. Based on market value in millions of U.S. dollars (share price on May 31, 1989 x number of shares outstanding, converted to dollars at May month-end exchange rates).

## Largest publicly-traded, nonfinancial corporations in West Germany

1. Daimler-Benz, with $39,323 million
2. Siemens, $31,768
3. Volkswagen, $31,686
4. Veba, $23,751
5. BASF, $23,472
6. Hoechst, $21,918
7. Bayer, $21,652

# BUSINESS CLASS

# BUSINESS CLASS

8. RWE, $20,851
9. Thyssen, $15,634
10. BMW, $11,061

*Where'd you hear that?*
Financial World, FW International 1000. Based on sales, in millions of dollars.

## Largest corporations in West Germany

1. Daimler-Benz Group, $41,848 million
2. Siemens Group, $34,148
3. Volkswagen Group, $33,721
4. VEBA Group, $25,276
5. BASF, $24,979
6. Hoechst Group, $23,325
7. Bayer Group, $23,043
8. Thyssen Group, $16,806
9. Allianz Worldwide, $16,625
10. RWE Group, $15,506

*Where'd you hear that?*
Forbes, Forbes Foreign Rankings. Based on 1988 revenues, in millions of U.S. dollars (converted from local currency at May 31, 1989 exchange rates). Ranks only publicly-traded, private-sector (non-government-owned) companies.

## Most valuable corporations in West Germany

1. Daimler-Benz, with $14,360 million
2. Siemens, $13,394
3. Allianz, $13,252
4. Deutsche Bank, $10,082
5. Bayer, $9,896
6. BASF, $8,962
7. Hoechst, $8,930
8. RWE, $6,352
9. VEBA, $5,922
10. Volkswagen, $5,826

*Where'd you hear that?*
Business Week, The Global 1000. Based on market value in millions of U.S. dollars (share price on May 31, 1989 x number of shares outstanding, converted to dollars at May month-end exchange rates).

## Largest publicly-traded, non-financial corporations in Great Britain

1. Shell Transport & Trading, with $78,394 million
2. British Petroleum, $42,251
3. Unilever PLC, $30,980
4. Imperial Chemical Industries PLC, $19,036
5. BAT Industries PLC, $18,796
6. British Telecom, $18,060
7. British Gas PLC, $12,277
8. Hanson PLC, $11,416
9. General Electric Co. PLC, $10,871
10. J. Sainsbury PLC, $9,649

*Where'd you hear that?*
Financial World, FW International 1000. Based on sales, in millions of dollars.

## Largest public companies in the United Kingdom

1. British Petroleum, with £15747.0 million
2. British Telecommunications, £15120.0
3. Shell Transport & Trading, £13757.0
4. Glaxo Holdings, £10112.0
5. BAT Industries PLC, £9877.3
6. Imperial Chemical Industries PLC, £8650.5
7. Hanson PLC, £8347.0
8. British Gas PLC, £7947.2
9. General Electric Co. PLC, £6808.5

## BUSINESS CLASS

10. BTR, £6681.0

*Where'd you hear that?*
Financial Times, FT Top 500. Based on market capitalization, in millions of British pounds.

### Most valuable corporations in Great Britain

1. British Telecommunications PLC, with $24,286 million
2. British Petroleum, $24,151
3. Shell Transport & Trading, $21,190
4. Glaxo Holdings, $15,921
5. BAT Industries PLC, $13,465
6. Imperial Chemical Industries PLC, $13,435
7. Hanson PLC, $12,248
8. British Gas PLC, $11,698
9. General Electric Co. PLC, $10,089
10. BTR, $9,890

*Where'd you hear that?*
Business Week, The Global 1000. Based on market value in millions of U.S. dollars (share price on May 31, 1989 x number of shares outstanding, converted to dollars at May month-end exchange rates).

### Largest manufacturing companies in Great Britain

1. British Petroleum, with £25,922,000 thousand
2. Unilever PLC, £17,116,000
3. Imperial Chemical Industries PLC, £11,699,000
4. BAT Industries PLC, £11,522,000
5. The Electricity Council, £11,366,500
6. BP International Ltd., £9,404,000
7. British Gas PLC, £7,526,000
8. Hanson PLC, £7,396,000
9. Grand Metropolitan PLC, £6,028,800
10. Ford Motor Co. Ltd., £5,936,000

*Where'd you hear that?*
U.K.'s 10,000 Largest Companies, Dun & Bradstreet. Based on 1988 sales, in thousands of British pounds.

### *Largest corporations in the United Kingdom*

1. British Petroleum, with $46,137 million
2. BAT Industries PLC, $20,021
3. Imperial Chemical Industries PLC, $19,898
4. British Telecommunications PLC, $19,587
5. Barclays PLC, $19,474
6. National Westminster, $18,920
7. British Gas PLC, $13,315
8. Hanson PLC, $13,109
9. Lloyds Bank Group, $12,309
10. Prudential Corp. PLC, $11,471

*Where'd you hear that?*
Forbes, Forbes Foreign Rankings. Based on 1988 revenues, in millions of U.S. dollars (converted from local currency at May 31, 1989 exchange rates). Ranks only publicly-traded, private-sector (non-government-owned) companies.

### Britain's largest private companies by assets

1. Littlewoods Organisation PLC, with £714,373 thousand
2. John Swire & Sons Ltd., £533,000
3. C. & J. Clark Ltd., £278,947
4. Hudson Place Investments Ltd., £185,100
5. Robert Stephen Holdings Ltd., £152,967
6. Linpac Group Ltd., £139,488

# BUSINESS CLASS

7. Andrew Weir & Co. Ltd., £132,118
8. D. C. Thomson & Co. Ltd., £125,289
9. Guardian & Manchester Evening News PLC, £112,415
10. Taylor Clark Ltd., £109,703

*Where'd you hear that?*
Britain's Privately Owned Companies, The Top 2000. Based on net tangible assets, in thousands of British pounds.

## Britain's largest private companies by sales

1. Littlewoods Organisation PLC., with £1,458,093 thousand
2. P & H Ltd., £847,586
3. C. & J. Clark, Ltd., £636,028
4. Robert Stephen Holdings Ltd., £487,374
5. Czarnikow, Holdings Ltd., £410,168
6. Hudson Place Investments Ltd., £409,300
7. Linpac Group Ltd., £406,725
8. Trebor Group Ltd., £375,867
9. C. Walker & Sons (Holdings) Ltd., £333,900
10. Premier Brands Ltd., £315,046

*Where'd you hear that?*
Britain's Privately Owned Companies, The Top 2000. Based on sales, in thousands of British pounds.

## Britain's most profitable private companies

1. Staple Holdings Ltd., with 874.95%
2. Bladon Lines Travel Ltd., 472.41%
3. Davis Wilkins Advertising Ltd., 330.69%
4. H. Page Engineering Services Ltd., 251.00%
5. Aqualisa Products Ltd., 247.57%
6. Ace Coin Equipment Ltd., 196.67%
7. Merrett Holdings PLC, 160.44%
8. J. Manning PLC, 142.76%
9. Orion Magnetic Media PLC, 139.00%
10. E. K. F. (Aluminium) Ltd., 129.40%

*Where'd you hear that?*
Britain's Privately Owned Companies, The Top 2000. Based on pre-tax profit/net tangible assets ratio, in percent.

## British companies paying the highest wages

1. J. & J. Fee Ltd., with £35,529
2. T. Costelloe & Co. Ltd., £33,780
3. James A. Jobling & Co. Ltd., £33,150
4. Lewis Rugg (Asburton) Ltd., £29,774
5. C. & S. Steels (Wolverhampton) Ltd., £28,785
6. Munro Corporate PLC, £29,015
7. Armstrong Capital Holdings Ltd., £28,785
8. Granville & Co. Ltd., £28,551
9. Grove Colourprint Ltd., £28,450
10. Bartle Bogle Hegarty Ltd., £26,634

*Where'd you hear that?*
Britain's Privately Owned Companies, The Top 2000. Based on average wage per annum, in British pounds.

# BUSINESS CLASS

### Scotland's top companies

1. United Biscuits (Holdings) PLC
2. Lasmo (TNS) Ltd.
3. Burmah Oil PLC
4. House of Fraser PLC
5. Grandmet Restaurants Ltd.
6. Scottish & Newcastle Breweries PLC
7. Coats Patons PLC
8. Britoil PLC
9. John Menzies PLC
10. Scottish and Universal Investments Ltd.

*Where'd you hear that?*
Scotland's Top 1000 Companies, Jordan's. Based on turnover (sales).

### Companies paying the highest wages in Scotland

1. Ireland Alloys (Holdings) Ltd., with £25,122
2. Nobel's Explosives Co. Ltd., £24,665
3. Britoil PLC, £24,121
4. Clyde Petroleum PLC, £23,183
5. Ivory & Sime PLC, £22,163
6. Scott Lithgow Ltd., £21,840
7. Scottish Television PLC, £21,187
8. Arthur D. Little Ltd., £21,082
9. Smith International (North Sea) Ltd., £18,801
10. Brown & Root-Wimpey Highlands Fabricators Ltd., £18,762

*Where'd you hear that?*
Scotland's Top 1000 Companies, Jordan's. Based on average wage per annum, in British pounds.

### Largest publicly-traded, non-financial corporations in Italy

1. Fiat SpA, with $32,491
2. STET, $12,687
3. Montedison, $10,355
4. SIP, $9,809
5. Eridania, $6,204
6. Olivetti, $6,165
7. Feruzzi Agricola, $3,692
8. Alitalia, $3,110
9. SME, $2,961
10. SELM, $2,926

*Where'd you hear that?*
Financial World, FW International 1000. Based on sales, in millions of dollars.

### Largest corporations in Italy

1. Fiat Group, with $34,040 million
2. Ferruzzi Group, $19,103
3. STET, $13,293
4. Generali Group, $10,015
5. Pirelli SpA, $7,007
6. Olivetti Group, $6,507
7. Alitalia, $3,227
8. SME, $2,869

*Where'd you hear that?*
Forbes, Forbes International 500. Based on 1988 revenues, in millions of U.S. dollars (converted from local currency at May 31, 1989 exchange rates). Ranks only publicly-traded, private-sector (non-government-owned) companies.

### Most valuable corporations in Italy

1. Assicurazioni Generali, with $14,791 million
2. Fiat Group, $13,325
3. STET, $4,652
4. Montedison, $3,621
5. RAS, $3,465

19

# BUSINESS CLASS

6. La Fondiaria, $3,274
7. Olivetti Group, $3,206
8. SIP, $3,176
9. Banca Commerciale Italiana, $2,981
10. Mediobanca, $2,924

*Where'd you hear that?*
Business Week, The Global 1000. Based on market value in millions of U.S. dollars (share price on May 31, 1989 x number of shares outstanding, converted to dollars at May month-end exchange rates).

### Largest publicly-traded, non-financial corporations in the Netherlands

1. Royal Dutch Petroleum, with $78,394 million
2. Unilever NV, $30,980
3. Philips, $26,626
4. Akzo, $7,874
5. Ahold, $7,250
6. DSM, $4,804
7. Hoogovens Groep, $3,734
8. Pirelli Tyre, $3,008
9. Heineken, $2,897
10. KLM, $2,829

*Where'd you hear that?*
Financial World, FW International 1000. Based on sales, in millions of dollars.

### Largest corporations in the Netherlands

1. Royal Dutch/Shell, with $78,380 million
2. Unilever, $31,367
3. Philips Group, $28,382
4. Nationale-Nederland, $9,510
5. Akzo Group, $8,393
6. Ahold, $7,728
7. NV DSM, $5,120
8. AEGON Insurance, $4,937
9. Schlumberger Ltd., $4,925
10. AMEV NV, $4,333

*Where'd you hear that?*
Forbes, Forbes Foreign Rankings. Based on 1988 revenues, in millions of U.S. dollars (converted from local currency at May 31, 1989 exchange rates). Ranks only publicly-traded, private-sector (non-government-owned) companies.

### Most valuable corporations in the Netherlands

1. Royal Dutch Petroleum, with $33,167 million
2. Unilever NV, $9,845
3. Philips' Gloeilampenfabrieken, $4,567
4. Nationale-Nederlanden, $3,852
5. Akzo, $2,737
6. DSM, $2,172
7. Algemene Bank Nederland, $2,156
8. Amro Bank, $2,049
9. Dordtsche Petroleum, $1,903
10. Elsevier, $1,863
11. Aegon, $1,767

*Where'd you hear that?*
Business Week, The Global 1000. Based on market value in millions of U.S. dollars (share price on May 31, 1989 x number of shares outstanding converted to dollars at May month-end exchange rates).

### Largest publicly-traded, non-financial corporations in Norway

1. Norsk Hydro, with $8,712 million
2. Aker, $2,418
3. Kvaerner Industrier, $1,264
4. Orkla-Borregaard, $1,126
5. DNL-Det Norske Luffart, $940

6. Kosmos, $855
7. Dyno Industrier, $811
8. Nora Inds, $805
9. Vard, $640

*Where'd you hear that?*
Financial World, FW International 1000. Based on sales, in millions of dollars.

## Largest publicly-traded, non-financial corporations in Spain

1. Repso, with $6,846 million
2. Telefonica, $5,201
3. Endesa, $3,962
4. Tabacalera, $3,758
5. Espanola Petroleos, $3,241
6. Hidroelectrica Espanola, $2,180
7. Iberduero, $2,146
8. Union Electrica-Fenosa, $1,722
9. Citroen Hispania, $1,592
10. Sevillana de Electricidad, $1,459

*Where'd you hear that?*
Financial World, FW International 1000. Based on sales, in millions of dollars.

## Largest corporations in Spain

1. Banco Central Group, with $9,936 million
2. Repsol SA, $8,089
3. Banco Bilbao-Vizcaya, $6,923
4. Telefonica, $5,219
5. Tabacalera, $3,563
6. Banco Santander, $3,292
7. Banco Hispano Americano, $3,140
8. CEPSA, $3,021

*Where'd you hear that?*
Forbes, Forbes Foreign Rankings. Based on 1988 revenues, in millions of U.S. dollars (converted from local currency at May 31, 1989 exchange rates). Ranks only publicly-traded, private-sector (non-government-owned) companies.

## Most valuable corporations in Spain

1. Banco Bilbao Vizcaya, with $7,323 million
2. Telefonica Nacional de Espana, $7,276
3. Banco de Santander, $5,135
4. Repsol, $4,932
5. Endesa, $4,713
6. Banco Espanol de Credito, $3,923
7. Banco Central, $3,817
8. Banco Hispano Americano, $2,813
9. Iberduero, $2,297
10. Banco Popular Espana, $2,183
11. Asland, $2,038

*Where'd you hear that?*
Business Week, The Global 1000. Based on market value in millions of U.S. dollars (share price on May 31, 1989 x number of shares outstanding, converted to dollars at May month-end exchange rates).

## Largest publicly-traded, non-financial corporations in Sweden

1. Asea, with $17,832 million
2. Volvo, $15,026
3. Electrolux, $11,510
4. Saab-Scania, $6,611
5. Stora Kopparbergs, $5,335
6. L. M. Ericsson, $4,869
7. Skanska, $3,592
8. Trelleborg, $3,348
9. Nobel Inds, $3,317

# BUSINESS CLASS

21

# BUSINESS CLASS

10. SKF, $3,305

*Where'd you hear that?*
Financial World, FW International 1000. Based on sales, in millions of dollars.

## Largest corporations in Sweden

1. Volvo Group, with $15,766 million
2. Electrolux Group, $12,077
3. Saab-Scania, $6,936
4. Stora Group, $5,598
5. L. M. Ericsson, $5,108
6. Skand Enskilda Bank, $4,985
7. PKbanken Group, $3,797
8. Svenska Handelsbank, $3,780
9. Skanska AB, $3,768
10. Trelleborg, $3,514

*Where'd you hear that?*
Forbes, Forbes Foreign Rankings. Based on 1988 revenues, in millions of U.S. dollars (converted from local currency at May 31, 1989 exchange rates). Ranks only publicly-traded, private-sector (non-government-owned) companies.

## Most valuable corporations in Sweden

1. Volvo, with $5,161 million
2. Skanska, $4,925
3. ASEA, $4,571
4. Stora Kopparbergs Bergslags, $3,698
5. Skandinaviska Enskilda Banken, $3,566
6. Electrolux, $3,530
7. Svenska Cellulosa Aktiebolaget, $3,050
8. L. M. Ericsson, $2,870

9. Astra, $2,815
10. SKF, $2,780

*Where'd you hear that?*
Business Week, The Global 1000. Based on market value in millions of U.S. dollars (share price on May 31, 1989 x number of shares outstanding, converted to dollars at May month-end exchange rates).

## Largest publicly-traded, non-financial corporations in Switzerland

1. Nestle, with $24,994 million
2. BBC Brown Boveri, $17,832
3. Ciba-Geigy Corp., $10,840
4. Sandoz, $6,235
5. Roche, $5,338
6. Jacobs Suchard, $3,921
7. AluSuisse, $3,672
8. Suize Brosr, $3,327
9. Swissair, $2,631
10. Oerlikon-Buehrle Hldg, $2,600

*Where'd you hear that?*
Financial World, FW International 1000. Based on sales, in millions of dollars.

## Largest corporations in Switzerland

1. Nestle, with $27,807 million
2. Asea Brown Boveri, $18,340
3. Ciba-Geigy Group, $12,060
4. Zurich Insurance, $10,506
5. Winterthur Group, $7,619
6. Union Bank of Switzerland, $7,411
7. Swiss Re Group, $7,154
8. Swiss Bank Corp., $7,021
9. Sandoz Group, $6,937
10. Roche/Sapac Group, $5,939

# BUSINESS CLASS

*Where'd you hear that?*
Forbes, Forbes Foreign Rankings. Based on 1988 revenues, in millions of U.S. dollars (converted from local currency at May 31, 1989 exchange rates). Ranks only publicly-traded, private-sector (non-government-owned) companies.

## Most valuable corporations in Switzerland

1. Nestle, with $13,388 million
2. Ciba-Geigy Corp., $8,968
3. F. Hoffmann-La Roche, $8,434
4. Sandoz, $7,525
5. Union Bank of Switzerland, $7,488
6. CS Holding, $6,438
7. Swiss Bank Corp., $5,523
8. Zurich Vers., $4,304
9. BBC Brown Boveri, $3,010
10. Schweiz. Ruck., $2,795

*Where'd you hear that?*
Business Week, The Global 1000. Based on market value in millions of U.S. dollars (share price on May 31, 1989 x number of shares outstanding, converted to dollars at May month-end exchange rates).

## Largest industrial, commercial, and service companies in Switzerland

1. Nestle, with 40,685 million francs
2. Metro International, 30,175
3. March Rich-Group, 30,000
4. ABB Asea, Brown Boveri, 27,640
5. Ciba-Geigy Corp., 17,647
6. Migros, 11,882
7. Pirelli, 10,210
8. Sandoz, 10,151
9. Maus Freres, 10,000
10. Michelin-Group, 9,836

*Where'd you hear that?*
Switzerland's Largest Companies, Union Bank of Switzerland. Based on 1988 consolidated sales, in millions of francs.

## Largest corporations in Brazil

1. Banco do Brasil, with $55,295 million
2. Banco Bradesco SA, $31,326
3. Banco Itau Group, $19,945
4. BANESPA Group, $18,881
5. Petrobras, $14,806
6. Unibanco Group, $8,865

*Where'd you hear that?*
Forbes, Forbes Foreign Rankings. Based on 1988 revenues, in millions of U.S. dollars (converted from local currency at May 31, 1989 exchange rates). Ranks only publicly-traded, private-sector (non-government-owned) companies.

## *Largest companies in Latin America*

1. Petrobras (Brazil), with $16,500 million
2. Petroleos Mexicanos, (Mexico), $12,928
3. Petroleos de Venezuela (Venezuela), $9,508
4. YPF (Argentina), $6,435
5. Corporacion Venezolana de Guayana (Venezuela), $5,852
6. Autolatina (Argentina/Brazil), $4,219
7. Codelco (Chile), $2,902
8. Souza Cruz (Brazil), $2,100
9. Petrobras Distribuidora (Brazil), $1,841
10. Grupo Industrial Alfa (Mexico), $1,816

*Where'd you hear that?*
Latin American Times. Based on 1989 sales/turnover, in millions of U.S. dollars.

# BUSINESS CLASS

### Canada's largest industrial companies

1. General Motors of Canada, with $19,668,377 thousand Canadian
2. BCE, $16,681,000
3. Ford Motor Co. of Canada Ltd., $15,311,800
4. Canadian Pacific, $11,020,200
5. Alcan Aluminium, $10,467,143
6. George Weston, $10,459,000
7. Imperial Oil Ltd., $10,007,000
8. Brascan Ltd., $9,622,000
9. Noranda, $9,158,000
10. Campeau Corp., $8,264,960

*Where'd you hear that?*
Canadian Business, Canadian Business 500. Based on 1989 sales, in thousands of Canadian dollars.

### Largest publicly-traded, non-financial corporations in Canada

1. BCE, with $12,893 million
2. Canadian Pacific, $10,157
3. George Weston, $9,156
4. Noranda, $7,340
5. Campeau Corp., $7,327
6. Alcan Aluminium, $7,210
7. Loblaw, $7,023
8. Provigo, $6,238
9. Imperial Oil Ltd., $6,090
10. Imasco, $5,073

*Where'd you hear that?*
Financial World, FW International 1000. Based on sales, in millions of dollars.

### Largest manufacturing companies in Canada

1. Moore, with $238,878 thousand
2. Reynolds Canada, $208,774
3. Varity, $108,889
4. CCL Industries, $78,495
5. General Electric Canada, $60,777
6. 3M Canada, $58,199
7. Rockwell International of Canada, $48,894
8. Finning, $42,197
9. PPG Industries, $40,437
10. Domtar, $33,000

*Where'd you hear that?*
Canadian Business, Canadian Business 500. Based on 1989 net income, in thousands of Canadian dollars.

### Most valuable corporations in Canada

1. BCE (Bell Canada Enterprises), with $9,292 million
2. Imperial Oil Ltd., $7,669
3. Seagram, $7,332
4. Canadian Pacific, $5,941
5. Toronto-Dominion Bank, $5,129
6. Alcan Aluminium, $5,044
7. Royal Bank of Canada, $4,847
8. International Thomson Organisation, $4,364
9. Canadian Imperial Bank of Commerce, $4,195
10. Shell Canada, $4,176

*Where'd you hear that?*
Business Week, The Global 1000. Based on market value in millions of U.S. dollars (share price on May 31, 1989 x number of shares outstanding, converted to dollars at May month-end exchange rates).

### Highest yielding foreign corporations (excludes US)

1. Partek, Finland, with 13.0%
2. British & Comm. Hldgs., United Kingdom, 12.4%
3. Next, United Kingdom, 11.5%

# BUSINESS CLASS

4. Storehouse, United Kingdom, 10.8%
5. British Steel, United Kingdom, 10.1%
6. Elders IXL Ltd., Australia, 9.5%
7. Barratt Devs., United Kingdom, 9.2%
8. Norcros, United Kingdom, 8.7%
9. Coats Viyella PLC, United Kingdom, 8.4%
10. Iberduero, Spain, 8.3%

*Where'd you hear that?*
Financial World, FW International 1000. Based on yield, in percent.

## Leading foreign corporations in sales (excludes US)

1. Mitsui, Japan, with $121,281 million
2. C. Itoh & Co. Ltd., Japan, $115,495
3. Mitsubishi, Japan, $113,151
4. Sumitomo, Japan, $107,247
5. Marubeni, Japan, $106,204
6. Nissho Iwai, Japan, $82,821
7. Royal Dutch/Shell, Netherlands/U.K., $78,394
8. Toyota Motor, Japan, $58,029
9. Hitachi Ltd., Japan, $46,309
10. NTT, Japan, $42,265

*Where'd you hear that?*
Financial World, FW International 1000. Based on sales, in millions of dollars.

## Leading foreign corporations in assets (excludes US)

1. Royal Dutch/Shell, Netherlands/U.K., with $85,280 million
2. NTT, Japan, $83,633
3. Tokyo Electric Power, Japan, $74,177
4. Mitsubishi, Japan, $68,824
5. Toyota Motor, Japan, $51,699
6. Hitachi Ltd., Japan, $50,194
7. Marubeni, Japan, $49,571
8. British Petroleum, United Kingdom, $47,847
9. Matsushita Elec. Ind., Japan, $46,316
10. Mitsui, Japan, $45,773

*Where'd you hear that?*
Financial World, FW International 1000. Based on assets, in millions of dollars.

## *Largest corporations in Canada*

1. BCE Inc., with $12,394 million
2. Canadian Pacific, $9,763
3. George Weston, $8,801
4. Alcan Aluminium, $8,529
5. Royal Bank of Canada, $8,488
6. Bank of Montreal, $7,355
7. Canadian Imperial Bank of Commerce, $7,337
8. Campeau Corp., $7,088
9. Noranda, $7,055
10. Provigo Inc., $6,034

*Where'd you hear that?*
Forbes, Forbes International 500. Based on 1988 revenues, in millions of U.S. dollars (converted from local currency at May 31, 1989 exchange rates). Ranks only publicly-traded, private-sector (non-government-owned) companies.

# BUSINESS CLASS

### Leading foreign corporations in profits (excludes US)

1. Royal Dutch/Shell, Netherlands/U.K., with $5,234 million
2. British Telecom, United Kingdom, $2,551
3. Toyota Motor, Japan, $2,503
4. Fiat SpA, Italy, $2,219
5. British Petroleum, United Kingdom, $1,974
6. NTT, Japan, $1,613
7. BAT Industries PLC, United Kingdom, $1,548
8. Matsushita Elec. Ind., Japan, $1,541
9. Unilever, Netherlands/U.K., $1,510
10. British Gas PLC, United Kingdom, $1,462

*Where'd you hear that?*
Financial World, FW International 1000. Based on profits, in millions of dollars.

### Industrial corporations outside the U.S. with greatest decrease in profits

1. Fried, Krupp, with -1,243.5%
2. Ruhrkohle, -820.2%
3. Aerospatiale, -146.8%
4. Empresa Colombiana, -145.3%
5. Pacific Dunlop, -143.1%
6. Amoco Canada Petroleum, -138.6%
7. Texaco (Britain), -99.5%
8. Arla, -96.5%
9. Nissan Diesel Motor, -94.3%
10. Valmet, -93.6%

*Where'd you hear that?*
Fortune, Fortune International 500. Based on 1988 percentage decrease in profits.

### Industrial corporations outside the U.S. with greatest decrease in sales

1. Turkiye Petrolleri, with -29.5%
2. McDermott International, -28.5%
3. Saint-Gobain, -24.7%
4. Feldmuhle Nobel, -17.8%
5. Charbonnages de France, -15.7%
6. Vale do Rio Doce, -15.5%
7. Showa Shell Sekiyu, -13.8%
8. Northern Foods, -13.7%
9. Hitachi Zosen, -10.9%
10. Mobil Oil (West Germany), -10.6%

*Where'd you hear that?*
Fortune, Fortune International 500. Based on 1988 percentage decrease in sales.

### Industrial corporations outside the U.S. with greatest increase in profits

1. Pemex, with 22,370.1%
2. General Motors of Canada, 7,521.3%
3. Zambia Industrial & Mining, 1,166.9%
4. Ebara, 1,123.3%
5. Kymmene Corp., 1,013.7%
6. Euroc, 746.1%
7. Rauma-Repola, 741.5%
8. Dillinger Huttenwerke, 650.4%
9. PT Astra International, 647.5%
10. Metsa-Serla, 622.6%

*Where'd you hear that?*
Fortune, Fortune International 500. Based on 1988 percentage increase in profits.

# BUSINESS CLASS

## Industrial corporations outside the U.S. with greatest increase in sales

1. Arbed, with 296.2%
2. Mo Och Domsjo, 177.7%
3. Bond Corp. Holdings, 143.6%
4. Redland, 110.8%
5. Williams Holdings, 93.9%
6. Huls, 86.5%
7. Nova, 82.5%
8. Inco, 82.3%
9. Bharat Petroleum, 79.0%
10. Siebe, 78.6%

*Where'd you hear that?*
Fortune, Fortune International 500. Based on 1988 percentage increase in sales.

## World's largest industrial corporations outside the U.S.

1. Royal Dutch/Shell Group (Britain/Netherlands), with $78,381.1 million
2. Toyota Motor (Japan), $50,789.9
3. British Petroleum (Britain), $46,174.0
4. IRI (Italy), $45,521.5
5. Daimler-Benz (West Germany), $41,817.9
6. Hitachi Ltd. (Japan), $41,330.7
7. Siemens (West Germany), $34,129.4
8. Fiat SpA (Italy), $34,039.3
9. Matsushita Electric Industrial (Japan), $33,922.5
10. Volkswagen (West Germany), $33,696.2

*Where'd you hear that?*
Fortune, Fortune International 500. Based on 1988 sales, in millions of U.S. dollars.

## Largest public companies outside the U.S.

1. Mitsui & Co. Ltd. (Japan), with $130,667 million
2. Sumitomo Corp. (Japan), $115,570
3. C. Itoh & Co. Ltd. (Japan), $112,327
4. Mitsubishi Corp. (Japan), $104,198
5. Marubeni Corp. (Japan), $99,475
6. Nissho Iwai Corp. (Japan), $81,371
7. Royal Dutch/Shell Group (Holland), $78,380
8. Banco do Brasil (Brazil), $55,295
9. Toyota Motor Corp. (Japan), $53,818
10. Hitachi Ltd. (Japan), $49,897

*Where'd you hear that?*
Forbes, Forbes Foreign Rankings. Based on 1988 sales, in millions of U.S. dollars (converted from local currency at May 31, 1989, exchange rates). Ranks only private sector (non-government-owned) companies.

## Largest privately-owned companies outside the U.S.

1. Nippon Life Insurance Co. (Japan), $48,062 million
2. Dai-Ichi Mutual Life Insurance (Japan), $28,344
3. Zenkyoren (Japan), $27,760
4. Samsung Group (Korea), $27,510
5. Renault Group (France), $27,101
6. Sumitomo Life Insurance Co. (Japan), $25,198
7. Credit Agricole (France), $21,275

# BUSINESS CLASS

8. Tengelmann Group (Germany), $20,208
9. Daewoo Group (Korea), $17,329
10. Meiji Mutual Life Insurance Co. (Japan), $16,766

*Where'd you hear that?*
Forbes, Forbes International 500. Based on 1988 sales, in millions of U.S. dollars (converted from local currency at May 31, 1989 exchange rates).

---

## Largest U.S. multinational corporations

1. Exxon Corp., with $48,192 million
2. Ford Motor Co., $41,842
3. IBM, $34,361
4. Mobil, $33,039
5. General Motors Corp., $29,128
6. Citicorp, $16,451
7. Texaco, $16,325
8. E. I. du Pont de Nemours & Co., $12,896
9. ITT Corp., $10,419
10. Dow Chemical Co., $9,185

*Where'd you hear that?*
Forbes, Forbes International 500. Based on 1988 foreign revenues, in millions of U.S. dollars (converted from local currency at May 31, 1989 exchange rates). Includes only sales generated by overseas operations, not exports from U.S.

---

## Largest conglomerates

1. General Electric Co., with $57,906 million
2. USX, $9,233
3. Tenneco, $8,598
4. ITT Corp., $6,650
5. Rockwell International, $5,524
6. Allied-Signal, $5,238
7. Teledyne, $3,831
8. TRW, $3,060
9. Whitman, $2,710
10. Textron, $2,113

*Where'd you hear that?*
Business Week, The Business Week 1000. Based on market value in millions of dollars.

## Most powerful U.S. corporations

1. General Motors Corp.
2. General Electric Co.
3. Exxon Corp.
4. IBM
5. Ford Motor Co.
6. Philip Morris Cos.
7. AT & T
8. Mobil
9. E. I. du Pont de Nemours & Co.
10. Sears, Roebuck

*Where'd you hear that?*
Forbes, Forbes 500s Annual Directory. Based on combination of *Forbes 500s* rankings for assets, profits, sales, and market value. Average is not stated.

## Largest corporate employers

1. General Motors Corp., with 775.1 thousand
2. Sears, Roebuck & Co., 510.0
3. IBM, 385.2
4. Ford Motor Co., 366.6
5. K mart Corp., 360.0

*Where'd you hear that?*
Forbes, Forbes 500s Annual Directory. Based on number of employees for 1989 in thousands.

# BUSINESS CLASS

## Largest companies traded on U.S. stock exchanges

1. IBM, with $62,508 million
2. Exxon Corp., $58,398
3. General Electric Co., $57,860
4. AT & T, $44,904
5. Philip Morris, $36,188
6. General Motors Corp., $28,675
7. Bristol-Myers Squibb Co., $27,638
8. Merck, $27,624
9. Amoco Corp., $27,599
10. E. I. du Pont de Nemours & Co., $27,455

*Where'd you hear that?*
Financial World, Financial World 1000. Based on market value as of March, 1990, in millions of dollars.

## Biggest U.S industrial corporations

1. General Motors Corp., with $126,974.3
2. Ford Motor Co., $96,932.6
3. Exxon Corp., $86,656.0
4. IBM, $63,438.0
5. General Electric Co., $55,264.0
6. Mobil, $50,976.0
7. Philip Morris, $39,069.0
8. Chrysler Corp., $36,156.0
9. E. I. du Pont de Nemours & Co., $35,209.0
10. Texaco, $32,416.0

*Where'd you hear that?*
Fortune, Fortune 500 Largest U.S. Industrial Corporations. Based on 1989 sales, in millions of dollars.

## Top corporations in the general manufacturing industry

1. Minnesota Mining & Manufacturing, with $18,537 million
2. Corning, $4,216
3. Illinois Tool Works, $2,654
4. Rubbermaid, $2,652
5. Hillenbrand Industries, $1,554
6. Newell, $1,550
7. Parker Hannifin, $1,447
8. Norton, $1,415
9. Avery International, $1,189
10. Jostens, Inc., $1,053

*Where'd you hear that?*
Business Week, The Business Week 1000. Based on market value as of March 16, 1990, in millions of dollars.

## Corporations with the highest sales

1. General Motors Corp., with $126,932 million
2. Ford Motor Co., $96,146
3. Exxon Corp., $86,656
4. IBM, $62,710
5. General Electric Co., $54,574
6. Sears, Roebuck, $53,794
7. Mobil, $50,220
8. Philip Morris Cos., $39,011
9. Citicorp, $37,970
10. AT & T, $36,112

*Where'd you hear that?*
Forbes, Forbes 500s Annual Directory. Based on 1989 sales, in millions of dollars.

## Corporations with the highest growth in sales

1. Primerica, with 500.0%
2. Maxxam, 366.7%

29

# BUSINESS CLASS

3. Ames Department Stores Inc., 135.5%
4. Penn Traffic, 128.8%
5. Panhandle Eastern, 120.4%

*Where'd you hear that?*
Forbes, Forbes 500s Annual Directory. Based on percentage change in 1989 sales over 1988.

## Top U.S. corporations in sales

1. General Motors Corp., with $126.9 billion
2. Ford Motor Co., $96.1
3. Exxon Corp., $88.1
4. IBM, $62.7
5. Mobil, $56.7
6. General Electric Co., $53.9
7. Sears, Roebuck, $53.8
8. Philip Morris, 444.8
9. Citicorp, $38.0
10. Salomon, $36.6

*Where'd you hear that?*
Business Week, The Business Week 1000. Based on 1989 sales, in billions of dollars.

## Industrial sales leaders for the 1980s

1. ConAgra, Inc., with 33.2%
2. Digital Equipment Corp., 21.7%
3. Philip Morris, 20.3%
4. Hewlett-Packard Co., 17.6%
5. Sequa, 16.0%
6. Sonoco Products, 14.7%
7. Dow Jones, 14.5%
8. Unisys, 13.7%
9. Anheuser-Busch Cos. Inc., 13.1%
10. Bristol-Myers Squibb Co., 12.8%

*Where'd you hear that?*
Fortune, Fortune 500 Largest U.S. Industrial Corporations. Based on percentage change from 1979 to 1989.

## Industrial corporations with the largest sales increases

1. Maxxam, with 366.7%
2. Doskocil, 350.3%
3. Conner Peripherals, 176.4%
4. Terex, 151.0%
5. Jefferson Smurfit Corp., 133.9%
6. Crystal Brands, 98.2%
7. Nacco Industries, 92.6%
8. Mark IV Industries Inc., 84.2%
9. Time Warner, 69.6%
10. Sun Microsystems, 68.2%

*Where'd you hear that?*
Fortune, Fortune 500 Largest U.S. Industrial Corporations. Based on 1989 increase in sales, in percent.

## Industrial corporations with the lowest sales increases

1. Fort Howard Paper Co., with 43.3%
2. Henley Group Inc., 41.7%
3. Beatrice Cos. Inc., 40.1%
4. Tyler, 39.6%
5. AM International Inc., 34.1%
6. International Minerals & Chemical, 33.2%
7. Hillsborough Holdings Corp., 31.9%
8. Tesoro Petroleum, 31.2%
9. Amstar, 27.6%
10. Armco Inc., 22.7%

*Where'd you hear that?*
Fortune, Fortune 500 Largest U.S. Industrial Corporations. Based on 1989 increase in sales, in percent.

# BUSINESS CLASS

## Corporations lagging in sales growth

1. Zenith Electronics, with -42.3%
2. Paramount Communications, -34.4%
3. Pinnacle West, -30.0%
4. Armco Inc., -24.9%
5. Interco, -24.3%

*Where'd you hear that?*
Forbes, Forbes 500s Annual Directory. Based on percentage change of 1989 performance from 1988.

## Industrial companies with the highest returns on sales

1. UST, with 28.4%
2. Lorillard, 27.0%
3. Marion Laboratories Inc., 23.5%
4. Eli Lilly & Co., 22.5%
5. Merck & Co., 22.3%
6. Newmont Mining, 20.9%
7. Coca-Cola Co., 18.8%
8. Dow Jones, 18.5%
9. Berkshire Hathaway, 18.0%
10. Sterling Chemicals, 17.9%

*Where'd you hear that?*
Fortune, Fortune 500 Largest U.S. Industrial Corporations. Based on 1989 percentage of returns on sales.

## Corporations with the highest market value

1. IBM, with $60,345 million
2. Exxon Corp., $57,676
3. General Electric Co., $57,193
4. AT & T, $44,646
5. Philip Morris Cos., $36,566
6. General Motors Corp., $31,307
7. Merck, $27,532
8. Bristol-Myers Squibb Co., $27,449
9. Amoco Corp., $26,666
10. Wal-Mart Stores, $26,325

*Where'd you hear that?*
Forbes, Forbes 500s Annual Directory. Based on market value for the 12 months ending March 23, 1990, in millions of dollars.

## Most valuable corporations in the United States

1. IBM, with $64,650 million
2. Exxon Corp., $54,923
3. General Electric Co., $49,391
4. AT & T, $38,115
5. Philip Morris, $32,142
6. Merck, $27,524
7. Du Pont Co., $26,077
8. General Motors Inc., $25,245
9. BellSouth Corp., $24,169
10. Ford Motor Co., $23,927

*Where'd you hear that?*
Business Week, The Global 1000. Based on market value in millions of U.S. dollars (share price on May 31, 1989 x number of shares outstanding, converted to dollars at May month-end exchange rates).

## Corporations with the highest growth in market value

1. Costco Wholesale Club, with 162.4%
2. Oracle Systems, 138.1%
3. Microsoft, 120.2%
4. Home Depot, 106.0%
5. Newell Co., 101.2%

*Where'd you hear that?*
Forbes, Forbes 500s Annual Directory. Based on percentage change in market value over 1988.

# BUSINESS CLASS

**Publicly-held corporations with highest growth rates**

1. Price Co., with 48.9%
2. Liz Claiborne, Inc., 45.4%
3. Consolidated Stores, 44.0%
4. The Limited Inc., 42.8%
5. Student Loan, 41.5%
6. Leucadia National, 39.7%
7. Cray Research, 39.4%
8. Hasbro Inc., 38.8%
9. Circuit City Stores, 38.6%
10. Oshkosh Truck, 38.5%

*Where'd you hear that?*
Forbes, Annual Report on American Industry. Based on 10-year average earnings per share, in percent.

**Top U.S. corporations in market value**

1. IBM, with $62.4 billion
2. Exxon Corp., $59.4
3. General Electric Co., $57.9
4. AT & T, $45.0
5. Philip Morris, $35.8
6. General Motors Corp., $28.8
7. Merck, $28.0
8. Bristol-Myers Squibb Co., $27.8
9. Amoco Corp., $27.5
10. Du Pont Co., $27.0

*Where'd you hear that?*
Business Week, The Business Week 1000. Based on 1989 market value, in billions of dollars.

**Corporations with the highest stock market value**

1. IBM, with $62,427 million
2. Exxon Corp., $59,389
3. General Electric Co., $57,906
4. AT & T, $45,049
5. Philip Morris, $35,832
6. General Motors Corp., $28,814
7. Merck, $27,975
8. Bristol-Myers Squibb Co., $27,843
9. Amoco Corp., $27,495
10. Du Pont Co., $26,985

*Where'd you hear that?*
Business Week, The Business Week 1000. Based on stock market value on March 17, 1990, in millions of dollars.

**Corporations lagging in market value**

1. Lyondell Petrochemical, with -40.0%
2. Shawmut National, -39.1%
3. McDonnell Douglas, -39.0%
3. Unisys, -39.0%
5. Chrysler Corp., -32.7%

*Where'd you hear that?*
Forbes, Forbes 500s Annual Directory. Based on percentage change of 1989 performance from 1988.

**Top U.S. corporations in assets**

1. Citicorp, with $230.6 billion
2. General Motors Corp., $173.3
3. Ford Motor Co., $160.9
4. American Express, $140.2
5. General Electric Co., $128.3
6. Federal National Mortgage Association, $124.3
7. Salomon, $117.0
8. Chase Manhattan Bank, $107.4
9. Bankamerica, $98.8
10. J. P. Morgan & Co., Inc., $89.0

*Where'd you hear that?*
Business Week, The Business Week 1000. Based on 1989 assets, in billions of dollars.

## Corporations with the highest growth in assets

1. First Financial Management Corp., with 500.0%
2. Time Warner, 404.6%
3. Black & Decker Corp., 220.2%
4. UA Entertainment, 176.9%
5. Stone Container, 161.1%

*Where'd you hear that?*
Forbes, Forbes 500s Annual Directory. Based on percentage change in assets over 1988.

## Corporations lagging in asset growth

1. Homestead Financial, with -47.5%
2. Northeast Savings FA, -34.2%
3. Meritor Savings Bank, -26.4%
4. SFFed Corp., -24.7%
5. Seamen's, -18.9%

*Where'd you hear that?*
Forbes, Forbes 500s Annual Directory. Based on percentage change of 1989 performance from 1988.

## Industrial companies with the highest return on assets

1. Lorillard, with 41.1%
2. Georgia Gulf, 40.6%
3. Sterling Chemical, 31.6%
4. UST, 29.9%
5. Lyondell Petrochemical, 29.5%
6. Marion Laboratories Inc., 29.0%
7. Merck, 22.1%
8. W. M. Wrigley, Jr., 21.3%
9. Vista Chemical, 21.2%
10. Coca-Cola Co., 20.8%

*Where'd you hear that?*
Fortune, Fortune 500 Largest U.S. Industrial Corporations. Based on 1989 percentage of returns on assets.

## Corporations with the highest profits

1. General Motors Corp., with $4,224.3 million
2. General Electric Co., $3,939.0
3. Ford Motor Co., $3,835.0
4. IBM, $3,758.0
5. Exxon Corp., $2,975.0
6. Philip Morris Cos., $2,946.0
7. AT & T, $2,697.0
8. Dow Chemical Co., $2,487.0
9. E. I. du Pont de Nemours & Co., $2,480.0
10. Texaco, $2,413.0

*Where'd you hear that?*
Forbes, Forbes 500s Annual Directory. Based on 1989 net profits, in millions of dollars.

## Corporations with the highest growth in profits

1. Continental Corp.
2. BHC Communications
3. Pacific Gas & Electric
4. Sun Co.
5. Unocal

*Where'd you hear that?*
Forbes, Forbes 500s Annual Directory. Based on percentage change in profits over 1988.

## Most profitable publicly-held corporations

1. Liz Claiborne, Inc., with 51.8%
2. Rollins, 47.2%
3. Price Co., 40.5%
4. The Limited Inc., 39.9%

# BUSINESS CLASS

# BUSINESS CLASS

5. Commerce Clearing House, 39.7%
6. Kellogg Co., 38.9%
7. General Motors EDS, 37.9%
8. Highland Superstores, 37.3%
9. Student Loan, 37.1%
10. Apple Computer Inc., 36.6%

*Where'd you hear that?*
Forbes, Annual Report on American Industry. Based on 10-year average return on equity, in percent.

## Top U.S. corporations in profits

1. General Motors Corp., with $4.2 billion
2. General Electric Co., $3.9
3. Ford Motor Co., $3.8
3. IBM, $3.8
5. Exxon Corp., $3.0
6. Philip Morris, $2.9
7. AT & T, $2.7
8. Dow Chemical Co., $2.5
8. Du Pont Co., $2.5
10. Texaco, $2.4

*Where'd you hear that?*
Business Week, The Business Week 1000. Based on 1989 profits, in billions of dollars.

## Industrial profit leaders for the 1980s

1. New York Times, 22.0%
2. Dow Jones, 20.0%
3. Dean Foods, 19.9%
4. Abbott Laboratories, 17.0%
5. H. J. Heinz, 14.8%
6. Sara Lee, 13.9%
7. Emerson Electric Co., 11.3%
8. Eli Lilly & Co., 11.1%
9. General Electric Co., 10.8%
9. American Home Products Corp., 10.8%

*Where'd you hear that?*
Fortune, Fortune 500 Largest U.S. Industrial Corporations. Based on percentage change from 1979 to 1989.

## Industrial corporations with the largest profit increases

1. Sun, with 1,300.0%
2. Pilgrim's Pride, 1.092.4%
3. Westmoreland and Coal, 661.9%
4. Maxxam, 568.5%
5. Amsted Industries, 475.2%
6. Arvin Industries Inc., 419.0%
7. Harnischfeger Industries, 389.5%
8. Gerber Products, 284.2%
9. Amerada Hess Corp., 283.5%
10. McCormick, 217.6%

*Where'd you hear that?*
Fortune, Fortune 500 Largest U.S. Industrial Corporations. Based on 1989 increase in profits, in percent.

## Industrial corporations with the largest profit decreases

1. Control Data Corp., with 40,123.5%
2. Prime Computer, 1,312.4%
3. Zenith Electronics, 684.6%
4. Mack Trucks, 683.3%
5. Finevest Foods, 657.9%

*Where'd you hear that?*
Fortune, Fortune 500 Largest U.S. Industrial Corporations. Based on 1989 decrease in profits, in percent.

## Corporations lagging in profit growth

1. Chevron Corp., with -85.8%
2. CBS Inc., -74.2%
3. UAL, -71.2%
4. Citicorp, -70.7%
5. Fund American Cos., -70.3%

# BUSINESS CLASS

*Where'd you hear that?*
Forbes, Forbes 500s Annual Directory. Based on percentage change of 1989 performance from 1988.

## Least admired corporations

1. Gibraltar Financial, with a rating of 2.24
2. Wang Laboratories, 3.08
3. Control Data Corp., 3.59
4. Meritor Financial Group, 3.61
5. Texas Air, 3.72
6. LTV Corp., 3.86
7. National Steel, 4.01
8. United Merchants & Manufacturers, 4.03
9. K-H Corp., 4.05
10. Unisys, 4.18

*Where'd you hear that?*
Fortune, America's Most Admired Corporations. Based on scores (0-10) derived from a survey of senior executives, outside directors, and financial analysts. Respondents ranked firms in their own industry on quality of management and products/services; innovation; long-term investment value; financial soundness; attraction and retention of talent; community and environmental responsibility; and use of assets.

## Biggest gains in reputation

1. BankAmerica, with a gain of 1.64
2. Texaco, 1.09
3. UST, 0.93
4. United Technologies, 0.85
5. American Brands Inc., 0.77
6. Tenneco, 0.75
7. American International Group, 0.68
8. Equitable Life Assurance, 0.65
9. American Standard, 0.63

9. Philip Morris, 0.63

*Where'd you hear that?*
Fortune, America's Most Admired Corporations. Based on point change on composite scores in surveys of senior executives, outside directors, and financial analysts for 1988 and 1989.

## Biggest money losers among U.S. corporations

1. RJR Nabisco Holdings, with $1,149,000,000
2. Control Data Corp., $680,400,000
3. Unisys, $639,300,000
4. Wang Laboratories, $424,300,000
5. Time Warner, $256,000,000
6. Fort Howard Paper Co., $239,400,000
7. Prime Computer, $230,200,000
8. Lone Star Technologies, $191,400,000
9. Henley Group Inc., $187,000,000
10. Hillsborough Holdings Corp., $186,300,000

*Where'd you hear that?*
Fortune, Fortune 500 Largest U.S. Industrial Corporations. Based on amount lost in sales, 1989.

## Biggest losses in reputation

1. RJR Nabisco, with a loss of -2.43
2. Wang Laboratories, -1.58
3. West Point-Pepperell, -1.46
4. Ohio Mattress, -1.45
5. Exxon Corp., -1.35
6. Interco, -1.20
7. Unisys, -1.15
8. Gibraltar Financial, -1.10
9. Mack Trucks, -0.99
10. Eastman Kodak Co., -0.77

# BUSINESS CLASS

*Where'd you hear that?*
Fortune, America's Most Admired Corporations. Based on point change on composite scores in surveys of senior executives, outside directors, and financial analysts for 1988 and 1989.

*Where'd you hear that?*
Fortune, America's Most Admired Corporations. Based on scores (0-10) derived from a survey of senior executives, outside directors, and financial analysts. Respondents ranked firms in their own industry.

## Corporations most admired for innovativeness

1. Merck, with a rating of 9.06
2. 3M, 8.53
3. Rubbermaid, 8.47

## Most admired corporations

1. Merck, with a rating of 8.90
2. Philip Morris, 8.78
3. Rubbermaid, 8.42
4. Procter & Gamble, 8.37
5. 3M, 8.21
6. PepsiCo, 8.16
6. Wal-Mart, 8.16
8. Coca-Cola Co., 8.15
9. Anheuser-Busch Cos. Inc., 7.96
10. Du Pont Co., 7.93

*Where'd you hear that?*
Fortune, America's Most Admired Corporations. Based on scores (0-10) derived from a survey of senior executives, outside directors, and financial analysts. Respondents ranked firms in their own industry on quality of management and products/services; innovation; long-term investment value; financial soundness; attraction and retention of talent; community and environmental responsibility; and use of assets.

*Where'd you hear that?*
Fortune, America's Most Admired Corporations. Based on scores (0-10) derived from a survey of senior executives, outside directors, and financial analysts. Respondents ranked firms in their own industry.

## Corporations most admired for community and environmental responsibility

1. Johnson & Johnson, with a rating of 8.23
2. Merck, 8.19
3. Du Pont Co., 7.99

*Where'd you hear that?*
Fortune, America's Most Admired Corporations. Based on scores (0-10) derived from a survey of senior executives, outside directors, and financial analysts. Respondents ranked firms in their own industry.

## Corporations most admired for attraction and retention of talent

1. Merck, with a rating of 8.89
2. Philip Morris, 8.82
3. 3M, 8.21

## Corporations most admired for long-term investment value

1. Philip Morris, with a rating of 9.42
2. Merck, 8.93
3. Berkshire Hathaway, 8.45

# BUSINESS CLASS

*Where'd you hear that?*
Fortune, America's Most Admired Corporations. Based on scores (0-10) derived from a survey of senior executives, outside directors, and financial analysts. Respondents ranked firms in their own industry.

## Corporations most admired for management quality

1. Philip Morris, with a rating of 9.42
2. Merck, 8.93
3. Berkshire Hathaway, 8.45

*Where'd you hear that?*
Fortune, America's Most Admired Corporations. Based on scores (0-10) derived from a survey of senior executives, outside directors, and financial analysts. Respondents ranked firms in their own industry.

## Corporations most admired for quality of products or services

1. Merck, with a rating of 9.18
2. Rubbermaid, 8.99
3. Philip Morris, 8.96

*Where'd you hear that?*
Fortune, America's Most Admired Corporations. Based on scores (0-10) derived from a survey of senior executives, outside directors, and financial analysts. Respondents ranked firms in their own industry.

## Most productive U.S industrial corporations by sales per employee

1. Lyondell Petrochemical, with $2,596,135
2. AG Processing, $1,561,293
3. Citgo Petroleum, $1,497,329
4. National Coop. Refinery Ass'n, $1,184,351
5. Louisiana Land & Exploration, $1,097,372
6. American Petrofina Inc., $913,548
7. Texaco, $874,525
8. Tosco, $857,452
9. Exxon Corp., $833,231
10. Georgia Gulf, $819,639

*Where'd you hear that?*
Fortune, Fortune 500 Largest U.S. Industrial Corporations. Based on 1989 sales per employee.

## Least productive U.S. industrial corporations by sales per employee

1. Seagate Technology, with $47,666
2. Kellwood Co., $50,245
3. Oxford Industries, $50,372
4. Russell, $50,659
5. Fruit of the Loom, $50,804

*Where'd you hear that?*
Fortune, Fortune 500 Largest U.S. Industrial Corporations. Based on 1989 sales per employee.

## Most productive U.S. industrial corporations by sales per dollar of stockholders' equity

1. Lyondell Petrochemical, $597.11
2. Reliance Electric, $128.27
3. Gillette Co., $54.99
4. American Standard, $49.28
5. National Gypsum, $37.58
6. Harvard Industries, $23.78
7. Thorn Apple Valley, $21.87
8. Lear Siegler Seating Corp., $20.55
9. Phillips-Van Heusen, $19.77
10. Cyclops Industries, $18.61

# BUSINESS CLASS

*Where'd you hear that?*
Fortune, Fortune 500 Largest U.S. Industrial Corporations. Based on sales per dollar of stockholders' equity.

## Least productive U.S. industrial corporations by sales per dollar of stockholders' equity

1. Berkshire Hathaway, with $.50
2. Seagold Vineyards Holding, $.71
3. Oryx Energy, $.83
4. St. Joe Paper, $.86
5. Penn Central, $1.00

*Where'd you hear that?*
Fortune, Fortune 500 Largest U.S. Industrial Corporations. Based on 1989 sales per dollar of stockholders' equity.

## Largest private companies in the U.S.

1. Cargill Inc., with $43,000 million
2. Koch Industries, $16,000
3. RJR Nabisco, $14,000
4. Safeway Stores, $13,612
5. Continental Grain Co., $13,500
6. United Parcel Service, $11,000
7. Mars, $8,541
8. Southland, $7,990
9. R. H. Macy & Co. Inc., $7,000
10. Supermarkets General, $5,962

*Where'd you hear that?*
Forbes, Largest Private Companies in the U.S. Based on revenues, in millions of dollars.

## Largest private companies ranked by sales

1. Continental Grain Co., with $15,100,000 thousand
2. United Parcel Service of America Inc., $11,000,000
3. Caltex Petroleum Corp., $9,100,000
4. Mars Inc., $7,360,000
5. United Parcel Service Inc. OH, $6,610,000
6. Supermarkets General Holdings Corp., $5,960,000
7. Supermarkets General Corp., $5,750,000
8. Star Enterprise, $5,470,000
9. Young & Rubicam Inc., $5,090,000
10. Kewit Peter Sons DE Corp., $4,920,000

*Where'd you hear that?*
Dun's Business Rankings, Dun & Bradstreet. Based on 1989 sales, in thousands of dollars.

## Largest private companies ranked by employment

1. United Parcel Service of America Inc., with 192,000
2. ARA Group Inc., 120,000
3. ARA Services Inc., 119,000
4. United Parcel Service. Inc. OH, 107,000
5. Prudential Insurance Co. of America, 93,400
6. HCA Hospital Corp. of America, 68,500
7. Farley Industries Inc., 65,000
8. United Parcel Service NY Corp., 64,100
9. Supermarkets General Corp., 53,000
9. Supermarkets General Holdings Corp., 53,000

*Where'd you hear that?*
Dun's Business Rankings, Dun & Bradstreet. Based on 1989 number of employees.

## America's fastest growing private companies

1. Cogentrix, with 96,716%
2. Ocean State Coordinated Health Services, 45,581%
3. CEBCOR, 20,803%
4. Adept Technology, 15,471%
5. Liuski International, 15,420%
6. Devon Direct Marketing & Advertising Inc., 11,974%
7. Bushman Press, 11,223%
8. OSP Consultants, 10,981%
9. Hall-Kimbrell Environmental Services, 10,774%
10. American Medical Imaging, 10,573%

*Where'd you hear that?*
Inc., America's Fastest Growing Private Companies. Based on sales growth, 1984-88, in percent.

## Largest takeovers of British quoted companies

1. Beecham Group PLC (target)/SmithKline (acquirer), for £4,665 million
2. Consolidated Gold Fields PLC (target)/Hanson PLC (acquirer), for £3,454
3. Gateway Corp. PLC (target)/Isosceles (acquirer), for £2,064
4. Plessey (target)/GEC Siemens (acquirer), for £2,006
5. Jaguar PLC (target)/Ford Motor Co. (acquirer), for £1,600
6. Pearl Assurance (target)/AMP (acquirer), for £1,240
7. Ward White (target)/Boots (acquirer), for £956
8. Morgan Grenfell (target)/Deutsche Bank (acquirer), for £950
9. Avis Europe (target)/Cilva Holdings (acquirer), for £896
10. DRG (target)/Pembridge (acquirer), for £697

*Where'd you hear that?*
Financial Times. Based on value, in millions of British pounds.

## Largest foreign acquisitions of U.S. interests

1. Beecham Group PLC (U.K.) acquired SmithKline Beckman Corp., for $8,279.3 million
2. Grand Metropolitan PLC (U.K.) acquired Pillsbury Co., $5,757.9
3. Sony Corp. (Japan) acquired Columbia Pictures Entertainment Inc., $3,477.8
4. Unilever NV (Netherlands) acquired Faberge cosmetics, toiletries, fragrances, $1,550.0
5. British Telecommunications PLC (U.K.) acquired McCaw Cellular Communications Inc. (20.04%), $1,372.4
6. Pechiney SA (France) acquired Triangle Industries Inc., $1,281.5
7. Dai-Ichi Kangyo Bank Ltd. (Japan) acquired CIT Group Holdings Inc., (60%) $1,280.0
8. Societe Nationale Elf Acquitaine (France) acquired Pennwalt Corp., $1,069.6
9. Polly Peck International PLC (U.K.) acquired Del Monte Tropical Fruit Co. (unit of RJR Nabisco), $875.0

# BUSINESS CLASS

# BUSINESS CLASS

10. Siemens AG (West Germany) acquired ROLM Corp. (manufacturing and development operations unit of IBM), $844.0

*Where'd you hear that?*
Mergers & Acquisitions, Mergers & Acquisitions Almanac & Index. Based on price, in millions of dollars.

## Largest U.S. acquisitions of foreign interests

1. Exxon Corp. acquired Texaco Canada Inc. (Canada), for $4,149.6 million
2. Stone Container Corp. acquired Consolidated-Bathurst Inc. (Canada), $2,203.5
3. PepsiCo Inc. acquired BSN SA (Walker's Crisps and Smith's Crisps) (France), $1,350.0
4. Newgateway PLC acquired Gateway Corp. PLC (increased stake to 33.89% from 10.4%) (U.K.), $1,123.6
5. Boone Co. (merchant bank controlled by T. Boone Pickens, Jr.) acquired Koito Manufacturing Co. (20.2%) (Japan), $800.0
6. Masco Corp. acquired Universal Furniture Ltd. (Hong Kong), $534.6
7. E. I. du Pont de Nemours & Co. acquired Howson-Algraphy (division of Vickers PLC (U.K.), $400.0
8. International Paper Co. acquired Aussedat Rey SA (France), $297.4
9. Southeastern Asset Management acquired Saatchi & Saatchi PLC (9.4%) (U.K.), $226.9

10. Owens-Corning Fiberglas Corp. acquired Fiberglas Canada Inc. (bought 50% to obtain full control) (Canada), $200.0

*Where'd you hear that?*
Mergers & Acquisitions, Mergers & Acquisitions Almanac & Index. Based on price, in millions of dollars.

## Countries most active in U.S. acquisitions

1. United Kingdom, with 158
2. Japan, 81
3. Canada, 76
4. West Germany, 28
5. Switzerland, 25

*Where'd you hear that?*
Mergers & Acquisitions, Mergers & Acquisitions Almanac & Index. Based on number of deals.

## Countries attracting most U.S. buyers

1. Canada, with 68
2. United Kingdom, 54
3. France, 17
4. Italy, 15
5. West Germany, 14

*Where'd you hear that?*
Mergers & Acquisitions, Mergers & Acquisitions Almanac & Index. Based on number of deals.

## Overseas industry areas attracting most U.S. buyers

1. Wholesale, with 22
2. Food and kindred products, 19
3. Business, professional, and social services, 16
3. Chemicals, 16
5. Machinery, 15
6. Transportation, 13

*Where'd you hear that?*
Mergers & Acquisitions, Mergers & Acquisitions Almanac & Index. Based on number of deals.

## Industry areas attracting most foreign buyers

1. Business, professional, and social services, with 38
2. Health care, 34
3. Media, 32
4. Electrical and electronic equipment, 31
5. Machinery, 26

*Where'd you hear that?*
Mergers & Acquisitions, Mergers & Acquisitions Almanac & Index. Based on numbers of deals.

## U.S. industries attracting the most foreign buyouts

1. Miscellaneous services, with 21
2. Printing & Publishing, 19
3. Electronics, 16
4. Chemicals, Paints & Coatings, 15
5. Banking & Finance, 13
6. Drugs, Medical supplies & Equipment, 12
6. Wholesale & Distribution, 12
8. Food processing, 11
8. Leisure & Entertainment, 11
10. Oil & Gas, 10

*Where'd you hear that?*
Mergerstat Review. Based on number of transactions in 1989.

## U.S. industries attracting the highest valued foreign buyouts

1. Leisure & Entertainment, with $4,023.4 million
2. Food processing, $3,925.1
3. Chemicals, Paints & Coatings, $3,203.9
4. Banking & Finance, $3,191.4
5. Printing & Publishing, $2,562.2
6. Toiletries & Cosmetics, $2,254.2
7. Miscellaneous services, $2,084.8
8. Fabricated metal products, $2,078.9
9. Communications, $1,912.0
10. Drugs, Medical supplies & Equipment, $1,679.9

*Where'd you hear that?*
Mergerstat Review. Based on 1989 total value, in millions of dollars.

## Countries with the most buyouts of U.S. companies

1. United Kingdom, with 69
2. Japan, 53
3. Canada, 50
4. West Germany, 18
5. France, 17
6. Netherlands, 14
7. Australia, 12
8. Switzerland, 8
9. Sweden, 7
10. South Africa, 6

*Where'd you hear that?*
Mergerstat Review. Based on number of transactions in 1989.

## Countries with the highest valued buyouts of U.S companies

1. Japan, with $10,373.0 million
2. United Kingdom, $7,845.1
3. France, $7,314.3
4. Netherlands, $3,216.0
5. Canada, $2,255.6
6. Sweden, $1,865.1
7. Switzerland, $1,711.1

# BUSINESS CLASS

# BUSINESS CLASS

8. Italy, $1,598.6
9. West Germany, $1,167.5
10. Australia, $1,121.1

*Where'd you hear that?*
Mergerstat Review. Based on 1989 total value, in millions of dollars.

## Industries attracting the most American buyers in 1989

1. Miscellaneous services, with 21
2. Wholesale & Distribution, 16
3. Retail, 12
4. Chemicals, Paints & Coatings, 11
4. Food processing, 11
4. Instruments & Photographic equipment, 11
7. Paper, 10
8. Industrial and farm equipment and machinery, 10
9. Brokerage, Investment & Management Consulting Services, 8
9. Mining & Minerals, 8

*Where'd you hear that?*
Mergerstat Review. Based on number of transactions in 1989.

## Industries attracting the highest valued American buyouts of foreign companies

1. Oil & gas, with $4,149.6 million
2. Retail, $3,927.7
3. Automobiles & trucks, $2,966.8
4. Paper, $2,659.4
5. Food processing, $1,646.0
6. Miscellaneous services, $636.0
7. Beverages, $614.0
8. Industrial and farm equipment and machinery, $595.5
9. Chemicals, Paints & Coatings, $594.2
10. Instruments & Photographic equipment, $545.6

*Where'd you hear that?*
Mergerstat Review. Based on 1989 total value, in millions of dollars.

## Countries with the most buyouts by U.S. companies

1. United Kingdom, with 71
2. Canada, 41
3. West Germany, 17
4. France, 16
5. Italy, 15
6. Australia, 13
7. Sweden, 8
8. Switzerland, 7
9. Netherlands, 4
9. Mexico, 4

*Where'd you hear that?*
Mergerstat Review. Based on number of transactions in 1989.

## Largest acquisitions of U.S. companies by foreign buyers

1. British Petroleum (buyer), Standard Oil Co. (seller), with $7,762.2 million
2. Campeau Corp. (buyer), Federated Department Stores Inc. (seller), $6,544.5
3. Grand Metropolitan PLC (buyer), Pillsbury Co. (seller), $5,635.6
4. Royal Dutch/Shell Group (buyer), Shell Oil Co. (seller), $5,467.9
5. B.A.T. Industries PLC (buyer), Farmers Group Inc. (seller), $5,168.8

*Where'd you hear that?*
Mergerstat Review. Based on price paid, in millions of dollars.

## BUSINESS CLASS

### Largest acquisitions of foreign companies by U.S. buyers

1. Amoco Corp. (buyer), Dome Petroleum Ltd. (seller), with $4,180.0 million
2. Exxon Corp. (buyer), Texaco Canada Inc. (seller), $4,149.6
3. Private Group Wasserstein Perella & Great APT (buyer), Gateway Corp. PLC seller), $3,280.0
4. Ford Motor Co. (buyer), Jaguar PLC (seller), $2,466.8
5. Sun Co. Inc. (buyer), Seagrams Co. Ltd. (seller), $2,300.0

*Where'd you hear that?*
Mergerstat Review. Based on price paid, in millions of dollars.

### Countries with the highest value of companies acquired by U.S. companies

1. United Kingdom, with $9,673.5 million
2. Canada, $7,318.2
3. France, $2,604.5
4. Australia, $667.3
5. Sweden, $569.0
6. Netherlands, $240.6
7. Japan, $178.6
8. Hungary, $150.0
9. New Zealand, $130.0
10. Israel, $65.0

*Where'd you hear that?*
Mergerstat Review. Based on 1989 total value, in millions of dollars.

### 10 most active industry areas by number of transactions

1. Business, professional, and social services, with 225
2. Media, 219
3. Banking, 213
4. Wholesale, 211
5. Health care, 181
6. Electrical and electronic equipment, 155
6. Computer and data processing services, 155
8. Machinery, 148
9. Retailing, 138
10. Food and tobacco products, 125

*Where'd you hear that?*
Mergers & Acquisitions, Mergers & Acquisitions Almanac & Index. Based on number of deals.

### 10 most active industry areas by dollar volume

1. Food and tobacco products, with $40,364.1 million
2. Health care, $38,177.1
3. Energy, $15,841.0
4. Media, $10,910.7
5. Transportation, $9,545.4
6. Electrical and electronic equipment, $8,897.3
7. Retailing, $8,302.4
8. Nonbank financial, $8,004.8
9. Banking, $6,709.4
10. Paper and packaging, $6,596.4

43

# BUSINESS CLASS

*Where'd you hear that?*
Mergers & Acquisitions, Mergers & Acquisitions Almanac & Index. Based on value, in millions of dollars.

### Leading industries in corporate buyouts by number of transactions, 1985-89

1. Banking & Finance, with 1,538
2. Miscellaneous services, 927
3. Wholesale & Distribution, 666
4. Computer Software, Supplies & Services, 630
5. Retail, 657
6. Brokerage, Investment, & Management Consulting Services, 272
7. Insurance, 353
8. Printing & Publishing, 441
9. Broadcasting, 430
10. Chemicals, Paints & Coatings, 383

*Where'd you hear that?*
Mergerstat Review. Based on number of transactions, 1985-89.

### Leading industries in corporate buyouts by dollar value paid

1. Drugs, Medical supplies & Equipment, with $34,556.9 million
2. Leisure & Entertainment, $24,368.0
3. Banking & Finance, $18,586.2
4. Retail, $10,181.8
5. Oil & Gas, $9,370.3
6. Broadcasting, $8,978.4
7. Food processing, $7,268.7
8. Paper, $7,164.7
9. Chemicals, Paints & Coatings, $7,107.7
10. Transportation, $6,975.7

*Where'd you hear that?*
Mergerstat Review. Based on 1989 dollar value paid in 1989, in millions of dollars.

### Leading industries in corporate buyouts by number of transactions

1. Banking & Finance, with 27
2. Broadcasting, 17
2. Retail, 17
4. Chemicals, Paints & Coatings, 15
4. Leisure & Entertainment, 15
6. Miscellaneous services, 14
7. Drugs, Medical supplies & Equipment, 13
8. Insurance, 12
9. Printing & Publishing, 11
9. Wholesale & Distribution, 11

*Where'd you hear that?*
Mergerstat Review. Based on number of transactions in 1989. All are for transactions of $100 million+.

### Largest corporate acquisitions in U.S. history

1. Kohlberg Kravis Roberts & Co. (buyer), RJR Nabisco (seller), $24,561.6 million
2. Chevron Corp. (buyer), Gulf Corp. (seller), $13,205.6
3. Phillip Morris Cos. (buyer), Kraft Inc. (seller), $13,099.8
4. Bristol-Myers Co. (buyer), Squibb Corp. (seller), $12,001.8
5. Time Inc. (buyer), Warner Communications Inc. (seller), $11,650.3

*Where'd you hear that?*
Mergerstat Review. Based on price paid, in millions of dollars.

44

## Largest acquisitions of publicly traded sellers in U.S. history

1. Kohlberg Kravis Roberts & Co. (buyer), RJR Nabisco (seller), $24,561.6 million
2. Chevron Corp. (buyer), Gulf Corp. (seller), $13,205.6
3. Phillip Morris Companies, Inc. (buyer), Kraft Inc. (seller), $13,099.8
4. Bristol-Myers Co. (buyer), Squibb Corp. (seller), $12,001.8
5. Time Inc. (buyer), Warner Communications Inc. (seller), $11,650.3

*Where'd you hear that?*
Mergerstat Review. Based on price paid, in millions of dollars.

## Largest statutory mergers in U.S. history

1. Beecham Group PLC (buyer), SmithKline Beckman Corp. (seller), $16,082.4 million
2. Santa Fe Industries Inc. (buyer), Southern Pacific Co. (seller), $5,099.1
3. Sovran Financial Corp. (buyer), Citizens & Southern Corp. (seller), $4,530.5
4. Connecticut General Corp. (buyer), INA Corp. (seller), $4,211.7
5. Kraft Inc. (buyer), Dart Industries Inc. (seller), $2,400.0

*Where'd you hear that?*
Mergerstat Review. Based on price paid, in millions of dollars.

# BUSINESS CLASS

## Largest corporate buyouts in history

1. Kohlberg Kravis Roberts & Co. (buyer), RJR Nabisco Inc. (seller), with $24,561.6 million
2. Beecham Group PLC - U.K. (buyer), SmithKline Beckman Corp. (seller), $16,082.4
3. Cheveron Corp. (buyer), Gulf Corp. (seller), $13,205.5
4. Phillip Morris Companies Inc. (buyer), Kraft Inc. (seller), $13,099.8
5. Bristol-Myers Co. (buyer), Squibb Corp. (seller), $12,001.8
6. Time Inc. (buyer), Warner Communications Inc. (seller), $11,650.3
7. Texaco Inc. (buyer), Getty Oil Co. (seller), $10,128.9
8. Du Pont Co. (buyer), Conoco Inc. (seller), $8,039.8
9. British Petroleum Co. - U.K. (buyer), Standard Oil Co. (seller), $7,762.2
10. U.S. Steel Corp. (buyer), Marathon Oil Corp. (seller), $6,618.5

*Where'd you hear that?*
Mergerstat Review. Based on approximate price paid, in millions of dollars.

# BUSINESS CLASS

### Largest acquisitions of privately owned sellers in U.S. history

1. General Motors Corp. (buyer), Hughes Aircraft Co. (seller), $5,025.0 million
2. Shell Oil Co. (buyer), Belridge Oil Co. (seller), $3,653.0
3. News Corp. Ltd. (buyer), Triangle Publications Inc. (seller), $3,000.0
4. Private Group (led by Tele-Comm, Inc.) (buyer), SCI Holdings Inc. (seller), $1,700.0
5. Rockwell International Corp. (buyer), Allen-Bradley Co. (seller), $1,650.0

*Where'd you hear that?*
Mergerstat Review. Based on price paid, in millions of dollars.

### Largest cancellations of acquisitions deals in U.S. history

1. Private Group - led by Shearson Lehman (buyer), RJR Nabisco Inc. (seller), $25,237.6 million
2. Private Group - led by Carl Icahn (buyer), Texaco Inc. (seller), $14,571.1
3. Paramount Communications Inc. (buyer), Time Inc. (seller), $11,395.4
4. Henley Group Inc. (buyer), Santa Fe Southern Pacific Corp. (seller), $9,897.7
5. Olympia & York Developments Ltd. (buyer), Santa Fe Southern Pacific Corp. (seller), $9,897.7

*Where'd you hear that?*
Mergerstat Review. Based on price offered, in millions of dollars.

### Largest non-oil corporate acquisition deals in U.S. history

1. Kohlberg Kravis Roberts & Co. (buyer), RJR Nabisco (seller), $24,561.6 million
2. Phillip Morris Cos., Inc. (buyer), Kraft Inc. (seller), $13,099.8
3. Bristol-Myers Co. (buyer), Squibb Corp. (seller), $12,001.8
4. Time Inc. (buyer), Warner Communications Inc. (seller), $11,650.3
5. Campeau Corp. (buyer), Federated Department Stores, Inc. (seller), $6,655.5

*Where'd you hear that?*
Mergerstat Review. Based on price paid, in millions of dollars.

### Best mergers and acquisitions of the decade

1. Dow Chemical/Merrell, Texize (1981, 1985)
2. General Electric/RCA (1986)
3. Grand Metropolitan/Heublein (1987)
4. May Department Stores/Associated Dry Goods (1986)
5. News Corp./Metromedia (1986)
6. Quaker Oats/Stokely-Van Camp (1984)
7. Triangle Industries/National, American CAM (1985, 1986)
8. UAL/Pan Am Pacific Routes (1986)
9. Unilever/Chesebrough-Pond's (1987)
10. Wells Fargo/Crocker National (1986)

# BUSINESS CLASS

*Where'd you hear that?*
Business Week. Based on subjective and objective judgment of *Business Week* editors.

## Leaders in corporate buyouts, 1980-1989

1. Alco Standard Corp., with 59
2. General Electric Co., 52
2. Merrill Lynch & Co., 52
4. Borden Inc., 51
5. ConAgra Inc., 50
6. Security Pacific Corp., 47
7. Kraft Inc., 45
8. American Express Co., 43
8. Banc One Corp., 43
10. W. R. Grace & Co., 41

*Where'd you hear that?*
Mergerstat Review. Based on number of transactions, 1980-89.

## States with the most corporate buyouts

1. New York, with 1,353
2. California, 1,000
3. Illinois, 581
4. Pennsylvania, 513
5. Ohio, 486
6. Texas, 464
7. New Jersey, 361
8. Connecticut, 338
9. Massachusetts, 291
10. Florida, 283

*Where'd you hear that?*
Mergerstat Review. Based on number of buyers, 1985-89.

## States with the most corporate mergers and acquisitions

1. California, with 1,323
2. New York, 1,006
3. Texas, 585
4. Illinois, 519
5. Florida, 426
5. Pennsylvania, 426
7. New Jersey, 394
8. Ohio, 390
9. Massachusetts, 388
10. Michigan, 322

*Where'd you hear that?*
Mergerstat Review. Based on number of sellers, 1985-89.

## *Worst mergers and acquisitions of the decade*

1. Baldwin United/MGIC (1982)
2. Beatrice/Esmark (1984)
3. Blue Arrow/Manpower (1987)
4. Campeau/Allied Stores, Federated Department Stores (1986, 1988)
5. Fluor/St. Joe Minerals (1981)
6. Honeywell/Sperry Aerospace (1986)
7. LTV/Republic Steel (1984)
8. Pan Am/National Airlines (1980)
9. Republicbank/Interfirst (1987)
10. Sohio/Kennecott (1981)

*Where'd you hear that?*
Business Week. Based on subjective and objective judgment of *Business Week* editors.

## Most aggressive divestitures, 1980-89

1. Beatrice Cos. Inc., with 55
2. General Electric Co., 45
3. Allied-Signal Inc., 43
4. Allegheny International Inc., 39
5. ITT Corp, 36
6. Textron, 29
7. Westinghouse Electric Inc., 28
7. WCI Holding Corp., 28
7. Armco Inc., 26

47

# BUSINESS CLASS

10. Control Data Corp., 25

*Where'd you hear that?*
Mergerstat Review. Based on number of divestitures, in 1980-89.

## Largest divestitures in the 1980s

1. Ford Motor Co. (buyer), Paramount Communications Inc. (seller), with $3,350.0 million
2. BSN SA (buyer), Kohlberg Roberts & Co. (seller), $2,500.0
3. Broken Hill Proprietary Co. (buyer), General Electric Co. (seller), $2,400.0
4. General Electric Co. (buyer), Borg Warner Corp. (seller), $2,310.0
5. Sun Co. Inc. (buyer), Seagram Co. Ltd. (seller), $2,300.0

*Where'd you hear that?*
Mergerstat Review. Based on price paid, in millions of dollars.

## 10 most active divesting industry areas

1. Energy, with $7,958.8 million
2. Media, $7,407.2
3. Nonbank financial, $5,731.5
4. Food and tobacco products, $4,339.4
5. Electrical and electronic equipment, $3,667.6
6. Machinery, $2,717.9
7. Insurance, $2,355.7
8. Retailing, $2,215.7
9. Consumer products, $1,998.7
10. Chemicals, $1,932.8

*Where'd you hear that?*
Mergers & Acquisitions, Mergers & Acquisitions Almanac & Index. Based on volume, in millions of dollars, for 1989.

## 10 most active divesting industry areas

1. Media, with 101
2. Electrical and electronic equipment, 70
3. Health care, 59
4. Energy, 57
5. Machinery, 56
5. Business, professional, and social services, 56
7. Wholesaling, 53
8. Food and tobacco products, 52
9. Retailing, 49
10. Computer and data processing services, 43

*Where'd you hear that?*
Mergers & Acquisitions, Mergers & Acquisitions Almanac & Index. Based on number of transactions, for 1989.

## Industries with the most divestitures

1. Miscellaneous Services, with 62
2. Broadcasting, 55
2. Retail, 55
4. Banking & Finance, 48
5. Printing & Publishing, 43
6. Brokerage, Investment & Management Consulting Services, 41
6. Chemicals, Paints & Coatings, 41
8. Food processing, 39
9. Computer Software, Supplies & Services, 38
9. Insurance, 38

*Where'd you hear that?*
Mergerstat Review. Based on number of divestitures in 1989.

## Industries with the most divestitures as a percentage of all activity

1. Automobiles & trucks, with 89%
2. Automotive products & accessories, 76%
3. Broadcasting, 75%
4. Aerospace, aircraft & defense, 69%
5. Food processing, 67%
6. Instruments & Photographic equipment, 63%
6. Mining & Minerals, 63%
8. Toiletries & Cosmetics, 60%
8. Primary metal processing, 60%
10. Electrical equipment, 58%

*Where'd you hear that?*
Mergerstat Review. Based on divestitures as a percentage of all activity in 1989.

## Largest unit management buyouts ever

1. Private group led by Kohlberg Kravis Roberts & Co. (buyer), Allied Corp. ( seller), for $1,700.0 million
2. Private group led by management of Mobil Corp. (buyer), Montgomery Ward & Co., $1,500.0
3. Private group led by division management of Exxon Corp. (buyer), Reliance Electric Co. (seller), $1,350.0
4. Private group led by Ford Motor Co. and Hertz management (buyer), Allegis Corp. (Hertz Corp.) (seller), $1,300.0
5. Private group led by Kohlberg Kravis Roberts & Co., $1,251.0

*Where'd you hear that?*
Mergerstat Review. Based on purchase price, in millions of dollars.

## Largest unit management buyout cancellations

1. Private group led by Shearson Lehman (buyer), RJR Nabisco Inc. (seller), for $25,237.6 million
2. Private group led by Carl Icahn (buyer), Texaco Inc. (seller), $14,571.1
3. Paramount Communications Inc. (buyer), Time Inc. (seller), $11,395.4
4. Henley Group Inc. (buyer), Santa Fe Southern Pacific Corp. (seller), $9,897.7
4. Olympia & York Developments Ltd. (buyer), Santa Fe Southern Pacific Corp. (seller), $9,897.7

*Where'd you hear that?*
Mergerstat Review. Based on purchase price, in millions of dollars.

## Biggest deals of the decade

1. RJR Nabisco, with $24.7 billion
2. Beatrice Cos. Inc., $6.3
3. Borg-Warner Corp., $4.4
4. Safeway, $4.2
5. Southland, $3.9
6. Montgomery Ward, $3.8
7. Owens-Illinois, $3.7

# BUSINESS CLASS

# BUSINESS CLASS

8. Fort Howard Paper Co., $3.6
9. R. H. Macy & Co. Inc., $3.5
10. Burlington Industries, $2.9

*Where'd you hear that?*
Business Week. Based on value of deal, in billions of dollars.

## Industries rated absolutely essential

1. Food, with 71%
2. Electric power, 62%
3. Banking, 57%
4. Oil, 50%
5. Steel, 41%
6. Automobiles, 37%
7. Nuclear Power, 27%
8. Insurance, 25%
9. Publishing, 22%
10. Cosmetics, 6%

*Where'd you hear that?*
Adweek's Marketing Week. Based on percentage of respondents to a Roper Organization survey.

## Industries with the highest confidence of American consumers

1. Drugs, with 31%
2. Banks, 30%
3. Automobiles, 29%
3. Food/grocery, 29%
5. Appliances, 27%
6. Clothing, 19%
7. Computers, 15%
8. Airlines, 13%
8. Publishing, 13%
10. Entertainment, 11%

*Where'd you hear that?*
Wall Street Journal. Based on percentage of respondents saying they had the most confidence in each industry; respondents were allowed to pick up to four industries.

## Top industries by employees

1. Electronics, with 1,551,991
2. Motor vehicles and parts, 1,528,850
3. Aerospace, 1,169,502
4. Food, 1,104,407
5. Computers (includes office equipment), 955,423
6. Chemicals, 854,259
7. Petroleum refining, 607,297
8. Forest products, 590,497
9. Industrial and farm equipment, 564,680
10. Scientific and Photographic equipment, 542,390

*Where'd you hear that?*
Fortune, Fortune 500 Largest U.S. Industrial Corporations. Based on employees in 1989.

## Top industries by sales

1. Petroleum refining, with $359,900
2. Motor vehicles and parts, $295,064
3. Food, $209,480
4. Electronics, $184,686
5. Chemicals, $173,509
6. Computers (includes office equipment), $136,424
7. Aerospace, $132,427
8. Forest products, $106,799
9. Industrial and Farm equipment, $73,644
10. Scientific and Photographic equipment, $69,425

# BUSINESS CLASS

*Where'd you hear that?*
Fortune, Fortune 500 Largest U.S. Industrial Corporations. Based on 1989 sales, in millions of dollars.

## Top industries by sales per employee

1. Petroleum refining, with $537,026
2. Mining, Crude-oil production, $314,563
3. Tobacco, $226,636
4. Food, $211,323
5. Soaps, Cosmetics, $209,117
6. Chemicals, $205,813
7. Metals, $195,750
8. Beverages, $194,426
9. Forest products, $177,000
10. Building materials, $155,000

*Where'd you hear that?*
Fortune, Fortune 500 Largest U.S. Industrial Corporations. Based on 1989 sales per employee. The Fortune 500 median is $146,887.

## Weakest industries by sales per employee

1. Apparel, with $58,232
2. Textiles, $80,901
3. Furniture, $95,280
4. Electronics, $101,190
5. Transportation equipment, $109,539
6. Industrial and Farm equipment, $112,091
7. Scientific and Photographic equipment, $112,718
8. Metal products, $114,869
9. Motor vehicles and parts, $117,941
10. Aerospace, $121,002

*Where'd you hear that?*
Fortune, Fortune 500 Largest U.S. Industrial Corporations. Based on 1989 sales per employee. The Fortune 500 median is $146,887.

## *Industries with the lowest confidence of American consumers*

1. Airlines, with 43%
2. Insurance, 27%
3. Banks, 23%
4. Oil and gas, 22%
4. Stockbrokers, 22%
6. Automobiles, 19%
7. Fast food, 18%
8. Drugs, 13%
8. Publishing, 13%
10. Toy manufacturers, 10%

*Where'd you hear that?*
Wall Street Journal. Based on percentage of respondents saying they had the least confidence in each industry; respondents were allowed to pick up to four industries.

## Top industries by return on sales

1. Pharmaceuticals, with 13.0%
2. Mining, Crude-oil production, 9.6%
3. Beverages, 8.1%
4. Forest products, 7.1%
5. Publishing, printing, 6.5%
6. Metal products, 6.2%
7. Chemicals, 6.1%
8. Computers (includes office equipment), 5.9%
9. Tobacco, 5.4%
10. Metals, 4.8%

# BUSINESS CLASS

*Where'd you hear that?*
Fortune, Fortune 500 Largest U.S. Industrial Corporations. Based on 1989 return on sales, in percent. The Fortune 500 median is 4.7%.

## Weakest industries by return on sales

1. Textiles, with 1.9%
2. Building materials, 2.2%
3. Food, 2.6%
4. Motor vehicles and parts, 2.7%
5. Transportation equipment, 3.0%
6. Petroleum refining, 3.3%
6. Aerospace, 3.3%
8. Industrial and farm equipment, 3.6%
9. Rubber and Plastics products, 4.1%
10. Electronics, 4.2%

*Where'd you hear that?*
Fortune, Fortune 500 Largest U.S. Industrial Corporations. Based on 1989 return on sales, in percent. The Fortune 500 median is 4.7%.

## Industries with the largest changes in sales

1. Soaps, Cosmetics, with 16.6%
2. Tobacco, 15.7%
3. Apparel, 14.2%
4. Petroleum refining, 13.8%
5. Furniture, 12.4%
6. Computers (includes office equipment), 10.1%
7. Pharmaceuticals, 10.0%
7. Beverages, 10.0%
9. Transportation equipment, 9.8%
10. Electronics, 8.7%

*Where'd you hear that?*
Fortune, Fortune 500 Largest U.S. Industrial Corporations. Based on 1989 increase in sales, in percent.

## Industries with the smallest change in sales

1. Motor vehicles and parts, with 2.4%
2. Aerospace, 3.0%
3. Mining, Crude-oil production, 3.6%
4. Rubber and Plastics products, 4.8%
5. Chemicals, 5.2%
6. Textiles, 5.7%
7. Building materials, 5.8%
8. Publishing, Printing, 6.9%
9. Metal products, 7.0%
10. Forest products, 7.2%

*Where'd you hear that?*
Fortune, Fortune 500 Largest U.S. Industrial Corporations. Based on 1989 increase in sales, in percent.

## Top industries by total return to investors

1. Mining, Crude-oil production, with 51.7%
2. Petroleum refining, 43.8%
3. Beverages, 41.0%
4. Soaps, Cosmetics, 39.7%
5. Pharmaceuticals, 37.6%
6. Food, 27.9%
7. Apparel, 25.3%
8. Metal products, 24.9%
9. Forest products, 19.8%
10. Chemicals, 17.6%

*Where'd you hear that?*
Fortune, Fortune 500 Largest U.S. Industrial Corporations. Based on 1989 total return to investors, in percent. The Fortune 500 median is 17.5%.

## Weakest industries by total return to investors

1. Computers (includes office equipment), with -17.1%
2. Transportation equipment, -10.4%
3. Motor vehicles and parts, -8.3%
4. Industrial and Farm equipment, -2.2%
5. Rubber and Plastics products, -1.6%
6. Furniture, 1.8%
7. Aerospace, 7.8%
8. Metals, 10.2%
9. Scientific and Photographic equipment, 11.9%
10. Tobacco, 12.3%

*Where'd you hear that?*
Fortune, Fortune 500 Largest U.S. Industrial Corporations. Based on 1989 total return to investors, in percent. The Fortune 500 median is 17.5%.

## Weakest industries by total return to investors, 1979-89 annual average

1. Mining, Crude-oil Production, with 6.5%
2. Computers (includes office equipment), 8.6%
3. Industrial and Farm equipment, 8.7%
4. Metals, 10.1%
5. Building materials, 11.4%
6. Aerospace, 12.0%
7. Scientific and Photographic equipment, 12.1%
8. Petroleum refining, 12.9%
9. Electronics, 13.0%
10. Motor vehicles and parts, 15.4%

*Where'd you hear that?*
Fortune, Fortune 500 Largest U.S. Industrial Corporations. Based on total return to investors, 1979-89 annual average, in percent. The Fortune 500 median is 16.3%.

# BUSINESS CLASS

## *Top industries by total return to investors, 1979-89 annual average*

1. Rubber and Plastics products, with 29.2%
2. Food, 27.1%
3. Beverages, 26.7%
4. Apparel, 24.0%
5. Tobacco, 22.7%
6. Publishing, Printing, 22.2%
7. Pharmaceuticals, 22.1%
7. Soaps, Cosmetics, 22.1%
9. Furniture, 21.9%
10. Textiles, 21.4%

*Where'd you hear that?*
Fortune, Fortune 500 Largest U.S. Industrial Corporations. Based on total return to investors, 1979-89 annual average, in percent. The Fortune 500 median is 16.3%.

## Most profitable industry groups

1. Health industry, with 18.7%
2. Food, drink, and tobacco companies, 18.4%
3. Entertainment and information industries, 17.3%
4. Business services and supplies companies, 16.7%
4. Retailers, 16.7%
6. Aerospace and defense industries, 15.7%
7. Consumer nondurables companies, 15.2%

# BUSINESS CLASS

8. Chemicals industry, 15.0%
9. Insurance industry, 14.4%
10. Financial services companies, 14.3%

*Where'd you hear that?*
Forbes, Annual Report on American Industry. Based on 10-year average return on equity. Rankings are based on performance of publicly held corporations.

## Top industries by profits

1. Petroleum refining, with $16,040 million
2. Chemicals, $11,680
3. Electronics, $9,960
4. Motor vehicles and parts, $9,353
5. Pharmaceuticals, $8,281
6. Food, $6,933
7. Forest products, $6,923
8. Computers (includes office equipment), $5,660
9. Aerospace, $4,296
10. Beverages, $4,136

*Where'd you hear that?*
Fortune, Fortune 500 Largest U.S. Industrial Corporations. Based on 1989 profits, in millions of dollars.

## Industries with the biggest increases in profits

1. Pharmaceuticals, with 19.6%
2. Beverages, 18.3%
3. Textiles, 15.3%
4. Food, 14.0%
5. Electronics, 10.0%
6. Metals, 9.7%
7. Publishing, Printing, 8.6%
8. Soaps, Cosmetics, 8.5%
8. Tobacco, 8.5%
10. Mining, Crude-oil production, 7.0%

*Where'd you hear that?*
Fortune, Fortune 500 Largest U.S. Industrial Corporations. Based on 1989 increases in profits, in percent.

## Industries with the biggest decreases in profits

1. Motor vehicles and parts, with a decrease of 25.0%
2. Aerospace, 12.5%
3. Petroleum refining, 11.8%
4. Transportation equipment, 9.4%
5. Computers (includes office equipment), 9.0%
6. Industrial and Farm equipment, 8.6%
7. Forest products, 5.3%
8. Furniture, 4.8%
9. Rubber and Plastics products, 2.2%

*Where'd you hear that?*
Fortune, Fortune 500 Largest U.S. Industrial Corporations. Based on 1989 decreases in profits, in percent.

## Top industries by assets

1. Motor vehicles and parts, with $414,076 million
2. Petroleum refining, $349,954
3. Electronics, $242,249
4. Food, $171,288
5. Chemicals, $164,519
6. Computers (includes office equipment), $140,446
7. Forest products, $115,809
8. Aerospace, $107,192
9. Scientific and Photographic equipment, $84,687
10. Industrial and Farm equipment, $72,563

*Where'd you hear that?*
Fortune, Fortune 500 Largest U.S. Industrial Corporations. Based on 1989 assets, in millions of dollars.

**BUSINESS CLASS**

**Top industries by return on assets**

1. Pharmaceuticals, with 14.0%
2. Furniture, 7.9%
3. Soaps, Cosmetics, 7.8%
4. Publishing, Printing, 7.7%
5. Forest products, 7.3%
6. Beverages, 6.8%
7. Metal products, 6.7%
7. Apparel, 6.7%
9. Chemicals, 6.5%
10. Rubber and Plastics products, 6.3%

*Where'd you hear that?*
Fortune, Fortune 500 Largest U.S. Industrial Corporations. Based on 1989 return on assets, in percent. The Fortune 500 median is 5.9%.

**Weakest industries by return on assets**

1. Motor vehicles and parts, with 2.5%
2. Building materials, 2.7%
3. Textiles, 3.0%
4. Industrial and farm equipment, 3.3%
5. Transportation equipment, 3.5%
6. Aerospace, 3.7%
6. Mining, Crude-oil production, 3.7%
8. Petroleum refining, 4.1%
9. Computers (includes office equipment), 5.0%
10. Food, 5.2%

*Where'd you hear that?*
Fortune, Fortune 500 Largest U.S. Industrial Corporations. Based on 1989 return on assets, in percent. The Fortune 500 median is 5.9%.

**Top industries by market value**

1. Petroleum refining, with $217,340
2. Pharmaceuticals, $156,742
3. Electronics, $141,070
4. Food, $120,587
5. Computers (includes office equipment), $114,543
6. Chemicals, $99,753
7. Motor vehicles and parts, $63,049
8. Forest products, $59,827
9. Publishing, Printing, $57,992
10. Scientific and photographic equipment, $55,811

*Where'd you hear that?*
Fortune, Fortune 500 Largest U.S. Industrial Corporations. Based on 1989 market value, in millions of dollars.

**Largest manufacturing industries**

1. Petroleum refining, with $207,960 million
2. Electronic computing equipment, $139,902
3. Motor vehicles and car bodies, $116,209
4. Miscellaneous plastic products, $64,474
5. Motor vehicle parts and accesories, $64,460
6. Radio and TV communication equipment, $48,648
7. Meat packing plants, $44,555
8. Semiconductors and related devices, $42,873
9. Steel mill products, $39,862
10. Industrial organic chemicals, $39,149

# BUSINESS CLASS

*Where'd you hear that?*
Facts & Figures of the U.S. Plastics Industry, Society of the Plastics Industry. Based on 1988 value of shipment, in millions of 1982 dollars.

### Best small businesses

1. J. Baker, 100%
2. Allwaste, 77.1%
3. Golden Valley Microwave, 59.1%
4. Tech-Ops Landauer, 54.5%
5. Franklin Resources, 53.5%
6. Quiksilver, 52.7%
7. Colonial Group, 50.9%
8. One Price Clothing Store, 47.4%
9. International Dairy Queen, 42.8%
10. Shorewood Packaging, 39.9%

*Where'd you hear that?*
Forbes. Based on 5-year average return on equity, in percent. All are publicly-traded companies.

### Fastest-growing small public companies

1. Network Equipment Technologies, with 413%
2. Digital Microwave, 325%
3. Encore Computer, 323%
4. Cirrus Logic, 312%
5. Rally's, 295%
6. Brajdas, 270%
7. Oxford Energy, 265%
8. Osicom Technologies, 253%
8. Adtec, 253%
10. Digi International, 243%

*Where'd you hear that?*
Inc., Inc. 100. Based on compound annual growth, 1985-89, in percent.

### Top public-sector growth companies

1. Rexhall Industries
2. Cabletron Systems
3. T2 Medical
4. American Power Conversion
5. Care Group
6. Tseng Laboratories
7. DIGI International
8. Adobe Systems
9. Datakey
10. Catalina Lighting

*Where'd you hear that?*
Business Week, Growth Companies. Based on three-year results in sales growth, earnings growth, and return on invested capital.

### Fastest growing companies

1. MMI Medical, with 212%
2. Horizon Industries, 147%
3. Gish Biomedical, 144%
4. Freeport-McMoRan, 138%
5. Trinity Industries, 136%
6. Applied Materials, 134%
7. Ohio Art, 131%
8. United Fire & Casualty, 123%
9. Pope & Talbot, 115%
10. Duriron, 112%

*Where'd you hear that?*
Financial World. Based on 5-year annual earnings per share growth rate, in percent.

# BUSINESS CLASS

## Fasting-growing small public companies

1. Newtwork Equipment Technologies, with 413%
2. Digital Microwave, 325%
2. Encore Computer, 323%
4. Cirrus Logic, 312%
5. Rally's, 295%
6. Brajdas, 270%
7. Oxford Energy, 265%
8. Osicom Technologies, 253%
8. Adtec, 253%
10. Digi International, 243%

*Where'd you hear that?*
Inc., Inc. 100. Based on compound annual growth, 1985-89, in percent.

## Most successful small growth companies

1. Rexhall Industries
2. Cabletron Systems Inc.
3. T2 Medical
4. American Power Conversion Corp.
5. Care Group
6. Tseng Laboratories
7. Digi International
8. Adobe Systems Inc.
9. Datakey
10. Catalina Lighting

*Where'd you hear that?*
Business Week, Growth Companies. Based on 1989 sales and earnings, growth computations, and return on capital.

## Leading growth companies by profitability

1. Care Group, with 61.8%
2. Rexhall Industries, 60.0%
3. Yes Clothing, 56.3%
4. National Media, 54.5%
5. Lund International Holdings, 53.3%

*Where'd you hear that?*
Business Week, Growth Companies. Based on percentage growth in average annual rate of profitability over last three years.

## Leading growth companies by sales

1. CSS Industries, with $146.9 million
2. Shorewood Packaging, $137.7
3. Adobe Systems Inc., $133.0
4. Stevens Graphics, $132.2
5. Superior Teletec, $130.9

*Where'd you hear that?*
Business Week, Growth Companies. Based on 1989 sales, in millions of dollars.

## America's fastest growing private companies

1. Cogentrix, with 96,716%
2. Ocean State Coordinated Health Services, 45,581%
3. CEBCOR, 20,803%
4. Adept Technology, 15,471%
5. Liuski International, 15,420%
6. Devon Direct Marketing & Advertising Inc., 11,974%
7. Bushman Press, 11,223%
8. OSP Consultants, 10,981%
9. Hall-Kimbrell Environmental Services, 10,774%
10. American Medical Imaging, 10,573%

*Where'd you hear that?*
Inc., America's Fastest Growing Private Companies. Based on sales growth, 1984-88, in percent.

# BUSINESS CLASS

**Leading growth companies by sales growth**

1. T2 Medical, with 177.1%
2. Network General, 144.8%
3. Rexhall Industries, 141.5%
4. American Power Conversion Corp., 139.2%
5. Software Toolworks, 130.4%

*Where'd you hear that?*
Business Week, Growth Companies. Based on percentage growth in average annual rate of sales, 1986-89.

**Leading growth companies by earnings**

1. Rayonier Timberlands, with $70.3 million
2. Adobe Systems Inc., $36.9
3. Cabletron Systems Inc., $22.5
4. Sanford, $21.8
5. Software Publishing, $19.6

*Where'd you hear that?*
Business Week, Growth Companies. Based on 1989 earnings, in millions of dollars.

**Leading growth companies by earnings growth**

1. Gish Biomedical, with 736.0%
2. Wietek, 531.9%
3. Serv-Tech, 397.9%
4. Oregon Metallurgical, 379.9%
5. Hurco Cos., 279.8%

*Where'd you hear that?*
Business Week, Growth Companies. Based on percentage growth in average annual rate of earnings, 1986-89.

**Leading growth companies by market value**

1. Adobe Systems Inc., with $773 million
2. Total System Services, $471
3. Rayonier Timberlands, $470
4. BMC Software, $422
5. Diagnostic Products, $416

*Where'd you hear that?*
Business Week, Growth Companies. Based on 1989 market value, in millions of dollars.

**Most active venture capital companies**

1. Warburg, Pincus Ventures Inc., with $644.00 million
2. First Chicago Venture Capital/First Capital Corp. of Chicago (SBIC), $246.01
3. Aeneas Venture Corp./Harvard Management Co. Inc., $202.20
4. Schroder Ventures, $164.24
5. BancBoston Capital Inc./BancBoston Ventures Inc. (SBIC), $144.76
6. Security Pacific Capital Corp./First SBIC of California, $120.42
7. Morgan Capital Corp./Morgan Investment Corp. (SBIC), $100.19
8. Clinton Capital Corp. (SBIC)/Columbia Capital Corp. (MESBIC), $98.13
9. Chemical Venture Partners/Chemical Venture Capital Associates LP (SBIC), $95.10

10. Boston Ventures Management Inc./Boston Ventures LP, $91.99

*Where'd you hear that?*
Venture, Venture Capital 100. Based on total 1988 investments, in millions of dollars.

## Top foreign companies in research and development spending

1. Siemens, with $3,684 million
2. Hitachi Ltd., $2,917
3. Matsushita Electric Industrial, $2,492
4. Philips' Gloeilampenfabrieken, $2,154
5. Fujitsu Ltd., $1,928
6. CIE Generale D'Electricite, $1,806
7. Toshiba, $1,799
8. Nippon Telegraph & Telephone, $1,731
8. NEC, $1,731
10. Honda Motor Co. Ltd., $1,731

*Where'd you hear that?*
Business Week. Based on r & D spending, in millions of U.S. dollars.

## Companies spending the most on research and development

1. General Motors Corp., with, $5,247 million
2. IBM, $5,201
3. Ford Motor Co., $3,167
4. AT & T, $2,652
5. Digital Equipment Corp., $1,525
6. Du Pont Co., $1,387
7. General Electric Co., $1,334
8. Hewlett-Packard Co., $1,269
9. Eastman Kodak Co., $1,253
10. United Technologies, $957

*Where'd you hear that?*
Business Week. Based on total 1989 R & D spending, in millions of dollars.

## U.S. companies with the highest research and development spending

1. IBM, with $5,925 million
2. Digital Equipment Corp., $1,307
3. Hewlett-Packard Co., $1,019
4. Xerox, $794
5. Unisys, $713
6. Motorola, $665
7. General Motors Hughes Electronics, $551
8. Texas Instruments, $494
9. NCR, $416
10. Control Data Corp., $336

*Where'd you hear that?*
Electronic Business. Based on 1988 total research and development spending, in millions of dollars.

## Companies spending the most on research and development as a percentage of sales

1. Chiron, with 108.9%
2. Genetics Institute, 92.6%
3. Centocor, 63.0%
4. Daisy Systems, 40.7%
5. Alza, 39.6%
6. Genentech, 38.0%
7. Amgen, 29.5%
8. Continuum, 29.1%
9. Phoenix Technologies, 28.2%
10. LTX, 26.7%

*Where'd you hear that?*
Business Week. Based on 1989 R & D expenditures as a percentage of sales.

**BUSINESS CLASS**

# BUSINESS CLASS

### Companies spending the most on research and development per employee

1. Chiron, with $84,575
2. Centocor, $82,460
3. Genentech, $81,454
4. Genetics Institute, $77,692
5. Bolar Pharmaceutical, $70,217
6. Chips & Technologies, $67,373
7. Daisy Systems, $51,813
8. Alza, $49,861
9. Ashton-Tate, $48,008
10. Phoenix Technologies, $46,431

*Where'd you hear that?*
Business Week. Based on 1989 R & D expenditures, in dollars per employee.

### U.S. companies with the highest research and development spending per employee

1. Chips & Technologies, with $60,828
2. Ashton-Tate, $42,490
3. Lotus Development Corp., $33,535
4. Amdahl, $26,626
5. Apple Computer Inc., $25,233
6. Microsoft, $24,982
7. MSA, $24,874
8. Applied Materials, $24,633
9. Quantum, $23,754
10. Cray Research, $22,485

*Where'd you hear that?*
Electronic Business. Based on 1988 per employee research and development spending.

### *U.S. companies with the greatest research and development spending growth*

1. Oracle Systems, with 226.4%
2. Chips & Technologies, 167.3%
3. Conner Peripherals, 144.0%
4. Computer Associates, 103.2%
5. Sun Microsystems, 101.1%
6. Loral, 100.7%
7. Maxtor, 90.4%
8. Ashton-Tate, 88.9%
9. Everex Systems, 86.4%
10. Microsoft, 83.3%

*Where'd you hear that?*
Electronic Business. Based on percentage change in research and development spending, 1987-88.

### Largest U.S. research and development spenders by R & D as a percentage of revenue

1. Cullinet Software, with 24.2%
2. Management Science America, 23.6%
3. Advanced Micro Devices, 18.5%
4. LTX, 18.1%
5. Lotus Development Corp., 17.9%
6. Ashton-Tate, 17.2%
7. Cray Research, 15.6%
8. Integrated Device Technology, 15.5%
9. Tektronix, 15.3%
10. GenRad, 14.9%

*Where'd you hear that?*
Electronic Business. Based on 1988 research and development spending as a percentage of revenue.

# BUSINESS CLASS

**U.S. government contractors with the highest research and development spending**

1. Motorola, with $665.0 million
2. General Motors Hughes Electronics, $550.9
3. Texas Instruments, $494.0
4. Honeywell Inc., $323.4
5. Litton Industries Inc., $227.9
6. Harris, $116.9
7. Varian Associates, $80.2
8. Loral, $64.1
9. M/A-COM, $25.0
10. Watkins-Johnson, $18.3

*Where'd you hear that?*
Electronic Business. Based on 1988 total R & D expenditures, in millions of dollars.

**Top 10 universities in all Research & Development spending**

1. Johns Hopkins University, with $510.9 million
2. Massachusetts Institute of Technology, $264.4
3. University of Wisconsin, Madison, $254.5
4. Cornell University, $244.8
5. Stanford University, $240.9
6. University of Michigan, $224.9
7. University of Minnesota, $222.4
8. Texas A & M University, $219.9
9. University of California, Los Angeles, $188.8
10. University of Illinois, Urbana, $188.7

*Where'd you hear that?*
Chemical & Engineering News, Facts & Figures for Chemical R & D. Based on total R & D spending, in millions.

**Top university-administrated, federally-funded Research & Development centers**

1. Jet Propulsion Lab, with $915.5 million
2. Lawrence Livermore Lab, $914.8
3. Los Alamos National Lab, $835.3
4. Lincoln Lab, $353.7
5. Argonne National Lab, $276.6
6. Brookhaven National Lab, $220.5
7. Lawrence Berkeley Lab, $178.1
8. Fermi National Accelerator Lab, $167.1
9. Plasma Physics Lab, $107.2
10. Stanford Linear Accelerator Center, $89.0
11. Others, total $144.1

*Where'd you hear that?*
Chemical & Engineering News, Facts & Figures for Chemical R & D. Based on total R & D spending, in millions.

**Products of the year**

Nintendo Game Boy
Sony CCD-TR5 Handycam
Mazda Miata MX-5
*Batman*
Compaq LTE
Cholesterol fighters
Motorola Micro TAC Personal Telephone
Epogen
Gillette Sensor
Arco EC-1
H-P LaserJet IIP

*Where'd you hear that?*
Fortune. Above items are listed, not ranked.

61

# BUSINESS CLASS

## Food companies that introduced the most new products

1. General Foods Corp., with 137
2. Kraft Inc., 116
3. H. J. Heinz, 106
4. Nestle, 99
5. Campbell Soup Co., 78
6. Borden, 77
7. General Mills Inc., 69
8. ConAgra, Inc., 69
9. Beatrice Cos. Inc., 62
10. Sara Lee, 56

*Where'd you hear that?*
Marketing & Media Decisions. Based on number of products introduced in 1988.

## Non-food companies that introduced the most new products

1. Revlon, with 66
2. Lever/Chesebrough-Pond's, 52
3. Schering, 49
4. Bristol-Myers Co., 31
5. Procter & Gamble, 30
6. Noxell, 26
7. Colgate-Palmolive Co., 25
7. Gillette Co., 25
9. Cosmair, 23
9. Pfizer, 23

*Where'd you hear that?*
Marketing & Media Decisions. Based on number of products introduced in 1988.

## U.S. universities receiving the most patents

1. Massachusetts Institute of Technology, with 102 patents
2. University of California, 81
3. California Institute of Technology, 59
4. University of Texas, 51
5. Stanford University, 43
6. University of Florida, 42
7. University of Minnesota, 41
8. Iowa State University, 28
8. University of Wisconsin, 28
10. Johns Hopkins University, 27

*Where'd you hear that?*
Wall Street Journal. Based on number of patents in 1989.

## Largest corporate law departments

1. AT & T, with 357
2. General Electric Co., 338
3. Exxon Corp., 320
4. IBM, 301
5. Sears, 292
6. Citicorp, 280
7. Chevron Corp., 260
8. Du Pont Co., 216
9. Prudential, 199
10. American Express, 187

*Where'd you hear that?*
Lawyers Almanac. Based on number of attorneys, 1988-89.

## Largest law firms in Great Britain

1. Clifford Chance, 1649
2. Linklaters & Paines, 1250
3. Lovell White Durant, 1076
4. Slaughter and May, 972
5. Denton Hall Burgin & Warrens, 854
6. Allen & Overy, 787
7. Freshfields, 762
8. Simmons & Simmons, 756
9. Herbert Smith, 729
10. Norton Rose, 660

*Where'd you hear that?*
Investors Chronicle. Based on total staff in 1988.

## Canada's largest law firms

1. Fasken Martineau Davis, with 481
2. McCarthy Tetrault, 471
3. Blake Cassels & Graydon, 314
4. Stikeman, Elliott, 240
5. Gowling, Strathy & Henderson, 217
6. Goodman Freeman Phillips & Vineberg, 213
7. Lang Michener Lawrence & Shaw, 188
8. Fraser & Beatty, 184
9. Tory, Tory, Deslauriers & Binnington, 153
10. Russell & DuMoulin, 148

*Where'd you hear that?*
Financial Post 500, Maclean Hunter, Ltd. Based on total number of lawyers.

## Largest law firms

1. Baker & McKenzie (Chicago), with 1294
2. Skadden, Arps, Slate, Meagher & Flom (New York), 958
3. Jones, Day, Reavis & Pogue (Cleveland), 945
4. Gibson, Dunn & Crutcher (Los Angeles), 677
5. Morgan, Lewis & Bockius (Phildelphia), 632
6. Sidley & Austin (Chicago), 610
7. Fulbright & Jaworski (Houston), 569
8. Shearman & Sterling (New York), 520
9. Pillsbury, Madison & Sutro (San Francisco), 506
10. Latham & Watkins (Los Angeles), 493

*Where'd you hear that?*
Lawyers Almanac. Based on total number of lawyers in 1989.

## Highest-grossing law firms

1. Skadden, Arps, Slate, Meagher & Flom (New York), with $440 million
2. Jones, Day, Reavis & Pogue (Cleveland), $260
3. Baker & McKenzie (Chicago), $255
4. Gibson, Dunn & Crutcher (Los Angeles), $230
5. Shearman & Sterling (New York), $220
6. Davis Polk & Wardwell (New York), $210
7. Sullivan & Cromwell (New York), $205
8. Cavath, Swaine & Moore (New York), $200
9. Fried, Frank, Harris, Shriver & Jacobson (New York), $195
10. Latham & Watkins (Los Angeles), $190

*Where'd you hear that?*
New York Times. Based on 1988 gross revenues, in millions of dollars.

## Highest paid trial lawyers in the U.S.

1. Joseph Dahr Jamail, with $450 million
2. Herbert Hafif, $40
3. Gerald Michaud, $18
4. Walter Umphrey, $14.5
5. Max Toberoff, $12
6. Ernest Cannon, $7
7. Ronald D. Krist, $9
8. John O'Quinn, $8
9. Stanley S. Schwartz, $7

# BUSINESS CLASS

# BUSINESS CLASS

10. Richard Warren Mithoff, $4.7

*Where'd you hear that?*
Forbes. Based on 1988 income, in millions of dollars.

## Highest paid corporate lawyers in the U.S.

1. Joseph Flom, with $5 million
2. Raoul Lionel Felder, $3.8
3. Harry (Skip) Brittenham, $3
3. Allen Grubman, $3
3. Martin Lipton, $3
3. Kenneth Ziffren, $3
3. John Eastman, $3
8. John Branca, $2.5
8. Arthur Fleischer, $2.5
10. Samuel Butler, $2.4

*Where'd you hear that?*
Forbes. Based on 1988 income, in millions of dollars.

## The most ethical occupations

1. Accountants
2. Dentists
3. Doctors
4. Officers of large corporations
5. Public relations practitioners
6. Lawyers
7. Funeral home operators
8. Advertising practitioners
9. TV repairmen
10. Realtors

*Where'd you hear that?*
Journal of Accountancy. Based on results of survey of business people.

## Leading corporate givers

1. IBM, with $135,400,000
2. AT & T, $59,532,000
3. General Motors Corp., $54,500,000
4. Hewlett-Packard Co., $50,400,000
5. Exxon Corp., $48,985,000
6. RJR Nabisco, $47,500,000
7. General Electric Co., $38,755,000
8. Merck & Co., $36,079,808
9. Ford Motor Co., $31,589,000
10. E. I. du Pont de Nemours & Co., $31,000,000

*Where'd you hear that?*
Across the Board. Based on total contributions.

## Corporations with biggest charitable spendings

1. IBM, with $135.4 million
2. General Motors Corp., $54.6
3. Exxon Corp., $53.0
4. Hewlett-Packard Co., $50.4
5. RJR Nabisco, $47.5
6. Du Pont Co., $36.7
7. AT & T, $36.5

*Where'd you hear that?*
Business Month. Based on total corporate giving in 1988, in millions of dollars.

## Leading Hispanic businesses

1. Eagle Brands, Inc., with $66.00 million
2. Precision Trading Corp., $61.00
3. Digitron Trading Co., $57.62
4. RJO Enterprises, Inc., $50.00
5. Generalbank FSB, $49.61
6. Infotec Development, Inc., $45.00

# BUSINESS CLASS

7. Ruiz Food Products, Inc., $42.00
8. Business Men's Insurance Corp., $40.30
9. Inner City Drywall Corp., $40.00
10. Computer Dynamics, Inc., $37.00

*Where'd you hear that?*
Hispanic Business, 100 Fastest Growing Companies. Based on 1988 sales, in millions of dollars. Enterprises in Puerto Rico excluded.

## Leading Hispanic business

1. Intercontinental Metals, with $4.33
2. Interamerican Trading and Produce, $1.90
3. Precision Trading Corp., $1.69
4. Rivasal International, $1.30
5. Government Micro Resources, $1.25
6. Design Build Team, Inc., $1.13
7. Orso Superior Enterprises Corp., $1.00
8. Greg's Trucking, Inc., $.69
9. Business Men's Insurance Corp., $.68
10. Reza Brothers Construction, Inc., $.66

*Where'd you hear that?*
Hispanic Business, 100 Fastest Growing Companies. Based on 1988 sales per employee, in dollars.

## Largest Hispanic-American businesses

1. Bacardi Imports Inc., with $500.000 million
2. Goya Foods, Inc., $320.00
3. Sedano's Supermarkets, $198.24
4. Handy Andy Supermarkets, $155.74
5. Galeana Van Dyke Dodge, $141.93
6. Pizza Management Inc., $134.50
7. Frank Parra Chevrolet Inc., $125.75
8. Ancira Enterprises Inc., $117.65
9. International Banchares Corp., $114.88
10. Capital Bancorp, $110.28

*Where'd you hear that?*
Hispanic Business, Hispanic Business 500. Based on 1989 sales, in millions of dollars.

## Largest Black-owned industrial/service companies

1. TLC Beatrice International Holdings Inc., with $1,514.000 million
2. Johnson Publishing Co. Inc., $241.327
3. Philadelphia Coca-Cola Bottling Co. Inc., $240.000
4. H. J. Russell & Co., $132.876
5. Gordy Co., $100.000
6. Soft Sheen Products Inc., $87.200
7. Trans Jones Inc./Jones Transfer Co., $78.555
8. Bing Group, $73.883
9. Maxima Corp., $58.383
10. Dick Griffey Productions, $50.162

*Where'd you hear that?*
Black Enterprise. Based on 1989 sales, in millions of dollars.

# BUSINESS CLASS

### Hispanic-American businesses with the most employees

1. Pizza Management Inc., with 4,500
2. El Chico Corp., 3,800
3. Handy Andy Supermarkets, 1,892
4. Vincam Group, 1,850
5. Goya Foods, Inc., 1,500
6. Sedano's Supermarkets, 1,360
7. Cantu Services, Inc., 1,150
8. Oscar Ortega Ranches, 1,000
9. Gator Industries, Inc., 985
10. Ninfa's Inc., 850

*Where'd you hear that?*
Hispanic Business, Hispanic Business 500. Based on number of employees in 1989.

### Fastest-growing Hispanic-owned firms by sales growth

1. JCI Environmental Services, with 113.04%
2. TAG Electric Co., 106.42%
3. Modern Sanitation Systems, Inc., 100.85%
4. Hugo's Cleaning Service, Inc., 99.97%
5. Cumbre, Inc., 92.31%
6. L & M Technologies, Inc., 91.18%
7. Gilram Supply, Inc., 89.66%
8. Ferrous Metal Processing, Inc., 88.24%
9. Campos Construction Co., 82.93%
10. Scientech, Inc., 80.0%

*Where'd you hear that?*
Hispanic Business, Hispanic Business 500. Based on percent increase of sales, 1989 over 1988.

### Fastest growing Hispanic businesses by sales

1. Pueblo Broadcasting Corp., with 276.72% growth in sales
2. NSI Research Group, 246.30%
3. C. V. I. Electric, 210.44%
4. Nick Mendoza Productions, 169.28%
5. CMA, Inc., 134.13%
6. Meta, Inc., 133.95%
7. RJO Enterprises, Inc., 132.88%
8. Chem-Tech Systems, Inc., 130.32%
9. Rosas Computer Co., Inc., 129.94%
10. Jason International Optical, Inc., 124.23%

*Where'd you hear that?*
Hispanic Business, 100 Fastest Growing Companies. Based on compounded annual rate of growth in sales, 1984-88, in percent.

### Fastest growing Hispanic businesses by employment

1. NSI Research Group, with 7400% growth rate
2. Fred Burgos Construction Co., 3880%
3. Pueblo Broadcasting Corp., 3400%
4. Rosas Computer Co., 3250%
5. Economy Laundries, Inc., 2800%
6. RJO Enterprises, 2800%
7. Atlantic Resources, 1900%
8. Ultraexpress Courier, 1850%
9. DCL Advertising, 1500%
10. Casanova Pendrill Publicidad, 1400%

*Where'd you hear that?*
Hispanic Business, 100 Fastest Growing Companies. Based on growth rate of employment, 1984-88, in percent.

## Leading Hispanic advertising markets

1. Los Angeles, CA, with $131.1 million
2. Miami, FL, $92.5
3. New York, NY, $90.4
4. Chicago, IL, $30.6
5. San Francisco/San Jose, CA, $24.8
6. San Antonio, TX, $19.8
7. Houston, TX, 18.9
8. San Diego, CA, $13.1
9. Phoenix, AZ, $10.9
10. El Paso, TX, $9.8

*Where'd you hear that?*
Hispanic Business. Based on 1989 media expenditures, in millions of dollars.

## Largest metropolitan areas ranked by Hispanic population

1. San Antonio, TX, with 51.4%
2. Miami-Hialeah, FL, 43.4%
3. Los Angeles-Long Beach, CA, 34.2%
4. Riverside-San Bernardino, CA, 21.8%
5. San Jose, CA, 20.8%
5. New York, NY, 20.8%
7. Anaheim-Santa Ana, CA, 19.1%
8. Houston, TX, 18.8%
9. San Diego, CA, 17.9%
10. Phoenix, AZ, 14.8%

*Where'd you hear that?*
Sales & Marketing Management, Survey of Buying Power. Based on percent of Hispanic population.

## Metropolitan areas with the largest Hispanic populations

1. Los Angeles-Long Beach, CA, with 2,974.1 thousand
2. New York, NY, 1,780.0
3. Miami-Hialeah, FL, 803.9
4. Chicago, IL, 674.7
5. San Antonio, TX, 667.0
6. Houston, TX, 601.1
7. Riverside-San Bernardino, CA, 497.7
8. Anaheim-Santa Ana, CA, 434.2
9. San Diego, CA, 425.7
10. El Paso, TX, 403.8

*Where'd you hear that?*
Sales & Marketing Management, Survey of Buying Power. Based on hispanic population, in thousands.

## BUSINESS CLASS

### Top 10 1989 Hispanic market advertisers

1. Procter & Gamble Co., with $29.3 million
2. Phillip Morris Cos., $8.6
3. Anheuser-Busch Cos. Inc., $8.4
4. Colgate-Palmolive Co., $7.8
5. McDonald's Corp., $6.9
6. Coca-Cola Co., $6.0
7. Adolph Coors Co., $5.2
8. Ford Motor Co., $5.0
8. Johnson & Johnson, $5.0
10. Sears, Roebuck & Co., $4.6

*Where'd you hear that?*
Advertising Age. Based on 1989 expenditures, in millions of dollars.

# BUSINESS CLASS

## Biggest corporations run by women

1. Estee Lauder Inc., Estee Lauder, with $1,600 million (est.)
2. Washington Post Co., Katharine Graham, $1,400
3. Wells, Rich, Greene, Mary Wells Lawrence, $836
4. Mary Kay Cosmetics, Inc., Mary Kay Ash, $825 (est.)
5. Warnaco, Inc., Linda J. Wachner, $649
6. Jockey International, Donna Wolf Steigerwaldt, $450 (est.)
7. Copley Press, Helen Copley, $381
8. Charles Levy Co., Barbara Levy Kipper $359
9. Diane Von Furstenberg Studio, Diane Von Furstenberg, $300 (est.)
10. Sunshine-Jr. Stores, Inc., Lana Jane Lewis-Brent, $173

*Where'd you hear that?*
Savvy Woman, Savvy 60. Based on 1988 revenues, in millions of dollars.

## The 10 top-paying professions for women

1. Lawyers
2. Engineers, architects, and surveyors
3. Computer systems analysts and scientists
4. Operations and systems researchers and analysts
5. Physicians
6. Personnel and labor relations managers
7. Teachers (college and university)
8. Natural scientists
9. Managers (health and medicine)
10. Social scientists and urban planners

*Where'd you hear that?*
Savvy Woman. Based on average salary.

## The 10 top-paying professions for men

1. Lawyers
2. Pilots
3. Management analysts
4. Physicians
5. Managers (marketing, advertising and PR)
6. Financial managers
7. Personnel and labor relations managers
8. Securities and financial services sales
9. Administrators (education and related fields)
10. Teachers (college and university)

*Where'd you hear that?*
Savvy Woman. Based on average salary.

## America's top-rated graduate business schools

1. Stanford University, with 100.0
2. Harvard University, 98.0
3. University of Pennsylvania, Wharton, 96.0
4. Northwestern University, Kellogg, 95.3
5. Massachusetts Institute of Technology, Sloan, 94.7
6. Dartmouth College, Tuck, 92.9
7. University of Michigan, 92.9
8. University of Chicago, 92.3
9. Duke University, Fuqua, 91.3

# BUSINESS CLASS

10. Columbia University, 90.5

*Where'd you hear that?*
U.S. News & World Report. Based on six factors: student selectivity, placement, graduation rates, instructional resources, research and academic reputation. Includes business schools selected from institutions that enroll 200 or more full-time graduate MBA candidates and are accredited by the American Assembly of Collegiate Schools of Business.

## Best finance business schools

1. University of Pennsylvania
2. University of Chicago
3. Stanford University
4. Massachusetts Institute of Technology
5. University of California, Los Angeles

*Where'd you hear that?*
U.S. News & World Report. Based on results of reputational survey of deans and heads of MBA programs.

## Best human resources business school

1. Cornell University
2. University of California, Berkeley
3. Harvard University
4. University of Michigan
5. Stanford University

*Where'd you hear that?*
U.S. News & World Report. Based on results of reputational survey of deans and heads of MBA programs.

## Best business information systems business schools

1. Massachusetts Institute of Technology
2. University of Minnesota
3. Carnegie-Mellon University
4. University of Arizona
5. New York University

*Where'd you hear that?*
U.S. News & World Report. Based on results of reputational survey of deans and heads of MBA programs.

## Best management business schools

1. Harvard University
2. Stanford University
3. Northwestern University
4. Dartmouth College
5. University of Pennsylvania

*Where'd you hear that?*
U.S. News & World Report. Based on results of reputational survey of deans and heads of MBA programs.

## Best international business business schools

1. University of South Carolina
2. University of Pennsylvania
3. New York University
4. Harvard University
5. Columbia University

*Where'd you hear that?*
U.S. News & World Report. Based on results of reputational survey of deans and heads of MBA programs.

## Best marketing business schools

1. Northwestern University
2. Stanford University
3. University of Pennsylvania
4. Harvard University
5. University of Michigan

# BUSINESS CLASS

*Where'd you hear that?*
U.S. News & World Report. Based on results of reputational survey of deans and heads of MBA programs.

### Best production management business schools

1. Massachusetts Institute of Technology
2. Carnegie-Mellon University
3. Stanford University
4. Harvard University
5. University of Michigan

*Where'd you hear that?*
U.S. News & World Report. Based on results of reputational survey of deans and heads of MBA programs.

### Best not-for-profit management business schools

1. Harvard University
2. Stanford University
3. Northwestern University
4. University of Pennsylvania
5. Cornell University

*Where'd you hear that?*
U.S. News & World Report. Based on results of reputational survey of deans and heads of MBA programs.

### Best real estate business schools

1. University of Pennsylvania
2. University of Wisconsin, Madison
3. University of California, Berkeley
4. University of Georgia
5. Ohio State University

*Where'd you hear that?*
U.S. News & World Report. Based on results of reputational survey of deans and heads of MBA programs.

### Canada's most powerful executives

1. Kenneth Roy Thomson, Thomson Corp.
2. Peter Bronfman, Edper Enterprises Ltd.
3. Albert Reichmann, Paul Reichmann, Ralph Reichmann, Olympia & York Developments Ltd.
4. Galen Weston, George Weston Ltd.
5. K. C. Irving, Irving Oil Ltd.
6. Fredrik Eaton, Eaton's of Canada Ltd.
7. James Pattison, Jim Pattison Group Inc.
8. Paul Desmarais, Power Corp. of Canada
9. Edward (Ted) Rogers, Rogers Communications Inc.
10. George Richardson, James Richardson & Sons Ltd.

*Where'd you hear that?*
Canadian Business. Based on an evaluation of 1989 performance, industrial leadership, diversity, proprietorship, regional dominance, community clout, and momentum.

### Highest paid non-CEOs

1. Frank G. Wells, President, Walt Disney, with $50,946,000
2. Gary Wilson, Former CEO, Walt Disney, $49,988,000
3. Wayne M. Perry, Vice-Chairman, McCaw Cellular, $24,061,000
4. Rufus W. Lumry, CFO, McCaw Cellular, $14,743,000
5. Sidney J. Sheinberg, President, MCA, $7,905,000

6. Ernst Weil, Executive Vice-President, Salomon Brothers, $7,400,000
7. John C. Pope, CFO, UAL, $6,571,000
8. Thomas P. Pollock, Executive Vice-President, MCA, $6,321,000
9. Donald R. Keough, President, Coca-Cola, $6,192,000
10. Robert F. Greenhill, Vice-Chairman, Morgan Stanley, $5,510,000

*Where'd you hear that?*
Business Week, Annual Survey of Executive Compensation. Based on total 1989 pay, including salary, bonus, and long-term compensation.

## Executives with the largest golden parachutes

1. John M. Richman, Vice-Chairman, Philip Morris, with $22,400,000
2. Robert M. Price, CEO, Control Data, $13,500,000
3. R. Gordon McGovern, CEO, Campbell Soup, $11,200,000
4. Garth H. Drabinsky, CEO, Cineplex Odeon, $7,400,000
5. Joseph G. Temple, Executive Vice-President, Dow Chemical, $6,500,000
6. Terrence D. Daniels, Vice-Chairman, W. R. Grace, $5,800,000
7. Jan Leschly, President, Squibb, $5,400,000
8. Myron I. Gottlieb, Vice-Chairman, Cineplex Odeon, $4,500,000
9. Horst W. Schroeder, President, Kellogg, $3,800,000
10. Kenneth J. Thygerson, Chairman, Imperial Corp., $2,600,000

*Where'd you hear that?*
Business Week, Annual Survey of Executive Compensation. Based on total package; 1989.

## Executives who gave shareholders the most for their pay, 1987-89

1. Albert L. Ueltschi, Flight Safety International, with a score of 437
2. George L. Lindemann, Metro Mobile CTS, 329
3. Lawrence J. Ellison, Oracle Systems, 326
4. Angelo J. Bruno, Bruno's, 227
5. Robert E. Price, Price, 206

*Where'd you hear that?*
Business Week, Annual Survey of Executive Compensation. Based on relative index of executive compensation and corporate performance.

## Executives who gave shareholders the least for their pay, 1987-89

1. Lee A. Iacocca, Chrysler, with a score of 3.6
2. Paul Fireman, Reebock, 4.1
3. Michael D. Eisner, Walt Disney, 4.6
4. W. Michael Blumenthal, Unisys, 5.3
5. William P. Stiritz, Ralston Purina, 6.4

*Where'd you hear that?*
Business Week, Annual Survey of Executive Compensation. Based on relative index of executive compensation and corporate performance.

# BUSINESS CLASS

# BUSINESS CLASS

**Executives whose companies did the best relative to their pay, 1987-89**

1. MacAllister Booth, Polaroid, with a score of 219
2. D. Euan Baird, Schlumberger, 199
3. Morton L. Mandel, 177
4. Albert L. Ueltschi, Flight Safety International, 150
4. Robert E. Price, Price, 150

*Where'd you hear that?*
Business Week, Annual Survey of Executive Compensation. Based on relative index of executive compensation and corporate performance.

**Executives whose companies did the worst relative to their pay, 1987-89**

1. Edwin Lupberger, Entergy, with a score of -63.6
2. Walter V. Shipley, Chemical Banking, -60.5
3. John F. McGillicuddy, Manufacturers Hanover, -58.0
4. William J. Catacosinos, Long Island Lighting Co., -48.9
5. Charles S. Sanford, Jr., Bankers Trust NY, -47.6

*Where'd you hear that?*
Business Week, Annual Survey of Executive Compensation. Based on relative index of executive compensation and corporate performance.

**Highest paid CEOs by deviation from compensation model**

1. James Wood, A & P, with 769%
2. Paul B. Fireman, Reebok International, 725%
3. Martin S. Davis, Paramount, 663%
4. Michael D. Eisner, Walt Disney, 386%
5. Richard K. Eamer, National Medical Enterprises, 284%
6. Roberto C. Goizueta, Coca-Cola, 230%
7. Alan C. Greenberg, Bear Stearns, 194%
8. S. Parker Gilbert, Morgan Stanley, 145%
9. Richard L. Gelb, Bristol-Myers Squibb, 138%
10. Anthony J. O'Reilly, H. J. Heinz, 134%

*Where'd you hear that?*
Fortune, Crystal Study/CEO Pay. Based on percentage deviation from computer-simulated compensation model.

**Biggest CEO money-makers, 1980-89**

1. Charles Lazarus, Toys 'R Us, with $156.2 million
2. Steven J. Ross, Time Warner, $84.6
3. Craig O. McCaw, McCaw Cellular Communications, $76.9
4. Lee A. Iacocca, Chrysler, $65.9
5. Michael D. Eisner, Walt Disney, $61.9
6. T. Boone Pickens, Jr., Mesa Petroleum, $56.9
7. Frederick W. Smith, Federal Express, $55.9
8. Paul B. Fireman, Reebok International, $54.5
9. Donald A. Pels, Lin Broadcasting, $49.8
10. Jim P. Manzi, Lotus Development, $47.9

# BUSINESS CLASS

*Where'd you hear that?*
Business Week. Based on total pay, 1980-89, in millions of dollars. Based on totals of annual income and long-term compensation from Executive Pay Scoreboards over the decade.

## Highest paid chief executives

1. Craig O. McCaw, McCaw Cellular, with $53,944,000
2. Steven J. Ross, Time Warner, $34,200,000
3. Donald A. Pels, Lin Broadcasting, $22,791,000
4. Jim P. Manzi, Lotus Development, $16,363,000
5. Paul Fireman, Reebok International, $14,606,000
6. Ronald K. Richey, Torchmark, $12,666,000
7. Martin S. Davis, Paramount, $11,635,000
8. Roberto C. Goizueta, Coca-Cola, $10,715,000
9. Michael D. Eisner, Walt Disney, $9,589,000
10. August A. Busch III, Anheuser-Busch, $8,861,000

*Where'd you hear that?*
Business Week, Annual Survey of Executive Compensation. Based on 1989 total pay, including salary, bonus, and long-term compensation.

## Most effective executive search consultants for general management

1. Gerard R. Roche, Heidrick & Struggles Inc., New York
2. Thomas J. Neff, Spencer Stuart, New York
3. Robert E. Lamalie, Robert Lamalie Inc, Marco Islands, FL
4. Frederick W. Wackerle, McFeely Wackerle Jett, Chicago
5. John F. Johnson, Lamalie Associates Inc., Cleveland
6. Leon A. Farley, Leon A. Farley Associates, San Francisco

*Where'd you hear that?*
Business Week. Based on resposes to a survey of 600 corporate clients and 311 headhunting firms (unspecified).

## Most productive business service corporations

1. FlightSafety International,O with $31.3 thousand
2. Kelly Services Inc., $18.5
3. PHH, $11.7

*Where'd you hear that?*
Forbes, Forbes 500s Annual Directory. Based on 1989 profits per employee, in thousands of dollars. Ranks U.S.-based corporations that were publicly traded as of March 23, 1990.

## Most profitable business service companies

1. Rollins, with 47.2% business services
2. Kelly Services Inc., 28.9%
3. Olsten, 22.1%
4. PHH, 16.7%
5. Wackenhut, 13.6%
6. American Building, 10.5%
7. Volt Information Sciences, 8.4%
8. Adia Services, NA

*Where'd you hear that?*
Forbes, Annual Report on American Industry. Based on 10-year average return on equity. Ranks publicly held corporations only.

# BUSINESS CLASS

### Leading exporters of services

1. United States, with 11.2%
2. France, 10.6%
3. United Kingdom, 8.6%
4. West Germany, 8.2%
5. Italy, 6.5%
6. Japan, 5.5%
7. Netherlands, 4.5%
8. Spain, 4.3%
9. Belgium-Luxembourg, 3.8%
10. Austria, 2.9%

*Where'd you hear that?*
Financial Times. Based on 1987 share of world exports, in percent.

### Leading importers of services

1. West Germany, with 12.4%
2. United States, 10.8%
3. Japan, 10.1%
4. France, 8.3%
5. United Kingdom, 6.4%
6. Italy, 5.0%
7. Netherlands, 4.5%
8. Belgium-Luxembourg, 3.3%
9. Canada, 3.1%
10. Switzerland, 2.3%

*Where'd you hear that?*
Financial Times. Based on 1987 share of world imports, in percent.

### Largest services companies in Europe

1. Veba Aktiengesellschaft, with 19,558,621,907 ECU
2. France Telecom, 13,601,417,187
3. Montecatini Edison SpA in Abbreviazione Montedison SpA, 9,433,496,000
4. Grand Metropolitan PLC, 8,858,067,610
5. Saatchi & Saatchi Co. PLC, 5,809,874,426
6. Post Office, 5,569,792,114
7. IBM France (Compagnie), 5,349,659,160
8. Ikea Deutschland Verkaufs Gmbh, 5,315,552,000
9. Feldmuehle Vermoegensverwaltung Aktiengesellschaft, 4,192,927,144
10. Ladbroke Group PLC, 4,184,543,616

*Where'd you hear that?*
Dun's Europa, Dun & Bradstreet. Based on sales, in European Currency Units.

### Largest transportation, communication, and power companies in Europe

1. Electricite de France, with 19,761,927,600 ECU
2. Rheinisch-Westfaelisches Elektrizitaetswerk Aktiengesellschaft, 18,846,048,000
3. British Telecommunications PLC, 14,964,739,020
4. Central Electricity Generating Board, 12,231,855,900
5. British Gas PLC, 10,819,866,288
6. Enel Ente Nazionale per L'Energia Elettrica, 10,235,119,380
7. Sip Societa Italiana per L'Esercizio della Telecomunicazioni SpA, 8,038,113,472
8. Deutsche Bundesbahn, 7,597,093,009
9. Eaux (Cie Generale), 7,541,239,846
10. Chemins de Fer Francais (Societe Nationale des), 6,779,280,855

# BUSINESS CLASS

*Where'd you hear that?*
Dun's Europa, Dun & Bradstreet. Based on sales, in European Currency Units.

## Largest diversified service companies

1. AT & T, with $36,345.0 million
2. Fleming Cos., Inc., $12,045.3
3. Super Valu Stores, $10,316.1
4. Enron, $9,869.6
5. Marriott, $8,382.01
6. United Telecommunications, $7,549.0
7. McKesson, $7,515.2
8. American Financial, $7,285.7
9. Sysco, $6,851.3
10. Pacific Enterprises, $6,797.0

*Where'd you hear that?*
Fortune, Service 500. Based on sales, fiscal year ended December 31, 1989, in millions of dollars.

## Most admired diversified service corporations

1. AT & T, with a rating of 7.30
2. MCI, 7.04
3. United Telecommunications, 6.52
4. McKesson, 6.33
5. Super Valu Stores, 6.31
6. Halliburton, 6.09
7. Fluor Daniel Inc., 5.92
8. Fleming Cos., Inc., 5.87
9. Ryder System, 5.69
10. American Financial, 5.63

*Where'd you hear that?*
Fortune, America's Most Admired Corporations. Based on scores (0-10) derived from a survey of senior executives, outside directors, and financial analysts. Respondents ranked firms in their own industry on quality of management and products/service; innovation; long-term investment value; financial soundness; attraction and retention of talent; community and environmental responsibility; and use of assets.

## Fastest growing job markets

1. Fort Myers, FL, with 4.67%
2. Naples, FL, 4.32%
3. Fort Pierce, FL, 4.12%
4. Anaheim-Santa Ana, CA, 4.00%
5. West Palm Beach-Boca Raton-Delray Beach, FL, 3.86%
6. Ocala, FL, 3.68%
7. Orlando, FL, 3.59%
8. Santa Rosa-Petaluma, CA, 3.49%
9. Bryan-College Station, TX, 3.48%
10. Fort Collins-Loveland, CO, 3.35%

*Where'd you hear that?*
Changing Times. Based on annual increase in employment, 1988-89 in percent.

## Top labor-related issues for the Business community in the 1990s: Management's view

1. Rising health-care costs/costs containment, with 22%
1. Labor-management cooperation/non-adversarial relationships, 22%

# BUSINESS CLASS

3. Retraining/education of workforce/preparation for new technology, 18%
4. Health-care benefits, 14%
4. Global competition/protection of U.S. jobs, 14%
4. Productivity improvement, 14%

*Where'd you hear that?*
National Underwriter, Property & Casualty/Risk & Benefits Management edition. Based on percent surveyed.

## Countries with highest labor productivity

1. United States, with $41,362
2. Canada, $39,125
3. France, $35,388
4. Italy, $35,206
5. West Germany, $33,489
6. Belgium, $33,067
7. Norway, $31,919
8. Netherlands, $31,776
9. Britain, $29,614
10. Japan, $29,575

*Where'd you hear that?*
U.S. News & World Report. Based on real output per worker in 1988, in U.S. dollars.

## Top labor-related issues for the business community in the 1990s: Labor's view

1. Health-care benefits, with 34%
2. Job security, 30%
3. Retirement/pension funds/benefits, 22%
4. Wage/pay increases, 20%
5. Rising health-care costs/cost-containment, 16%
5. Global competition/protection of U.S. jobs, 16%

*Where'd you hear that?*
National Underwriter, Property & Casualty/Risk & Benefits Management edition. Based on percent surveyed.

## Largest tax-exempt union funds

1. Teamsters, Western Conference, with $8,604,561 thousand
2. Teamsters, Central States Southeast & Southwest Areas Pension Fund, $6,534,000
3. United Mine Workers of America Health & Retirement Funds, $5,195,300
4. Electrical Workers, National Contractors Assoc., $3,432,720
5. Boilermakers-Blacksmiths National Pension Trust, $2,132,349
6. Engineers, Operating, International, $2,033,715
7. Food & Commercial Workers, Joint Trust Funds, $1,994,700
8. Bakery, Confectionary International Union, $1,815,400
9. Plumbers, National Headquarters, $1,598,936
10. Machinists, IAM, National Pension Fund, $1,461,884

*Where'd you hear that?*
Money Market Directory of Pension Funds and Their Investment Managers. Based on 1989 assets, in thousands of dollars.

## Most hazardous industries

1. Shipbuilding, with 44.9
2. Meatpacking, 39.2
3. Sawmills, 31.0
4. Gray iron foundries, 30.3
5. Auto stampings, 30.0
6. Primary aluminum, 29.6
7. Mobile homes, 28.7
8. Vitreous plumbing, 28.4
9. Lumber, timbers, 28.3
9. Truck trailers, 28.3

*Where'd you hear that?*
AFL-CIO News. Based on number of illnesses and injuries per 100 workers in 1988.

## Most frequently-occurring work-force health problems

1. Stress
2. High blood pressure
3. Cigarette smoking
4. Back injuries/pain
5. Overweight
6. Alcohol abuse
7. High cholesterol
8. Drug abuse
9. Depression
10. Mental health problems

*Where'd you hear that?*
Business & Health.number of illnesses and injuries per 100 workers in 1988.

## Largest pension funds/sponsors

1. TIAA-CREF, with $81,000 million
2. California Public Employees, $54,000
3. New York City, $45,422
4. New York State & Local, $44,238
5. AT & T, $42,700
6. General Motors Corp., $40,900
7. California State Teachers' Retirement System, $30,335
8. General Electric Co., $28,912
9. New York State Teachers, $28,130
10. IBM, $25,775

*Where'd you hear that?*
Pensions & Investment Age, Top 1000 Funds. Based on assets, in millions of dollars, in 1989.

## Leading tax-exempt corporation funds

1. General Motors Corp. (New York), with $39,575,374 thousand
2. AT & T (Berkeley Heights, NJ), $38,485,014
3. General Electric Investment Corp. (Stamford, CT), $30,631,000
4. IBM (Stamford, CT), $24,465,000
5. Ford Motor Co. (Dearborn, MI), $21,000,000
6. E. I. du Pont de Nemours & Co. (Wilmington, DE), $16,658,364
7. NYNEX Corp. (New York, NY), $15,205,957
8. BellSouth Corp. (Atlanta, GA), $12,819,000
9. Ameritech (Chicago, IL), $12,515,600
10. Bell Atlantic Corp. (Philadelphia, PA), $11,500,000

*Where'd you hear that?*
Money Market Directory of Pension Funds and Their Investment Managers. Based on 1989 assets, in thousands of dollars.

# BUSINESS CLASS

# BUSINESS CLASS

**Leading tax-exempt union funds**

1. Teamsters, Western Conference (Seattle, WA), with $8,604,561 thousand
2. Teamsters, Central States Southeast & Southwest Areas Pension Fund (Chicago, IL), $6,534,000
3. United Mine Workers of America Health & Retirement Funds (Washington, DC), $5,195,300
4. Electrical Workers, National Contractors Association (Washington, DC), $3,432,720
5. Boilermakers-Blacksmith National Pension Trust (Kansas City, KS), $2,132,349
6. Engineers, Operating, International (Washington, DC), $2,033,715
7. Food & Commercial Workers, Joint Trust Funds, Southern California (Cypress, CA), $1,994,700
8. Bakery, Confectionary International Union (Kensington, MD), $1,815,400
9. Plumbers, National Headquarters (Washington, DC), $1,598,936
10. Machinists, IAM, National Pension Fund (Washington, DC), $1,461,884

*Where'd you hear that?*
Money Market Directory of Pension Funds and Their Investment Managers. Based on 1989 assets, in thousands of dollars.

**Leading tax-exempt government funds**

1. California Employees' Retirement Systems (Sacramento, CA), with $48,059,866 thousand
2. New York State & Local Retirement Systems (Albany, NY), $40,280,644
3. New York City Retirement Systems (New York, NY), $37,918,000
4. California State Teachers' Retirement System (Sacramento, CA), $28,984,000
5. New Jersey Division of Investment (Trenton, NJ), $24,694,000
6. New York State Teachers' Retirement System (Albany, NY), $22,688,713
7. Wisconsin Investment Board (Madison, WI), $22,179,830
8. Teacher Retirement System of Texas (Austin, TX), $22,000,000
9. Ohio Public Employees' Retirement System (Columbus, OH), $19,400,000
10. Florida State Board of Administration (Tallahassee, FL), $17,505,544

*Where'd you hear that?*
Money Market Directory of Pension Funds and Their Investment Managers. Based on 1989 assets, in thousands of dollars.

## BUSINESS CLASS

### Leading tax-exempt endowment funds

1. Texas Permanent School Fund (Austin, TX), with $8,500,000 thousand
2. Howard Hughes Medical Institute (Bethesda, MD), $5,600,000
3. Harvard University (Boston, MA), $3,435,000
4. Princeton University (Princeton, NJ), $2,539,000
5. University of Texas, Austin $2,151,614
6. Yale University (New Haven, CT), $2,111,000
7. Stanford University (Palo Alto, CA), $1,700,000
8. Columbia University (New York, NY), $1,460,356
9. Washington University (St. Louis, MO), $1,315,467
10. The Texas A & M University System (College Station, TX), $1,178,850

*Where'd you hear that?*
Money Market Directory of Pension Funds and Their Investment Managers. Based on 1989 assets, in thousands of dollars.

### Leading tax-exempt foundation funds

1. Ford Foundation (New York, NY), with $5,407,711 thousand
2. J. Paul Getty Trust (Los Angeles, CA), $3,200,000
3. Lilly Endowment Inc. (Indianpolis, IN), $3,000,000
4. The Pew Charitable Trust (Philadelphia, PA), $3,000,000
5. Shriners Hospitals for Crippled Children, Inc. (Tampa, FL), $2,689,052
6. John D. and Catherine T. MacArthur Foundation (Chicago, IL), $2,500,000
7. Robert Wood Johnson Foundation (Princeton, NJ), $2,200,000
8. Rockefeller Foundation (New York, NY), $2,000,000
9. W. K. Kellogg Foundation (Battle Creek, MI), $1,901,386
10. Andrew W. Mellon Foundation (New York, NY), $1,402,110

*Where'd you hear that?*
Money Market Directory of Pension Funds and Their Investment Managers. Based on 1989 assets, in thousands of dollars.

### Largest group annuity writers

1. Metropolitan, with $8.2 billion
2. Aetna Life, $5.6
3. Equitable Life, $3.9
4. New York Life, $3.2
5. John Hancock, $2.9
6. Principal Mutual Life, $2.8
7. Prudential, $2.5
8. Mutual Life of New York, $1.9
9. Provident National Life, $1.6
10. Hartford Life, $1.4

*Where'd you hear that?*
Pensions & Investments. Based on total amount, year-end, 1988, in billions of dollars.

### Leading writers of annuities

1. Metropolitan Life Insurance Co., with $8,853,994,754
2. Aetna Life Insurance Co., $5,653,457,534

# BUSINESS CLASS

3. Equitable Life Assurance Society, $3,980,245,036
4. Prudential Insurance Co. of America, $3,629,754,304
5. New York Life Insurance Co., $3,341,408,120
6. John Hancock Mutual Life Insurance Co., $2,976,193,251
7. Teachers Insurance Annuity, $2,900,447,435
8. Principal Mutual Life, $2,826,429,423
9. Allstate Life Insurance Co., $2,471,566,379
10. Mutual Life Insurance Co. of NY, $1,942,224,743

*Where'd you hear that?*
Best's Review, Life/Health edition. Based on 1988 total premiums and deposits.

## Leading individual annuity writers

1. Teachers Insurance & Annuity, $2,869,305,718
2. Allstate Life Insurance Co., $1,609,474,465
3. Keystone Provident Life, $1,433,390,560
4. IDS Life, $1,430,335,764
5. Jackson National Life Insurance Co., $1,253,790,814
6. Lincoln National Pension, $1,239,090,664
7. Prudential, $1,144,144,603
8. Tandem Insurance Group, $1,003,336,155
9. Fidelity & Guaranty, $902,677,107
10. New York Life & Annuity, $877,780,576

*Where'd you hear that?*
Best's Review, Life/Health edition. Based on 1988 premiums and deposits.

## Leading group annuity writers

1. Metropolitan, with $8,204,937,861
2. Aetna Life, $5,653,393,622
3. Equitable Life Assurance, $3,942,238,946
4. New York Life, $3,156,947,690
5. John Hancock Mutual Life, $2,863,638,927
6. Principal Mutual Life, $2,815,632,661
7. Prudential, $2,485,609,701
8. Mutual Life of New York, $1,935,720,150
9. Provident National Life, $1,554,194,278
10. Hartford Life, $1,405,722,262

*Where'd you hear that?*
Best's Review, Life/Health edition. Based on 1988 total premiums and deposits.

## Largest group insurance companies in insurance issued

1. Metropolitan Life Insurance Co., with $56,791,929,000
2. Prudential Insurance Co. of America, $33,259,388,000
3. Equitable Life Assurance Society, $19,346,988,000
4. Sun Life Assurance Co. of CN, $14,629,952,563
5. Travelers Insurance Co., $14,253,103,000
6. Hartford Life & Accident Insurance Co., $12,321,573,000

80

7. Confederation Life Insurance Co., $11,704,925,036
8. Aetna Life Insurance Co., $11,238,377,000
9. Great-West Life Assurance Co., $10,843,904,428
10. Mutual Life Insurance Co. of NY, $10,618,392,000

*Where'd you hear that?*
Best's Review, Life/Health edition. Based on current insurance issued, in dollars.

## Largest international reinsurers

1. Munich Reinsurance Co., with $5,706,773 thousand
2. Swiss Re Group, $4,541,244
3. General Reinsurance Corp., $1,626,645
4. The Yasuda Fire & Marine Insurance Co. Ltd., $1,576,881
5. Employers Reinsurance Corp., $1,312,390
6. Skandia International Insurance Corp., $1,239,000
7. Cologne Reinsurance Co., $1,147,094
8. American Re-Insurance Co., $976,399
9. Mercantile & General Reinsurance Co. PLC, $971,484
10. Gerling-Konzern Globale Reinsurance Group, $917,609

*Where'd you hear that?*
Business Insurance. Based on amount of net reinsurance premiums written in 1988, in thousands of dollars.

## Leading European reinsurers

1. Munich Reinsurance, with $6.54 billion
2. Swiss Reinsurance, $2.56
3. Skandia International, $1.29
4. Hannover Ruck, $1.19
5. Scor/UAP Reinsurance, $1.16
6. M & G Reinsurance, $1.14
7. Generali Group, $1.11
8. Cologne Reinsurance Co., $1.07
9. Gerling-Konzern Globale Reinsurance Group, $1.06
10. Frankona Ruck, $0.81

*Where'd you hear that?*
Financial Times. Based on 1988 net premiums, in billions of dollars.

## *Leading national insurance underwriters*

1. Japan, with $178.3 billion
2. United States, $165.4
3. Great Britain, $40.2
4. West Germany, $36.4
5. France, $21.2
6. Soviet Union, $15.5
7. Canada, $11.1
8. South Korea, $9.2
9. Switzerland, $8.9
10. Netherlands, $7.1

*Where'd you hear that?*
National Underwriters Life/Health edition. Based on 1987 premiums, in billions of U.S. dollars.

# BUSINESS CLASS

# BUSINESS CLASS

### Largest world business insurance brokers

1. Marsh & McLennan Cos. Inc., with $2,455,400,000
2. Alexander & Alexander Services Inc., $1,248,900,00
3. Sedgwick Group PLC, $1,042,153,000
4. Johnson & Higgins, $785,945,000
5. Corroon & Black Corp., $456,826,000
6. Willis Faber PLC, $452,100,000
7. Frank B. Hall & Co. Inc., $383,712,000
8. Rollins Burdick Hunter Group, $316,400,000
9. Minet Holdings PLC, $285,100,000
10. Jardine Insurance Brokers Group, $241,286,000

*Where'd you hear that?*
Business Insurance. Based on 1989 gross revenues.

### Largest U.S. commercial insurance brokers

1. Marsh & McLennan Cos. Inc., with $2,455,400,000
2. Alexander & Alexander Services Inc., $1,248,900,000
3. Johnson & Higgins, $785,945,000
4. Sedgwick James North America, $489,155,000
5. Corroon & Black Corp., $456,826,000
6. Frank B. Hall & Co. Inc., $383,712,000
7. Rollins Burdick Hunter Group Inc., $316,400,000
8. Arthur J. Gallagher & Co., $173,206,000
9. Jardine Insurance Brokers Inc., $100,000,000
10. Hilb, Rogal & Hamilton Co., $78,310,541

*Where'd you hear that?*
Business Insurance. Based on 1989 gross revenues.

### World's largest securities firms

1. Prudential (U.S.), with $153,023 million
2. Nippon Life (Japan), $145,131
3. Dai-Ichi Mutual Life Insurance (Japan), $99,664
4. Metropolitan Life (U.S.), $94,232
5. Sumitomo Life (Japan), $83,651
6. Aetna (U.S.), $81,415
7. Equitable Life (U.S.), $58,028
8. Cigna Corp. (U.S.), $55,825
9. Prudential Corp. (U.K.), $55,770
10. Meiji Mutual (Japan), $54,3650

*Where'd you hear that?*
Wall Street Journal, Annual Global Ranking. Based on fiscal year 1988 capital, in millions of dollars.

### Leading international non-life insurance companies

1. State Farm, with $18.4 billion
2. Allstate Insurance Co., $10.7
3. Tokyo, $10.3
4. Yasuda, $8.5
5. Aetna Life & Casualty, $7.5
6. AIG, $6.9
7. Royal, $6.0
8. Taisho, $5.5
9. General Accident, $4.0

82

10. Allianz, $3.9

*Where'd you hear that?*
National Underwriter, Property & Casualty/Risk & Benefits Management edition. Based on 1987 premiums, in billions of U.S. dollars.

## Asia's largest quoted insurance companies

1. Tokio Marine & Fire Insurance Co. Ltd., with $29,163,426 thousand
2. The Yasuda Fire & Marine Insurance Co. Ltd., $22,273,020
3. Taisho Marine & Fire Insurance Co. Ltd., $14,434,876
4. Sumitomo Marine & Fire Insurance Co. Ltd., $12,712,032
5. Nichido Fire & Marine Isurance Co. Ltd., $10,844,446
6. Nippon Fire & Marine Insurance Co. Ltd., $10,792,598
7. Dai-Tokyo Fire & Marine Insurance Co. Ltd., $7,600,869
8. Fuji Fire & Marine Insurance Co. Ltd., $7,415,036
9. Chiyoda Fire & Marine Insurance Co. Ltd., $7,157,474
10. The Koa Fire & Marine Insurance Co. Ltd., $7,037,251

*Where'd you hear that?*
Asia's 7500 Largest Companies, Dun & Bradstreet. Based on 1988 assets, in thousands of U.S. dollars.

## Largest insurance companies in western Europe

1. Allianz Welt (Munchen), with 29,211 million DM
2. Zurich Versicherung (Zurich), 16,786
3. Union Assurance de Paris (Paris), 16,392
4. Generali Gruppe (Roma), 14,677
5. Schweizer Ruck (Zurich), 12,564
6. Nationale-Nederlanden (Den Haag), 12,461
7. Winterthur (Winterthur), 12,440
8. Axa Midi (Paris), 12,347
9. Assurance Generale de France (Paris), 11,944
10. Prudential (London), 11,871

*Where'd you hear that?*
Commerzbank. Based on 1988 premium income, in millions of Deutschmarks.

## Britain's largest insurance companies

1. Prudential Corp. PLC, with £30,837,600 thousand
2. Legal & General Group PLC, £13,826,200
3. Royal Insurance Holdings PLC, £13,656,100
4. The Standard Life Assurance Co., £12,770,800
5. Commercial Union Assurance Co. PLC, £12,432,400
6. Sun Alliance & London Insurance PLC, £12,192,300
7. Legal & General Assurance Society Ltd., £11,884,600
8. General Accident Fire & Life Assurance Corp. PLC, £10,862,300

# BUSINESS CLASS

# BUSINESS CLASS

9. Guardian Royal Exchange PLC, £10,003,500
10. The Norwich Union Life Insurance Society, £9,379,300

*Where'd you hear that?*
U.K.'s 10,000 Largest Companies, Dun & Bradstreet. Based on 1988 assets, in thousands of British pounds

## Largest general insurance companies in Switzerland

1. Zurich, with 6,594 million francs
2. Winterthur, 4,372
3. SUVA, 2,025
4. Baloise, 1,415
5. Swiss Mobiliar, 1,059
6. Helvetia, 918
7. Elvia, 892
8. Switzerland General, 882
9. Swiss National, 547
10. Alpina, 465

*Where'd you hear that?*
Switzerland's Largest Companies, Union Bank of Switzerland. Based on 1988 gross premium income, in millions of francs.

## Top U.S insurance corporations

1. American International Group, with $15,584 million
2. General Reinsurance Corp., $7,612
3. Aetna Life & Casualty, $5,669
4. CNA Financial Corp., $4,661
5. Chubb Group of Insurance Cos., $4,259
6. Cigna Corp., $4,027
7. Traveler's, $3,533
8. American General, $3,472
9. St. Paul, $3,032
10. Torchmark, $2,663

*Where'd you hear that?*
Business Week, The Business Week 1000. Based on market value as of March 16, 1990, in millions of dollars.

## Most productive diversified insurance corporations

1. General Reinsurance Corp., with $252.4 thousand
2. Cincinnati Financial, $67.3
3. American International Group, $42.6
4. American General, $34.9
5. Safeco, $34.5
6. Kemper, $30.7
7. Aon, $26.6
8. Old Republic International, $20.9
9. Transamerica, $18.5
10. Lincoln National, $16.9

*Where'd you hear that?*
Forbes, Forbes 500s Annual Directory. Based on 1989 profits per employee, in thousands of dollars. Ranks U.S.-based corporations that were publicly traded as of March 23, 1990.

## Most profitable diversified insurance companies

1. Marsh & McLennan Cos., with 34.8%
2. Corroon & Black Corp., 34.6%
3. Leucadia National, 20.4%
4. Zenith National Insurance, 19.7%
5. American International Group, 19.3%
6. Aon, 18.6%
7. Cincinnati Financial, 18.5%
8. Safeco, 16.6%
8. General Reinsurance Corp., 16.6%
10. Old Republic International, 16.1%

*Where'd you hear that?*
Forbes, Annual Report on American Industry. Based on 10-year average return on equity. Ranks publicly held corporations only.

## Largest Black-owned insurance companies

1. North Carolina Mutual Life Insurance Co.
2. Atlanta Life Insurance Co.
3. Golden State Mutual Life Insurance Co.
4. Universal Life Insurance Co.
5. Supreme Life Insurance Co. of America
6. Chicago Metropolitan Mutual Insurance Co.
7. Booker T. Washington Insurance Co.
8. Mammoth Life & Accident Insurance Co.
9. Pilgrim Health & Life Insurance Co.
10. Protective Industrial Co. of Alabama, Inc.

*Where'd you hear that?*
Black Enterprise. Based on total assets as of December 31, 1989, in millions of dollars.

## Highest paid commercial insurance CEOs

1. Saul P. Steinberg (Reliance Group Holdings Inc.), with $4,498,000
2. Marshall Manley (AmBase Corp.), $1,803,444
3. Robert D. Kilpatrick (CIGNA Corp.), $1,587,000
4. Edward J. Noha (CNA Financial Corp), $1,373,607
5. James R. Harvey (Transamerica Corp.), $1,300,000
6. James T. Lynn (Aetna Life & Casualty Co.), $1,136,538
7. John J. Byrne (Fireman's Fund Corp.), $1,124,539
8. Harold S. Hook (American General Corp.), $1,089,000
9. Ronald E. Ferguson (General Re Corp.), $979,351
10. Maurice R. Greenberg (American International Group Inc.), $975,000

*Where'd you hear that?*
Business Insurance. Based on 1988 cash compensation.

## Largest Lloyd's syndicates

1. Marine 418, Merrett Underwriting Agency Management Ltd., with £242.1 million
2. Marine 206, R. W. Sturge & Co., £193.8
3. Non-marine 210, R. W. Sturge & Co., £176.4
4. Non-marine 190, Three Quays Underwriting Management Ltd., £158.8
5. Non-marine 362, Murray Lawrence & Partners, £143.3
6. Marine 367, F. L. P. Secretan & Co. Ltd., £142.5
7. Marine 448, Wellington (Underwriting Agencies) Ltd., £130.1
8. Marine 483, Methuen (Lloyd's Underwriting Agents) Ltd., £124.9
9. Marine 932, Janson Green Management Ltd., £123.6
10. Non-marine 510, R. J. Klin & Co. Ltd., £114.9

*Where'd you hear that?*
Business Insurance, Lloyd's of London. Based on 1989 gross allocated capacity, in millions of British pounds.

# BUSINESS CLASS

# BUSINESS CLASS

### Largest Lloyd's brokerage groups

1. Sedgwick Group PLC, with £164.9 billion
2. Willis Faber PLC, £159.3
3. Marsh & McLennan Cos. Inc., £134.7
4. Alexander & Alexander Services Inc., £86.4
5. Inchcape PLC, £54.9
6. C. E. Heath PLC, £39.8
7. Jardine Matheson Holdings Ltd., £39.1
8. Hogg Robinson & Gardner Mountain PLC, £36.8
9. Frizzell Group PLC, £36.1
10. Lowndes Lambert Group Ltd., £30.1

*Where'd you hear that?*
Business Insurance, Lloyd's of London. Based on 1989 Lloyd's brokerage revenues, in billions of British pounds.

### Leading fire insurance underwriters

1. American Intern Group, with $221,793 thousand
2. Travelers Insurance Group, $200,205
3. Aetna Life & Casualty Group, $124,511
4. Hartford Insurance Group, $117,667
5. St. Paul Group, $97,372
6. Farmers Insurance Group, $89,928
7. Allstate Insurance Group, $78,556
8. Continental Insurance Cos., $73,953
9. Nationwide Group, $71,164
10. United States F & G Group, $60,009

*Where'd you hear that?*
Best's Review, Property/Casualty edition. Based on 1988 direct premiums, in thousands of dollars.

### Market share of smoke detectors

1. Pittway, with 55%
2. Black & Decker, 10%
2. Jameson, 10%
2. Probe, 10%
5. Others, total, 15%

*Where'd you hear that?*
Appliance Manufacturer. Based on 1989 market share, in percent.

### Largest guard companies

1. Pinkerton's
2. Burns International Security Services
3. Wackenhut
4. Wells Fargo Guard Services
5. American Protection Industries
6. Globe Security Systems
7. Guardmark
8. Stanley Smith Security Services
9. Allied Security
10. Advance Security

*Where'd you hear that?*
New York Times. Based on total revenues.

### Cities with the highest robbery rates

1. New York, NY, with 1,271.1
2. Detroit, MI, 1,095.2
3. Washington, DC, 1,055
4. Baltimore, MD, 1,042.8
5. New Orleans, LA, 1,012.7
6. Boston, MA, 1,011.5
7. Dallas, TX, 927.7
8. Los Angeles, CA, 91.3
9. Cleveland, OH, 742.9

10. San Francisco, CA, 663.9

*Where'd you hear that?*
Daily News. Based on reported robberies per 100,000 people.

## Cities reporting the most violent crime

1. Atlanta, GA, with 1,919
2. Miami, FL, 1,645
3. Newark, NJ, 1,437
4. St. Louis, MO, 1,386
5. Chicago, IL, 1,110
6. Los Angeles, CA, 1,074
7. New York, NY, 1,067
8. Detroit, MI, 1,038
9. Boston, MA, 993
10. Portland, OR, 966

*Where'd you hear that?*
U.S. News & World Report. Based on violent crimes per 100,000 residents in 1989.

## 10 most overburdened state prison systems

1. California, with 29,892
2. Ohio, 7,379
3. Michigan, 5,582
4. Pennsylvania, 4,957
5. New York, 4,465
6. Massachusetts, 3,037
7. Maryland, 2,902
8. North Carolina, 2,527
9. Oklahoma, 1,840
10. New Jersey, 1,593

*Where'd you hear that?*
City & State. Based on number of inmates over capacity as of January 1, 1989.

## States rated the most hospitable to business

1. Nevada, with 87.02
2. New Hampshire, 81.15
3. Virginia, 79.84
4. Maryland, 75.75
5. Georgia, 74.39
6. Florida, 73.56
7. Delaware, 72.39
8. North Carolina, 67.78
9. Tennessee, 66.93
10. California, 66.69

*Where'd you hear that?*
Inc.. Based on composite score based on 9 categories reflecting new jobs, new companies, and the climate for growth for 1988.

# BUSINESS CLASS

## *Most important security threats to business*

1. Accidents and errors, with 55%
2. Employee dishonesty, 15%
2. Fire, 15%
4. Employee revenge, 10%
5. Flood damage, 3%
6. Earthquakes, etc., 2%

*Where'd you hear that?*
Information Center. Based on share of total, in percent.

## States with the lowest labor costs

1. South Dakota
2. North Dakota
3. Mississippi
4. New Mexico
5. Arkansas
6. South Carolina
7. Nebraska
8. Iowa
9. Idaho
10. Florida

# BUSINESS CLASS

*Where'd you hear that?*
Grant Thornton, Grant Thornton Manufacturing Climates Study. Based on average labor costs.

### States with the lowest state-regulated employment costs

1. North Carolina
2. Indiana
3. South Dakota
4. Mississippi
5. New Jersey
6. Virginia
7. Nevada
8. Tennessee
9. Utah
10. South Carolina

*Where'd you hear that?*
Grant Thornton, Grant Thornton Manufacturing Climates Study. Based on average employment costs. The following factors are considered: unemployment compensation, unemployment compensation trust fund, average worker compensation per case, and workers' compensation levels.

### Metropolitan areas rated most hospitable to industry

1. Las Vegas, NV
2. Washington, DC
3. Orlando, FL
4. Tallahassee, FL
5. San Jose, CA
6. Atlanta, GA
7. Charleston, SC
8. Lincoln, NE
9. Raleigh-Durham, NC
10. Anaheim, CA

*Where'd you hear that?*
Inc., Annual Ranking of Metropolitan Economies. Based on 3 criteria used: business birthrate, percentage growth in private employment and percentage of young companies experiencing high growth. For each place a relative score for each factor was calculated based on a 4-year pe.

### Top 10 metropolitan areas for business

1. Dallas/Fort Worth, TX
2. Atlanta, GA
3. Kansas City, MO
4. Los Angeles, CA
5. Baltimore, MD
6. New York, NY
7. Bay Area, CA
8. Pittsburgh, PA
9. Portland, OR
10. Minneapolis/St. Paul, MN

*Where'd you hear that?*
Fortune. Based on various factors.

### States with highest corporate income tax revenues

1. Connecticut, with $2,877.7
2. Alaska, $312.3
3. California, $181.6
4. Michigan, $175.1
5. New Jersey, $146.4
6. Indiana, $136.0
7. Delaware, $131.1
8. North Carolina, $119.0
9. Minnesota, $108.7
10. New Hampshire, $102.8

*Where'd you hear that?*
City & State, State Financial Report. Based on estimated fiscal 1990 per capita corporate income tax revenues.

# BUSINESS CLASS

**States with highest corporate tax rates**

1. Connecticut, with 11.5%
2. Minnesota, 9.5%
2. Massachusetts, 9.5%
4. West Virginia, 9.45%
5. California, 9.3%

*Where'd you hear that?*
City & State, State Financial Report. Based on corporate tax rate for fiscal year 1990.

**States with the largest corporate income tax collections per capita**

1. Alaska, with $268.70
2. Connecticut, $211.85
3. Massachusetts, $205.63
4. Delaware, $187.88
5. Michigan, $178.77
6. California, $172.03
7. New Hampshire, $143.61
8. New Jersey, $141.85
9. New York, $120.25
10. Minnesota, $99.62

*Where'd you hear that?*
P.E.L. Factbook, Pennsylvania Economic League. Based on fiscal year 1987 state corporate income tax collections per capita.

**States with the largest corporate income tax collections per $1000 personal income**

1. Alaska, with $14.73
2. Michigan, $11.61
3. Delaware, $11.25
4. Massachusetts, $10.74
5. Connecticut, $9.96
6. California, $9.65
7. New Hampshire, $8.19
8. New Jersey, $6.97
9. New York, $6.68
10. Wisconsin, $6.64

*Where'd you hear that?*
P.E.L. Factbook, Pennsylvania Economic League. Based on fiscal year 1987 state corporate income tax collections per $1000 personal income.

**States with the most new companies, 1984-1988**

1. California, with 12,352
2. Texas, 8,289
3. New York, 6,734
4. Florida, 6,540
5. Illinois, 3,788
6. Pennsylvania, 3,469
7. Ohio, 3,240
8. New Jersey, 3,237
9. Georgia, 2,983
10. Michigan, 2,752

*Where'd you hear that?*
Florida Trend. Based on number of new companies, 1984-1988.

## *Most productive states*

1. Massachusetts
2. Colorado
3. Texas
4. Minnesota
5. Utah
6. Kansas
7. Delaware
8. North Dakota
9. Washington
10. Arizona

*Where'd you hear that?*
Grant Thornton, Grant Thornton Manufacturing Climates Study. Based on availability and productivity of resources. The following factors are considered: available work force, manhours lost, value-added, and energy costs.

# BUSINESS CLASS

### States with the highest business birthrate, 1984-1988

1. Florida, with 2.88%
2. Arizona, 2.87%
3. Georgia, 2.79%
4. Texas, 2.58%
5. Nevada, 2.57%
6. Maryland, 2.55%
7. Tennessee, 2.41%
8. California, 2.38%
9. New Hampshire, 2.32%
10. Colorado, 2.26%

*Where'd you hear that?*
Florida Trend. Based on total number of new companies divided by the total number of business establishments in the state.

### Oldest science parks

1. Stanford Research Park (Palo Alto, CA), 1952
2. Research Triangle Park (NC), 1955
3. Ann Arbor Research Park (MI), 1961
4. Cummings Research Park (Huntsville, AL), 1962
5. University City Science Center (Philadelphia, PA), 1964

*Where'd you hear that?*
Site Selection. Based on year opened.

### Most active markets for factory space construction, 1988-98

1. New York, NY, with 96.6 million sq. ft.
2. Los Angeles, CA, 93.7
3. Chicago, IL, 49.5
4. Detroit, MI, 35.5
5. San Francisco, CA, 27.8
6. Dallas-Fort Worth, TX, 26.1
7. Philadelphia, PA, 26.0
8. Boston, MA, 23.0
9. Minneapolis, MN, 21.1
10. Houston, TX, 19.6

*Where'd you hear that?*
Urban Land. Based on estimated total space, 1988-98, in millions of square feet.

### Most productive heavy equipment corporations

1. Illinois Tool Works, with $11.0 thousand
2. Deere & Co., $10.6
3. Caterpillar Inc., $8.2
4. Dover, $7.1
5. Ingersoll-Rand, $6.5
6. Stanley Works, $6.4
7. Tenneco, $6.3
8. Crane, $5.2
8. Norton $5.2
10. Cooper Industries, $5.1

*Where'd you hear that?*
Forbes, Forbes 500s Annual Directory. Based on 1989 profits per employee, in thousands of dollars. Ranks U.S.-based corporations that were publicly traded as of March 23, 1990.

### Most profitable heavy equipment companies

1. Nacco Industries, with 20.2%
2. Dover, 19.8%
3. Illinois Tool Works, 18.0%

# BUSINESS CLASS

4. Goulds Pumps, 15.8%
5. L. B. Foster, 15.6%
6. Stanley Works, 15.1%
7. Tecumseh Products, 13.9%
8. Parker Hannifin, 13.8%
9. Trinova, 12.8%
10. Lincoln Electric, 12.6%

*Where'd you hear that?*
Forbes, Annual Report on American Industry. Based on 10-year average return on equity. Ranks publicly held corporations only.

## Most productive industrial service corporations

1. Waste Management, with $14.3 thousand
2. Browning-Ferris Industries, $11.5
3. Safety-Kleen, $9.7
4. JWP, $3.0
5. Ogden, $1.6

*Where'd you hear that?*
Forbes, Forbes 500s Annual Directory. Based on 1989 profits per employee, in thousands of dollars. Ranks U.S.-based corporations that were publicly traded as of March 23, 1990.

## Most active office developers

1. Maguire Thomas Partners, with 10,500,000 sq. ft.
2. Prudential Property Co., 9,809,609
3. John W. Galbreath & Co., 8,800,000
4. Trammell Crow Co.–Commercial, 5,646,314
5. BetaWest Properties, Inc., 5,310,400
6. Equitable Real Estate Investment Management, Inc., 5,100,500
7. Gerald D. Hines Interests, 4,843,100
8. JMB/Urban Development Co., 4,700,000
9. Metropolitan Structures, 4,100,000
10. Ahmanson Commercial Development Co., 4,025,000

*Where'd you hear that?*
National Real Estate Investor, Office Developer Survey. Based on square feet under construction in 1989.

## Cities with the highest commercial vacancy rates worldwide

1. San Antonio, TX, with 30.5%
2. Stamford, CT, 29.7%
3. Houston, TX, 27.5%
4. Phoenix, AZ, 27.2%
5. Dallas, TX, 26.9%
6. Tampa, FL, 26.8%
7. Fort Lauderdale, FL, 26.3%
8. Denver, CO, 26.1%
9. New Orleans, LA, 25.7%
10. Fort Worth, TX, 24.6%

*Where'd you hear that?*
Crain's New York Business. Based on commercial vacancy rates, in percent.

## Cities with the lowest commercial vacancy rates worldwide

1. Vienna, Austria, 0.8%
2. Munich, West Germany, 1.3%
3. Cologne, West Germany, 1.6%
4. Dusseldorf, West Germany, 1.9%
4. Frankfurt, West Germany, 1.9%
6. Copenhagen, Denmark, 2.4%
6. London, England, 2.4%
6. Stuttgart, West Germany, 2.4%

# BUSINESS CLASS

9. Hamburg, West Germany, 3.0%
10. Amsterdam, Netherlands, 8.5%

*Where'd you hear that?*
Crain's New York Business. Based on commerical vacancy rates, in percent.

## Most admired computer and office equipment corporations

1. Hewlett-Packard Co., with a rating of 7.62
2. IBM, 7.26
3. Apple Computer Inc., 7.16
4. Digital Equipment Corp., 6.70
5. NCR, 6.11
6. Pitney Bowes, 5.74
7. Zenith Electronics, 4.82
8. Unisys, 4.18
9. Control Data Corp., 3.59
10. Wang Laboratories, 3.08

*Where'd you hear that?*
Fortune, America's Most Admired Corporations. Based on scores (0-10) derived from a survey of senior executives, outside directors, and financial analysts. Respondents ranked firms in their own industry on quality of management and products/services; innovation; long-term investment value; financial soundness; attraction and retention of talent; community and environmental responsibility; and use of assets.

## U.S. office equipment providers with the highest research and development spending

1. IBM, with $5,925.0 million
2. Xerox, 794.0
3. NCR, $416.4
4. Wang Laboratories, $246.0
5. Harris, $116.9

*Where'd you hear that?*
Electronic Business. Based on 1988 total R & D expenditures, in millions of dollars.

## Largest U.S. corporations in the business machines & services industry

1. Pitney Bowes, with $3,634 million
2. Deluxe, $2,567
3. Esselte Business Systems Inc., $959
4. John H. Harland Co., $948
5. Hon Industries, $616
6. Diebold, $594
7. Wallace Computer Services, $541
8. Herman Miller, $485
9. Standard Register, $466
10. General Binding, $384

*Where'd you hear that?*
Business Week, The Business Week 1000. Based on market value as of March 16, 1990, in millions of dollars.

## Most profitable office equipment companies

1. Diebold, with 7.7%
2. NCR, 6.9%
3. Pitney Bowes, 6.3%

*Where'd you hear that?*
Electronic Business, Most Profitable Companies. Based on 1989 profit as a percentage of sales.

## Most reliable copiers

1. Xerox
2. Canon
3. Sharp
4. Minolta
5. Mita Copystar
6. IBM

# BUSINESS CLASS

7. Harris/3M (now Lanier Worldwide)
8. Toshiba
9. Ricoh
10. Savin

*Where'd you hear that?*
Office World News. Based on results of survey of users.

## Most recognized copier brands

1. Xerox
2. Canon
3. Sharp
4. Minolta
5. Harris/3M (now Lanier Worldwide)
6. IBM
7. Mita Copystar
8. Savin
9. Ricoh
10. Toshiba

*Where'd you hear that?*
Office World News. Based on results of survey of users.

## Most productive business supply corporations

1. Comdisco, with $65.8 thousand
2. Minnesota Mining & Manufacturing, $14.4
3. Deluxe, $9.1
4. Avery International, $7.4
5. Alco Standard Corp., $6.5
6. Xerox, $6.3
7. Pitney Bowes, $6.2

*Where'd you hear that?*
Forbes, Forbes 500s Annual Directory. Based on 1989 profits per employee, in thousands of dollars. Ranks U.S.-based corporations that were publicly traded as of March 23, 1990.

## Largest companies in the Japanese workstation market

1. Sony, with 19.6%
2. Sun Microsystems, 19.3%
3. Hewlett-Packard Co., 14.0%
4. Hitachi Ltd., 8.2
5. Apollo, 8.1%
6. NEC, 6.3%
7. Digital Equipment Corp., 5.3%
8. Others, total 19.0%

*Where'd you hear that?*
Business Week. Based on 1988 market share, in percent.

## Largest manufacturers of business forms

1. Star Forms, with $168,440 thousand
2. SCM Allied Paper, $160,000
3. Ennis Business Forms, Inc., $128,170
4. Vanier Graphics, $120,000
5. CST Group, $101,000
6. General Business Forms, $84,000
7. Transkrit, $83,296
8. Shade Informations Systems, $76,788
9. Better Business Forms, $57,000
10. Paris Business Forms, $53,000

*Where'd you hear that?*
Business Forms, Labels & Systems. Based on sales, in thousands of dollars.

## Largest distributors of business forms

1. Data Supplies, with $45,635 thousand
2. GBS, $38,121
3. Standard Forms, $31,400

93

# BUSINESS CLASS

4. VanGuard Group, $28,260
5. Forms Group, $20,856
6. Woodbury Business Systems, $20,146
7. Cosmos Forms, $19,481
8. Superior Business Forms, $19,141
9. Consolidated Business Forms, $18,000
10. ImageTek, $17,490

*Where'd you hear that?*
Business Forms, Labels & Systems. Based on sales, in thousands of dollars.

### Largest convention bureaus in the U.S.

1. Tucson, AZ, with 85
2. San Antonio, TX, 84.5
3. Phoenix, AZ, 82
4. New Orleans, LA, 80
5. Palm Springs, CA, 79
5. Seattle, WA, 79
7. Atlanta, GA, 78
7. St. louis, MO, 78
9. Cincinnati, OH, 76
9. Denver, CO, 76

*Where'd you hear that?*
Successful Meetings. Based on survey results scores.

### Largest convention facilities in the U.S.

1. McCormick Place, Chicago, with 1.7 million sq. ft.
2. Jacob Javits Convention Center, New York City, 750,000
3. Las Vegas Convention Center, 737,000
4. Cobo Center, Detroit, 700,000
5. Kentucky Fair & Exposition Center, Louisville, 650,000
6. Georgia World Congress Center, Atlanta, 640,000
7. Dallas Convention Center, 525,000
8. George R. Brown Convention Center, Houston, 471,000

*Where'd you hear that?*
Crain's Detroit Business. Based on convention center exhibit space, in square feet.

### Largest business travel companies

1. AMR Corp., with $11,026,000 thousand
2. UAL Corp., $9,800,000
3. Delta Air Lines, $8,571,709
4. Travel Trust International, $7,200,000
5. Northwest Airlines, $6,553,827
6. Woodside Travel Management Corp., $6,500,000
7. USAir Group, $6,252,000
8. Texas Air Corp., $5,570,000
9. The Carlson Cos., $5,000,000
10. Holiday Inn Hotels, $4,800,000

# BUSINESS CLASS

*Where'd you hear that?*
Business Travel News, Business Travel Survey. Based on 1989 revenues, in thousands of dollars.

## Most expensive cities for business travel

1. New York, NY
2. Chicago, IL
3. Boston, MA
4. Washington, DC
5. Newark, NJ
6. San Francisco, CA
7. Los Angeles, CA
8. Dallas, TX
9. Baltimore, MD
10. Detroit, MI

*Where'd you hear that?*
Corporate Travel. Based on index of per diem costs.

## Most expensive cities for lodging

1. New York, NY, with $162.78
2. Chicago, IL, $134.83
3. Boston, MA, $123.94
4. Washington, DC, $107.98
5. Newark, NJ, $104.01
6. San Francisco, CA, $91.73
7. Dallas, TX, $88.31
8. Oakland, CA, $87.03
9. Philadelphia, PA, $86.67
10. Baltimore, MD, $84.53

*Where'd you hear that?*
Corporate Travel. Based on average lodging costs.

## Most expensive cities for food

1. New York, NY, with $74.84
2. San Francisco, CA, $63.74
3. Washington, DC, $61.69
4. Los Angeles, CA, $60.68
5. Chicago, IL, $57.19
6. Boston, MA, $57.18
7. Seattle, WA, $54.56
8. Atlanta, GA, $54.25
9. Honolulu, HI, $54.09
10. New Orleans, LA, $53.78

*Where'd you hear that?*
Corporate Travel. Based on average food costs.

## Most expensive cities for car rental

1. New York, NY, $74.39
2. Boston, MA, $70.75
3. Newark, NJ, $67.01
4. Detroit, MI, $66.95
5. Chicago, IL, $63.75
6. Atlanta, GA, $60.44
7. Charlotte, NC, $60.22
8. Hartford, CT, $59.74
9. Greensboro, NC, $59.12
10. Mobile, AL, $58.50

*Where'd you hear that?*
Corporate Travel. Based on average car rental.

## Best watches

1. Rolex, with 45%
2. Seiko, 10%
3. Don't know, 9%
4. Cartier, 7%
5. Gucci, 6%
6. Longines, 5%

*Where'd you hear that?*
Wall Street Journal. Based on percent of respondents when asked to pick the 'finest, most elegant.'.

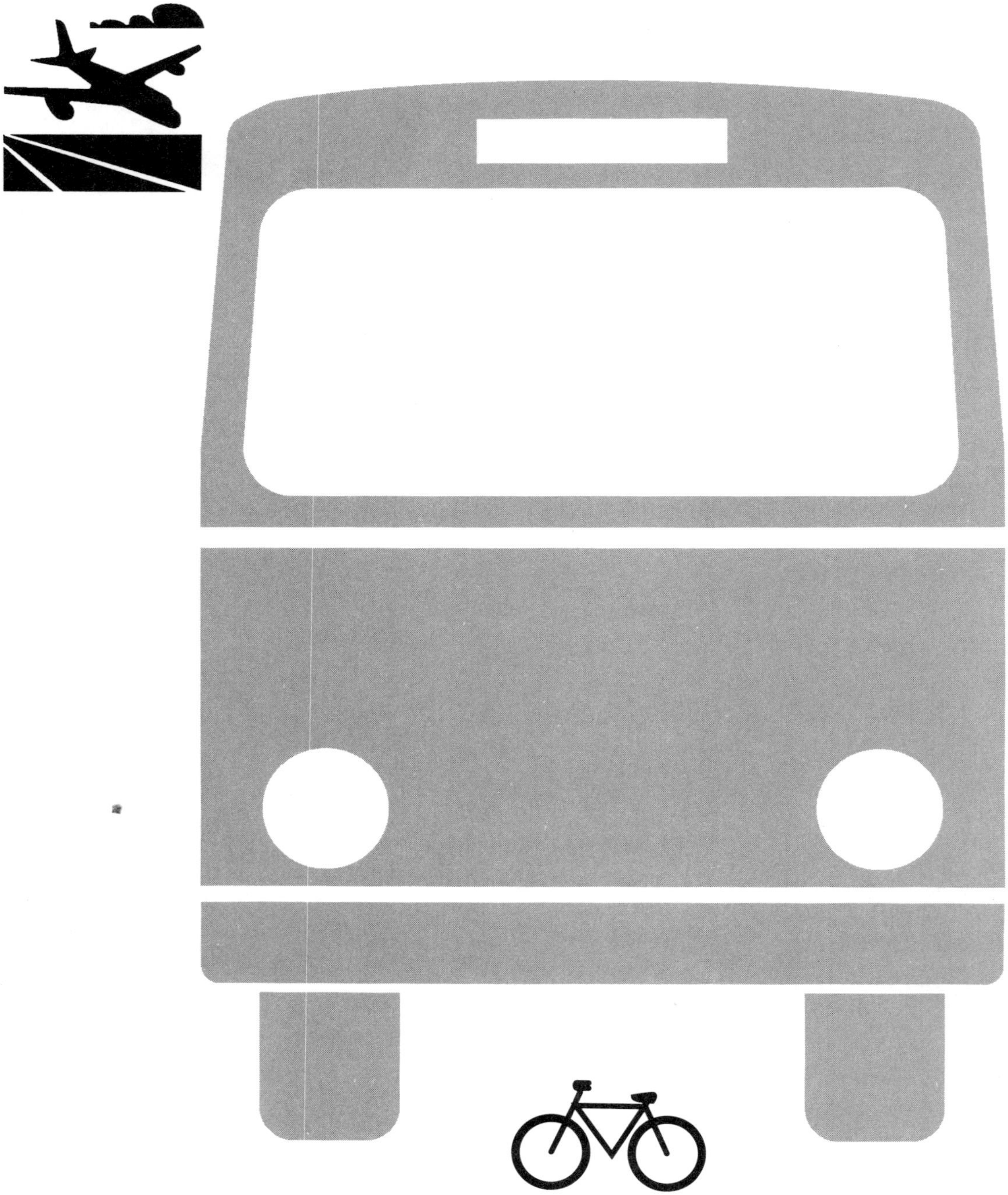

# Getting Somewhere

**Top states in mass transit lines and tunnel construction markets**

1. New York, with $116 million
2. Pennsylvania, $50
3. New Jersey, $45
4. Illinois, $44
5. Maryland, $38
6. California, $37
7. Georgia, $30
8. Massachusetts, $20
9. Michigan, $18
10. Louisiana, $10

*Where'd you hear that?*
ENR, Top 20 States in Major Construction Markets. Based on eleven-month cumulative contract awards, 1989 vs. 1988, in millions of dollars.

**Largest quoted companies in transportation and allied services**

1. Nippon Express Co. Ltd., Japan, with $9,650,486 thousand
2. Japan Air Lines Co. Ltd., Japan, $8,697,753
3. Kinki Nippon Railway Co. Ltd., Japan, $5,821,753
4. Nippon Yusen, Japan, $5,175,315
5. All Nippon Airways Co. Ltd, Japan, $4,966,143
6. Mitsui O. S. K. Lines Ltd., Japan, $3,562,550
7. Swire Pacific Ltd., Hong Kong, $3,214,802
8. Seibu Railway Co. Ltd., Japan, $3,158,430
9. Nagoya Railroad Co. Ltd., Japan, $3,152,502
10. Kawasaki Kisen Kaisha Ltd., Japan, $3,102,685

# GETTING SOMEWHERE

*Where'd you hear that?*
Asia's 7500 Largest Companies, Dun & Bradstreet. Based on sales in thousands of U.S. dollars.

## Most admired transportation corporations

1. United Parcel Service, with a rating of 7.56
2. American Airlines, 7.16
3. Delta Air Lines, 6.89
4. Union Pacific, 6.30
5. USAir Group, 6.13
6. Burlington Northern, 6.04
7. United Airlines, 5.73
8. CSX, 5.47
9. Santa Fe Pacific, 5.08
10. Texas Air, 3.72

*Where'd you hear that?*
Fortune, America's Most Admired Corporations. Based on scores (0-10) derived from a survey of senior executives, outside directors, and financial analysts. Respondents ranked firms in their own industry on quality of management and products/services; innovation; long-term investment value; financial soundness; attraction and retention of talent; community and environmental responsibility; and use of assets.

## Canada's largest transportation companies

1. Canadian National Railway Co., with $4,203,520 thousand Canadian
2. Air Canada, $3,676,000
3. P W A Corp., $2,667,817
4. Canadian Airlines, $2,517,500
5. Bombardier Inc., $2,093,800
6. Laidlaw Inc., $1,673,719
7. Canadian Pacific Express & Transport, $533,433
8. Purolator Courier Ltd., $488,000
9. Fednav Ltd., $357,628
10. Trimac Ltd., $338,635

*Where'd you hear that?*
Financial Post 500. Based on 1989 sales, in thousands of Canadian dollars.

## Largest transportation companies

1. United Parcel Service, with $12,380.7 million
2. American Airlines, $10,589.5
3. United Airlines, $9,914.5
4. Delta Air Lines, $8,089.5
5. CSX $7,821.0
6. Texas Air, $6,768.7
7. Union Pacific, $6,768.7
8. Northwest Airlines, $6,553.8
9. USAir Group, $6,257.3
10. Federal Express, $5,183.3

*Where'd you hear that?*
Fortune, Service 500. Based on 1989 operating revenues, in millions of dollars.

## Largest U.S. corporations in the transportation services industry

1. Federal Express, with $2,847 million
2. Flightsafety International, $1,653
3. Ryder System, $1,494
4. International Lease Finance, $762
5. GATX, $629
6. PHH, $566
7. Trinity Industries, $506
8. Agency Rent-A-Car, $347

# GETTING SOMEWHERE

*Where'd you hear that?*
Business Week, The Business Week 1000. Based on market value as of March 16, 1990, in millions of dollars.

## Biggest corporations in the transportation equipment industry

1. Brunswick, with $2,826 million
2. Outboard Marine, $1,678
3. Trinity Industries, $1,002
4. Harley-Davidson, $831
5. Avondale Industries, $708

*Where'd you hear that?*
Fortune, Fortune 500 Largest U.S. Industrial Corporations. Based on 1989 sales, in millions of dollars.

## Most admired transportation equipment corporations

1. Trinity Industries, with a rating of 6.93
2. Fleetwood Enterprises, Inc., 6.89
3. Outboard Marine, 6.62
4. Brunswick, 6.49
5. Avondale Industries, 6.37
6. Minstar, 5.95

*Where'd you hear that?*
Fortune, America's Most Admired Corporations. Based on scores (0-10) derived from a survey of senior executives, outside directors, and financial analysts. Respondents ranked firms in their own industry on quality of management and products/services; innovation; long-term investment value; financial soundness; attraction and retention of talent; community and environmental responsibility; and use of assets.

## World's busiest subway systems

1. Moscow, U.S.S.R., with 2.6 billion
2. Tokyo, Japan, 2.5 billion
3. New York, NY, 1.5 billion
3. Mexico City, Mexico, 1.5 billion
5. Paris, France, 1.2 billion
6. Osaka, Japan, 948 million
7. Leningrad, U.S.S.R., 821 million
8. London, England, 815 million
9. Seoul, South Korea, 810 million
10. Hong Kong, 630 million

*Where'd you hear that?*
U.S. News & World Report. Based on 1989 ridership.

## Largest U.S. corporations in the railroad industry

1. Union Pacific, with $7,124 million
2. Norfolk Southern, $6,347
3. CSX, $3,383
4. Santa Fe Pacific, $3,195
5. Burlington Northern, $2,691
6. Consolidated Rail Corp., $2,221
7. Florida East Coast Industries, Inc., $553
8. Kansas City Southern Industries, $393

*Where'd you hear that?*
Business Week, The Business Week 1000. Based on market value as of March 16, 1990, in millions of dollars.

## Most productive railroads

1. Norfolk Southern, with $18.2 thousand
2. Union Pacific, $12.4
3. CSX, $8.5
4. Burlington Northern, $7.4
5. Consolidated Rail Corp., $4.7
6. Santa Fe Pacific, -$10.2

# GETTING SOMEWHERE

*Where'd you hear that?*
Forbes, Forbes 500s Annual Directory. Based on 1989 profits per employee, in thousands of dollars. Ranks U.S.-based corporations that were publicly traded as of March 23, 1990.

## Most profitable railroads

1. Norfolk Southern, with 10.9%
2. Union Pacific, 9.4%
3. CSX, 7.0%
4. Santa Fe Pacific, 5.4%
5. Kansas City Southern Industries, 4.3%
6. Soo Line, 1.8%
7. Burlington Northern, NA
8. Consolidated Rail Corp., NA

*Where'd you hear that?*
Forbes, Annual Report on American Industry. Based on 10-year average return on equity. Ranks publicly held corporations only.

## World's largest producers of motor vehicles

1. Japan, with 26.1%
2. United States, 23%
3. West Germany, 9.5%
4. France, 7.6%
5. Italy, 4.3%
6. Canada, 4.1%
7. Spain, 3.8%
8. United Kingdom, 3.2%
9. South Korea, 2.2%
9. Brazil, 2.2%
11. Sweden, 1%
12. Others, total 13%

*Where'd you hear that?*
Financial Times. Based on 1988 market share, in percent.

## World's largest motor vehicle producers

1. General Motors Corp., with 7,497,063
2. Ford Motor Co., 5,892,267
3. Toyota, 3,729,719
4. Nissan, 2,658,255
5. Peugeot-Citroen, 2,511,502
6. Volkswagen, 2,475,347
7. Chrysler Corp., 2,187,706
8. Renault, 2,053,444
9. Fiat SpA, 1,880,408
10. VAZ, 1,604,740

*Where'd you hear that?*
Motor Vehicle Manufacturers Association, Motor Vehicle Facts and Figures. Based on 1987 total vehicle production.

## Biggest corporations in the motor vehicles and parts industry

1. General Motors Corp., with $126,974 million
2. Ford Motor Co., $96,933
3. Chrysler Corp., $36,156
4. Dana Corp., $5,157
5. Navistar International, $4,296
6. Eaton Corp., $4,249
7. Paccar, $3,373
8. Mack Trucks, $1,958
9. Masco Industries, $1,687
10. Fleetwood Enterprises, Inc., $1,632

*Where'd you hear that?*
Fortune, Fortune 500 Largest U.S. Industrial Corporations. Based on 1989 sales, in millions of dollars.

# GETTING SOMEWHERE

## Most admired motor vehicles and parts corporations

1. Ford Motor Co., with a rating of 7.69
2. Eaton Corp., 6.80
3. Dana Corp., 6.66
4. Paccar, 6.60
5. General Motors Corp., 6.08
6. Chrysler Corp., 5.84
7. Borg-Warner Corp., 5.58
8. Navistar International, 5.03
9. Mack Trucks, 4.49
10. K-H Corp., 4.05

*Where'd you hear that?*
Fortune, America's Most Admired Corporations. Based on scores (0-10) derived from a survey of senior executives, outside directors, and financial analysts. Respondents ranked firms in their own industry on quality of management and product/services; innovation; long-term investment value; financial soundness; attraction and retention of talent; community and environmental responsibility; and use of assets.

## Most popular imported trucks

1. Toyota, with 280,168
2. Nissan, 168,856
3. Mazda, 99,020
4. Isuzu, 86,369
5. Others, 217,440

*Where'd you hear that?*
Ward's Automotive Yearbook. Based on number of new registrations in 1988.

## Largest producers of heavy trucks

1. Navistar with 23.9%
2. Paccar, 23.7%
3. Freightliner, 16.1%
4. Mack Trucks, 13.1%
5. Volvo-GM, 12%
6. Ford Motor Co., 9.6%
7. Others total, 1.6%

*Where'd you hear that?*
Wall Street Journal. Based on 1989 market share, in percent.

## Largest refrigerated truck companies

1. KLLM Inc. (Jackson, MS), with $97,410 thousand
2. FFE Transportation Services (Dallas, TX), $88,699
3. Midwest Coast Transport (Sioux Falls, SD), $69,174
4. National Carriers (Liberal, KS), $68,118
5. Marten Transport (Mondovi, WI), $67,173

*Where'd you hear that?*
Transport Topics, Annual Report. Based on 1988 revenues, in thousands of dollars.

## *States with the most deficient interstate highway systems*

1. Missouri, with 56%
2. Nevada, 52%
3. Alaska, 42%
4. Arizona, 40%
5. Oklahoma, 34%
6. Oregon, 33%
7. Rhode Island, 24%
8. Kansas, 22%
9. Tennessee, 21%
10. Ohio, 19%

*Where'd you hear that?*
Financial World. Based on percentage of urban interstates rated deficient.

# GETTING SOMEWHERE

### Largest less-than-truckload trucking companies

1. Yellow Freight System, with $1,991,602 thousand
2. Consolidated Freightways Motor Freight, $1,749,180
3. Roadway Express, $1,693,597
4. Overnite Transportation Co., $638,486
5. ABF Freight System, $616,774
6. Carolina Freight Carriers, $531,557
7. P-I-E Nationwide, $498,799
8. ANR Freight System, $468,009
9. Preston Trucking Co., $368,044
10. Central Transport, $309,642

*Where'd you hear that?*
Transport Topics, Annual Report. Based on 1988 revenues, in thousands of dollars.

### Largest bulk trucking companies

1. Matlack Inc., with $227,694 thousand
2. Chemical Leaman Tank Lines, $214,424
3. Koch Service, $91,956
4. Groendyke Transport, $76,357
5. Miller Transporters, $74,048

*Where'd you hear that?*
Transport Topics, Annual Report. Based on 1988 revenues, in thousands of dollars.

### Largest heavy specialized trucking companies

1. Tri-State Motor Transit Co., with $93,721 thousand
2. Ligon Nationwide, $89,330
3. Anderson Trucking Service, $83,822
4. International Transport, $71,730
5. Ace Transportation, $64,532

*Where'd you hear that?*
Transport Topics, Annual Report. Based on 1988 revenues, in thousands of dollars.

### Largest auto haulers

1. Anchor Motor Freight, with $272,209 thousand
2. Complete Auto Transit, $247,180
3. Allied Systems, $200,822
4. Commercial Carriers, $198,043
5. Nu-Car Carriers, $145,847

*Where'd you hear that?*
Transport Topics, Annual Report. Based on 1988 revenues in thousands of dollars.

### Largest general freight trucking companies

1. J. B. Hunt Transport Services, with $392,553 thousand
2. Schneider National Carriers, $302,919
3. North American Van Lines Commercial Transport Div., $277,485
4. Ranger Transportation, $209,926
5. Builders Transport, $203,861
6. Werner Enterprises, $191,438

# GETTING SOMEWHERE

7. Schneider Transport, $152,224
8. National Freight, $143,647
9. Independent Freightway, $130,802
10. Stoops Express, $104,533

*Where'd you hear that?*
Transport Topics, Annual Report. Based on 1988 revenues, in thousands of dollars.

## Fastest growing private trucking companies

1. Gainey Transportation Services (Grand Rapids, MI)
2. D. D. F. Transportation (Tonawanda, NY)
3. Roadshow Services (San Francisco, CA)
4. Quicksilver Express Courier (Minneapolis, MN)
5. Unique Transportation Systems (Lewisville, TX)
6. Guaranteed Overnight Delivery (Kearny, NJ)
7. Pride Transport (Salt Lake City, UT)
8. Arizona Freight System (Phoenix, AZ)
9. Landair Transport (Greeneville, TN)

*Where'd you hear that?*
Transport Topics. Based on sales growth 1984-88, in percent, as tallied in *Inc.*, December 1989. Numerical rank is position in the *Inc.* list.

## Largest U.S. corporations in the trucking & shipping industry

1. Roadway Services, with $1,536 million
2. Alexander & Baldwin, $1,394

3. Overseas Shipholding Group, $938
4. Yellow Freight System, $756
5. Consolidated Freightways Motor Freight, $647
6. J. B. Hunt Transport Services, $514
7. American President, $505
8. OMI, $381

*Where'd you hear that?*
Business Week, The Business Week 1000. Based on market value as of March 16, 1990, in millions of dollars.

## Most profitable trucking and shipping companies

1. Alexander & Baldwin, with 19.5%
2. Ryder System, 16.0%
3. Yellow Freight System, 15.8%
4. Consolidated Freightways Motor Freight, 15.3%
5. Carolina Freight Carriers, 15.2%
6. Roadway Services, 14.7%
7. Preston, 6.3%
8. American President, NA
9. Avondale Industries, NA

*Where'd you hear that?*
Forbes, Annual Report on American Industry. Based on 10-year average return on equity. Ranks publicly held corporations only.

## Most productive trucking and shipping corporations

1. Alexander & Baldwin with $63.7 thousand
2. Roadway Services, $2.9
3. American President, $2.4
4. Ryder System, $1.2
5. Yellow Freight System, $0.6
6. Consol Freightways, $0.2

103

# GETTING SOMEWHERE

*Where'd you hear that?*
Forbes, Forbes 500s Annual Directory. Based on 1989 profits per employee, in thousands of dollars. Ranks U.S.-based corporations that were publicly traded as of March 23, 1990.

## Countries with most cars on the road

1. United States, with 179,044,449
2. Japan, 49,901,936
3. West Germany, 30,105,249
4. France, 24,854,000
5. Italy, 24,716,000
6. United Kingdom, 23,520,551
7. Soviet Union, 21,573,000
8. Canada, 15,340,269
9. Spain, 12,130,484
10. Brazil, 11,937,283

*Where'd you hear that?*
World Automotive Market. Based on number of cars on the road as of January 1, 1988.

## Top 10 states for new car registrations

1. California, with 1,206,552
2. Florida, 800,834
3. New York, 729,601
4. Illinois, 602,656
5. Texas, 553,958
6. Pensylvania, 527,242
7. Ohio, 495,316
8. Michigan, 473,457
9. New Jersey, 462,645
10. Massachusetts, 362,780

*Where'd you hear that?*
Ward's Automotive Yearbook. Based on number of registrations in 1988.

## Best-selling American cars

1. Ford Escort
2. Chevrolet Corsica/Beretta
3. Ford Taurus
4. Chevrolet Cavalier
5. Ford Tempo
6. Chevrolet Celebrity
7. Honda Accord (U.S.)
8. Oldsmobile Cutless Ciera
9. Pontiac Grand AM
10. Chevrolet Caprice

*Where'd you hear that?*
Ward's Automotive Yearbook. Based on 1988 dealer sales.

## New cars with best resale value

1. Honda Prelude Coupe S, with 52%
2. BMW 325i (convertible), 49%
2. Porsche 911 Carrera, 49%
4. Acura Integra, 47%
4. Honda Accord DX, 47%
4. Mercedes-Benz 300E sedan, 47%
7. Lexus Infiniti Q45, 45%
7. Lexus ES250, 45%
9. Nissan Maxima, 43%
9. Toyota Camry, 43%

*Where'd you hear that?*
Changing Times. Based on retained value in 1994, in percent.

## Most popular cars among people age 50 and over

1. Chevrolet, with 19%
2. Ford, 16%
3. Buick, 12%

# GETTING SOMEWHERE

4. Oldsmobile, 10%
5. Pontiac, 7%
6. Mercury, 6%
7. Cadillac, 4%
7. Chrysler Corp., 4%
9. Toyota, 3%
10. others, total 19%

*Where'd you hear that?*
Advertising Age. Based on percentage of car owners aged 50+ buying the brand.

## Favorite car colors

1. Blue, with 22%
2. Red, 17%
3. White, 14%
4. Gray, 13%
5. Black, 11%
6. Other, 21%

*Where'd you hear that?*
Adweek's Marketing Week. Based on color's percent of all cars.

## The 10 most fuel-efficient cars

1. Geo Metro XFI, with 58 MPG highway
2. Honda Civic CRX HF, 52
3. Geo Metro, 50
3. Geo Metro LSI, 50
3. Suzuki Swift (1-L I-3 engine), 50
6. Honda Civic CRX HF, 49
7. Suzuki Swift (1.3 L I-4 engine), 44
8. Volkswagen Jetta, 43
9. Daihatsu Charade, 42
10. Suzuki Swift (1-L I-3 with A3 transmission), 39

*Where'd you hear that?*
Automotive News. Based on 1990 EPA highway fuel-economy estimates, in miles per gallon.

## *Most complained-about cars*

1. Oldsmobile Delta 88, with 10.5
2. Plymouth Horizon, 10.1
3. Acura Legend, 10.0
4. Pontiac Bonneville, 9.8
5. Buick LeSabre, 9.7
6. Oldsmobile 98, 6.7
7. Mercury Sable, 6.6
8. Nissan Maxima, 5.5
9. Mazda 626, 5.4
10. Ford Tempo, 5.2

*Where'd you hear that?*
Chilton's Automotive Industries. Based on complaints per 10,000 cars, 1987-88.

## The 10 least fuel-efficient cars

1. Lamborghini Countach, with 10 MPG highway
2. Bentley Continental, 13
2. Rolls-Royce Corniche III, 13
2. Rolls-Royce Silver Spirit/Spur, 13
2. Bentley Eight/Mulsanne 13
6. Ferrari Testarossa, 15
7. Audi V8, 18
7. BMW 750IL, 18
9. Porsche 928-S4, 19
9. Maserati 228, 19

*Where'd you hear that?*
Automotive News. Based on 1990 EPA highway fuel-economy estimates, in miles per gallon.

# GETTING SOMEWHERE

## Cars with the highest occupant death rates

1. Chevrolet Corvette, with 5.2
2. Chevrolet Camaro, 4.9
2. Dodge Charger/Shelby, 4.5
4. Ford Mustang, 4.4
5. Nissan 300ZX, 4.2
6. Chevrolet Chevette 4-door, 4.1
6. Chevrolet Sprint 2-door, 4.1
8. Honda Civic CRX, 3.9
9. Pontiac Firebird, 3.8
10. Plymouth Turismo, 3.6
10. Pontiac Fiero, 3.6

*Where'd you hear that?*
U.S. News & World Report. Based on occupant death rates per 10,000 cars over the 1986-88 period.

## Cars with the lowest occupant death rates

1. Volvo 740/760 4-door, with 0.6
2. Ford Taurus station wagon, 0.7
3. Lincoln Town Car, 0.8
4. Audi 5000 4-door, 1.1
4. Volkswagen Jetta 4-door, 1.1
4. Toyota Cressida 4-door, 1.1
4. Olds Cutlass Ciera station wagon, 1.1
4. Chevrolet Cavalier station wagon, 1.1
4. Cadillac Fleetwood/DeVille 2-door, 1.1
4. Cadillac Fleetwood/DeVille 4-door, 1.1

*Where'd you hear that?*
U.S. News & World Report. Based on occupant death rates per 10,000 cars over the 1986-88 period.

## World's largest auto manufacturers

1. General Motors Corp., U.S., with 17.7%
2. Ford Motor Co., U.S., 14.6%
3. Toyota, Japan, 9.4%
4. Volkswagen, West Germany, 6.6%
5. Nissan, Japan, 6.4%
6. Chrysler Corp., U.S., 5.4%
6. Fiat SpA, Italy, 5.4%
8. Peugeot, France, 4.6%
9. Renault, France, 4.2%
10. Honda Motor Co. Ltd., Japan, 4.0%

*Where'd you hear that?*
Business Week, Business Week Global Auto Scoreboard. Based on 1989 world market share of units sold, in percentage.

## World's largest producers of passenger cars

1. Japan, with 23.6%
2. United States, 20.5%
3. West Germany, 12.5%
4. France, 9.3%
5. Italy, 5.4%
6. Spain, 4.3%
7. United Kingdom, 3.5%
8. Canada, 3.0%
9. South Korea, 2.5%
10. Brazil, 2.2%
11. Sweden, 1.2%
12. Others, total 12%

*Where'd you hear that?*
Financial Times. Based on 1988 market share, in percent.

# GETTING SOMEWHERE

**Largest advertisers among auto companies in Great Britain**

1. Rover 200 Series, with £11,295 thousand
2. Ford Fiesta, £10,508
3. Vauxhall Nova, £9,875
4. Citroen AX, £8,585
5. Peugeot 405, £8,396
6. Renault 19, £7,113
7. Citroen BX, £6,970
8. Fiat Uno, £6,903
9. Ford Sierra, £6,493
10. Volvo 440, £6,362

*Where'd you hear that?*
Marketing, Top 500 Brands. Based on 1989 advertising expenditures, in thousands of British pounds.

**Most popular cars in Britain**

1. Ford, with 608,617
2. Vauxhall/Opel, 349,901
3. Rover group, 312,306
4. Peugeot/Citroen, 205,367
5. Nissan, 138,437
6. Audi/VW/Seat, 138,030
7. Renault, 88,111
8. Volvo, 81,706
9. Fiat/Alfa/Lancia, 77,485

*Where'd you hear that?*
Financial Times. Based on 1989 car registrations.

**States with the highest penetration of imported new cars**

1. Hawaii, with 59.0%
2. California, 55.7%
3. Washington, DC, 50.0%
4. Oregon, 48.7%
5. Washington, 48.7
6. Alaska, 45.2%
7. Colorado, 44.2%
8. Idaho, 44.1%
9. New Hampshire, 43.7%
10. Connecticut, 43.6%

*Where'd you hear that?*
Ward's Automotive Yearbook. Based on percentage of state registrations in 1988.

**Most popular imported cars**

1. Honda, with 662,138
2. Toyota, 644,763
3. Nissan, 471,981
4. Hyundai, 263,248
5. Mazda, 253,272
6. Volkswagen, 166,344
7. Subaru, 159,894
8. Acura, 129,589
9. Volvo, 98,672
10. Mercedes-Benz, 84,557

*Where'd you hear that?*
Ward's Automotive Yearbook. Based on 1988 new car registrations.

---

***Most popular cars in Western Europe***

1. Volkswagen AG, with 14.9%
2. Fiat Group, 14.8%
3. Peugeot SA, 12.9%
4. Ford, 11.3%
4. Japanese brands, 11.3%
6. General Motors/Opel, 10.4%
7. Renault, 10.1%
8. Mercedes, 3.4%
8. Rover, 3.4%
10. BMW, 2.7%

*Where'd you hear that?*
Financial Times. Based on percentage of total car registrations, 1988.

# GETTING SOMEWHERE

## Most productive automobile and truck corporations

1. Paccar, with $18.1 thousand
2. Ford Motor Co., $10.5
3. General Motors Corp., $5.5
4. Fleetwood Enterprises, Inc., $4.9
5. Chrysler Corp., $2.9
6. Navistar International, $2.2
7. Subaru of America, -$17.6
8. Mack Trucks, -$21.4

*Where'd you hear that?*
Forbes, Forbes 500s Annual Directory. Based on 1989 profits per employee, in thousands of dollars. Ranks U.S.-based corporations that were publicly traded as of March 23, 1990.

## Largest U.S. corporations in the automotive industry

1. General Motors Corp., with $28,814 million
2. Ford Motor Co., $22,990
3. Chrysler Corp., $4,147
4. Paccar, $1,596
5. Navistar International, $1,099

*Where'd you hear that?*
Business Week, The Business Week 1000. Based on market value on March 16, 1990, in millions of dollars.

## Most profitable automobile and truck companies

1. Oshkosh Truck, with 29.2%
2. Subaru of America, 24.7%
3. Chrysler Corp., 24.5%
4. Ford Motor Co., 23.0%
5. Paccar, 14.3%
6. General Motors Corp., 13.2%
7. Mack Trucks, deficit
8. Navistar International, deficit
9. K-H Corp., NA

*Where'd you hear that?*
Forbes, Annual Report on American Industry. Based on 10-year average return on equity. Ranks publicly held corporations only.

## Predicted auto industry leaders in 1994

1. General Motors Corp., with 32.7%
2. Ford Motor Co., 20.4%
3. Chrysler Corp., 9.4%
4. Honda Motor Co. Ltd., 9.1%
5. Toyota, 7.6%
6. Nissan, 6.1%
7. European makes, 4.7%
8. Hyundai Motor Co. Ltd., 3.0%
9. Mazda, 2.9%
10. Mitsubishi, 1.6%

*Where'd you hear that?*
Automobile News. Based on projected 1994 share of U.S. new car sales, in percent.

## Leading luxury car makers

1. Cadillac, with 26.9%
2. Lincoln-Mercury, 19.5%
3. Buick-Oldsmobile, 18.8%
4. Mercedes-Benz, 7.3%
5. Acura, 7.2%
6. Volvo, 5.9%
7. Chrysler Corp., 5.2%
8. Audi, 3.1%
9. Jaguar PLC, 1.6%
10. BMW, 1.4%
11. Others, total 3.2%

*Where'd you hear that?*
Wall Street Journal. Based on 1988 market share, in percent.

# GETTING SOMEWHERE

## Largest auto dealerships

1. Jordan Auto Mall (Mishawaka, IN)
2. Prospect Motors (Jackson, CA)
3. Luke Potter Dodge Inc. (Winter Park, FL)
4. Ed Morse Chevrolet Inc. (Lauderhill, FL)
5. Longo Toyota (El Monte, CA)
6. Libertyville Lincoln-Mercury (Libertyville, IL)
7. Bayview Cadillac (Ft Lauderdale, FL)
8. Polkowitz Motors (Perth Amboy, NJ)
9. McInerney Ford (Orlando, FL)
10. Ricart Ford (Columbus, OH)

*Where'd you hear that?*
Ward's Auto Dealer, Ward's Auto Dealer Diamond 500. Based on 1989 sales, plus other factors; see magazine for explanation.

## Largest auto dealers

1. Jordan Motors, Inc., $560.5 million
2. Prospect Motors, Inc., $470.6
3. Luke Potter Dodge, Inc., $411.8
4. Ed Morse Chevrolet Inc., $403.5
5. Longo Toyota, $338.0
6. Libertyville Lincoln-Mercury, $330.2
7. Bayview Cadillac, $271.4
8. Polkowitz Motors, $245.3
9. McInerney Ford, $244.8
10. Stephen Pontiac, Inc., $233.7

*Where'd you hear that?*
Automotive News. Based on 1989 sales, in millions of dollars.

## Largest auto dealerships in retail sales

1. Longo Toyota, with $205,914,073
2. Ricart Ford, $167,588,238
3. #1 Cochran, $102,926,712
4. Galpin Motors Inc., $95,575,597
5. Jordan Auto Mall, $91,175,348
6. Frontier Ford, $90,852,779
7. Lawrence Marshall Chevrolet, $88,051,162
8. Don Kott Ford, $84,606,317
9. Varsity Ford, $80,186,291
10. Herb Gordon Auto World Inc., $76,399,591

*Where'd you hear that?*
Ward's Auto Dealer, Ward's Auto Dealer Diamond 500. Based on 1989 retail sales, in dollars.

## Largest auto dealerships in fleet sales

1. Jordan Auto Mall, with $474,315,686
2. Prospect Motors Inc., $455,809,561
3. Luke Potter Dodge Inc., $387,387,703
4. Ed Morse Chevrolet Inc., $338,952,596
5. Libertyville Lincoln Mercury, $282,859,634
6. Polkowitz Motors, $228,614,976
7. McInerney Ford Inc., $216,302,000
8. Bayview Cadillac, $184,871,265
9. Island Lincoln Mercury, $171,379,222
10. Marty Franich Ford, $161,534,218

## GETTING SOMEWHERE

*Where'd you hear that?*
Ward's Auto Dealer, Ward's Auto Dealer Diamond 500. Based on 1989 fleet sales, in dollars.

### Largest auto dealerships in used car sales

1. Davis Moore Automotive Inc., with $35,826,281
2. Don Davis Oldsmobile Inc., $31,602,585
3. Riverside Chevrolet Inc., $30,291,278
4. Ricart Ford, $29,957,646
5. Ernie Von Schledorn Ltd., $28,611,566
6. C & O Motors Inc., $26,343,455
7. Earnhardt Ford, $25,476,327
8. Don Sanderson Ford Inc., $25,462,861
9. Wagstaff's House of Toyota, $22,361,229
10. Terry Schulte Chevrolet Geo, $21,914,439

*Where'd you hear that?*
Ward's Auto Dealer, Ward's Auto Dealer Diamond 500. Based on 1989 used car sales.

### Largest auto dealerships in service/parts sales

1. Lustine Chevrolet, with $39,383,356
2. Chuck Hutton Chevrolet Co., $29,148,501
3. Jim Slemons Imports, $25,490,520
4. Friendly Chevrolet, $23,798,881
5. Herb Gordon Auto World Inc., $23,364,103
6. Fred Jones Ford of Tulsa, $20,544,194
7. Don Sanderson Ford Inc., $19,749,636
8. Courtesy Chevrolet, $19,246,627
9. Chapman Chevrolet Inc., $18,767,364
10. Longo Toyota, $18,700,441

*Where'd you hear that?*
Ward's Auto Dealer, Ward's Auto Dealer Diamond 500. Based on 1989 service/parts sales.

### Largest auto dealerships in body shop sales

1. Jim Slemons Imports, with $4,993,904
2. Nalley Chevrolet, $4,958,000
3. Buick Mart Inc., $4,938,890
4. Ed Voyles Oldsmobile Sterling, $4,450,471
5. Art Moran Pontiac GMC Inc., $4,296,508
6. Coggin Pontiac Inc., $4,217,305
7. Tamaroff Buick Inc., $4,020,000
8. John Hine Pontiac Mazda, $3,312,178
9. Herb Gordon Auto World Inc., $3,203,891
10. Dan Young Chevrolet Honda, $3,172,608

*Where'd you hear that?*
Ward's Auto Dealer, Ward's Auto Dealer Diamond 500. Based on 1989 body shop sales.

### Metropolitan areas with the most automotive dealer sales

1. Los Angeles-Long Beach, CA, with $12,643,489 thousand
2. Philadelphia, PA, $8,532,686
3. Chicago, IL, $8,224,093
4. Detroit, MI, $7,596,254

5. Washington, DC, $7,370,231
6. New York, NY, $7,231,904
7. Boston-Lawrence-Salem-Lowell-Brockton, MA, $7,166,193
8. Houston, TX, $5,762,120
9. Atlanta, GA, $5,530,856
10. Nassau-Suffolk, NY, $5,121,143

*Where'd you hear that?*
Sales & Marketing Management, Survey of Buying Power. Based on automotive dealer sales, in thousands of dollars.

## Largest Acura franchises

1. Val Strough Acura (Pleasanton, CA), 1,800
2. Stevens Creek Acura (Santa Clara, CA), 1,600
3. Tustin Acura (Tustin, CA), 1,575
4. Cerritos Acura (Cerritos, CA), 1,437
5. Radley Acura (Falls Church, VA), 1,342
6. Acura of Westchester (Larchmont, NY), 1,263
7. Acura of Seattle (Seattle, WA), 1,200
8. Claremont Acura (Claremont, CA), 1,175
9. Rosenthal Acura (Gaithersburg, MD), 1,150
10. Pflueger Acura (Honolulu, HI), 1,078

*Where'd you hear that?*
Automotive News, Automotive News Market Data Book. Based on 1989 sales of new vehicles per outlet, by number of units sold.

# GETTING SOMEWHERE

## Largest Black-owned automobile dealers

1. Shack-Woods & Associates, with $138.000 millions
2. Jerry Watkins Cadillac-GMC Truck Inc., $107.916
3. S & J Enterprises, $97.882
4. Dick Gidron Cadillac & Ford Inc., $57.500
5. Mel Farr Automotive Group, $52.100
6. Baranco Lincoln-Mercury, Inc., $50.424
7. Gulf Freeway Dodge Inc., $50.127
8. Mort Hall Ford Inc., $47.000
9. Al Bennett Inc., $46.492
10. Baranco Pontiac-GMC Truck-Subaru Inc., $45.096

*Where'd you hear that?*
Black Enterprise. Based on 1989 sales, in millions of dollars.

## Largest Alfa Romeo franchises

1. Suburban Auto Imports (Maywood, IL), with 144
2. Robert Ruehman Inc. (North Hollywood, CA), 84
3. Beach Imports (Newport Beach, CA), 73
4. Beverly Hills Alfa (Los Angeles, CA), 69
5. E. E. R. Enterprises, Inc. (San Juan, PR), 61
6. Burlingame Alfa (Burlingame, CA), 51
7. Alfredo's Foreign Car (Larchmont, NY), 48
8. Paul Spruell Alfa (Chamblee, GA), 46

111

# GETTING SOMEWHERE

9. Southwest Alfa (Houston, TX), 45
10. Bobcor Motors (Hackensack, NJ), 36

*Where'd you hear that?*
Automotive News, Automotive News Market Data Book. Based on 1989 sales of new vehicles per outlet, by number of units sold.

## Largest Audi franchises

1. Carousel Automobiles (Golden Valley, MN), with 365
2. Jack Daniels Motors (Fairlawn, NJ), 329
3. Annis Corp. (Natick, MA), 284
4. Audi Exchange (Highland Park, IL), 263
5. Bill Cook Audi (Farmington Hills, MI), 211
6. Town Motor Car Corp. (Englewood, NJ), 209
7. O'Hare International Autos, Inc. (Elk Grove Village, IL), 196
8. Pray Audi Corp. (Greenwich, CT), 192
9. Audi Manhattan, Inc. (New York, NY), 187
10. Paul Miller, Inc. (Parsippany, NJ), 181

*Where'd you hear that?*
Automotive News, Automotive News Market Data Book. Based on 1989 sales of new vehicles per outlet, by number of units sold.

## Largest BMW franchises

1. Crevier BMW (Santa Ana, CA), 1,004
2. BMW South (Miami, FL), 885
3. Saddleback BMW (Irvine, CA), 817
4. BMW Concord (Concord, CA), 790
5. Pacific BMW (Glendale, CA), 779
6. Weatherford Motors (Berkeley, CA), 769
7. Braman Motors Inc. (Miami, FL), 716
8. Century Motor Sales (Alhambra, CA), 707
9. Nick Alexander Imports (Los Angeles, CA), 667
10. Sterling Motors Ltd. (Newport Beach, CA), 663

*Where'd you hear that?*
Automotive News, Automotive News Market Data Book. Based on 1989 sales of new vehicles per outlet, by number of units sold.

## Largest Buick franchises

1. Orange Buick-GMC Truck Co. (Orlando, FL), with 5,060
2. Wilkins Buick, Inc. (Glen Burnie, MD), 4,473
3. Lupient Buick (Minneapolis, MN), 4,042
4. Loren Buick, Inc. (Glenview, IL), 3,774
5. William Lehman Buick, Inc. (Miami, FL), 3,660
6. Prospect Motors, Inc. (Jackson, CA), 3,564
7. Grant Dean Buick, Inc. (Highland Park, IL), 3,160
8. Polkowitz Motors (Perth Amboy, NJ), 3,029
9. Ron Smith Buick Jeep-Eagle (Merced, CA), 2,464
10. Buick Mart Inc. (Cerritos, CA), 2,297

*Where'd you hear that?*
Automotive News, Automotive News Market Data Book. Based on 1989 sales of new vehicles per outlet, by number of units sold.

# GETTING SOMEWHERE

**Largest Cadillac franchises**

1. Bayview Cadillac (Fort Lauderdale, FL), with 9,257
2. Polkowitz Motors (Perth Amboy, NJ), 8,025
3. Long Cadillac (Roseville, MN), 5,055
4. Prospect Motors (Jackson, CA), 3,772
5. Penske Cadillac (Downey, CA), 3,691
6. Martin Cadillac Co., Inc. (Los Angeles, CA), 2,650
7. Roger Meier Cadillac Co. (Dallas, TX), 2,465
8. Premier Cadillac Inc. (Kansas City, MO), 1,650
9. Cashman Cadillac (Las Vegas, NV), 1,600
10. Coral Cadillac Inc. (Pompano Beach, FL), 1,556

*Where'd you hear that?*
Automotive News, Automotive News Market Data Book. Based on 1989 sales of new vehicles per outlet, by number of units sold.

**Largest Chevrolet franchises**

1. Ed Morse Chevrolet, Inc. (Lauderhill, FL), with 37,489
2. Prospect Motors, Inc. (Jackson, CA), 18,319
3. Del'Orme Chevrolet (Alhambra, CA), 12,058
4. Z Frank Chevrolet (Chicago, IL), 11,430
5. Bob Brest Chevrolet (Lynn, MA), 10,495
6. Bast Chevrolet, Inc. (Seaford, NY), 9,334
7. Harold Chevrolet (Bloomington, MN), 7,630
8. Friendly Chevrolet (Dallas, TX), 7,090
9. Povey Chevrolet (Red Bluff, CA), 6,860
10. Celozzi-Ettleson Chevrolet (Elmhurst, IL), 6,404

*Where'd you hear that?*
Automotive News, Automotive News Market Data Book. Based on 1989 sales of new vehicles per outlet, by number of units sold.

**Largest Chrysler-Plymouth franchises**

1. Precision Chrysler-Plymouth-Dodge (Winter Haven, FL), with 8,644
2. Forest Lake Chrysler-Plymouth-Dodge (Forest Lake, MN), 7,160
3. Lake Forest Chrysler-Plymouth (Gaithersburg, MD), 6,536
4. Hollywood Chrysler-Plymouth, Inc. (Hollywood, FL), 5,367
5. Massey Yardley Chrysler-Plymouth (Plantation, FL), 5,351
6. Galena Chrysler-Plymouth, Inc. (Fort Myers, FL), 4,738
7. Allen Cubbage Chrysler-Plymouth-Dodge (Stanley, VA), 4,159
8. South Bay Chrysler-Plymouth Jeep-Eagle (Torrance, CA), 3,846
9. Russ Darrow Chrysler-Plymouth (Waukesha, WI), 3,567
10. Tate Chrysler-Plymouth (Glen Burnie, MD), 3,549

*Where'd you hear that?*
Automotive News, Automotive News Market Data Book. Based on 1989 sales of new vehicles per outlet, by number of units sold.

# GETTING SOMEWHERE

### Largest Dodge franchises

1. Luke Potter Dodge Inc. (Winter Park, FL), with 20,272
2. Precision Chrysler-Plymouth-Dodge (Winter Haven, FL), 12,704
3. Tate Dodge Inc. (Glen Burnie, MD), 12,125
4. Colonial Dodge, Inc. (Kensington, MD), 9,076
5. Freeway Dodge, Inc. (Bloomington, MN), 9,010
6. Haggerty Dodge (Chicago, IL), 7,601
7. Ed Morse Dodge (Coconut Creek, FL), 6,668
8. Forest Lake Chrysler-Plymouth-Dodge (Forest Lake, MN), 5,214
9. Dodge World Kissimmee (Kissimmee, FL), 4,888
10. Amador Motors, Inc. (Sutter Creek, CA), 4,608

*Where'd you hear that?*
Automotive News, Automotive News Market Data Book. Based on 1989 sales of new vehicles per outlet, by number of units sold.

### Largest Ford franchises

1. Jordan Motors, Inc. (Mishawaka, IN), 47,652
2. McInerney Ford (Orlando, FL), 20,985
3. Al Piemonte Ford Sales, Inc. (Melrose Park, IL), 18,009
4. Santa Monica Ford (Santa Monica, CA), 15,333
5. Highland Park Ford (Highland Park, IL), 12,425
6. Pacifico Ford, Inc. (Philadelphia, PA), 12,389
7. Fairway Ford (Latrobe, PA), 12,050
8. Rice and Holman Ford (Mt. Laurel, NJ), 11,679
9. Ricart Ford Inc. (Columbus, OH), 11,344
10. S & C Ford (San Francisco, CA), 11,160

*Where'd you hear that?*
Automotive News, Automotive News Market Data Book. Based on 1989 sales of new vehicles per outlet, by number of units sold.

### Largest Honda franchises

1. Gardena Honda (Gardena, CA), 6,071
2. Norm Reeves Honda, Inc. (Cerritos, CA), 4,301
3. Robertson Honda (North Hollywood, CA), 3,850
4. Plaza Honda (Brooklyn NY), 3,330
5. Penske Honda (Downey, CA), 2,970
6. Herson's Honda (Rockville, MD), 2,775
7. Rosenthal Honda (Vienna, VA), 2,450
8. Honda of Lisle (Lisle, IL), 2,418
9. Showcase Honda (Phoenix, AZ), 2,240
10. Pacific Honda (San Diego, CA, 1,735

*Where'd you hear that?*
Automotive News, Automotive News Market Data Book. Based on 1989 sales of new vehicles per outlet, by number of units sold.

### Largest Isuzu franchises

1. Sam White Isuzu (Houston, TX), 1,396
2. Courtesy Isuzu (Lafayette, LA), 1,178

3. Fountain Isuzu (Orlando, FL), 1,082
4. Fletcher Jones Isuzu (Las Vegas, NV), 949
5. Covert Isuzu (Austin, TX), 802
6. Royal Isuzu (Tampa, FL), 794
7. J. K. J. Isuzu (Woodbridge, PA), 789
8. Fresno Isuzu (Fresno, CA), 757
9. Henderson-Sellers (Baton Rouge, LA), 726
10. Biddulph Isuzu (Santa Rosa, CA), 709

*Where'd you hear that?*
Automotive News, Automotive News Market Data Book. Based on 1989 sales of new vehicles per outlet, by number of units sold.

## Largest Jaguar franchises

1. Hempstead Auto Co. (Hempstead, NY), 706
2. Newport Imports, Inc. (Newport Beach, CA), 641
3. Hornburg Jaguar, Inc. (Los Angeles, CA), 534
4. Jaguar Collection (Coral Gables, FL), 431
5. Bauer Jaguar (Anaheim, CA), 376
6. Rosenthal Jaguar (Vienna, VA), 375
7. Sportique Motors Ltd. (Huntington, NY), 341
8. Rallye Motors, Inc. (Paramus, NJ), 338
9. Dominion Jaguar (Houston, TX), 332
10. Crown Jaguar (St. Petersburg, FL), 331

*Where'd you hear that?*
Automotive News, Automotive News Market Data Book. Based on 1989 sales of new vehicles per outlet, by number of units sold.

# GETTING SOMEWHERE

## Largest Hyundai franchises

1. Cormier Hyundai (Long Beach, CA), with 2,158
2. Kim-Hankey Hyundai (Los Angeles, CA), 1,951
3. Bauer Hyundai (Tinley Park, IL), 1,929
4. Olympic Hyundai (Chicago, IL), 1,640
5. O'Connor Hyundai (Chicago, IL), 1,625
6. Galpin Hyundai (Sepulvela, CA), 1,594
7. Garden Grove Hyundai (Garden Grove, CA), 1,377
8. Savage Hyundai (Monrovia, CA), 1,361
9. Lee Hyundai (Fayetteville, NC), 1,346
10. Woodfield Hyundai (Hoffman Estates, IL), 1,264

*Where'd you hear that?*
Automotive News, Automotive News Market Data Book. Based on 1989 sales of new vehicles per outlet, by number of units sold.

## Largest Jeep-Eagle franchises

1. Don-A-Vee Jeep Eagle (Bellflower, CA), 2,453
2. Jasper Jeep Sales (Jasper, GA), 2,258
3. Manhattan Jeep Eagle (New York, NY), 1,926
4. South Bay Chrysler-Plymouth Jeep-Eagle (Torrance, CA), 1,804
5. Buerge Jeep-Eagle (West Los Angeles, CA), 1,735

# GETTING SOMEWHERE

6. Pete Ellis Dodge, Inc. (South Gate, CA), 1,724
7. Royal Jeep/Eagle, Inc. (Fern Park, FL), 1,473
8. Salerno Duane Pontiac-Har (Summit, NJ), 1,360
9. Broadway Jeep-Eagle (Littleton, CO), 1,356
10. Heritage Chrysler-Plymouth (Alexandria, VA), 1,330

*Where'd you hear that?*
Automotive News, Automotive News Market Data Book. Based on 1989 sales of new vehicles per outlet, by number of units sold.

## Largest Lincoln-Mercury franchises

1. Libertyville Lincoln-Mercury (Libertyville, IL), 21,014
2. Island Lincoln-Mercury (Merritt Island, FL), 7,715
3. Marty Franich Lincoln-Mercury (Watsonville, CA), 7,450
4. O'Conner Lincoln-Mercury (Los Angeles), 5,525
5. Arnold Palmer Ford, Lincoln-Mercury (Blufton, SC), 5,296
6. Northgate Lincoln-Mercury (Tampa, FL), 4,366
7. Stu Evans Lincoln-Mercury Inc. (Garden City, MI), 3,880
8. North Park Lincoln-Mercury (San Antonio, TX), 3,358
9. Holman Lincoln-Mercury (Mapleshade, NJ), 3,329
10. Stu Evans Lincoln-Mercury Inc. (Southgate, MI), 3,071

*Where'd you hear that?*
Automotive News, Automotive News Market Data Book. Based on 1989 sales of new vehicles per outlet, by number of units sold.

## Largest Mazda franchises

1. Puente Hills Mazda (City of Industry, CA), with 2,452
2. Frank Bommarito Mazda (Ellisville, MO), 2,281
3. Gunther Mazda (Ft. Lauderdale, FL), 2,276
4. Billy Barrett Mazda (Dallas, TX), 2,236
5. Freeman Mazda (Irving, TX), 2,147
6. Roger Beasley Mazda (Austin, TX), 1,709
7. Mapleshade Mazda (Mapleshade, NJ), 1,654
8. Red McCombs Mazda (San Antonio, TX), 1,601
9. Oak Tree Imports (San Jose, CA), 1,567
10. Jim Ellis Mazda (Marietta, GA), 1,527

*Where'd you hear that?*
Automotive News, Automotive News Market Data Book. Based on 1989 sales of new vehicles per outlet, by number of units sold.

## Largest Mercedes-Benz franchises

1. Downtown L.A. Motors (Los Angeles, CA), with 1,483
2. Ray Catena Motor Car (Edison, NJ), 1,182
3. Jim Slemons Imports (Newport Beach, CA), 1,135
4. Rallye Motors (Roslyn, NY), 1,080
5. Benzel-Busch Motorcar (Englewood, NJ), 1,053
6. Mercedes Benz Manhattan (New York, NY), 1,050
7. RBW of Atlanta (Atlanta, GA), 905
8. Smythe European (San Jose, CA), 825

9. Park Place Motorcars (Dallas, TX), 804
10. Prestige Motors (Paramus, NJ), 765

*Where'd you hear that?*
Automotive News, Automotive News Market Data Book. Based on 1989 sales of new vehicles per outlet, by number of units sold.

## Largest Mitsubishi franchises

1. Michael Mitsubishi (Fresno, CA), with 2,060
2. Frank Parra Mitsubishi (Irving, TX), 2,013
3. Boch Mitsubishi (Norwood, MA), 1,999
4. Century Mitsubishi (Warwick, RI), 1,560
5. Bob King Mitsubishi (Winston-Salem, NC), 1,363
6. Paul York Mitsubishi (Corpus Cristi, TX), 1,238
7. Serramonte Mitsubishi (Colma, FL), 1,196
8. Manhasset Mitsubishi (Manhasset, NY), 1,176
9. Jim Hudson Mitsubishi (Columbia, SC), 1,129
10. Rockland Mitsubishi (Nyack, NY), 1,058

*Where'd you hear that?*
Automotive News, Automotive News Market Data Book. Based on 1989 sales of new vehicles per outlet, by number of units sold.

## Largest Nissan franchises

1. Northwestern Nissan (Fridley, MN), with 6,130
2. Nissan of Downey (Downey, CA), 5,479
3. ABC Nissan Inc. (Phoenix, AZ), 4,812
4. Duarte Nissan (Duarte, CA), 3,959
5. Mossy Nissan (National City, CA), 3,939
6. West Covina Nissan (West Covina, CA), 3,419
7. Universal City Nissan (Los Angeles, CA), 3,386
8. Bob Brest Nissan (Lynn, MA), 3,000
9. Winner Nissan (Newark, DE), 2,838
10. Rosenthal Nissan (Vienna, VA), 2,672

*Where'd you hear that?*
Automotive News, Automotive News Market Data Book. Based on 1989 sales of new vehicles per outlet, by number of units sold.

## Largest Oldsmobile franchises

1. Jim Lupient Oldsmobile (Minneapolis, MN), with 11,285
2. Dale Oldsmobile-Pontiac (Houston, TX), 10,900
3. Browning Oldsmobile (Cerritos, CA), 7,320
4. Prospect Motors, Inc. (Jackson, CA), 6,981
5. Larry Faul Oldsmobile (Schaumburg, IL), 5,079
6. Anderson Oldsmobile (Baltimore, MD), 4,985
7. Sam White Oldsmobile (Houston, TX), 4,699
8. Fountain Oldsmobile (Orlando, FL), 4,685
9. Z Frank Oldsmobile (Chicago, IL), 4,300
10. Henry Faulkner Inc. (Philadelphia, PA), 4,052

# GETTING SOMEWHERE

# GETTING SOMEWHERE

*Where'd you hear that?*
Automotive News, Automotive News Market Data Book. Based on 1989 sales of new vehicles per outlet, by number of units sold.

## Largest Peugeot franchises

1. Peugeot of Union County (Rahway, NJ), with 172
2. Autos Vega, Inc. (San Juan, PR), 154
3. Fred's Peugeot (Philadelphia, PA), 110
4. Imported Car Center (Williston, VT), 97
5. Foreign Motors West, Inc. (Natick, MA), 94
6. Overseas Auto Corp. (Hastings-on-Hudson, NY), 86
7. Trans-Atlantic Motors Inc. (Stamford, CT), 76
8. Maplewood Peugeot (Maplewood, NJ), 73
9. Tenafly Foreign Cars (Tenafly, NJ), 68
10. Clair Peugeot (West Roxbury, MA), 67

*Where'd you hear that?*
Automotive News, Automotive News Market Data Book. Based on 1989 sales of new vehicles per outlet, by number of units sold.

## Largest Pontiac franchises

1. Stephen Pontiac-Cadillac, Inc. (Bristol, CT), with 15,030
2. J. M. Pontiac (Hollywood, FL), 14,072
3. Prospect Motors (Jackson, CA), 12,620
4. Hansford Pontiac-GMC (Minneapolis, MN), 9,090
5. Patrick Pontiac-GMC (Libertyville, IL), 8,100
6. Wiesner Pontiac (Conroe, TX), 5,550
7. Dale Oldsmobile-Pontiac (Bronx, NY), 4,340
8. Dave Gill Pontiac-GMC Inc. (Columbus, OH), 4,086
9. Larry Faul Pontiac, Inc. (Schaumburg, IL), 3,416
10. Cochran Pontiac, Inc. (Monroeville, PA), 3,214

*Where'd you hear that?*
Automotive News, Automotive News Market Data Book. Based on 1989 sales of new vehicles per outlet, by number of units sold.

## Largest Porsche franchises

1. Champion Porsche (Pompano Beach, FL), with 242
2. Max Dial Porsche (Inglewood, CA), 223
3. Porsche Exchange (Highland Park, IL), 215
4. Rainbow Porsche (North Miami, FL), 185
5. Jim Ellis Atlanta (Atlanta, GA), 184
6. Lipshy Motors (Dallas, TX), 179
7. Deel Porsche (Miami, FL), 175
8. Zipper Porsche (Beverly Hills, CA), 157
9. Brumos Atlanta, Inc. (Atlanta, GA), 149
10. Jack Daniels Motors (Fairlawn, NJ), 128

*Where'd you hear that?*
Automotive News, Automotive News Market Data Book. Based on 1989 sales of new vehicles per outlet, by number of units sold.

**Largest Range Rover franchises**

1. Range Rover Land (Passapequa, NY), with 209
2. Range Rover of Darien (Darien, CT), 184
3. Terry York Motor Cars (Encino, CA), 177
3. Hornburg Jaguar Inc. (Los Angeles, CA), 177
5. Prestige Motors Inc. (Paramus, NJ), 149
6. Newport Imports, Inc (Newport Beach, CA), 140
7. Foreign Motors West, Inc. (Natick, MA), 138
8. Paul Miller Inc. (Parsippany, NJ), 134
9. Zumbach Sports Cars (New York, NY), 126
10. H. B. L. Inc. (Vienna, VA), 107

*Where'd you hear that?*
Automotive News, Automotive News Market Data Book. Based on 1989 sales of new vehicles per outlet, by number of units sold.

**Largest Saab franchises**

1. Zumbach Sportscars, Ltd. (New York, NY), with 560
2. Ramsey Saab (Ramsey, NJ), 522
3. Lindquist Motors (Culver City, CA), 419
4. Saab of Westport (Westport, CT), 384
5. Clews & Strawbridge Inc. (Frazer, PA), 300
5. Fields Saab (Glenview, IL), 300
7. Wigwam Inc. (North Providence, RI), 290
8. Charles River Saab (Watertown, MA), 273
9. Mitchell Saab (Simsbury, CT), 251
10. Stohlman Saab (Alexandria, VA), 246

*Where'd you hear that?*
Automotive News, Automotive News Market Data Book. Based on 1989 sales of new vehicles per outlet, by number of units sold.

# GETTING SOMEWHERE

**Largest Rolls Royce franchises**

1. Carriage House Motor Cars Ltd. (New York, NY), with 140
2. Gregg Motors Beverly Hills (Beverly Hills, CA), 130
3. Newport Auto Center (Newport Beach, CA), 125
4. Terry York Motor Cars, Ltd. (Encino, CA), 70
5. Lauderdale Imports (Ft. Lauderdle, FL), 59
6. Braman Motorcars (West Palm Beach, FL), 55
7. Rusnak/Pasadena (Pasadena, CA), 54
8. Braman Motors Inc. (Miami, FL), 35
9. Carriage House Motor Cars (Greenwich, CT), 34
10. Whitehouse Imported (Whitehouse Station, NJ), 33

*Where'd you hear that?*
Automotive News, Automotive News Market Data Book. Based on 1989 sales of new vehicles per outlet, by number of units sold.

**Largest Subaru franchises**

1. Continental Motor Co. (Anchorage, AK), 1,417
2. Burt Subaru (Englewood, CT), 1,176

# GETTING SOMEWHERE

3. Shortline Subaru, Inc. (Aurora, CO), 980
4. Long Subaru (West Chicago, IL), 600
5. Norwood Subaru (Norwood, MA), 548
6. Brown's Subaru of Alexandria (Alexandria, VA), 527
7. Tischer Subaru (Silver Spring, MD), 517
8. Carter Subaru (North Seattle, WA), 513
9. Appleway Subaru (Spokane, WA), 490
10. Stohlman Subaru (Vienna, VA), 478

*Where'd you hear that?*
Automotive News, Automotive News Market Data Book. Based on 1989 sales of new vehicles per outlet, by number of units sold.

## Largest Toyota franchises

1. Longo Toyota (El Monte, CA), 23,058
2. Kendall Toyota (Miami, FL), 17,313
3. Toyota of Hollywood (Hollywood, FL), 6,388
4. Toyota of Orange (Orange, CA), 6,186
5. Sterling McCall Toyota (Houston, TX), 5,355
6. Downey Toyota (Downey, CA), 4,937
7. Delray Toyota (Delray Beach, FL), 4,744
8. Gateway Toyota (Toms River, NJ), 4,493
9. Hudson Toyota, Inc. (Jersey City, NJ), 4,187
10. Toyota of Cerritos (Cerritos, CA), 4,041

*Where'd you hear that?*
Automotive News, Automotive News Market Data Book. Based on 1989 sales of new vehicles per outlet, by number of units sold.

## Largest Volkswagen franchises

1. Jim Ellis Volkswagen, Inc. (Atlanta, GA), with 1,238
2. South County Motors (Huntington Beach, CA), 1,112
3. Volkswagen Santa Monica, Inc. (Santa Monica, CA), 942
4. Gunther Volkswagen (Fort Lauderdale, FL), 830
5. Douglas Motors Corp. (Summit, NJ), 824
6. Annis Corp. (Natick, MA), 761
7. Stohlman Volkswagen (Vienna, VA), 729
8. Libon Motors Inc. (Boston, MA), 705
9. Volkswagen of Downtown LA (Los Angeles, CA), 693
10. Queensboro Volkswagen, Inc. (Woodside, NY), 643

*Where'd you hear that?*
Automotive News, Automotive News Market Data Book. Based on 1989 sales of new vehicles per outlet, by number of units sold.

## Largest Volvo franchises

1. Volvoville, USA (Massapequa, NY), with 1,480
2. Dyer & Dyer (Chamblee, GA), 1,280
3. Warren Henry Volvo (Miami, FL), 1,148
4. Deel Volvo (Miami, FL), 1,110
5. Point West Volvo (Irving, TX), 1,096

6. San Diego Volvo (San Diego, CA), 1,057
7. Martin Motor Sales (New York, NY), 910
8. Volvo of Lisle (Lisle, IL), 821
9. Kramer Motors (Santa Monica, CA), 795
10. Karp Volvo (Rockville Center, NY), 746

*Where'd you hear that?*
Automotive News, Automotive News Market Data Book. Based on 1989 sales of new vehicles per outlet, by number of units sold.

## Top car rental companies ranked by number of locations

1. Hertz Rent a Car, with 1,400
2. Avis Rent a Car, 1,300
3. Budget Car and Truck Rental, 1,242
4. National Car Rental, 1,012
5. Dollar Rent a Car, 762
6. Agency Rent-A-Car, 701
7. Enterprise Rent-a-Car, 650
8. Thrifty Car Rental, 382
9. Rent A Wreck, 322
10. Snappy Car Rental, 244

*Where'd you hear that?*
Business Travel News, Business Travel Survey. Based on number of U.S. locations.

## Top car rental companies ranked by revenues

1. Hertz Rent a Car, with $3,100,000 thousand
2. Avis Rent a Car, $2,800,000
3. National Car Rental, $2,300,000
4. Budget Car and Truck Rental, $2,000,000
5. Dollar Rent a Car, $800,000
6. Alamo Rent A Car Inc., $510,000
7. Enterprise Rent-a-Car, $500,000
8. American International Rent a Car, $350,000
9. Thrifty Car Rental, $300,000
10. Agency Rent-A-Car, $270,000

*Where'd you hear that?*
Business Travel News, Business Travel Survey. Based on systemwide revenues, in thousands of dollars.

## Top automobile parts brands

1. Quaker State, with 39%
2. Pennzoil, 28%
3. Valvoline, 18%
4. Fram, 17%
5. Havoline, 14%
6. STP, 12%
7. Prestone, 9%
8. Castrol/Castroil, 8%
9. AC-Delco, 5%
9. Turtle Wax, 5%

*Where'd you hear that?*
Discount Store News. Based on percentage of discount store managers naming brand as top performer in 1989.

## Largest U.S. corporations in the automotive parts industry

1. Eaton Corp., with $2,039 million
2. Dana Corp., $1,427
3. Echlin, Inc., $732
4. Pep Boys-Manny, Moe & Jack, $623
5. Masco Industries, $491
6. Cummins Engine Co., Inc., $421
7. Federal-Mogul, $401
8. SPX, $395
9. Danaher, $361

# GETTING SOMEWHERE

# GETTING SOMEWHERE

*Where'd you hear that?*
Business Week, The Business Week 1000. Based on market value on March 16, 1990, in millions of dollars.

## Most productive automotive parts corporations

1. Bandag, with $31.8 thousand
2. SPX, $16.3
3. Snap-on Tools, $14.3
4. PPG Industries, $13.1
5. Genuine Parts Co., $12.8
6. Eaton Corp., $5.9
7. Dana Corp., $3.4
8. Masco Industries, $3.2
9. Johnson Controls, $2.8
10. Goodyear Tire & Rubber Co., $1.7
11. Arvin Industries Inc., $1.1
12. Cummins Engine Co., Inc., $-0.2

*Where'd you hear that?*
Forbes, Forbes 500s Annual Directory. Based on 1989 profits per employee, in thousands of dollars. Ranks U.S.-based corporations that were publicly traded as of March 23, 1990.

## Most profitable automotive parts companies

1. Bandag, with 33.0%
2. Standard Products, 25.3%
3. TBC, 22.6%
4. Snap-on Tools, 21.6%
5. Genuine Parts Co., 19.8%
6. PPG Industries, 17.4%
7. Cooper Tire & Rubber, 17.1%
8. Goodyear Tire & Rubber Co., 16.3%

*Where'd you hear that?*
Forbes, Annual Report on American Industry. Based on 10-year average return on equity. Ranks publicly held corporations only.

## Largest publicly-owned manufacturers of miscellaneous automobile parts ranked by revenues

1. Echlin, Inc., with $1,294.30 million
2. Federal-Mogul Corp., $1,176.90
3. SPX Corp., $877.70
4. Intermark, Inc., $573.40
5. Bearings, Inc., $542.90
6. Standard Products Co., $508.30
7. Standard Motor Products, $398.40
8. Modine Manufacturing Co., $395.20
9. Lamson & Sessions Co., $388.20
10. Allen Group, Inc., $344.40

*Where'd you hear that?*
Jobber Topics, Annual Marketing Directory. Based on 1988 revenues, in millions of dollars.

## Largest publicily-owned manufacturers of miscellaneous automobile parts ranked by net income

1. Echlin, Inc., with $62.10 million
2. SPX Corp., $44.90
3. Federal-Mogul Corp., $43.40
4. Standard Products Co., $34.10
5. Lamson & Sessions Co., $26.90
6. Modine Manufacturing Co., $25.00
7. Bearings, Inc., $17.00
8. Intermark, Inc., $13.40
9. Neoax, Inc., $10.60
10. Simpson Industries, Inc., $10.50

*Where'd you hear that?*
Jobber Topics, Annual Marketing Directory. Based on 1988 net income, in millions of dollars.

**Largest publicly-owned manufacturers of major automobile parts ranked by revenues**

1. Dana Corp., with $4,895.60 million
2. Eaton Corp., $3,468.50
3. Cummins Engine Co., Inc., $3,310.10
4. Genuine Parts Co., $2,942.00
5. Trinova Corp., $1,918.60
6. Timken Co., $1,554.10
7. Arvin Industries Inc., $1,313.30
8. A. O. Smith Corp., $970.40
9. Champion Spark Plug Co., $738.00
10. Barnes Group, Inc., $496.10

*Where'd you hear that?*
Jobber Topics, Annual Marketing Directory. Based on 1988 revenues, in millions of dollars.

**Largest publicly-owned manufacturers of major automobile parts ranked by net income**

1. Eaton Corp., with $227.70 million
2. Genuine Parts Co., $181.40
3. Dana Corp., $162.20
4. Trinova Corp., $87.80
5. Timken Co., $65.90
6. Champion Spark Plug Co., $22.10
7. Barnes Group, Inc., $18.80
8. Arvin Industries Inc., $16.50
9. A. O. Smith Corp., $15.50
10. Walbro Corp., $5.90

*Where'd you hear that?*
Jobber Topics, Annual Marketing Directory. Based on 1988 net income, in millions of dollars.

**Most profitable publicly-owned manufacturers of miscellaneous automobile parts ranked by profit margin**

1. Larizza Industries, Inc., with 14.30%
2. Valley Forge Corp., 11.60%
3. Cascade Corp., 11.50%
4. Modine Manufacturing Co., 11.00%
4. Standard Products Co., 11.00%
6. Howell Industries, Inc., 10.70%
7. SPX Corp., 10.50%
8. Kysor Industrial Corp., 10.20%
9. Superior Industries, 9.50%
10. Standard Motor Products, 9.10%

*Where'd you hear that?*
Jobber Topics, Annual Marketing Directory. Based on 1987 operating profit margin, in percent.

**Most profitable publicly-owned manufacturers of miscellaneous automobile parts ranked by return on capital**

1. Howell Industries, Inc., with 21.34%
2. Larizza Industries, Inc., 21.00%
3. Standard Products Co., 19.68%
4. Kysor Industrial Corp., 14.52%
5. Raytech Corp., 13.20%
6. Bearings, Inc., 12.76%

# GETTING SOMEWHERE

# GETTING SOMEWHERE

7. Modine Manufacturing Co., 11.97%
8. Radlaw Industries, Inc., 11.25%
9. Cascade Corp., 11.09%
10. Superior Industries, 10.65%

*Where'd you hear that?*
Jobber Topics, Annual Marketing Directory. Based on 1987 return on capital, in percent.

## Most profitable publicly-owned manufacturers of major automobile parts ranked by profit margin

1. Eaton Corp., with 12.00%
2. Walbro Corp., 10.70%
3. Genuine Parts Co., 9.90
4. Defiance Precision, 9.30%
5. Mr. Gasket Co., 9.30%
6. Timken Co., 9.00%
7. Barnes Group, Inc., 8.80%
8. Trinova Corp., 8.70%
9. Arvin Industries Inc., 7.10%
10. Dana Corp., 7.00%

*Where'd you hear that?*
Jobber Topics, Annual Marketing Directory. Based on 1988 operating profit margin, in percent.

## Most profitable publicly-owned manufacturers of major automobile parts ranked by return on capital

1. Genuine Parts Co., with 19.94%
2. Eaton Corp., 9.52%
3. Trinova Corp., 8.81%
4. Dana Corp., 8.44%
5. Barnes Group, Inc., 8.43%
6. Arvin Industries Inc., 7.23%
7. Walbro Corp., 7.05%
8. Timken Co., 5.43%

9. Defiance Precision, 4.29%
10. Champion Spark Plug Co., 3.70%

*Where'd you hear that?*
Jobber Topics, Annual Marketing Directory. Based on 1988 return on capital, in percent.

## Top states in garages and service stations construction markets

1. California, with $636 million
2. Illinois, $219
3. Florida, $215
4. Texas, $173
5. Ohio, $168
6. Georgia, $135
7. Pennsylvania, $134
8. Nevada, $133
9. Michigan, $127
10. Massachusetts, $112

*Where'd you hear that?*
ENR, Top 20 States in Major Construction Markets. Based on eleven-month cumulative contract awards, 1989 vs. 1988, in millions of dollars.

## 10 largest chains of gasoline stations

1. Texaco, with 15,389 in 45 states
2. Exxon Corp., 12,456 in 37 states
3. Chevron Corp., 11,969 in 33 states
4. Mobil, 11,074 in 36 states
5. Unocal, 10,926 in 43 states
6. Shell, 10,847 in 41 states
7. Amoco Corp., 10,246 in 30 states
8. Phillips, 9,757 in 36 states
9. Citgo, 7,697 in 40 states
10. BP America, 7,413 in 28 states

# GETTING SOMEWHERE

*Where'd you hear that?*
New York Times. Based on number of stations.

## Oil companies with the most service stations

1. Texaco, with 15,389
2. Exxon Corp., 12,456
3. Chevron Corp., 11,969
4. Mobil, 11,074
5. Unocal, 10,926
6. Shell, 10,847
7. Amoco Corp., 10,246
8. Phillips, 9,757
9. Citgo, 7,697
10. BP America, 7,413

*Where'd you hear that?*
National Petroleum News. Based on number of branded retail outlets in 1988.

## Top 10 auto auctions

1. Florida Auto Auction of Orlando, with $741.6 million
2. Southern California Auto Auction, $519.3
3. Nashville Auto Auction, $489.9
4. Aptco Auto Auction, Detroit, $471.7
5. Manheim Auto Auction, PA, $461.8
6. Metro Auto Auction of Kansas City, $459.0
7. National Auto Dealers Exchange, NJ, $416.4
8. California Auto Dealers Exchange, $400.9
9. Bay Cities Auto Auction, CA, $392.6
10. Greater Chicago Auto Auction, $383.5

*Where'd you hear that?*
Automotive News, Top 10 Auto Auctions. Based on 1988 volume, in millions of dollars.

## *Metropolitan Statistical Areas with largest gasoline service station sales*

1. Los Angeles-Long Beach, CA, with $3,565,594 thousand
2. Chicago, IL, $2,465,638
3. Detroit, MI, $2,218,151
4. Washington, DC, $1,994,624
5. Philadelphia, PA, $1,852,132
6. Boston-Lawrence-Salem-Lowell-Brockton, MA, $1,653,106
7. Minneapolis-St. Paul, MN, $1,529,401
8. Atlanta, GA, $1,527,064
9. New York, NY, $1,501,611
10. St. Louis, MO, $1,361,821

*Where'd you hear that?*
Sales & Marketing Management, Survey of Buying Power. Based on sales per MSA, in thousands of dollars.

## Leading commercial automobile insurance writers

1. American International Group, with $902.133 thousand
2. Liberty Mutual Group, $880,854
3. Aetna Life & Casualty Group, $694,443
4. Travelers Insurance Group, $656,959
5. CNA Insurance Cos., $615,304

125

# GETTING SOMEWHERE

6. Hartford Insurance Group, $606,624
7. American Road Insurance Group, $591,629
8. Zurich Insurance Group—U.S., $512,663
9. USF & G, $496,068
10. State Farm Group, $475,140

*Where'd you hear that?*
Best's Review, Property/Casualty edition. Based on 1988 direct premiums, in thousands of dollars.

## Leading automobile insurance writers

1. State Farm Group, with $14,136,636 thousand
2. Allstate Insurance Group, $8,529,614
3. Farmers Insurance Group, $3,801,409
4. Nationwide Group, $3,199,199
5. Aetna Life & Casualty Group, $2,634,014
6. Liberty Mutual Group, $2,247,922
7. Travelers Insurance Group, $1,946,520
8. USAA Group, $1,881,660
9. Hartford Insurance Group, $1,757,267
10. Progressive Group, $1,232,727

*Where'd you hear that?*
Best's Review, Property/Casualty edition. Based on amount of 1988 direct premiums, in thousands of dollars.

## Leading private passenger auto insurance writers

1. State Farm Group, with $13,661,496 thousand
2. Allstate Insurance Group, $8,211,105
3. Farmers Insurance Group, $3,579,228
4. Nationwide Group, $2,791,980
5. Aetna Life & Casualty Group, $1,939,571
6. USAA Group, $1,881,414
7. Liberty Mutual Group, $1,367,068
8. Travelers Insurance Group, $1,289,560
9. Geico Corp. Group, $1,153,893
10. Hartford Insurance Group, $1,150,644

*Where'd you hear that?*
Best's Review, Property/Casualty edition. Based on 1988 direct premiums, in thousands of dollars.

## States with the highest automobile insurance premiums

1. Massachusetts, with $834.76
2. New Jersey, $733.66
3. Nevada, $691.05
4. California, $673.18
5. Pennsylvania, $620.33
6. Arkansas, $613.58
7. Washington, DC, $606.39
8. Maryland, $604.41
9. Rhode Island, $604.28
10. New York, $601.84

*Where'd you hear that?*
Best's Review, Property/Casulty. Based on 1988 average premium per passenger vehicle.

## GETTING SOMEWHERE

### Largest transit bus fleets

1. New York City Transit Authority, with 3800
2. New Jersey Transit Corp., 2761
3. Southern California Rapid Transit District, 2469
4. Chicago Transit Authority, 2200
5. Montreal Urban Community Transit Corp., 1955
6. Toronto Transit Commission, 1948
7. Washington Metropolitan Area Transit Authority, 1611
8. Southeastern Pennsylvania Transportation Authority, 1610
9. Massachusetts Bay Transportation Authority, 1475
10. Seattle Metro, 1096

*Where'd you hear that?*
Metro magazine. Based on 1989 fleet size.

### Largest private motorcoach fleets

1. Greyhound Lines, with 3,940
2. Academy Lines, Inc., 434
3. Greyhound Lines of Canada, 425
4. Robert's Hawaii Inc., 381
5. Voyageur Enterprises, Ltd., 324
6. Suburban Transit Corp., 261
7. Shortline Companies, 236
8. Gray Line of Ft. Lauderdale, 191
9. Rockland Coaches, Inc., 182
10. Starline Tours, 170

*Where'd you hear that?*
Metro magazine, Largest Private Motorcoach Fleets. Based on number of motorcoaches owned or leased.

### World's largest tire manufacturers

1. Michelin, with 22%
2. Goodyear Tire & Rubber Co., 18%
3. Bridgestone, 17%
4. Continental, 7.5%
5. Pirelli, 7%
6. Sumitomo, 6%
7. Yokohama, 5%
8. Toyo, 3%
9. Others, total, 14,5%

*Where'd you hear that?*
New York Times. Based on 1989 world market share, in percent.

### Largest U.S. corporations in the tire and rubber industry

1. Goodyear Tire & Rubber Co., with $2,167 million
2. Bandag, $1,249
3. Cooper Tire & Rubber, $761

*Where'd you hear that?*
Business Week, The Business Week 1000. Based on market value on March 16, 1990, in millions of dollars.

127

# GETTING SOMEWHERE

### Largest aerospace companies

1. Boeing Co., with $20,276.0 million
2. United Technologies Corp., $19,613.7
3. McDonnell Douglas Corp., $14,581.0
4. Rockwell International Corp., $12,518.1
5. Allied Signal Inc., $11,942.0
6. General Dynamics Corp., $10,042.9
7. Lockheed Corp., $9,891.0
8. Textron Inc., $7,440.1
9. LTV Corp., $6,362.1
10. Martin Marietta Corp., $5,796.2

*Where'd you hear that?*
Aviation Week & Space Technology, Aerospace/Defense Financial Report. Based on 1989 sales, in millions of dollars.

### Top aerospace companies

1. Boeing Co., with $20,276 million
2. United Technologies, $19,766
3. McDonnell Douglas, $14,995
4. Rockwell International, $12,633
5. Allied-Signal, $12,021
6. General Dynamics Corp., $10,053
7. Lockheed Corp., $9,932
8. Textron, $7,440
9. Martin Marietta, $5,814
10. Northrop, $5,200

*Where'd you hear that?*
Fortune, Fortune 500 Largest U.S. Industrial Corporations. Based on 1989 sales, in millions of dollars.

### Largest U.S. corporations in the aerospace industry

1. Boeing Co., with $16,074 million
2. United Technologies, $6,781
3. Lockheed Corp., $2,235
4. McDonnell Douglas, $2,174
5. Martin Marietta, $2,115
6. General Dynamics Corp., $1,575
7. Sundstrand, $1,313
8. Northrop, $780
9. Sequa, $678
10. Grumman Corp., $478

*Where'd you hear that?*
Business Week, The Business Week 1000. Based on market value on March 16, 1990, in millions of dollars.

### America's best aerospace engineering schools

1. Massachusetts Institute of Technology
2. California Institute of Technology
3. Stanford University
4. Purdue University
5. University of Michigan

*Where'd you hear that?*
U.S. News & World Report. Based on results of reputational survey of engineering-school deans and academic-affairs deans.

### NASA'S largest contractors

1. Rockwell International, with $1,714 million
2. Lockheed Corp., $811
3. Morton Thiokol, $423
4. Martin Marietta, $341
5. Boeing Co., $302
6. McDonnell Douglas, $299
7. General Electric Co., $218

# GETTING SOMEWHERE

*Where'd you hear that?*
Fortune. Based on 1988 contract value, in millions of dollars.

## Fastest growing avionics/military electronics companies

1. Sun Microsystems Inc., with 101.139%
2. Mark IV Industries Inc., 89.733%
3. Cypress Semiconductor Corp., 75.123%
4. Computer Associates International Inc., 63.101%
5. UTL Corp., 60.108%
6. Integrated Device Technology Inc., 57.904%
7. Tech-Sym Corp., 56.996%
8. Convex Computer Corp., 50.038%
9. Logicon Inc., 49.146%
10. Apple Computer Inc., 46.043%

*Where'd you hear that?*
Aviation Week & Space Technology, Aerospace/Defense Financial Report. Based on 5-year research and development growth rate, in percent.

## Largest avionics companies

1. Honeywell Inc., with 43%
2. Collins, 29%
3. Bendix/King, 18%
4. Others, total 10%

*Where'd you hear that?*
New York Times. Based on 1989 market share of commercial and military instruments (estimated).

## Largest manufacturers of new turbine-powered helicopters

1. Aerospatiale, with 72
1. Bell, 72
3. MDHC, 32
4. MBB, 19
5. Sikorsky, 10
6. Agusta, 4

*Where'd you hear that?*
Interavia Aerospace Review. Based on number of helicopters manufactured in 1989.

## Most admired aerospace corporations

1. Boeing Co., with a rating of 7.92
2. Martin Marietta, 7.27
3. United Technologies, 6.54
4. General Dynamics Corp., 6.47
5. Rockwell International, 6.44
6. Lockheed Corp., 6.27
7. McDonnell Douglas, 5.82
8. Textron, 5.77
9. Allied-Signal, 5.76
10. Northrop, 4.88

*Where'd you hear that?*
Fortune, America's Most Admired Corporations. Based on scores (0-10) derived from a survey of senior executives, outside directors, and financial analysts. Respondents ranked firms in their own industry on quality of management and products/services; innovation; long-term investment value; financial soundness; attraction and retention of talent; community and environmental responsiblility; and use of assets.

## Leading turbine-powered helicopter companies

1. Bell, with 50.47%
2. Aerospatiale, 21.62%
3. McDonnell-Douglas, 12.98%
4. MBB, 5.87%
5. Sikorsky, 4.81%
6. Agusta, 1.71%
7. Fairchild-Hiller, 1.04%
8. Hiller, 0.69%

# GETTING SOMEWHERE

9. Boeing-Vertol, 0.33%
10. Westland, 0.32%

*Where'd you hear that?*
Interavia Aerospace Review. Based on world fleet share of turbine-powered helicopters on December 31, 1989, in percent.

## Leading principal piston-powered helicopter companies

1. Bell, with 31.91%
2. Hughes Aircraft Co., 22.30%
3. Robinson, 15.42%
4. Hiller, 12.64%
5. Enstrom, 10.2%
6. Sikorsky, 4.68%
7. Brantly, 2.46%
8. Piasecki, 0.26%
9. Boeing-Vertol, 0.23%
10. Kaman, 0.08%

*Where'd you hear that?*
Interavia Aerospace Review. Based on world fleet share of principal piston-powered helicopters on December 31, 1989, in percent.

## World's largest airlines in passengers

1. Aeroflot, with 132,051 thousand
2. American Airlines, 72,074
3. Delta Air Lines, 68,258
4. USAir, 61,345
5. United Airlines, 54,951
6. Northwest Airlines, 38,860
7. Continental Airlines, 35,350
8. All Nippon, 29,693
9. TWA, 25,346
10. British Airways, 24,700

*Where'd you hear that?*
Air Transport World. Based on 1989 passengers, in thousands.

## World's largest airlines in passenger-kilometers

1. Aeroflot, with 228,794 million
2. American Airlines, 118,223
3. United Airlines, 112,049
4. Delta Air Lines, 95,554
5. USAir, 89,475
6. Northwest, 75,863
7. British Airways, 64,300
8. Continental Airlines, 62,384
9. TWA, 56,572
10. Japan Air Lines Co. Ltd., 53,329

*Where'd you hear that?*
Air Transport World. Based on 1989 passenger-kilometers, in millions.

## World's largest airlines in employees

1. Aeroflot, with 400,000
2. American Airlines, 75,470
3. United Airlines, 71,170
4. Delta Air Lines, 60,413
5. British Airways, 50,959
6. Lufthansa, 43,565
7. Northwest Airlines, 40,000
8. Air France, 37,122
9. Continental Airlines, 33,000
10. Eastern Airlines, 30,000

*Where'd you hear that?*
Air Transport World. Based on 1989 employees.

# GETTING SOMEWHERE

## World's largest airlines in fleet size

1. Aeroflot, with 2,442
2. American Airlines, 500
3. USAir, 446
4. United Airlines, 429
5. Delta Air Lines, 405
6. UPS, 356
7. Continental Airlines, 328
8. Northwest Airlines, 323
9. Federal Express, 297
10. British Airways, 218

*Where'd you hear that?*
Air Transport World. Based on 1988 number of aircraft.

## World's largest airlines in operating revenue

1. American Airlines, with $9,961 billion
2. United Airlines, $9,642
3. Delta Air Lines, $8,648
4. British Airways, $7,726
5. Lufthansa, $6,700
6. Northwest Airlines, $6,554
7. Federal Express, $6,455
8. USAir, $6,251
9. Continental Airlines, $4,944
10. TWA, $4,507

*Where'd you hear that?*
Air Transport World. Based on 1989 operating revenue, in millions of dollars.

## World's largest airlines in operating profit

1. Korean Airlines, with $797 million
2. American Airlines, $731
3. Singapore Airlines, $691
4. Delta Air Lines, $677
5. British Airways, $628
6. Cathay Airlines, $486
7. United Airlines, $457
8. Federal Express, $444
9. SAS, $353
10. Northwest Airlines, $290

*Where'd you hear that?*
Air Transport World. Based on 1989 operating profit, in millions of dollars.

## World's largest air carriers

1. American Airlines, with 64,296 thousand
2. United Airlines, 56,326
3. Continental Airlines, 37,401
4. Eastern Airlines, 35,493
5. TWA, 25,311
6. British Airways, 22,516
7. JAL, 19,989
8. Lufthansa, 17,791
9. Pan Am, 16,755
10. Iberia, 15,109

*Where'd you hear that?*
Air Transport World, Leading IATA Airlines. Based on number of passengers in 1988, in thousands.

## World's largest airline employers

1. American Airlines, with 65,340
2. United Airlines, 60,139
3. Federal Express, 58,761
4. British Airways, 48,656
5. Lufthansa, 40,684
6. Air France, 37,122
7. Eastern Airlines, 32,542
8. TWA, 31,520
9. Continental Airlines, 30,113
10. Iberia, 28,003

*Where'd you hear that?*
Air Transport World, Leading IATA Airlines. Based on number of employees in 1988.

# GETTING SOMEWHERE

## World's largest airlines

1. United Airlines, with 111,081 million
2. American Airlines, 104,207
3. Continental Airlines, 65,154
4. British Airways, 56,939
5. TWA, 56,399
6. JAL, 49,328
7. Pan Am, 47,166
8. Eastern Airlines, 46,336
9. Air France, 34,333
10. Lufthansa, 34,033

*Where'd you hear that?*
Air Transport World, Leading IATA Airlines. Based on 1988 revenue passenger kilometers, in millions.

### Largest commercial owners of DC-10s in the world

1. American Airlines, with 59
2. United Airlines, 55
3. Federal Express, 24
4. Northwest Airlines, 20
5. JAL, 18
6. Continental Airlines, 15
7. Canadian Airlines International, 12
7. Varig, 12
9. Lufthansa, 11
9. SAS, 11
11. Swiss Air, 10

*Where'd you hear that?*
Wall Street Journal. Based on number of DC-10s. Original source: McDonell Douglas.

### Europe's largest air carriers

1. British Airways, with 22.5 million
2. Lufthansa (West Germany), 17.8
3. Air France, 14.8
4. Iberia (Spain), 14.5
5. SAS (Scandinavia), 13.3
6. Alitalia (Italy), 9.2
7. Swissair, 7.1
8. Olympic Airways (Greece), 6.7
9. KLM (The Netherlands), 6.2
10. JAT (Yugoslavia), 3.9

*Where'd you hear that?*
New York Times. Based on passengers carried in 1988, in millions.

### Largest airlines ranked by revenue

1. American Airlines, with $10,476,000 thousand
2. United Airlines, $9,793,635
3. Delta Air Lines, $8,571,709
4. Northwest Airlines, $6,553,827
5. USAir, $6,252,000
6. Continental Airlines, $5,100,000
7. TWA, $4,507,348
8. Pan Am, $3,284,146
9. Air Canada, $2,640,325
10. Canadian Airlines, $2,241,022

*Where'd you hear that?*
Business Travel News, Business Travel Survey. Based on 1989 revenue, in thousands of dollars.

### Largest airlines ranked by revenue passenger miles

1. American Airlines, with 73,475,000 thousand
2. United Airlines, 69,639,000
3. Delta Air Lines, 59,347,600

# GETTING SOMEWHERE

4. Northwest Airlines, 45,663,051
5. Continental Airlines, 38,700,000
6. TWA, 35,046,000
7. USAir, 33,700,000
8. Pan Am, 28,904,000
9. Air Canada, 16,278,000
10. Canadian Airlines, 14,732,000

*Where'd you hear that?*
Business Travel News, Business Travel Survey. Based on 1989 revenue passenger miles, in thousands.

## Largest U.S. corporations in the airline industry

1. AMR, with $4,104 million
2. Delta Air Lines, $3,661
3. UAL, $3,109
4. USAir Group, $1,363
5. Southwest Airlines, $711
6. Pan Am, $440

*Where'd you hear that?*
Business Week, The Business Week 1000. Based on market value as of March 16, 1990, in millions of dollars.

## Largest U.S. airlines' market share

1. American Airlines, with 18.6%
2. United Airlines, 17.6%
3. Delta Air Lines, 15.0%
4. Northwest Airlines, 11.5%
5. Continental Airlines, 9.8%
6. Trans World, TWA, 8.8%
7. USAir, 8.5%
8. Pan Am, 7.3%
9. Eastern Airlines, 2.9%

*Where'd you hear that?*
New York Times. Based on 1989 market share.

## Leading domestic airline markets

1. New York–Boston, with 3,300,400 passengers
2. New York–Los Angeles, 3,044,050
3. New York–Washington, 2,970,670
4. New York–Chicago, 2,789,550
5. New York–Miami, 2,169,240
6. Los Angeles–San Francisco, 2,036,190
7. Dallas-Fort Worth–Houston, 1,984,280
8. New York–San Francisco, 1,933,930
9. New York–Ft. Lauderdale, 1,860,130
10. New York–Orlando, 1,677,770

*Where'd you hear that?*
Air Transport, Air Transport Association. Based on passengers (outbound plus inbound), twelve months ended September, 1988.

## Most profitable airlines

1. United Airlines, with 17.5%
2. Alaska Air Group, 17.3%
3. Southwest Airlines, 14.5%
4. USAir Group, 14.1%
5. Delta Air Lines, 12.6%
6. American Airlines, 11.7%
7. Midway Airlines, deficit
8. Texas Air, deficit
9. Pan Am, deficit
10. American West Airlines, NA

*Where'd you hear that?*
Forbes, Annual Report on American Industry. Based on 10-year average return on equity. Ranks publicly held corporations only.

# GETTING SOMEWHERE

## Most productive airlines

1. Delta Air Lines, with $8.3 thousand
2. American Airlines, $6.5
3. United Airlines, $4.8
4. Federal Express, $2.0
5. Pittston, $0.3
6. USAir Group, -$1.2
7. Pan Am, -$12.8
8. Texas Air -$13.0

*Where'd you hear that?*
Forbes, Forbes 500s Annual Directory. Based on 1989 profits per employee, in thousands of dollars. Ranks U.S.-based corporations that were publicly traded as of March 23, 1990.

## Largest publicly traded commuter airlines

1. Westair, with $185
2. Atlantic Southeast, $181
3. Air Wisconsin, $169
4. Metro Airlines, 147
5. Comair, $118
6. Skywest, $84

*Where'd you hear that?*
Business Week. Based on 1989 sales, in millions of dollars.

## Most efficient advertisers among airlines

1. Eastern Airlines, with $3.94
2. Pan Am, $6.08
3. Piedmont Airlines, $7.18
4. Continental Airlines, $8.12
5. TWA, $8.17
6. American Airlines, $10.65
7. Delta Air Lines, $14.07
8. Alaska Airlines, $15.25
9. United Airlines, $15.80
10. Northwest Airlines, $20.77
11. USAir, $22.68

*Where'd you hear that?*
Adweek's Marketing Week, Annual Measure of Efficiency. Based on efficiency quotient (average weekly cost of television advertising divided by average number of retained impressions).

## Largest international air freight carriers by ton-kilometer

1. Lufthansa, with 3,815 million
2. Japan Air Lines, 3,402
3. Air France, 3,123
4. Federal Express, 2,957
5. Korean Air, 2,364
6. British Airways, 2,173
7. KLM, 1,994
8. Alitalia, 1,086
9. Quantas Airways, 1,033
10. Swissair, 880

*Where'd you hear that?*
World Air Transport Statistics. Based on 1989 scheduled freight ton-kilometers performed, in millions.

## Largest total air freight carriers by ton-kilometers

1. Federal Express, with 6,049 million
2. Lufthansa, 3,840
3. Japan Air Lines, 3,632
4. Air France, 3,261
5. Aeroflot, 2,645
6. Korean Air, 2,403
7. British Airways, 2,183
8. KLM, 1,994
9. United Airlines, 1,470
10. Alitalia, 1,116

*Where'd you hear that?*
World Air Transport Statistics. Based on 1989 scheduled freight ton-kilometers performed, in millions, for domestic and international carriers.

# GETTING SOMEWHERE

## Largest international air freight carriers by tons carried

1. Federal Express, with 825 thousand
2. Lufthansa, 611
3. Air France, 463
4. Japan Air Lines, 456
5. Korean Air, 373
6. British Airways, 332
7. KLM, 325
8. Swissair, 198
9. Alitalia, 184
10. El Al, 165

*Where'd you hear that?*
World Air Transport Statistics. Based on 1989 scheduled freight tons carried, in thousands.

## Largest total air freight carriers by tons carried

1. Aeroflot, with 3,230 thousand
2. Federal Express, 2,680
3. Japan Air Lines, 741
4. Lufthansa, 672
5. Air France, 489
6. Korean Air, 475
7. United Airlines, 426
8. All Nippon, 351
9. British Airways, 340
10. American Airlines, 327

*Where'd you hear that?*
World Air Transport Statistics. Based on 1989 scheduled freight tons carried, in thousands, for domestic and international carriers.

## World's largest airlines in air freight

1. Federal Express, with 6,323 million
2. Lufthansa, 3,905
3. Japan Air Lines Co. Ltd., 3,650
4. Air France, 3,279
5. Aeroflot, 2,760
6. Northwest Airlines, 2,441
7. Korean Airlines, 2,410
8. British Airways, 2,186
9. UPS, 2,095
10. KLM, 1,999

*Where'd you hear that?*
Air Transport World. Based on 1989 FTKs, in millions.

## Most profitable air freight companies

1. Air Express International, 20.5%
2. Federal Express, 16.3%
3. Airborne Freight, 11.3%
4. Pittston, deficit

*Where'd you hear that?*
Forbes, Annual Report on American Industry. Based on 10-year average return on equity. Ranks publicly held corporations only.

## Largest domestic air freight carriers by ton-kilometer

1. Federal Express, with 3,092 million
2. Aeroflot, 2,279
3. United Airlines, 945
4. American Airlines, 505
5. All Nippon, 293
6. TWA, 266
7. Air Canada, 240
8. Japan Air Lines, 230
8. VARIG, 230
10. Continental Airlines, 212

*Where'd you hear that?*
World Air Transport Statistics. Based on 1989 scheduled freight ton-kilometers performed, in millions.

# GETTING SOMEWHERE

## Largest domestic air freight carriers by tons carried

1. Aeroflot, with 3,162 thousand
2. Federal Express, 1,855
3. United Airlines, 345
4. All Nippon, 323
5. Japan Air Lines, 286
6. American Airlines, 229
7. VARIG, 146
8. Continental Airlines, 120
9. Korean Air, 102
10. Indian Airlines, 101

*Where'd you hear that?*
World Air Transport Statistics. Based on 1989 scheduled freight tons carried, in thousands.

## Leading U.S. airports in cargo

1. Kennedy, New York, with 1,299,104 tons
2. Los Angeles International Airport, 1,099,522
3. O'Hare, Chicago, 906,928
4. Miami International Airport, $740,280
5. Standiford Field Airport, Louisville, $701,502
6. Hartsfield, Atlanta, 598,365
7. San Francisco International Airport, 575,249
8. James M. Cox Dayton International Airport, 500,031
9. Newark International Airport, 454,681
10. Logan, Boston, 355,201

*Where'd you hear that?*
Air Transport, Air Transport Association. Based on cargo tons (enplaned and deplaned) in 1988.

## Busiest U.S. airports

1. O'Hare, Chicago, with 59.1 million passengers
2. Dallas-Fort Worth International Airport, 47.6
3. Los Angeles International Airport, 45.0
4. Hartsfield, Atlanta, 43.3
5. John F. Kennedy, New York, 30.3
6. San Francisco International, 29.9
7. Stapleton, Denver, 27.6
8. Miami International, 23.4
9. Laguardia, NY, 23.2
10. Honolulu, HI, 22.6

*Where'd you hear that?*
Fortune. Based on total number of passengers, in millions.

## Leading U.S. airports in passengers

1. O'Hare, Chicago, with 56,678,991 passengers
2. Hartsfield, Atlanta, 45,900,098
3. Los Angeles International Airport, 44,398,611
4. Dallas-Fort Worth International Airport, 44,271,038
5. Kennedy, New York, 31,165,676
6. San Francisco International Airport, 30,506,794
7. Stapleton, Denver, 30,011,8021
8. Miami International Airport, 24,525,302
9. Laguardia, NY, 24,158,780
10. Logan, Boston, 23,732,959

*Where'd you hear that?*
Air Transport, Air Transport Association. Based on passengers (arriving and departing) in 1988.

**Top states in airport paving and lighting construction markets**

1. Florida, with $109 million
2. California, $60
3. Pennsylvania, $49
4. Nevada, $38
5. Alaska, $35
6. Hawaii, $32
6. Texas, $32
6. Tennessee, $32
9. Kentucky, $31
10. Maryland, $30

*Where'd you hear that?*
ENR, Top 20 States in Major Construction Markets. Based on eleven-month cumulative contract awards, 1989 vs. 1988, in millions of dollars.

**Top states in docks, piers, and dredging construction markets for 1989**

1. California, with $80 million
2. Texas, $78
3. New York, $61
4. Florida, $52
5. Virginia, $48
6. Washington, $47
7. Alaska, $46
8. Oregon, $43
9. Michigan, $40
10. New Jersey, $35

*Where'd you hear that?*
ENR, Top 20 States in Major Construction Markets. Based on eleven-month cumulative contract awards, 1989 vs. 1988, in millions of dollars.

**Busiest U.S. ports**

1. New Orleans, LA, with 167,917,822
2. New York/New Jersey, 154,536,680
3. Houston, TX, 112,546,187
4. Valdez, AK, 106,867,415
5. Baton Rouge, LA, 73,401,202
6. Hampton Roads, VA, 59,491,077
7. Corpus Christi, TX, 53,539,806
8. Long Beach, CA, 45,898,541
9. Tampa, FL, 44,303,389
10. Los Angeles, CA, 40,460,556

*Where'd you hear that?*
Area Development. Based on 1987 short tons.

# GETTING SOMEWHERE

## *Top airports*

1. O'Hare, Chicago, with 56,280,545
2. Hartsfield, Atlanta, 47,649,470
3. Los Angeles International Airport, 44,873,113
4. Dallas/Ft. Worth International Airport, 41,875,444
5. Heathrow, London, 34,742,100
6. Stapleton, Denver, 32,355,000
7. Kennedy International Airport, New York, 30,192,477
8. Tokyo International Airport, 29,927,027
9. San Francisco International Airport, 29,812,440
10. La Guardia, New York, 24,225,913

*Where'd you hear that?*
Travel Industry World Yearbook: The Big Picture. Based on worldwide airport traffic, in total passengers.

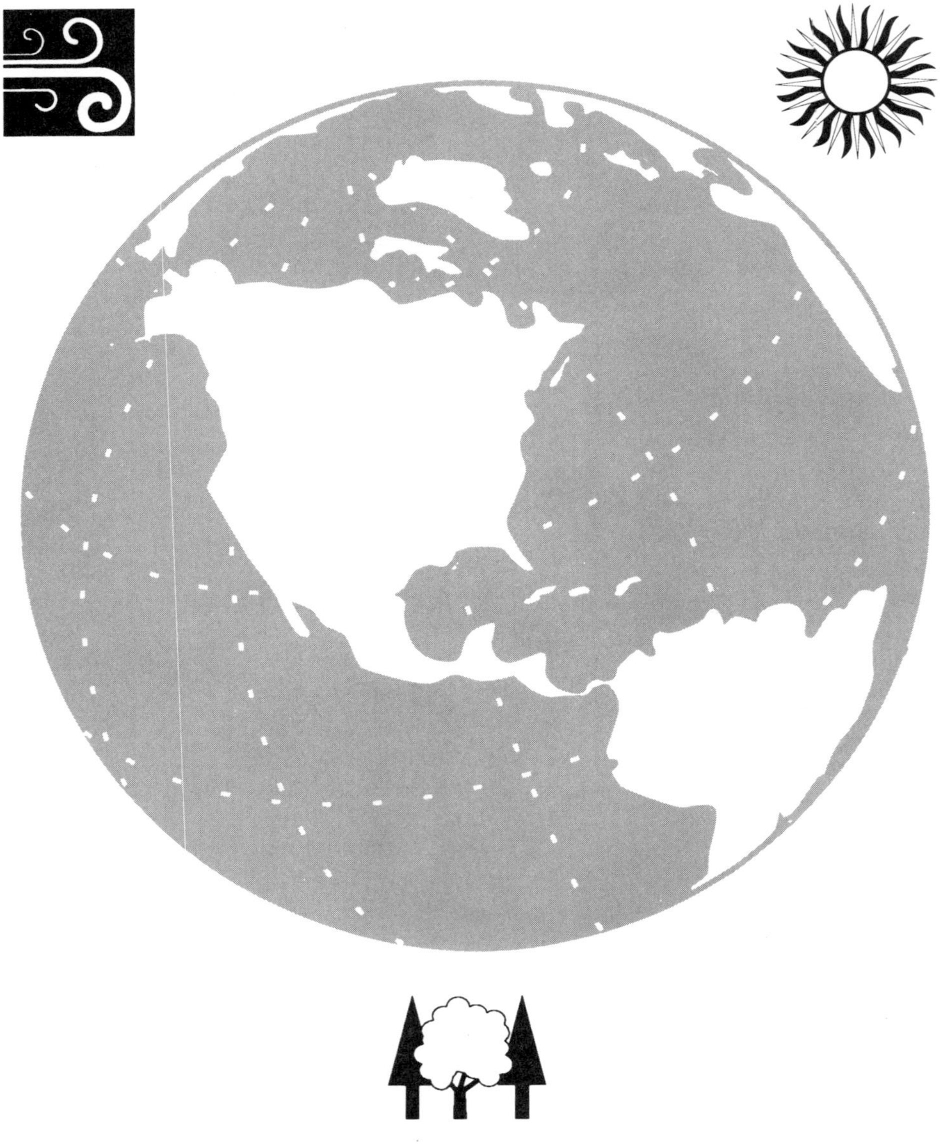

# RESOURCES

**Biggest corporations in the oil & gas industry**

1. Exxon Corp., with $59,389 million
2. Amoco Corp., $27,495
3. Mobil, $25,839
4. Chevron Corp., $24,896
5. Atlantic Richfield Co., $19,146
6. Texaco, $15,681
7. Occidental Petroleum, $7,487
8. Unocal, $7,166
9. Phillips Petroleum, $6,250
10. Burlington Resources, $5,967

*Where'd you hear that?*
Business Week, The Business Week 1000. Based on market value as of March 16, 1990, in millions of dollars.

**Most productive miscellaneous oil and gas corporations**

1. Union Texas Petroleum, with $91.3 thousand
2. Atlantic Richfield Co., $72.6
3. Louisiana Land & Exploration, $71.8
4. Anadarko Petroleum, 65.5
5. Amerada Hess Corp., $54.5
6. American Petrofina Inc., $32.7
7. Tosco, $32.0
8. Mapco, $21.1
9. Kerr-McGee, $19.9
10. USX, $18.0

*Where'd you hear that?*
Forbes, Forbes 500s Annual Directory. Based on 1989 profits per employee, in thousands of dollars. Ranks U.S.-based corporations that were publicly traded as of March 23, 1990.

**Largest utilities companies in Canada**

1. TransAlta Utilities, with $136,900 thousand
2. Canadian Utilities, $110,324
3. Consumers' Gas, $102,807
4. Noverco, $65,996
5. ICG Utilities, $37,561

# RESOURCES

*Where'd you hear that?*
Canadian Business, Canadian Business 500. Based on 1989 net income, in thousands of Canadian dollars.

## Largest U.S. public utilities

1. GTE Corp., with $31,986.5 million
2. Bellsouth Corp., $30,049.8
3. Bell Atlantic Corp., $26,219.7
4. NYNEX, $25,909.0
5. US West, $25,425.9
6. Pacific Gas & Electric, $21,352.0
7. Pacific Telesis Group, $21,194.0
8. Southwestern Bell, $21,160.5
9. Southern, $20,086.0
10. American Information Technology, $19,833.0

*Where'd you hear that?*
Fortune, Service 500. Based on assets as of December 31, 1989, in millions of dollars.

## Most admired utilities

1. BellSouth Corp., with a rating of 7.65
2. Bell Atlantic Corp., 7.33
3. Pacific Telesis Group, 7.30
4. Ameritech, 7.09
5. Southwestern Bell, 6.93
6. US West, 6.84
7. GTE Corp., 6.58
8. Pacific Gas & Electric, 6.54
9. NYNEX, 6.32
10. Southern, 6.21

*Where'd you hear that?*
Fortune, America's Most Admired Corporations. Based on scores (0-10) derived from a survey of senior executives, outside directors, and financial analysts. Respondents ranked firms in their own industry on quality of management and products/services; innovation; long-term investment value; financial soundness; attraction and retention of talent; community and environmental responsibility; and use of assets.

## Biggest corporations in the coal industry

1. Nerco, with $944 million
2. Pittston, $697
3. Nacco Industries, $464

*Where'd you hear that?*
Business Week, The Business Week 1000. Based on market value as of March 16, 1990, in millions of dollars.

## Most profitable coal and other energy companies

1. Nacco Industries, with 20.2%
2. Pittston, deficit
3. Westmoreland Coal, deficit
4. Cyprus Minerals Co., NA

*Where'd you hear that?*
Forbes, Annual Report on American Industry. Based on 10-year average return on equity. Ranks publicly held corporations only.

## World's largest oil companies

1. Saudi Aramco
2. Royal Dutch/Shell
3. Exxon Corp.
4. Petroleos de Venezuela
5. National Iranian Oil Co.
6. Chevron Corp.
7. Mobil
8. British Petroleum
9. Texaco

# RESOURCES

*Where'd you hear that?*
New York Times. Based on based on *Petroleum Intelligence Weekly*'s index.

## Most profitable international oil companies

1. Exxon Corp., with 17.7%
2. Amoco Corp., 15.1%
3. E. I. du Pont de Nemours & Co., 12.7%
4. Chevron Corp., 12.5%
5. Mobil, 11.9%
6. Occidental Petroleum, 9.4%
7. Texaco, 3.1%

*Where'd you hear that?*
Forbes, Annual Report on American Industry. Based on 10-year average return on equity. Ranks publicly held corporations only.

## Most productive international oil corporations

1. Texaco, with $61.2 thousand
2. Amoco Corp., $30.1
3. Exxon Corp., $29.0
4. Mobil, $26.3
5. Occidental Petroleum, $4.8
6. Chevron Corp., $4.6

*Where'd you hear that?*
Forbes, Forbes 500s Annual Directory. Based on 1989 profits per employee, in thousands of dollars. Ranks U.S.-based corporations that were publicly traded as of March 23, 1990.

## Largest oil and gas producers in Canada

1. Imperial Oil Ltd., with $456,000 thousand
2. Shell Canada, $212,000
3. Chevron Canada Resources, $137,183
4. PanCanadian Petroleum, $133,001
5. Interhome Energy, $116,200
6. Norcen Energy Resources, $110,213
7. Union Gas, $59,690
8. Total Petroleum, $57,078
9. Gulf Canada Resources Ltd., $52,000
10. Suncor, $49,000

*Where'd you hear that?*
Canadian Business, Canadian Business 500. Based on 1989 net income, in thousands of Canadian dollars.

## Largest U.S. petroleum companies in total revenue

1. Exxon Corp., with $88,563.0
2. Mobil Corp., $54,361.0
3. Texaco Inc., $35,138.0
4. Chevron Corp., $28,857.0
5. Amoco Corp., $23,919.0
6. Shell Oil Co., $21,399.0
7. Occidental Petroleum Corp., $19,417.0
8. ARCO (Atlantic Richfield Corp.), $18,868.0
9. BP America, $16,661.0
10. Conoco Inc., $12,806.0

*Where'd you hear that?*
Oil & Gas Journal, Oil & Gas Journal 400. Based on total revenue, in millions of dollars.

## Largest oil companies in net income

1. Exxon Corp., with $5,260.0
2. BP America, $2,129.0
3. Mobil Corp., $2,087.0
4. Amoco Corp., $2,063.0
5. Chevron Corp., $1,768.0
6. ARCO (Atlantic Richfield Corp.), $1,583.0
7. Penzoil Co., $1,475.4
8. Texaco Inc., $1,304.0
9. Shell Oil Co., $1,239.0

# RESOURCES

10. Phillips Petroleum Co., $650.0

*Where'd you hear that?*
Oil & Gas Journal, Oil & Gas Journal 400. Based on net income, in millions of dollars.

## Largest petroleum companies in assets

1. Exxon Corp., with $74,293,000 thousand
2. Mobil Corp., $38,820,000
3. Chevron Corp., $33,968,000
4. Amoco Corp., $29,919,000
5. Shell Oil Co., $27,169,000
6. Texaco Inc., $26,337,000
7. BP America, $22,452,000
8. ARCO (Atlantic Richfield Corp.), $21,514,000
9. Occidental Petroleum Corp., $20,747,000
10. Phillips Petroleum Co., $11,968,000

*Where'd you hear that?*
Oil & Gas Journal, Oil & Gas Journal 400. Based on total assets, in thousands of dollars.

## Largest oil companies in net wells drilled

1. Shell Oil Co., with 883.0
2. Amoco Corp., 607.0
3. Mobil Corp., 568.0
4. Texaco Corp., 532.0
5. Exxon Corp., 502.0
6. ARCO (Atlantic Richfield Corp.), 462.0
7. USX (Oil & Gas segment), 448.0
8. Oryx Energy Co., 347.0
9. Chevron Corp., 342.0
10. Meridian Oil Inc., 260.7

*Where'd you hear that?*
Oil & Gas Journal, Oil & Gas Journal 400. Based on number of U.S. net wells drilled.

## Largest oil companies in capital exploratory spending

1. Exxon Corp., with $7,508.0
2. Mobil Corp., $3,915.0
3. Amoco Corp., $3,697.0
4. Shell Oil Co., $3,318.0
5. ARCO (Atlantic Richfield Corp.), $3,038.0
6. BP America, $2,496.0
7. Chevron Corp., $2,459.0
8. Texaco Inc., $2,435.0
9. Conoco Inc., $2,069.0
10. Unocal Corp., $1,193.0
10. Occidental Petroleum Corp., $1,193.0

*Where'd you hear that?*
Oil & Gas Journal, Oil & Gas Journal 400. Based on capital exploratory spending, in millions of dollars.

## Most profitable non-international oil and gas companies

1. Holly Corp., with 32.9%
2. Getty Petroleum Corp., 21.7%
3. Mapco, 16.8%
4. Atlantic Richfield Co., 16.1%
5. Phillips Petroleum, 15.7%
6. Ashland Oil, 12.1%
7. Unocal, 11.0%
8. PS Group, 10.5%
9. American Petrofina Inc., 9.1%
9. Charter, 9.1%

*Where'd you hear that?*
Forbes, Annual Report on American Industry. Based on 10-year average return on equity. Ranks publicly held corporations only.

## RESOURCES

### Top oil and gas marketing companies

1. Exxon Corp.
2. Mobil
3. Chevron Corp.
4. Amoco Corp.
5. Shell
6. Texaco
7. BP America
8. ARCO
9. Philips
10. Conoco Inc.

*Where'd you hear that?*
National Petroleum News, NPN Factbook. Based on 1988 total assets amounts unstated.

### Petroleum companies with the most active purchasing departments

1. Exxon Corp., with $6,417 million
2. Tenneco, $5,811
3. Shell Oil Co., $4,965
4. Mobil Corp., $4,800
5. Texaco USA, $2,348
6. Chevron Corp., $2,094
7. Amoco Corp., $1,692
8. Unocal Corp., $1,558
9. Occidental Petroleum, $1,553
10. ARCO (Atlantic Richfield Corp.), $1,400

*Where'd you hear that?*
Purchasing, Purchasing Top 100. Based on 1988 dollars spent by industrial purchasing departments, in millions.

### Most admired petroleum refining corporations

1. Shell Oil, with a rating of 7.58
2. Amoco Corp., 7.70
3. ARCO, 7.47
4. Mobil, 6.96
5. Chevron Corp., 6.81
6. Exxon Corp., 6.70
7. Phillips Petroleum, 6.21
8. Unocal, 5.97
9. Texaco, 5.73
10. USX, 5.50

*Where'd you hear that?*
Fortune, America's Most Admired Corporations. Based on scores (0-10) derived from a survey of senior executives, outside directors, and financial analysts. Respondents ranked firms in their own industry on quality of management and products/services; innnovation; long-term investment value; financial soundness; attraction and retention of talent; community and environmental responsibility; and use of assets.

### Top corporations in the pertroleum industry by spending on information systems

1. Exxon Corp., with $79,557 million
2. Mobil Corp., $48,198
3. Texaco, $33,544
4. Chevron Corp., $25,196
5. Amoco Corp., $21,150
6. Shell Oil Co., $21,070
7. ARCO (Atlantic Richfield Corp.), $17,626
8. USX, $15,792
9. Phillips Petroleum, $11,304
10. Unocal Corp., $8,853

# RESOURCES

*Where'd you hear that?*
Datamation, Spending Survey. Based on 1988 revenue, in millions of dollars.

## Petroleum companies that are the most effective users of information systems

1. Union Texas Petroleum, with 26,905
2. ARCO (Atlantic Richfield Corp.), 26,195
3. Unocal Corp., 25,440
4. Mobil Corp., 25,030
5. Amoco Corp., 24,990
6. American Petrofina, Inc., 23,040
7. Shell Oil Co., 22,830
8. Diamond Shamrock R & M, 22,710
9. Chevron Corp., 22,025
10. Sun Co., Inc., 21,195

*Where'd you hear that?*
Computerworld, Premier 100. Based on 1988 Computerworld Index. See magazine for details.

## America's best petroleum engineering schools

1. University of Texas, Austin
2. Texas A & M University
3. Stanford University
4. Louisiana State University
5. University of Oklahoma

*Where'd you hear that?*
U.S. News & World Report. Based on results of reputational survey of engineering-school deans and academic-affairs deans.

## Leaders in world petroleum reserves

1. Exxon Corp., with 6,551.0 barrels
2. Chevron Corp., 3,317.0
3. ARCO (Atlantic Richfield Co.), 3,093.0
4. Shell Oil Co., 3,058.0
5. Texaco Inc., 2,992.0
6. Amoco Corp., 2,798.0
7. BP America, 2,752.0
8. Mobil Corp., 2,553.0
9. Unocal Corp., 1,520.0
10. Conoco Inc., 1,036.0

*Where'd you hear that?*
Oil & Gas Journal, Oil & Gas Journal 400. Based on world liquids reserves, in billions of barrels.

## Leaders in world oil reserves

1. Arabian American Oil Co., with 169,970.0 million barrels
2. Iraq National Oil Co., 100,000.0
3. National Iranian Oil Co., 92,850.0
4. Abu Dhabi National Oil Co., 92,205.0
5. Kuwait Oil Co., 91,920.0
6. Petroleos de Venezuela SA, 58,504.0
7. Petroleos Mexicanos, 53,012.0
8. Royal Dutch/Shell, 8,839.0
9. Sonatrach (Algeria), 8,400.0
10. Oil and Natural Gas Commission (India), 6,354.0

*Where'd you hear that?*
Oil & Gas Journal, Oil & Gas Journal 400. Based on oil reserves, in millions of barrels.

## Biggest corporations in the petroleum services industry

1. Schlumberger, with $11,942 million
2. Halliburton, $4,810
3. Baker Hughes, $3,694
4. Dresser Industries, $3,345
5. Ocean Drilling & Exploration, $1,391
6. NL Industries, $1,338
7. Rowan, $929
8. Helmerich & Payne, $882
9. CBI Industries, $754
10. Noble Affiliates, $700

*Where'd you hear that?*
Business Week, The Business Week 1000. Based on market value as of March 16, 1990, in millions of dollars.

## Most profitable oilfield service companies

1. Schlumberger, with 10.3%
2. Dresser Industries, 4.2%
3. Halliburton, 4.1%
4. Smith International, deficit
5. Baker Hughes, NA
6. Baroid, NA
7. Valhi, NA

*Where'd you hear that?*
Forbes, Annual Report on American Industry. Based on 10-year average return on equity. Ranks publicly held corporations only.

## Most productive oilfield service corporations

1. Dresser Industries, with $5.2 thousand
2. Baker Hughes, $4.4

3. Halliburton, $2.1

*Where'd you hear that?*
Forbes, Forbes 500s Annual Directory. Based on 1989 profits per employee, in thousands of dollars. Ranks U.S.-based corporations that were publicly traded as of March 23, 1990.

# RESOURCES

## Leaders in U.S. petroleum reserves

1. Shell Oil Co., with 2,851.0 billion barrels
2. ARCO (Atlantic Richfield Co.), 2,829.0
3. BP America, 2,678.0
4. Exxon Corp., 2,630.0
5. Chevron Corp., 1,806.0
6. Amoco Corp., 1,736.0
7. Texaco Inc., 1,623.0
8. Mobil Corp., 1,140.0
9. Unocal Corp., 639.0
10. Oryx Energy Co., 601.0

*Where'd you hear that?*
Oil & Gas Journal, Oil & Gas Journal 400. Based on U.S. liquids reserves, in billions of barrels.

## Biggest corporations in the petroleum refining industry

1. Exxon Corp., with $86,656 million
2. Mobil, $50,976
3. Texaco, $32,416
4. Chevron Corp., $29,443
5. Amoco Corp., $24,214
6. Shell Oil, $21,703
7. USX, $17,755
8. Atlantic Richfield Co., $15,905
9. Phillips Petroleum, $12,492
10. Unocal, $10,417

# RESOURCES

*Where'd you hear that?*
Fortune, Fortune 500 Largest U.S. Industrial Corporations. Based on 1989 sales, in millions of dollars.

## Largest liquid pipeline companies ranked by mileage

1. Amoco Pipeline Co., with 12,297
2. Mobil Pipe Line Co., 9,683
3. Exxon Pipeline Co., 9,378
4. Chevron Pipe Line Co., 8,130
5. Mid-America Pipeline Co., 8,100
6. Conoco Pipe Line Co., 7,895
7. Shell Pipe Line Corp., 7,235
8. ARCO Pipe Line Co., 6,839
9. Williams Pipe Line Co., 6,780
10. Texaco Pipeline Co., 6,275

*Where'd you hear that?*
Oil & Gas Journal. Based on 1988 mileage.

## Largest liquids pipeline companies in crude oil deliveries

1. Alyeska Pipeline Service Co., with 744,107 thousand barrels
2. Lakehead Pipe Line Co. Inc., 473,075
3. Exxon Pipeline Co., 428,041
4. Marathon Pipe Line Co., 414,891
5. Shell Pipe Line Corp., 404,224
6. ARCO Pipe Line Co., 403,694
7. BP Pipelines (Alaska) Inc., 380,879
8. Texaco Pipeline Inc., 360,599
9. Amoco Pipeline Co., 343,593
10. Chevron Pipe Line Co., 338,133

*Where'd you hear that?*
Pipeline & Gas Journal, Pipeline & Gas Journal 500. Based on 1988 crude oil deliveries, in thousands of barrels.

## Most productive gas and pipelines corporations

1. Burlington Resources, with $73.9 thousand
2. Enron, $34.6
3. Sonat, $23.4
4. Transco Energy, $22.8
5. Williams Cos., $15.4
6. Coastal Corp., $13.4
7. Panhandle Eastern, $12.5

*Where'd you hear that?*
Forbes, Forbes 500s Annual Directory. Based on 1989 profits per employee, in thousands of dollars. Ranks U.S.-based corporations that were publicly traded as of March 23, 1990.

## Most productive integrated gas corporations

1. Consolidated Natural Gas, with $24.5 thousand
2. Columbia Gas System, 13.5
3. Enserch Corp., $6.5
4. Pacific Enterprises, $5.0
5. Arkla, -$12.8

*Where'd you hear that?*
Forbes, Forbes 500s Annual Directory. Based on 1989 profits per employee, in thousands of dollars. Ranks U.S.-based corporations that were publicly traded as of March 23, 1990.

## Most profitable integrated gas companies

1. Equitable Resources, with 16.2%
2. Consolidated Natural Gas, 13.6%
3. National Fuel Gas, 12.8%
4. Arkla, 12.6%

# RESOURCES

5. Pacific Enterprises, 11.9%
6. Questar, 11.2%
7. Oneok, 9.6%
8. Columbia Gas System, 7.1%
9. KN Energy, 6.9%
10. Enserch Corp., deficit

*Where'd you hear that?*
Forbes, Annual Report on American Industry. Based on 10-year average return on equity. Ranks publicly held corporations only.

## Most productive gas distributors

1. Nicor, with $31.1 thousand
2. Peoples Energy, $24.9
3. Kansas Power & Light, $16.0
4. Southwest Gas, $15.0

*Where'd you hear that?*
Forbes, Forbes 500s Annual Directory. Based on 1989 profits per employee, in thousands of dollars. Ranks U.S.-based corporations that were publicly traded as of March 23, 1990.

## Most profitable gas distributors

1. UtilCorp United, with 16.4%
2. Peoples Energy, 15.8%
3. Laclede Gas, 15.7%
4. Kansas Power & Light, 15.5%
5. Washington Gas Light, 15.1%
6. Piedmont Natural Gas, 14.3%
7. Brooklyn Union Gas Co., 14.2%
8. Southwest Gas, 13.7%
9. Midwest Energy, 12.9%
10. Wicor, 12.1%

*Where'd you hear that?*
Forbes, Annual Report on American Industry. Based on 10-year average return on equity. Ranks publicly held corporations only.

## *World leaders in gas production*

1. Mobil Corp., with 1,519.0 billion cubic feet
2. Exxon Corp., 1,514.0
3. Amoco Corp., 1,066.0
4. Texaco Inc., 912.0
5. Chevron Corp., 839.0
6. Shell Oil Co., 590.0
7. ARCO (Atlantic Richfield Corp.), 564.0
8. Unocal Corp., 448.0
9. Phillips Petroleum Co., 448.0
10. USX (Oil & Gas segment), 411.6

*Where'd you hear that?*
Oil & Gas Journal, Oil & Gas Journal 400. Based on worldwide gas production, in billions of cubic feet.

## Leaders in world gas reserves

1. Exxon Corp., with 22,797.0 cubic ft.
2. Mobil Corp., 19,637.0
3. Amoco Corp., 19,487.0
4. Chevron Corp., 10,710.0
5. ARCO (Atlantic Richfield Corp.), 7,622.0
6. Texaco Inc., 7,238.0
7. Shell Oil Co., 6,583.0
8. Unocal Corp., 6,137.0
9. Phillips Petroleum Co., 5,509.0
10. USX (oil & gas segment), 4,655.2

*Where'd you hear that?*
Oil & Gas Journal, Oil & Gas Journal 400. Based on world gas reserves, in billions of cubic feet.

# RESOURCES

### World's major gas reserves

1. Soviet Union, with 37.9%
2. Iran, 12.5%
3. United States, 4.7%
4. Abu Dhabi, 4.6%
5. Qatar, 4.0%
6. Saudi Arabia, 3.7%
7. Algeria, 2.6%
7. Venezuela, 2.6%
9. Canada, 2.4%
9. Iraq, 2.4%

*Where'd you hear that?*
Oil & Gas Journal, Annual Gas Processing Report. Based on share of estimated proved reserves.

### World's leading gas companies

1. L'Air Group (Paris), with $2,650 million
2. BOC Group (Windlesham, UK), $2,381
3. Union Carbide (Danbury, CT), $2,076
4. Air Products & Chemicals (Allentown, PA), $1,403
5. AGA (Stockholm), $1,015
6. Messer Griesheim (Frankfurt), $868
7. Nippon Sanso (Tokyo), $641
8. Linde AG (Wiesbaden, West Germany), $598
9. Liquid Carbonic (Chicago), $551

*Where'd you hear that?*
Chemicalweek. Based on fiscal 1987 sales, in millions of dollars.

### Largest suppliers of gas to the European market

1. L'Air Liquide Group, with 25%
2. BOC Group, 14%
2. Air Products & Chemicals, 14%
4. Messer Griesheim 11%
4. AGA, 11%
6. Linde AG 10%
7. Union Carbide 4%
8. Others, total 11%

*Where'd you hear that?*
Chemicalweek. Based on 1988 market share, in percent.

### Leaders in U.S. gas production

1. Texaco Inc., with 780.0 billion cubic feet
2. Exxon Corp., 571.0
3. Chevron Corp., 740.0
4. Mobil Corp., 658.0
5. Amoco Corp., 605.0
6. Shell Oil Co., 581.0
7. ARCO (Atlantic Richfield Corp.), 508.0
8. USX (Oil & Gas segment), 313.5
9. Phillips Petroleum Co., 312.0
10. Occidental Petroleum Corp., 282.0

*Where'd you hear that?*
Oil & Gas Journal, Oil & Gas Journal 400. Based on U.S. gas production, in billions of cubic feet.

### Leaders in U.S. gas reserves

1. Amoco Corp., with 12,371.0 cubic ft.
2. Exxon Corp., 9,341.0
3. Chevron Corp, 8,274.0
4. Mobil Corp., 7,515.0
5. ARCO (Atlantic Richfield Corp.), 6,373.0
6. Shell Oil Co., 6,248.0
7. Texaco Inc., 4,655.0
8. Unocal Corp., 4,320.0
9. Meridian Oil Inc., 3,365.0
10. Philips Petroleum Corp., 3,047.7

*Where'd you hear that?*
Oil & Gas Journal, Oil & Gas Journal 400. Based on U.S. gas reserves, in billions of cubic feet.

## Top U.S. gas & transmission companies

1. Consolidated Natural Gas, with $3,693 million
2. Pacific Enterprises, $3,191
3. Enron, $2,718
4. Panhandle Eastern, $2,378
5. Columbia Gas System, $2,168
6. Arkla, $2,085
7. Sonat, $2,042
8. Enserch Corp., $1,509
9. Williams, $1,348
10. Transco Energy, $1,265

*Where'd you hear that?*
Business Week, The Business Week 1000. Based on market value as of March 16, 1990, in millions of dollars.

## Largest gas-pipeline companies ranked by mileage

1. Northern Natural, Div. of Enron, with 23,924
2. El Paso Natural Gas Co., 21,709
3. Columbia Gas Transmission Corp., 18,804
4. Tennessee Gas Pipeline Co., 14,171
5. Natural Gas Pipeline of America, 12,771
6. Panhandle Eastern Pipe Line Co., 12,660
7. K N Energy Inc., 12,233
8. ANR Pipeline Co., 11,534
9. Transcontinental Gas Pipe Line Corp., 10,728
10. Enserch Corp., 10,583

*Where'd you hear that?*
Oil & Gas Journal. Based on 1988 mileage.

## Largest gas pipelines by gas moved for other companies

1. Transcontinental Gas Pipe Line, with 1,245,800 million cubic feet
2. EL Paso Natural Gas Co., 1,121,964
3. Natural Gas Pipeline Co. of America, 1,042,406
4. ANR Pipeline Co., 922,822
5. United Gas Pipe Line Co., 729,852
6. Texas Gas Transmission Corp., 634,591
7. Texas Oil & Gas Corp., 353,937
8. United Texas Tranmission Corp., 353,897
9. Southern Natural Gas Co., 350,000
10. Arkla Energy Resources, 347,113

*Where'd you hear that?*
Pipeline & Gas Journal, Pipeline & Gas Journal 500. Based on gas moved for others in 1988, in millions of cubic feet.

## Largest gas utilities by miles of piping

1. Southern California Gas Co., with 78,865 miles
2. Pacific Gas & Electric Co., 64,079
3. Northern Illinois Gas Co., 46,763
4. Atlanta Gas Light Co., 41,119
5. Entex, 38,597
6. Arkla Inc., 30,232
7. Consolidated Gas Distribution Cos., 29,275
8. Lone Star Gas Co., 28,336
9. Public Service Electric & Gas Co., 27,642

# RESOURCES

149

# RESOURCES

10. Michigan Consolidated Gas Co., 27,591

*Where'd you hear that?*
Pipeline & Gas Journal, Pipeline & Gas Journal 500. Based on miles of distribution piping.

## Largest gas utilities by gas sold

1. Pacific Gas & Electric, with 775,889 million cubic feet
2. Southern California Gas Co., 654,225
3. Michigan Consolidated Gas Co., 341,535
4. Northern Illinois Gas Co., 332,266
5. Consolidated Gas Distribution Cos., 291,225
6. Northern Indiana Public Service Co., 251,647
7. The Peoples Gas Light & Coke Co., 250,650
8. Consumers Power Co., 227,712
9. Public Service Electric & Gas Co., 223,341
10. DPL Gas Service, 216,846

*Where'd you hear that?*
Pipeline & Gas Journal, Pipeline & Gas Journal 500. Based on 1988 gas sales, in millions of cubic feet.

## Largest combination gas/electric utilities

1. Pacific Gas & Electric, with 4,026,701 electric; 3,299,844 gas
2. Public Service Electric & Gas Co., 1,832,681 electric; 1,432,636 gas
3. Niagara Mohawk Power Corp., 1,470,108 electric; 452,702 gas
4. Consumers Power Co., 1,430,560 electric; 1,313,132 gas
5. Northern States Power Co., 1,269,252 electric; 333,862 gas
6. Union Electric Co., 1,067,170 electric; 109,825 gas
7. San Diego Gas & Electric Co., 1,032,591 electric; 642,770 gas
8. Baltimore Gas & Electric Co., 991,105 electric; 518,753 gas
9. Long Island Lighting Co., 989,097 electric; 421,429 gas
10. Public Service Co. of Colorado, 974,043 electric; 841,429 gas

*Where'd you hear that?*
Pipeline & Gas Journal, Pipeline & Gas Journal 500. Based on number of gas and electric customers in 1988.

## Biggest U.S. electric & water companies

1. Pacific Gas & Electric, with $9,223 million
2. SCEcorp, $8,384
3. Southern, $8,325
4. Commonwealth Edison Co., $7,494
5. Texas Utilities, $6,320
6. Consolidated Edison Co. of New York, $6,074

7. American Electric Power, $5,951
8. Duke Power Co., $5,684
9. Public Service Enterprise Group, $5,541
10. Pacificorp, $5,412

*Where'd you hear that?*
Business Week, The Business Week 1000. Based on market value as of March 16, 1990, in millions of dollars.

## Largest state and local publicly-owned electric systems by electric customers served

1. Los Angeles Department of Water and Power, with 1,315,644
2. Puerto Rico Electric Power Authority, 1,128,278
3. Salt River Project, Phoenix, 506,478
4. San Antonio, TX, City Public Service, 462,469
5. Sacramento, CA, Municipal Utility District, 420,396
6. Memphis, TN, Light, Gas & Water Division, 332,296
7. Seattle City Light, 313,353
8. Jacksonville, FL, Electric Authority, 284,628
9. Nashville, TN, Electric Service, 268,186
10. Austin, TX, Electric Utility, 254,895

*Where'd you hear that?*
Public Power, Directory Issue. Based on 1988 electric customers served.

## Largest state and local publicly-owned electric systems by kilowat hour sales

1. New York Power Authority, with 38,833,247,000
2. Los Angeles Department of Water and Power, 21,345,000,000
3. Salt River Project, Phoenix, 17,572,031,608
4. Nebraska Public Power District, 12,695,024,506
5. South Carolina Public Service Authority, 12,290,341,937
6. Puerto Rico Electric Power Authority, 12,000,913,000
7. Intermountain Power Agency, 11,623,111,000
8. San Antonio, TX, City Public Service, 10,989,731,180
9. Memphis, TN, Light, Gas & Water Division, 10,400,996,676
10. Nashville, TN, Electric Service, 9,378,256,249

*Where'd you hear that?*
Public Power, Directory Issue. Based on 1988 kilowatt hour sales.

## Largest state and local publicly-owned electric systems ranked by electric revenues

1. Los Angeles Department of Water and Power, with $1,585,946,000
2. New York Power Authority, $1,049,094,000
3. Salt River Project, Phoenix, $1,022,299,000
4. Puerto Rico Electric Power Authority, $904,941,000
5. San Antonio, TX, Light, Gas & Water Division, $583,314,000

# RESOURCES

# RESOURCES

6. Memphis, TN, Electric Service, $583,314,000
7. Sacramento, CA, Municipal Utility District, $580,528,000
8. Nashville, TN, Electric Service, $509,217,000
9. South Carolina Public Service Authority, $500,306,000
10. Jacksonville, FL, Electric Authority, $487,233,000

*Where'd you hear that?*
Public Power, Directory Issue. Based on 1988 electric revenues.

## Top states in electric powerplant construction markets

1. New York, with $557 million
2. Rhode Island, $274
3. Massachusetts, $259
4. California, $234
5. North Carolina, $108
6. Connecticut, $65
7. Alaska, $64
8. Virginia, $61
9. West Virginia, $55
10. Alabama, $54

*Where'd you hear that?*
ENR, Top 20 States in Major Construction Markets. Based on eleven-month cumulative contract awards, 1989 vs. 1988, in millions of dollars.

### Leading electric power municipal bond issuers

1. Washington Public Power Supply System, with $1,552,500 thousand
2. Puerto Rico Electric Power Authority, $1,000,100
3. Southern California Public Power Authority, $841,000
4. San Antonio, TX, $576,600
5. North Carolina East Municipal Power Agency, $429,600
6. Jacksonville, FL, Electric Authority, $355,800
7. Los Angeles Department of Water & Power, CA, $335,800
8. Northern Municipal Power Agency, MN, $302,800
9. Georgia Municipal Electric Authority, $274,300
10. Intermountain Power Agency, UT, $270,700

*Where'd you hear that?*
Bond Buyer, Bond Buyer Yearbook. Based on 1989 dollar amount, in thousands.

### 10 most expensive companies for 500 kilowatt hours

1. Consolidated Edison Co. of New York, with $0.128 kwh
2. Kauai Electric Co., $0.126
3. Philadelphia Electric Co., $0.123
4. Long Island Lighting Co., $0.122
5. Orange & Rockland Utilities, Inc., $0.121
6. Northern Indiana Public Service, $0.117
6. Hawaii Electric Light Co., $0.117
8. Ohio Edison, $0.113
9. Commonwealth Edison Co., $0.112
10. United Illuminating Co., $0.111

*Where'd you hear that?*
Public Utilities Fortnightly. Based on winter 1988-89 average cost, in dollars/kwh.

# RESOURCES

## 10 least expensive companies for 500 kilowatt hours

1. Washington Water Power Co., Lewiston, with $0.042
2. Washington Water Power Co., Spokane, $0.043
2. Pacific Power & Light Co., $0.043
4. Potomac Electric Power Co., $0.045
4. Idaho Power Co., Boise, $0.45
6. Idaho Power Co., Ontario, OR, $0.048
7. Portland General Electric Co., $0.051
8. Kentucky Utilities Co., $0.52
8. Minnesota Power & Light Co., $0.052
10. Puget Sound Power & Light Co., $0.053

*Where'd you hear that?*
Public Utilities Fortnightly. Based on winter 1988-89 average cost, in dollars/kwh.

## Most productive electrical equipment corporations

1. W. W. Grainger, with $16.1 thousand
2. Hubbell, $15.1
3. Honeywell Inc., $8.9
4. Emerson Electric Co., $8.2
5. Westinghouse, $7.6
6. Square D, $5.0
7. National Service, $4.7

*Where'd you hear that?*
Forbes, Forbes 500s Annual Directory. Based on 1989 profits per employee, in thousands of dollars. Ranks U.S.-based corporations that were publicly traded as of March 23, 1990.

## Most profitable electrical equipment companies

1. Emerson Electric Co., with 19.7%
2. Westinghouse, 19.2%
3. General Electric Co., 18.7%
4. Hubbell, 18.3%
5. National Service, 17.9%
6. Square D, 17.6%
7. W. W. Grainger, 16.6%
8. Raychem, 15.7%
9. AVX Corp., 6.5%
10. Genlyte Group, NA

*Where'd you hear that?*
Forbes, Annual Report on American Industry. Based on 10-year average return on equity. Ranks publicly held corporations only.

## Largest corporations in the electric products industry

1. Westinghouse Electric, with $10,875 million
2. Emerson Electric Co., $9,004
3. Cooper Industries, $4,565
4. Square D, $1,642
5. National Service Industries, $1,367
6. Hubbell, $1,199
7. Raychem, $998
8. Ametek, $564

*Where'd you hear that?*
Business Week, The Business Week 1000. Based on market value as of March 16, 1990, in millions of dollars.

## Europe's largest electrical and electronic machinery, equipment, and supplies

1. NV Philips Gloeilampenfabrieken, with 24,040,450,431
2. Siemens Aktiengesellschaft, 20,061,859,712

153

# RESOURCES

3. Thomson Sa, 8,539,202,952
4. General Electric Co. PLC, 8,260,506,553
5. Robert Bosch Gmbh, 6,891,502,508
6. AEG International Ag, 5,352,922,230
7. Thomson C.S.F., 5,087,557,341
8. Thorn EMI PLC, 4,487,217,768
9. Allgemeine Deutsche Philips Industries Gmbh, 4,156,744,268
10. AEG Aktiengesellschaft, 3,446,893,856

*Where'd you hear that?*
Dun's Europa, Dun & Bradstreet. Based on sales, in European currency units.

## Europe's largest machinery (except electrical) companies

1. Mannesmann Anlagenbau Aktien-Gesellschaft, with 8,048,371,997 ECU
2. Fried Krupp Gesellschaft mit Beschraenkter Haftung, 6,816,227,043
3. Lurgi Gmbh, 6,441,167,493
4. Ing. C. Olivetti & C. Spa, 5,615,876,000
5. IBM Deutschland Gesellschaft mit Beschraenkter Haftung, 5,495,513,879
6. IBM United Kingdom Holdings Ltd., 4,522,333,847
7. English Electric Co. Ltd., 4,136,791,626
8. IBM Italia Spa, 3,544,220,960
9. Thyssen Maschinebau Gmbh, 2,163,922,137
10. International Computers Ltd., 1,988,099,005

*Where'd you hear that?*
Dun's Europa, Dun & Bradstreet. Based on sales, in European currency units.

## Top corporations in the machine & hand tools industry

1. Stanley Works, with $1,565 million
2. Snap-On Tools, $1,321
3. Black & Decker Corp., $1,083
4. Clark Equipment, $772
5. Cincinnati Milacron, $438

*Where'd you hear that?*
Business Week, The Business Week 1000. Based on market value as of March 16, 1990, in millions of dollars.

## Top corporations in the special machinery industry

1. Caterpillar Inc., with $6,161 million
2. Deere & Co., $5,574
3. Ingersoll-Rand, $2,947
4. Dover, $2,319
5. Tyco Laboratories, $2,066
6. FMC Corp., $1,211
7. McDermott International, $976
8. Timken, $962
9. Harnischfeger Industries, $719
10. Nordson, $470

*Where'd you hear that?*
Business Week, The Business Week 1000. Based on market value as of March 16, 1990, in millions of dollars.

## Biggest corporations in the rubber and plastic products industry

1. Goodyear Tire & Rubber Co., with $11,045 million
2. Premark International, $2,601
3. Uniroyal Goodrich, $2,267

# RESOURCES

4. Rubbermaid, $1,349
5. Raychem, $1,104
6. Cooper Tire & Rubber, $870
7. Tredegar Industries, $638
8. A. Schulman, $626
9. Standard Products, $560
10. Carlisle, $558

*Where'd you hear that?*
Fortune, Fortune 500 Largest U.S. Industrial Corporations. Based on 1989 sales, in millions of dollars.

## Most admired rubber products corporations

1. Rubbermaid, with a rating of 8.42
2. Millipore, 7.07
3. Johnson Controls, 7.01
4. Cooper Tire & Rubber, 6.91
5. Standard Products, 6.71
6. Premark International, 6.67
7. Ferro, 6.65
8. Goodyear Tire & Rubber Co., 6.61
9. Carlisle, 6.08
10. Constar International, 5.71

*Where'd you hear that?*
Fortune, America's Most Admired Corporations. Based on scores (0-10) derived from a survey of senior executives, outside directors, and financial analysts. Respondents ranked firms in their own industry on quality of management and products/services; innovation; long-term investment value; financial soundness; attraction and retention of talent; community and environmental responsibility; and use of assets.

## Most productive cement and gypsum corporations

1. CalMat, with $25.2 thousand
2. Lafarge, $13.2
3. USG, $2.0

*Where'd you hear that?*
Forbes, Forbes 500s Annual Directory. Based on 1989 profits per employee, in thousands of dollars. Ranks U.S.-based corporations that were publicly traded as of March 23, 1990.

## Most profitable cement and gypsum companies

1. USG, with 22.2%
2. Florida Rock Industries, 19.9%
3. Southdown, 17.5%
4. CalMat, 11.9%
5. Lone Star Industries, 8.3%
6. Lafarge, 7.0%
7. Ideal Basic Industries, deficit

*Where'd you hear that?*
Forbes, Annual Report on American Industry. Based on 10-year average return on equity. Ranks publicly held corporations only.

## Largest forest products companies in Canada

1. MacMillan Bloedel Inc., with $246,700 thousand
2. CP Forest Products, $220,164
3. Noranda Forest, $189,000
4. Fletcher Challenge Canada Ltd., $120,045
5. Canfor Corp., $96,351
6. Repap Enterprises, $93,100
7. Weldwood of Canada, $65,390
8. Crown Forest Industries, $59,531

155

# RESOURCES

9. Abitibi-Price, $54,200
10. Donohue, $44,250

*Where'd you hear that?*
Canadian Business, Canadian Business 500. Based on 1989 net income, in thousands of Canadian dollars.

## Biggest corporations in the forest products industry

1. International Paper Co., with $11,378 million
2. Georgia-Pacific Corp., $10,171
3. Weyerhaeuser, $10,106
4. James River Corp., $5,902
5. Kimberly-Clark, $5,777
6. Stone Container, $5,361
7. Champion International Corp., $5,254
8. Scott Paper, $5,066
9. Mead, $4,647
10. Boise Cascade, $4,338

*Where'd you hear that?*
Fortune, Fortune 500 Largest U.S. Industrial Corporations. Based on 1989 sales, in millions of dollars.

## Largest U.S. corporations in the forest products industry

1. Weyerhaeuser, with $5,477 million
2. Georgia-Pacific Corp., $4,014
3. Louisiana-Pacific Corp., $1,715
4. Boise Cascade, $1,598
5. Willamette Industries, $1,379

*Where'd you hear that?*
Business Week, The Business Week 1000. Based on market value as of March 16, 1990, in millions of dollars.

## Most admired forest products corporations

1. Kimberly-Clark, with a rating of 7.39
2. Scott Paper, 7.14
3. Mead, 6.83
4. Georgia-Pacific Corp., 6.72
5. James River Corp., 6.45
6. International Paper Co., 6.32
7. Boise Cascade, 5.94
7. Weyerhauser, 5.94
9. Stone Container, 5.92
10. Champion International Corp., 5.54

*Where'd you hear that?*
Fortune, America's Most Admired Corporations. Based on scores (0-10) derived from a survey of senior executives, outside directors, and financial analysts. Respondents ranked firms in their own industry on quality of management and products/services; innovation; long-term investment value; financial soundness; attraction and retention of talent; community and environmental responsibility; and use of assets.

## Biggest lumber producers in the U.S. and Canada

1. Weyerhauser Co. (Tacoma, WA), with 2,942 million board feet
2. Louisiana-Pacific Corp. (Portland, OR), 2,438
3. Georgia-Pacific Corp. (Atlanta, GA), 2,323
4. Fletcher Challenge Canada Ltd. (Vancouver, BC), 1.735
5. Weldwood of Canada Ltd. (Vancouver, BC), 1,107
6. West Fraser Mills Ltd. (Vancouver, BC), 1,085
7. Canfor Corp. (Vancouver, BC), 1,040

8. WTD Industries Inc. (Portland, OR), 1,039
9. MacMillan Bloedel Ltd. (Vancouver, BC), 925
9. Sierra Pacific Industries (Redding, CA), 925

*Where'd you hear that?*
Forest Industries. Based on 1988 production, in millions of board feet.

## World's largest pulp and paper companies

1. Weyerhaeuser (Tacoma, WA), with $10,004.0 million
2. International Paper Co. (New York, NY), $9,533.0
3. Georgia-Pacific Corp. (Atlanta, GA), $9,509.0
4. James River Corp. (Richmond, VA), $5,871.8
5. Stora (Falun, Sweden), $5,590.8
6. Kimberly-Clark (Dallas, TX), $5,393.5
7. Champion International Corp. (Stamford, CT), $5,128.5
8. Scott Paper (Philadelphia, PA), $4,726.4
9. Oji Paper (Tokyo, Japan), $4,690.6
10. Boise Cascade (Boise, ID), $4,094.6

*Where'd you hear that?*
Financial Times. Based on 1988 sales, in millions of U.S. dollars.

## Asia's largest paper, printing, and publishing companies

1. Dai Nippon Printing Co. Ltd., with $8,025,669 thousand
2. Toppan Printing Co. Ltd., $7,292,884
3. Oji Paper Co. Ltd., $4,789,410
4. Sanyo-Kokusaku Pulp Co. Ltd., $3,517,761
5. Honshu Paper Co. Ltd., $3,435,530
6. Jujo Paper Co. Ltd., $2,923,378
7. Daishowa Paper Manufacturing Co. Ltd., $2,899,195
8. Rengo Co. Ltd., $2,160,032
9. Mitsubishi Paper Mills Ltd., $1,858,837
10. Taio Paper Manufacturing Co. Ltd., $1,836,127

*Where'd you hear that?*
Asia's 7500 Largest Companies, Dun & Bradstreet. Based on 1989 sales, in thousands of U.S. dollars.

## Largest U.S. corporations in the paper products industry

1. International Paper Co., with $5,663 million
2. Kimberly-Clark, $5,234
3. Great Northern Nekoosa Corp., $3,603
4. Scott Paper, $3,337
5. Champion International Corp., $2,696
6. Union Camp, $2,462
7. Mead, $2,041
8. James River Corp. of Virginia, $1,968
9. Westvaco, $1,828
10. Consolidated Papers, $1,799

*Where'd you hear that?*
Business Week, The Business Week 1000. Based on market value as of March 16, 1990, in millions of dollars.

## Most profitable paper and lumber companies

1. P. H. Glatfelter, with 21.9%
2. Consolidated Papers, 20.1%

# RESOURCES

# RESOURCES

3. James River Corp. of Virginia, 17.8%
4. Pentair, 17.3%
5. Federal Paper Board, 17.0%
5. Bowater, 17.0%
7. Willamette Industries, 16.3%
8. Great Northern Nekoosa Corp., 14.6%
9. Union Camp, 14.2%
10. Pope & Talbot, 13.5%

*Where'd you hear that?*
Forbes, Annual Report on American Industry. Based on 10-year average return on equity. Ranks publicly held corporations only.

## Most productive paper and lumber corporations

1. Consolidated Papers, with $36.8 thousand
2. Federal Paper Board, $34.5
3. Bowater, $28.3
4. P. H. Glatfelter, $27.0
5. Willamette Industries, $20.4
6. Potlatch, $18.7
7. Union Camp, $16.1
8. Georgia-Pacific Corp., $15.0
9. Westvaco, $14.9
10. Louisiana-Pacific Corp., $14.8

*Where'd you hear that?*
Forbes, Forbes 500s Annual Directory. Based on 1989 profits per employee, in thousands of dollars. Ranks U.S.-based corporations that were publicly traded as of March 23, 1990.

## Largest corporations in the paper container industry

1. Temple-Inland, with $1,729 million
2. Sonoco Products, $1,476
3. Stone Container, $1,348
4. Potlatch, $1,186
5. Federal Paper Board, $932
6. Bemis Co. Inc., $789
7. Longview Fibre, $652
8. Greif Bros., $519

*Where'd you hear that?*
Business Week, The Business Week 1000. Based on market value on March 16, 1990, in millions of dollars.

## Leading paperboard packagers

1. Philip Morris
2. RJR Nabisco
3. Anheuser-Busch Cos. Inc.
4. Procter & Gamble
5. Coca-Cola Enterprises

*Where'd you hear that?*
Packaging, Top 100 Packaging Giants. Based on 1988 consumption of packaging materials.

## Most productive packaging corporations

1. Temple-Inland, with $18.0 thousand
2. Stone Container, $10.3
3. Crown Cork & Seal Co. Inc., $6.9
3. Sonoco Products, $6.9

*Where'd you hear that?*
Forbes, Forbes 500s Annual Directory. Based on 1989 profits per employee, in thousands of dollars. Ranks U.S.-based corporations that were publicly traded as of March 23, 1990.

## Most profitable packaging companies

1. Sonoco Products, with 19.2%
2. Stone Container, 19.1%
3. Longview Fibre, 17.4%
4. Ball Corp., 15.6%
5. Bemis Co. Inc., 13.6%
6. Crown Cork & Seal Co. Inc., 13.4%
7. Constar International, 11.7%
8. International Paper Co., 9.8%

9. Kerr Glass Manufacturing, deficit
10. Gaylord Container, NA

*Where'd you hear that?*
Forbes, Annual Report on American Industry. Based on 10-year average return on equity. Ranks publicly held corporations only.

## Largest corporations in the glass, metal, and plastic container industry

1. Crown Cork & Seal Co. Inc., with $1,393 million
2. Ball, $664

*Where'd you hear that?*
Business Week, The Business Week 1000. Based on market value on March 16, 1990, in millions of dollars.

## Leading glass packagers

1. Anheuser-Busch Cos. Inc.
2. Joseph E. Seagram & Sons
3. Philip Morris
4. Coca-Cola Enterprises
5. PepsiCo

*Where'd you hear that?*
Packaging, Top 100 Packaging Giants. Based on 1988 consumption of packaging materials.

## Leading plastic packagers

1. Procter & Gamble
2. Philip Morris
3. PepsiCo
4. Kraft Inc.
5. Coca-Cola Co.

*Where'd you hear that?*
Packaging, Top 100 Packaging Giants. Based on 1988 consumption of packaging materials.

## Leading metal packagers

1. Anheuser-Busch Cos. Inc.
2. Philip Morris
3. RJR Nabisco
4. Coca-Cola Enterprises
5. Coca-Cola Co.

*Where'd you hear that?*
Packaging, Top 100 Packaging Giants. Based on 1988 consumption of packaging materials.

## *Largest corporate consumers of packaging materials*

1. Anheuser-Busch Cos. Inc., with $2,253,757,000
2. Philip Morris, $1,981,450,000
3. RJR Nabisco, $1,232,000,000
4. Coca-Cola Enterprises, $1,084,832,000
5. PepsiCo, $1,054,573,000
6. Coca-Cola Co., $1,031,400,000
7. Procter & Gamble, $934,527,000
8. Kraft Inc., $587,000,000
9. Joseph E. Seagram & Sons, $567,000,000
10. Sara Lee, $471,120,000

*Where'd you hear that?*
Packaging, Top 100 Packaging Giants. Based on 1988 packaging expenditures.

## Largest South African mining companies in the Mining House League

1. Anglo American, with 1,809 million rand
2. Gencor, 475
3. JCI, 324
4. GFSA, 321
5. Rand Mines, 165

# RESOURCES

# RESOURCES

6. Anglovaal, 145

*Where'd you hear that?*
Financial Mail, Financial Mail Special Survey of Top Companies. Based on 1988 net profits, in millions of rand.

## Largest South African mining companies not in the Mining House League

1. De Beers, with 2,090.0 million rand
2. Rusplats, 388.9
3. Implats, 299.8
4. Samancor, 293.4
5. Palamin, 174.6
6. G. F. Namibia, 58.1
7. Ass Mang, 57.0
8. Lebowa Plats, 14.8
9. GEFCO, 13.1
10. Msauli, 11.4

*Where'd you hear that?*
Financial Mail, Financial Mail Special Survey of Top Companies. Based on 1988 net profits, in millions of rand.

## Largest mining companies in Canada

1. Inco, with $892,181 thousand
2. Falconbridge, $394,711
3. Brascan Ltd., $281,000
4. Cominco Ltd., $214,615
5. Brascade Resources, $127,300
6. Placer Dome, $125,100
7. Teck, $106,400
8. Rio Algom, $104,602
9. Potash Corp. of Saskatchewan, $82,475
10. Westmin Resources, $63,555

*Where'd you hear that?*
Canadian Business, Canadian Business 500. Based on 1989 net income, in thousands of Canadian dollars.

## Biggest corporations in mining and crude oil production industries

1. Asarco, with $2,249 million
2. Freeport-McMoran, $2,015
3. Oryx Energy, $1,237
4. Union Texas, $1,160
5. Vulcan Materials, $1,076
6. Louisiana Land and Exploration, $752
7. Nerco, $713
8. Maxus Energy, $608
9. Westmoreland Coal, $605
10. Mitchell Energy, $577

*Where'd you hear that?*
Fortune, Fortune 500 Largest U.S. Industrial Corporations. Based on 1989 sales, in millions of dollars.

## Most admired mining and crude oil production corporations

1. Burlington Resources, with a rating of 6.89
2. Cyprus Minerals Co., 6.42
3. Union Texas, 6.33
4. Louisiana Land & Exploration, 6.31
5. Vulcan Materials, 6.28
6. Mitchell Energy, 6.17
7. Nerco, 6.04
8. Maxus Energy, 5.68
9. Westmoreland Coal, 5.50

*Where'd you hear that?*
Fortune, America's Most Admired Corporations. Based on scores (0-10) derived from a survey of senior executives, outside directors, and financial analysts. Respondents ranked firms in their own industry on quality of management and products/services; innovation; long-term investment value; financial soundness; attraction and retention of talent; community and environmental responsibility; and use of assets.

## Largest companies in Asia manufacturing ferrous and non-ferrous metals

1. Nippon Steel Corp., with $20,997,793 thousand
2. N K K Corp., $10,992,932
3. Nippon Kokan K. K., $10,297,004
4. Kobe Steel Ltd., $9,948,414
5. Sumitomo Metal Industries, $9,748,056
6. Kawasaki Steel Corp., $9,092,048
7. Sumitomo Electric Industries Ltd., $6,920,040
8. Mitsubishi Metal Corp., $6,783,155
9. Furukawa Electric Co., Ltd., $5,688,406
10. Nippon Light Metal, $4,211,084

*Where'd you hear that?*
Asia's 7500 Largest Companies, Dun & Bradstreet. Based on 1989 sales, in thousands of U.S. dollars.

## Biggest corporations in the metal industry

1. Aluminum Co. of America, with $11,162 million
2. LTV Corp., $6,362
3. Reynolds Metals, $6,201
4. Bethlehem Steel, $5,306
5. Inland Steel Industries, $4,147
6. Amax, $3,915
7. Phelps Dodge, $2,726
8. National Steel, $2,577
9. Armco Inc., $2,494
10. Maxxam, $2,423

*Where'd you hear that?*
Fortune, Fortune 500 Largest U.S. Industrial Corporations. Based on 1989 sales, in millions of dollars.

## Top corporations in the metals industry

1. Newmont Gold, with $5,493 million
2. Newmont Mining, $3,477
3. Phelps Dodge, $2,151
4. Homestake Mining, $2,063
5. Freeport-McMoran Copper, $1,265
6. Asarco, $1,238
7. Amax Gold, $1,095
8. Cyprus Minerals Co., $1,033
9. Battle Mountain Gold, $999
10. FMC Gold, $786

*Where'd you hear that?*
Business Week, The Business Week 1000. Based on market value as of March 16, 1990, in millions of dollars.

## Most admired metals corporations

1. Alcoa, with a rating of 7.13
2. Reynolds Metals, 6.84
3. Phelps Dodge, 6.29
4. Inland Steel Industries, 6.06
5. Amax, 5.96
6. Asarco, 5.48
7. Armco Inc., 5.19
8. Bethlehem Steel, 4.67
9. National Steel, 4.01
10. LTV Corp., 3.86

*Where'd you hear that?*
Fortune, America's Most Admired Corporations. Based on scores (0-10) derived from a survey of senior executives, outside directors, and financial analysts. Respondents ranked firms in their own industry on quality of management and products/services; innovation; long-term investment value; financial soundness; attraction and retention of talent; community and environmental responsibility; and use of assets.

# RESOURCES

# RESOURCES

### Biggest corporations in the metal products industry

1. Gillette Co., with $3,850 million
2. Masco, $3,151
3. Illinois Tool Works, $2,173
4. McDermott, $2,121
5. Stanley Works, $1,981
6. Crown Cork & Seal Co. Inc., $1,910
7. Harsco, $1,351
8. Ball, $1,222
9. Hillenbrand Industries, $1,144
10. Newell, $1,123

*Where'd you hear that?*
Fortune, Fortune 500 Largest U.S. Industrial Corporations. Based on 1989 sales, in millions of dollars.

### Most admired metal products corporations

1. Illinois Tool Works, with a rating of 7.19
2. Stanley Works, 7.05
3. Hillenbrand Industries, 6.89
4. Gillette Co., 6.84
4. Newell, 6.84
6. Crown Cork & Seal Co. Inc., 6.63
7. Ball, 6.59
8. Harsco, 6.04
9. Combustion Engineering, 5.85
10. Tyler, 5.69

*Where'd you hear that?*
Fortune, America's Most Admired Corporations. Based on scores (0-10) derived from a survey of senior executives, outside directors, and financial analysts. Respondents ranked firms in their own industry on quality of management and products/services; innovation; long-term investment value; financial soundness; attraction and retention of talent; community and environmental responsibility; and use of assets.

### Most productive nonferrous metals corporations

1. Newmont Mining, with $44.9 thousand
2. Cyprus Minerals Co., $31.5
3. Asarco, $26.3
4. Homestake Mining, $25.4
5. Phelps Dodge, $22.2
6. AMAX, $18.0
7. Reynolds Metals, $17.5
8. Alcoa, $15.8
9. Maxxam, $11.1
10. Engelhard, -$9.4

*Where'd you hear that?*
Forbes, Forbes 500s Annual Directory. Based on 1989 profits per employee, in thousands of dollars. Ranks U.S.-based corporations that were publicly traded as of March 23, 1990.

### Most profitable nonferrous metals companies

1. Maxxam, with 14.4%
2. Engelhard, 12.4%
3. Alcan Aluminium, 10.0%
4. Alcoa, 9.1%
5. Reynolds Metals, 8.0%
6. Handy & Harman, 6.9%
7. Newmont Mining, 6.8%
8. Phelps Dodge, 6.5%
9. Inco, 5.7%
10. Asarco, 4.4%

*Where'd you hear that?*
Forbes, Annual Report on American Industry. Based on 10-year average return on equity. Ranks publicly held corporations only.

### Top corporations in the aluminum industry

1. Aluminum Co. of America, with $5,866 million
2. Reynolds Metals, $3,351
3. Amax, $2,236

4. Maxxam, $336

*Where'd you hear that?*
Business Week, The Business Week 1000. Based on market value as of March 16, 1990, in millions of dollars.

## World's largest steel producers

1. Nippon Steel (Japan), with 31.3 million tons
2. Usinor Sacilor (France), 25.4
3. Pohang Iron & Steel (South Korea), 17.1
4. British Steel (Britain), 15.6
5. USX (U.S.), 14.2
6. NKK (Japan), 13.6

*Where'd you hear that?*
Business Week. Based on 1989 output of crude steel, in millions of U.S. tons.

## Largest steel companies in Canada

1. Dofasco, with $217,900 thousand
2. Stelco, $93,869
3. Co-Steel, $45,139
4. Ivaco, $32,654
5. Ipsco, $19,300

*Where'd you hear that?*
Canadian Business, Canadian Business 500. Based on 1989 net income, in thousands of Canadian dollars.

## Top corporations in the steel industry

1. Bethlehem Steel, with $1,483 million
2. Nucor, $1,289
3. Inland Steel Industries, $1,198
4. Allegheny Ludlum, $946
5. Armco Inc., $940
6. Worthington Industries, $863
7. Carpenter Technology, $454

*Where'd you hear that?*
Business Week, The Business Week 1000. Based on market value as of March 16, 1990, in millions of dollars.

## Most productive steel corporations

1. Allegheny Ludlum, with $23.9 thousand
2. Wheeling-Pittsburgh, $20.3
3. Armco Inc., $15.7
4. Nucor, $11.0
5. Bethlehem Steel, $8.1
6. LTV Corp., $6.9
7. Inland Steel Industries, $5.8
8. Lone Star Technologies, -$78.9

*Where'd you hear that?*
Forbes, Forbes 500s Annual Directory. Based on 1989 profits per employee, in thousands of dollars. Ranks U.S.-based corporations that were publicly traded as of March 23, 1990.

## Most profitable steel companies

1. Worthington Industries, with 21.4%
2. Nucor, 18.0%
3. Valmont Industries, 12.7%
4. Central Steel & Wire, 12.3%
5. A. M. Castle & Co., 11.1%
6. Texas Industries, 9.6%
7. Carpenter Technology, 7.8%
8. Lukens, 7.5%
9. Quanex, 4.9%
10. Earle M. Jorgensen, 4.8%

*Where'd you hear that?*
Forbes, Annual Report on American Industry. Based on 10-year average return on equity. Ranks publicly held corporations only.

# RESOURCES

# RESOURCES

### World's largest tin-in-concentrates producers

1. Brazil, with 44,000 tons
2. Indonesia, 30,500
3. Malaysia, 28,866
4. Thailand, 14,500
5. Bolivia, 9,900
6. Australia, 7,000
7. Others, total, 20,934

*Where'd you hear that?*
Financial Times. Based on world production, in tons.

### Leading states in silver mining

1. Nevada, with 18,216,295
2. Idaho, 10,868,209
3. Montana, 6,206,290
4. Arizona, 4,661,734
5. Missouri, 1,440,946
6. Colorado, 840,996
7. California, 471,881
8. Others, total, 8,770,590

*Where'd you hear that?*
Jewelers' Circular Keystone Directory. Based on preliminary 1988 Troy ounces mined.

### Top 10 gold producers in the Western World

1. South Africa, with 608.3
2. United States, 259.1
3. Australia, 197.0
4. Canada, 158.4
5. Brazil, 96.9
6. Philippines, 37.1
7. Papua New Guinea, 33.7
8. Colombia, 30.7
9. Chile, 26.1
10. Zimbabwe, 16.0

*Where'd you hear that?*
Gold 1990, Consolidated Gold Fields PLC. Based on 1989 metric tons.

### Largest South African gold mines

1. Freegold, with 106.5 thousand kilograms
2. Vaal Reefs, 80.4
3. Drie Cons, 60.6
4. Western Deep Levels, 39.2
5. Harties, 32.2
6. Kloof, 29.1
7. Randfontein, 27.8
8. Harmony, 27.4
9. Buffels, 15.5
10. Beatrix, 12.9

*Where'd you hear that?*
Financial Mail, Financial Mail Special Survey of Top Companies. Based on kilograms of fine gold produced in 1988, in thousands.

### North America's largest gold producers

1. Placer Dome, with 1,941 thousand ounces
2. Newmont Gold, 1,750
3. Newmont Mining, 1,600
4. Homestake Mining, 1,225
5. American Barrick, 1,175
6. Echo Bay mines, 1,088
7. Lac Minerals, 921
8. Corona, 763
9. Bond International Gold, 725
10. Amax Gold, 453

*Where'd you hear that?*
Barron's. Based on 1993 estimated net adjusted gold output, in thousands of ounces.

### Countries exporting the most gold to the U.S. in 1988

1. Canada, with 1,023,774 Troy ounces
2. Chile, 222,354
3. Uruguay, 220,039

# RESOURCES

4. Switzerland, 152,780
5. Mexico, 57,743
6. Bolivia, 36,009
7. Belgium, 28,260
8. Yugoslavia, 27,810
9. Brazil, 22,506
10. Others, total 60,477

*Where'd you hear that?*
Jewelers' Circular Keystone Directory. Based on 1988 volume, in Troy ounces.

## Countries that imported the most U.S. gold in 1988

1. Taiwan, with 5,436,780 Troy ounces
2. Hong Kong, 1,207,805
3. Switzerland, 917,517
4. Canada, 491,552
5. Netherlands, 269,841
6. China, 166,766
7. Japan, 84,749
8. France, 61,151
9. Peru, 60,315
10. Others, total 27,134

*Where'd you hear that?*
Jewelers' Circular Keystone Directory. Based on 1988 volume, in Troy ounces.

## Leading gold fabrication countries in electronics

1. Japan, with 56.1
2. United States, 42.2
3. Germany, 9.5
4. United Kingdom & Ireland, 9.4
5. Switzerland, 4.0
6. South Korea, 3.5
7. France, 2.6
8. Netherlands, 2.1
9. Singapore, 1.4
10. Yugoslavia, 1.3

*Where'd you hear that?*
Gold 1990, Consolidated Gold Fields PLC9, 1990, p. 46. Based on 1989 metric tons.

## Leading gold fabrication countries for dentistry

1. Japan, with 14.0
2. United States, 11.1
3. Germany, 8.8
4. Italy, 4.8
5. Switzerland, 3.4
6. South Korea, 2.0
7. Netherlands, 0.9
8. France, 0.7
9. Austria, 0.6
10. Sweden, 0.5
10. Yugoslavia, 0.5

*Where'd you hear that?*
Gold 1990, Consolidated Gold Fields PLC. Based on 1989 metric tons.

## Leading gold fabrication countries in industrial and decorative applications

1. United States, with 22.4
2. Japan, 14.7
3. Germany, 7.1
4. Switzerland, 3.3
5. South Korea, 3.0
6. France, 2.6
7. Italy, 2.4
8. United Kingdom & Ireland, 1.6
9. Spain, 0.8
10. Brazil, 0.7
10. India, 0.7

*Where'd you hear that?*
Gold 1990, Consolidated Gold Fields PLC. Based on 1989 metric tons.

# RESOURCES

**Leading gold fabrication countries in official coins**

1. Canada, with 35.6
2. Mexico, 29.1
3. United States, 16.2
4. Austria, 13.0
5. Australia, 9.4
6. South Africa, 6.5
7. Belgium, 5.6
8. United Kingdom & Ireland, 3.4
9. Spain, 2.0
10. France, 0.8

*Where'd you hear that?*
Gold 1990, Consolidated Gold Fields PLC. Based on 1989 metric tons.

**Leading gold fabrication countries in medals, medallions, and fake coins**

1. Italy, 5.5
2. Saudi Arabia & Yemen, 4.0
3. South Korea, 2.0
3. Pakistan & Afghanistan, 2.0
5. Turkey, 1.3
6. Japan, 1.0
7. Switzerland, 0.7
8. Arabian Gulf States, 0.5
8. Kuwait, 0.5
10. Singapore, 0.4

*Where'd you hear that?*
Gold 1990, Consolidated Gold Fields PLC. Based on 1989 metric tons.

**Leading gold fabricating countries in Europe**

1. Italy, with 358.8
2. Germany, 77.6
3. Switzerland, 42.6
4. UK & Ireland, 40.6
5. Spain, 33.6
6. France, 32.1
7. Austria, 18.9
8. Greece, 8.7
9. Yugoslavia, 8.5
10. Belgium, 8.0

*Where'd you hear that?*
Gold 1990, Consolidated Gold Fields PLC. Based on 1989 metric tons. Includes scrap.

**Leading gold fabricating countries in Europe (carat jewelry)**

1. Italy, with 345.0
2. Germany, 51.9
3. Switzerland, 31.2
4. Spain, 30.0
5. United Kingdom & Ireland, 25.7
6. France, 25.1
7. Greece, 8.6
8. Yugoslavia, 6.5
9. Portugal, 5.3
10. Austria, 4.4

*Where'd you hear that?*
Gold 1990, Consolidated Gold Fields PLC. Based on 1989 metric tons. Includes Scrap.

**Leading gold fabricating countries in the Middle East**

1. Turkey, with 100.2
2. Saudi Arabia & Yemen, 70.0
3. Egypt, 26.9
4. Arabian Gulf States, 23.5
5. Kuwait, 18.2
6. Iraq, Syria & Jordan, 11.0
7. Israel, 10.7
8. Lebanon, 3.7
9. Iran, 0.5

*Where'd you hear that?*
Gold 1990, Consolidated Gold Fields PLC. Based on 1989 metric tons. Includes scrap.

## Leading gold fabricating countries in the Middle East (carat jewelry)

1. Turkey, with 98.1
2. Saudi Arabia & Yemen, 66.0
3. Egypt, 26.9
4. Arabian Gulf States, 23.0
5. Kuwait, 17.7
6. Iraq, Syria & Jordan, 11.0
7. Israel, 10.4
8. Lebanon, 3.7
9. Iran, 0.5

*Where'd you hear that?*
Gold 1990, Consolidated Gold Fields PLC. Based on 1989 metric tons. Includes Scrap.

## Leading gold fabricating countries in the Indian sub-continent

1. India, with 222.3
2. Pakistan & Afghanistan, 30.0
3. Bangladesh & Nepal, 6.5
4. Sri Lanka, 2.5

*Where'd you hear that?*
Gold 1990, Consolidated Gold Fields PLC. Based on 1989 metric tons. Includes scrap.

## Leading gold fabricating countries in the Indian sub-continent (carat jewelry)

1. India, with 221.5
2. Pakistan & Afghanistan, 28.0
3. Bangladesh & Nepal, 6.5
4. Sri Lanka, 2.5

*Where'd you hear that?*
Gold 1990, Consolidated Gold Fields PLC. Based on 1989 metric tons. Includes Scrap.

## Leading gold fabricating countries in the Far East

1. Japan, with 198.3
2. Taiwan, 107.2
3. Thailand, 95.0
4. South Korea, 84.1
5. Indonesia, 66.5,
6. Hong Kong, 65.9
7. Singapore, 22.9
8. Malaysia, 21.6
9. Philippines, 2.1
10. Vietnam, 1.0
10. Burma, Laos & Cambodia, 1.0

*Where'd you hear that?*
Gold 1990, Consolidated Gold Fields PLC. Based on 1989 metric tons. Includes scrap.

## Leading gold fabricating countries in the Far East (carat jewelry)

1. Japan, with 112.5
2. Taiwan, 106.0
3. Thailand, 95.0
4. South Korea, 73.6
5. Indonesia, 66.5
6. Hong Kong, 65.0
7. Malaysia, 21.6
8. Singapore, 21.0
9. Philippines, 2.0
10. Vietnam, 1.0
10. Burma, Laos & Cambodia, 1.0

*Where'd you hear that?*
Gold 1990, Consolidated Gold Fields PLC. Based on 1989 metric tons. Includes scrap.

# RESOURCES

# RESOURCES

### Leading gold fabricating countries in Africa

1. Morocco, with 15.5
2. South Africa, 12.9
3. Algeria, 7.0
4. Libya, 4.5
5. Tunisia, 0.7
6. Others, total, 4.0

*Where'd you hear that?*
Gold 1990, Consolidated Gold Fields PLC. Based on 1989 metric tons. Inclues scrap.

### Leading gold fabricating countries in Africa (carat jewelry)

1. Morocco, with 15.5
2. Algeria, 7.0
3. Libya, 4.5
4. South Africa, 2.1
5. Tunisia, 0.7
6. Others, total, 33.8

*Where'd you hear that?*
Gold 1990, Consolidated Gold Fields PLC. Based on 1989 metric tons. Includes Scrap.

### Leading gold fabricating countries in Latin America

1. Mexico, 36.4
2. Peru, 9.4
3. Brazil, 7.9
4. Colombia, 2.5
5. Ecuador, 1.8
6. Argentina, 1.6
7. Venezuela, 0.8
8. Chile, 0.3
9. Others, total, 60.9

*Where'd you hear that?*
Gold 1990, Consolidated Gold Fields PLC. Based on 1989 metric tons. Includes scrap.

### Leading gold fabricating countries in Latin America (carat jewelry)

1. Peru, with 9.4
2. Mexico, 6.5
3. Brazil, 6.0
4. Colombia, 2.2
5. Ecuador, 1.8
6. Argentina, 1.5
7. Venezuela, 0.7
8. Chile, 0.3
9. Others, total 0.2

*Where'd you hear that?*
Gold 1990, Consolidated Gold Fields PLC. Based on 1989 metric tons. Includes Scrap.

### Leading gold fabricating countries in North America

1. United States, with 201.3
2. Canada, 47.0

*Where'd you hear that?*
Gold 1990, Consolidated Gold Fields PLC. Based on 1989 metric tons. Includes scrap.

### Leading gold fabricating countries in North America (carat jewelry)

1. United States, with 108.8
2. Canada, 10.4

*Where'd you hear that?*
Gold 1990, Consolidated Gold Fields PLC. Based on 1989 metric tons. Includes Scrap.

# RESOURCES

**Leading uses of gold in the United States**

1. Jewelry and arts, with 1,820 thousand Troy ounces
2. Industrial, 1,101
3. Dental, 240
4. Small items for investment, 3 Jewelers' Circular

*Where'd you hear that?*
Keystone Directory. Based on 1988 volume, in thousands of Troy ounces.

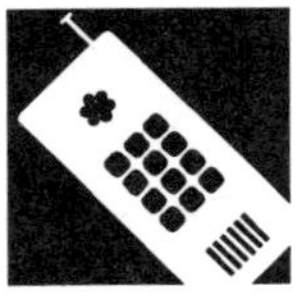

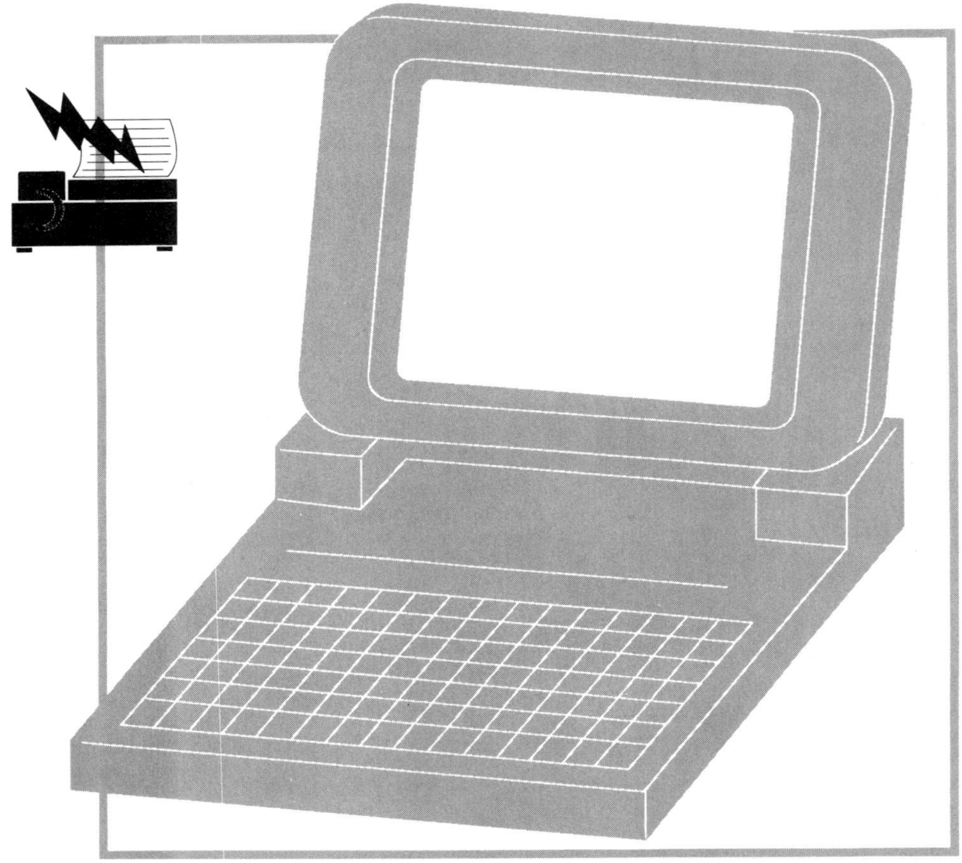

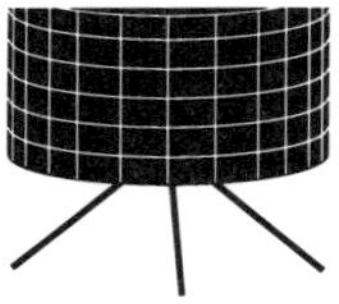

# GO TECH

## Top 10 high-tech industries

1. Guided missiles and spacecraft
2. Communication equipment and electronic components
3. Aircraft and parts
4. Office computing and accounting machines
5. Ordinance and accessories
6. Drugs and medicines
7. Industrial inorganic chemicals
8. Professional and scientific instruments
9. Engines, turbines and parts
10. Plastic materials and synthetic resins, rubber, and fibers

*Where'd you hear that?*
Journal of Advertising Research. Based on total research and development expenditures.

## Largest high technology companies in Canada

1. IBM Canada, with $349,000 thousand
2. Digital Equipment of Canada, $47,654
3. CAE Industries, $42,755
4. NCR Canada, $30,000
5. SNC Group, $28,134
6. Canadian Marconi, $23,210
7. Federal Pioneer, $22,823
8. Mitel, $22,200
9. Allied-Signal Canada, $20,123
10. Honeywell Inc., $12,431

*Where'd you hear that?*
Canadian Business, Canadian Business 500. Based on 1989 net income, in thousands of Canadian dollars.

## Largest Hispanic-American high tech companies

1. CTA Inc. (Rockville, MD), with $68.00 million
2. Colsa, Inc. (Huntsville, AL), $50.00

# GO TECH

2. RJO Enterprises, Inc. (Lanham, MD), $50.00
4. Infotec Development, Inc. (Santa Ana, CA), $45.00
5. Computer Dynamics, Inc. (Virginia Beach, VA), $37.00
6. Magnet Industrial Group, Inc. (Milford, CT), $28.20
7. Pacifica Services, Inc. (Pasadena, CA), $25.90
8. Advanced Sciences, Inc. (Albuquerque, NM), $25.50
9. J. T. Slocomb Co. (Glastonbury, CT), $24.00
10. Omniplan Corp. (Culver City, CA), $18.44

*Where'd you hear that?*
Hispanic Business. Based on 1988 sales, in millions of dollars.

## Top communications companies

1. Capital Cities/ABC Inc., with $3,900.0 million
2. General Electric Co., $3,410.0
3. CBS Inc., $2,959.9
4. Time Warner, $2,401.0
5. TCI, $2,330.0
6. Sony, $1,921.9
7. Viacom, $1,436.2
8. News Corp., $1,050.0
9. Turner Broadcasting, $1,032.6
10. Saatchi & Saatchi, $1,003.6

*Where'd you hear that?*
Broadcasting. Based on 1989 electronic communications revenue, in millions of dollars.

## Fastest growing communications companies

1. Novell, with 89.1%
2. 3Com, 81.0%
3. Stanford Telecommunications, 29.9%
4. Digital Communications Associates, 28.8%
5. Inmac, 25.0%
6. Data Switch, 24.9%
7. Bolt Beranek and Newman, 22.3%
8. Dynascan, 19.9%
9. Dynatech, 18.2%
10. ADC Telecommunications, 17.5%

*Where'd you hear that?*
Electronic Business, Fastest Growing Companies. Based on 1989 5-year compounded annual sales growth rate, in percent.

## Largest communications companies by employee revenues

1. Dynascan, with $482.7 thousand
2. Inmac, $327.7
3. 3Com, $186.9
4. Novell, $177.5
5. TIE/communications, $170.2
6. DCA, $158.7
7. Scientific-Atlanta, $147.6
8. Datapoint, $122.8
8. DSC Communications, $122.8
10. Dynatech, $120.2

*Where'd you hear that?*
Electronic Business, Electronic Business 200. Based on 1988 per employee revenues, in thousands of dollars.

## Canada's largest communications industries

1. Northern Telecom Ltd., with $7,230,133 thousand (Canadian dollars)
2. Thomson Corp., $6,054,000
3. Quebecor Inc., $1,755,482

172

4. Southam Inc., $1,677,154
5. Maclean Hunter Ltd., $1,426,200
6. Torstar Corp., $982,589
7. Hollinger Inc., $754,867
8. Rogers Communications Inc., $600,839
9. G.T.C. Transcontinental Group Ltd., $366,382
10. Canadian Broadcasting Corp., $363,046

*Where'd you hear that?*
Financial Post 500. Based on 1989 revenues, in thousands of Canadian dollars.

## World's top 10 telecommunications equipment manufacturers

1. AT & T Technologies (U.S.), with $10.2 billion
2. Alcatel NC (Belgium), $8.0
3. Siemens (West Germany), $5.4
4. NEC (Japan), $4.5
5. Northern Telecom (Canada), $4.4
6. IBM (U.S.), $3.3
7. Motorola (U.S.), $3.1
7. L. M. Ericsson (Sweden), $3.1
9. Fujitsu Ltd. (Japan), $2.1
10. Philips (Netherlands), $2.0

*Where'd you hear that?*
Financial Times. Based on 1986 sales, in billions of dollars.

## World's largest telecommunication companies

1. Northern Telecom, with 19.3%
2. AT & T, 18.0%
3. Alcatel, 15.5%
4. L. M. Ericsson, 8.7%
5. GPT, 7.5%
5. NEC, 7.5%
7. Others, total 23.5%

*Where'd you hear that?*
Electronic Business. Based on share of total local digital lines placed in service in 1988, in percent.

## Countries spending the most on telecommunications equipment

1. United States, with $24,081.1 million
2. Japan, $12,142.9
3. West Germany, $9,836.1
4. Italy, $6,666.7
5. France, $5,967.7
6. United Kingdom, $3,761.6
7. Canada, $3,658.3
8. Australia, $2,346.2
9. South Korea, $2,238.8
10. Switzerland, $1,817.3

*Where'd you hear that?*
Telephony. Based on 1990 telecommunications equipment spending, in millions of dollars.

## Most productive telecommunications corporations

1. Citizens Utilities, with $52.0 thousand
2. Centel Corp., $34.5
3. MCI Communications, $32.8
4. Alltel, $19.9
5. Pacific Telesis, $18.0
6. BellSouth Corp., $16.8
7. Southwestern Bell, $16.7
8. US West, $15.8
8. Ameritech, $15.8

**GO TECH**

# GO TECH

10. Southern New England Telecom, $14.3

*Where'd you hear that?*
Forbes, Forbes 500 Annual Directory. Based on 1989 profits per employee, in thousands of dollars. Ranks U.S.-based corporations that were publicly traded as of March 23, 1990.

## Most profitable telecommunications companies

1. Alltel, with 15.6%
2. Centel Corp., 15.5%
3. Cincinnati Bell, 14.9%
4. Rochester Telephone, 14.3%
4. Contel, 14.3%
6. Southern New England Telecom, 13.7%
7. United Telecom, 13.0%
8. GTE Corp., 12.8%
8. MCI Communications, 12.8%
10. Western Union, deficit

*Where'd you hear that?*
Forbes, Annual Report on American Industry. Based on 10-year average return on equity. Ranks publicly held corporations only.

## Largest U.S. corporations in the telephone industry

1. BellSouth Corp., with $26,187 million
2. GTE Corp., $20,974
3. Pacific Telesis Group, $18,378
4. Bell Atlantic Corp., $17,945
5. Ameritech, $16,414
6. NYNEX, $15,960
7. Southwestern Bell, $15,846
8. US West, $13,534
9. Contel, $4,424
10. Centel Corp., $2,859

*Where'd you hear that?*
Business Week, The Business Week 1000. Based on market value as of March 16, 1990, in millions of dollars.

## Largest U.S. corporations in the telecommunications equipment & services industry

1. AT & T, with $45,049 million
2. MCI Communications, $8,969
3. United Telecommunications, $7,922
4. McCaw Cellular Communications, $6,309
5. Contel Cellular, $2,148
6. Citizens Utilities, $1,770
7. US West New Vector Group, $1,756
8. Metro Mobile Cts., $1,438
9. Cellular Communications, $1,364
10. Telephone & Data Systems, $1,072

*Where'd you hear that?*
Business Week, The Business Week 1000. Based on market value as of March 16, 1990, in millions of dollars.

## Market share of office and business equipment

1. AT & T, with 35.2%
2. Siemens, 23.0%
3. NEC, 17.0%
4. GTE Corp., 16.4%
5. Fujitsu Ltd., 16.3%
6. British Telecom, 16.2%
7. BCE, Inc., 15.0%
8. Alcatel, 11.1%
9. Motorola, 7.1%
10. L. M. Ericsson, 6.0%

*Where'd you hear that?*
Appliance Manufacturer. Based on 1989 market share, in percent.

## Countries with the most telephone lines

1. United States, with 121,475,000
2. Japan, 46,325,000
3. Soviet Union, 29,475,000
4. West Germany, 26,399,284
5. France, 23,911,097
6. United Kingdom, 22,137,000
7. Italy, 18,252,973
8. Canada, 12,250,680
9. Spain, 9,801,009
10. South Korea, 7,659,000

*Where'd you hear that?*
Financial Times. Based on number of main telephone lines.

## Largest long-distant telephone companies

1. AT & T, with 69%
2. MCI, 12%
3. US Sprint, 8%
4. Telecom U.S.A., 1.4%
5. Others, total 9.6%

*Where'd you hear that?*
New York Times. Based on percentage of market based on 1989 revenues.

## Most used long distance services

1. Dial '1' (Residential-business inter/intrastate), with 49%
2. WATS, 11%
2. 800 Services, 11%
2. International, 11%
5. Data/Private line, 9%
6. Pay phone, 4%
6. Operator Service/Credit Card, 4%
8. 900 Services, 1%

*Where'd you hear that?*
Wall Street Journal. Based on estimated share of 1989 long-distance market.

# GO TECH

## Top 10 metropolitan areas in percentage of telephone numbers that are unlisted

1. Las Vegas, NV, with 60.3%
2. Los Angeles-Long Beach, CA, 56.0%
3. Oakland, CA, 53.6%
4. Fresno, CA, 52.6%
5. Jersey City, NJ, 51.7%
6. San Jose, CA, 50.6%
7. Sacramento, CA, 49.6%
8. Riverside-San Bernardino, CA, 48.7%
9. Bakersfield, CA, 48.6%
10. San Francisco, CA, 47.7%

*Where'd you hear that?*
American Demographics. Based on percentage of telephone numbers that are unlisted.

## Most popular types of 900 telephone numbers

1. Entertainment, with 68%
2. Live conversation, 15%
3. Polling, 10%
4. Product & event promotion, 5%
5. News, financial and other, 2%

175

# GO TECH

*Where'd you hear that?*
Wall Street Journal. Based on 1989 market share, in percent.

## Leading cordless phone companies

1. AT & T, with 38%
2. Panasonic, 19%
3. Cobra, 10%
4. Uniden, 7%
5. Tandy, 5%
6. Southwestern Bell, 4%
7. General Electric Co., 3%
8. GTE Corp., 2%
9. Others, total 12%

*Where'd you hear that?*
New York Times. Based on 1989 market share, in percent.

## Largest manufacturers of mobile telephones

1. Motorola, with 13.2%
2. Matsushita, 12.6%
3. Mitsubishi, 10.8%
4. Uniden, 10.6%
5. Toshiba, 9.5%
6. NEC, 8.7%
7. OKI, 6.8%
8. Tandy, 6.6%
9. Nokia, 4.8%
10. Shintom, 4.3%

*Where'd you hear that?*
Phone+. Based on 1988 average market share of mobile transportable telephones.

## Top 10 cellular radio service companies

1. McCaw/Lin Cellular, with 611 thousand
2. BellSouth Corp., 419
3. Southwestern Bell, 382
4. PacTel Cellular, 381
5. GTE Mobilnet, 303
6. Ameritech, 242
7. NYNEX, 213
8. Bell Atlantic Corp., 189
9. U.S. West New Vector, 135
10. Contel, 95

*Where'd you hear that?*
New York Times. Based on number of subscribers as of December 31, 1989, in thousands.

## Leading cellular radio service companies

1. PacTel, with 262 thousand
2. McCaw, 258
3. BellSouth Corp., 255
4. Southwestern Bell, 244
5. Lin Broadcasting Inc., 228
6. Ameritech, 146
7. GTE Mobilnet, 127
7. NYNEX, 127
9. Bell Atlantic Corp., 100
10. US West Newvector, 83

*Where'd you hear that?*
New York Times. Based on number of cellular telephone subscribers in 1988, in thousands.

## Largest voice mail systems

1. Boston Technology, with 23%
2. Octel, 20%
3. VMX, 14%
4. Digital Sound, 12%
5. Unisys, 9%
6. Centigram, 8%
7. Comverse Tech, 7%
8. Glenayre, 2%
9. Others, total, 5%

*Where'd you hear that?*
Voice Processing Magazine. Based on 1989 market share, in percent.

## Largest manufacturers of facsimile machines

1. Sharp, with 20.8%
2. Murata Business Systems, 15.0%
3. Canon, 10.5%
4. Ricoh, 9.9%
5. Pitney Bowes, 5.6%
6. Panafax, 5.3%
7. Toshiba, 5.0%
8. Fujitsu Ltd., 3.2%
9. Harris/3M, 3.0%
9. Xerox, 3.0%

*Where'd you hear that?*
Direct Marketing. Based on market share, in percent.

## Leading foreign electronics companies

1. Matsushita Electric Ltd., with $40,511,000,000
2. NEC Ltd., $24,861,000,000
3. Hitachi Ltd., $20,853,000,000
4. N.V. Philips GMB, $20,300,000,000
5. Fujitsu Ltd., $18,086,000,000
6. Toshiba Ltd., $17,276,000,000
7. Siemens AG, $15,190,000,000
8. Compagnie Generale D'Electricite, $14,377,000,000
9. Alcatel N.V., $12,000,000,000
10. General Electric Co. PLC, $7,798,300,000

*Where'd you hear that?*
Electronic News, Financial Fact Book & Directory. Based on 1989 electronic sales in latest available four quarters, in dollars.

## Largest electronics companies in Europe

1. Philips, with $20,803 million
2. IBM, $20,520
3. Siemens, $17,389
4. CGE, $12,226
5. Thomson, $11,149
6. GEC, $6,795
7. Olivetti, $6,375
8. Robert Bosch, $6,265
9. Groupe Bull, $5,296
10. Digital Equipment Corp., $5,130

*Where'd you hear that?*
Electronic Business. Based on 1988 electronics sales, in millions of dollars.

## Top U.S. electronics companies in Japan

1. IBM Japan, with $6,894 million
2. Fuji Xerox, $3,553 (50% owned by Rank Xerox)
3. Nihon Unisys, $2,026 (33.3% owned by Unisys)
4. Yamatake Honeywell, $970 (26.5% owned by Honeywell)
5. Yokogawa HP, $933 (75% owned by Hewlett-Packard)
6. NCR Japan, $730
7. DEC Japan, $689
8. Texas Instruments, $610
9. Nippon Motorola, $475
10. AMP Japan, $400

*Where'd you hear that?*
Electronic Business. Based on 1989 sales in Japan, in millions of dollars.

## Japan's largest electronics companies

1. Matsushita, with $30,400 million
2. NEC, $23,355

# GO TECH

# GO TECH

3. Toshiba, $20,300
4. Hitachi Ltd., $19,400
5. Fujitsu Ltd., $18,087
6. Sony, $13,700
7. Mitsubishi Electric, $12,500
8. NTT, $9,700
9. Canon, $8,200
10. Sharp, $7,700

*Where'd you hear that?*
Electronic Business. Based on 1988 electronics revenue, in millions of U.S. dollars.

## Biggest corporations in the U.S. electronics industry

1. General Electric Co., with $55,264 million
2. Westinghouse Electric, $12,844
3. Motorola, $9,620
4. Raytheon, $8,796
5. TRW, $7,408
6. Honeywell Inc., $7,242
7. Emerson Electric Co., $7,071
8. Texas Instruments, $6,592
9. Whirlpool, $6,289
10. North American Philips, $6,203

*Where'd you hear that?*
Fortune, Fortune 500 Largest U.S. Industrial Corporations. Based on 1989 sales, in millions of dollars.

## Largest corporations in the electronics industry

1. Motorola, with $8,873 million
2. Raytheon, $4,109
3. General Motors Hughes Electronics, $1,914
4. Litton Industries Inc., $1,806
5. Harris, $1,311
6. E-Systems, $1,005
7. General Instrument, $969
8. Loral, $790
9. Varian Associates, $487
10. Sensormatic Electronics, $366

*Where'd you hear that?*
Business Week, The Business Week 1000. Based on market value as of March 16, 1990, in millions of dollars.

## Top electronics businesses

1. IBM, with $5,390.0 million
2. Digital Equipment Corp., $1,517.6
3. Xerox, $1,399.0
4. Motorola, $873.0
5. Unisys, $669.9
6. Hewlett-Packard Co., $648.0
7. Texas Instruments, $628.1
8. General Motors Hughes Electronics, $533.0
9. Intel Corp., $477.5
10. NCR, $420.4

*Where'd you hear that?*
Electronic Business, Top Electronics Capital Spenders. Based on 1988 total capital expenditures, in millions of dollars, on components. Only companies from Electronic Business 200 that derive at least 70% of their total revenue from electronics are eligible for this list.

## Fastest growing electronics companies

1. Cypress Semiconductor Corp., with 127.8%
2. Silicon Graphics, 117.9%
3. Oracle Systems, 115.0%
4. Sun Microsystems, 114.5%
5. Cadence Design Systems, 89.8%
6. Novell, 89.1%
7. Maxtor, 84.4%
8. 3Com, 81.0%
9. Informix Corp., 72.1%
10. Integrated Device Technology, 66.4%

*Where'd you hear that?*
Electronic Business, Fastest Growing Companies. Based on 1989 5-year compounded annual sales growth rate, in percent.

## Most admired electronics corporations

1. General Electric Co., with a rating of 7.62
2. Motorola, 7.24
3. Emerson Electric Co., 7.08
4. Westinghouse, 6.56
5. Texas Instruments, 6.55
6. Raytheon, 6.40
7. Whirlpool, 6.32
8. TRW, 6.28
9. North American Phillips, 6.04
10. Honeywell Inc., 5.65

*Where'd you hear that?*
Fortune, America's Most Admired Corporations. Based on scores (0-10) derived from a survey of senior executives, outside directors, and financial analysts. Respondents ranked firms in their own industry on quality of management and products/services; innovation; long-term investment value; financial soundness; attraction and retention of talent; community and environmental responsibility; and use of assets.

## Most profitable electronics companies

1. Micron Technology, with 23.8%
2. Microsoft, 21.2%
3. Cadence Design Systems, 19.4%
4. Computer Associates International Inc., 15.9%
5. Cypress Semiconductor Corp., 15.4%
6. Chips and Technologies, 15.2%
7. Measurex, 14.3%
8. Oracle Systems, 14.0%
9. Octel Communications, 13.5%
10. Medtronic, 13.1%
11. Intel Corp., 12.5%
12. Lotus Development Corp., 12.2%
13. Network Systems, 12.0%
14. Teradata, 11.9%
15. Mentor Graphics, 11.8%

*Where'd you hear that?*
Electronic Business, Most Profitable Companies. Based on fiscal year 1989 profits as a percentage of sales.

## Most profitable electronics companies

1. IBM, with $3,758 million
2. DEC, $1,073
3. Hewlett-Packard Co., $829
4. General Motors Hughes Electronics, $663
5. Honeywell Inc., $550
6. Raytheon, $529
7. Motorola, $498
8. Apple Computer Inc., $454
9. NCR, $412
10. Intel Corp., $391

*Where'd you hear that?*
Electronic Business, Most Profitable Companies. Based on fiscal year 1989 profits, in millions of dollars.

## Top electronic businesses for 1988

1. IBM, with $59,681 million
2. AT & T, $14,377
3. Digital Equipment Corp., $12,285
4. General Motors Hughes Electronics, $11,244
5. Xerox, $11,152
6. Hewlett-Packard Co., $10,296
7. Unisys, $9,902
8. General Electric Co., $9,300

# GO TECH

179

# GO TECH

9. Motorola, $8,250
10. Rockwell International, $7,148

*Where'd you hear that?*
Electronic Business, Electronic Business 200. Based on 1988 electronics revenues, in millions of dollars.

## Top net income/sales electronics companies

1. Micron Technology, with 32.6%
2. Microsoft, 21.0%
3. Cray Research, 20.7%
4. Eli Lilly & Co., 18.7%
5. Digital Communications, 18.6%
6. Intel Corp., 15.8%
7. Chips & Technologies, 15.6%
8. Ashton-Tate, 15.5%
9. Oracle Systems, 15.2%
10. Computer Associates, 14.4%

*Where'd you hear that?*
Electronic Business, Electronic Business 200. Based on 1988 net income/sales, in percent.

## Top return on equity electronics companies

1. Reliance Electric, with 58.7%
2. Atari, 47.3%
3. Apple Computer Inc., 39.9%
4. Micron Technology, 34.0%
5. Chips & Technologies, 33.2%
6. Microsoft, 33.0%
7. Oracle Systems, 31.9%
8. Compaq Computer Corp., 31.3%
9. Marshall Industries, 29.0%
10. MAI Basic Four, 27.6%

*Where'd you hear that?*
Electronic Business, Electronic Business 200. Based on 1988 return on equity, in percent.

## Top return on investment electronics companies

1. Apple Computer Inc., with 35.4%
2. Micron Technology, 31.4%
3. Microsoft, 31.3%
3. Chips & Technologies, 31.3%
5. Oracle Systems, 29.3%
6. Compaq Computer Corp., 23.4%
7. Atari, 22.3%
8. Premier Industrial, 21.7%
9. Digital Communications, 20.8%
10. Eli Lilly & Co., 20.3%

*Where'd you hear that?*
Electronic Business, Electronic Business 200. Based on 1988 return on investment, in percent.

## Largest electronics distributors

1. Anthem Electronics, with $529.3 thousand
2. Arrow Electronics Inc., $362.7
3. Pioneer-Standard, $292.6
4. Marshall Industries, $280.3
5. Wyle Laboratories, $188.9
6. Avnet Inc., $182.9

*Where'd you hear that?*
Electronic Business, Electronic Business 200. Based on 1988 per employee revenues, in thousands of dollars.

## Fastest growing distribution companies

1. Emerson Radio, with 33.2%
2. Anthem Electronics, 27.4%
3. Western Micro Technology, 22.5%
4. Marshall Industries, 16.8%

*Where'd you hear that?*
Electronic Business, Fastest Growing Companies. Based on 1989 5-year compounded annual sales growth rate, in percent.

### Electronics businesses spending the most on distribution projects

1. Avnet Inc., with $24.7 million
2. Marshall Industries, $10.8
3. Wyle Laboratories, $9.4

*Where'd you hear that?*
Electronic Business, Top Electronics Capital Spenders. Based on capital expenditures, in millions of dollars, on distribution projects.

### Most profitable capital equipment companies

1. Gerber Scientific, with 11.0%
2. Applied Materials, 10.3%
3. Fluke, 9.3%
4. BTU International, 7.3%
4. Silicon Valley Group, 7.3%
6. MTS Systems, 7.2%
7. KLA Instruments, 7.1%
8. Hewlett-Packard Co., 7.0%
9. Kulicke & Soffa, 6.0%
10. Keithley Instruments, 4.7%

*Where'd you hear that?*
Electronic Business, Most Profitable Companies. Based on fiscal year 1989 profits as a percentage of sales.

### Fastest growing capital equipment companies

1. Silicon Valley Group, with 33.9%
2. KLA Instruments, 31.0%
3. Applied Materials, 24.4%
4. MTS Systems, 15.3%
5. Hewlett-Packard Co., 14.5%

6. Keithley Instruments, 14.3%

*Where'd you hear that?*
Electronic Business, Fastest Growing Companies. Based on 1989 5-year compounded annual sales growth rate, in percent.

### Most profitable electronics industry segments

1. Software, with 15.5%
2. Distribution, 9.3%
3. Computer-based systems, 9.2%
4. Components, 8.8%
5. Semiconductors, 8.0%
6. Capital equipment, 7.2%
7. Computers, 6.8%
7. Office equipment, 6.8%
9. Peripherals, 6.5%
10. Government, 6.4%

*Where'd you hear that?*
Electronic Business, Most Profitable Companies. Based on fiscal year 1989 profits as a percentage of sales.

### Most profitable electronics government contractors

1. Honeywell Inc., with 9.1%
2. Watkins-Johnson, 6.0%
2. Raytheon, 6.0%
4. General Motors Hughes Electronics, 5.8%
4. Aydin, 5.8%
6. Harris, 5.2%
7. E-Systems, 5.1%
7. Loral, 5.1%
9. Cubic, 5.0%

# GO TECH

# GO TECH

*Where'd you hear that?*
Electronic Business, Most Profitable Companies. Based on fiscal year 1989 profits as a percentage of sales.

## Electronics businesses spending the most on government projects

1. Motorola, with $873.0 million
2. Texas Instruments, $628.1
3. General Motors Hughes Electronics, $533.0
4. Honeywell Inc., $327.7
5. Litton Industries Inc., $230.1
6. Harris, $81.2
7. E-Systems, $53.7
8. Loral, $50.9
9. Varian Associates, $43.2
10. SCI Systems, $42.8

*Where'd you hear that?*
Electronic Business, Top Electronics Capital Spenders. Based on capital expenditures, in millions of dollars, on government projects.

## Largest electronics components companies

1. AMP, with $112.0 thousand
2. LPL Investment Group, $89.9
3. Augat, $89.2
4. BRIntec, $86.5
5. Molex, $85.1
6. AVX Corp., $77.2
7. Cherry Electrical Products, $68.7
8. Sprague Technologies, $61.5
9. Oak Industries, $52.4
10. CTS, $43.2

*Where'd you hear that?*
Electronic Business, Electronic Business 200. Based on 1988 per employee revenues, in thousands of dollars.

## Most profitable electronic components companies

1. Molex, with 10.1%
2. AMP, 10.0%
3. CTS, 5.4%
4. Augat, 4.9%
5. Eldec, 4.7%
6. Vishay Intertechnology, 4.3%

*Where'd you hear that?*
Electronic Business, Most Profitable Companies. Based on fiscal year 1989 profits as a percentage of sales.

## Fastest growing components (other than semiconductors) companies

1. Vishay Intertechnology, with 53.7%
2. Microsemi, 27.9%
3. Molex, 17.8%
4. Cherry, 15.6%
5. Methode Electronics, 13.0%

*Where'd you hear that?*
Electronic Business, Fastest Growing Companies. Based on 1989 5-year compounded annual sales in growth rate, in percent.

## Electronics businesses spending the most on components projects

1. AMP, with $220.3 million
2. Molex, $68.7
3. Sprague Technologies, $38.1
4. AVX Corp., $32.5
5. Cherry Electrical Products, $17.8
6. Augat, $17.7
7. CTS, $10.0

*Where'd you hear that?*
Electronic Business, Top Electronics Capital Spenders. Based on capital expenditures, in millions of dollars, on components projects.

## Most taxed electronics companies

1. IBM, with $3,542.0 million
2. Xerox, $470.0
3. DEC, $435.2
4. General Motors Hughes Electronics, $349.3
5. NCR, $347.9
6. Hewlett-Packard Co., $326.0
7. Unisys, $278.0
8. Apple Computer Inc., $255.9
9. Honeywell Inc., $234.0
10. AMP, $210.1

*Where'd you hear that?*
Electronic Business. Based on 1988 total income tax provision, in millions of dollars.

## U.S. electronic capital equipment providers with the highest research and development spending

1. Hewlett-Packard Co., with $1,019.0 million
2. Tektronix, $215.6
3. Perkin-Elmer, $98.6
4. Varian Associates, $80.2
5. Teradyne $61.9
6. Applied Materials, $43.5
7. LTX, $31.6
8. GenRad, $30.7
9. Fluke, $23.4
10. Gerber Scientific, $17.1

*Where'd you hear that?*
Electronic Business. Based on 1988 total R & D expenditures, in millions of dollars.

## U.S. electronic communications providers with the highest research and development spending

1. Motorola, with $665.0 million
2. DSC Communications, $45.0
3. Dynatech, $34.4
4. Scientific-Atlanta, $30.0
5. Digital Communications, $25.7
6. 3Com, $23.4
7. General DataComm, $23.3
8. ADC Telecommunications, $17.4
9. Novell, $16.0
10. Bolt Beranek and Newman, $14.7

*Where'd you hear that?*
Electronic Business. Based on 1988 total R & D expenditures, in millions of dollars.

## U.S. electronic components providers with the highest research and development spending

1. AMP, with $238.0 million
2. Molex, $26.6
3. Sprague Technologies, $25.1
4. Augat, $13.1
5. Cherry Electrical Products, $11.0

*Where'd you hear that?*
Electronic Business. Based on 1988 total R & D expenditures, in millions of dollars.

# GO TECH

# GO TECH

## America's best electric/electronic engineering schools

1. Stanford University
2. Massachusetts Institute of Technology
3. University of Illinois, Urbana
4. University of California, Berkeley
5. University of Michigan

*Where'd you hear that?*
U.S. News & World Report. Based on results of reputational survey of engineering-school deans and academic-affairs deans.

## Highest paid U.S. electronics executives

1. John Sculley (Apple Computer), with $2,479,000
2. Joseph R. Canion (Compaq Computer), $1,866,839
3. Charles B. Wang (Computer Associates), $1,794,000
4. W. Michael Blumenthal (Unisys), $1,662,886
5. John F. Akers (IBM), $1,525,500
6. Anthony W. Wang (Computer Associates), $1,521,000
7. Lawrence J. Ellison (Oracle Systems), $1,362,500
8. John A. Young (Hewlett-Packard), $1,342,232
9. Melvin Howard (Xerox), $1,269,153
10. Charles E. Exley, Jr. (NCR), $1,069,390

*Where'd you hear that?*
Electronic Business. Based on 1988 salary.

## Top independent North American printed circuit board makers

1. Hadco, with $157 million
2. Diceon, $110
2. Photocircuits, $110
4. Zycon, $90
5. Sheldahl, $88
6. Tyco, $84
7. Circo Craft (Quebec), $78
8. Advance Circuits, $75
9. Continental, $65
10. ACD Litton, $63

*Where'd you hear that?*
Electronic Business. Based on 1989 value of North American printed circuit board production and interconnect value added in millions of dollars.

## Top 10 semiconductor equipment companies

1. Tokyo Electron Ltd., with $633.9 million
2. Nikon, $582.2
3. Applied Materials, $523.3
4. Advantest, $398.8
5. Canon, $383.6
6. General Signal, $353.7
7. Varian, $335.0
8. Hitachi Ltd., $210.0
9. Teradyne, $199.9
10. ASM International, $186.8

*Where'd you hear that?*
Electronics News. Based on 1989 world wide sales, in millions of dollars.

## Largest corporations in the semiconductor industry

1. Intel Corp., with $7,765 million
2. AMP, $5,350
3. Texas Instruments, $3,056
4. Molex, $1,053

5. Thomas & Betts, $944
6. National Semiconductor, $820
7. Advanced Micro Devices, $751
8. Micron Technology, $492
9. Cypress Semiconductor Corp., $479
10. Analog Devices, $387
11. LSI Logic, $375

*Where'd you hear that?*
Business Week, The Business Week 1000. Based on market value as of March 16, 1990, in millions of dollars.

## Most profitable semiconductor companies

1. Micron Technology, 23.8%
2. Cypress Semiconductor Corp., 15.4%
3. Chips and Technologies, 15.2%
4. Intel Corp., 12.5%
5. Integrated Device Technology, 9.9%
6. Richardson Electronics, 7.6%
7. Analog Devices, 6.1%
8. Burr-Brown Corp., 5.1%
9. Texas Instruments, 4.5%

*Where'd you hear that?*
Electronic Business, Most Profitable Companies. Based on 1989 profit as a percentage of sales.

## U.S. semiconductor providers with the highest research and development spending

1. Motorola, with $665.0 million
2. Texas Instruments, $494.0
3. Intel Corp., $318.3
4. National Semiconductor, $280.2
5. Advanced Micro Devices, $208.3
6. Western Digital, $67.7
7. Analog Devices, $60.5

8. LSI Logic, $37.0
9. VLSI Technology, $21.2
10. Integrated Device Technology, $18.8

*Where'd you hear that?*
Electronic Business. Based on 1988 total R & D expenditures, in millions of dollars.

## *World's largest computer companies*

1. IBM, with $55,003 million
2. Digital Equipment Corp., $12,742
3. Fujitsu Ltd., $11,674
4. NEC, $10,039
5. Unisys, $8,912
6. Hitachi Ltd., $8,486
7. Hewlett-Packard Co., $6,300
8. Siemens, $5,611
9. Olivetti, $5,393
10. NCR, $5,324

*Where'd you hear that?*
Financial World. Based on fiscal year 1989 computer revenues, in millions of dollars.

## Leading U.S. semiconductor manufacturers

1. Motorola, with $3.3 billion
2. Texas Instruments, $2.8 billion
3. Intel Corp., $2.4 billion
4. National Semiconductor, $1.6 billion
5. Advanced Micro Devices, $1.1 billion
6. AT & T, $873 million

*Where'd you hear that?*
New York Times. Based on revenues.

# GO TECH

# GO TECH

### Most profitable computer companies

1. Teradata, with 11.9%
2. Compaq Computer Corp., 11.6%
3. Cray Research, 11.3%
4. Stratus Computer, 10.4%
5. Sequent Computer, 9.5%
6. Apple Computer Inc., 8.6%
7. Digital Equipment Corp., 8.4%
8. Pyramid Technology, 8.1%
9. Tandy, 7.7%
10. Amdahl, 7.3%

*Where'd you hear that?*
Electronic Business, Most Profitable Companies. Based on 1989 profit as a percentage of sales.

### Fastest growing computer companies

1. Silicon Graphics, with 117.9%
2. Sun Microsystems, 114.5%
3. Tandon, 57.6%
4. Compaq Computer Corp., 54.3%
5. Pyramid Technology, 53.5%
6. Stratus Computer, 51.9%
7. Rexon, 48.5%
8. Apple Computer Inc., 28.4%
9. Cray Research, 28.0%
10. Tandem Computers, 25.1%

*Where'd you hear that?*
Electronic Business, Fastest Growing Companies. Based on 1989 5-year compounded annual sales growth rate, in percent.

### Largest computer-based systems companies

1. Ask Computer Systems, with $206.7 thousand
2. Mentor Graphics, $176.0
3. Gerber Scientific, $142.7
4. Hewlett-Packard Co., $113.0
5. Coherent, $110.8
6. Intergraph, $109.6
7. Measurex, $101.2
8. Recognition Equipment, $96.3
9. Sun Electric, $77.7

*Where'd you hear that?*
Electronic Business, Electronic Business 200. Based on 1988 revenue per employee, in thousands of dollars.

### Most profitable computer-based systems companies

1. Measurex, with 14.3%
2. Mentor Graphics, 11.8%
3. Telxon, 9.3%
4. Intergraph, 9.2%
5. Symbol Technologies, 8.5%
6. Electro Scientific, 7.6%
7. ASK Computer Systems, 7.2%
8. BancTec, 6.2%
9. Valid Logic Systems, 5.8%
10. Coherent, 4.2%

*Where'd you hear that?*
Electronic Business, Most Profitable Companies. Based on 1989 profit as a percentage of sales.

### Fastest growing computer-based systems companies

1. Mentor Graphics, with 34.0%
2. Telxon, 30.9%
3. Symbol Technologies, 30.5%
4. Bank Tec, 29.3%
5. ASK Computer Systems, 23.4%
6. Valid Logic Systems, 21.2%
7. Daisy Systems, 17.3%
8. Intergraph, 16.3%
9. Evans & Sutherland, 14.6%
10. Recognition Equipment, 12.8%
10. Finnigan, 12.8%

# GO TECH

*Where'd you hear that?*
Electronic Business, Fastest Growing Companies. Based on 1989 5-year compounded annual sales growth rate, in percent.

## Largest computer peripherals companies

1. Quantum, with $371.1 thousand
2. AST Research, $229.3
3. QMS, $196.3
4. Everex Systems, $166.7
5. Rexon, $133.3
6. Micropolis, $110.4
7. Wyse Technology, $109.0
8. Storage Technology, $102.8
9. Dataproducts, $97.3
10. Cipher Data Products, $90.2

*Where'd you hear that?*
Electronic Business, Electronic Business 200. Based on 1988 revenue per employee, in thousands of dollars.

## Most profitable computer peripheral companies

1. Iomega, with 10.3%
2. Emulex, 8.9%
3. Archive, 8.4
4. Quantum, 6.2%
5. Intermec, 5.9%
6. Conner Peripherals, 5.9%
7. Everex Systems, 5.6%
7. Cipher Data Products, 5.6%

*Where'd you hear that?*
Electronic Business, Most Profitable Companies. Based on 1989 profit as a percentage of sales.

## Fastest growing peripherals companies

1. Maxtor, with 84.4%
2. AST Research, 48.2%
3. EMC, 47.7%
4. Wyse Technology, 47.6%
5. QMS, 38.6%
5. Micropolis, 38.6%
7. Archive, 36.6%
8. Intermec, 34.6%
9. Seagate Technology, 31.9%
10. Quantum, 25.4%

*Where'd you hear that?*
Electronic Business, Fastest Growing Companies. Based on 1989 5-year compounded annual sales growth rate, in percent.

## Most productive computer and communications hardware corporations

1. Compaq Computer Corp., with $42.6 thousand
2. Apple Computer Inc., $34.6
3. Micron Technology, $27.8
4. Amdahl, $18.7
5. Intel Corp., $18.2
6. Cray Research, $17.9
7. Premier Industrial, $15.9
8. Tandem Computers, $13.0
9. Penn Central, $12.0
10. AMP, $11.6

*Where'd you hear that?*
Forbes, Forbes 500s Annual Directory. Based on 1989 profits per employee, in thousands of dollars. Ranks U.S.-based corporations that were publicly traded as of March 23, 1990.

## Most profitable computer and communications hardware companies

1. Apple Computer Inc., with 36.6%
2. Mark IV Industries Inc., 29.0%
3. Cray Research, 28.9%
4. EG & G, 26.7%
5. Intergraph, 25.2%

# GO TECH

6. Molex, 25.1%
7. Premier Industrial, 21.7%
8. AMP, 20.7%
9. IBM, 20.2%
10. Thomas & Betts, 18.1%

*Where'd you hear that?*
Forbes, Annual Report on American Industry. Based on 10-year average return on equity. Ranks publicly held corporations only.

## Biggest U.S. corporations in the computer industry

1. IBM, with $63,438 million
2. Digital Equipment Corp., $12,866
3. Hewlett-Packard Co., $11,899
4. Unisys, $10,097
5. NCR, $5,956
6. Apple Computer Inc., $5,284
7. Wang Laboratories, $3,078
8. Pitney Bowes, $2,959
9. Control Data Corp., $2,952
10. Compaq Computer Corp., $2,876

*Where'd you hear that?*
Fortune, Fortune 500 Largest U.S. Industrial Corporations. Based on 1989 sales, in millions of dollars.

## Largest U.S. corporations in the computers & peripherals industry

1. IBM, with $62,427 million
2. Hewlett-Packard Co., $10,785
3. Digital Equipment Corp., $9,444
4. Xerox, $5,168
5. Apple Computer Inc., $5,039
6. NCR, $4,862
7. Compaq Computer Corp., $3,883
8. Tandem Computers, $2,986
9. Tandy, $2,820
10. Unisys, $2,495

*Where'd you hear that?*
Business Week, The Business Week 1000. Based on market value as of March 16, 1990, in millions of dollars.

## Largest mainframe computer companies by revenue

1. IBM, with $5,390.0 million
2. Unisys, $669.9
3. NCR, $420.4
4. Amdahl, $278.9
5. Control Data Corp., $169.8
6. Cray Research, $82.0

*Where'd you hear that?*
Electronic Business, Top Electronics Capital Spenders. Based on total revenue derived from mainframes, in millions of dollars.

## Largest computer mainframe companies by revenue per employee

1. Amdahl, with $217.1 thousand
2. IBM, $154.2
3. Cray Research, $144.4
4. Control Data Corp., $108.3
5. Unisys, $106.5
6. NCR, $99.8

*Where'd you hear that?*
Electronic Business, Electronic Business 200. Based on 1988 revenue per employee, in thousands of dollars.

## U.S. computer-based system providers with the highest research and development spending

1. Hewlett-Packard Co., with $1,019.0 million
2. Intergraph, $89.2

3. Mentor Graphics, $33.8
4. Coherent, $19.7
5. Measurex, $19.2
6. Gerber Scientific, $17.1
7. Ask Computer Systems, $11.9

*Where'd you hear that?*
Electronic Business. Based on 1988 total R & D expenditures, in millions of dollars.

## U.S. mainframe computer providers with the highest research and development spending

1. IBM, with $5,925.0 million
2. Unisys, $713.0
3. NCR, $416.4
4. Control Data Corp., $335.7
5. Amdahl, $221.0
6. Cray Research, $117.8

*Where'd you hear that?*
Electronic Business. Based on 1988 total R & D expenditures, in millions of dollars.

## U.S. peripherals providers with the highest research and development spending

1. Storage Technology, with $67.5 million
2. Seagate Technology, $50.1
3. Micropolis, $28.4
4. Dataproducts, $26.7
5. Wyse Technology, $24.2
6. Maxtor, $24.0
7. Applied Magnetics, $22.7
8. Cipher Data Products, $17.4
9. AST Research, $15.7
10. Everex Systems, $15.6

*Where'd you hear that?*
Electronic Business. Based on 1988 total R & D expenditures, in millions of dollars.

## America's best computer engineering schools

1. Massachusetts Institute of Technology
2. Stanford University
3. University of Illinois, Urbana
4. University of California, Berkeley
5. Carnegie-Mellon University

*Where'd you hear that?*
U.S. News & World Report. Based on results of reputational survey of engineering-school deans and academic-affairs deans.

## World's largest merchant disk drive manufactuers

1. Seagate, with $2,450 million
2. Conner Peripherals, $660
3. Fujitsu Ltd., $600
4. Maxtor, $440
5. MiniScribe, $400
5. Quantum, $400
7. NEC, $375
8. Micropolis, $300
9. Hitachi Ltd., $240

*Where'd you hear that?*
Electronic Business. Based on estimated 1989 worldwide shipment revenue, in millions of dollars.

# GO TECH

# GO TECH

## World's largest captive disk drive manufacturers

1. IBM, with $6,500 million
2. DEC, $1,000
2. NEC, $1,000
4. Fujitsu Ltd., $850
5. Hewlett-Packard Co., $400
6. Hitachi Ltd., $275

*Where'd you hear that?*
Electronic Business. Based on estimated 1989 worldwide shipment revenue, in millions of dollars.

## World's largest microcomputer companies

1. IBM, with 16%
2. NEC, 5%
3. Amstrad, 4.3%
4. Zenith, 4.0%
4. Compaq Computer Corp., 4.0%
6. Olivetti, 3.3%
7. Tandy, 3.0%
8. Epson, 2.8%
9. Acer, 2.0%
10. Toshiba, 1.8%

*Where'd you hear that?*
CFO. Based on worldwide market share of PC compatible shipments, in percent.

## Largest microcomputer producers in Europe

1. IBM, with 26.6%
2. Olivetti, 8.6%
3. Apple Computer Inc., 7.4%
4. Compaq Computer Corp., 7.1%
5. Hewlett-Packard Co., 3.2%
6. Tandon, 3.0%
7. Toshiba, 2.6%
7. Victor, 2.6%
9. Nokia Data, 2.1%
9. Bull, 2.1%

*Where'd you hear that?*
Financial Times. Based on market share of European PC market, in percent.

## Largest microcomputer companies

1. Apple Computer Inc., with $377.0 thousand
2. Compaq Computer Corp., $299.4
3. Atari, $254.0
4. AST Research, $229.3
5. Dell Computer, $214.8
6. Tandon, $208.5
7. Everex Systems, $166.7
8. IBM, $154.2
9. Tandy, $102.5
10. Zenith Electronics, $74.6

*Where'd you hear that?*
Electronic Business, Electronic Business 200. Based on 1988 revenue per employee, in thousands of dollars.

## Electronics businesses spending the most on microcomputer projects

1. IBM, with $5,390.0 million
2. Compaq Computer Corp., $273.5
3. Apple Computer Inc., $144.0
4. Tandy, $94.2
5. Zenith Electronics, $32.9
6. AST Research, $14.6

*Where'd you hear that?*
Electronic Business, Top Electronics Capital Spenders. Based on capital expenditures, in millions of dollars, on microcomputer projects.

# GO TECH

**U.S. microcomputer providers with the highest research and development spending**

1. IBM, with $5,925.0 million
2. Apple Computer Inc., $272.5
3. Zenith Electronics, $100.6
4. Compaq Computer Corp., $74.9
5. Atari, $21.4
6. AST Research, $15.7
7. Everex Systems, $15.6
8. Tandon, $13.7

*Where'd you hear that?*
Electronic Business. Based on 1988 total R & D expenditures, in millions of dollars.

**Largest minicomputer companies**

1. Stratus Computer, with $155.1 thousand
2. IBM, $154.2
3. Tandem Computers, $152.4
4. Sun Microsystems, $148.3
5. Apollo Computer, $147.0
6. Prime Computer, $128.7
7. Hewlett-Packard Co., $113.0
8. MAI Basic Four, $94.1
9. Digital Equipment Corp., $91.4
10. Data General, $88.5

*Where'd you hear that?*
Electronic Business, Electronic Business 200. Based on 1988 revenue per employee, in thousands of dollars.

**Electronics businesses spending the most on minicomputer projects**

1. IBM, with $5,390.0 million
2. Digital Equipment Corp., $1,517.6
3. Hewlett-Packard Co., $648.0
4. Tandem Computers, $185.1
5. Prime Computer, $140.9
6. Sun Microsystems, $117.3
7. Data General, $96.6
8. Apollo Computer, $60.3
9. Concurrent Computer, $20.4
10. Stratus Computer, $17.8

*Where'd you hear that?*
Electronic Business, Top Electronics Capital Spenders. Based on capital expenditures, in millions of dollars, on minicomputer projects.

**U.S. minicomputer providers with the highest research and development spending**

1. IBM, with $5,925.0 million
2. Digital Equipment Corp., $1,306.5
3. Hewlett-Packard Co., $1,019.0
4. Prime Computer, $174.3
5. Tandem Computers, $169.4
6. Data General, $165.2
7. Sun Microsystems, $139.9
8. Apollo Computer, $76.9
9. Concurrent Computer, $32.0
10. Stratus Computer, $30.6

*Where'd you hear that?*
Electronic Business. Based on 1988 total R & D expenditures, in millions of dollars.

**World's largest manufacturers of local area networks (LAN)**

1. DEC, with 26.6%
2. IBM, 12.7%
3. 3COM, 9.8%
4. Novell, 9.1%
5. Excelan, 2%
6. Others, total, 39.8%

*Where'd you hear that?*
Electronic News. Based on 1988 market share of revenues, in percent.

# GO TECH

## Biggest users of supercomputers

1. Research, with 24%
2. Universities, 18%
3. Defense, 16%
4. Aerospace, 12%
5. Petroleum, 10%
6. Environmental, 7%
6. Nuclear energy, 7%
8. Service bureaus, 3%
8. Others, total, 3%

*Where'd you hear that?*
Datamation. Based on share of total users, in percent.

## Largest manufacturers of bridge and router installed bases

1. Digital Equipment Corp., with 28%
2. 3Com Corp., 19%
3. Vitalink Communications, 12%
4. Ungermann-Bass Inc., 5%
5. Proteon Inc., 4%
5. Cisco Systems Inc., 4%
7. Others, total, 28%

*Where'd you hear that?*
Data Communications. Based on 1988 market share, in percent.

## Largest U.S. corporations in the computer software & services industry

1. Microsoft, with $6,347 million
2. Automatic Data Processing, $3,934
3. Oracle Systems, $3,445
4. Computer Associates International Inc., $2,768
5. Electronic Data Systems, $2,639
6. Lotus Development Corp., $1,487
7. Novell, $1,438
8. Autodesk, $1,170
9. Intergraph, $1,126
10. Comdisco, $1,111

*Where'd you hear that?*
Business Week, The Business Week 1000. Based on market value as of March 16, 1990, in millions of dollars.

## Largest computer software companies by employee revenues

1. Ultimate, with $283.4 thousand
2. Ashton-Tate, $245.8
3. Microsoft, $211.5
4. Lotus Development Corp., $187.4
5. Computer Associates, $158.7
6. Oracle Systems, $127.8
7. Management Science America, $105.5
8. Cullinet Software, $90.3

*Where'd you hear that?*
Electronic Business, Electronic Business 200. Based on 1988 per employee revenues, in thousands of dollars.

## Most profitable software companies

1. Microsoft, 21.2%
2. Cadence Design Systems, 19.4%
3. Computer Associates International Inc., 15.9%
4. Oracle Systems, 14.0%
5. Lotus Development Corp., 12.2%

6. Systematics, 9.1%
7. Informix Corp., 4.4%

*Where'd you hear that?*
Electronic Business, Most Profitable Companies. Based on 1989 profit as a percentage of sales.

## U.S. software providers with the highest research and development spending

1. Lotus Development Corp., with $83.8 million
2. Computer Associates, $81.5
3. Microsoft, $69.8
4. Management Science America, $58.9
5. Ashton-Tate, $52.9
6. Cullinet Software, $52.4
7. Oracle Systems, $25.7

*Where'd you hear that?*
Electronic Business. Based on 1988 total expenditures, in millions of dollars.

## Leaders in the U.S. modem market

1. Codex, with 18%
2. Racal-Milgo, 11%
3. IBM, 9%
4. UDS, 8%
4. AT & T, 8%
6. Hayes, 7%
7. Others, total, 39%

*Where'd you hear that?*
Electronic News. Based on market share, in percent.

## Leading videotex vendors

1. Compuserve Information Service, H & R Block, with 575,000
2. Dow Jones News Retrieval Service, 280,000
3. Eastlink, Western Union, 200,000
4. Genie, General Electric Information Service Co., 165,000
5. Quantumlink PC-Link, Quantum Computer Services, 94,000
6. Prodigy Service Co., IBM/Sears, 75,000
7. Delphi, General Videotext Corp., 50,000

*Where'd you hear that?*
New York Times. Based on number of subscribers.

## Leading on-line information companies

1. Lexis, Nexis, Medis, with $307.5 million
2. Dialog Information Service Inc., $113.0
3. Compuserve Information Service Co., $86.5
4. Dow Jones News Retrieval Service, $60.0

*Where'd you hear that?*
Wall Street Journal. Based on sales as of December 31, 1988, in millions of dollars.

## Largest information systems companies in the world

1. IBM, with $60,805.0 million
2. Digital Equipment Corp., $12,936.7
3. NEC, $11,480.4
4. Fujitsu Ltd., $11,378.9
5. Unisys, $9,390.0
6. Hitachi Ltd., $8,719.0
7. Hewlett-Packard Co., $7,800.0
8. Groupe Bull, $6,465.4
9. Siemens, $6,010.6
10. Olivetti, $5,573.3

# GO TECH

# GO TECH

*Where'd you hear that?*
Datamation, Datamation 100. Based on 1989 worldwide IS revenues, in millions of dollars.

### Largest information systems companies in Scandinavia

1. Nokia, with $1,191.9 million
2. Norsk Data, $358.1

*Where'd you hear that?*
Datamation, Datamation 100. Based on 1989 worldwide IS revenues, in millions of dollars.

## *Who can be trusted with private data?*

1. Hospitals, with 81%
1. U.S. Bureau of the Census, 81%
3. Employers, 77%
4. Social Security Administration, 76%
4. Telephone companies, 76%
6. Internal Revenue Service, 67%
7. Companies that investigate job applicants, 65%
8. Credit bureaus 59%
9. Direct marketing firms, 34%

*Where'd you hear that?*
Computerworld. Based on survey results; percent of respondents having moderate or high degree of trust. Original source: Louis Harris and Associates, Inc.

### Largest information systems companies in Great Britain

1. STC, with $2,643.4 million
2. Amstrad, $717.0
3. British Telecom, $692.5
4. Racal, $573.9
5. SD-Scicon, $431.5
6. Sema Group, $378.6

*Where'd you hear that?*
Datamation, Datamation 100. Based on 1989 worldwide IS revenues, in millions of dollars.

### Largest information systems companies in France

1. Groupe Bull, with $6,465.4 million
2. Alcate, $1,800.3
3. Cap Gemini, $1,103.4
4. Silgos, $400.7

*Where'd you hear that?*
Datamation, Datamation 100. Based on 1989 worldwide IS revenues, in millions of dollars.

### Largest information systems companies in West Germany

1. Siemens, with $6,010.6 million
2. Nixdorf, $2,792.6
3. Mannesmann, $819.1
4. Comparex, $566.0

*Where'd you hear that?*
Datamation, Datamation 100. Based on 1989 worldwide IS revenues, in millions of dollars.

### Largest information systems companies in the Netherlands

1. NV Philips, with $2,814.8 million
2. Memorex, $2,056.6

*Where'd you hear that?*
Datamation, Datamation 100. Based on 1989 worldwide IS revenues, in millions of dollars.

### Largest information systems companies in Japan

1. NEC, with $11,480.4 million
2. Fujitsu Corp., $11,378.9

3. Hitachi Ltd., $8,719.0
4. Toshiba, $4,595.1
5. Canon, $3,783.3
6. Matsushita, $3,663.7
7. NTT, $2,254.0
8. Nihon Unisys, $2,112.7
9. Mitsubishi, $2,025.7
10. Oki, $1,952.0

*Where'd you hear that?*
Datamation, Datamation 100. Based on 1989 worldwide IS revenues, in millions of dollars.

## Largest robotics manufacturers

1. GMFanuc Robotics, with $114 million
2. ABB Robotics, $40-42
2. Cincinnati Milacron, $40-42
4. Adept Technology, $30
5. Prab Robots, $20
5. Graco Robotics, $20
7. Westinghouse, $15
8. Cimcorp, $14
9. Kawasaki, $10

*Where'd you hear that?*
Metalworking News. Based on 1988 sales, in millions of dollars.

## Largest corporations in the instrument industry

1. Honeywell Inc., with $3,500 million
2. Johnson Controls, $1,196
3. Perkin-Elmer, $1,038
4. General Signal, $1,018
5. Millipore, $759
6. Henley Group Inc., $695
7. Beckman Instruments, $431
8. Measurex, $394
9. Tektronix, $391

*Where'd you hear that?*
Business Week, The Business Week 1000. Based on market value as of March 16, 1990, in millions of dollars.

## Biggest corporations in the scientific and photographic equipment industry

1. Eastman Kodak Co., with $18,398 million
2. Xerox, $17,635
3. Minnesota Mining, $11,990
4. Baxter International Inc., $7,399
5. Polaroid, $1,942
6. Becton, Dickinson & Co., $1,921
7. EG & G, $1,655
8. Tektronix, $1,439
9. Bausch & Lomb, $1,231
10. Perkin-Elmer, $1,105

*Where'd you hear that?*
Fortune, Fortune 500 Largest U.S. Industrial Corporations. Based on 1989 sales, in millions of dollars.

## Most admired scientific and photographic equipment corporations

1. 3M, with a rating of 8.21
2. Xerox, 6.58
3. Eastman Kodak Co., 6.49
4. Baxter International Inc., 6.43
5. Becton, Dickinson & Co., 6.42
6. Polaroid, 6.02
7. Perkin-Elmer, 5.95
8. Tektronix, 5.66

# GO TECH

195

# GO TECH

9. Litton Industries Inc., 5.56
10. Henley Group Inc., 5.36

*Where'd you hear that?*
Fortune, America's Most Admired Corporations. Based on scores (0-10) derived from a survey of senior executives, outside directors, and financial analysts. Respondents ranked firms in their own industry on quality of management and products/services; innovation; long-term investment value; financial soundness; attraction and retention of talent; community and environmental responsibility; and use of assets.

## Electronics businesses spending the most on medical projects

1. Medtronic, with $33.5 million
2. Westmark International, $11.3
3. Diasonics Inc., $10.5

*Where'd you hear that?*
Electronic Business, Top Electronics Capital Spenders. Based on capital expenditures, in millions of dollars, on medical projects.

## Largest medical electronics companies

1. Diasonics Inc., with $169.6 thousand
2. Westmark International, $113.2
3. Medtronic, $111.2

*Where'd you hear that?*
Electronic Business, Electronic Business 200. Based on 1988 per employee revenues, in thousands of dollars.

## U.S. medical electronics providers with the highest research and development spending

1. Medtronic, with $53.1 million
2. Westmark International, $37.8
3. Diasonics Inc., $20.3

*Where'd you hear that?*
Electronic Business. Based on 1988 total R & D expenditures, in millions of dollars.

## America's best biomedical engineering schools

1. Johns Hopkins University
2. Duke University
3. Massachusetts Institute of Technology
4. Case Western Reserve University
5. University of Pennsylvania

*Where'd you hear that?*
U.S. News & World Report. Based on results of reputational survey of engineering-school deans and academic-affairs deans.

## Largest biotechnology companies

1. Genentech, with $383.2 million
2. Applied Biosystems, $158.8
3. Alza, $92.7
4. Centocor, $72.0

5. Amgen, $70.2
6. Genetics Institute, $43.6
7. Genzyme, $32.8
8. Biotechnica, $30.1
9. Biogen, $28.5
10. Cetus, $25.2

*Where'd you hear that?*
Chemicalweek, Chemicalweek 300. Based on 1989 sales, in millions of dollars.

## Largest advertisers in lab/pathology publications

1. Abbott
2. Boehringer-Mannheim
3. Syva
4. Ciba-Corning
5. Roche Diagnostics
6. Coulter
7. Behring
8. Eastman-Kodak Co.
9. Dade Pharmaceuticals Inc.
10. Beckman

*Where'd you hear that?*
Medical Marketing & Media, Healthcare Advertising Review. Based on 1989 expenditures.

## Leading advertisers in radiology journals

1. Siemens Medical
2. Mallinckrodt
3. General Electric Co.
4. Berlex
5. Eastman-Kodak Co.
6. Toshiba
7. Winthrop
8. Philips Medical
9. Picker International
10. Konica

*Where'd you hear that?*
Medical Marketing & Media, Healthcare Advertising Review. Based on 1989 expenditures.

## Most productive medical supply corporations

1. St. Jude Medical, with $121.8 thousand
2. Medtronic, $17.1
3. Becton, Dickinson & Co., $10.8
4. Bausch & Lomb, $10.2
5. Corning, $9.6
6. Hillenbrand Industries, $8.3
7. Baxter International Inc., $6.9
8. Henley Group Inc., -$6.4

*Where'd you hear that?*
Forbes, Forbes 500s Annual Directory. Based on 1989 profits per employee, in thousands of dollars. Ranks U.S.-based corporations that were publicly traded as of March 23, 1990.

## Most profitable medical supply companies

1. C. R. Bard, with 20.8%
2. Medtronic, 20.2%
3. Hillenbrand Industries, 19.2%
4. Bausch & Lomb, 16.8%
5. Becton, Dickinson & Co., 14.5%
6. Baxter International Inc., 12.9%
7. Owens & Minor, 12.7%
8. Corning, 12.5%
9. Healthco International, 10.6%
10. Beckman Instruments, NA

*Where'd you hear that?*
Forbes, Annual Report on American Industry. Based on 10-year average return on equity. Ranks publicly held corporations only.

# GO TECH

197

# GO TECH

## Biggest corporations in the drugs & research industry

1. Merck, with $27,975 million
2. Bristol-Myers Squibb Co., $27,843
3. Eli Lilly & Co., $17,670
4. American Home Products Corp., $15,763
5. Pfizer, $9,671
6. Schering-Plough, $8,952
7. Warner-Lambert, $6,970
8. Upjohn, $6,920
9. Marion Merrell Dow, $6,005
10. Syntex, $5,674

*Where'd you hear that?*
Business Week, The Business Week 1000. Based on market value as of March 16, 1990, in millions of dollars.

## Largest Japanese drug companies

1. Takeda Chemical, with $4,905 million
2. Sankyo, $3,043
3. Shionogi, $2,082
4. Yamanouchi Pharmaceutical, $1,790
5. Tanabe Seiyaku, $1,655
6. Fujisawa Pharmaceutical, $1,606

*Where'd you hear that?*
Forbes. Based on sales for fiscal year March, 1989, in millions of dollars.

## Largest U.S. drug companies

1. Johnson & Johnson, with $9,486 million
2. Bristol-Myers Squibb Co., $8,973
3. Merck, $6,324
4. American Home Products Corp., $5,729
5. Pfizer, $5,546
6. Eli Lilly & Co., $4,434

*Where'd you hear that?*
Forbes. Based on worldwide drug sales, in millions, for the preceding 12 months.

## Largest pharmaceutical companies

1. Johnson & Johnson, with $9,757.0 million
2. Baxter International Inc., $7,399.0
3. American Home Products Corp., $6,747.0
4. Merck, $6,550.5
5. Pfizer, $5,671.5
6. Abbott Laboratories, $5,379.8
7. Warner-Lambert, $4,195.8
8. Eli Lilly & Co., $4,175.6
9. Schering-Plough, $3,157.9
10. Upjohn, $2,916.3

*Where'd you hear that?*
Chemicalweek, Chemicalweek 300. Based on 1989 sales, in millions of dollars.

## Leading pharmaceutical companies

1. Johnson & Johnson, with $9,844 million
2. Bristol-Myers Squibb Co., $9,422
3. American Home Products Corp., $6,747
4. Merck, $6,698
5. Pfizer, $5,904
6. Abbott Laboratories, $5,454
7. Warner-Lambert, $4,272
8. Eli Lilly & Co., $4,176
9. Schering-Plough, $3,243
10. Upjohn, $2,916

*Where'd you hear that?*
Fortune, Fortune 500 Largest U.S. Industrial Corporations. Based on 1989 sales, in millions of dollars.

## Most productive drug corporations

1. Merck, with $45.0 thousand
2. Eli Lilly & Co., $34.2
3. ALZA Corp, $29.0
4. Genentech, $25.0
5. Abbott Laboratories, $21.6
5. American Home Products Corp., $21.6
5. Schering-Plough, $21.6
8. Pfizer, $16.4
9. Bergen Brunswig Corp., $14.7
10. Bristol-Myers Squibb Co., $13.9

*Where'd you hear that?*
Forbes, Forbes 500s Annual Directory. Based on 1989 profits per employee, in thousands of dollars. Ranks U.S.-based corporations that were publicly traded as of March 23, 1990.

## Most profitable drug companies

1. American Home Products Corp., with 35.0%
2. Syntex, 31.2%
3. Merck & Co., 30.8%
4. Abbott Laboratories, 30.4%
5. Marion Laboratories Inc., 30.0%
6. Cardinal Distribution, 24.1%
7. Eli Lilly & Co., 23.1%
8. Rorer Group, 21.8%
9. Pfizer, 20.4%
10. Warner-Lambert, 19.9%

*Where'd you hear that?*
Forbes, Annual Report on American Industry. Based on 10-year average return on equity. Ranks publicly held corporations only.

## Leading pharmaceutical packagers

1. Johnson & Johnson
2. Eastman Kodak Co.
3. Bristol-Myers Co.
4. American Home Products Corp.

*Where'd you hear that?*
Packaging, Top 100 Packaging Giants. Based on 1988 consumption of packaging materials.

## *Most admired pharmaceutical corporations*

1. Merck, with a rating of 8.90
2. Johnson & Johnson, 7.91
3. Bristol-Myers Co., 7.51
4. Eli Lilly & Co., 7.47
5. Abbott Laboratories, 7.25
6. Schering-Plough, 7.00
7. Warner-Lambert, 6.60
8. American Home Products Corp., 6.51
9. Pfizer, 6.41
10. SmithKline Beckman, 5.26

*Where'd you hear that?*
Fortune, America's Most Admired Corporations. Based on scores (0-10) derived from a survey of senior executives, outside directors, and financial analysts. Respondents ranked firms in their own industry on quality of management and products/services; innovation; long-term investment value; financial soundness; attraction and retention of talent; community and environmental responsibility; and use of assets.

## Biggest corporations in the drug distribution industry

1. Walgreen, with $2,638 million
2. McKesson, $1,438
3. Rite Aid, $1,364
4. Medco Containment Services, $916

# GO TECH

# GO TECH

5. Longs Drug Stores, Inc., $865
6. Bergen Brunswig Corp., $813

*Where'd you hear that?*
Business Week, The Business Week 1000. Based on market value as of March 16, 1990, in millions of dollars.

## Largest advertisers in pharmacy publications

1. Upjohn, with 2.80
2. Parke-Davis, 2.70
3. Whitehall, 2.65
4. Glaxo, 2.45
5. Merck, 2.25
6. Searle, 2.14
7. Lederle, 2.13
8. Eli Lilly & Co., 2.11
9. SmithKline & French, 1.91
10. Pfizer, 1.61

*Where'd you hear that?*
Medical Marketing & Media, Healthcare Advertising Review. Based on 1989 share of ad dollars.

## Most advertised pharmacy products/services

1. Rogaine Topical Solution (Upjohn), with 1.80
2. Inst-Mylan (Mylan), 1.00
3. Epogen (Amgen Inc.), .92
4. Norethin (Searle), .81
4. Cytotec 200 Tabs (Searle), .81
6. Advil Tabs (Whitehall), .80
7. Lopid Family (Parke-Davis), .75
8. Pepcid Tabs & Susp (Merck), .74
9. Cholybar (Parke-Davis), .71
10. Inst-Geneva Gen (Geneva Gen), .70

*Where'd you hear that?*
Medical Marketing & Media, Healthcare Advertising Review. Based on 1989 share of ad dollars.

## Drug companies that issued the most patents in 1988

1. Merck, with 125
2. Warner-Lambert, 113
3. Squibb, 74
4. American Home Products Corp., 69
5. Eli Lilly & Co., 68
6. Pfizer, 63
7. Hoffmann-LaRoche, 59
8. SmithKline Beckman, 56
9. Upjohn, 15

*Where'd you hear that?*
Chemical & Engineering News, Facts & Figures for Chemical R & D. Based on number of patents issued in 1988.

## World's largest chemical companies

1. BASF (West Germany), with $24.4 billion
2. Hoechst (West Germany), $23.4
3. Bayer (West Germany), $22.2
4. ICI (UK), $20.8
5. Du Pont Co. (US), $19.6
6. Dow Chemical Co. (US), $16.7
7. Ciba-Geigy Corp. (Switzerland), $11.4
8. Shell (UK/Netherlands), $11.3
9. Rhone-Poulenc (France), $11.0

9. Eminont (Italy), $11.0

*Where'd you hear that?*
Financial Times. Based on 1988 sales, in billions of U.S. dollars.

## Asia's largest quoted companies in chemicals, plastics, and petroleum

1. Maruzen Oil Co. Ltd., with $13,210,287 thousand
2. Showa Shell Sekiyu K.K., $10,052,635
3. Daikyo Oil Co. Ltd., $9,558,263
4. Asahi Chemical Industry Co. Ltd., $8,069,163
5. Sumitomo Chemical Co. Ltd., $7,149,522
6. Fuji Photo Film Co. Ltd., $6,983,928
7. Nippon Mining Co., $6,878,693
8. Toray Industries Co., $6,275,291
9. Dainippon Ink & Chemicals Inc., $5,673,952
10. Takeda Chemical Industries Ltd., $5,471,833

*Where'd you hear that?*
Asia's 7500 Largest Companies, Dun & Bradstreet. Based on sales, in thousands of U.S. dollars.

## Europe's largest chemical and allied products companies

1. Imperial Chemical Industries PLC, with 17,189,247,108 ECU
2. Ciba-Geigy Werke Schwiezerhalle AG, 9,933,019,831
3. BASF Aktiengesellschaft, 8,962,697,197
4. Bayer AG, 8,626,657,664
5. Hoechst Aktiengesellschaft, 7,694,986,368
6. Akzo NV, 7,107,877,964
7. Solvay & Cie SA, 5,850,571,458
8. Sandoz Holding AG, 5,713,723,823
9. Dow (Europe) SA, 4,366,205,861
10. Naamloze Vennootschap DSM, 4,338,761,369

*Where'd you hear that?*
Dun's Europa, Dun & Bradstreet. Based on sales, in European currency units.

## Largest industrial chemical companies

1. Dow Chemical Co., with $17,600.0 million
2. Union Carbide, $8,744.0
3. Monsanto, $8,681.0
4. Lyondell Petrochemical, $5,358.0
5. American Cyanamid Co., $4,825.0
6. Hercules, $3,091.7
7. Quantum Chemical, $2,671.0
8. ARCO Chemical, $2,663.0
9. Rohm and Haas, $2,661.0
10. Air Products & Chemicals, $2,641.8

*Where'd you hear that?*
Chemicalweek, Chemicalweek 300. Based on 1989 sales, in millions of dollars.

## Leading industrial chemical companies

1. E. I. du Pont de Nemours & Co., with $35,209 million
2. Dow Chemical Co., $17,730
3. Union Carbide, $8,744
4. Monsanto, $8,681

# GO TECH

**201**

# GO TECH

5. W. R. Grace & Co., $6,115
6. Hoechst Celanese, $6,016
7. Hanson Industries NA, $5,933
8. PPG Industries, $5,825
9. Bayer USA, $5,425
10. BASF, $5,422

*Where'd you hear that?*
Fortune, Fortune 500 Largest U.S. Industrial Corporations. Based on 1989 sales, in millions of dollars.

## Largest corporations in the chemical industry

1. Du Pont Co., with $26,985 million
2. Dow Chemical Co., $18,279
3. Monsanto, $7,023
4. American Cyanamid Co., $5,039
5. ARCO Chemical, $3,548
6. Union Carbide, $3,132
7. Ethyl, $3,073
8. Air Products & Chemicals, $2,719
9. W. R. Grace & Co., $2,596
10. Rohm & Haas, $2,032

*Where'd you hear that?*
Business Week, The Business Week 1000. Based on market value as of March 16, 1990, in millions of dollars.

## Largest diversified chemical companies

1. Du Pont Co., with $35,534.0 million
2. Allied-Signal, $11,942.2
3. W. R. Grace & Co., $6,114.6
4. PPG Industries, $5,734.1
5. FMC Corp., $3,414.5
6. Engelhard, $2,403.0
7. Sequa, $1,959.2
8. Cabot, $1,936.9
9. Inspiration Resources, $1,419.6
10. Vulcan Materials, $1,076.2

*Where'd you hear that?*
Chemicalweek, Chemicalweek 300. Based on 1989 sales, in millions of dollars.

## Most productive diversified chemical corporations

1. Dow Chemical Co., with $42.3 thousand
2. Quantum Chemical, $23.6
3. E. I. du Pont de Nemours & Co., $17.3
4. Monsanto, $15.5
5. BF Goodrich, $14.3
6. Rohm & Haas, $13.8
7. Union Carbide, $12.7
8. American Cyanamid Co., $8.2
9. Olin, $7.8
10. FMC Corp., $6.5

*Where'd you hear that?*
Forbes, Forbes 500s Annual Directory. Based on 1989 profits per employee, in thousands of dollars. Ranks U.S.-based corporations that were publicly traded as of March 23, 1990.

## Most profitable diversified chemical companies

1. Valspar, with 20.8%
2. Union Carbide, 19.4%
3. A. Schulman, 18.8%
4. Dow Chemical Co., 18.0%
5. Rohm & Haas, 17.3%
6. Hercules, 17.0%
7. Quantum Chemical, 16.7%
8. American Cyanamid Co., 12.9%
9. E. I. du Pont de Nemours & Co., 12.7%
10. Monsanto, 10.3%

*Where'd you hear that?*
Forbes, Annual Report on American Industry. Based on 10-year average return on equity. Ranks publicly held corporations only.

## Most admired chemical corporations

1. Du Pont Co., with a rating 7.93
2. Dow Chemical Co., 7.85
3. Monsanto, 7.03
4. Bayer USA, 6.89
5. PPG Industries, 6.88
6. BASF, 6.60
7. Hoechst Celanese, 6.49
8. Hanson Industries NA, 5.46
9. W. R. Grace & Co., 5.22
10. Union Carbide, 5.21

*Where'd you hear that?*
Fortune, America's Most Admired Corporations. Based on scores (0-10) derived from a survey of senior executives, outside directors, and financial analysts. Respondents ranked firms in their own industry on quality of management and products/services; innovation; long-term investment value; financial soundness; attraction and retention of talent; community and environmental responsibility; and use of assets.

## Leading specialty chemical companies

1. Dow Corning, with $1,574.5 million
2. Morton International, $1,406.6
3. Lubrizol, 1,227.9
4. Ferro, $1,083.6
5. Nalco Chemical, $1,070.8
6. International Flavors & Fragrances, $869.5
7. Dexter, $848.7
8. Great Lakes Chemical, $792.3
9. H. B. Fuller Co., $753.4
10. Betz Laboratories, $516.7

*Where'd you hear that?*
Chemicalweek, Chemicalweek 300. Based on 1989 sales, in millions of dollars.

# GO TECH

## Top chemical products

1. Sulfuric acid, with 86.80 billion lbs.
2. Nitrogen, 53.77
3. Oxygen, 37.75
4. Ethylene, 34.95
5. Ammonia, 33.76
6. Lime, 32.99
7. Phosphoric acid, 23.12
8. Chlorine, 22.32
9. Sodium hydroxide, 22.15
10. Propylene, 20.23

*Where'd you hear that?*
Chemical & Engineering News. Based on 1989 production, in billions of pounds.

## Most productive specialized chemical corporations

1. Lyondell Petrochemical, with $186.9 thousand
2. Georgia Gulf, $141.3
3. Vista Chemical, $59.6
4. Ethyl, $39.9
5. International Flavors & Fragrances, $33.0
6. Great Lakes Chemical, $32.8
7. Freeport-McMoran, Inc., $23.1
8. Nalco Chemical, 22.1
9. IMC Fertilizer Group, $19.3
10. Lubrizol, $18.6

203

# GO TECH

*Where'd you hear that?*
Forbes, Forbes 500s Annual Directory. Based on 1989 profits per employee, in thousands of dollars. Ranks U.S.-based corporations that were publicly traded as of March 23, 1990.

## Most profitable specialized chemical companies

1. Chemed, with 25.1%
2. Betz Laboratories, 22.0
3. Freeport-McMoRan, 21.3%
4. Nalco Chemical, 21.1%
5. International Flavors & Fragrances, 20.1%
6. Great Lakes Chemical, 20.0%
7. Loctite, 18.7%
8. Lubrizol, 16.3%
9. H. B. Fuller Co., 15.3%
10. Dexter, 15.0%

*Where'd you hear that?*
Forbes, Annual Report on American Industry. Based on 10-year average return on equity. Ranks publicly held corporations only.

## Largest multi-industry chemical companies with chemical process operations

1. General Electric Co., with $53,884.0 million
2. ITT Corp., $20,054.0
3. Eastman Kodak Co., $18,398.0
4. Tenneco, $14,083.0
5. Minnesota Mining & Manufacturing, $11,990.0
6. McKesson Corp., $7,046.4
7. Martin Marietta, $5,796.2
8. Johnson Controls, $3,683.6
9. Greyhound, $3,536.9
10. Teledyne, $3,531.2

*Where'd you hear that?*
Chemicalweek, Chemicalweek 300. Based on 1989 sales, in millions of dollars.

## America's best chemical engineering schools

1. Massachusetts Institute of Technology
2. University of California, Berkeley
3. University of Minnesota
4. University of Illinois, Urbana
5. University of Wisconsin, Madison

*Where'd you hear that?*
U.S. News & World Report. Based on results of reputational survey of engineering-school deans and academic-affairs deans.

## Largest university research and development centers

1. Jet Propulsion Laboratory, with $915.5 million
2. Lawrence Livermore Laboratory, $914.8
3. Los Alamos National Laboratory, $853.3
4. Lincoln Laboratory, $353.7
5. Argonne National Laboratory, $276.6
6. Brookhaven National Laboratory, $220.5
7. Lawrence Berkeley Laboratory, $178.1

8. Fermi National Accelerator Laboratory, $167.1
9. Plasma Physics Laboratory, $107.2
10. Stanford Linear Accelerator Center, $89.0

*Where'd you hear that?*
Chemical & Engineering News, Facts & Figures for Chemical R & D. Based on total 1988 spending, in millions of dollars.

## Top universities in spending for research and development

1. Johns Hopkins University, with $510.9 million
2. Massachusetts Institute of Technology, $264.4
3. University of Wisconsin, Madison, $254.5
4. Cornell University, $244.8
5. Stanford University, $240.9
6. University of Michigan, $224.9
7. University of Minnesota, $222.4
8. Texas A & M University, $219.9
9. University of California, Los Angeles, $188.8
10. University of Illinois, Urbana, $188.7

*Where'd you hear that?*
Chemical & Engineering News, Facts & Figures for Chemical R & D. Based on total 1988 research and development spending, in millions.

## Top universities in spending for chemical research and development

1. University of +California, Berkeley, with $12,490 thousand
2. Massachusetts Institute of Technology, $11,471
3. University of Texas, Austin, $11,420
4. California Institute of Technology, $10,870
5. University of +California, Los Angeles, $10,099
6. University of Maryland, College Park, $9,258
7. University of +Illinois, Urbana-Champaign, $9,035
8. Stanford University, $8,916
9. Harvard University, $8,895
10. Cornell University, $8,095

*Where'd you hear that?*
Chemical & Engineering News, Facts & Figures for Chemical R & D. Based on total spending in 1987, in thousands of dollars.

## Universities with the most federal support for chemical research and development

1. University of +California, Berkeley, with $11,160 thousand
2. Massachusetts Institute of Technology, $10,656
3. California Institute of Technology, $9,922
4. University of +California, Los Angeles, $9,414
5. Harvard University, $8,309
6. Stanford University, $7,918
7. Cornell University, $6,753
8. Columbia University, main division, $6,625
9. University of Chicago, $6,499
10. University of Texas, Austin, $6,405

*Where'd you hear that?*
Chemical & Engineering News, Facts & Figures for Chemical R & D. Based on total federal funding in 1987, in thousands of dollars.

**GO TECH**

# GO TECH

**Companies spending the most on chemical research and development**

1. Du Pont Co., with $1,319 million
2. Dow Chemical Co., $772
3. Monsanto, $648
4. American Cyanamid Co., $365
5. Union Carbide, $159
6. Rohm & Haas, $156
7. W. R. Grace & Co., $119
8. Hercules, $74
9. Lubrizol, $65
10. Olin, $58

*Where'd you hear that?*
Chemical & Engineering News, Facts & Figures for Chemical R & D. Based on 1988 spending, in millions of dollars.

## Chemical companies that issued the most patents in 1988

1. Dow Chemical Co., with 421
2. Du Pont Co., 375
3. Ciba-Geigy Corp., 279
4. Union Carbide, 141
5. PPG Industries, 118
6. American Cyanamid Co., 101
7. Dow Corning, 82
8. Monsanto, 76
9. Stauffer Chemical, 69
10. Olin, 59

*Where'd you hear that?*
Chemical & Engineering News, Facts & Figures for Chemical R & D. Based on number of patents issued in 1988.

**Largest U.S. PVC producers**

1. Occidental, with 1900 million lb. per year
2. BF Goodrich, 1750
3. Shintech, 1500
4. Formosa Chemicals & Fibre Corp., 1090
5. Georgia-Gulf, 870
6. Vista, 850
7. Borden, 750
8. Air Products, 500
9. CertainTeed, 270
10. Union Carbide, 140

*Where'd you hear that?*
Plastics World. Based on operating capacity as of January 1, 1990.

**Largest fertilizer companies**

1. IMC Fertilizer Group, with $1,221.7 million
2. Freeport-McMoran, $1,173.2
3. First Mississippi, $433.5
4. Mississippi Chemical, $208.6

*Where'd you hear that?*
Chemicalweek, Chemicalweek 300. Based on 1989 sales, in millions of dollars.

**America's best nuclear engineering schools**

1. Massachusetts Institute of Technology
2. University of Michigan
3. University of California, Berkeley
4. University of Illinois, Urbana
5. Texas A & M University

*Where'd you hear that?*
U.S. News & World Report. Based on results of reputational survey of engineering-school deans and academic-affairs deans.

**Most hazardous toxic waste sites**

1. Lipari Landfill (Pitman, NJ)
2. Tybouts Corner Landfill (New Castle County, DE)

## GO TECH

3. Bruin Lagoon (Bruin Borough, PA)
4. Helen Kramer Landfill (Mantua Township, NJ)
5. Industri-Plex (Woburn, MA)
6. Price Landfill (Pleasantville, NJ)
7. Pollution Abatement Services (Oswego, NY)
8. LaBounty Site (Charles City, IA)
9. Army Creek Landfill (New Castle County, DE)
10. CPS/Madison Industries (Old Bridge Township, NJ)

*Where'd you hear that?*
Corporate Travel. Based on risk presented by toxic waste.

### Largest waste-burning companies

1. Ogden Projects, with 13
2. Wheelabrator Technologies, 10
3. Foster Wheeler Corp., 3
3. Combustion Engineering, 3
5. Westinghouse Electric, 2
6. American Ref-Fuel, 1

*Where'd you hear that?*
Fortune. Based on number of facilities in operation.

### Largest U.S. corporations in the pollution control industry

1. Waste Management, with $15,778 million
2. Browning-Ferris Industries, $5,033
3. Chemical Waste Management, $4,269
4. Chambers Development Co., Inc., $956
5. Calgon Carbon, $942
6. Rollins Environmental Services, $773
7. Metcalf & Eddy, $381

*Where'd you hear that?*
Business Week, The Business Week 1000. Based on market value as of March 16, 1990, in millions of dollars.

### Largest categories of disposable waste

1. Packaging, with 30.3%
2. Non durable goods, 25.1%
3. Yard waste, 20.1%
4. Durable goods, 13.6%
5. Food, 8.9%
6. Others, total 1.8%

*Where'd you hear that?*
Packaging. Based on percentage of all refuse and waste disposed of in 1988.

### America's best environmental engineering schools

1. Stanford University
2. University of California, Berkeley
3. University of Illinois, Urbana
4. University of Michigan
5. University of Texas, Austin

*Where'd you hear that?*
U.S. News & World Report. Based on results of reputational survey of engineering-school deans and academic-affairs deans.

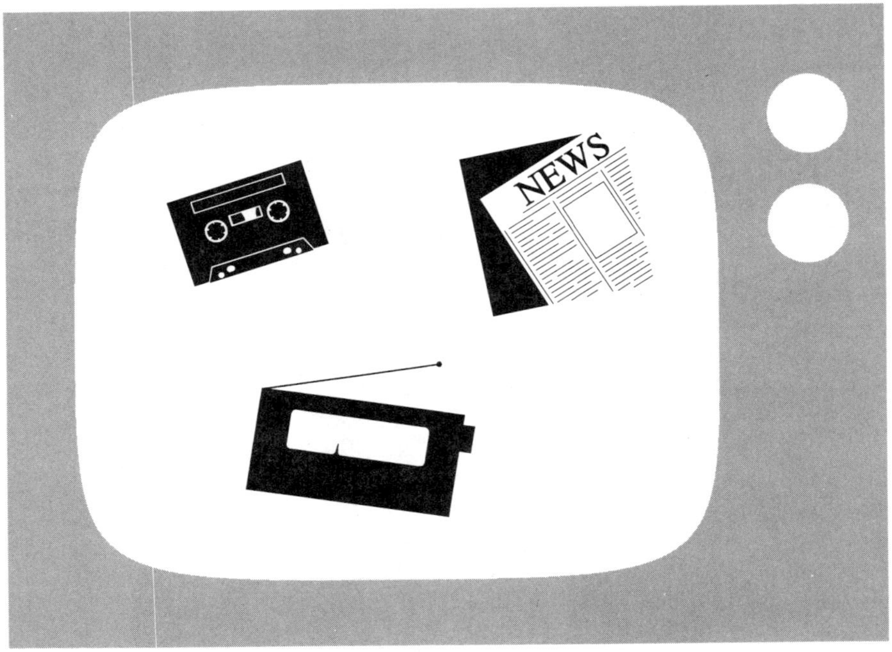
NEWS

# Mass Appeal

**Europe's largest media companies**

1. Bertelsmann, with $1.665 billion
2. Reed International, $1.649
3. Fininvest, $1.468
4. Axel Springer Verlag, $1.425
5. Hachette, $1.382
6. Havas, $1.286
7. United Newspaper, $1.212
8. Hersant, $1.176
9. Heinrich Bauer Verlag, $1.142
10. RCS, $1.092

*Where'd you hear that?*
Advertising Age. Based on media revenue, in billions of dollars.

**Largest media and communications companies in Canada**

1. Thomson, with $497,364 thousand
2. Torstar, $95,285
3. Southam, $91,177
4. Maclean Hunter Ltd., $90,300
5. Hollinger Inc., $73,087

*Where'd you hear that?*
Canadian Business, Canadian Business 500. Based on 1989 net income, in thousands of Canadian dollars.

**Largest media companies**

1. Capital Cities/ABC Inc., with $4,767.0 million
2. Time Warner, $4,575.0
3. Gannett Co. Inc., $3,518.2
4. General Electric Co., $3,392.0
5. CBS Inc., $2,959.9
6. Advance Publications, $2,881.7
7. Times Mirror Co., $2,807.1
8. TCI, $2,353.0
9. Knight-Ridder, Inc., $2,261.8
10. News Corp., $2,203.0

*Where'd you hear that?*
Advertising Age, 100 Leading Media Companies. Based on 1989 media revenue, in millions of dollars.

# MASS APPEAL

### Largest media companies

1. General Electric Co., with $50,089.0
2. Gulf & Western Inc., $5,107.8
3. Capital Cities/ABC Inc., $4,773.5
4. Time Inc., $4,507.0
5. News Corp. Ltd., $4,354.5
6. Warner Communications Inc., $4,206.1
7. Walt Disney Co., $3,438.2
8. Times Mirror Co., $3,332.6
9. Gannett Co. Inc., $3,314.5
10. MCA Inc., $3,023.7

*Where'd you hear that?*
Channels, Channels Achievers. Based on 1988 revenues, in millions of dollars.

### Fastest growing media companies

1. Carolco
2. CVN Companies
3. Jones Intercable
4. Tele-Communications Inc.
5. Reeves Communication
6. New Line Cinema
7. Orion Pictures
8. Warner Communications Inc.
9. Republic Pictures
10. King World Productions

*Where'd you hear that?*
Channels, Channels Achievers. Based on achievers Index. The index is comprised of two measures: annual growth in revenue and net income. Two rankings are added together and company with the lowest number is labeled number 1.

### Most profitable public media companies

1. Chris-Craft Industries, with 176.9%
2. LIN Broadcasting Inc., 22.9%
3. Dow Jones & Co., 18.8%
4. Berkshire Hathaway, 18.0%
5. Thomson Corp, 17.5%
6. Lee Enterprises, 16.0%
7. Reuters Holdings PLC, 15.3%
8. New York Times Co., 15.1%
9. Washington Post Co., 13.7%
10. Park Communications, 12.3%

*Where'd you hear that?*
Advertising Age, 100 Leading Media Companies. Based on 1989 return on sales, in percent.

### Most profitable media companies

1. Pulitzer Publishing, with 0.58
2. Warner Communications Inc., 0.24
3. Walt Disney Co., 0.22
3. Westinghouse, 0.22
5. Gannett Co. Inc., 0.20
6. Times Mirror, 0.19
6. New York Times, 0.19
6. Washington Post, 0.19
6. Knight-Ridder, Inc., 0.19
10. General Electric Co., 0.18

*Where'd you hear that?*
Channels, Channels Achievers. Based on 1988 return on equity.

### Ten best business books

*Down to the Wire: UPI's Fight for Survival*, by Gregory Gordon and Ronald E. Cohen
*Liar's Poker: Rising Through the Wreckage on Wall Street*, by Michael Lewis

*One Up on Wall Street: How to Use What You Already Know to Make Money in the Market*, by Peter Lynch with John Rothchild
*Rude Awakening: The Rise, Fall, and Struggle for Recovery of General Motors*, by Maryann Keller
*The Debt and the Deficit: False Alarms/Real Possibilities*, by Robert Heilbroner and Peter Bernstein
*The Enigma of Japanese Power*, by Karelvan Wolferen
*The New Competitors: How Foreign Investors Are Changing the U.S. Economy*, by Douglas P. Woodward and Norman J. Glickman
*The New Realities: In Goverment and Politics/In Economics and Business/In Society and World View*, by Peter F. Drucker
*West of Eden: The End of Innocence of Apple Computer*, by Frank Rose
*When the Machine Stopped: A Cautionary Tale from Industrial America*, by Max Holland

*Where'd you hear that?*
Business Week. Above items are listed, not ranked. Lists books published in 1989.

## Most admired publishing and printing corporations

1. Berkshire Hathaway, with a rating of 7.70
2. Dow Jones, 7.34
3. New York Times, 7.15
4. Gannett Co. Inc., 7.13
5. R. R. Donnelley & Sons, 6.94
6. Tribune, 6.80
7. Times Mirror, 6,72
8. Knight-Ridder Inc., 6.61
9. Time Warner, 6.36
10. McGraw-Hill, 5.97

*Where'd you hear that?*
Fortune, America's Most Admired Corporations. Based on scores (0-10) derived from a survey of senior executives, outside directors, and financial analysts. Respondents ranked firms in their own industry on quality of management and products/services; innovation; long-term investment value; financial soundness; attraction and retention of talent; community and environmental responsibility; and use of assets.

### Biggest corporations in the publishing and printing industry

1. Time Warner, with $7,642 million
2. Gannett Co. Inc., $3,523
3. Times Mirror, $3,517
4. R. R. Donnelley & Sons, $3,128
5. Berkshire Hathaway, $2,484
6. Tribune, $2,455
7. Knight-Ridder, Inc., $2,343
8. Reader's Digest, $1,871
9. New York Times, $1,807
10. McGraw-Hill, $1,789

*Where'd you hear that?*
Fortune, Fortune 500 Largest U.S. Industrial Corporations. Based on 1989 sales, in millions of dollars.

## Largest U.S. corporations in the publishing industry

1. Dun & Bradstreet Corp., with $8,680 million
2. Gannett Co. Inc., $6,640
3. Time Warner, $5,510
4. Times Mirror, $4,875

**MASS APPEAL**

# MASS APPEAL

5. Tribune, $3,670
6. Washington Post, $3,278
7. Knight-Ridder, Inc., $2,908
8. Reader's Digest Association, $2,843
9. Dow Jones, $2,811
10. McGraw-Hill, $2,586

*Where'd you hear that?*
Business Week, The Business Week 1000. Based on market value as of March 16, 1990, in millions of dollars.

## America's biggest publishers

1. Simon & Schuster, with $1300 million
2. Time Inc. Book Co., $988
3. Harcourt Brace Jovanovich, $879.7
4. Random House, $800
5. Reader's Digest, N/A
6. McGraw-Hill, $727.2
7. Encyclopaedia Britannica, $624
8. Bantam Doubleday Dell, $600
9. Times Mirror, $520
10. Thomson Corp., $500

*Where'd you hear that?*
Publishers Weekly. Based on revenues, in millions of dollars.

## Most productive publishing corporations

1. Dow Jones, with $33.5 thousand
2. Washington Post, $31.4
3. New York Times, $25.0
4. Readers Digest Association, $23.1
5. Tribune, $14.2
6. Knight-Ridder, Inc., $11.7
7. Gannett Co. Inc., $10.8
8. Times Mirror, $10.5
9. Harcourt Brace, $9.8
10. E. W. Scripps, $9.1

*Where'd you hear that?*
Forbes, Forbes 500s Annual Directory. Based on 1989 profits per employee, in thousands of dollars. Ranks U.S.-based corporations that were publicly traded as of March 23, 1990.

## Most profitable publishing companies

1. Commerce Clearing House, with 39.7%
2. Washington Post, 32.4%
3. Dun & Bradstreet Corp., 31.0%
4. Dow Jones, 29.7%
5. Times Mirror, 22.6%
6. New York Times, 22.0%
7. Gannett Co. Inc., 21.9%
8. McGraw-Hill, 21.5%
9. R. R. Donnelley & Sons, 18.2%
10. Banta, 17.9%

*Where'd you hear that?*
Forbes, Annual Report on American Industry. Based on 10-year average return on equity. Ranks publicly held corporations only.

## Largest parent companies of magazines

1. Time Warner, with $2,500.3 million
2. News Corp., $1,247.9
3. Advance Publications, $1,141.0
4. Hearst Corp., $1,019.2
5. New York Times Co., $669.7
6. Meredith Corp., $627.7
7. Hachette Publications, $573.0
8. Reader's Digest, $507.0
9. McGraw-Hill, $470.8
10. Reed International, $428.5

212

# MASS APPEAL

*Where'd you hear that?*
Advertising Age, Ad Age 300. Based on 1989 total revenues, in millions of dollars.

## Largest magazine publishers

1. Time Inc. magazines, with $1412.7
2. Newhouse/Conde Nast, $874.7
3. Hearst magazines, $602.3
4. Murdoch magazines, $479.7
5. New York Times, 440.0
6. Family Media, $385.2
7. Diamandis Communications, $321.2
8. Meredith Corp., $314.2
9. Times Mirror, $228.2
10. Forbes Inc., $161.5

*Where'd you hear that?*
Adweek's Marketing Week, Hottest Magazines. Based on 1989 ad revenue, in millions of dollars.

## Largest magazines ranked by gross revenues

1. *TV Guide*, with $928.3 million
2. *Time*, $636.5
3. *People*, $605.6
4. *Sports Illustrated*, $565.9
5. *Reader's Digest*, $419.2
6. *Newsweek*, $397.8
7. *Parade*, $314.5
8. *Business Week*, $298.7
9. *Better Homes & Gardens*, $275.7
10. *Family Circle*, $249.3

*Where'd you hear that?*
Advertising Age, Ad Age 300. Based on 1989 gross revenues, in millions of dollars.

## Largest magazines ranked by circulation revenues

1. *TV Guide*, with $605.4 million
2. *Reader's Digest*, $305.6
3. *People*, $279.4
4. *Time*, $263.1
5. *Sports Illustrated*, $229.3
6. *National Geographic*, $192.9
7. *National Enquirer*, $174.9
8. *Star Magazine*, $154.9
9. *Newsweek*, $141.9
10. *Better Homes & Gardens*, $123.3

*Where'd you hear that?*
Advertising Age, Ad Age 300. Based on 1989 circulation revenues, in millions of dollars.

## Fastest growing magazines

1. *PC Computing*, with 311.6%
2. *Victoria*, 80.3%
3. *Lear's*, 78.3%
4. *Discount Store News*, 76.5%
5. *Financial World*, 45.4%
6. *European Travel & Life*, 44.5%
7. *Nation's Restaurant News*, 42.5%
8. *Premiere*, 41.1%
9. *Alfred Hitchcock & Ellery Queen*, 39.2%
10. *RN*, 37.6%

*Where'd you hear that?*
Advertising Age, Ad Age 300. Based on circulation revenue growth, 1988-89, in percent.

## Largest magazines ranked by ad revenues

1. *Time*, with $373.4 million
2. *Sports Illustrated*, $336.7
3. *People*, $326.2
4. *TV Guide*, $323.0

# MASS APPEAL

5. *Parade*, $314.5
6. *Business Week*, $260.6
7. *Newsweek*, $255.9
8. *Fortune*, $168.7
9. *Forbes*, $157.7
10. *U.S. News & World Report*, $152.8

*Where'd you hear that?*
Advertising Age, Ad Age 300. Based on 1989 ad revenues, in millions of dollars.

## *Where magazines are sold*

1. Food stores, with 54%
2. News stands, 11%
3. Convenience stores, 10%
4. Drug stores, 9%
5. Book stores, 7%
6. Discount stores, 2%
7. Others, total, 7%

*Where'd you hear that?*
Non-Foods Merchandising. Based on market share, in percent.

### Largest magazines ranked by ad revenue growth

1. *PC Computing*, with 337.2%
2. *Victoria*, 235.4%
3. *Lear's*, 174.7%
4. *National Examiner*, 168.1%
5. *Golf Illustrated*, 110.7%
6. *Premiere*, 99.4%
7. *Easyriders*, 81.5%
8. *Globe*, 80.4%
9. *Conde Nast Traveler*, 78.0%
10. *Cooking Light*, 75.9%

*Where'd you hear that?*
Advertising Age, Ad Age 300. Based on ad revenue growth, 1988-89, in percent.

### Magazine ad page leaders

1. *Business Week*, with 4,914,15
2. *Forbes*, 3,905.84
3. *Fortune*, 3,775.00
4. *People*, 3,770.81
5. *Bride's*, 3,358.86
6. *Vogue*, 3,321.86
7. *TV Guide*, 3,255.13
8. *New York Magazine*, 3,094.86
9. *Sports Illustrated*, 2,981.90
10. *Time*, 2,733.86

*Where'd you hear that?*
Advertising Age. Based on number of ad pages in 1989.

### Best-selling magazines

1. *Modern Maturity*, with 21,430,990
2. *Reader's Digest*, 16,343,599
3. *TV Guide*, 15,867,750
4. *National Geographic Magazine*, 10,890,660
5. *Better Homes and Gardens*, 8,005,311
6. *Family Circle*, 5,461,786
7. *Good Housekeeping*, 5,152,245
8. *McCalls*, 5,088,686
9. *Ladies' Home Journal*, 5,038,297
10. *Woman's Day*, 4,705,288

*Where'd you hear that?*
Advertising Age. Based on 1989 circulation; per-issue averages for six-months ending December 31, 1989.

# MASS APPEAL

## Hottest magazines

1. *Conde Nast Traveler*, with 634
2. *Entrepreneur*, 541
3. *Vanity Fair*, 449
4. *Parade*, 360
5. *Muscle & Fitness*, 343
6. *USA Weekend*, 339
7. *Forbes*, 305
7. *Country Home*, 305
9. *Fortune*, 303
10. *Ladies' Home Journal*, 286

*Where'd you hear that?*
Adweek's Marketing Week, Hottest Magazines. Based on adweek performance index, assessing 1989 performance.

## Favorite magazines among college students

1. *Cosmopolitan*, with 424
2. *Sports Illustrated*, 399
3. *Time*, 325
4. *Rolling Stone*, 317
5. *Glamour*, 315
6. *Vogue*, 261
7. *Newsweek*, 199
8. *People Weekly*, 190
9. *Mademoiselle*, 174
10. *Elle*, 168

*Where'd you hear that?*
Advertising Age. Based on survey results, in points. Students were asked to list their three favorite magazines in descending order. First place mentions received three points; second, two points; third, one point.

## Largest medical/surgical publications

1. *Medical Economics*
2. *JAMA*
3. *New England Journal of Medicine*
4. *American Medical News*
5. *Diversion*
6. *Postgraduate Medicine*
7. *American Family Physician*
8. *Patient Care*
9. *Hospital Practice*
10. *Emergency Medicine*

*Where'd you hear that?*
Medical Marketing & Media, Healthcare Advertising Review. Based on 1989 estimated advertising revenues.

## Largest newspaper groups

1. MI Newspapers Inc., with 1,871,067
2. UNYT, 596,359
3. Boston Area Newspapers, 552,362
4. Booth Newspapers, 538,752
5. Bees Inland V Group, 471,658
6. Tampa Bay Best B, 436,740
7. Philadelphia ADI NN, 376,891
8. Greater Cleveland NT, 344,332
9. Georgia Group, 343,147
10. Key Market Newspaper Group, 339,645

*Where'd you hear that?*
Newspaper Circulation Analysis, Standard Rate & Data Service. Based on total daily circulation.

## Largest combined daily newspapers

1. St. Joseph News-Press/Gazette, with 104.1%
2. Muncie Press Star, 78.2%
3. Enid News & Eagle, 77.6%
4. Lewiston Sun Journal, 77.2%
5. Wheeling Intelligencer-News Register, 75.0%
6. Charleston Gazette Mail, 73.9%
7. Roanoke Times-World News, 72.5%
8. Hagerstown Herald-Daily Mail, 70.6%
9. Milwaukee Journal-Sentinel, 70.3%

# MASS APPEAL

10. Kansas City Star Times, 70.2%

*Where'd you hear that?*
Newspaper Circulation Analysis, Standard Rate & Data Service. Based on 1989 metropolitan area penetration ratio within their own metro area, in percent.

## Largest all day newspapers

1. Buffalo News, with 73.6%
2. Peoria Journal-Star, 60.4%
3. Lynchburg News & Advertiser, 59.5%
4. Long Island Newsday, 57.6%
5. Southern Connecticut Newspaper, 56.2%
6. Yakima Herald-Republic, 52.7%
7. Springfield Union-News, 51.1%
8. New Orleans Time-Picayune, 50.7%
9. Fort Smith Times Register, 48.8%
10. Portland Oregonian, 47.9%

*Where'd you hear that?*
Newspaper Circulation Analysis, Standard Rate & Data Service. Based on 1989 metropolitan area penetration ratio within their own metro area, in percent.

## Largest daily newspapers

1. New York Daily News, with 1,282,046
2. Los Angeles Times, 1,122,952
3. New York Times, 1,039,304
4. Washington Post, 788,752
5. Chicago Tribune, 765,702
6. Philadelphia Inquirer News, 753,632
7. New York Post, 713,786
8. San Francisco Chronicle, 702,506
9. Detroit News, 684,098
10. Detroit Free Press, 648,217

*Where'd you hear that?*
Newspaper Circulation Analysis, Standard Rate & Data Service. Based on 1989 total circulation.

## Largest morning newspapers by circulation

1. New York Daily News, with 1,282,046
2. Los Angeles Times, 1,122,952
3. New York Times, 1,039,304
4. Washington Post, 788,752
5. Chicago Tribune, 765,702
6. Detroit Free Press, 648,217
7. Chicago Sun-Times, 614,212
8. San Francisco Chronicle, 561,130
9. Philadelphia Inquirer News, 505,834
10. Boston Globe, 499,661

*Where'd you hear that?*
Newspaper Circulation Analysis, Standard Rate & Data Service. Based on 1989 total circulation.

## Largest morning newspapers by market penetration ratio

1. Buffalo News, with 73.7%
2. Victoria Advocate, 70.9%
3. Bangor News, 70.6%
4. Pueblo Chieftain, Star-Journal, 69.8%
5. St. Joseph News-Press, Gazette, 68.8%
6. Owensboro Messenger Inquirer, 68.5%
7. Bloomington Pantagraph, 68.4%
8. Colorado Springs Gazette Telegraph, 67.0%
9. Grand Forks Herald 66.9%
10. Glens Falls Post-Star 66.6%

# MASS APPEAL

*Where'd you hear that?*
Circulation, American Newspaper Markets, Inc. Based on market penetration ratio, in percent.

## Largest morning newspapers by penetration ratio in metro area

1. Victoria Advocate, with 75.8%
2. Pueblo Chieftain, 75.6%
3. Casper Star-Tribune, 71.6%
4. Springfield/Lincoln Journal, 67.9%
5. Bloomington Pantagraph, 67.8%
6. Bangor News, 67.7%
7. St. Joseph News-Press Gazette, 67.0%
8. Elmira Star-Gazette, 66.7%
9. Owensboro Messenger Inquirer, 66.5%
10. Sioux City Journal, 66.4%

*Where'd you hear that?*
Newspaper Circulation Analysis Standard Rate & Data Service. Based on 1989 metropolitan area penetration ratio within their own metro area, in percent.

## Largest evening newspapers by circulation

1. Portland This Week-Weekly, with 461,724
2. Milwaukee Journal-Sentinel, 285,888
3. Philadelphia Inquirer News, 247,798
4. Seattle Times Post-Intelligencer, 236,432
5. Pittsburgh Press-Post Gazette, 229,539
6. Macromedia Inc. Newspapers, 207,933
7. Kansas City Star Tribune, 206,533
8. Atlanta Constitution-Journal, 184,324
9. Baltimore Sun, 176,877
10. Greater Chicago Newspapers, 170,794

*Where'd you hear that?*
Newspaper Circulation Analysis, Standard Rate & Data Service. Based on 1989 total circulation.

## Largest evening newspapers by market penetration ratio

1. Dubuque Telegraph-Herald, with 70.2%
2. Williamsport Sun-Gazette, 69.9%
3. Burlington Times-News, 68.4%
4. Muskegon Chronicle, 65.7%
5. Rochester Post-Bulletin, 65.4%
6. Mansfield News Journal, 64.3%
7. South Bend Tribune, 64.0%
8. Jackson Citizen Patriot, 63.8%
9. Kenosha News, 63.6%
10. Redding Record Searchlight, 63.5%

*Where'd you hear that?*
Circulation, American Newspaper Markets, Inc. Based on market penetration ratio, in percent.

## Largest evening newpapers by penetration ratio in metro area

1. Portland This Week-Weekly, with 93.6%
2. Williamsport Sun-Gazette, 71.2%
3. Dubuque Telegraph-Herald, 69.7%

# MASS APPEAL

4. Burlington Times-News, 69.2%
5. Kankakee Journal, 65.8%
6. Mansfield News-Journal, 65.5%
7. Muskegon Chronicle, 64.1%
8. Jackson City Patriot, 63.3%
9. Redding Record Searchlight, 63.0%
10. Kenosha News, 62.9%

*Where'd you hear that?*
Newspaper Circulation Analysis, Standard Rate & Data Service. Based on 1989 metropolitan area penetration ratio within their own metro area, in percent.

## Largest Sunday or weekend newspapers by circulation

1. New York Daily News, with 1,622,966
2. New York Times, 1,615,135
3. Los Angeles Times, 1,400,603
4. Chicago Tribune, 1,123,693
5. Washington Post, 1,122,375
6. Philadelphia Inquirer News, 992,116
7. Detroit News, 836,287
8. Boston Globe, 784,611
9. Detroit Free Press, 727,299
10. San Francisco Chronicle, 710,758

*Where'd you hear that?*
Newspaper Circulation Analysis, Standard Rate & Data Service. Based on 1989 total circulation.

## Top Sunday newspapers by market penetration

1. Buffalo News, with 81.3%
2. Bangor Daily News, 80.3%
3. Sarasota Herald-Tribune, 77.9%
4. Erie Times, News, 77.7%
5. St. Joseph News-Press, Gazette, 76.2%
6. Dubuque Telegraph-Herald, 76.0%
7. Pueblo Chieftain, Star-Journal, 75.4%
8. Wichita Falls Record News, Times, 74.9%
9. Great Falls Tribune, 74.4%
10. Wichita Eagle-Beacon, 73.2%
10. Victoria Advocate, 73.2%

*Where'd you hear that?*
Circulation, American Newspaper Markets Inc. Based on market penetration.

## Largest Sunday or weekend newspapers by penetration ratio in metro area

1. Wheeling Intelligencer-News Register, with 82.0%
2. Pueblo Chieftain, 81.5%
3. Buffalo News, 81.2%
4. Erie News Times, 78.7%
5. Victoria Advocate, 78.1%
6. Casper Star-Tribune, 77.2%
7. Bangor News, 76.9%
8. Sarasota Herald-Tribune, 76.7%
9. Dubuque Telegraph-Herald, 75.5%
9. Wichita Falls Record News, 75.5%

*Where'd you hear that?*
Newspaper Circulation Analysis, Standard Rate & Data Service. Based on 1989 metropolitan area penetration ratio within their own metro area, in percent.

## Largest English-language publishers

1. News Corporation (Australia), with $1,417 million
2. Paramount Communications (U.S.), $1,300
3. Hachette (France), $1,089

# MASS APPEAL

4. Reed (Britain), $925
5. Pearson (Britain), $905
6. Harcourt Brace Jovanovich (U.S.), $879
7. Bertelsmann (West Germany), $843
7. Reader's Digest (U.S.), $843
7. Time Warner (U.S.), $843
10. Times Mirror (U.S.), $650

*Where'd you hear that?*
Economist. Based on worldwide sales, in millions of dollars.

## Largest U.S. corporations in the printing & advertising industry

1. R. R. Donnelley & Sons, with $3,496 million
2. Interpublic Group, $1,161
3. Omnicom Group, $607

*Where'd you hear that?*
Business Week, The Business Week 1000. Based on market value as of March 16, 1990, in millions of dollars.

## Printing companies with greatest numbers of employees

1. R. R. Donnelley & Sons, with 24,000
2. Deluxe Corp., 16,628
3. Lawson Mardon, 7,800
4. Dennison Manufacturing, Co., 7,600
5. Arcata, 7,200
6. World Color, 6,700
7. Quebecor, 6,000
8. John H. Harland Co., 5,600
9. Taylor Industries, 5,000
10. Sullivan Graphics, Inc., 4,800

*Where'd you hear that?*
graphic arts monthly, GAM 101. Based on number of employees in 1988-89.

## Printing companies with highest sales

1. R. R. Donnelley & Sons (Chicago, IL), with $2,878,432 thousand
2. Deluxe Corp. (St. Paul, MN), $1,200,000
3. Lawson Mardon (Mississauga, ON), $928,378
4. Maxwell Communications (St. Paul, MN), $730,000
5. Dennison Manufacturing Co. (Framingham, MA), $721,776
6. World Color Press (Effingham, IL), $670,000
7. Quebecor Printing (Montreal, Quebec), $627,000
8. Sullivan Graphics, Inc. (Nashville, TN), $575,000
9. Treasure Chest Advertising (Glendora, CA), $540,000
10. Banta Corp. (Menasha, WI), $526,000

*Where'd you hear that?*
graphic arts monthly, GAM 101. Based on 1988 sales, in thousands of dollars.

## *Where books are sold*

1. Book stores, with 54%
2. Discount stores, 15%
2. Food stores, 15%
4. Drug stores, 8%
5. News stands, 2%
6. Convenience stores, 1%
7. Others, total, 5%

*Where'd you hear that?*
Non-Foods Merchandising. Based on market share, in percent.

# MASS APPEAL

### Largest financial printers

1. Browne & Co. (New York, NY), with $187,826 thousand
2. Chas. P. Young (New York, NY), $90,000
3. Sorg (New York, NY), $80,000

*Where'd you hear that?*
graphic arts monthly, GAM 101. Based on 1988 sales, in thousands of dollars.

### Largest color trade printing shops

1. Applied Graphics Technologies (New York, NY), with $100,000 thousand
2. Techtron Imaging Network (Chicago, IL), $92,000
3. Parkway USA (New York, NY), $75,000
4. Jannock Imaging (Toronto, Ontario), $74,050
5. American Color (Phoenix, AZ), $55,000
6. Schawk (Des Plaines, IL), $55,000
7. Enteron Group (Chicago, IL), $40,000
8. Black Dot Graphics (Crystal Lake, IL), $28,500
9. Lincoln Graphics, Inc. (Cherry Hill, NJ), $19,125
10. Kwik International (New York, NY), $18,900

*Where'd you hear that?*
graphic arts monthly, GAM 101. Based on 1988 sales, in thousands of dollars.

### Most productive broadcasting corporations

1. BHC Communications, with $961.8 thousand
2. LIN Broadcasting Corp., $63.7
3. CBS Inc., $44.3
4. Viacom, $28.2
5. Capital Cities/ABC Inc., $24.5
6. Tele-Communications, -$8.3
6. Turner Broadcasting -$8.3
8. Comcast -$24.8

*Where'd you hear that?*
Forbes, Forbes 500s Annual Directory. Based on 1989 profits per employee, in thousands of dollars. Ranks U.S.-based corporations that were publicly traded as of March 23, 1990.

### Most profitable broadcasting and cable companies

1. CBS Inc., with 35.4%
2. Capital Cities/ABC Inc., 18.3%
3. Multimedia, 8.7%
4. Tele-Communications, 8.3%
5. Comcast, 5.9%
6. Cablevision Systems Corp., NA
7. Turner Broadcasting, NA
8. Viacom, NA

*Where'd you hear that?*
Forbes, Annual Report on American Industry. Based on 10-year average return on equity. Ranks publicly held corporations only.

### Most successful radio communications companies

1. Osborn Communications, with 0.52
2. Clear Channel Communications, 0.16
3. Satellite Music Network, 0.12
4. Durham Corp., 0.06
5. Westwood One, 0.01

# MASS APPEAL

6. Jacor Communications, -0.48
7. Faircom, -0.60
8. Southern Starr Broadcasting, -0.90
9. Olympia Broadcasting, NM
10. Sun Group, -3.57

*Where'd you hear that?*
Channels, Channels Achievers. Based on return on equity in 1988.

## Top radio broadcasting companies by share of Hispanic market

1. Caballero, with 41%
2. Katz Hispanic Radio, 29%
3. Spanish Broadcasting System, 19%
4. Lotus Hispanic Reps, 11%

*Where'd you hear that?*
Hispanic Business. Based on national market share.

## Top Hispanic radio stations

1. KLVE (FM)/KTNQ (AM), Los Angeles, with $17.5 million
2. WCMQ (AM & FM), Miami, $11.5
3. WQBA (AM & FM), Miami, $10.0
3. WIND-WOJO (AM & FM), Chicago, $10.0
5. WSKQ (AM), New York, $9.0
6. KWKW (AM), Los Angeles, $8.1
7. WADO (AM), New York, $6.0
8. KSKQ (AM), Los Angeles, $5.5
9. WAQI (AM), Miami, $5.0
10. KALI (AM), Los Angeles, $4.0

*Where'd you hear that?*
Hispanic Business. Based on ad billings, in millions.

## Most profitable production companies

1. King World Productions, with 1.22
2. Dick Clark Productions, 0.14
3. All American Television, 0.11
4. Carolco Pictures, 0.10
5. Orion Pictures, 0.08
6. Spelling Entertainment, 0.06
7. Republic Pictures, 0.05
8. New Line Cinema, 0.03
8. Imagine Films Entertainment, 0.03
10. Columbia Pictures Entertainment, 0.02

*Where'd you hear that?*
Channels, Channels Achievers. Based on 1989 return on equity.

## *Largest U.S. corporations in the broadcasting industry*

1. Capital Cities/ABC Inc., with $9,026 million
2. Tele-Communications, $5,028
3. Lin Broadcasting Inc., $4,394
4. CBS Inc., $4,212
5. American Television & Communications Corp., $3,652
6. Viacom, $2,828
7. Turner Broadcasting, $2,312
8. Comcast, $1,641
9. Multimedia, $910
10. Chris-Craft Industries, $799

*Where'd you hear that?*
Business Week, The Business Week 1000. Based on market value as of March 16, 1990, in millions of dollars.

# MASS APPEAL

## Favorite TV shows among college students

1. *Cheers*, with 649
2. *Thirtysomething*, 414
3. *Cosby*, 393
4. *Wonder Years*, 383
5. *L.A. Law*, 350
6. *Letterman*, 135
7. *Roseanne*, 134
8. *Knots Landing*, 124
9. *Football telecasts*, 103
9. *Married... with Children*, 103

*Where'd you hear that?*
Advertising Age. Based on survey results, in points. Students were asked to list their three favorite TV shows in descending order. First place mentions received three points; second, two points; third, one point.

## 10 top-rated PBS shows

1. National Geographic, 'Sharks', January, 1982, with 17.4%
2. National Geographic, 'Grizzlies', March, 1987, 17.0%
3. National Geographic, 'Land of the Tiger', January, 1985, 16.5%
4. National Geographic, 'Incredible Machine', October, 1975, 16.0%
5. National Geographic, 'National Geographic', March, 1985, 15.7%
6. 'Best of Wild America: The Babies', March 1987, 14.7%
6. 'Music Man', March 1985, 14.7%
8. 'Live from the Grand Ole Opry', March, 1979, 14.6%
9. 'Live from the Grand Ole Opry', March 1980, 14.2%
10. National Geographic, 'Lions of...African Night', January 1987, 13.8%

*Where'd you hear that?*
Wall Street Journal. Based on audience share: percentage of U.S. TV homes viewing at least six minutes of the program.

## Most profitable television broadcasting companies

1. Pulitzer Publishing, with 0.31
2. Lee Enterprises, 0.24
3. CBS Inc., 0.12
3. LIN Broadcasting, 0.12
5. A. H. Belo, 0.10
5. Park Communications, 0.10
5. American Family, 0.10
5. Gray Communications, 0.10
9. Stauffer Communications, 0.07
9. New York Times, 0.07

*Where'd you hear that?*
Channels, Channels Achievers. Based on 1989 return on equity.

## Television's top syndicators

1. Warner, with $377 million
2. King World Productions, $370
3. MCA, $347
4. Paramount, $338
5. Columbia, $304
6. Viacom, $290
7. Fox, $230
8. Camelot, $185
9. Turner, $168
10. LBS, $134

*Where'd you hear that?*
Channels, Top 20 Syndicators. Based on gross revenues from U.S. domestic syndication, from both barter ad sales and cash sales, to stations for the 1988-89 season, in millions of dollars.

## MASS APPEAL

### Designated market areas with the most TV households

1. New York, NY, with 7,020,030
2. Los Angeles, CA, 4,931,560
3. Chicago, IL, 3,119,920
4. Philadelphia, PA, 2,669,210
5. San Francisco-Oakland, CA, 2,209,770
6. Boston, MA, 2,131,780
7. Washington, DC, 1,727,830
8. Detroit, MI, 1,720,420
9. Dallas-Fort Worth, TX, 1,716,160
10. Cleveland, Akron, OH, 1,458,520

*Where'd you hear that?*
Broadcasting Cablecasting Yearbook. Based on number of TV households.

### Designated market areas with the most cable TV households

1. New York, NY, with 3,449,530
2. Los Angeles, CA, 2,356,900
3. Philadelphia, PA, 1,636,720
4. Chicago, IL, 1,347,600
5. Boston, MA, 1,333,020
6. San Francisco-Oakland, CA, 1,291,150
7. Detroit, MI, 834,690
8. Pittsburgh, PA, 820,320
9. Washington, DC, 793,990
10. Tampa-St. Petersburg, Sarasota, FL, 766,510

*Where'd you hear that?*
Broadcasting Cablecasting Yearbook. Based on number of cable TV households.

### Designated market areas by highest cable penetration

1. Palm Springs, CA, with 88.7%
2. Santa Barbara-Santa Maria, CA, 85.3%
3. San Angelo, CA, 84.0%
4. Biloxi-Gulfport, MS, 82.5%
5. Victoria, BC, 82.5%
6. Hartford & New Haven, CT, 80.9%
7. Honolulu, HI, 80.4%
8. Laredo, TX, 79.9%
9. Tuscaloosa, AL, 77.4%
10. San Diego, CA, 77.0%

*Where'd you hear that?*
Broadcasting Cablecasting Yearbook. Based on percent of cable penetration in market area.

### Largest cable networks

1. HBO, with 54%
2. Showtime, 35%
3. Prism, 6%
4. SelecTV, 3%
5. Disney Channel, 1%
6. Others, 1%

*Where'd you hear that?*
Cable World, September 1, 1989, p. 3. Based on 1988 market share, in percent.

### Top cable networks ranked by ad billings

1. TBS, with 26.7%
2. ESPN, 20.7%
3. USA, 17.1%
4. CNN, 14.4%
5. MTV, 11.0%
6. FAM, 10.1%

# MASS APPEAL

*Where'd you hear that?*
Cable World. Based on 1989 share of national billings, in percent.

## Top cable networks ranked by local ad sales revenue

1. ESPN, with 32.1%
2. CNN, 25.7%
3. USA, 15.7%
4. MTV, 5.4%
5. TNT, 4.6%
6. Others, total, 16.5%

*Where'd you hear that?*
Cable World. Based on 1989 local ad sales revenue share, in percent.

## Largest multiple-system cable television operators

1. Tele-Communications Inc., with 6,228,526
2. American Television & Communications Corp., 4,202,000
3. UA Entertainment, 2,530,000
4. Continental Cablevision Inc., 2,486,358
5. Warner Cable Communications, 1,700,000
6. Storer Cable Communications, 1,531,000
7. Cox Cable Communications, 1,500,000
8. Comcast, 1,490,000
9. Cablevision Systems Corp., 1,387,771
10. Jones Intercable/Spacelink, 1,325,552

*Where'd you hear that?*
Cable TV Facts. Based on number of basic subscribers, 1989.

## Largest cable television systems

1. Long Island, NY (Cablevision Systems), with 479,594
2. Orlando/Central Complex, FL (ATC), 400,000
3. San Diego, CA (Cox Cable), 303,637
4. San Antonio, TX (KBLCOM), 234,835
5. Manhattan, NY (ATC), 231,864
6. Puget Sound, WA (Viacom), 225,800
7. Phoenix, AZ (Times Mirror), 220,968
8. East Orange, NJ (Maclean Hunter), 212,000
9. Honolulu, HI (ATC), 206,251
10. Chicago, IL (suburbs) (Continental), 181,537

*Where'd you hear that?*
Cable TV Facts. Based on number of basic subscribers, 1989.

## Largest cable television interconnects

1. New York Interconnect, with 3,100,000
2. Adlink (Los Angeles, CA), 1,200,000
2. Greater Philadelphia Cable, 1,200,000
4. Boston Interconnect, 1,032,000
5. Bay Area Interconnect, 1,025,000
6. Detroit Interconnect, 760,000
7. Tampa Bay Interconnect, 711,000
8. Cable AdNet-North Carolina, 630,000
9. Metrobase Cable Advertising (Philadelphia, PA), 602,100

10. News 12 Long Island, 601,000

*Where'd you hear that?*
Cable TV Facts. Based on number of subscribers, 1989.

## Most profitable cable television companies in 1988

1. Jones Intercable, with 0.34%
2. QVC Network, 0.27%
2. American Television & Communications Corp., 0.27%
4. Time, 0.21%
5. Maclean Hunter Ltd., 0.17%
6. TCA Cable, 0.16%
6. Financial News Network Inc., 0.16%
8. Centel Corp., 0.15%
9. Home Shopping Network Inc., 0.13%
10. Playboy, 0.08%
10. CVN Companies, 0.08%

*Where'd you hear that?*
Channels, Channels Achievers. Based on return on equity.

## Largest cable television advertising agencies

1. Saatchi & Saatchi Advertising, with $62.7 million
2. Lintas:Campbell-Ewald Co., $60.3
3. Foote, Cone & Belding Communications Inc., $57
4. DDB Needham Worldwide Inc., $56
5. D'Arcy Masius Benton & Bowles Inc., $45
6. Grey Advertising Inc., $38.9
7. J. Walter Thompson Co., $35
8. McCann-Erickson, $30.4
9. BBDO, $30
10. Ogilvy & Mather, $28
11. N. W. Ayer, $27.7

*Where'd you hear that?*
Marketing & Media Decisions. Based on 1989 cable television billings, in millions of dollars.

## Largest cable television network advertisers

1. Procter & Gamble Co., with $36,096.7 thousand
2. Time Inc., $29,823.0
3. Anheuser-Busch Cos. Inc., $26,300.2
4. General Mills Inc., $21,305.6
5. General Motors Corp., $21,039.3
6. Philip Morris Cos. Inc., $20,491.8
7. RJR Nabisco Inc., $19,149.1
8. Mars Inc., $13,984.4
9. Sears, Roebuck & Co., $13,343.8
10. Chrysler Corp., $11,765.4

*Where'd you hear that?*
LNA Ad Dollars Summary, Leading National Advertisers. Based on 1989 cable television network advertising expenditures, in thousands of dollars.

## Top media advertising categories

1. Network TV, with $5,117.0 million
2. Spot TV, $2,655.6
3. Magazine, $1,754.6
4. Newspaper, $1,479.7
5. Syndicated TV, $505.5
6. Cable TV networks, $306.7
7. Network radio, $285.7
8. Outdoor, $190.4
9. Sunday magazine, $132.6

*Where'd you hear that?*
Advertising Age, Top 200 Brands. Based on 1989 measured ad spending, in millions of dollars.

# MASS APPEAL

# MASS APPEAL

### Top advertising categories

1. Passenger car, with $2,424.2 million
2. Retail, non-food, $1,243.4
3. Restaurants, $1,171.2
4. Cereals (food), $643.6
5. Beer, $549.2
6. Airline, $486.2
7. Movies, $462.9
8. Trucks & vans, $455.5
9. Cigarettes, $432.3
10. Telephone companies, $400.0

*Where'd you hear that?*
Advertising Age, Top 200 Brands. Based on 1989 measured ad spending, in millions of dollars.

### Product brand loyalty

1. Cigarettes, with 71%
2. Mayonnaise, 65%
3. Toothpaste, 61%
4. Coffee, 58%
5. Headache remedy, 56%
5. Film, 56%
7. Bath soap, 53%
8. Ketchup, 51%
9. Laundry detergent, 48%
9. Beer, 48%

*Where'd you hear that?*
Wall Street Journal. Based on percentage of users who are loyal to one brand.

### Product categories spending the most on advertising

1. Department stores, with $2,031,108 thousand
2. Restaurants, hotel dining, and night clubs, $1,496,634
3. Car dealers and services, including used cars, $1,448,732
4. Passenger cars, imported, $1,170,873
5. Passenger cars, domestic, $1,153,273
6. Cereals, $835,825
7. Miscellaneous retail, $818,886
8. Beer, $885,913
9. Food stores, $740,483
10. Motion pictures, $675,700

*Where'd you hear that?*
Marketing & Media Decisions, Top 200 Brands. Based on 1988 total media investments, thousands of dollars.

### Parent companies that advertised the most in 1989

1. General Motors Corp., with $778.7 million
2. Philip Morris Cos., $753.7.
3. McDonald's Corp., $424.8
4. Ford Motor Co., $416.1
5. Sears, Roebuck & Co., $404.6
6. PepsiCo Inc., $401.3
7. Kellogg Co., $373.3
8. Chrysler Corp., $355.5
9. AT & T, 314.3
10. Anheuser-Busch Cos. Inc., $297.2

*Where'd you hear that?*
Advertising Age, Top 200 Brands. Based on 1989 measured ad spending, in millions of dollars.

### Biggest advertisers of brands, products, and services

1. McDonald's restaurants, $424,789.9 million
2. Kellogg's cereals, $373,331.3
3. Sears, Roebuck & Co. stores, $363,714.4
4. AT & T, $314,333.7
5. Ford passenger cars, $197,361.3
6. Budweiser beer, $183,074.6

7. Chevrolet passenger cars, $180,551.0
8. Nissan passenger cars, $173,595.1
9. Burger King Corp., $170,358.5
10. Toyota passenger cars, $162,014.8

*Where'd you hear that?*
Advertising Age, Top 200 Brands. Based on 1989 measured ad spending, in millions of dollars.

**Top spending advertisers**

1. McDonald's Restaurants, with $404,951,827
2. Burger King Corp., $161,310,866
3. Budweiser Beer, $134,020,888
4. Ford Dealers Association Franchise, $113,583,802
5. American Airlines Passenger Service, $101,205,800
6. Kentucky Fried Chicken Food Service, $100,523,154
7. American Express Credit Card Services, $98,713,730
8. AT & T, Co. General Promotion, $93,913,900
9. Wendy's Restaurants, $86,836,432
10. Red Lobster Restaurants, $85,399,700

*Where'd you hear that?*
Marketing & Media Decisions, Top 200 Brands. Based on 1988 total media investments.

**World's largest advertisers, excluding U.S. advertising**

1. Unilever NV/PLC, with $1,207,509 thousand
2. Procter & Gamble Co., $932,724
3. Nestle SA, $600,586
4. Renault SA, $370,056
5. Matsushita Electric Industrial Co., $365,252
6. Fiat SpA, $354,568
7. Mars Inc., $352,983
8. Kao Corp., $344,233
9. Nissan Motor Co., $333,215
10. Toyota Motor Co., $322,598

*Where'd you hear that?*
Advertising Age, Global Marketing & Media. Based on 1988 advertising expenditures outside the U.S., in thousands of U.S. dollars.

## *World's top 10 advertising markets*

1. United States, with $75.8 billion
2. Japan, $28.0
3. United Kingdom, $12.1
4. West Germany, $9.5
5. France, $6.9
6. Italy, $5.1
6. Canada, $5.1
8. Spain, $4.6
9. Australia, $3.1
10. Netherlands, $2.6

*Where'd you hear that?*
Financial Times. Based on 1988 advertising spending, in billions of U.S. dollars.

# MASS APPEAL

# MASS APPEAL

### Biggest agency mega groups

1. WPP Group PLC (London), with $2,404 million
2. Saatchi & Saatchi PLC (London), $2,300
3. Interpublic Group of Cos. Inc. (New York), $1,355
4. Omnicom Group (New York), $1,210
5. FCB Publicis (Chicago/Paris), $689
6. Eurocom (Paris), $507
7. WCRS Group PLC (London), $280
8. Lowe Group PLC (London), $230
9. BJK & E (New York), $201
10. Lopex PLC (London), $161
11. BDDP Group (Paris), $119
12. GGK Holding AG (Basel), $82
13. Gold Greenlees Trott (London), $67

*Where'd you hear that?*
Advertising Age, Agency Income Report. Based on 1989 worldwide gross income, in millions of dollars.

### Top agencies worldwide

1. Dentsu Inc. (Tokyo), with $1,316.4 million
2. Saatchi & Saatchi Advertising Worldwide (New York), $890.0
3. Young & Rubicam (New York), $865.4
4. Backer Spielvogel Bates Worldwide (New York), $759.8
5. McCann-Erickson Worldwide (New York), $715.5
6. Ogilvy & Mather Worldwide (New York), $699.7
7. BBDO Worldwide (New York), $656.6
8. J. Walter Thompson Co. (New York), $626.4
9. Lintas:Worldwide (New York), $593.3
10. Hakuhodo Inc. (Tokyo), $585.5
11. DDB Needham Worldwide Inc. (New York), $552.9
12. Foote, Cone & Belding Communications Inc. (Chicago), $510.9
13. Grey Advertising Inc. (New York), $498.9
14. Leo Burnett Co. (Chicago), $483.8
15. D'Arcy Masius Benton & Bowles Inc. (New York), $417.5

*Where'd you hear that?*
Advertising Age, Agency Income Report. Based on 1989 worldwide gross income, in millions of dollars.

### World's largest advertising holding companies

1. WPP Group PLC, London, with $16,052,000 thousand
2. Saatchi & Saatchi Co. PLC, London, $11,193,123
3. Dentsu Inc., Tokyo, $9,431,184
4. Interpublic Group of Cos. Inc., New York, $9,035,055
5. Omnicom, New York, $8,645,433
6. Young & Rubicam Inc, New York, $6,565,000
7. FCB-Publicis, Chicago, $4,599,000
8. D'Arcy Masius Benton & Bowles Inc., New York, $3,803,108
9. Grey Advertising Inc., New York, $3,682,900
10. Leo Burnett Co., Chicago, $3,245,464

# MASS APPEAL

*Where'd you hear that?*
Adweek, Eastern edition, Regional Agency Report Card. Based on 1989 worldwide billings, in thousands of dollars.

## World's largest advertising agencies

1. Saatchi & Saatchi Advertising, New York, with $5,176,351 thousand
2. McCann-Erickson, New York, $4,632,105
3. J. Walter Thompson Co., New York, $4,407,500
4. Ogilvy & Mather Worldwide, New York, $4,167,752
5. Backer Spielvogel Bates Worldwide, New York, $4,166,504
6. Young & Rubicam, New York, $4,137,000
7. FCB-Publicis, Chicago, $4,122,000
8. Lintas:Worldwide, New York, $3,795,662
9. D'Arcy Masius Benton & Bowles Inc., New York, $3,408,656
10. Leo Burnett Co., Chicago, $3,245,464

*Where'd you hear that?*
Adweek, Eastern edition, Regional Agency Report Card. Based on 1989 worldwide billings, in thousands of dollars.

## Largest advertisers in Argentina

1. Philip Morris Cos., with $25,091 thousand
2. Aurora SAICIF, $17,423
3. BAT Industries PLC, $16,420
4. Mastellone Hermanos, $14,302
5. Unilever NV/PLC, $12,092
6. Sancor Coop, $10,046
7. Bagley & Cia, $7,900
8. Renault SA, $7,208
9. S. C. Johnson & Son, $7,091
10. Molinos Rio de la Plata, $7,006

*Where'd you hear that?*
Advertising Age, Global Marketing & Media. Based on 1988 ad spending, in thousands of dollars. Top advertisers need not be domestic companies.

## Biggest agencies in Argentina

1. J. Walter Thompson Argentina (Buenos Aires), with $18,933 thousand
2. Lautrec/Saatchi & Saatchi (Buenos Aires), $12,862
3. Funes, Straschnoy, Dreyfuss Y & R (Buenos Aires), $12,213
4. Colonnese:Lintas (Buenos Aires), $11,701
5. Graffiti DMB & B (Buenos Aires), $11,340
6. McCann-Erickson (Buenos Aires), $9,245
7. Ortiz, Scopesi y Cia (Buenos Aires, $8,686
8. Pragma/FCB Publicidade (Buenos Aires), $7,425
9. Leo Burnett Co. (Buenos Aires), $6,313
10. Fontanarrosa, Capurro & Asociados (Capital Federal), $4,947

*Where'd you hear that?*
Advertising Age, Agency Income Report. Based on 1989 gross income, in thousands of U.S. dollars.

# MASS APPEAL

### Largest advertisers in Australia

1. Coles Meyer, with $80,107 thousand
2. Unilever NV/PLC, $41,592
3. Amatil Ltd., $24,915
4. Mars Inc., $23,833
5. Australian Government, $21,987
6. Nestle SA, $18,365
7. PepsiCo, $17,825
8. News Corp., $17,739
9. Bond Corp. Holdings, $17,229
10. Cadbury Schweppes PLC, $16,959

*Where'd you hear that?*
Advertising Age, Global Marketing & Media. Based on 1988 ad spending, in thousands of dollars. Top advertisers need not be domestic companies.

### Biggest agencies in Australia

1. George Patterson Pty. (Sydney), with $76,883 thousand
2. Clemenger/BBDO (Melbourne), $52,011
3. Chiat/Day/Mojo (Sydney), $32,157
4. Young & Rubicam (Sydney), $30,401
5. HDM Mattingly (Melbourne), $29,695
6. DDB Needham (Sydney), $29,164
7. Neville Jeffress Advertising (Sydney), $20,781
8. McCann-Erickson (Sydney), $20,117
9. DMB & B (Sydney), $18,553
10. Saatchi & Saatchi Advertising (Sydney), $17,334

*Where'd you hear that?*
Advertising Age, Agency Income Report. Based on 1989 gross income, in thousands of U.S. dollars.

### Largest advertisers in Austria

1. Unilever NV/PLC, with $33,118 thousand
2. Billa Konzern, $12,183
3. Henkel, $11,107
4. Procter & Gamble Co., $10,716
5. Mars Inc., $10,537
6. Raiffeisenverband, $10,423
7. Konsum Oesterreich, $9,958
8. Jacobs Suchard, $8,426
9. Spar Warenhandels AG, $8,418
10. Porsche, $8,304

*Where'd you hear that?*
Advertising Age, Global Marketing & Media. Based on 1988 ad spending, in thousands of dollars. Top advertisers need not be domestic companies.

### Biggest agencies in Austria

1. GGK Vienna/Salzburg (Vienna/Salzburg), with $8,386 thousand
2. Demner & Merlicek (Vienna), $8,016
3. Lintas:Austria (Vienna/Salzburg), $7,611
4. Werbeagentur Wirz (Vienna), $7,404
5. Ogilvy & Mather (Vienna), $5,811
6. Saatchi & Saatchi Advertising (Vienna), $5,213
7. McCann-Erickson (Vienna), $4,876
8. HDM Dorland (Vienna), $4,261
9. Grey Austria (Vienna), $4,163

10. Dr. Puttner & Ted Bates (Vienna), $4,049

*Where'd you hear that?*
Advertising Age, Agency Income Report. Based on 1989 gross income, in thousands of U.S. dollars.

## Largest advertisers in Bahrain

1. Philip Morris Cos., with $201 thousand
2. Gulf Air, $173
3. Procter & Gamble Co., $147
4. Bank of Bahrain & Kuwait, $94
5. Rothmans International, $81
6. Anchor Powder Milk, $75
7. Gulf Hotel, $74
8. Unilever NV/PLC, $73

*Where'd you hear that?*
Advertising Age, Global Marketing & Media. Based on 1988 advertising spending, in thousands of U.S. dollars. Top advertisers need not be domestic companies.

## Biggest agencies in Bahrain

1. Fortune Promoseven (Manama), with $9,414 thousand
2. Radius Advertising (Manama), $1,242
3. Madco Bahrain (Manama), $945

*Where'd you hear that?*
Advertising Age, Agency Income Report. Based on 1989 gross income, in thousands of U.S. dollars.

## Largest advertisers in Belgium and Luxembourg

1. Procter & Gamble Co., with $14,295 thousand
2. GIB, $13,882
3. Mars Inc., $13,195
4. L'Oreal SA, $12,920
5. Henkel, $12,371
5. Gervais Danone, $12,371
7. Belgian Government, $12,096
8. Nestle SA, $11,683
9. Ford Motor Co., $10,996
9. Tabacofina, $10,996

*Where'd you hear that?*
Advertising Age, Global Marketing & Media. Based on 1988 ad spending, in thousands of dollars. Top advertisers need not be domestic companies.

## Biggest agencies in Belgium

1. McCann-Erickson Belgium (Brussels), with $15,232 thousand
2. BSB Brussels (Brussels), $14,702
3. HHD Ogilvy & Mather (Brussels), $13,466
4. DMB & B (Brussels), $11,984
5. HDM Belgium (Brussels), $9,003
6. Lintas:Brussels (Brussels), $8,460
7. Young & Rubicam Belgium (Brussels), $7,473
8. J. Walter Thompson Co. (Brussels), $6,949
9. Lowe Troost (Brussels), $6,913
10. Publicis.FCB (Brussels), $6,761

*Where'd you hear that?*
Advertising Age, Agency Income Report. Based on 1989 gross income, in thousands of U.S. dollars.

## Largest advertisers in Brazil

1. Nestle SA, $29,013 thousand
2. Unilever NV/PLC, $27,622

# MASS APPEAL

# MASS APPEAL

3. Grupo Fenicia, $18,396
4. Pao de Acucar, $17,406
5. Cx. Economica Federal, $15,672
6. Manufatura Brinquedo Estrela, $14,990
7. Philips NV, $14,504
8. Whirlpool, $13,085
9. Sao Paulo Alpargatas, $12,973
10. Mappin-Casa Anglo Br, $12,473

*Where'd you hear that?*
Advertising Age, Global Marketing & Media. Based on 1988 ad spending, in thousands of dollars. Top advertisers need not be domestic companies.

## Biggest agencies in Brazil

1. MPM Propaganda (Sao Paulo), with $83,876 thousand
2. Alcantara Machado, Periscinoto/BBDO (Sao Paulo), $37,969
3. Duailibi, Petit, Zaragoza (Sau Paulo), $34,616
4. Standard Ogilvy & Mather (Sao Paulo), $31,200
5. Lintas:Brazil (Sao Paulo), $25,521
6. McCann-Erickson Brazil (Sao Paulo), $25,233
7. Norton Publicidade (Sao Paulo), $24,202
8. Salles/Inter-Americana (Sao Paulo), $21,986
9. J. Walter Thompson Publicidade (Sao Paulo), $16,880
10. Young & Rubicam do Brasil (Sao Paulo), $12,146

*Where'd you hear that?*
Advertising Age, Agency Income Report. Based on 1989 gross income, in thousands of U.S. dollars.

## Largest advertisers in Canada

1. Government of Canada, with $73,009 thousand
2. Procter & Gamble Co., $46,533
3. General Motors Corp., $41,720
4. Gulf & Western Inc., $35,301
5. John Labatt, $33,697
5. RJR Nabisco, $33,697
7. Molson Cos., $32,894
8. Thomson Group, $32,092
8. Philip Morris Cos., $32,092
10. Cineplex, $30,487

*Where'd you hear that?*
Advertising Age, Global Marketing & Media. Based on 1988 ad spending, in thousands of dollars. Top advertisers need not be domestic companies.

## Biggest agencies in Canada

1. McCann-Erickson (Toronto), with $29,132 thousand
2. Cossette Communications-Marketing (Quebec City), $28,256
3. MacLaren:Lintas Inc. (Toronto), $28,226
4. Young & Rubicam (Toronto), $24,671
5. Ogilvy & Mather (Toronto), $22,974
6. McKim Advertising (Toronto), $22,648
7. J. Walter Thompson Co. (Toronto), $21,896
8. Grey Canada (Toronto), $17,957
9. Baker Lovick Ltd. (Toronto), $17,745
10. FCB/Ronalds-Reynolds (Toronto), $17,134

# MASS APPEAL

*Where'd you hear that?*
Advertising Age, Agency Income Report. Based on 1989 gross income, in thousands of U.S. dollars.

## Largest advertising agencies in Canada

1. MacLaren:Lintas Inc., with $33,321 thousand Canadian
2. Cossette Communications-Marketing, $32,300
3. McKim Advertising Ltd., $29,300
4. Young & Rubicam Ltd., $28,689
5. McCann-Erickson Advertising of Canada, $28,500
6. Ogilvy & Mather (Canada) Ltd., $27,400
7. J. Walter Thompson Co. Ltd., $26,904
8. Vickers & Benson Advertising Ltd., $25,360
9. Baker Lovick Ltd., $24,200
10. Saffer Advertising Inc., $23,504

*Where'd you hear that?*
Financial Post 500. Based on 1989 revenue, in thousands of Canadian dollars.

## Largest advertising agencies in Canada

1. MacLaren:Lintas Inc., with $220 million
2. Cossette Communications-Marketing, $215.4
3. FCB/Ronalds-Reynolds Ltd., $202
4. J. Walter Thompson Co. Ltd., $195
5. Young & Rubicam Ltd., $193.8
6. McCann-Erickson Advertising of Canada Ltd., $190.9
7. McKim Advertising Ltd., $185.3
8. Ogilvy & Mather (Canada) Ltd., $183
9. Saffer Advertising Inc., $180
10. Vickers & Benson Advertising Ltd., $169.1

*Where'd you hear that?*
Marketing (Canada). Based on 1989 billings, in millions of Canadian dollars.

## Largest advertisers in Chile

1. Unilever NV/PLC, with $13,382 thousand
2. Nestle SA, $8,790
3. Cervezarias de Chile Unidas, $5,834
4. Coca-Cola Co., $4,801
5. Corona, $3,608
6. Sociedad Productora de Leche, $3,190
7. Campania Manufacturera de Papeles, $3,132
8. Campania de Tabacos Chilenos, $2,870
9. Reckitt & Colman PLC, $2,718
10. Philips NV, $2,079

*Where'd you hear that?*
Advertising Age, Global Marketing & Media. Based on 1988 ad spending, in thousands of dollars. Top advertisers need not be domestic companies.

## Biggest agencies in Chile

1. J. Walter Thompson Chilena (Santiago), with $3,819 thousand
2. McCann-Erickson (Santiago), $3,658
3. BBDO de Chile (Santiago), $3,144
4. A. M. W. de Publicidad (Santiago), $2,358

# MASS APPEAL

5. Northcote/Ogilvy & Mather (Santiago), $1,768
6. Lintas:Chile (Santiago), $1,723
7. Leo Burnett-Chile (Santiago), $1,481
8. Porta Publicidad (Santiago), $1,317
9. Grey Chile (Santiago), $1,277
10. Israel & De Bianchi (Santiago), $1,171

*Where'd you hear that?*
Advertising Age, Agency Income Report. Based on 1989 gross income, in thousands of U.S. dollars.

## Largest advertisers in France

1. Renault SA, with $128 million
2. Peugeot SA, $107
3. Nestle SA, $82
4. Henkel, $67
5. Procter & Gamble Co., $62
6. France Loto, $59
7. Fiat SpA, $45
7. Colgate-Palmolive Co., $45
9. Ford Motor Co., $44
10. Volkswagen AG, $40

*Where'd you hear that?*
Advertising Age, Global Marketing & Media. Based on 1988 ad spending, in millions of dollars. Top advertisers need not be domestic companies.

## Biggest agencies in France

1. Publicis Conseil (Paris), with $131,200 thousand
2. HDM France (Paris), $109,208
3. RSCG France (Issy-les-Moulineaux), $107,000
4. BDDP (Paris), $79,159
5. Young & Rubicam France (Paris), $56,077
6. Lintas:Paris (Paris), $42,582
7. DDB Needham (Paris), $37,455
8. Ogilvy & Mather France (Paris), $34,718
9. Saatchi & Saatchi Advertising (Paris), $33,651
10. McCann-Erickson France (Paris), $32,009

*Where'd you hear that?*
Advertising Age, Agency Income Report. Based on 1989 gross income, in thousands of U.S. dollars.

## Largest advertisers in West Germany

1. Procter & Gamble Co., with $172 million
2. Unilever NV/PLC, $151
3. C & A NV, $137
4. Nestle SA, $107
5. Henkel, $105
6. Mars Inc., $91
7. Volkswagen AG, $84
8. General Motors Corp., $78
9. Jacobs Suchard, $77
10. Bundesministerium Fuer Post, $76

*Where'd you hear that?*
Advertising Age, Global Marketing & Media. Based on 1988 ad spending, in millions of dollars. Top advertisers need not be domestic companies.

## Biggest agencies in West Germany

1. Lintas:Germany (Hamburg), with $52,322 thousand
2. Ogilvy & Mather Germany (Frankfurt), $46,200
3. BBDO Group Germany (Duesseldorf), $46,062
4. McCann-Erickson Germany (Frankfurt), $44,552
5. Young & Rubicam (Frankfurt), $39,561

# MASS APPEAL

6. HDM Germany (Duesseldorf), $39,062
7. Grey Gruppe Deutschland (Duesseldorf), $38,008
8. BSB Deutschland Holding (Frankfurt), $31,500
9. DMB & B (Duesseldorf/Frankfurt), $31,215
10. Saatchi & Saatchi Advertising (Frankfurt), $31,082

*Where'd you hear that?*
Advertising Age, Agency Income Report. Based on 1989 gross income, in thousands of U.S. dollars.

## Largest advertisers in Great Britain

1. Unilever NV/PLC, with $209 million
2. Procter & Gamble Co., $137
3. British Government, $135
4. Mars Inc., $130
5. Nestle SA, $127
6. British Telecom, $83
7. Kingfisher, $82
8. Electricity Council, $76
9. Kellogg Co., $73
10. General Motors Corp., $59

*Where'd you hear that?*
Advertising Age, Global Marketing & Media. Based on 1988 ad spending, in millions of dollars. Top advertisers need not be domestic companies.

## Biggest spenders on advertising in Great Britain

1. Unilever, with £81,356 thousand
2. Procter & Gamble, £71,422
3. Kellogg Co., £48,353
4. Kingfisher, £47,974
5. Mars, £46,009
6. Water Authorities, £38,738
7. News International, £36,531
8. Nestle, £31,405
9. Rover Group, £31,147
10. British Telecom, £30,442

*Where'd you hear that?*
Marketing, Top 500 Brands. Based on 1989 billings, in thousands of British pounds sterling.

## British companies that spent the most on press advertising

1. Currys, with £13,706 thousand
2. Benson & Hedges Special Kingsize, £13,617
3. B & Q, £13,041
4. Sky, £12,940
5. MFI/Hygena, £12,494
6. Dixons, £11,718
7. Woolworths, £11,635
8. Water Share Offer, £10,840
9. Texas Homecare, £10,517
10. Tesco, £10,193

*Where'd you hear that?*
Marketing, Top 500 Brands. Based on 1989 press expenditures, in thousands of British pounds.

## Top 10 brands using TV advertising in Great Britain

1. McDonald's, with £14,028 thousand
2. Water Sewage Businesses, £12,019
3. Water Share Offer, £11,633
4. BT Call Stimulation, £10,944
5. Woolworths, £9,486
6. Ariel Automatic Powder, £8,978
7. Yellow Pages, £8,909
8. Carlsberg Pilsner Lager, £8,485
9. NDC/MMB Milk, £8,063
10. Maxwell House, £7,847

# MASS APPEAL

*Where'd you hear that?*
Marketing, Top 500 Brands. Based on 1989 TV ad expenditures, in thousands of British pounds.

## Biggest agencies in Great Britain

1. Saatchi & Saatchi Advertising (London), with $156,347 thousand
2. Ogilvy Group (London), $90,451
3. J. Walter Thompson Co. (London), $84,792
4. Young & Rubicam Holdings (London), $82,527
5. Grey Communications Group (London), $81,072
6. BSB Dorland (London), $79,575
7. DMB & B (London), $66,126
8. McCann-Erickson U.K. (London), $60,033
9. BMP DDB Needham (London), $53,050
10. Lowe Howard-Spink (London), $43,018

*Where'd you hear that?*
Advertising Age, Agency Income Report. Based on 1989 gross income, in thousands of U.S. dollars.

## Largest ad agencies in Great Britain

1. Saatchi & Saatchi, with £137,573 thousand
2. J. Walter Thompson Co., £134,620
3. DMB & B, £132,466
4. BSB Dorland, £114,555
5. Ogilvy & Mather, £96,010
6. Lowe Howard-Spink, £73,580
7. Collett Dickenson Pearce, £71,740
8. Young & Rubicam, £65,663
9. Leo Burnett Co., £64,810
10. BMP DDB Needham, £58,563

*Where'd you hear that?*
Marketing, Top 500 Brands. Based on 1989 billings, in thousands of British pounds sterling.

## Largest advertisers in Hong Kong

1. Philip Morris Cos., with $13,974 thousand
2. BAT Industries PLC, $8,024
3. RJR Nabisco, $6,205
4. Matsushita Electric Industrial Co., $5,316
5. Hutchinson Whampoa, $5,205
6. Hong Tai Travel, $5,123
7. Japan Tobacco International, $4,967
8. McDonald's Corp., $4,871
9. Sunflower Travel, $4,822
10. Hattori Corp., $4,344

*Where'd you hear that?*
Advertising Age, Global Marketing & Media. Based on 1988 ad spending, in thousands of dollars. Top advertisers need not be domestic companies.

## Biggest agencies in Hong Kong

1. Ogilvy & Mather (Hong Kong), with $12,402 thousand
2. Leo Burnett Ltd. (Hong Kong), $8,706
3. J. Walter Thompson Co. (Hong Kong), $7,340
4. HDM Hong Kong (Hong Kong), $6,859
5. Backer Spielvogel Bates (Hong Kong), $6,511
6. Ball Partnership (Hong Kong), $6,022
7. BBDO Hong Kong (Hong Kong), $4,631
8. DDB Needham (Hong Kong), $4,292

9. McCann-Erickson (Hong Kong), $4,249
10. People & Grey (Hong Kong), $3,673

*Where'd you hear that?*
Advertising Age, Agency Income Report. Based on 1989 gross income, in thousands of U.S. dollars.

**Largest advertisers in Israel**

1. Bank Leumi, with $4,100 thousand
2. Bank Hapoalim, $3,600
3. Mifal Hapayis, $3,100
4. Osem Foods, $3,000
5. Elite, $2,900
6. Israel Discount Bank, $2,600
7. Hamashbir, $2,500
8. First International Bank, $2,400
9. Tnuva Dairy, $2,200
10. Coca-Cola Co., $2,000

*Where'd you hear that?*
Advertising Age, Global Marketing & Media. Based on 1988 advertising spending, in thousands of U.S. dollars. Top advertiser is not necessarily a domestic one.

**Biggest agencies in Israel**

1. Ariely Communications (Tel Aviv), with $5,537 thousand
2. Gitam Image (Ramat-Gan), $3,250
3. Fogel Levin (Tel Aviv), $1,972
4. Pelled Advertising (Tel Aviv), $1,700
5. Bing Linial Advertising (Tel Aviv), $1,479

*Where'd you hear that?*
Advertising Age, Agency Income Report. Based on 1989 gross income, in thousands of U.S. dollars.

**Largest advertisers in Italy**

1. Unilever NV/PLC, with $373 million
2. Procter & Gamble Co., $293
3. Ferrero SpA, $133
4. Fiat SpA, $121
5. Barilla SpA, $106
6. Colgate-Palmolive Co., $95
7. Henkel, $85
8. Philips NV, $83
9. Renault SA, $79
9. Saipo, $79

*Where'd you hear that?*
Advertising Age, Global Marketing & Media. Based on 1988 ad spending, in millions of dollars. Top advertisers need not be domestic companies.

**Biggest agencies in Italy**

1. Publicis.FCB/Mac (Milan), with $54,550 thousand
2. Gruppo Armando Testa (Turin/Milan/Rome), $50,232
3. Young & Rubicam Italia (Milan), $46,980
4. McCann-Erickson Italiana (Milan), $38,090
5. J. Walter Thompson Italia (Milan), $28,756
6. Italia/BBDO (Milan), $27,664
7. EWDB Italia (Milan), $24,424
8. Saatchi & Saatchi Advertising (Rome), $24,170
9. DMB & B (Milan/Rome), $21,130
10. Milano & Grey (Milan), $20,206

*Where'd you hear that?*
Advertising Age, Agency Income Report. Based on 1989 gross income, in thousands of U.S. dollars.

# MASS APPEAL

# MASS APPEAL

### Largest advertisers in Japan

1. Kao Corp., with $338 million
2. Matsushita Electric Industrial Co., $334
3. Hitachi Ltd., $257
4. Mitsubishi Motors Corp., $249
5. Nissan Motor Co., $248
6. NEC Corp., $231
7. Honda Motor Co. Ltd., $229
8. Toyota Motor Co., $220
9. Suntory, $211
10. Toshiba Corp., $199

*Where'd you hear that?*
Advertising Age, Global Marketing & Media. Based on 1988 ad spending, in millions of dollars. Top advertisers need not be domestic companies.

### Biggest agencies in Japan

1. Dentsu Inc. (Tokyo), with $1,314,400 thousand
2. Hakuhodo Inc. (Tokyo), $585,457
3. Tokyu Agency (Tokyo), $156,222
4. Dai-Ichi Kikaku (Tokyo), $155,795
5. Daiko Advertising (Osaka), $152,064
6. Asatsu (Tokyo), $113,879
7. Yomiko Advertising (Tokyo), $100,302
8. I & S Corp. (Tokyo), $94,734
9. McCann-Erickson Hakuhodo Japan (Tokyo), $92,712
10. Asahi Advertising (Tokyo), $82,888

*Where'd you hear that?*
Advertising Age, Agency Income Report. Based on 1989 gross income, in thousands of U.S. dollars.

### Largest advertisers in South Korea

1. Pacific Chemical, with $29,346 thousand
2. Lucky, $28,408
3. Samsung Electronics, $25,728
4. GoldStar Electronics, $24,924
5. Cheil Sugar, $16,616
6. Lotte Confectionary, $14,338
7. Daewong Pharmaceutical, $13,802
8. Nhongshim, $13,668
9. HaiTai Confectionary, $12,998
9. Dongguh Foods, $12,998

*Where'd you hear that?*
Advertising Age, Global Marketing & Media. Based on 1988 advertising spending, in thousands of U.S. dollars. Top advertiser is not necessarily a domestic one.

### Biggest agencies in South Korea

1. Cheil Communications (Seoul), with $64,018 thousand
2. Oricom (Seoul), $45,112
3. LG Ad (Seoul), $24,102
4. Korad Ogilvy & Mather (Seoul), $18,794
5. Daehong Ad (Seoul), $16,185
6. Diamond Ad (Seoul), $12,456
7. Seoul Advertising (Seoul), $7,120
8. Nara Communications (Seoul), $3,944
9. Eastern Advertising Co. (Seoul), $1,366

*Where'd you hear that?*
Advertising Age, Agency Income Report. Based on 1989 gross income, in thousands of U.S. dollars.

## Largest advertisers in Kuwait

1. Philip Morris Cos., with $1,935 thousand
2. NBK, $714
3. CBK, $712
4. Rothmans International, $584
5. Gulf Bank, $465
6. Superlights, $412
7. Mild Seven, $367
8. GoldStar Electronics, $351
9. BKME, $350

*Where'd you hear that?*
Advertising Age, Global Marketing & Media. Based on 1988 advertising spending, in thousands of U.S. dollars. Top advertiser is not necessarily a domestic one.

## Biggest agencies in Kuwait

1. Madco Kuwait (Al Kuwait), with $365 thousand
2. Hiba (Al Kuwait), $227

*Where'd you hear that?*
Advertising Age, Agency Income Report. Based on 1989 gross income, in thousands of U.S. dollars.

## Largest advertisers in Malaysia

1. BAT Industries PLC, with $12,321 thousand
2. Rothmans International, $11,402
3. Nupro, $7,722
4. RJR Nabisco, $6,091
5. Unilever NV/PLC, $5,063
6. Colgate-Palmolive Co., $4,587
7. Malaysian Breweries/F&N, $1,871
8. Philip Morris Cos., $1,859
9. Royal Dutch Shell, $1,667
10. Peter Stuyvesant, $1,531

*Where'd you hear that?*
Advertising Age, Global Marketing & Media. Based on 1988 ad spending, in thousands of dollars. Top advertisers need not be domestic companies.

## Biggest agencies in Malaysia

1. Ogilvy & Mather (Petaling Jaya), with $3,846 thousand
2. McCann-Erickson Malaysia (Kuala Lumpur), $3,301
3. Leo Burnett Co. (Kuala Lumpur), $2,730
4. BSB (Malaysia) (Kuala Lumpur $2,719
5. PTM Thompson Advertising (Kuala Lumpur), $2,370
6. HDM (Kuala Lumpur), with $2,225 thousand
7. Lintas:Malaysia (Kuala Lumpur), $1,870
8. AP-Foote, Cone & Belding (Kuala Lumpur), $1,866
9. Wings/BBDO (Petaling Jaya), $1,415
10. Bozell (Petaling Jaya), $1,224

*Where'd you hear that?*
Advertising Age, Agency Income Report. Based on 1989 gross income, in thousands of U.S. dollars.

## Largest advertisers in Mexico

1. Direccion Corporativa Impulsora, with $35,819 thousand
2. Procter & Gamble Co., $33,863
3. Industrias Vitivinicolas Domecq, $28,144
4. PepsiCo, $25,736
5. Colgate-Palmolive Co., $22,876
6. Unilever NV/PLC, $21,973
7. Bacardi Corp., $21,672
8. Kimberly-Clark Corp., $18,211

# MASS APPEAL

# MASS APPEAL

9. Nestle SA, $17,910
10. Kellogg Co., $13,696

*Where'd you hear that?*
Advertising Age, Global Marketing & Media. Based on 1988 advertising spending, in thousands of U.S. dollars. Top advertisers need not be domestic companies.

## Biggest agencies in Mexico

1. McCann-Erickson (Mexico City), with $8,203 thousand
2. Publicidad Ferrer (Mexico City), $8,080
3. J. Walter Thompson de Mexico (Mexico City), $5,651
4. Publicidad Augusto Elias (Mexico City), $5,178
5. Leo Burnett Co. (Mexico City), $4,961
6. Panamericana Ogilvy & Mather (Mexico City), $4,861
7. Bozell S. A. (Mexico City), $4,750
8. Garcia Patto (Mexico City), $4,061
9. DMB & B (Mexico City), $3,933
10. Publicidade Oscar Leal (Mexico City), $3,744

*Where'd you hear that?*
Advertising Age, Agency Income Report. Based on 1989 gross income, in thousands of U.S. dollars.

## Largest advertisers in the Netherlands

1. Unilever NV/PLC, with $15,354 thousand
2. Procter & Gamble Co., $11,030
3. Mars Inc., $10,414
4. Rijksvoorlichtings, $10,190
5. PTT, $10,114
6. Heineken Netherlands, $8,891
7. Philips NV, $8,333
8. Sara Lee Corp., $7,921
9. Postbank, $6,500
10. Nestle SA, $6,461

*Where'd you hear that?*
Advertising Age, Global Marketing & Media. Based on 1988 advertising spending, in thousands of U.S. dollars. Top advertiser is not necessarily a domestic one. Also notes 1987 spending and currency conversion rates.

## Biggest agencies in the Netherlands

1. FHV/BBDO Group (Amstelveen), with $32,076 thousand
2. PMSvW/Young & Rubicam (Amsterdam), $23,396
3. Ogilvy & Mather (Amsterdam), $18,604
4. Lintas:Netherlands (Amsterdam), $17,816
5. PPGH/JWT Group (Amsterdam), $17,650
6. Prad Alliance (Amsterdam/Eindhoven), $13,451
7. ARA/BDDP (Rotterdam), $13,215
8. Saatchi & Saatchi Advertising (Amsterdam), $12,880
9. Publicis FCB Holland (Amsterdam/Eindhoven), $10,619
10. TBWA Groep (Amstelveen), $10,536

*Where'd you hear that?*
Advertising Age, Agency Income Report. Based on 1989 gross income, in thousands of U.S. dollars.

## Largest advertisers in New Zealand

1. Lion Nathan Group, with $15,249 thousand
2. Unilever NV/PLC, $9,267
3. Foodstuffs Co-op, $8,666
3. FTC Farmers, $8,666
5. Goodman Fielder Wattie, $8,658
6. Fletcher Challenge, $6,739
7. Cadbury Schweppes PLC, $6,486
8. RJR Nabisco, $6,055
9. Nissan Motor Co., $5,008
10. Colgate-Palmolive Co., $4,983

*Where'd you hear that?*
Advertising Age, Global Marketing & Media. Based on 1988 ad spending, in thousands of dollars. Top advertisers need not be domestic companies.

## Biggest agencies in New Zealand

1. Clemenger/BBDO New Zealand (Auckland) with $16,516 thousand
2. Saatchi & Saatchi Advertising (Wellington), $14,036
3. J. Walter Thompson New Zealand (Wellington), $5,030
4. Ogilvy & Mather (Wellington), $4,971
5. DDB Needham (Auckland), $4,654
6. Ted Bates New Zealand (Wellington), $4,215
7. DMB & B (Auckland), $3,631
8. Lintas:New Zealand (Auckland), $3,094
9. Young & Rubicam (Auckland), $2,728
10. Dobbs-Wiggins McCann-Erickson (Auckland), $2,692

*Where'd you hear that?*
Advertising Age, Agency Income Report. Based on 1989 gross income, in thousands of U.S. dollars.

## Largest advertisers in Norway

1. Norwegian Dairy Association, with $5,852 thousand
2. Toyota Motor Co., $5,713
3. Denofa & Lilleborg Fabr., $5,436
4. State Information Service, $5,267
5. General Motors Corp., $5,005
6. Volkswagen AG, $4,805
7. Ford Motor Co., $4,789
8. Mitsubishi, $3,742
9. Ernst G. Mortensens Forlag AS, $3,711
10. TBK AS, $3,496

*Where'd you hear that?*
Advertising Age, Global Marketing & Media. Based on 1988 advertising spending, in thousands of U.S. dollars. Top advertiser is not necessarily a domestic one. Also notes 1987 spending and currency conversion rates.

## Biggest agencies in Norway

1. BSB Batesgruppen Norway (Oslo), with $21,095 thousand
2. Scaneco-Young & Rubicam (Oslo), $12,508
3. DMB & B Lund & Lommer (Oslo), $5,444
4. Myres/Lintas (Oslo), $5,062
5. Art & Copy.FCB Group (Oslo), $4,990
6. Ogilvy & Mather (Oslo), $4,513
7. Nordskar & Thorkildsen Leo Burnett (Olso), $4,101
8. Jenssen & Borkenhagen/BBDO (Oslo), $3,119

# MASS APPEAL

# MASS APPEAL

9. ScanPartner Norge (Oslo), $2,975
10. Reklamens Hus/McCann (Oslo), $2,743

*Where'd you hear that?*
Advertising Age, Agency Income Report. Based on 1989 gross income, in thousands of U.S. dollars.

## Largest advertisers in the Philippines

1. San Miguel Corp., with $9,255 thousand
2. Nestle SA, $8,913
3. Philippine Refining Co., $6,582
4. Colgate-Palmolive Co., $5,144
5. Procter & Gamble Co., $4,418
6. United Laboratories, $4,093
7. Coca-Cola Co., $3,745
8. Fortune Tobacco Corp., $3,393
9. LaSuerte Cigar & Cigarette, $2,943
10. Asia Brewery, $2,582

*Where'd you hear that?*
Advertising Age, Global Marketing & Media. Based on 1988 advertising spending, in thousands of U.S. dollars. Top advertiser is not necessarily a domestic one. Also notes 1987 spending and currency conversion rates.

## Biggest agencies in the Philippines

1. McCann-Erickson (Manila), with $3,869 thousand
2. J. Walter Thompson Co. (Manila), $3,111
3. Ace/Saatchi & Saatchi (Manila), $2,683
4. Basic/FCB (Manila), $2,533
5. Amacon (Manila), $2,513
6. Hemisphere-Leo Burnett Co. (Manila), $1,659
7. HDM-Alcantara (Manila), $1,647
8. Lintas:Manila (Manila), $1,585
9. PAC/BBDO Worldwide (Manila), $1,401
10. Olbes, Ogilvy & Mather (Manila), $1,248

*Where'd you hear that?*
Advertising Age, Agency Income Report. Based on 1989 gross income, in thousands of U.S. dollars.

## Largest advertisers in Saudi Arabia

1. Philip Morris Cos., with $1,239 thousand
2. Saudia, $1,126
3. Procter & Gamble Co., $996
4. PepsiCo, $817
5. Toyota Motor Co., $761
6. Afia, $668
7. CPC International, $633
8. Arrojol, $601
9. Nido, $559
10. Sony Corp., $552

*Where'd you hear that?*
Advertising Age, Global Marketing & Media. Based on 1988 advertising spending, in thousands of U.S. dollars. Top advertiser is not necessarily a domestic one. Also notes 1987 spending and currency conversion rates.

## Biggest agencies in Saudi Arabia

1. Saatchi & Saatchi Advertising (Jeddah), with $2,100 thousand
2. Targets Advertising (Jeddah), $1,592
3. Madco Saudi Arabia (Jeddah), $810
4. Orientations (Jeddah), $750
5. DMB & B (Jeddah), $46

*Where'd you hear that?*
Advertising Age, Agency Income Report. Based on 1989 gross income, in thousands of U.S. dollars.

## Largest advertisers in Singapore

1. McDonald's Corp., with $2,078 thousand
2. Yaohan, $2,068
3. PepsiCo, $1,604
4. Singapore Airlines, $1,209
5. American Express Co., $1,190
6. Metro, $1,101
7. Tiger Beer, $1,091
8. Courts Furniture, $1,002
9. Family Life campaign, $992
10. NTUC Fairprice, $908

*Where'd you hear that?*
Advertising Age, Global Marketing & Media. Based on 1988 advertising spending, in thousands of U.S. dollars. Top advertiser is not necessarily a domestic one. Also notes 1987 spending and currency conversion rates.

## Biggest agencies in Singapore

1. Batey Communications (Singapore), with $6,750 thousand
2. Ogilvy & Mather (Singapore), $5,055
3. McCann-Erickson Singapore (Singapore), $3,999
4. Saatchi & Saatchi Advertising (Singapore), $3,073
5. Leo Burnett Ltd. (Singapore), $2,881
6. HDM Singapore (Singapore), $2,877
7. J. Walter Thompson Singapore (Singapore), $2,446
8. Ko Advertising (Singpore), $2,253
9. Lintas:Singapore (Singapore), $1,706
10. Grey Advertising Inc. (Singapore), $1,613

*Where'd you hear that?*
Advertising Age, Agency Income Report. Based on 1989 gross income, in thousands of U.S. dollars.

## Largest advertisers in South Africa

1. Unilever NV/PLC, with $18,750 thousand
2. OK Bazaars, $14,973
3. Pick 'n Pay, $13,425
4. Checkers, $11,332
5. SA Breweries, $8,783
6. Toyota SA, $7,782
7. BAT Industries PLC, $$5,825
8. Volkswagen AG, $5,643
8. Nissan SA, $5,643
10. SmithKline Beecham, $4,733

*Where'd you hear that?*
Advertising Age, Global Marketing & Media. Based on 1988 ad spending, in thousands of dollars. Top advertisers need not be domestic companies.

## Biggest agencies in South Africa

1. Grey Holdings (Johannesburg), with $14,784 thousand
2. Ogilvy & Mather Rightford (Cape Town), $14,124
3. Lindsay Smithers-FCB (Johannesburg), $11,334
4. Young & Rubicam South Africa (Cape Town), $8,574
5. Klerck & McCormac (Johannesburg), $7,682
6. McCann-Erickson DeVilliers (Johannesburg), $6,489
7. Lintas:South Africa (Johannesburg), $6,324

# MASS APPEAL

# MASS APPEAL

8. J. Walter Thompson South Africa (Johannesburg), $4,625
9. Bernstein, Loxton, Golding & Klein (Johannesburg), $2,364
10. Partnership in Advertising (Johannesburg), $1,874

*Where'd you hear that?*
Advertising Age, Agency Income Report. Based on 1989 gross income, in thousands of U.S. dollars.

## Largest advertisers in Spain

1. Peugeot SA, with $87,157 thousand
2. Renault SA, $73,111
3. El Corte Ingles, $57,839
4. Volkswagen AG, $57,479
5. Unilever NV/PLC, $47,846
6. Spanish Ministry of Economy, $47,435
7. Nestle SA, $43,356
8. Grupo Repsol, $39,859
9. Fiat SpA, $34,726
10. Henkel, $31,649

*Where'd you hear that?*
Advertising Age, Global Marketing & Media. Based on 1988 advertising spending, in thousands of U.S. dollars. Top advertiser is not necessarily a domestic one.

## Biggest agencies in Spain

1. Grupo BSB (Madrid), with $37,907 thousand
2. TAPSA/ N W Ayer (Madrid), $27,198
3. McCann-Erickson S. A. Group (Madrid), $26,626
4. BBDO Espana (Barcelona), $25,966
5. Lintas:Spain (Madrid), $24,686
6. J. Walter Thompson Co. (Madrid), $23,240
7. TAPSA Ayer (Madrid), $22,315
8. Bassat Ogilvy & Mather (Madrid), $22,088
9. Young & Rubicam Espana (Madrid), $21,681
10. RCP-Saatchi & Saatchi (Barcelona), $18,375

*Where'd you hear that?*
Advertising Age, Agency Income Report. Based on 1989 gross income, in thousands of U.S. dollars.

## Largest advertisers in Sweden

1. Kooperativa Forbundet, with $76,983 thousand
2. ICA AB, $75,343
3. Ahlens AB, $22,496
4. State Telephone Co., $12,753
5. Hennes & Mauritz AB, $12,654
6. Volvo AB, $12,642
7. Government Information Service, $10,683
8. Philipson Bil AB, $10,523
9. B & W Sormarknad AB, $10,209
10. Volkswagen AG, $9,614

*Where'd you hear that?*
Advertising Age, Global Marketing & Media. Based on 1988 ad spending, in thousands of dollars. Top advertisers need not be domestic companies.

## Biggest agencies in Sweden

1. Young & Rubicam (Stockholm), with $19,879 thousand
2. Swedish Communications (Stockholm),$14,815
3. BSB Sweden (Stockholm), $13,945
4. Intermarco/FCB (Stockholm), $8,453

5. McCann-Erickson Sweden (Stockholm), $7,996
6. HLR & Co./BBDO (Stockholm), $5,189
7. Carlsson & Broman/DDB Needham (Stockholm), $4,338
8. Soren Blanking (Malmo/Stockholm), $4,242
9. Lintas:Sweden (Stockholm), $4,186
10. KREAB (Stockholm), $3,736

*Where'd you hear that?*
Advertising Age, Agency Income Report. Based on 1989 gross income, in thousands of U.S. dollars.

## Largest advertisers in Switzerland

1. Migros, with $46,440 thousand
2. Co-op, $39,519
3. Denner, $17,233
4. Toyota Motor Co., $16,403
5. General Motors Corp., $15,988
6. Ringier/Blick, $14,742
7. Unilever NV/PLC, $14,603
8. Amag (VW & BMW), $12,319
9. Ford Motor Co., $9,897
10. Maus Brothers, $9,551

*Where'd you hear that?*
Advertising Age, Global Marketing & Media. Based on 1988 ad spending, in thousands of dollars. Top advertisers need not be domestic companies.

## Biggest agencies in Switzerland

1. Advico Young & Rubicam (Zurich), with $16,147 thousand
2. GGK (Basel/Zurich), $13,585
3. ASGS/BBDO (Zurich), $10,816
4. Wirz Advertising (Zurich), $10,603
5. HDM Marketing Kommunication (Zurich), $9,782
6. Farner Publicis.FCB (Zurich), $8,758
7. McCann-Erickson Switzerland (Geneva/Zurich), $8,523
8. Lintas:Zurich (Zurich), $5,670
9. Marti, Ogilvy & Mather (Zurich), $5,523
10. Impuls (Zurich), $5,227

*Where'd you hear that?*
Advertising Age, Agency Income Report. Based on 1989 gross income, in thousands of U.S. dollars.

## Largest advertisers in Taiwan

1. President Food Co., with $10,831 thousand
2. Nestle SA, $7,818
3. Matsushita Electric Industrial Co., $6,826
4. Ta Tung Electric, $6,605
5. Kuo Lien Chemical Industry, $5,744
6. Wei Chuan Food Co., $5,497
7. Sampo Electric, $5,453
8. Ko Lin Electric, $4,939
9. Sam Shin Trading, $4,591
10. Kao Corp., $4,451

*Where'd you hear that?*
Advertising Age, Global Marketing & Media. Based on 1988 ad spending, in thousands of dollars. Top advertisers need not be domestic companies.

## Biggest agencies in Taiwan

1. McCann-Erickson (Taiwan) (Taipei), with $6,107 thousand
2. Ogilvy & Mather (Taiwan) (Taipei), $5,174
3. Hwa Wei & Grey (Taipei), $4,618

**MASS APPEAL**

# MASS APPEAL

4. Leo Burnett Co. (Taipei), $3,295
5. Bozell CCAA (Taipei), $3,181
6. Eastern Advertising Co. (Taipei), $3,179
7. J. Walter Thompson Taiwan (Taipei), $3,060
8. Saatchi & Saatchi Gaynor (Taipei), $3,002
9. International Advertising (Taipei), $2,750
10. Regal International (Taipei), $2,694

*Where'd you hear that?*
Advertising Age, Agency Income Report. Based on 1989 gross income, in thousands of U.S. dollars.

## Largest advertisers in Thailand

1. Unilever NV/PLC, with $12,369 thousand
2. Colgate-Palmolive Co., $8,844
3. Osothsapha Co., $7,766
4. Saha Pathanapibul Co., $5,249
5. Nestle SA, $4,447
6. T.C. Pharmaceutical Industrial Co., $3,858
7. Matsushita Electric Industrial Co., $2,883
8. Toyota Motor Co., $2,642
9. Boon Rawd Brewery, $2,451
10. Nissan Motor Co., $2,365

*Where'd you hear that?*
Advertising Age, Global Marketing & Media. Based on 1988 ad spending, in thousands of dollars. Top advertisers need not be domestic companies.

## Biggest agencies in Thailand

1. Lintas:Thailand (Bangkok), with $7,197 thousand
2. Ogilvy & Mather (Bangkok), $5,611
3. Far East Advertising (Bangkok), $4,271
4. Spa Advertising Co. (Bangkok), $3,365
5. Saatchi & Saatchi Advertising (Bangkok), $3,015
6. Leo Burnett Ltd. (Bangkok), $2,818
7. Prakit & FCB (Bangkok), $2,739
8. McCann-Erickson Thailand (Bangkok), $2,167
9. HDM (Bangkok), $2,113
10. J. Walter Thompson Co. (Bangkok), $1,971

*Where'd you hear that?*
Advertising Age, Agency Income Report. Based on 1989 gross income, in thousands of U.S. dollars.

## Largest advertisers in the U.S.

1. McDonald's Restaurants, with $404,951,827
2. Burger King Corp., $161,310,866
3. Budweiser Beer, Anheuser-Bush, Inc., $134,020,888
4. Ford Dealers Association Franchise, Ford Motor Division, $113,583,802
5. American Airlines Passenger Service, American Airlines, Inc., $101,205,800
6. Kentucky Fried Chicken Food Service, PepsiCo Inc., $100,523,154
7. American Express Credit Card Services, American Express Co., $98,713,730
8. AT & T, American Telephone & Telegraph Co., $93,913,900

9. Wendy's Restaurants, Wendy's International Inc., $86,836,432
10. Red Lobster Restaurants, Red Lobster Inns of America, $85,399,700

*Where'd you hear that?*
Marketing & Media Decisions, Top 200 Brands. Based on 1988 total media investments.

## Companies with the highest combined media advertising expenditures

1. Philip Morris Cos., Inc., with $1,081,920.3 thousand
2. General Motors Corp., $959,639.5
3. Procter & Gamble Co., $869,429.3
4. Sears, Roebuck & Co., $525,336.5
5. PepsiCo Inc., $473,042.3
6. Ford Motor Co., $447,266.0
7. Kellogg Co., $428,047.8
8. McDonalds Corp., $425,081.0
9. RJR Nabisco Inc., $407,788.3
10. Unilever NV, $376,462.3

*Where'd you hear that?*
LNA Ad Dollars Summary, Leading National Advertisers. Based on 1989 nine-media total advertising expenditures, in thousands of dollars.

## Largest advertisers in the U.S.

1. Philip Morris Cos., with $2,058.2 million
2. Procter & Gamble Co., $1,506.9
3. General Motors Corp., $1,294.0
4. Sears, Roebuck & Co., $1,045.2
5. RJR Nabisco, $814.5
6. Grand Metropolitan PLC, $773.9
7. Eastman Kodak Co., $735.9
8. McDonald's Corp., $728.3
9. PepsiCo Inc., $712.3
10. Kellogg Co., $683.1

*Where'd you hear that?*
Advertising Age, 100 Leading National Advertisers. Based on 1988 ad spending, in millions of dollars.

## Top 10 association advertisers

1. General Motors Corp. Dealers Association, with $220,320 thousand
2. Ford Auto Dealers Association, $140,116
3. Chrysler Corp. Dealers Association, $113,648
4. American Dairy Association, $82,031
5. Toyota Auto Dealers Association, $67,521
6. Hyundai Group, $38,409
7. Toyo Kogyo Co. Auto Dealers Association, $37,589
8. Honda Dealers Association, $37,096
9. National Live Stock & Meat Board, $36,611
10. Blue Cross & Blue Shield Association, $36,181

*Where'd you hear that?*
Public Relations Journal, Annual Review of Corporate Advertising Expenditures. Based on 9-media advertising total, in thousands of dollars.

## Top U.S. agency brands

1. Leo Burnett Co. (Chicago), with $1,945.3 million
2. J. Walter Thompson Co. (New York), $1,786.0

# MASS APPEAL

# MASS APPEAL

3. Saatchi & Saatchi Advertising (New York), $1,706.3
4. D'Arcy Masius Benton & Bowles Inc. (New York), $1,595.6
5. Foote, Cone & Belding Communications Inc. (Chicago), $1,578.5
6. Young & Rubicam (New York), $1,453.9
7. Grey Advertising Inc. (New York), $1,434.1
8. Ogilvy & Mather Worldwide (New York), $1,419.2
9. DDB Needham Worldwide Inc. (New York), $1,316.5
10. McCann-Erickson Worldwide (New York), $1,299.8
11. BBDO Worldwide (New York), $1,214.9
12. Backer Spielvogel Bates Worldwide (New York), $1,177.8
13. Lintas:Worldwide (New York), $1,070.9
14. Bozell Inc. (New York), $950.4
15. Wells Rich Greene (New York), $883.0

*Where'd you hear that?*
Advertising Age, Agency Income Report. Based on 1989 U.S. brand billings, in millions. The 'brand' chart ranks agencies by pure advertising billings.

## Top U.S. agencies by productivity

1. Admarketing Inc., with 1.89
2. Towne, Silverstein, Rotter, 1.84
3. Tarlow Advertising, 1.48
4. Partners & Shevack, 1.42
5. Messner Vetere Berger Carey Schmetterer, 1.39
6. Ally & Gargano, 1.37
7. Avrett, Free & Ginsberg, 1.26
8. Jordan, McGrath, Case & Taylor, 1.12
9. Devon Direct Marketing & Advertising Inc., 1.08
10. Kern/Mathai Direct Mail Advertising, 1.05
10. Lois/GGK New York, 1.05
12. Slater Hanft Martin, 1.03
12. Wells, Rich, Greene, 1.03
14. Levine, Huntley, Schmidt & Beaver, 1.02
15. Thomas G. Ferguson Associates Inc., 1.01

*Where'd you hear that?*
Advertising Age, Agency Income Report. Based on one million dollars billed per employee.

## Top U.S.-based agencies

1. Young & Rubicam (New York), with $409.5 thousand
2. Saatchi & Saatchi Advertising Worldwide (New York), $395.2
3. BBDO Worldwide (New York), $373.6
4. Backer Spielvogel Bates Worldwide (New York), $310.7
5. Ogilvy & Mather Worldwide (New York), $305.1
6. DDB Needham Worldwide Inc. (New York), $302.9
7. Leo Burnett Co. (Chicago), $288.8
8. Foote, Cone & Belding Communications Inc. (Chicago), $280.5
9. J. Walter Thompson Co. (New York), $266.5
10. Grey Advertising Inc. (New York), $240.7

11. D'Arcy Masius Benton & Bowles Inc. (New York), $232.3
12. Lintas:Worldwide (New York), $224.9
13. McCann-Erickson Worldwide (New York), $209.1
14. Bozell Inc. (New York), $155.4
15. Wells, Rich, Greene (New York), $132.5

*Where'd you hear that?*
Advertising Age, Agency Income Report. Based on 1989 domestic gross income, in thousands.

## Hottest ad agencies

1. Tarlow, with 175.1%
2. Lord Einstein O'Neill & Partners, 140.3%
3. Wieden & Kennedy, 58.1%
4. Kresser Craig, 51.8%
5. Messner Vetere Berger Carey Schmetterer, 46.1%
6. Chiat/Day/Mojo, 28.2%
7. Slater Hanft Martin, 40.0%
8. D'Arcy Masius Benton & Bowles Inc., 16.6%
9. Foote Cone & Belding Communications Inc., 15.3%
10. Wyse Advertising, 32.8%

*Where'd you hear that?*
Adweek, Eastern edition, Agency Report Card. Based on percent increase in billings, 1988-89.

## Largest advertising agencies

1. Young & Rubicam, New York, with $2,026,500
2. Leo Burnett Co., Chicago, $1,945,282
3. Saatchi & Saatchi DFS Advertising, New York, $1,905,300
4. Foote, Cone & Belding Communications Inc., Chicago, $1,790,000
5. J. Walter Thompson Co., New York, $1,660,810
6. D'Arcy Masius Benton & Bowles Inc., New York, $1,660,810
7. DDB Needham, New York, $1,479,000
8. Ogilvy & Mather, New York, $1,445,289
9. Grey Advertising Inc., New York, $1,434,000
10. McCann-Erickson, New York, $1,345,750

*Where'd you hear that?*
Adweek, Eastern edition, Agency Report Card. Based on 1989 total domestic billings.

## Top 10 agencies in network TV

1. Saatchi & Saatchi Advertising Worldwide, with $918.6 million
2. Leo Burnett Co., $855.1
3. Backer Spielvogel Bates Worldwide, $845.7
4. Young & Rubicam, $646.8
5. D'Arcy Masius Benton & Bowles Inc., $645.8
6. Grey Advertising Inc., $532.9
7. Lintas:Worldwide, $532.3
8. Ogilvy & Mather Worldwide, $512.4
9. J. Walter Thompson Co., $507.6
10. BBDO Worldwide, $501.8

*Where'd you hear that?*
Advertising Age, Agency Income Report. Based on 1989 billings for ads in this medium, in millions of dollars.

# MASS APPEAL

# MASS APPEAL

### Top 10 agencies in cable TV

1. Saatchi & Saatchi Advertising Worldwide, with $72.2 million
2. DDB Needham Worldwide Inc., $60.3
3. Foote, Cone & Belding Communications Inc., $60.2
4. Grey Advertising Inc., $47.8
5. D'Arcy Masius Benton & Bowles Inc., $45.6
6. Lintas:Worldwide, $43.9
7. Leo Burnett Co., $38.4
8. Jordan, McGrath, Case & Taylor, $33.1
9. Ogilvy & Mather Worldwide, $32.2
10. Young & Rubicam, $32.0

*Where'd you hear that?*
Advertising Age, Agency Income Report. Based on 1989 billings for ads in this medium, in millions of dollars.

### Top 10 agencies in syndicated TV

1. Leo Burnett Co., with $130.5 million
2. D'Arcy Masius Benton & Bowles Inc., $80.1
3. McCann-Erickson Worldwide, $42.0
4. Jordan, McGrath, Case & Taylor, $41.6
5. Foote, Cone & Belding Communications Inc., $40.0
6. DDB Needham Worldwide Inc., $29.1
7. Wells, Rich, Greene, $27.0
8. Young & Rubicam, $21.6
9. Towne, Silverstein, Rotter, $10.0
10. Burrell Communications Group, $7.0

*Where'd you hear that?*
Advertising Age, Agency Income Report. Based on 1989 billings for ads in this medium, in millions of dollars.

### Top 10 agencies in spot TV

1. Saatchi & Saatchi Advertising Worldwide, with $622.4 million
2. Backer Spielvogel Bates, $525.2
3. Chiat/Day/Mojo, $471.0
4. BBDO Worldwide, $413.9
5. Foote, Cone & Belding Communications Inc., $361.6
6. D'Arcy Masius Benton & Bowles Inc., $358.0
7. Young & Rubicam, $342.0
8. J. Walter Thompson Co., $332.5
9. Grey Advertising Inc., $321.2
10. DDB Needham Worldwide Inc., $252.3

*Where'd you hear that?*
Advertising Age, Agency Income Report. Based on 1989 billings for ads in this medium, in millions of dollars.

### Top 10 agencies in radio

1. BBDO Worldwide, with $138.4 million
2. DDB Needham Worldwide Inc., $132.3
3. Backer Spielvogel Bates Worldwide, $131.6
4. D'Arcy Masius Benton & Bowles Inc., $101.5
5. Bozell Inc., $96.0
6. Ogilvy & Mather Worldwide, $95.6
7. McCann-Erickson Worldwide, $93.2
8. Foote, Cone & Belding Communications Inc., $93.1
9. Saatchi & Saatchi Advertising Worldwide, $90.2

# MASS APPEAL

10. Young & Rubicam, $78.6

*Where'd you hear that?*
Advertising Age, Agency Income Report. Based on 1989 billings for ads in this medium, in millions of dollars.

## Top 10 agencies in newspapers

1. DDB Needham Worldwide Inc., with $240.5 million
2. J. Walter Thompson Co., $226.5
3. BBDO Worldwide, $190.4
4. Nationwide Advertising Service, $173.7
5. Young & Rubicam, $144.4
6. Saatchi & Saatchi Advertising Worldwide, $127.4
7. Lintas:Worldwide, $127.0
8. Grey Advertising Inc., $102.8
9. D'Arcy Masius Benton & Bowles Inc., $94.5
10. Backer Spielvogel Bates Worldwide, $92.3

*Where'd you hear that?*
Advertising Age, Agency Income Report. Based on 1989 billings for ads in this medium, in millions of dollars.

## Largest newspaper advertisers

1. News Corp. Ltd., with $247,450.1 thousand
2. May Department Stores Co., $230,874.4
3. Valassis Inserts, $226,653.3
4. R. H. Macy & Co. Inc., $183,640.2
5. Sears, Roebuck & Co., $153,559.8
6. Campeau Corp., $144,003.4
7. General Motors Corp. Local Dealers, $110,255.4
8. Ford Motor Co. Local Dealers, $88,237.3
9. American Stores Co., $81,877.3
10. J. C. Penney Co. Inc., $81,387.7

*Where'd you hear that?*
LNA Ad Dollars Summary Leading National Advertisers. Based on 1989 newspaper advertising expenditures, in thousands of dollars.

## Largest advertisers in newspapers

1. May Department Stores Co., with $224,282 thousand
2. Macy Acquiring Corp., $182,212
3. Sears, Roebuck & Co., $160,969
4. Campeau Corp., $124,488
5. Dayton-Hudson Corp., $90,630
6. General Motors Corp., $86,835
7. Texas Air Corp., $82,441
8. Philip Morris Cos., $76,711
9. Carter Hawley Hale Stores Inc., $75,554
10. J. C. Penney Co. Inc., $74,568

*Where'd you hear that?*
Advertising Age. Based on 1988 newspaper advertising expenditures, in thousands of dollars.

## Largest advertisers in newspaper supplements

1. National Paragon Corp., with $41,404 thousand
2. Franklin Mint, $29,683
3. Sony Corp., $18,243
4. Philip Morris Cos., $16,868

# MASS APPEAL

5. General Motors Corp., $12,233
6. Loews Corp., $10,908
7. Hallmark Cards, $9,659
8. Bertelsmann AG, $8,902
9. American Brands Inc., $8,829
10. Primerica Corp., $8,052

*Where'd you hear that?*
Advertising Age. Based on 1988 newspaper supplement advertising expenditures, in thousands of dollars.

## 10 most popular print campaigns

1. Ford Motor Co. by J. Walter Thompson
2. Pepsi-Cola by BBDO
3. Chevrolet by Lintas:Campbell-Ewald
4. McDonald's by Leo Burnett Co.
5. Budweiser Beer by D'Arcy Masius Benton & Bowles
6. Marlboro by Leo Burnett Co.
7. General Motors Corp. by N. W. Ayer
8. Virginia Slims by Leo Burnett Co.
9. Toyota by Saatchi & Saatchi DFS
9. Calvin Klein's Obsession by CRK (in-house)

*Where'd you hear that?*
Adweek's Marketing Week. Based on from Video Storyboard tests.

## Largest magazine advertisers

1. Philip Morris Cos. Inc., with $281,453.5 thousand
2. General Motors Corp., $213,523.6
3. RJR Nabisco Inc., $154,052.1
4. Ford Motor Co., $135,238.8
5. Chrysler Corp., $95,741.6

6. Procter & Gamble Co., $95,741.6
7. Nestle SA, $77,202.4
8. Unilever NV, $72,963,8
9. AT & T, $71,050.6
10. Grand Metropolitan PLC, $69,285.6

*Where'd you hear that?*
LNA Ad Dollars Summary, Leading National Advertisers. Based on 1989 magazine advertising expenditures, in thousands of dollars.

## Largest magazine advertisers

1. Philip Morris Cos., with $270,251 thousand
2. General Motors Corp., $190,799
3. RJR Nabisco, $131,463
4. Ford Motor Co., $125,532
5. Chrysler Corp., $104,527
6. Procter & Gamble Co., $79,279
7. AT & T, $66,193
8. Time Warner, $64,989
9. Nestle SA, $63,477
10. Grand Metropolitan PLC, $59,545

*Where'd you hear that?*
Advertising Age. Based on 1988 magazine expenditures, in thousands of dollars.

## Top 10 agencies in consumer magazines

1. Saatchi & Saatchi Advertising Worldwide, with $422.1 million
2. Young & Rubicam, $280.7
3. J. Walter Thompson Co., $233.1
4. Backer Spielvogel Bates Worldwide, $226.2
5. DDB Needham Worldwide Inc., $220.0

6. Leo Burnett Co, $207.4
7. Bozell Inc., $199.5
8. Wells, Rich, Greene, $197.0
9. Lintas:Worldwide, $191.4
10. BBDO Worldwide, $187.9

*Where'd you hear that?*
Advertising Age, Agency Income Report. Based on 1989 billings for ads in this medium, in millions of dollars.

## Top 10 agencies in Sunday magazines

1. Nationwide Advertising Service, with $22.7 million
2. Lois/GGK New York, $10.0
3. Ogilvy & Mather Worldwide, $9.9
4. TBWA Advertising, $9.3
5. Saatchi & Saatchi Advertising Worldwide, $8.5
6. Valentine-Radford, $8.4
7. Noble Communications, $6.5
8. Ross Roy Group, $5.0
9. Laurence, Charles, Free & Lawson, $4.9
10. BBDO Worldwide, $4.3

*Where'd you hear that?*
Advertising Age, Agency Income Report. Based on 1989 billings for ads in this medium, in millions of dollars.

## Top 10 agencies in business publications

1. BBDO Worldwide, with $89.2 million
2. Saatchi & Saatchi Advertising Worldwide, $54.3
3. J. Walter Thompson Co., $51.2
4. Ketchum Communications, $43.7
5. Young & Rubicam, $40.5
6. Ogilvy & Mather Worldwide, $38.9
7. McCann-Erickson Worldwide, $36.4
7. Della Femina, McNamee/EWDB, $36.4
9. Ingalls, Quinn & Johnson, $21.3
10. Backer Spielvogel Bates Worldwide, $19.2

*Where'd you hear that?*
Advertising Age, Agency Income Report. Based on 1989 billings for ads in this medium, in a millions of dollars.

## Top 10 agencies in medical journals

1. BBDO Worldwide (Lavey/Wolff/Swift), with $69.3 million
2. McCann-Erickson Worldwide, $65.0
3. Saatchi & Saatchi Advertising (Klemtner), $59.6
4. William Douglas McAdams Inc., $44.0
5. Young & Rubicam (Sudler & Hennessey), $35.1
6. Dorritie & Lyons, $31.5
7. Ketchum Communications, $26.0
8. Foote, Cone & Belding Communications Inc., $25.2
9. Robert A. Becker EWDB, $25.0
10. Gross Townsend Frank Hoffman, $20.0

*Where'd you hear that?*
Advertising Age, Agency Income Report. Based on 1989 billings for ads in this medium, in millions of dollars.

# MASS APPEAL

# MASS APPEAL

### Largest network radio advertisers

1. Sears, Roebuck & Co., with $70,987.6 thousand
2. General Motors Corp., $35,308.9
3. Procter & Gamble Co., $24,217.1
4. AT & T, $19,757.7
5. City Investing Co., $17,425.3
6. Cotter & Co., $16,001.8
7. U.S. Government, $14,854.3
8. Warner-Lambert Co., $14,338.5
9. Campbell Soup Co., $13,966.7
10. K mart Corp., $13,587.5

*Where'd you hear that?*
LNA Ad Dollars Summary, Leading National Advertisers. Based on 1989 network radio advertising expenditures, in thousands of dollars.

### Largest U.S. network radio advertisers

1. Sears, Roebuck & Co., with $67,612 thousand
2. General Motors Corp., $38,255
3. Procter & Gamble Co., $25,534
4. Bayer AG, $18,701
5. Campbell Soup Co., $18,572
6. Cotter & Co., $18,284
7. Warner-Lambert Co., $16,911
8. Anheuser-Busch Cos. Inc., $15,391
9. AT & T, $12,311
10. Ford Motor Co., $12,043

*Where'd you hear that?*
Advertising Age, 100 Leading National Advertisers. Based on 1988 network radio expenditures, in thousands of dollars.

### Largest U.S. spot radio advertisers

1. Anheuser-Busch Cos. Inc., with $42,696 thousand
2. General Motors Corp., $40,185
3. Philip Morris Cos., $28,092
4. PepsiCo Inc., $28,198
5. Sears, Roebuck & Co., $25,431
6. Southland Corp., $22,108
7. Grand Metropolitan PLC, $21,090
8. Delta Air Lines, $19,948
9. Chrysler Corp., $19,412
10. Procter & Gamble Co., $15,777

*Where'd you hear that?*
Advertising Age, 100 Leading National Advertisers. Based on 1988 spot radio expenditures, in thousands of dollars.

### Largest network television advertisers

1. General Motors Corp., with $443,402 thousand
2. Philip Morris Cos., $388,602
3. Procter & Gamble Co., $370,175
4. Kellogg Co., $297,740
5. McDonald's Corp. $245,389
6. Anheuser-Busch Cos. Inc., $207,278
7. Unilever NV, $189,652
8. Ford Motor Co., $175,688
9. RJR Nabisco, $174,002
10. AT & T, $173,912

*Where'd you hear that?*
Advertising Age, 100 Leading National Advertisers. Based on 1988 network TV advertising expenditures, in thousands of dollars.

# MASS APPEAL

## Largest spot television advertisers

1. PepsiCo Inc., with $257,957 thousand
2. Procter & Gamble Co., $222,883
3. Philip Morris Cos., $157,578
4. General Mills Inc., $145,945
5. Grand Metropolitan PLC, $130,339
6. McDonald's Corp., $128,102
7. General Motors Corp., $115,286
8. Anheuser-Busch Cos. Inc., $87,486
9. Hasbro Inc., $78,681
10. Time Warner, $78,368

*Where'd you hear that?*
Advertising Age, 100 Leading National Advertisers. Based on 1988 spot TV advertising expenditures, in thousands of dollars.

## Companies with the highest network television advertising expenditures

1. General Motors Corp., with $506,513.5 thousand
2. Procter & Gamble Co., $404,828.4
3. Philip Morris Cos. Inc., $368,373.0
4. Kellogg Co., $324,822.8
5. McDonalds Corp., $252,066.2
6. Ford Motor Co., $201,371.7
7. Unilever NV, $190,394.4
8. Sears, Roebuck & Co., $187,511.3
9. Anheuser-Busch Cos. Inc., $181,467.0
10. Johnson & Johnson, $169,945.3

*Where'd you hear that?*
Leading National Advertisers, LNA Ad Dollar Summary. Based on 1989 network television expenditures, in thousands of dollars.

## Companies with the highest spot television advertising expenditures

1. PepsiCo. Inc., with $264,649.7 thousand
2. General Motors Corp. Dealers Association, $259,639.7
3. Procter & Gamble Co., $218,062.3
4. Philip Morris Cos. Inc., $180,414.2
5. General Mills Inc., $150,256.7
6. McDonalds Corp., $141,268.1
7. Ford Auto Dealers Association, $127,905.4
8. Chrysler Corp. Dealers Association, $114,211.3
9. Nissan Motor Co. Ltd., $113,502.0
10. Anheuser-Busch Cos. Inc., $94,834.9

*Where'd you hear that?*
Leading National Advertisers, LNA Ad Dollars Summary. Based on 1989 spot television expenditures, in thousands of dollars.

## Companies with the highest syndicated television advertising expenditures

1. Philip Morris Cos. Inc., with $106,800.5 thousand
2. Procter & Gamble Co., $82,897.0
3. Kellogg Co., $50,676.5
4. Unilever NV, $38,942.0
5. Bristol-Myers Squibb Co., $34,252.1
6. Nestle SA, $33,290.9

255

# MASS APPEAL

7. H. J. Heinz, $27,151.9
8. Grand Metropolitan PLC, $25,351.3
9. Warner-Lambert Co., $24,743.3
10. Mars Inc., $22,282.9

*Where'd you hear that?*
Leading National Advertisers, LNA Ad Dollars Summary. Based on 1989 syndicated television expenditures, in thousands of dollars.

## Largest prime-time television advertiser categories

1. Restaurants & drive-ins, with $459.9 million
2. Domestic cars, $330.0
3. Cereals, $305.6
4. Imported cars, $293.9
5. Movies, $161.7
6. Cold/cough remedies, $134.7
7. Headache remedies, $110.4
8. Trucks, $107.3
9. Department stores, $104.1
10. Soft drinks, $101.3

*Where'd you hear that?*
Marketing & Media Decisions. Based on 1989 advertising expenditures, in millions of dollars.

## Largest prime-time television advertising clients

1. General Motors Corp., with $289.7 million
2. Kellogg Co., $199.7
3. Procter & Gamble, $196.7
4. McDonald's, $169.7
5. Philip Morris, $157.6
6. PepsiCo, $128.4
7. Unilever, $121.6
8. Grand Metropolitan PLC, $115.3
9. Ford Motor Co., $109.5
10. Kohlberg Kravis Roberts & Co., $102.3

*Where'd you hear that?*
Marketing & Media Decisions. Based on 1989 advertising expenditures, in millions of dollars.

## Largest daytime television advertiser categories

1. Cold remedies, with $43.4 million
2. Underwear/apparel, $39.2
3. Cereals, $35.1
4. Games/toys, $34.1
5. Headache remedies, $33.0
6. Cleaners, $32.2
7. Dental supplies, $31.0
8. Coffee/tea, $30.0
9. Candy/gum, $28.9
10. Pet food, $28.4

*Where'd you hear that?*
Marketing & Media Decisions. Based on 1989 advertising expenditures, in millions of dollars.

## Largest daytime television advertising clients

1. Procter & Gamble, with $139.3 million
2. Philip Morris, $47.0
3. Unilever, $46.5
4. Kohlberg Kravis Roberts & Co., $42.9
5. Johnson & Johnson, $37.6
6. Bristol-Myers Co., $34.2
7. Quaker Oats, $33.6
8. American Home Products Corp., $32.3
9. Eastman Kodak Co., $30.9

10. Nestle, $22.6

*Where'd you hear that?*
Marketing & Media Decisions. Based on 1989 advertising expenditures, in millions of dollars.

## Largest early morning television advertiser categories

1. Coffee/tea/cocoa, with $34.0 million
2. Cereals, $19.7
3. Dental products, $11.2
4. Financial, $7.3
5. Headache remedies, $6.6
6. Fruit juices, $6.3
7. Health/diet foods, $6.1
8. Media, $5.9
9. Furniture, $5.6
10. Cold/cough remedies, $5.2

*Where'd you hear that?*
Marketing & Media Decisions. Based on 1989 advertising expenditures, in millions of dollars.

## Largest early morning television advertising clients

1. Procter & Gamble, with $30.8 million
2. Philip Morris, $20.9
3. Kellogg Co., $7.4
4. H. J. Heinz, $6.2
5. Johnson & Johnson, $5.6
6. Seagrams, $5.5
7. American Home Products Corp., $5.3
8. Quaker Oats, $5.2
8. Sears, $5.3
10. General Motors Corp., $4.8

*Where'd you hear that?*
Marketing & Media Decisions. Based on 1989 advertising expenditures, in millions of dollars.

## Largest latenight advertiser categories

1. Imported cars, with $43.4 million
2. Beer, $34.2
3. Domestic cars, $23.5
4. Candy/gum, $19.8
5. Movies, $18.6
6. Restaurants/drive-ins, $13.9
7. Headache remedies, $13.3
8. Long-distance services, $13.0
9. Financial, $12.2
10. Health/diet foods, $11.0

*Where'd you hear that?*
Marketing & Media Decisions. Based on 1989 advertising expenditures, in millions.

## Largest latenight television advertising clients

1. Anheuser-Busch Cos. Inc., with $22.6 million
2. Philip Morris, $21.1
3. General Motors Corp., $18.5
4. Bristol-Myers Co., $18.0
5. AT & T, $15.7
6. Ford Motor Co., $11.9
7. Sears, $11.1
8. Procter & Gamble, $11.0
9. Monsanto, $10.1
10. Toyota, $9.7

*Where'd you hear that?*
Marketing & Media Decisions. Based on 1989 advertising expenditures, in millions of dollars.

## Largest television news advertiser categories

1. Cereals, with $73.9 million
2. Institutional/corporate, $49.4
3. Headache remedies, $44.5
4. Domestic cars, $30.9
5. Digestive aids, $28.8

# MASS APPEAL

# MASS APPEAL

6. Imported cars, $27.4
7. Long distance services, $24.7
8. Dental products, $22.8
9. Cold/cough remedies, $19.7
10. Financial, $19.6

*Where'd you hear that?*
Marketing & Media Decisions. Based on 1989 advertising expenditures, in millions of dollars.

## Largest television news advertising clients

1. Kellogg Co., with $44.3 million
2. American Home Products Corp., $35.4
3. Philip Morris, $25.9
4. Bristol-Myers Co., $23.8
5. General Mills Inc., $23.5
6. Procter & Gamble, $23.3
7. Eastman-Kodak Co., $20.9
8. AT & T, $20.6
9. General Motors Corp., $19.7
10. Johnson & Johnson, $19.6

*Where'd you hear that?*
Marketing & Media Decisions. Based on 1989 advertising expenditures, in millions of dollars.

## Most popular television commercials

1. McDonald's ad by Leo Burnett Co.
2. Pepsi/Diet Pepsi, by BBDO
3. California Raisins, by Foote, Cone & Belding Communications Inc.
4. Energizer, by Chiat/Day/Mojo
5. Isuzu, by Della Femina, McNamee WCRS
6. Bud Light, by DDB/Needham
7. Coca-Cola, by McCann-Erickson
8. Miller Lite, by Backer Spielvogel Bates
9. Lexus Infiniti, by Hill, Holliday, Connors, Cosmopulos
10. Nike, by Wieden & Kennedy

*Where'd you hear that?*
Wall Street Journal. Based on viewers preference, based on an interviewee pool of 24,000 persons (results not specified).

## 10 favorite television campaigns

1. Pepsi-Cola by BBDO
2. Miller Lite by Backer Spielvogel Bates
3. McDonald's by Leo Burnett Co.
4. California Raisins by Foote, Cone & Belding
5. Bud Light by DDB Needham
6. Coca-Cola by McCann-Erickson
7. Michelin Tires by DDB Needham
8. Kodak by J. Walter Thompson
9. Levi's by Foote, Cone & Belding
10. Isuzu by Della Femina, McNamee WCRS

*Where'd you hear that?*
Adweek's Marketing Week. Based on surveys of Video Storyboard test.

## Top 10 corporation advertisers

1. AT & T, with $93,190 thousand
2. Ford Motor Co., $45,397
3. General Electric Co., $40,013
4. Dow Chemical Co., $34,625
5. IBM, $34,029
6. Citicorp, $33,842
7. General Motors Corp., $30,963
8. Sears, Roebuck & Co., $30,623

9. K mart Corp., $29,918
10. Macy Acquiring Corp., $29,906

*Where'd you hear that?*
Public Relations Journal, Annual Review of Corporate Advertising Expenditures. Based on 9-media advertising total, in thousands of dollars.

## Leading Hispanic market advertisers

1. Procter & Gamble Co., with $29.3
2. Philip Morris Cos., $8.6
3. Anheuser-Busch Cos. Inc., $8.4
4. Colgate-Palmolive Co., $7.8
5. McDonald's Corp., $6.9
6. Coca-Cola Co., $6.0
7. Adolph Coors Co., $5.2
8. Ford Motor Co., $5.0
8. Johnson & Johnson, $5.0
10. Sears, Roebuck & Co., $4.6

*Where'd you hear that?*
Hispanic Business. Based on 1989 media expenditures, in millions of dollars.

## Leading Hispanic advertising markets

1. Los Angeles, CA, with $131.1 million
2. Miami, FL, $92.5
3. New York, NY, $90.4
4. Chicago, IL, $30.6
5. San Francisco/San Jose, CA, $24.8
6. San Antonio, TX, $19.8
7. Houston, TX, $18.9
8. San Diego, CA $13.1
9. Phoenix, AZ, $10.9
10. El Paso, TX, $9.8

*Where'd you hear that?*
(Hispanic Business, December, 1989, p. 18. Based on 1989 media expenditures, in millions of dollars.

## Largest Hispanic advertising agencies

1. Sosa & Associates (San Antonio), with $53.5 million
2. Mendoza, Dillon (Newport Beach, CA), $48.6
3. Castor GS & B (New York), $44.0
4. Bravo Group (New York), $34.9
5. Font & Vaamonde (New York), $32.5
6. Bermudez Associates (Los Angeles), $29.6
7. Noble y Asociados (Irvine, CA), $24.6
8. Casanova-Pendrill Publicidad (Irvine, CA), $23.3
9. Publicidad Siboney (New York), $21.2
10. Conill Advertising (New York), $20.0

*Where'd you hear that?*
Hispanic Business. Based on 1989 Hispanic billings, in millions of dollars.

## Largest advertisers in Puerto Rico

1. Procter & Gamble Co., with $19,700 thousand
2. Unilever NV/PLC, $14,700
3. Sears, Roebuck & Co., $8,200
4. Colgate-Palmolive Co., $7,000
5. PepsiCo, $6,000
6. American Home Products Corp., $5,900
7. J. C. Penney Co. Inc., $4,400
8. AT & T, $4,200

# MASS APPEAL

# MASS APPEAL

9. Banco de Ponce, $3,800
10. Food & Spirits, $1,000

*Where'd you hear that?*
Advertising Age, Global Marketing & Media. Based on 1988 advertising spending, in thousands of U.S. dollars. Top advertisers need not be domestic companies.

## Biggest agencies in Puerto Rico

1. Badillo/Saatchi & Saatchi (San Juan), with $12,200 thousand
2. Marti, Flores, Prieto & Wachtel (San Juan), $7,850
3. Young & Rubicam Puerto Rico (San Juan), $6,272
4. West Indies & Grey (San Juan), $5,275
5. BBDO Puerto Rico (Hato Rey), $4,181
6. FCB Puerto Rico (Isla Verde), $3,864
7. McCann-Erickson (San Juan), $3,558
8. Leo Burnett Co. (San Juan), $3,356
9. De la Cruz & Goachet (San Juan), $2,283
10. Bozell/CPV Advertising (Santurce), $989

*Where'd you hear that?*
Advertising Age, Agency Income Report. Based on 1989 gross income, in thousands of U.S. dollars.

# To Market

## Largest market research firms in the United Kingdom

1. AGB, with £44,906 thousand
2. Nielsen Marketing Research, £30,580
3. Taylor Nelson/MAS Group, £17,031
4. Millward Brown, £16,728
5. Research International UK, £16,156
6. MRB Group, £15,676
7. MIL Research Group, £15,200
8. NOP Group, £14,809
9. MORI, £8,523
10. The Research Business Group Research Services, £8,452

*Where'd you hear that?*
Financial Times. Based on 1989 turnover, in thousands of British pounds.

## Largest U.S. market research firms

1. Nielsen, with $950.0 million
2. IMS International Inc., $390.0
3. The Arbitron Co., $238.0
4. Information Resources Inc., $136.4
5. Westat Inc., $65.7
6. M/A/R/C Inc., $53.3
7. Maritz Marketing Research Inc., $46.1
8. MRB Group Inc., $44.6
9. NFO Research Inc., $43.1
10. Market Facts Inc., $39.1

*Where'd you hear that?*
Marketing News, The Honomichl 50. Based on 1989 total research revenues, in millions of dollars.

## Leading U.S. research organizations

1. A. C. Nielsen Co. (Northbrook, IL), with $426.0 million
2. Arbitron Co. (New York, NY), $290.0
3. IMS International Inc. (New York, NY), $181.0
4. Information Resources Inc. (Chicago, IL), $113.8
5. Westat (Rockville, MD), $65.9

# TO MARKET

6. M/A/R/C Inc. (Irving, TX), $53.2
7. Maritz Marketing Research Inc. (Fenton, MO), $46.1
8. MRB Group (New York, NY), $44.6
9. NFO Research (Greenwich, CT), $42.0
10. Market Facts Inc. (Chicago, IL), $39.0

*Where'd you hear that?*
Advertising Age. Based on 1989 gross research revenues, in millions of dollars.

## Largest telemarketing companies in Great Britain

1. BT Connections in Business, with £20 million
2. Programmes Group, £6.56
3. Decisions Group, £3.3
4. PBA Direct, £2.8
5. Audiotext, £2.5
5. Golley Slater Telephone Marketing, £2.5
7. Adlink, £2.3
8. Merit Direct, £2
9. FKB Telephone Marketing, £1.45
10. Contact 24, £1.15

*Where'd you hear that?*
Marketing, Direct Marketing League Table. Based on 1989 turnover, in millions of British pounds.

## Leading U.S. telemarketing companies

1. Pioneer Tele-Technologies, Inc., with 4,890
2. Precision Software, Inc., 3,500
3. Telecom USA Direct, 3,425
4. DialAmerica Marketing, Inc., 2,880
5. AT & T American Trans-tech, 2,200
6. Matrixx Marketing, Inc., 2,094
7. Idelman Telemarketing, Inc., 1,744
8. NDC Telemarketing, 1,458
9. Audiotext PLC, 1,150
10. Phone Marketing America, Inc., 930

*Where'd you hear that?*
Telemarketing, Telemarketing's Top 50 Service Agency Ranking & Industry Profile. Based on number of lines.

## Largest direct marketing companies in Great Britain

1. Watson Ward, Albert Varndell, £25.6 million
2. Grey Direct, £22
3. Ogilvy and Mather Direct, £18.26
4. Brann Direct Marketing, £13.9
5. SML, £13
6. Wunderman Worldwide, N/A
7. RCF Marketing Group, £11.7
8. DDM Advertising, £9.8
9. Evans Hunt Scott, N/A
10. Judith Donovan Associates, £7

*Where'd you hear that?*
Marketing, Direct Marketing League Table. Based on 1989 turnover, in millions of British pounds.

## Largest U.S. direct marketing agencies

1. Ogilvy & Mather Direct, with $304,900 thousand
2. Wunderman Worldwide, $270,000
3. FCB Direct, $227,800
4. Rapp Collins Marcoa, $226,000
5. The Direct Marketing Group, $149,600

# TO MARKET

6. Grey Direct, $119,000
7. Kobs & Draft, $116,900
8. Barry Blau, $101,175
9. HDM Worldwide Direct, $92,400
10. Devon Direct Marketing & Advertising Inc., $82,000

*Where'd you hear that?*
Adweek, Eastern edition, Agency Report Card. Based on 1989 billings, in thousands of dollars.

## Highest-paid direct marketing executives

1. Leslie H. Wexner (The Limited), with $1,030,753
2. John Shea (Spiegel), $889,434
3. R. B. Gill, (J. C. Penney), $728,205
4. Michael Bozic (Sears, Roebuck & Co.), $701,910
5. William B. Snyder (GEICO), $700,000
6. Lillian Vernon Katz (Lillian Vernon), $656,145
7. Charles M. Leighton (CML Group), $550,000
8. Richard Thalheimer (The Sharper Image), $532,071
9. Donald Schupak (Horn & Hardart), $519,077
10. Richard Merrill (Commerce Clearing House), $437,703

*Where'd you hear that?*
Target Marketing, Target Marketing 400. Based on combination of salary, bonuses, and deferred compensation.

## Student response to direct mail

1. J. Crew, with 10.4%
2. Citibank Visa, 10.0%
3. American Express, 7.1%
4. L. L. Bean, 6.3%
5. Credit cards, 5.6%
6. Magazine subscriptions, 4.8%
7. Lands End, 3.7%
8. MasterCard, 3.3%
9. Catalogs, 2.2%
9. Publishers Clearing House, 2.2%

*Where'd you hear that?*
Advertising Age. Based on percent of responses.

## Largest mail order businesses

1. United Services Automobile Association, with $2,180.4 million
2. Time, Inc., $1,997.1
3. Sears, Roebuck & Co., $1,596.7
4. Tele-Communications, $1,468.0
5. Geico Corp. Group, $1,429.6
6. Reader's Digest, $1,420.0
7. Otto Versand (Spiegel), $1,384.1
8. Primerica (Fingerhut), $1,145.5
9. AT & T, $1,132.2
10. American Cable & Communications, $1,066.8

*Where'd you hear that?*
Direct Marketing, Mail Order Top 250. Based on mail order sales for 1988, in millions of dollars.

## Leading catalogs

1. Spiegel, with 3.8 million
2. L'eggs, 3.7
3. Fingerhut, 3.2
4. Lillian Vernon, 3.1
5. Avon Fashions, 3.0
6. L. L. Bean, 1.9
7. Harriet Carter, 1.8

# TO MARKET

8. Miles Kimball, 1.7
8. Current, 1.7
10. Warshawsky/Whitney, 1.6

*Where'd you hear that?*
Target Marketing, Target Marketing 400. Based on number of 12-month buyers, in millions.

## Top 10 consumer catalogs

1. Spiegel, with $1,134.0 million
2. J. C. Penney Co. Inc., $928.0
3. Sears, Roebuck & Co., $880.3
4. Fingerhut, $600.0
5. L. L. Bean, $588.0
6. The Limited Inc., $500.0
7. Lands' End, $455.8
8. Hanover House, $316.8
9. New Hampton Inc., $295.0
10. Current, $169.0

*Where'd you hear that?*
Catalog Age. Based on 1988 sales, in millions of dollars.

## Leading catalog showrooms

1. Service Merchandise, with $3.5 billion
2. Best Products, $2.1 billion
3. Consumers (USA), $330 million
4. Brendle's, $295 million
5. L. Luria & Son, $232.5 million
6. K's Merchandise, $184 million
7. David Weis, $145 million
8. W. Bell & Co., $125 million
9. Present Co., $100 million
10. Dahlkempers, $88 million

*Where'd you hear that?*
Upscale Discounting, Annual Study of the World of Upscale Discounting. Based on 1989 projected dollar volume.

## Largest catalog showroom chains

1. Service Merchandise, with $3,093 million
2. Best Products, $2,088
3. Consumers Distributing, $300
4. Brendles, $261
5. L. Luria & Son, $216
6. K's Merchandise, $165
7. David Weis, $130
8. Dahlkemper's, $80
9. W. Bell & Co., $79
10. Present Co., $77

*Where'd you hear that?*
Discount Store News, Discount Industry Annual Report. Based on 1988 sales, in millions of dollars.

## Top catalog showroom chains in electronics sales

1. Service Merchandise, with $1.25 billion
2. Best Products, $585 million
3. Consumers Distributing, $100 million
4. Sharper Image, $95 million
5. L. Luria & Son, $50 million

*Where'd you hear that?*
HFD, Focus 200 Consumer Electronics' Top Retailers. Based on 1988 electronics sales volume.

## Europe's largest wholesale trade companies in durable goods

1. Marubeni U K PLC, with 4,748,623,916 ECU
2. Nissho IWAI (UK) Ltd., 4,709,198,403
3. Thyssen Handelsunion Aktien-Gesellschaft, 4,368,079,018
4. Degussa Aktiengesellschaft, 3,960,333,172

# TO MARKET

5. Metallgesellschaft Aktien-Gesellschaft, 3,943,670,366
6. S T C PLC, 3,462,827,386
7. Lex Service PLC, 2,692,036,802
8. Dalgety U K Ltd., 2,540,405,868
9. Sumitomo Corporation (UK) Ltd., 2,136,294,735
10. Federazione Italiana Dei Consorzi Agrari Soc. Coop A.R.L. Federconsorzi, 2,035,230,336

*Where'd you hear that?*
Dun's Europa, Dun & Bradstreet. Based on sales, in European Currency Units.

## Europe's largest wholesale trade companies in non-durable goods

1. Nv Kon. Nederlandse Petroleum Maatschappij, with 68,332,795,108 ECU
2. Groupement D'Achats Edouard Leclerc (Ste Coope), 9,282,980,400
3. Dalgety PLC, 6,616,221,876
4. Koninklijke Ahold NV, 6,275,001,684
5. Promodes, 4,940,875,145
6. ASDA Group PLC, 4,009,110,151
7. Magasins B. (Grands) Loceda Import, 3,844,179,000
8. Co-operative Wholesale Society Ltd., 3,759,624,370
9. Esso Petroleum Co. Ltd., 3,510,138,588
10. MRH, Mineraloel-Rohstoff-Handel Gesellschaft MBH, 3,382,624,000

*Where'd you hear that?*
Dun's Europa, Dun & Bradstreet. Based on sales, in European Currency Units.

## Top states in manufacturer warehouse construction markets

1. California, with $139 million
2. Ohio, $78
3. Texas, $58
4. Michigan, $57
5. Tennessee, $33
6. Indiana, $32
6. Georgia, $32
8. Illinois, $28
9. Minnesota, $25
9. Wisconsin, $25

*Where'd you hear that?*
ENR, Top 20 States in Major Construction Markets. Based on eleven-month cumulative contract awards, 1989 vs. 1988, in millions of dollars.

## Leading warehouse clubs

1. Sam's, with $5.3 billion
2. Price Club, $5.0
3. Costco Wholesale Club, $2.8
4. Pace, $1.7
5. BJ's Wholesale Club, $968
6. Price Savers, $807
7. The Wholesale Club, $582
8. Markro, $402
9. Warehouse Club, $271
10. Buyers Club, $70

*Where'd you hear that?*
Upscale Discounting, Annual Study of the World of Upscale Discounting. Based on 1989 projected dollar volume.

# TO MARKET

## Largest membership warehouse clubs

1. Price Club, with $4,053 million
2. Sam's, $3,829
3. Costco Wholesale Club, $1,989
4. PACE, $1,271
5. BJ's Wholesale Club, $800
6. Price Savers, $600
7. Wholesale Club, $402
8. Makro Self-Service Wholesale Club, $300
9. Warehouse Club, $249
10. Buyer's Club, $100

*Where'd you hear that?*
Discount Store News, Discount Industry Annual Report. Based on 1988 sales, in millions of dollars.

## Largest wholesale clubs

1. Price Co., with $4,901,000 thousand
2. Sams Wholesale Club, $4,841,000
3. Costco Wholesale Club, $2,900,000
4. PACE Membership Warehouse, $1,600,000
5. BJ's Wholesale Club, $950,000
6. Price Savers Wholesale Club, $725,000
7. Makro Self-Service Wholesale Club, $700,000
8. Wholesale Club, $570,000
9. Warehouse Club, $267,000
10. Club Wholesale, $85,000

*Where'd you hear that?*
Discount Merchandiser, True Look of the Discount Industry. Based on 1989 volume, in thousands of dollars.

## Leading teleshopping direct discounters

1. Home Shopping Network Inc., with $765 million
2. Cable Value Network, $486
3. QVC Network, $410
4. CompuServe, $350
5. Family Shopping Network, $14
6. J. C. Penney Shopping Channel, $11

*Where'd you hear that?*
Upscale Discounting, Annual Study of the World of Upscale Discounting. Based on 1989 projected dollar volume, in millions of dollars.

## Largest passive cable shopping networks

1. Home Shopping Network Inc., with $730.1 million
2. Cable Value Network, $345.2
3. QVC, $193.2
4. J. C. Penney Shopping Channel, $7.9
5. Fashion Channel, NA
6. America's Shopping Channel, NA

*Where'd you hear that?*
Discount Store News, Discount Industry Annual Report. Based on 1988 sales, in millions of dollars.

## Largest direct interactive computer shopping services

1. CompuServe, with 500,000
2. Prodigy Services Co., 20,000
3. Genie, G. E. Information Service Co., 115,000
4. Quantum, 80,000
5. Minitel, NA

*Where'd you hear that?*
Discount Store News, Discount Industry Annual Report. Based on number of subscribers.

# TO MARKET

**Largest telephone gateway computer shopping services**

1. INFO-LOOK
2. Gateway
3. SourceLine
4. Community Link

*Where'd you hear that?*
Discount Store News, Discount Industry Annual Report. Based on number of customers.

**Largest interactive kiosk shopping services**

1. Gift Host USA, with 19
2. Gift Sender, 10

*Where'd you hear that?*
Discount Store News, Discount Industry Annual Report. Based on number of kiosks.

**Largest companies in retail trade in the European Economic Community, Austria, and Switzerland**

1. Hanson PLC, with 10,866,883,632 ECU
2. Aldi Gmbh & Co. Kommandit-Gesellschaft, 9,664,640,000
3. Carrefour France, 8,044,727,631
4. Compagnies Europeennes Reunies, 7,696,473,489
5. Gateway Corp. PLC, 7,558,184,977
6. J. Sainsbury PLC, 7,360,418,274
7. Guichard Perrachon et Cie (Ets Economiques du Casino), 7,316,668,604
8. Tesco PLC, 6,931,678,868
9. Marks & Spencer PLC, 6,725,831,059
10. Rewe Handelsgesellschaft Leibbrand Ohg, 5,946,276,636

*Where'd you hear that?*
Dun's Europa, Dun & Bradstreet. Based on sales in the European Community in European Currency units.

**Largest advertisers among retail brands in Great Britain**

1. Woolworths, with £21,121 thousand
2. B & Q, £15,242
3. McDonald's, £14,312
4. MFI/Hygena, £14,155
5. Currys, £14,050
6. Tesco, £13,298
7. Dixons, £12,293
8. Texas Homecare, £12,058
9. Comet, £11,611
10. Asda, £9,642

*Where'd you hear that?*
Marketing, Top 500 Brands. Based on 1989 advertising expenditures, in thousands of British pounds.

---

## *Largest factory outlet chains*

1. Van Heusen Factory Store, with 218
2. Hanes, 180
3. Bass Shoe Outlet, 156
4. Banister Shoe, 140
5. Little Red Shoe House (Wolverine), 128
6. Kuppenheimer Men's Clothiers, 125
6. Aileen Stores, 125
8. Kids Port USA (Health-Tex), 110
9. Prestige Fragrance & Cosmetics, 105
10. Old Mill (Country Miss), 94

*Where'd you hear that?*
Discount Store News. Based on number of units as of January 1, 1990.

# TO MARKET

## Cities with the most shoppers

1. Milwaukee, WI, with 59.3%
2. Detroit, MI, 59.0%
3. Houston, TX, 57.0
4. Chicago, IL, 56.8%
5. Kansas City, MO, 55.9%
6. New York, NY, 53.8%
7. San Francisco, CA, 53.0%
8. Atlanta, GA, 52.4%
9. Salt Lake City, UT, 50.5%
10. Denver, CO, 50.4%

*Where'd you hear that?*
Advertising Age. Based on 1989 percent of consumers 18 and older surveyed who like to shop in their spare time.

## Largest retail companies in Canada

1. Canadian Tire, with $149,616 thousand Canadian
2. Hudson's Bay, $121,908
3. Sears Canada, $106,100
4. Loblaw, $70,000
5. Oshawa Group, $69,600
6. Woolworth, $64,311
7. Steinberg, $55,199
8. Gendis, $25,175
9. InterTAN Canada, $21,650
10. Jean Coutu Group, $18,495

*Where'd you hear that?*
Canadian Business, Canadian Business 500. Based on 1989 net income, in thousands of Canadian dollars.

## Metropolitan areas with highest total retail sales

1. Los Angeles-Long Beach, CA, $59,291,182 thousand
2. New York, NY, $52,563,406
3. Chicago, IL, $42,741,467
4. Philadelphia, PA, $35,844,743
5. Boston-Lawrence-Salem-Lowell-Brockton, MA, $32,195,958
6. Washington, DC, $31,471,548
7. Detroit, MI, $30,775,120
8. Nassau-Suffolk, NY, $24,431,910
9. Houston, TX, $23,194,911
10. Atlanta, GA, $22,255,492

*Where'd you hear that?*
Sales & Marketing Management, Survey of Buying Power. Based on amount of sales in 1988, in thousands of dollars.

## Metroplitan areas with highest general merchandise store sales

1. Los Angeles-Long Beach, CA, with $5,986,334 thousand
2. New York, NY, $5,566,938
3. Chicago, IL, $4,987,995
4. Philadelphia, PA, $4,023,558
5. Detroit, MI, $3,562,211
6. Washington, DC, $3,539,120
7. Minneapolis-St. Paul, $3,125,944
8. Boston-Lawrence-Salem-Lowell-Brockton, MA, $3,101,728
9. Atlanta, GA, $2,741,863
10. Houston, TX, $2,736,521

*Where'd you hear that?*
Sales & Marketing Management, Survey of Buying Power. Based on amount of sales in 1988, in thousands of dollars.

## Metropolitan areas with highest per household retail sales

1. Laredo, TX, with $33,992
2. Portland, ME, $31,644
3. Odessa, TX, $30,961
4. Midland, TX, $28,715
5. Manchester-Nashua, NH, $28,168
6. Nassau-Suffolk, NY, $27,846
7. Bridgeport-Stamford-Norwalk-Danbury, CT, $27,718
8. St. Cloud, MN, $27,557
9. Abilene, TX, $25,778
10. Portsmouth-Dover-Rochester, NH, $25,615

*Where'd you hear that?*
Sales & Marketing Management, Survey of Buying Power. Based on amount of sales per household in 1988.

## Largest owners of shopping center space

1. Edward J. DeBartolo Corp. (Youngstown, OH), with 69,107,396 sq. ft.
2. JMB/Urban Development Co. (Chicago, IL), 68,838,357
3. Melvin Simon & Associates Inc. (Indianapolis, IN), 60,997,145
4. Equitable Real Estate (Atlanta, GA), 60,560,072
5. Rouse Co. (Columbia, MD), 45,000,000
6. Jacobs, Visconsi & Jacobs Co. (Cleveland, OH), 35,762,911
7. Hahn Co. (San Diego, CA), 35,303,000
8. Crown American Corp. (Johnstown, PA), 33,075,730
9. Cafaro Co. (Youngstown, OH), 31,795,406
10. Leo Eisenberg Co. (Kansas City, MO), 26,885,235

*Where'd you hear that?*
Shopping Center World, Top Owners Survey. Based on 1989 square footage owned.

## Largest shopping center developers

1. Edward J. DeBartolo Corp., with 74,715,396 sq. ft.
2. Melvin Simon & Associates Inc., 61,549,045
3. Homart Development Co., 56,460,300
4. General Growth/Center Cos., 52,836,000
5. Hahn Co., 44,253,000
6. Crown American Corp., 37,375,983
7. HSW Investments Inc., 33,500,000
8. Cafaro Co., 31,795,406
9. Taubman Co. Inc., 31,000,000
10. Jacobs, Visconsi & Jacobs Co., 30,963,380

*Where'd you hear that?*
Shopping Center World. Based on total gross leasable area, in square feet.

## Largest companies in shopping center development

1. Crown American Corp., 14,682,889
2. HSW Investments Inc., 11,770,000
3. Trammell Crow Co., 11,647,194
4. Melvin Simon & Associates Inc., 11,478,656
5. Leo Eisenberg Co., 10,666,173
6. Edward J. DeBartolo Corp., 10,274,402

# TO MARKET

# TO MARKET

7. MaceRich Co., 9,510,000
8. Ramco-Gershenson Inc., 9,413,831
9. Developers Diversified, 6,489,451
10. J. J. Gumberg Co., 6,208,000

*Where'd you hear that?*
Monitor. Based on gross leasing area developed as of December 31, 1989.

## Largest companies in open center development

1. Trammell Crow Co., with 11,647,194 sq. ft.
2. HSW Investments Inc., 11,245,000
3. Leo Eisenberg Co., 10,666,173
4. Ramco-Gershenson Inc., 8,698,831
5. Developers Diversified, 5,149,911
6. Kornwasser & Friedman S.C. Prop., 4,805,000
7. Aronov Realty Co. Inc., 4,435,816
8. Melvin Simon & Associates Inc., 4,433,286
9. J. J. Gumberg Co., 4,408,000
10. Bronson & Hutensky, 4,200,764

*Where'd you hear that?*
Monitor. Based on gross leasing area developed between January 1, 1987 and December 31, 1989, in square feet.

## Largest companies in shopping center acquisition

1. JMB/Urban Development Co., 14,091,144
2. O'Connor Group, 11,781,116
3. Kimco Development Corp., 10,656,678
4. General Growth/Center Cos., 9,912,100
5. Edward J. DeBartolo Corp., 8,562,486
6. Equity Properties and Development Co., 8,426,477
7. Sizeler Cos., 6,989,400
8. Roebling Investment Co., 6,515,341
9. Equitable Real Estate Investment Management Inc., 6,408,387
10. Westfield Inc., 6,324,000

*Where'd you hear that?*
Monitor. Based on gross leasing area acquired as of December 31, 1989.

## Largest companies in open center acquisitions

1. Kimco Development Corp., with 10,656,678 sq. ft.
2. Jerry J. Moore Investments, 5,963,179
3. Roebling Investment Co., 5,439,763
4. J. J. Gumberg Co., 4,390,045
5. National Property Analysts Inc., 4,000,000
6. Leo Eisenberg Co., 3,800,000
7. Sizeler Co., 3,609,000
8. Brookhill Group, 3,473,068
9. Benderson Development, 3,215,000
10. Hopkins Development Co., 3,200,000

*Where'd you hear that?*
Monitor. Based on gross leasing area acquired between January 1, 1987 and December 31, 1989, in square feet.

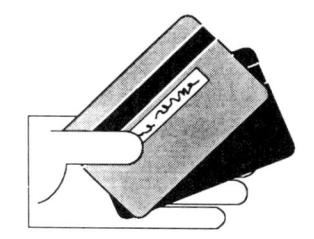

# TO MARKET

## Largest retail shell construction companies

1. Tribble & Stephens Co., with 14,234,097 sq. ft.
2. McDevitt & Street, 14,003,925
3. Hoar Construction, 9,381,548
4. Pinkerton & Laws Co., 8,215,621
5. Hale-Mills Construction Inc., 7,365,000
6. EMJ Corp., 6,835,354
7. Bencor Corp., 6,364,659
8. Pepper Cos. Inc., 5,711,400
9. Walbridge Aldinger, 5,441,000
10. Rentenbach Constructors Inc., 4,835,160

*Where'd you hear that?*
Shopping Center World, Top Contractors Survey. Based on retail shell construction square footage, June, 1984 to June, 1989.

## Largest interior construction companies

1. Pinkerton & Laws Co., with 8,215,621 sq. ft.
2. De Jager Construction Inc., 7,444,400
3. Bencor Corp., 6,364,659
4. Hale-Mills Construction Inc., 6,228,000
5. Herbert & Boghosian Inc., 5,586,700
6. Tribble & Stephens Co., 5,509,422
7. McCrory Construction Co. Inc., 5,492,000
8. Weekes Construction Inc., 4,815,300
9. Tony Crawford Construction, 4,795,000
10. Trio Construction Services, 4,737,000

*Where'd you hear that?*
Shopping Center World, Top Contractors Survey. Based on interior construction square footage, June, 1984 to June, 1989.

## Largest shopping center builders and contractors

1. Tribble & Stephens Co., with 9,324,843 sq. ft.
2. McDevitt & Street Co., 9,063,087
3. EMJ Corp., 5,910,927
4. Hale-Mills Construction Inc., 5,645,257
5. Pinkerton & Laws Co., 5,617,947
6. Hoar Construction, 5,341,750
7. Pepper Co. Inc., 5,210,056
8. De Jager Construction Inc., 5,193,000
9. Inland Construction Co., 4,820,000
10. John S. Clark Co., 4,616,150

*Where'd you hear that?*
Monitor, Top Builders and Contractors. Based on 1988 square footage.

## Largest companies in shopping center management

1. Edward J. DeBartolo Corp., with 75,749,655
2. Melvin Simon & Associates Inc., 73,546,142
3. General Growth/Center Cos., 50,200,300
4. JMB/Urban Development Co., 49,626,921
5. Rouse Co., 44,648,000
6. Jacobs, Visconsi & Jacobs Co., 39,989,265
7. Hahn Co., 34,882,000
8. Crown American Corp., 32,199,362
9. Cafaro Co., 31,795,406

# TO MARKET

10. Kravco Co., 26,854,916

*Where'd you hear that?*
Monitor. Based on gross leasing area managed as of December 31, 1989.

## Largest types of retail chains

1. Supermarkets, with 34.7%
2. Discount stores, 15.9%
3. Sears, Penney, Ward, 12%
4. Department stores, 9.8%
5. Drug stores, 6.1%
6. Apparel stores, 4.4%
7. Hard lines stores, 4.1%
8. Warehouse wholesale clubs, 3%
9. Home centers, 2.7%
10. Shoe stores, 2%

*Where'd you hear that?*
Chain Store Age Executive, Exec 100. Based on 1988 percentage of market share.

## Largest retailing companies

1. Sears, Roebuck & Co., with $53,912.9 million
2. K mart Corp., $29,557.0
3. Wal-Mart Stores, $25,921.8
4. American Stores Co., $22,004.2
5. Kroger Co., $19,087.8
6. J. C. Penney Co. Inc., $16,405.0
7. Safeway Stores, $14,324.6
8. Dayton-Hudson Corp., $13,644.7
9. May Department Stores, $12,043.0
10. Great Atlantic & Pacific Tea Co., $10,072.7

*Where'd you hear that?*
Fortune, Service 500. Based on 1989 sales, in millions of dollars.

## Most admired retailers

1. Wal-Mart, with a rating of 8.16
2. Dayton-Hudson Corp., 6.84
3. J. C. Penney Co. Inc., 6.54
4. May Department Stores, 6.51
5. Great Atlantic & Pacific Tea Co., 6.11
6. Kroger Co., 5.74
7. K mart Corp., 5.65
8. American Stores Co., 5.55
9. Safeway, 5.45
10. Sears, Roebuck & Co., 5.17

*Where'd you hear that?*
Fortune, America's Most Admired Corporations. Based on scores (0-10) derived from a survey of senior executives, outside directors, and financial analysts. Respondents ranked firms in their own industry on quality of management and products/services; innovation; long-term investment value; financial soundness; attraction and retention of talent; community and environmental responsibility; and use of assets.

## Largest retailer credit card programs

1. Sears, Roebuck and Co., with $14,758,600,000
2. J. C. Penney Co. Inc., $4,376,000,000
3. May Department Stores Co., $2,100,000,000
4. Campeau Corp./Federated Department Stores, $1,550,000,000
5. Dayton Hudson Corp., $1,216,000,000
6. Dillard Department Stores, $654,333,000

# TO MARKET

7. The Limited Inc., $486,193,000
8. Nordstrom Inc., $484,861,000
9. Carter Hawley Hale Stores Inc., $436,900,000
10. The Neiman Marcus Group, $162,442,000

*Where'd you hear that?*
Card Industry Directory. Based on dollar amount outstanding.

## Retail merchandise chains with greatest capital expenditures for expansion

1. Dayton-Hudson Corp., with $700,000 thousand
2. May Co., $700,000
3. Sears, Roebuck & Co., $631,000
4. K mart Corp., $600,000
5. Wal-Mart, $592,756
6. American Stores Co., $550,000
7. J. C. Penney Co. Inc., $500,000
8. Albertson's Inc., $369,000
9. Toys 'R' Us, $325,000
10. The Limited Inc., $325,000

*Where'd you hear that?*
Chain Store Age Executive. Based on 1989 capital expenditures for expansion, in thousands of dollars.

## Best-performing retail chains

1. Sears, Roebuck & Co.
2. K mart Corp.
3. Wal-Mart
4. Kroger Co.
5. American Stores Co.
6. J. C. Penney Co. Inc.
7. Safeway
8. Dayton-Hudson Corp.
9. May

10. A & P

*Where'd you hear that?*
Chain Store Age Executive, Exec 100. Based on performance Index. Index includes compound annual sales and profits growth, and return on assets, based on total assets of the end of the most recent fiscal year.

## Largest convenience store chains

1. Southland Corp., with 7,205
2. Circle K Corp., 4,664
3. Emro Marketing, 1,673
4. Convenient Food Mart Inc., 1,258
5. Silcorp, 1,168
6. National Convenience Stores, 1,147
7. Dairy Mart Convenience Stores, 1,145
8. Cumberland Farms, 1,100
9. Chevron Corp., 1,042
10. Amoco Corp., 1,000

*Where'd you hear that?*
Convenience Store News. Based on number of units in 1989.

## Leading convenience stores

1. Southland Corp., with $701 million
2. Circle K Corp., $263.4
3. Convenient Food Mart Inc., $80.0

*Where'd you hear that?*
Restaurants & Institutions, Restaurants & Institutions 400. Based on 1988 sales, in millions of dollars.

## Most productive supermarkets and convenience stores

1. Weis Markets, with $6.0 thousand
2. Giant Food Inc., $4.3

# TO MARKET

3. McDonald's, $4.1
4. Albertson's Inc., $3.7
4. Food Lion, $3.7
6. Bruno's, $3.0
7. Hannaford Bros. Co., $2.8
8. Smith's Food & Drug, $1.9
9. Great Atlantic & Pacific Tea Co., $1.6
9. Winn-Dixie Stores, $1.6

*Where'd you hear that?*
Forbes, Forbes 500s Annual Directory. Based on 1989 profits per employee, in thousands of dollars. Ranks U.S.-based corporations that were publicly traded as of March 23, 1990.

## Most profitable supermarkets

1. Food Lion, with 30.8%
2. Bruno's, 24.6%
3. Giant Food Inc., 23.2%
4. Arden Group, 21.4%
5. Albertson's Inc., 21.3%
6. American Stores Co., 19.6%
7. Hannaford Bros. Co., 19.5%
8. Weis Markets, 19.1%
9. Circle K Corp., 18.9%
10. Winn-Dixie Stores, 18.1%

*Where'd you hear that?*
Forbes, Annual Report on American Industry. Based on 10-year average return on equity. Ranks publicly held corporations only.

## Metropolitan areas with the highest food sales

1. New York, NY, with $10,632,951 thousand
2. Los Angeles-Long Beach, CA, $10,610,928
3. Chicago, IL, $7,422,292
4. Philadelphia, PA, $7,350,426
5. Washington, DC, $5,660,260
6. Boston-Lawrence-Salem-Lowell-Brockton, MA, $5,651,504
7. Detroit, MI, $5,613,719
8. Nassau-Suffolk, NY, $5,046,861
9. Houston, TX, $4,930,033
10. Dallas, TX, $3,935,305

*Where'd you hear that?*
Sales & Marketing Management, Survey of Buying Power. Based on sales, in thousands of dollars.

## Big 5 co-ops

1. Wakefern Food Corp., with $4.3 billion
2. Certified Grocers of California Ltd., $2.33
3. Roundy's, $2.25
4. Associated Wholesale Grocers, Inc., $1.94
5. Spartan Stores, $1.73

*Where'd you hear that?*
Supermarket News. Based on volume, in billions of dollars.

## Leading retail grocery chains

1. Kroger Co., with $19,100,000 thousand
2. American Stores Co., $18,478,354
3. Safeway Stores, Inc., $13,612,393
4. Atlantic & Pacific Tea Co., $10,067,776
5. Winn Dixie Stores, Inc., $9,007,707
6. Albertson's, Inc., $6,773,061
7. Supermarkets General Corp., $5,800,000
8. Publix Super Markets, Inc., $4,742,607
9. Stop & Shop Supermarket Co., $4,624,110
10. Vons Companies, Inc., $3,916,600

# TO MARKET

*Where'd you hear that?*
Progressive Grocer's Marketing Guidebook. Based on 1988 sales, in thousands of dollars.

## 10 largest supermarket chains ranked by dollar volume

1. American Stores Co., with $19.48 billion
2. Kroger Co., $18.8
3. Safeway, $14.3
4. A & P, $11.1
5. Winn-Dixie, $9.15
6. Albertson's Inc., $7.42
7. SGC, $6.15
8. Publix, $5.30
9. Vons, $5.22
10. Food Lion, $4.72

*Where'd you hear that?*
Mass Market Retailers, Annual Report of the Mass Market Industries. Based on 1989 dollar volume, in billions of dollars.

## 10 largest supermarket chains ranked by store count

1. Kroger Co., with 1,235
2. Winn-Dixie, 1,229
3. American Stores Co., 1,222
4. A & P, 1,215
5. Safeway, 1,117
6. Food Lion, 663
7. Albertson's Inc., 523
8. Publix, 370
9. Vons, 328
10. Grand Union, 305

*Where'd you hear that?*
Mass Market Retailers, Annual Report of the Mass Market Industries. Based on 1989 store count.

## Largest food/drug combo operators

1. Kroger Co., with 485
2. American Stores Co., 445
3. Safeway, 415
4. Albertson's Inc., 250
5. SGC, 142
6. Giant Food Inc., 101
7. Vons, 93
8. H. E. Butt, 87
9. A & P, 75
10. King Soopers, 64

*Where'd you hear that?*
Mass Market Retailers, Hybrid Formats. Based on number of combos.

## Leading supermarket companies with pharmacies

1. Kroger Co., with 473
2. Safeway, 415
3. Albertson's Inc., 226
4. Jewel Food Stores/Osco, 141
5. Pathmark, 131
6. Vons, 117
7. H. E. Butt, 107
8. Giant Food Inc., 97
9. Smith's Management, 88
10. Skaggs Alpha Beta, 87

*Where'd you hear that?*
Drug Store News, Annual Report of the Drug Chain Industry. Based on number of stores with prescription departments.

## Largest grocery wholesale companies

1. Fleming Cos., Inc., with $10,467 million
2. Super Valu Stores Inc., $10,296
3. Scrivner Inc.. $4,900
4. Wetterau Inc., $4,608
5. Wakefern Food Corp., $2,700

275

# TO MARKET

6. Roundy's Inc., $2,036
7. Certified Grocers of California Ltd., $2,000
8. Spartan Stores Inc., $1,725
9. Associated Wholesale Grocers Inc., $1,700
10. Super Food Services Inc., $1,530

*Where'd you hear that?*
U.S. Distribution Journal. Based on latest fiscal year sales, in millions of dollars.

## Largest supermarket wholesalers

1. Fleming Cos., Inc., with $12.5 billion
2. Super Valu Stores, $11.1
3. Scrivner Inc., $5.7
4. Wetterau Inc., $5.4
5. Wakefern Food Corp., $4.3
6. McLane Co., $2.7
7. Certified Grocers of California Ltd., $2.33
8. Roundy's Inc., $2.25
9. Nash Finch Co., $2.22
10. Associated Wholesale Grocers, $1.94

*Where'd you hear that?*
Supermarket News. Based on 1989 sales, in billions of dollars.

## Leading hypermarkets

1. Hypermart USA, with $360 million
2. Biggs, $220
3. Auchan, $100
4. Carrefour, $85
5. American Fare, $75
6. Twin Value, $55

*Where'd you hear that?*
Upscale Discounting, Annual Study of the World of Upscale Discounting. Based on 1989 projected dollar volume, in millions of dollars.

## Largest hypermarkets in the U.S.

1. Hypermart USA, with $275 million
2. Bigg's, $150
3. Big Bear Plus, $75
4. Carrefour, $60
5. Auchan, $5
6. Twin Valu, $0
6. American Fare, $0

*Where'd you hear that?*
Discount Store News, Discount Industry Annual Report. Based on 1988 sales, in millions of dollars.

## Leading upscale discount department stores

1. Sears, Roebuck & Co., with $32.1 billion
2. K mart Corp., $23.7
3. Wal-Mart, $20.4
4. Target Stores, $7.2
5. Montgomery Ward, $5.1
6. Ames Department Stores Inc., $5
7. Meijer, $2.42
8. Fred Meyer, Inc., $2.4
9. Bradlees, $2.1
10. Hills Department Stores Inc., $1.9
11. Caldor, $1.6

*Where'd you hear that?*
Upscale Discounting, Annual Study of the World of Upscale Discounting. Based on projected 1989 dollar volume of sales, in billions.

# TO MARKET

### Largest discount stores

1. K mart Corp., with $24,400,000,000
2. Wal-Mart, $20,969,800,000
3. Target, $7,500,000,000
4. Ames Department Stores Inc., $5,065,000,000
5. Meijer Thrifty Acres, $2,300,000,000
6. Best, $2,090,000,000
7. Hills Department Stores Inc., $2,075,000,000
8. Marshalls, $1,939,300,000
9. Bradlees, $1,750,000,000
10. Caldor, $1,650,000,000

*Where'd you hear that?*
Discount Merchandiser, True Look of the Discount Industry. Based on 1989 discount store sales.

### Largest full line discount store chains

1. K mart Corp., with $22,940,000 thousand
2. Wal-Mart, $16,820,000
3. Target, $6,331,000
4. Ames Department Stores Inc., $3,362,865
5. Meijer, $3,000,000
6. Bradlees, $2,106,747
7. Fred Meyer, Inc., $2,073,544
8. Hills Department Stores Inc., $1,670,866
9. Caldor, $1,574,000
10. Rose's, $1,439,279

*Where'd you hear that?*
Chain Store Age Executive, Exec 100. Based on 1988 sales, in thousands of dollars.

### Leading full-line discounters in sales

1. K mart Corp., with $22,940 million
2. Wal-Mart, $16,820
3. Target, $6,331
4. Montgomery Ward, $4,784
5. Ames Department Stores Inc., $3,363
6. Meijer, $3,000
7. Zayre, $2,600
8. Bradlees, $2,107
9. Fred Meyer, Inc., $2,074
10. Hills Department Stores Inc., $1,671

*Where'd you hear that?*
Discount Store News, Discount Industry Annual Report. Based on 1988 sales, in millions of dollars.

### Largest discount store chains

1. K mart Corp., with $22,940 million
2. Wal-Mart, $16,820
3. Target, $6,331
4. Montgomery Ward, $4,784
5. Price Club, $4,053
6. Sam's, $3,829
7. Toys 'R' Us, $3,645
8. Ames Department Stores Inc., $3,363
9. Service Merchandise, $3,093
10. Meijer, $3,000

*Where'd you hear that?*
Discount Store News, Discount Industry Annual Report. Based on 1988 sales, in millions of dollars.

### Largest specialty discounters

1. Toys 'R' Us, with $4.4 billion
2. Circuit City Stores, $2.0 billion
3. Highland Superstores, $1.1 billion

# TO MARKET

4. Silo, $938 million
5. Kay Bee, $890 million
6. Child World, $871 million
7. Thrifty Corp., $737 million
8. Herman's, $735 million
9. Best Buy, $573 million
10. Lionel, $470 million

*Where'd you hear that?*
Upscale Discounting, Annual Study of the World of Upscale Discounting. Based on 1989 projected dollar volume.

## Discounters' top traffic builders

1. Candy, with 9.2%
2. Household paper products, 7.9%
3. Hair care/Personal care items, 7.0%
4. Toys/games, 5.6%
5. Household cleaners, 5.4%
6. Laundry products, 5.1%
7. Food, 4.0%
8. Sheets, Comforters, Bedspreads, 3.5%
9. Halloween costumes/Decor, 3.3%
10. Women's blouses/shirts, 3.1%
10. Women's jeans, 3.1%

*Where'd you hear that?*
Discount Store News, Traffic Builders Survey. Based on percent of total number of products mentioned by shoppers as traffic builders at discount stores. Survey is based on interviews with shoppers in market areas covering major regions of the country. Survey is conducted to find out about consumer awareness of promotions carried out to increase sales traffic in stores.

### Leading discount store chains in sales

1. K mart Corp., $22,940 million
2. Wal-Mart, $16,820
3. Target, $6,331
4. Montgomery Ward, $4,784
5. Price Club, $4,053
6. Sam's, $3,829
7. Toys 'R' Us, $3,645
8. Ames Department Stores Inc., $3,363
9. Service Merchandise, $3,093
10. Meijer, $3,000

*Where'd you hear that?*
Discount Store News, Discount Industry Annual Report. Based on 1988 sales, in millions of dollars.

### Fastest growing discount chains in sales

1. Wal-Mart, $3,572 million
2. Ames Department Stores Inc., $1,251
3. Sam's, $1,118
4. Target, $1,025
5. Price Club, $817
6. Toys 'R' Us, $758
7. K mart Corp., $699
8. Costco Wholesale Club, $619
9. Service Merchandise, $374
10. Circuit City Stores, $371

*Where'd you hear that?*
Discount Store News, Discount Industry Annual Report. Based on sales growth, 1987-88, in millions of dollars.

### Fastest growing discount chains in percentage of sales growth

1. Office Depot, with 288.2%
2. Staples, 197.5%
3. Price Savers, 100.0%
4. Whitlock, 73.3%
5. Ames Department Stores Inc., 59.2%
6. Northern Automotive, 56.4%
7. Bigg's, 50.0%
8. Wholesale Club, 47.8%
9. Costco Wholesale Club, 45.2%

# TO MARKET

10. Kids 'R' Us, 42.0%

*Where'd you hear that?*
Discount Store News, Discount Industry Annual Report. Based on sales growth, 1987-88, in percent.

## Leading discount store chains in profits

1. K mart Corp., with $1,436.0 million
2. Wal-Mart, $1,325.0
3. Toys 'R' Us, $428.8
4. Target, $341.0
5. Price Club, $156.6
6. Montgomery Ward, $130.0
7. Service Merchandise, $121.3
8. Circuit City Stores, $114.5
9. Hills Department Stores Inc., $97.7
10. Bradlees, $84.9

*Where'd you hear that?*
Discount Store News, Discount Industry Annual Report. Based on 1988 earnings, in millions of dollars.

## Largest discount chains ranked by dollar volume

1. K mart Corp., with $29.5 billion
2. Wal-Mart, $25.8
3. Target, $7.5
4. Ames Department Stores Inc., $5.1
5. Hills Department Stores Inc., $2.1
6. Bradlees, $1.8
7. Caldor, $1.7
8. Rose's, $1.5
9. Venture, $1.3
10. Jamesway, $0.9

*Where'd you hear that?*
Mass Market Retailers, Annual Report of the Mass Market Industries. Based on 1989 dollar volume, in billions of dollars.

## Largest discount chains ranked by store count

1. K mart Corp., with 2,315
2. Wal-Mart, 1,402
3. Ames Department Stores Inc., 606
4. Target, 399
5. Rose's, 258
6. Hills Department Stores Inc., 208
7. Jamesway, 130
8. Bradlees, 129
9. Caldor, 118
10. Shopko, 99

*Where'd you hear that?*
Mass Market Retailers, Annual Report of the Mass Market Industries. Based on 1989 store count.

## Fastest growing discount chains in store count growth

1. Northern Automotive, with 391
2. Ames Department Stores Inc., 332
3. Family Dollar Stores, 159
4. Wal-Mart, 145
5. Whitlock, 90
6. Champs Sports, 87
7. Nationwise, 85
8. Dress Barn, 76
9. Thrifty Corp., 73

*Where'd you hear that?*
Discount Store News, Discount Industry Annual Report. Based on number of new stores in 1988.

# TO MARKET

## Leading discount store chains in selling space

1. K mart Corp., 124,410 thousand sq. ft.
2. Wal-Mart, 100,720
3. Ames Department Stores Inc., 52,644
4. Target, 34,100
5. Montgomery Ward, 25,920
6. Toys 'R' Us, 18,860
7. Service Merchandise, 17,435
8. Hills Department Stores Inc., 13,360
9. Best Products, 12,610
10. Fred Meyer, Inc., 11,760

*Where'd you hear that?*
Discount Store News, Discount Industry Annual Report. Based on total footage, in thousands of square feet.

## Fastest growing discount chains in earnings growth

1. Wal-Mart, with $257.0 million
2. Toys 'R' Us, $82.9
3. Service Merchandise, $76.7
4. K mart Corp., $52.0
5. Bradlees, $27.9
6. Circuit City Stores, $25.3
7. Costco Wholesale Club, $20.3
8. Ross Stores, $18.0
8. Target, $18.0
10. Price Club, $16.9

*Where'd you hear that?*
Discount Store News, Discount Industry Annual Report. Based on earnings growth, 1987-88, in millions of dollars.

## Largest mass market retailers ranked by dollar volume

1. K mart Corp., with $29.5 billion
2. Wal-Mart, $25.8
3. American Stores Co., $22.0
4. Kroger Co., $18.8
5. Safeway, $14.3
6. A & P, $11.1
7. Winn-Dixie, $9.2
8. Target Stores, $7.5
9. Albertson's Inc., $7.5
10. Walgreens, $5.6

*Where'd you hear that?*
Mass Market Retailers, Annual Report of the Mass Market Industries. Based on 1989 dollar volume, in billions of dollars.

## Largest mass market retailers ranked by net income

1. Wal-Mart, with $1.1 billion
2. K mart Corp., $322.7 million
3. Albertson's Inc., $196.6 million
4. Walgreens, $154.2 million
5. A & P, $146.7 million
6. Food Lion, $139.8 million
7. Winn-Dixie, $134.5 million
8. American Stores Co., $118.1 million
9. Giant Food Inc., $108.4 million
10. Rite Aid, $81.9 million

*Where'd you hear that?*
Mass Market Retailers, Annual Report of the Mass Market Industries. Based on 1989 net income.

## Largest corporations in the discount retailing industry

1. Wal-Mart Stores, with $26,750 million
2. Sears, Roebuck & Co., $14,342
3. J. C. Penney Co. Inc., $8,280
4. Toys 'R' Us, $7,713
5. The Limited Inc., $7,323
6. K mart Corp., $7,017

7. May Department Stores, $6,078
8. Melville, $4,954
9. Dayton-Hudson Corp., $4,857
10. Woolworth, $4,104

*Where'd you hear that?*
Business Week, The Business Week 1000. Based on market value as of March 16, 1990, in millions of dollars.

## Largest department stores

1. Mervyn's (Hayward, CA), with $3,411 million
2. Macy's Northeast (New York), $3,315
3. Nordstrom (Seattle), $2,327.9
4. Dayton-Hudson Corp. (Minneapolis), $1,693
5. Macy's California (San Francisco), $1,465
6. Bloomingdale's (New York), $1,188.9
7. Saks Fifth Avenue (New York), $1,154
8. The Broadway (Los Angeles), $1,125
9. Marshall Field's (Chicago), $1,024
10. Neiman-Marcus (Dallas), $1,020

*Where'd you hear that?*
Stores. Based on 1988 sales volume, in millions of dollars.

## Most productive department stores

1. General Cinema Corp., $37.7 thousand
2. Mercantile Stores, $5.9
3. Dillard Department Stores, $5.6
4. Equitable of Iowa, $5.0
5. J. C. Penney Co. Inc., $4.1
6. May Department Stores, $4.0
7. Sears, Roebuck, $3.0
8. Carter Hawley Hale Stores Inc., $0.2

*Where'd you hear that?*
Forbes, Forbes 500s Annual Directory. Based on 1989 profits per employee, in thousands of dollars. Ranks U.S.-based corporations that were publicly traded as of March 23, 1990.

## Most profitable department stores

1. General Cinema Corp., with 27.5%
2. Dillard Department Stores, 19.2%
3. Mercantile Stores, 16.7%
4. May Department Stores, 16.2%
5. Strawbridge, 14.4%
6. J. C. Penney Co. Inc., 14.0%
7. Sears, Roebuck, 11.1%
8. Equitable of Iowa, 9.9%
9. Alexander's, 2.1%
10. Carter Hawley Hale Stores Inc., NA

*Where'd you hear that?*
Forbes, Annual Report on American Industry. Based on 10-year average return on equity. Ranks publicly held corporations only.

## Top 10 department stores in electronics sales

1. Macy's Northeast, with $275 million
2. Macy's California, $161
3. Dillard Department Stores, $130
4. Hills Department Stores Inc., $100
5. Dayton-Hudson Corp., $78
6. Foley's, $72
7. Lazarus, $70

# TO MARKET

# TO MARKET

8. Abraham & Straus, $68
9. Burdines, $66
10. Boscov's, $62

*Where'd you hear that?*
HFD, Focus 200 Consumer Electronics' Top Retailers. Based on 1988 electronics sales volume.

## Top Canadian franchises

1. Uniglobe Travel
2. Mr. Submarine
3. First Choice Haircutters
4. Treats
5. The Second Cup Ltd.
6. Japan Camera Centre 1 Hour Photo
7. Mike's Restaurant
8. Grandma Lee's
9. Baskin-Robbins 31 Ice Cream/Silcorp
10. Yogen Fruz

*Where'd you hear that?*
Entrepreneur, Entrepreneur Annual Franchise 500. Based on industrial ranking, 1989.

## Top U.S. franchises

1. Subway
2. Domino's Pizza Inc.
3. McDonald's
4. Little Caesars Pizza
5. Burger King Corp.
6. International Dairy Queen
7. Arby's Inc.
8. Chem-Dry
9. Hardee's Inc.
10. Century 21 Real Estate Corp.

*Where'd you hear that?*
Entrepreneur, Entrepreneur Annual Franchise 500. Based on scores in overall weighted ranking, listed by industrial rank.

## Fastest-growing franchises

1. Subway
2. Domino's Pizza Inc.
3. West Coast Video
4. McDonald's
5. Little Caesars Pizza
6. TCBY
7. Chem-Dry
8. Burger King Corp.
9. Jazzercise Inc.
10. Mail Boxes Etc. USA

*Where'd you hear that?*
Entrepreneur, Entrepreneur Annual Franchise 500. Based on number of new franchises added, 1989.

## Top new franchises

1. West Coast Video
2. General Nutrition Franchising Inc.
3. Red Carpet Real Estate Services Inc.
4. Fax-9
5. Rally's Hamburgers
6. Winchell's Donut House
7. O.P.E.N. Cleaning Systems
8. Jackson Hewitt Tax Service
9. Freshens Premium Yogurt
10. The Pro Image

*Where'd you hear that?*
Entrepreneur, Entrepreneur Annual Franchise 500. Based on industrial ranking. Ranks companies that began franchising since 1985.

## Top low-investment retail-trade franchises

1. Jazzercise Inc.
2. H & R Block
3. Packy the Hipper, Pack 'N Ship
4. Coverall North America Inc.
5. Novus Windshield Repair
6. Fax-9

## TO MARKET

7. Triple Check Income Tax Service
8. O.P.E.N. Cleaning Systems
9. *Homes & Land Magazine*
10. National Maintenance Contractors

*Where'd you hear that?*
Entrepreneur, Entrepreneur Annual Franchise 500. Based on weighted rating for franchises with a minimum total investment of less than $10,000 as of 1989.

### Largest black-owned franchises

1. McDonald's Corp., with 418
2. Burger King Corp., 174
3. Popeye's Famous Fried Chicken and Biscuits Inc., 150
4. Kentucky Fried Chicken Corp., 135
5. Subway Sandwiches and Salads, 126
6. The Southland Corp. (7-Eleven), 103
7. Almost Heaven Ltd., 87
8. Wendy's International Inc., 65
9. Church's Fried Chicken Inc., 56
10. American Speedy Printing Centers Inc., 46

*Where'd you hear that?*
Black Enterprise, Top 50 Franchises. Based on number of black-owned franchise units in 1989.

### Largest office supply megastores

1 Office Depot, with $132 million
2 Staples, $120
3 Super City, $100
3 Arvey Paper & Office Products, $100
5 Office Club, $51
6 Jaffe's, $40
7 WORKplace, $25
7 Office Place, $25
9 BizMart, $20
10 O. P. Club, $15

*Where'd you hear that?*
Discount Store News, Discount Industry Annual Report. Based on 1988 sales, in millions of dollars.

### Top 10 eyewear retailers

1. Pearle Inc., with $599 million
2. U.S. Shoe (Lens Crafters), $489
3. Cole National (Cole Vision, Eyelab), $311
4. Sterling Optical, $120
5. Royal International, $101
6. D & K Optical, $75
7. Eye Care Centers of America, $73
8. Benson Optical, $70
9. NuVision, $58
10. Eckerd Vision Group, $57

*Where'd you hear that?*
New York Times. Based on sales for the 12 months ended September 30, 1989, in millions of dollars.

### Most productive drug and discount stores

1. Longs Drug Stores, Inc., $4.6 thousand
2. Wal-Mart Stores, $4.4

283

# TO MARKET

3. Rite Aid, $3.6
4. Walgreen, $3.3
5. Dayton-Hudson Corp., $2.9
6. K mart, $0.9
7. Rose's Stores, $0.4
8. Ames Department Stores Inc., $0.0
8. Hills Department Stores Inc., $0.0
10. Fred Meyer, Inc., $-0.3

*Where'd you hear that?*
Forbes, Forbes 500s Annual Directory. Based on 1989 profits per employee, in thousands of dollars. Ranks U.S.-based corporations that were publicly traded as of March 23, 1990.

## Largest drugstore chains

1. Walgreen Co., with $4,751 million
2. American Stores Co., $3,190
3. Imasco Ltd., $3,405.6
4. Jack Eckerd Corp., $2,800
5. Rite Aid Corp., $2,700
6. Revco Drug Stores, $2,400
7. Longs Drug Stores, Inc., $1,925
8. Melville Corp., $1,817.9
9. Pacific Enterprises, $1,800
10. K mart Corp., $1,500

*Where'd you hear that?*
Private Label. Based on 1989 chain sales, in millions of dollars.

## Largest American drug chains

1. Walgreens (Deerfield, IL), with $5,380 million
2. American Stores Co. (Oak Brook, IL), $3,520
3. Eckerd Drug (Clearwater, FL), $3,200
4. Thrifty (Los Angeles, CA), $3,100
5. Rite Aid (Shiremanstown, PA), $3,012
6. Revco (Twinsburg, OH), $2,701
7. Longs Drug Stores, Inc. (Walnut Creek, CA), $2,111
8. CVS (Woonsocket, RI), $1,950
9. Hook-SupeRx, Inc. (Cincinnati, OH), $1,730
10. Pay Less NW (Wilsonville, OR), $1,600

*Where'd you hear that?*
Drug Store News, Report of the Drug Chain Industry. Based on 1989 dollar volume, in millions.

## Largest American drug chains

1. Rite Aid (Shiremanstown, PA), with 2,353
2. Revco (Twinsburg, OH), 1,888
3. Eckerd Drug (Clearwater, FL), 1,630
4. Walgreens (Deerfield, IL), 1,484
5. Hook-SupeRx, Inc., (Cincinnati, OH), 1,040
6. Medicine Shoppe (St. Louis, MO), 821
7. Thrifty (Los Angeles, CA), 809
8. CVS (Woonsocket, RI), 789
9. American Stores Co. (Oak Brook, IL), 675
10. Peoples (Alexandria, VA), 486

*Where'd you hear that?*
Drug Store News, Report of the Drug Chain Industry. Based on number of stores in 1989.

## Largest private label drugstore chains

1. Rite Aid, with $378.0 million
2. Walgreen, $332.6
3. Eckerd Drug, $224.0
4. American Stores Co., $223.3
4. Imasco Ltd., $221.8

**TO MARKET**

6. Melville, $171.4
7. Revco, $144.0
8. Longs Drug Stores, Inc., $115.5
9. Thrifty Drug, $99.0
10. Hook-SupeRx, Inc., $78.0

*Where'd you hear that?*
Private Label. Based on 1989 private label sales, in millions of dollars.

## Largest deep discount drug store chains

1. Drug Emporium, with $880 million
2. Phar-Mor, $752
3. F & M Distributors Inc., $402
4. Rockbottom, $200
5. Marc's, $197
6. Freddy's, $130
7. Drug Palace, $78
8. dot, $70
9. A. L. Price, $49
10. Rx Place, $46

*Where'd you hear that?*
Discount Store News, Discount Industry Annual Report. Based on 1988 sales, in millions of dollars.

## Largest deep discount drug operators

1. Drug Emporium, with 193
2. Phar-Mor, 167
3. F & M Distributors Inc., 80
4. Drug Palace (Rite Aid), 40
4. Pic 'N Save (National Merchandise), 40
6. Rockbottom, 28
7. Freddy's (Melville), 25
8. Marc's, Bernie Shulman's Expect (Marc Glassman), 19
9. Drugs for Less (Big B), 18
10. A. L. Price (Perry), 16

*Where'd you hear that?*
Mass Market Retailers, Hybrid Formats. Based on number of outlets.

## Largest drugstore markets

1. Los Angeles-Long Beach, CA, with $2,433,310 thousand
2. Chicago, IL, $2,028,626
3. New York, NY, $1,870,802
4. Detroit, MI, $1,433,077
5. Philadelphia, PA, $1,262,465
6. Washington, DC, $1,260,519
7. Boston-Lawrence-Salem-Lowell-Brockton, MA, $1,056,789
8. Atlanta, GA, $808,777
9. Miami-Hialeah, FL, $774,337
10. Houston, TX, $692,772
11. Oakland, CA, $662,512

*Where'd you hear that?*
Sales & Marketing Management, Survey of Buying Power. Based on sales, in thousands of dollars.

## Best-selling general merchandise at drugstores ranked by unit movement

1. Bounty paper towels
2. Clorox bleach gal
3. Kodak VRG 100 135-24
4. Kodak VRG 200 SP 135-24
5. Eveready AA Energizer 4 pk
6. Polaroid 600 film
7. Arm & Hammer baking soda 16 oz.
8. Dove liquid 48 oz.
9. Dawn liquid 22 oz.
10. Duracell AA 4 pk

# TO MARKET

*Where'd you hear that?*
Drug Store News, Drug Store News Triple-A Product Performance Survey. Based on number of units sold in 1988.

## Product categories with highest number of items in drug stores

1. Natural vitamins, mineral, supplements, with 1,956
2. Shampoo, 1,525
3. Synthetic vitamins, 1,251
4. Hair conditioning rinses, 1,134
5. Hand & body cream/lotions, 999
6. Internal analgesics, 949
7. Chocolate candy bars, 928
8. Facial preparations, 884
9. Hair dressing needs, 853
10. Cold remedies, 849

*Where'd you hear that?*
Drug Store News. Based on number of different items in category for the year ending May 19, 1989.

## Best-selling general merchandise at drugstores ranked by sales

1. Polaroid 600 High Spd film
2. Polaroid SX 70 Time Zero
3. Polaroid 600 High Spd film twin
4. Kodak VRG 200 135-24
5. Kodak VRG 100 print film 135-24
6. Duracell AA 8 pk
7. Kodak HR disc 2 pk
8. Kodak VRG 400 carded 135-24
9. Eveready AA Energizer 4 pk
10. Kodak VRG 100 carded 3 pk/135

*Where'd you hear that?*
Drug Store News, Drug Store News Triple-A Product Performance Survey. Based on 1988 dollar volume.

## Product categories with highest annual sales per item in drug stores

1. Home testing kits, with $2.2 million
2. Formula baby food, $1.6
3. Measured diet meals, $1.4
4. Disposable baby diapers, $1.3
4. Chest rubs, $1.3
6. Packaged candy covered chocolate, $1.1
7. Tampons, $1.0
7. Eye care products, $1.0
9. Contraceptives, $0.9
9. Internal analgesics, $0.9

*Where'd you hear that?*
Drug Store News. Based on retail sales for the year ending May 19, 1989, in millions of dollars.

## Best-selling health and beauty aids at drugstores ranked by unit movement

1. Fleet adult enema 4.5 oz.
2. B & L saline solution sensitive eyes 12 oz.
3. Chap Stick
4. Advil tablets 24
5. Tylenol extra strength caplets 50
6. Blistik lip balm
7. Plax dental rinse
8. Q-tips 300
9. Tylenol extra strength caplets 24
10. Mylanta 12 oz.

*Where'd you hear that?*
Drug Store News, Drug Store News Triple-A Product Performance Survey. Based on number of units sold in 1988.

## Best-selling health and beauty aids at drugstores ranked by sales

1. Tylenol extra strength caplets 100
2. Listerine mouthwash 32 oz.
3. Tylenol extra strength caplets 50
4. Plax dental rinse original 16 oz.
5. Centrum vitamins 130
6. Plax dental rinse mint 16 oz.
7. Pampers Ultra Plus large 32
8. AoSept disinfecting solution 12 oz.
9. Huggies Supertrim large 32
10. AoSept disinfecting solution 8 oz.

*Where'd you hear that?*
Drug Store News, Drug Store News Triple-A Product Performance Survey. Based on 1988 dollar volume.

## Housewares sales distribution

1. Discounters, with 27.5%
2. Supermarkets, 11.2%
3. Wholesalers, 10.6%
4. National chains, 7.9%
5. Department stores, 7.7%
6. Catalog showrooms, 5.8%
7. Mail order, 4.7%
8. Drug stores, 4.4%
9. Warehouse clubs, 3.9%
10. Hardware stores, 3.6%

*Where'd you hear that?*
Non-Foods Merchandising. Based on 1988 sales share, in percent.

## Metropolitan areas with top building material and hardware store sales

1. Los Angeles-Long Beach, CA, with $2,499,301 thousand
2. Chicago, IL, $1,929,215
3. New York, NY, $1,647,076
4. Detroit, MI, $1,624,914
5. Philadelphia, PA, $1,525,513
6. Boston-Lawrence-Salem-Lowell-Brockton, MA, $1,458,665
7. Houston, TX, $1,278,580
8. Nassau-Suffolk, NY, $1,249,103
9. Washington, DC, $1,245,580
10. Atlanta, GA, $1,188,773

*Where'd you hear that?*
Sales & Marketing Management, Survey of Buying Power. Based on sales, in thousands of dollars.

## Largest automotive specialty chains

1. Western Auto, with $1,107 million
2. Northern Automotive, $660
3. Pep Boys, $656
4. AutoZone, $440
5. Chief Auto Parts, $312
6. Nationwise, $262
7. Whitlock, $260
8. Trak Auto, $243
9. PACCAR, $190

*Where'd you hear that?*
Discount Store News, Discount Industry Annual Report. Based on 1988 sales, in millions of dollars.

## Largest appliance retailers

1. Sears, Roebuck & Co., with $5.6 billion
2. Montgomery Ward & Co., $650 million

# TO MARKET

# TO MARKET

3. Circuit City Stores, $344 million
4. Silo, $206 million
5. Highland Superstores, $200 million
6. Lowe's Cos., $163 million
7. P. C. Richard & Son, $132 million
8. ABC Appliance Center, $120 million
9. Tops Appliance City, $119 million
10. Price Club, $106 million

*Where'd you hear that?*
HFD. Based on 1988 major appliance dollar volume.

## Metropolitan statistical areas with the most furniture, home furnishing, and appliance store sales

1. Los Angeles-Long Beach, CA, with $4,957,395 thousand
2. New York, NY, $4,457,969
3. Chicago, IL, $2,798,436
4. Washington, DC, $2,162,941
5. Nassau-Suffolk, NY, $1,988,274
6. Detroit, MI, $1,804,245
7. Boston-Lawrence-Salem-Lowell-Brockton, MA, $1,742,487
8. Philadelphia, PA, $1,674,431
9. Atlanta, GA, $1,195,034
10. Houston, TX, $1,152,880

*Where'd you hear that?*
Sales & Marketing Management, Survey of Buying Power. Based on 1988 sales, in thousands of dollars.

## Metropolitan Statistical Areas with the most furniture and sleep equipment sales

1. New York, NY, with $1,658,942 thousand
2. Los Angeles-Long Beach, CA, $1,559,137
3. Chicago, IL, $1,147,098
4. Washington, DC, $799,542
5. Boston-Lawrence-Salem-Lowell-Brockton, MA, $730,247
6. Philadelphia, PA, $728,590
7. Detroit, MI, $683,890
8. Nassau-Suffolk, NY, $651,020
9. Atlanta, GA, $513,736
10. Houston, TX, $505,470

*Where'd you hear that?*
Sales & Marketing Management. Based on 1988 sales, in thousands of dollars.

## Largest retailers of furniture and lighting

1. Levitz Furniture Corp., with $921 million
2. Sears, Roebuck & Co., $812
3. Ethan Allen Inc., $620
4. Montgomery Ward, $610
5. J. C. Penney Co. Inc., $600
6. Spiegel, $300
7. Heilig-Meyers, $295
8. Seaman's, $268
9. W. S. Badcock, $261
10. Rhodes, $250

*Where'd you hear that?*
HFD. Based on 1988 sales volume, in millions of dollars.

## Largest textile market share by store type

1. National chains, with 39.0%
2. Mass merchants, 32.7%
3. Department stores, 19.3%

# TO MARKET

4. Specialty stores, 5.2%
5. Catalog houses, 2.2%
6. Warehouse clubs, 1.6%

*Where'd you hear that?*
HFD, HFD Top 100 Retailers of Home Textiles. Based on 1988 market share, in percent.

## Best performing textile retailing companies

1. Woodward & Lothrup, with 24.5%
2. Belk, 21.0%
3. J. C. Penney Co. Inc., 20.0%
4. Jacobson's, 10.1%
5. Beall's, 10.0%
6. Bradlees, 9.7%
7. Stern's, 9.0%
8. Bloomingdale's, 8.9%
9. Emporium-Capwell, 8.8%
10. McRae's, 8.3%

*Where'd you hear that?*
HFD, HFD Top 100 Retailers of Home Textiles. Based on 1988 textile sales as a percentage of total sales.

## Retailers with the largest textile sales volume

1. J. C. Penney Co. Inc., with $2,790.2 thousand
2. Sears, Roebuck & Co., $2,294.0
3. K mart Corp., $1,366.4
4. Wal-Mart, $1,008.0
5. Target Stores, $506.4
6. Mervyn's, $272.7
7. Ames/Zayre, $262.0
8. Montgomery Ward, $239.0
9. Bradlees, $222.0
10. Belk, $216.0

*Where'd you hear that?*
HFD, HFD Top 100 Retailers of Home Textiles. Based on 1988 textile sales volume, in thousands of dollars.

## Fastest growing textile retailers by percent increase

1. Luxury Linens, with 328.0%
2. Costco Wholesale Club, 83.3%
3. Goudchaux, 66.6%
4. Domestications, 66.0%
5. Dayton-Hudson Corp., 60.3%
6. Hess's, 40.5%
7. Meijer, 40.0%
8. Sam's Wholesale, 39.0%
9. Beall's, 36.0%
10. Kohl's, 33.8%

*Where'd you hear that?*
HFD, HFD Top 100 Retailers of Home Textiles. Based on 1988 increase in sales, in percent.

## Fastest growing textile retailers by dollar increase

1. Wal-Mart, with $216.0 million
2. Sears, Roebuck & Co., $128.0
3. K mart Corp., $85.1
4. Target, $81.6
5. Dayton-Hudson Corp., $38.0
6. Belk, $36.0
7. Luxury Linens, $23.0
8. Costco Wholesale Club, $22.9
9. Dillard Department Stores, $22.1
10. Bradlees, $22.0

*Where'd you hear that?*
HFD, HFD Top 100 Retailers of Home Textiles. Based on 1988 dollar increase in sales, in millions.

# TO MARKET

### Largest full price apparel chains

1. The Limited Inc., $4,070,777 thousand
2. U.S. Shoe, $1,151,400
3. The Gap, Inc., $1,252,097
4. Petrie Stores, $1,218,341
5. Charming Shoppes, $725,200
6. Hartmarx, $627,600
7. F. W. Woolworth Co., $577,400
8. Melville, $469,300
9. Edison Brosthers Stores, $459,000
10. Kids 'R' Us, $360,000

*Where'd you hear that?*
Chain Store Age Executive, Exec 100. Based on 1988 sales, in thousands of dollars.

### Most productive apparel retailers

1. The Limited Inc., with $5.8 thousand
2. The Gap, Inc., $4.6
3. Nordstrom, $4.3
4. Melville, $4.0
5. TJX Cos., $3.0
6. Petrie Stores, $1.4
7. Brown Group, $1.2
8. US Shoe, $1.1

*Where'd you hear that?*
Forbes, Forbes 500s Annual Directory. Based on 1989 profits per employee, in thousands of dollars. Ranks U.S.-based corporations that were publicly traded as of March 23, 1990.

### Most profitable apparel stores

1. The Limited Inc., with 39.9%
2. Charming Shoppes, 28.8%
3. The Gap, Inc., 26.7%
4. Burlington Coat, 24.2%
5. Melville, 23.4%
6. Nordstrom, 19.8%
7. Petrie Stores, 15.5%
8. Hartmarx, 11.9%
9. US Shoe, 11.6%
10. Brown Group, 11.5%

*Where'd you hear that?*
Forbes, Annual Report on American Industry. Based on 10-year average return on equity. Ranks publicly held corporations only.

### Largest off-price apparel specialty chains

1. Marshalls, with $1,753 million
2. T. J. Maxx, $1,490
3. Burlington Coat, $639
4. Ross Stores, $634
5. Hit or Miss, $370
6. Kids 'R' Us, $355
7. Loehmann's, $334
8. Filene's Basement, $300
9. Syms, $283
10. Dress Barn, $204

*Where'd you hear that?*
Discount Store News, Discount Industry Annual Report. Based on 1988 sales, in millions of dollars.

### Largest markets for women's and girls' clothing sales

1. New York, NY, with $4,167,766 thousand
2. Los Angeles-Long Beach, CA, $3,357,027
3. Chicago, IL, $3,080,092
4. Philadelphia, PA, $2,230,818
5. Boston-Lawrence-Salem-Lowell-Brockton, MA, $1,916,613
6. Washington, DC, $1,802,314
7. Detroit, MI, $1,719,333
8. Nassau-Suffolk, NY, $1,390,801
9. Houston, TX, $1,283,946
10. Atlanta, GA, $1,228,453

*Where'd you hear that?*
Sales & Marketing Management, Survey of Buying Power. Based on sales, in thousands of dollars.

## Largest markets for apparel and accessory store sales

1. New York, NY, with $4,642,312 thousand
2. Los Angeles-Long Beach, CA, $3,585,100
3. Chicago, IL, $2,940,586
4. Philadelphia, PA, $2,135,791
5. Boston-Lawrence-Salem-Lowell-Brockton, MA, $1,845,217
6. Detroit, MI, $1,718,434
7. Washington, DC, $1,715,775
8. Nassau-Suffolk, NY, $1,444,341
9. Houston, TX, $1,350,439
10. Anaheim-Santa Ana, CA, $1,235,820

*Where'd you hear that?*
Sales & Marketing Management, Survey of Buying Power. Based on sales, in thousands of dollars.

## Leading sporting goods retailers

1. Foot Locker, with $1,070 million
2. Herman's, $647
3. Oshman's, $305
4. Athlete's Foot, $253
5. Big 5, $200
6. REI, $183
7. Sportmart, $117
8. Champs, $110
9. MC Sports, $94
10. Athletic Express, $91

*Where'd you hear that?*
Sports Market Place, Market Statistics Report. Based on 1988 sales, in millions of dollars.

## Largest sporting goods specialty chains

1. Herman's, with $700 million
2. Thrifty Corp., $635
3. Oshman's, $305
4. Sportmart, $165
5. Champs Sports, $88
6. Academy, $82
7. Modell's Sporting Goods, $71
8. Sports Authority, $40
9. Sports Town, $20
10. Irving's Sport Shops, $16

*Where'd you hear that?*
Discount Store News, Discount Industry Annual Report. Based on 1988 sales, in millions of dollars.

## Top 10 electronics chains

1. Radio Shack, with $2.968 billion
2. Curtis Mathes, $367 million
3. The Federated Group, $253 million
4. The Wiz, $220 million
5. The Good Guys, $160 million
6. Erol's Inc., $155 million
7. Wall to Wall Sound & Video, $95 million
8. SaveMart, $95 million
9. Western Auto, $78 million
10. Leo's Stereo, $70 million

*Where'd you hear that?*
HFD, Focus 200 Consumer Electronics' Top Retailers. Based on 1988 electronics sales volume.

# TO MARKET

# TO MARKET

## Top 10 electronics/appliance chains in electronics sales

1. Circuit City Stores, with $1.377 billion
2. Highland Superstores, $641 million
3. Silo Inc., $610 million
4. Best Buy, $330 million
5. Tandy Name Brand, $300 million
6. Lechmere, $300 million
7. Crazy Eddie, $253 million
8. ABC Appliance Center, $235 million
9. Fretter Inc., $190 million
10. American of Madison, $185 million

*Where'd you hear that?*
HFD, Focus 200 Consumer Electronics' Top Retailers. Based on 1988 electronics sales volume.

## Market-share of types of electronic retailers

1. Mass merchants, with 29.0%
2. Electronics/Appliance chains, 25.0%
3. Electronics chains, 22.1%
4. Catalog showrooms, 8.1%
5. Department stores, 6.1%
6. Others, total 9.7%

*Where'd you hear that?*
HFD, Focus 200 Consumer Electronics' Top Retailers. Based on percentage market share of total 1988 sales of Focus 200.

## Largest electronics retailers

1. Radio Shack, with $3,175 million
2. Sears, Roebuck & Co., $3,000
3. K mart Corp., $2,950
4. Circuit City Stores, $1,828
5. Service Merchandise, $1,200
6. Wal-Mart Stores, $848
7. Montgomery Ward, $830
8. Silo, $800
9. Highland Superstores, $743
10. Best Products, $600

*Where'd you hear that?*
Consumer Electronics, Consumer Electronics Top 300 Retailers. Based on projected 1989 sales volume, in millions of dollars.

## Top electronics retailers of all types

1. Radio Shack, with $2,968 million
2. K mart Corp., $2,475
3. Sears, Roebuck & Co., $2,063
4. Circuit City Stores, $1,377
5. Service Merchandise, $1,250
6. Montgomery Ward, $750
7. Wal-Mart Stores, $655
8. Target, $650
9. Highland Superstores, $641
10. Silo, $610

*Where'd you hear that?*
HFD, Focus 200 Consumer Electronics' Top Retailers. Based on 1988 electronics sales volume.

## Top 10 mass merchandisers for electronics sales

1. K mart Corp., with $2.475 billion
2. Sears, $2.063 billion
3. Montgomery Ward, $750 million
4. Wal-Mart Stores, $655 million
5. Target, $650 million
6. Venture Stores, $132 million
7. Caldor, $126 million
8. Ames Department Stores Inc., $125 million

292

9. Zayre, $125 million
10. Rose's Stores, $120 million

*Where'd you hear that?*
HFD, Focus 200 Consumer Electronics' Top Retailers. Based on 1988 electronics sales volume.

## Largest computer storefront companies

1. Radio Shack (Fort Worth, TX), with $2,991,631,000
2. ComputerLand (Pleasanton, CA), $2,630,000,000
3. ASCII Group, Inc. (Washington, DC), $1,500,000,000
4. Intelligent Electronics (Exton, PA), $1,200,000,000
5. Businessland, Inc. (San Jose, CA), $1,188,741,000
6. NYNEX Business Centers (Atlanta, GA), $410,000,000
7. CompuAdd Corp. (Austin, TX), $400,000,000
8. Computer Factory (Elmsford, NY), $369,002,000
9. MicroAge, Inc. (Tempe, AZ), $363,942,000
10. ValCom Computer Center (Omaha, NE), $359,100,000

*Where'd you hear that?*
Directory of Computer & Software Storefront Dealers. Based on 1989 sales volume.

## Largest video chains

1. Blockbuster (FL), with $600,000,000
2. West Coast/National (PA), $180,000,000
3. Erol's Inc. (VA), $159,888,000
4. RKO Warner Video (NY), $42,500,000
5. Palmer Video (NJ), $34,000,000
6. Video Store (OH), $30,000,000
7. Applause Video (NE), $28,428,000
8. Video Galaxy (CT), $27,000,000
9. Video Xpress (AL), $24,000,000
10. Video Update (MN), $19,211,294

*Where'd you hear that?*
Video Store, Video Store 100. Based on 1989 estimated revenues.

## Most popular type of vending machine items

1. Foods, with 38.2%
2. Cold beverages, 22.9%
3. Confections, 17.8%
4. Hot beverages, 12.7%
5. Cigarettes, 5.6%
6. Dairy, 2.0%
7. Others, total 0.8%

*Where'd you hear that?*
American Automatic Merchandiser. Based on 1989 percentage market share.

# TO MARKET

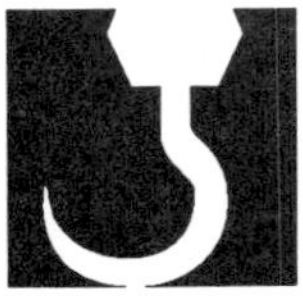

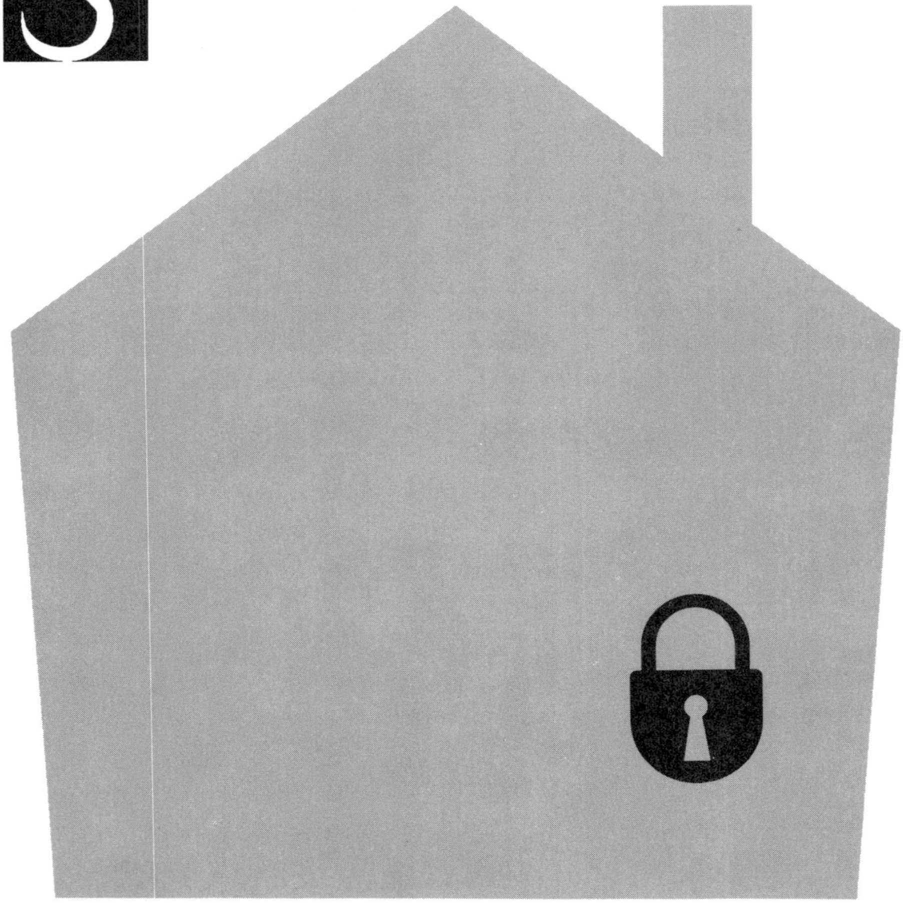

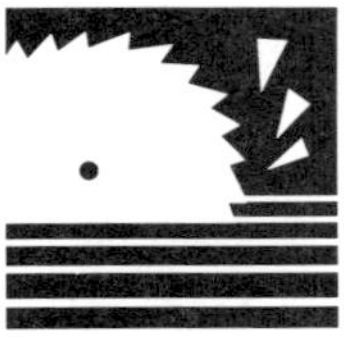

# Gimme Shelter

**World's most expensive cities**

1. Tokyo, Japan, with 160.2
2. Sofia, Bulgaria, 159.1
3. Osaka, Japan, 156.8
4. Oslo, Norway, 132.5
5. Brazzaville, Congo, 132.1
6. Helsinki, Finland, 128.7
7. Taipei, Taiwan, 126.5
8. Tripoli, Libya, 121.8
9. Stockholm, Sweden, 121.3
10. Geneva, Switzerland, 118.6

*Where'd you hear that?*
Financial Times. Based on living cost index, London=100.

**World's largest urban agglomerations in 2000**

1. Mexico City, Mexico, with 25.8 million
2. Sao Paulo, Brazil, 24.0
3. Tokyo/Yokohama, Japan, 20.2
4. Calcutta, India, 16.5
5. Bombay, India, 16.0
6. New York, NY, 15.8
7. Shanghai, China, 14.3
8. Seoul, Korea, 13.8
9. Teheran, Iran, 13.6
10. Rio de Janerio, Brazil, 13.3

*Where'd you hear that?*
Challenge. Based on projected 2000 population, in millions.

**Most populous U.S. cities**

1. New York, NY, with 7,284,280
2. Los Angeles, CA, 3,667,221
3. Chicago, IL, 2,828,020
4. Houston, TX, 1,770,913
5. San Fernando Valley, CA, 1,561,763
6. Philadelphia, PA, 1,557,637
7. Dallas, TX, 1,081,823
8. San Diego, CA, 1,079,510
9. Phoenix, AZ, 1,024,152
10. Detroit, MI, 1,015,457

*Where'd you hear that?*
Editor & Publisher Market Guide. Based on 1988 population estimates.

# GIMME SHELTER

### U.S. cities with the highest disposable income

1. New York, NY, with $126,209,485 thousand
2. Los Angeles, CA, $39,036,888
3. Chicago, IL, $34,914,818
4. Philadelphia, PA, $22,563,259
5. Houston, TX, $20,473,804
6. San Jose, CA, $18,194,154
7. San Francisco, CA, $17,809,438
8. San Diego, CA, $17,506,767
9. Dallas, TX, $17,362,497
10. San Fernando Valley, CA, $17,297,381

*Where'd you hear that?*
Editor & Publisher Market Guide. Based on 1988 disposable income, in thousands of dollars.

### U.S. cities with the highest income per household

1. Newport Beach, CA, with $86,978
2. San Francisco, CA, $79,481
3. Palo Alto, CA, $78,152
4. Trumbull, CT, $69,632
5. Thousand Oaks, CA, $67,795
6. Pleasanton, CA, $67,377
7. Greenwich, CT, $66,740
8. Dublin, CA, $66,642
9. Wakefield, MA, $65,849
10. Dedham, MA, $65,481

*Where'd you hear that?*
Editor & Publisher Market Guide. Based on 1988 income per household.

### Top U.S. cities by advertising agency local billings

1. New York, NY, with $22,025.4 million
2. Chicago, IL, $6,293.6
3. Los Angeles, CA, $4,026.9
4. Detroit, MI, $3,457.6
5. San Francisco, CA, $1,635.7
6. Minneapolis, MN, $1,085.4
7. Dallas, TX, $992.3
8. Boston, MA, $847.1
9. Atlanta, GA, $726.2
10. Cleveland, OH, $697.0

*Where'd you hear that?*
Advertising Age, Agency Income Report. Based on total local shop billings in 1989, in millions of dollars.

### Cities with the most tax audits

1. Las Vegas, NV, with 1.92%
2. Cheyenne, WY, 1.46%
3. Anchorage, AK, 1.45%
4. San Francisco, CA, 1.44%
5. New York, NY, 1.36%
6. Oklahoma City, OK, 1.34%
7. Laguna Niguel, CA, 1.25%
8. Los Angeles, CA, 1.22%
9. Dallas, TX, 1.18%
10. San Jose, CA, 1.17%

*Where'd you hear that?*
Barron's. Based on 1988 percentage of returns audited.

### Most populous suburban areas

1. Los Angeles-Long Beach, CA, with 4,506.0 thousand
2. Philadelphia, PA, 3,149.8
3. Detroit, MI, 3,121.9
4. Chicago, IL, 3,067.4
5. Washington, DC, 2,909.2
6. Nassau-Suffolk, NY, 2,669.2
7. Boston-Lawrence-Salem-Lowell-Brockton, MA, 2,500.4
8. Atlanta, GA, 2,265.7
9. Riverside-San Bernardino, CA, 1,888.1
10. St. Louis, MO, 1,851.4

# GIMME SHELTER

*Where'd you hear that?*
Sales & Marketing Management, Survey of Buying Power. Based on 1988 population, in thousands.

## Largest metropolitan areas

1. Los Angeles-Long Beach, CA, with 9,180,324
2. New York, NY, 8,534,969
3. Chicago, IL, 6,280,2331
4. Boston-Lawrence-Salem-Lowell-Brockton, MA, 4,974,786
5. Philadelphia, PA-NJ, 4,933,415
6. Detroit, MI, 4,456,056
7. Washington, DC-MD-VA, 3,781,946
8. Houston, TX, 3,368,741
9. Atlanta, GA, 2,911,583
10. Nassau-Suffolk, NY, 2,798,361

*Where'd you hear that?*
Editor & Publisher Market Guide. Based on estimated 1990 population.

## Most densely populated metropolitan areas

1. Jersey City, NJ, with 11,880
2. New York, NY, 7,491
3. Chicago, IL, 3,261
4. Bergen-Passaic, NJ, 3,056
5. Anaheim-Santa Ana, CA, 2,849
6. Nassau-Suffolk, NY, 2,226
7. Los Angeles-Long Beach, CA, 2,139
8. San Francisco, CA, 1,580
9. Newark, NJ, 1,552
10. Boston-Lawrence-Salem-Lowell-Brockton, MA, 1,534

*Where'd you hear that?*
Sales & Marketing Management, Survey of Buying Power. Based on total population per square mile.

## *Boom towns for the 1990s*

1. Marietta/Roswell, GA, with 30,697 indexed growth
2. Dallas-Richardson, TX, 21,929
3. Troy/Warren, MI, 21,661
4. Scottsdale/Sun City, AZ, 20,847
5. Newport Beach/Laguna, CA, 19,773
6. Herndon/Manassas, VA, 19,252
7. Santa Ana/Costa Mesa, CA, 18,887
8. Virginia Beach/Chesapeake, VA, 18,443
9. East Brunswick, NJ, 17,171
10. Orlando/Kissimmee, FL, 16,885

*Where'd you hear that?*
Building. Based on indexed growth (predicted absolute job growth, 1988-89, times the percent change, 1988-93).

## Metropolitan areas with the highest disposable incomes

1. New York, NY, with $151,239,153 thousand
2. Los Angeles-Long Beach, CA, $122,635,432
3. Boston-Lawrence-Salem-Lowell-Brockton, MA, $103,706,645
4. Chicago, IL, $102,517,826
5. Washington, DC-MD-VA, $87,369,844
6. Detroit, MI, $71,819,579
7. Anaheim-Santa Ana, CA, $68,056,640
8. Philadelphia, PA-NJ, $59,892,272
9. Houston, TX, $55,917,859
10. Nassau-Suffolk, NY, $52,602,766

# GIMME SHELTER

*Where'd you hear that?*
Editor & Publisher Market Guide. Based on estimated 1990 disposable income, in thousands of dollars.

## Metropolitan areas with the highest income per household

1. San Jose, CA, with $73,896
2. Vallejo-Fairfield-Napa, CA, $69,508
3. Anaheim-Santa Ana, CA, $68,274
4. Santa Barbara-Santa Maria-Lompoc, CA, $65,552
5. Santa Cruz, CA, $63,198
6. Sacramento, CA, $62,992
7. Oakland, CA, $62,417
8. San Diego, CA, $62,381
9. Oxnard-Ventura, CA, $62,359
10. Bridgeport-Stamford-Norwalk-Danbury, CT, $62,268

*Where'd you hear that?*
Editor & Publisher Market Guide. Based on estimated 1990 income per household.

## Fastest growing metropolitan areas, 1988-93

1. Naples, FL, with 17.1%
1. Ocala, FL, 17.1%
3. Fort Myers-Cape Coral, FL, 16.8%
3. Riverside-San Bernardino, CA, 16.8%
5. Fort Pierce, FL, 16.7%
6. West Palm Beach-Boca Raton-Delray Beach, FL, 16.4%
7. Melbourne-Titusville-Palm Bay, FL, 16.3%
7. Orlando, FL, 16.3%
9. Austin, TX, 16.2%
10. Fort Walton Beach, FL, 16.0%

*Where'd you hear that?*
Sales & Marketing Management, Survey of Buying Power. Based on projected population growth rate, 1988-93, in percent.

## Largest projected metropolitan areas, 1993

1. Los Angeles-Long Beach, CA, with 9,441.1 thousand
2. New York, NY, 8,765.1
3. Chicago, IL, 6,253.6
4. Philadelphia, PA, 5,013.3
5. Detroit, MI, 4,386.0
6. Washington, DC, 4,008.5
7. Boston-Lawrence-Salem-Lowell-Brockton, MA, 3,766.1
8. Houston, TX, 3,422.5
9. Atlanta, GA, 3,086.5
10. Dallas, TX, 2,757.4

*Where'd you hear that?*
Sales & Marketing Management, Survey of Buying Power. Based on projected 1993 population, in thousands.

## Wealthiest American counties

1. Fairfax, VA, with $51,147
2. Fairfax City, VA, $50,616
3. Morris, NJ, $48,380
4. Montgomery, MD, $47,082
5. Somerset, NJ, $46,994
6. Nassau, NY, $45,944
7. Falls Church City, VA, $45,390
8. Rockland, NY, $45,358
9. Washington, MN, $45,088
10. Los Alamos, NM, $43,791

*Where'd you hear that?*
Jewelers' Circular Keystone Directory. Based on median household income for 1988.

**GIMME SHELTER**

**Counties with the largest revenues**

1. Los Angeles, CA, with $6,831.7 million
2. Montgomery, MD, $2,150.0
3. Fairfax, VA, $1,927.0
4. Orange, CA, $1,844.5
5. Nassau, NY, $1,552.5
6. Prince George's, MD, $1,376.9
7. Dade, FL, $1,359.1
8. San Diego, CA, $1,256.1
9. Westchester, NY, $1,118.1
10. Suffolk, NY, $1,072.0

*Where'd you hear that?*
City & State, Annual County Financial Report. Based on fiscal year 1989 estimates of all governmental funds revenue, in millions of dollars.

**Counties with the lowest unemployment**

1. Fairfax, VA, with 1.7%
2. Prince William, VA, 2.0%
3. Henrico, VA, 2.3%
4. Montgomery, MD, 2.6%
5. Mecklenburg, NC, 2.7%

*Where'd you hear that?*
City & State, Annual County Financial Report. Based on 1988 unemployment rate, in percent.

**Counties with the highest unemployment**

1. Fresno, CA, with 10.6%
2. Kern, CA, 10.2%
3. San Joaquin, CA, 9.7%
4. Wayne, MI, 8.6%
5. Harris, TX, 6.9%

*Where'd you hear that?*
City & State, Annual County Financial Report. Based on 1988 unemployment rate, in percent.

**Counties with the most job growth**

1. Prince William, VA, with 15.19%
2. Clark, NV, 13.09%
3. Fairfax, VA, 12.23%
4. Palm Beach, FL, 12.15%
5. Orange, FL, 11.85%

*Where'd you hear that?*
City & State, Annual County Financial Report. Based on job growth, 1986-88, in percent.

### *Fastest declining metropolitan areas, 1988-93*

1. Kankakee, IL, with -2.1%
1. Kokomo, IN, -2.1%
1. Terre Haute, IN, -2.1%
4. Pittsburgh, PA, -2.3%
5. Anderson, IN, -2.4%
5. Casper, WY, -2.4%
5. Dubuque, IA, -2.4%
5. Duluth, MN, -2.4%
5. Great Falls, MT, -2.4%
5. Peoria, IL, -2.4%

*Where'd you hear that?*
Sales & Marketing Management, Survey of Buying Power. Based on projected population decline, 1988-93, in percent.

**Counties with the least job growth**

1. Kern, CA, with -1.65%
2. Westchester, NY, 0.03%
3. Essex, NJ, 0.25%
4. Cuyahoga, OH, 2.05%
5. Cook, IL, 2.67%

# GIMME SHELTER

*Where'd you hear that?*
City & State, Annual County Financial Report. Based on job growth, 1986-88, in percent.

## Counties receiving the most federal spending

1. Los Angeles, CA, with $30,511.4
2. Cook, IL, $14,699.2
3. San Diego, CA, $10,963.6
4. Orange, CA, $7,325.3
5. Santa Clara, CA, $7,235.4
6. Nassau, NY, $6,555.3
7. King, WA, $6,424.2
8. Wayne, MI, $6,420.3
9. Maricopa, AZ, $6,191.6
10. Sacramento, CA, $5,984.5

*Where'd you hear that?*
City & State, Annual County Financial Report. Based on 1988 federal spending in each county, in millions of dollars.

## Counties receiving the most federal defense spending

1. Los Angeles, CA, with $10,931.3 million
2. San Diego, CA, $6,243.0
3. Santa Clara, CA, $4,167.6
4. Nassau, NY, $3,502.3
5. Orange, CA, $3,461.6
6. King, WA, $2,313.2
7. Orange, FL, $2,270.9
8. Hamilton, OH, $2,020.9
9. Fairfax, VA, $1,958.1
10. Maricopa, AZ, $1,905.0

*Where'd you hear that?*
City & State, Annual County Financial Report. Based on 1988 federal defense spending in each county, in millions of dollars.

## Largest counties

1. Los Angeles, CA, with 9,180,324
2. Cook, IL, 5,261,417
3. Harris, TX, 2,880,473
4. Orange, CA, 2,651,856
5. San Diego, CA, 2,472,250
6. Kings, NY, 2,219,459
7. Maricopa, AZ, 2,189,856
8. Wayne, MI, 2,098,189
9. Dallas, TX, 2,015,205
10. Dade, FL, 2,001,010

*Where'd you hear that?*
Editor & Publisher Market Guide. Based on estimated 1990 population.

## Smallest counties

1. Henrico, VA, with 200,000
2. Prince William, VA, 216,000
3. Anne Arundel, MD, 418,000
4. San Joaquin, CA, 443,000
5. Onondaga, NY, 463,000

*Where'd you hear that?*
City & State, Annual County Financial Report. Based on 1988 population.

## Fastest growing states, 1980-88

1. Nevada, with an increase of 31.7%
2. Alaska, 30.5%
3. Arizona, 28.4%
4. Florida, 26.6%
5. California, 19.6%
6. Texas, 18.4%
7. New Hampshire, 17.9%
8. Georgia, 16.1%
9. Utah, 15.7%
10. New Mexico, 15.6%

*Where'd you hear that?*
Current Population Reports. Based on increase in populations, 1980-88, by percent.

## States with highest estimated revenues

1. California, with $69,639.1 million
2. New York, $47,091.0
3. Texas, $21,878.6
4. Florida, $20,634.8
5. Illinois, $19,892.0
6. Ohio, $19,466.0
7. Michigan, $17,408.5
8. New Jersey, $17,405.6
9. Pennsylvania, $15,879.7
10. Massachusetts, $12,417.9

*Where'd you hear that?*
City & State, State Financial Report. Based on estimated fiscal 1990 all funds revenues, in millions of dollars.

## States with lowest unemployment

1. Hawaii, with 2.6%
2. Nebraska, 3.1%
3. North Carolina, 3.5%
3. New Hampshire, 3.5%
3. Delaware, 3.5%

*Where'd you hear that?*
City & State, State Financial Report. Based on 1989 unemployment rate. U.S. average is 5.0%.

## States with lowest job growth, 1988-90

1. Oklahoma, with -1.62%
2. Missouri, -1.30%
3. Rhode Island, -1.25%
4. Massachusetts, -0.84%
5. North Dakota, -0.30%
5. New Jersey, -0.30%

*Where'd you hear that?*
City & State, State Financial Report. Based on percentage rate of job growth, 1988-90. U.S. average is 5.07%.

## States with highest spending for public safety

1. Alaska, with $496
2. Connecticut, $202
3. Delaware, $184
4. New Jersey, $139
5. California, $130
6. Maryland, $119
7. North Carolina, $115
8. New York, $112
9. Georgia, $105
9. Pennsylvania, $105

*Where'd you hear that?*
City & State, State Financial Report. Based on estimated fiscal 1990 per capita spending in this category.

## *States with the highest per capita personal income*

1. Connecticut, with $21,266
2. District of Columbia, $20,457
3. New Jersey, $20,352
4. Massachusetts, $19,142
5. Alaska, $18,230
6. Maryland, $18,124
7. New York, $18,004
8. California, $17,821
9. New Hampshire, $17,529
10. Delaware, $16,696

*Where'd you hear that?*
P.E.L. Factbook Pennsylvania Economic League. Based on 1987 per capita personal income.

# GIMME SHELTER

# GIMME SHELTER

### States with highest spending for public education

1. Alaska, with $1,528
2. Washington, $837
3. North Carolina, $836
4. Delaware, $794
5. Georgia, $778
6. Minnesota, $765
7. Wisconsin, $761
8. New Mexico, $760
9. Hawaii, $759
10. California, $719

*Where'd you hear that?*
City & State, State Financial Report. Based on estimated fiscal 1990 per capita spending in this category.

### States with highest spending for social services

1. Massachusetts, with $707
2. Wisconsin, $558
3. Connecticut, $506
4. Washington, $443
5. Alaska, $413
6. Illinois, $379
7. Georgia, $370
8. Iowa, $369
9. California, $364
10. New York, $360

*Where'd you hear that?*
City & State, State Financial Report. Based on estimated fiscal 1990 per capita spending in this category.

### States with highest spending for public health

1. Louisiana, with $371
2. Tennessee, $350
3. Alaska, $347
4. Rhode Island, $234
5. Delaware, $229
6. Connecticut, $217
7. New Jersey, $200
8. Florida, $194
9. New York, $191
10. Maryland, $154

*Where'd you hear that?*
City & State, State Financial Report. Based on estimated fiscal 1990 per capita spending in this category.

### States where people have the longest life span

1. Hawaii, 77.0%
2. Minnesota, 76.2%
3. Iowa, 75.8%
3. Utah, 75.8%
5. North Dakota, 75.7%

*Where'd you hear that?*
Changing Times. Based on average life span, in years.

### States where people have the shortest life span

1. Louisiana, 71.7%
2. South Carolina, 71.9%
3. Mississippi, 72.0%
4. Georgia, 72.2%
4. Alaska, 72.2%

*Where'd you hear that?*
Changing Times. Based on average life span, in years.

### States with the most consumers age 45 to 64

1. California, with 5,107 thousand
2. New York, 3,694
3. Texas, 2,801
4. Florida, 2,601
5. Pennsylvania, 2,439
6. Illinois, 2,214
7. Ohio, 2,113
8. Michigan, 1,714
9. New Jersey, 1,644
10. North Carolina, 1,249

*Where'd you hear that?*
LDB/Interior Textiles. Based on number of people age 45-64, in thousands.

## States with the most consumers age 65 and over

1. California, with 3,011 thousand
2. New York, 2,328
3. Florida, 2,201
4. Pennsylvania, 1,793
5. Texas, 1,666
6. Illinois, 1,421
7. Ohio, 1,372
8. Michigan, 1,076
9. New Jersey, 1,009
10. Massachusetts, 806

*Where'd you hear that?*
LDB/Interior Textiles, October, 1989, p. 106. Based on number of people age 65 and older, in thousands.

## States with the lowest tax burdens

1. New Hampshire
2. Florida
3. Alaska
4. Texas
5. Nevada
6. Washington
7. Connecticut
8. Wyoming
9. South Dakota
10. Tennessee

*Where'd you hear that?*
Money. Based on tax rates, 1980-88.

## States with the highest tax burdens

1. Hawaii
2. Oregon
3. District of Columbia
4. Maryland
5. Idaho
6. Utah
7. New York
8. Wisconsin
9. Minnesota
10. Maine

*Where'd you hear that?*
Money. Based on tax rates, 1980-88.

## *States with the most men*

1. Alaska, with 52.9%
2. Wyoming, 51.4%
3. Hawaii, 50.9%
4. Nevada, 50.7%
5. North Dakota, 50.3%
6. Idaho, 50.0%
7. Montana, 50.0%
8. Washington, 49.9%
9. Utah, 49.8%
10. Colorado, 49.8%

*Where'd you hear that?*
Current Population Reports. Based on percent male population as of July 1, 1988.

## States with the best 'quality of life'

1. North Dakota
2. Minnesota
3. Iowa
4. Connecticut
5. Massachusetts
6. Nebraska
7. Kansas
8. Wisconsin
9. South Dakota
10. Washington

# GIMME SHELTER

# GIMME SHELTER

*Where'd you hear that?*
Grant Thornton, Grant Thornton Manufacturing Climates Study. Based on selected quality of life issues: education, health care, cost of living, and transportation.

## Best places to live in the U.S.

1. Seattle, WA
2. Danbury, CT
3. San Francisco, CA
4. Denver, CO
5. Nashua, NH
6. Boston, MA
7. Boston's North Shore, MA
8. Central New Jersey
9. Minneapolis/St. Paul, MN
10. Pittsburgh, PA

*Where'd you hear that?*
Money, Best Places to Live. Based on composite ranking derived from nine categories: health, economy, housing, crime, transit, education, weather, leisure and arts.

## Largest household relocation magnet states

1. District of Columbia, with 73.0%
2. Rhode Island, 64.3%
3. Hawaii, 63.5%
4. Nevada, 62.2%
5. Maine, 61.6%
5. Vermont, 61.6%
7. Oregon, 61.2%
8. Washington, 60.1%
9. Georgia, 59.0%
10. South Carolina, 58.1%

*Where'd you hear that?*
WG & L Real Estate Outlook. Based on 1988 percentage of allied-service household relocations into the state.

## Largest household relocation outbound states

1. North Dakota, with 72.8%
2. South Dakota, 63.6%
3. Wyoming, 60.0%
4. Oklahoma, 58.3%
5. New Jersey, 58.2%
6. Idaho, 57.9%
6. West Virginia, 57.9%
8. New York, 57.1%
9. Louisiana, 56.5%
10. Utah, 56.1%

*Where'd you hear that?*
WG & L Real Estate Outlook. Based on 1988 percentage of allied-service household relocations out of the state.

## States with highest relocation activity

1. California, with 32,118
2. Florida, 24,424
3. Texas, 22,525
4. Illinois, 15,997
5. New York, 14,233
6. Pennsylvania, 12,855
7. Virginia, 12,685
8. Ohio, 11,094
9. New Jersey, 9,801
10. Georgia, 9,777

*Where'd you hear that?*
WG & L Real Estate Outlook. Based on total number of allied-service household relocations in/out of state in 1988.

# GIMME SHELTER

## Leading household goods movers

1. North American Van Lines, with $540,411 thousand
2. United Van Lines, $440,284
3. Allied Van Lines, $383,626
4. Mayflower Transit, $314,226
5. Bekins Van Lines Co. $212,650

*Where'd you hear that?*
Transport Topics. Based on 1988 revenue, in thousands of dollars.

## Largest metropolitan areas for total households

1. New York, NY, with 3,458.7 thousand
2. Los Angeles-Long Beach, CA, 3,162.1
3. Chicago, IL, 2,303.2
4. Philadelphia, PA, 1,823.6
5. Detroit, MI, 1,625.7
6. Boston-Lawrence-Salem-Lowell-Brockton, MA, 1,406.0
7. Washington, DC, 1,401.6
8. Houston, TX, 1,176.6
9. Atlanta, GA, 1,033.6
10. Dallas, TX, 934.8

*Where'd you hear that?*
Sales & Marketing Management, Survey of Buying Power. Based on numbers, in thousands.

## Largest one-person household market areas

1. New York, NY, with 1,100.0 thousand
2. Los Angeles-Long Beach, CA, 843.5
3. Chicago, IL, 591.9
4. Philadelphia, PA, 457.7
5. Detroit, MI, 385.5
6. Boston-Lawrence-Salem-Lowell-Brockton, MA, 384.6
7. Washington, DC, 359.5
8. Houston, TX, 281.4
9. Atlanta, GA, 234.0
10. Nassau-Suffolk, NY, 132.1

*Where'd you hear that?*
Long Island Almanac. Based on number of one-person households, in thousands.

## Largest metropolitan areas for single-person households

1. New York, NY, with 1,100.0 thousand
2. Los Angeles-Long Beach, CA, 843.5
3. Chicago, IL, 591.9
4. Philadelphia, PA, 457.7
5. Detroit, MI, 385.5
6. Boston-Lawrence-Salem-Lowell-Brockton, MA, 384.6
7. Washington, DC, 359.5
8. Houston, TX, 281.4
9. Minneapolis-St. Paul, 239.9
10. Atlanta, 234.0

*Where'd you hear that?*
Sales & Marketing Management, Survey of Buying Power. Based on numbers, in thousands.

## Most affordable housing markets

1. Houston, TX, with 10%
2. San Antonio, TX, 11%
3. Grand Rapids, MI, 12%
3. Akron, OH, 12%
3. El Paso, TX, 12%
6. Portland, OR, 13%
6. Pittsburgh, PA, 13%
6. Greenville, SC, 13%
9. Cleveland, OH, 14%
9. Mobile, AL, 14%
9. Dayton, OH, 14%

# GIMME SHELTER

9. Cincinnati, OH, 14%
9. Fort Lauderdale, FL, 14%
9. Columbus, OH, 14%

*Where'd you hear that?*
U.S. News & World Report. Based on share of the average monthly household income spent on the monthly mortgage payment.

## Housing markets with the highest rates of home price appreciation

1. West Palm Beach, FL, with 24.1%
2. Akron, OH, 22.0%
3. Greenville, SC, 20.7%
4. Mobile, AL, 19.9%
5. Sacramento, CA, 19.3%
6. Honolulu, HI, 18.1%
7. El Paso, TX, 17.6%
8. Chicago, IL, 16.4%
9. Houston, TX, 16.3%
10. Los Angeles, CA, 15.7%

*Where'd you hear that?*
U.S. News & World Report. Based on growth in housing prices, first quarter, 1989 to first quarter, 1990, in percent.

## Areas with greatest change in median existing home prices

1. Houston, TX, with 24.8%
2. Honolulu, HI, 22.2%
3. Seattle/Tacoma, WA, 19.7%
4. Sacramento, CA, 19.6%
5. San Francisco Bay Area, CA, 18.1%
6. Los Angeles, CA, 17.5%
7. Tampa/St. Petersburg, FL, 14.9%
8. Akron, OH, 14.0%
9. Riverside/San Bernardino, CA, 13.7%
10. Dayton/Springfield, OH, 13.5%

*Where'd you hear that?*
Mortgage Market Statistical Annual. Based on april, 1988 - March, 1989 increase in median existing home prices, expressed as percentage change.

## Top ten multi-family markets

1. Los Angeles/Long Beach, CA, with 7,670
2. Las Vegas, NV, 3,980
3. Miami/Hialeah, FL, 3,910
4. Atlanta, GA, 3,210
5. West Palm Beach/Boca Raton, FL, 3,180
6. Seattle, WA, 3,140
7. New York, NY, 3,120
8. Chicago, IL, 2,900
9. Orlando, FL, 2,730
10. Riverside/San Bernardino, CA, 2,590

*Where'd you hear that?*
Builder. Based on permits filed, January-April, 1989.

## Busiest housing markets

1. Los Angeles/Long Beach, CA, with 10,504
2. Riverside/San Bernardino, CA, 9,795
3. Washington, DC/MD/VA, 9,236
4. Atlanta, GA, 8,892
5. Las Vegas, NV, 8,112
6. Chicago, IL, 6,833
7. Portland, OR, 5,735
8. Detroit, MI, 5,529
9. Philadelphia, PA/NJ, 5,238
10. Baltimore, MD, 5,195

*Where'd you hear that?*
Realty. Based on number of dwelling unit starts.

# GIMME SHELTER

## Leading producers of housing starts

1. Trammell Crow Residential, with 11,491
2. Ryland Group, 9,622
3. Centex Corp., 7,989
4. William Lyon Co., 6,490
5. Weyerhaeuser Real Estate, 6,270
6. NVR, 6,070 (est.)
7. Kaufman and Broad Home Corp., 6,043
8. U.S. Home Corp., 5,437
9. Jim Walter Homes Inc., 5,400
10. PHM Corp., 4,450

*Where'd you hear that?*
Professional Builder, Professional Builder Giant 100. Based on number of starts in 1988.

## Biggest corporations in the construction & real estate industry

1. Rouse, with $1,199 million
2. Rockefeller Center Properties, $717
3. Koger Properties, $598
4. New Plan Realty Trust, $597
5. Centex Corp., $575
6. Weingarten Realty Investors, $427
7. Kaufman & Broad Home Corp., $356
8. Federal Realty Investment Trust, $341

*Where'd you hear that?*
Business Week, The Business Week 1000. Based on market value as of March 16, 1990, in millions of dollars.

## *Top ten single-family housing markets*

1. Riverside/San Bernardino, CA, with 12,280
2. Atlanta, GA, 8,200
3. Washington, DC, 7,810
4. Los Angeles/Long Beach, CA, 7,000
5. Philadelphia, PA, 4,970
6. Orlando, FL, 4,500
7. Sacramento, CA, 4,480
8. Tampa/St. Petersburg, 4,390
9. Las Vegas, NV, 4,170
10. San Diego, CA, 4,050

*Where'd you hear that?*
Builder. Based on permits filed, January-April, 1989.

## Largest real estate developers

1. Trammell Crow Co., with 43,537,444 sq. ft.
2. Melvin Simon & Associates, Inc., 15,245,352
3. Prudential Property Co., 13,704,544
4. Maguire Thomas Partners, 12,500,000
5. Edward J. DeBartolo Corp., 12,337,048
6. Crown American Corp., 10,021,618
7. Rouse & Associates, 9,200,000
8. John W. Galbreath & Co., 9,150,000
9. Ahmanson Commercial Development Co., 8,740.540

# GIMME SHELTER

10. Equitable Real Estate Investment Management, Inc., 8,540,381

*Where'd you hear that?*
National Real Estate Investor, Top Developer Survey. Based on amount of square footage under construction in 1989, in the office, industrial, retail, multifamily, hotel, and business park sectors.

## Biggest owners of U.S. commercial real estate

1. Corporations, with $2.6 trillion
2. Financial institutions, $700 billion
3. Limited partnerships and investment trusts, $95 billion
4. Pension funds, $70 billion
5. Foreign investors, $32 billion

*Where'd you hear that?*
Wall Street Journal. Based on ownership of commercial real estate in the U.S. in 1989.

## Most profitable real estate investment trusts

1. American Health Properties, with 39.7%
2. Health Care Property Investors, 33.2%
3. Meditrust, 30.7%
4. Weingarten Realty Investors, 30.3%
5. New Plan Realty Trust, 24.3%
6. Western Investment Real Estate Trust, 16.1%
7. Rockefeller Center Properties, 14.6%
8. Federal Realty Investment Trust, 10.7%
9. Santa Anita Realty Enterprises, 3.6%
10. First Union Real Estate Equity, -2.1%
11. Washington Real Estate Investment, -4.7%

*Where'd you hear that?*
Wall Street Journal. Based on total return, in percent.

## Largest real estate mortgage investment conduits

1. Fannie Mae, $41,250.38 million
2. Freddie Mac, $39,373.65
3. Ryland Acceptance Corp., $2,024.65
4. Prudential-Bache Capital, $1,500.22
5. Salomon Brothers, $1,416.55
6. Bear, Stearns & Co., $1,132.50
7. PaineWebber, $800.10
8. Merrill Lynch, $800.00
9. First Boston Corp., $750.02
10. Goldman, Sachs & Co., $750.00

*Where'd you hear that?*
Mortgage Market Statistical Annual. Based on 1989 volume of issues, in millions of dollars.

## Top banks in commercial real estate loans

1. Citibank NA, with $16,270 million
2. Wells Fargo Bank NA, $9,064
3. Chase Manhattan Bank NA, $7,576
4. Security Pacific National Bank, $6,611
5. Bank of America NT & SA, $5,401
6. Chemical Bank, $3,468
7. First National Bank, $3,231

# GIMME SHELTER

8. Bank of New England NA, $3,194
9. NCNB National Bank of North Carolina, $2,991
10. First National Bank, $2,923

*Where'd you hear that?*
American Banker. Based on commercial real estate loans as of December 31, 1989, in millions of dollars.

## Largest brokerage firms ranked by revenue.

1. Coldwell Banker, with $460.2 million
2. Grubb & Ellis, $380
3. Burke Commercial, $350
4. Cushman & Wakefield Inc., $260
5. Marcus & Millichap, $155

*Where'd you hear that?*
Land Use Digest. Based on 1989 revenue, in millions of dollars.

## Largest brokerage firms ranked by number of transactions

1. Coldwell Banker, with 25,000
2. Grubb & Ellis, 11,282
3. Helmsley-Spear, 7,000
4. Cushman & Wakefield Inc., 5,200
5. Daum Commercial, 4,000

*Where'd you hear that?*
Land Use Digest. Based on number of transactions in 1989.

## Largest federal home loan mortgage (Freddie Mac) sellers

1. Citicorp Mortgage, Inc. (St. Louis, MO)
2. First Nationwide Bank (San Francisco, CA)
3. Marine Midland Bank, N.A. (Buffalo, NY)
4. Weyerhaeuser Mortgage Co. (Walnut Creek, CA)
5. IMCO Realty Services, Inc. (Santa Rosa, CA)
6. Sears Mortgage Corp. (Riverwoods, IL)
7. Norwest Mortgage, Inc. (Des Moines, IA)
8. First Union Mortgage Corp. (Raleigh, NC)
9. Home Owners Savings Bank (Burlington, MA)
10. Household Mortgage Services (Prospect Heights, IL)

*Where'd you hear that?*
Mortgage Market Statistical Annual. Based on 1989 sales.

## States with the most nonperforming real estate loans

1. Arizona, with 11.80%
2. Texas, 10.34%
3. Massachusetts, 6.89%
4. Connecticut, 6.12%
5. Alaska, 5.29%
6. Oklahoma, 5.01%
7. Louisiana, 4.82%
8. New Hampshire, 4.43%
9. New York, 4.14%
10. New Mexico, 3.73%

*Where'd you hear that?*
American Banker. Based on percent of nonperforming real estate loans on 12/31/89.

# GIMME SHELTER

### Largest federal home loan mortgage (Freddie Mac) servicers

1. Marine Midland Bank (Buffalo, NY)
2. American Savings & Loan Association (Irvine, CA)
3. Countrywide Funding Corp. (Pasadena, CA)
4. Fireman's Fund Mortgage Corp. (Farmington Hills, MI)
5. Shearson Lehman Mortgage Corp. (Newport Beach, CA)
6. Great Western Savings (Chatsworth, CA)
7. General Motors Acceptance Corp. Mortgage Corp. (Elkins Park, PA)
8. Standard Federal Savings Bank (Gaithersburg, MD)
9. Citicorp Mortgage, Inc. (St. Louis, MO)
10. Foster Mortgage Corp. (Fort Worth, TX)

*Where'd you hear that?*
Mortgage Market Statistical Annual. Based on service at the end of 1989.

### Largest Ginnie Mae issuers

1. Fleet Mortgage Corp. (Milwaukee, WI), with $4,013,362,722
2. First Union Mortgage Corp. (Raleigh, NC), $2,406,705,083
3. Fleet Real Estate Funding Corp. (Florence, SC), $1,768,221,149
4. General Motors Acceptance Corp. Mortgage Corp. (Philadelphia, PA), $1,739,682,569
5. BancBoston Mortgage Corp. (Jacksonville, FL), $1,688,622,348
6. Citicorp Mortgage, Inc. (St. Louis, MO), $1,518,632,385
7. America's Mortgage Co. (Gaithersburg, MD), $1,209,401,368
8. Foster Mortgage Corp. (Fort Worth, TX), $1,163,750
9. Fireman's Fund Mortgage Corp. (Farmington Hills, MI), $920,264,971
10. Empire of America Realty Credit (Buffalo, NY), $893,769,456

*Where'd you hear that?*
Mortgage Market Statistical Annual. Based on 1989 sales volume of Ginnie Maes (Government National Mortgage Association MBS Securities).

### States with the greatest change in mortgage originations

1. Idaho, with 34%
2. Rhode Island, 19%
3. District of Columbia, 10%
4. California, 1%
5. Alaska, -6%
6. Kentucky, -11%
6. Pennsylvania, -11%
8. South Dakota, -12%
8. Florida, -12%
10. Alabama, -13%

*Where'd you hear that?*
Mortgage Market Statistical Annual. Based on percentage change in dollar amounts of originations, 1987-88.

# GIMME SHELTER

## Largest mortgage originators

1. Home Savings of America, with $13.4 billion
2. Citicorp Mortgage and affiliates, $11.9
3. Great Western Financial Corp., $10.5
4. First Nationwide Bank, $7.4
5. CalFed, $7.0
6. GlenFed, $5.7
7. Fleet/Norstar Financial Group, Inc., $5.4
8. Golden West Financial Corp., $4.7
9. Coast Savings and Loan, $3.8
10. Sears Mortgage and affiliates, $3.7

*Where'd you hear that?*
Mortgage Market Statistical Annual. Based on volume of mortgages, in billions of dollars in 1988.

## Leading homeowners insurance writers

1. State Farm Group, with $3,187,833 thousand
2. Allstate Insurance Group, $2,012,173
3. Farmers Insurance Group, $778,514
4. Aetna Life & Casualty Group, $676,859
5. Nationwide Group, $461,054
6. USAA Group, $434,025
7. Chubb Group of Insurance Cos., $375,966
8. Travelers Insurance Group, $363,569
9. Hartford Insurance Group, $354,827
10. Prudential of America Group, $284,059

*Where'd you hear that?*
Best's Review, Property/Casualty edition. Based on 1988 direct premiums, in thousands of dollars.

## The 10 most costly insured hurricanes

1. Hugo, Sept. 17-18, 21-22, 1989, with $3,984,000,000
2. Frederic, Sept. 12-14, 1979, $752,510,000
3. Betsy, Sept. 7-10, 1965, $715,000,000
4. Alicia, Aug. 18, 1983, $675,520,000
5. Elena, Aug. 30 - Sept. 3, 1985, $543,300,000
6. Gloria, Sept. 26-27, 1985, $418,750,000
7. Celia, Aug. 3, 1970, $309,950,000
8. Camille, Aug. 17-18, 1969, $225,000,000
9. Iwa, Nov. 23-24, 1982, $137,000,000
10. Carol, Aug. 30-31, 1954, $129,700,000

*Where'd you hear that?*
Insurance Review. Based on estimated insured loss.

## Largest construction companies in Asia

1. Taisei Corp., with $12,050,231 thousand
2. Kajima Corp., $10,587,339

# GIMME SHELTER

3. Shimizu Construction Co. Ltd., $10,330,454
4. Samsung Co. Ltd., $9,957,753
5. Ohbayashi Corp., $7,561,578
6. Daewoo Corp., $6,914,121
7. Ohbayashi-Gumi Ltd., $6,394,558
8. Sekisui House Ltd., $6,097,163
9. Daiwa House Industry Co. Ltd., $4,479,012
10. Fujita Corp., $4,366,661

*Where'd you hear that?*
Asia's 7500 Largest Companies Dun & Bradstreet. Based on 1988 sales, in thousands of U.S. dollars.

## Largest European construction companies

1. Bouygues, with 6,639,751,395 ECU
2. Alsthom, 4,020,299,349
3. Tarmac PLC, 3,178,225,525
4. Dumez Sa., 3,128,734,575
5. Entreprises, 2,935,683,180
6. Auxilliaire D Entreprise, 2,666,204,809
7. Spie Batignolles, 2,545,073,020
8. George Wimpey PLC, 2,488,980,648
9. John Laing PLC, 1,975,463,094
10. Beazer PLC, 1,973,699,944

*Where'd you hear that?*
Dun's Europa, Dun & Bradstreet. Based on sales, in European Currency Units. Includes 12 EEC member countries, Austria, and Switzerland.

## Largest U.S. construction companies

1. Trammell Crow Residential, with 11,491
2. Ryland Group, Inc., 8,167
3. Centex Corp., 7,924
4. William Lyon Co., 7,148
5. Weyerhaeuser Real Estate Co., 6,270
6. Pulte Home Corp., 6,187
7. NVR L.P., 6,069
8. Jim Walter Homes, Inc., 5,257
9. U.S. Home Corp., 4,793
10. Lewis Homes Management Corp., 4,055

*Where'd you hear that?*
Builder. Based on 1989 starts.

## Largest construction companies ranked by units

1. Fleetwood Enterprises, Inc., with 36703 units
2. Redman Homes, 16038
3. Skyline Corp., 14640
4. Champion Home Builders Co., 13953
5. Trammell Crow Co., 12932
6. Ryland Group, 9354
7. Clayton Homes, Inc., 9350
8. NVR L. P., 8556
9. William Lyon Co., 8082
10. PHM Corp., 7249

*Where'd you hear that?*
Professional Builder, Annual Report of Housing Giants. Based on total units.

## Largest construction companies ranked by revenues

1. Trammell Crow Co., with $3,018,500 thousand
2. Lincoln Property Co., $2,126,997

# GIMME SHELTER

3. Centex Corp., $1,845,484
4. William Lyon Co., $1,401,000
5. NVR L. P., $1,321,275
6. Ryland Group Inc., $1,271,875
7. PHM Corp., $1,179,164
8. Kaufman & Broad, $903,399
9. M. D. C. Holdings Inc., $840,597
10. Weyerhaeuser Real Estate Co., $819,000

7. John W. Galbreath & Co., $337.60
8. Zeckendorf Co. Inc., $298.44
9. Paragon Group Inc., $287.47
10. Weitz Corp., $270.27

*Where'd you hear that?*
Building Design & Construction, Building Design & Construction Owner/Developer 300. Based on volume of construction and reconstruction put in place in 1989 or most recent fiscal year, in millions of dollars.

*Where'd you hear that?*
Professional Builder, Annual Report of Housing Giants. Based on 1988 revenues, in thousands of dollars.

## Top construction management firms

1. Bechtel Group Inc.
2. Fluor Daniel Inc.
3. CRSS Inc.
4. Lehrer McGovern Bovis Inc.
5. ICF-Kaiser Engineers Group Inc.
6. Metcalf & Eddy Cos. Inc.
7. Rust International Corp.
8. Holmes & Narver Inc.
9. Parsons Corp.
10. IT Corp.

*Where'd you hear that?*
ENR, Top CM Firms. Based on construction management fees billed for 1989, by ranges of fees (individual fees not stated).

## Largest diversified developers

1. Maguire Thomas Partners, with $2,194.00 million
2. Trammell Crow Co., $1,600.00
3. Lincoln Property Co., $894.59
4. Webb Companies, $811.23
5. Koll Co., $450.00
6. Taubman Co. Inc., $350.00

## *Largest U.S. corporations in the construction & engineering industry*

1. Fluor Daniel Inc., with $3,262 million
2. Wheelabrator Technologies, $1,395
3. EG & G, $1,135
4. Foster Wheeler Corp., $844
5. Thermo Electron, $600
5. Morrison Knudsen, $600
7. Stone & Webster, $568
8. Zurn Industries, $488

*Where'd you hear that?*
Business Week, The Business Week 1000. Based on market value as of March 16, 1990, in millions of dollars.

## Most productive commercial builders

1. Centex Corp., with $13.4 thousand
2. Fluor Daniel Inc., $6.1
3. Wheelabrator Tech, $5.9
4. CBI Industries, $2.9
5. Morrison Knudsen, $2.5
6. Rouse, $1.9
7. Turner Corp., $0.8

313

# GIMME SHELTER

*Where'd you hear that?*
Forbes, Forbes 500s Annual Directory. Based on 1989 profits per employee, in thousands of dollars. Ranks U.S.-based corporations that were publicly traded as of March 23, 1990.

## Largest retail developers

1. May Department Stores Co., with $482.00 million
2. Dayton Hudson Corp., $396.00
3. Melvin Simon & Associates, $344.49
4. Albertson's Inc., $327.25
5. K mart Corp., $228.00
6. Wal-Mart Stores Inc., $226.76
7. Sears, Roebuck & Co., $206.80
8. Leo Eisenberg Co., $190.00
9. Kroger Co., $180.00
10. J. C. Penney Co. Inc., $158.00

*Where'd you hear that?*
Building Design & Construction, Building Design & Construction Owner/Developer 300. Based on volume of construction and reconstruction put in place in 1989 or most recent fiscal year, in millions of dollars.

## Largest industrial developers

1. AT & T Technologies, with $686.00 million
2. IBM, $536.00
3. Argonaut AEC, $448.00
4. E. I. du Pont de Nemours & Co., $400.00
5. Boeing Co., $300.00
5. International Paper Co., $300.00
7. Minnesota Mining & Manufacturing Co., $260.00
8. Bristol-Myers Squibb Co., $250.00
8. Hewlett-Packard Co., $250.00
10. Philip Morris Cos. Inc., $244.00

*Where'd you hear that?*
Building Design & Construction, Building Design & Construction Owner/Developer 300. Based on volume of construction and reconstruction put in place in 1989 or most recent fiscal year, in millions of dollars.

## Largest developers of hotels/motels and restaurants

1. Marriott Corp., with $954.30 million
2. McDonald's Corp., $475.44
3. Hilton Hotels Corp., $350.00
4. Holiday Corp., $290.36
5. General Mills Restaurants Inc., $183.00
6. Hemmeter Development Corp., $181.00
7. Golden Nugget Inc., $179.00
8. Cardinal Industries, $159.00
9. Sheraton Corp., $150.00
10. Days Inn of America Inc., $140.00

*Where'd you hear that?*
Building Design & Construction, Building Design & Construction Owner/Developer 300. Based on volume of construction and reconstruction put in place in 1989 or most recent fiscal year, in millions of dollars.

## Largest health care construction developers

1. Kaiser Foundation Hospital & Health Plans, with $375.00 million
2. New York State Facilities Development Corp., $182.53
3. National Medical Enterprises Inc., $175.00

4. Charter Medical Corp., $165.00
5. Humana Inc., $160.00
6. Hospital Corp. of America, $150.00
7. American Medical International Inc., $129.00
8. Massachusetts General Hospital, $98.00
9. Life Care Services Corp., $65.60
10. Universal Medical Buildings, $64.00

*Where'd you hear that?*
Building Design & Construction, Building Design & Construction Owner/Developer 300. Based on volume of construction and reconstruction put in place in 1989 or most recent fiscal year, in millions of dollars.

## Most productive residential builders

1. Kaufman & Broad, with $82.9 thousand
2. PHM, $27.0
3. Ryland Group, $16.4

*Where'd you hear that?*
Forbes, Forbes 500s Annual Directory. Based on 1989 profits per employee, in thousands of dollars. Ranks U.S.-based corporations that were publicly traded as of March 23, 1990.

## Largest developers of multi-family housing

1. Trammell Crow Residential Co., with $807.50 million
2. Pacific Coast, $620.00
3. Robertson Homes, $230.00
4. Hovnanian Enterprises Inc., $217.74
5. A. G. Spanos Construction Inc., $212.00
6. Pulte Home Corp., $205.45
7. Oxford Development Corp., $180.00
8. U.S. Home Corp., $175.31
9. Fogelman Properties, $158.25
10. Picerne Properties, $94.73

*Where'd you hear that?*
Building Design & Construction, Building Design & Construction Owner/Developer 300. Based on volume of construction and reconstruction put in place in 1989 or most recent fiscal year, in millions of dollars.

## Leaders in for-sale housing

1. NVR L.P., with $984,082,000
2. William Lyon Co., $861,000,000
3. PHM Corp., $823,667,000
4. Ryland Group Inc., $810,684,000
5. Centex Corp., $769,364,000
6. Kaufman & Broad, $693,815,000
7. M. D. C. Holdings Inc., $640,677,000
8. U.S. Home Corp., $636,944,000
9. Weyerhaeuser Real Estate Co., $609,000,000
10. Watt Industries Inc., $532,000,000

*Where'd you hear that?*
Professional Builder, Annual Report of Housing Giants. Based on 1988 dollar volume.

## Leaders in rental housing

1. Trammell Crow Co., with $620,325,000
2. Lincoln Property Co., $265,414,000
3. Oxford Development, $240,000,000
4. William Lyon Co., $239,000,000

# GIMME SHELTER

315

# GIMME SHELTER

5. Forest City Development, $206,348,265
6. Robertson Homes, $197,000,000
7. A. G. Spanos Construction Inc., $195,900,000
8. Homestead Group Assoc., $190,000,000
9. Fogelman Properties, $189,000,000
10. CoastFed Properties, $185,267,000

*Where'd you hear that?*
Professional Builder, Annual Report of Housing Giants. Based on 1988 dollar volume.

## Leaders in mobile homes

1. Fleetwood Enterprises, Inc., with $535,300,000
2. Redman Homes, $268,014,000
3. Champion Home Builders, $263,761,000
4. Skyline Corp., $240,627,304
5. Palm Harbor Group, $157,017,000
6. Clayton Homes Inc., $137,368,000
7. Commodore Corp., $104,713,000
8. Schult Homes Corp., $103,213,000
9. Horton Homes Inc., $103,000,000
10. Cavalier Homes Inc., $91,807,630

*Where'd you hear that?*
Professional Builder, Annual Report of Housing Giants. Based on 1988 dollar volume.

## Leaders in manufactured housing

1. North American Housing, with $81,000,000
2. Ryland Group, $70,000,000
3. Wausau Homes Inc., $67,950,000
4. Nanticoke Homes Inc., $60,708,525
5. National Enterprises Inc., $59,341,000
6. Ritz-Craft Corp of Pennsylvania, $57,000,000
7. Coachmen Housing, $51,303,928
8. Contempri Homes Inc., $44,550,000
9. Lindal Cedar Homes Inc., $40,000,000
10. DeLuxe Homes of Pennsylvania Inc., $25,751,174

*Where'd you hear that?*
Professional Builder, Annual Report of Housing Giants. Based on 1988 dollar volume.

## Government agencies with the largest volume of construction

1. U.S. Department of Energy, with $2,298.03 million
2. U.S. Naval Facilities Engineering Command, $2,252.33
3. U.S. Army Corps of Engineers Resource Management Office (CERM-FC), $1,808.00
4. U.S. Postal Service, $1,408.00
5. Ohio Division of Public Works, $1,353.96
6. U.S. Air Force HQ USAF/LEE, $1,251.90
7. U.S. Veterans Administration, $622.34

8. U.S. General Services Administration (GSA), $528.00
9. New York City Department of General Services, $450.00
10. New York State Dormitory Authority, $432.00

*Where'd you hear that?*
Building Design & Construction, Building Design & Construction Owner/Developer 300. Based on volume of construction and reconstruction put in place in 1989 or most recent fiscal year, in millions of dollars.

**Asia's largest quoted companies in engineering, electrical, and transport equipment**

1. Toyota Motor Corp., with $57,496,398 thousand
2. Hitachi Ltd., $51,007,307
3. Matsushita Electric Industrial Co. Ltd., $43,858,566
4. Nissan Motor Co. Ltd., $38,340,167
5. Toshiba Corp., $30,285,713
6. Honda Motor Co. Ltd., $27,802,853
7. NEC Corp., $24,914,454
8. Mitsubishi Electric Corp., $21,647,952
9. Fujitsu Ltd., $19,023,442
10. Mitsubishi Heavy Industries Ltd., $15,061,665

*Where'd you hear that?*
Asia's 7500 Largest Companies, Dun & Bradstreet. Based on 1989 sales, in thousands of U.S. dollars.

**Largest foreign engineering consultants in Asia**

1. Nippon Koei Co. Ltd., Japan
2. NEDECO, Netherlands
3. Lavalin Inc., Canada
4. Louis Berger Group, U.S.
5. Pacific Consultants International, Japan
6. Holmes & Narver Inc., U.S.
7. Maunsell Consultancy Services Ltd., England
8. Mott MacDonald Group, England
9. Sargent & Lundy, U.S.
10. Ove Arup Partnership, England

*Where'd you hear that?*
ENR, Top International Design Firms. Based on billings.

---

***Top international design firms***

1. Lavalin Inc., Montreal, Canada
2. CRSS Inc., Houston, TX
3. Louis Berger Group, East Orange, NJ
4. NEDECO, The Hague, Netherlands
5. Holmes & Narver Inc., Orange, CA
6. Nethconsult, Hague, Netherlands
7. Jaakko Poyry Oy, Helsinki, Finland
8. Tractebel, Brussels, Belgium
9. Simons International Corp., Vancouver, Canada
10. Nippon Koei Co. Ltd., Tokyo, Japan

*Where'd you hear that?*
ENR, Top International Design Firms. Based on foreign billings.

---

**Largest foreign engineering consultants in Africa**

1. Lavalin Inc., Canada
2. Tractebel, Belgium
3. Louis Berger Group, U.S.
4. BCEOM, France
5. NEDECO, Netherlands
6. Bonifica SpA, Italy
7. SOGELERG, France

# GIMME SHELTER

# GIMME SHELTER

8. Norconsult AS, Norway
9. WLPU Consultants, England
10. Gauff Ingenieure GmbH & Co., West Germany

*Where'd you hear that?*
ENR, Top International Design Firms. Based on billings.

## Largest foreign engineering consultants in the Middle East

1. CRSS Inc., U.S.
2. Holmes & Narver Inc., U.S.
3. Energoprojekt Consulting & Engineering Co., Yugoslavia
4. Dar Al-Handasah Consultants, Egypt
5. Rail India Technical & Economic Services Ltd., India
6. Ewbank Preece Group Ltd., England
7. Electrowatt Engineering Services Ltd., Switzerland
8. Acer Consultants Ltd., England
9. De Leuw, Cather & Co., U.S.
10. Lahmeyer International GmbH, West Germany

*Where'd you hear that?*
ENR, Top International Design Firms. Based on billings.

## Largest foreign engineering consultants in Europe

1. Lavalin Inc., Canada
2. Jaakko Poyry Oy, Finland
3. Nethconsult, Netherlands
4. Hill International Inc., U.S.
5. Louis Berger Group, U.S.
6. Lester B. Knight & Associates Inc., U.S.
7. Fugro-McClelland BV, Netherlands
8. Tractebel, Belgium
9. Suter & Suter Corp., Switzerland
10. Tribble Harris & Li, U.S.

*Where'd you hear that?*
ENR, Top International Design Firms. Based on billings.

## Largest foreign engineering consultants in Latin America

1. Lavalin Inc., Canada
2. Jaakko Poyry Oy, Finland
3. Harza Engineering Co., U.S.
4. Louis Berger Group, U.S.
5. Frederic R. Harris Inc., U.S.
6. Salzgitter Consult GmbH, West Germany
7. NEDECO, Netherlands
8. Bonifica SpA, Italy
9. Italconsult SpA, Italy
10. Williams Brothers Engineering Co., U.S.

*Where'd you hear that?*
ENR, Top International Design Firms. Based on billings.

## Largest construction and engineering companies in Canada

1. Con-Drain, with $38,000 thousand
2. Pomerleau, $12,653
3. Delta Catalytic, $4,983
4. Sandwell, $4,680
5. Canadian Energy Services, $3,205
6. UMA Goup, $2,224
7. Majestic Contractors, $1,599
8. Bird Construction, $1,007
9. Gestion Bemacon, $1,000
10. Lambert Somec, $610

*Where'd you hear that?*
Canadian Business, Canadian Business 500. Based on 1989 net income, in thousands of Canadian dollars.

# GIMME SHELTER

## Largest foreign consultants in Canada

1. CH2M Hill Inc., U.S.
2. ENSR Corp., U.S.
3. ICF-Kaiser Engineers Group Inc., U.S.
4. Giffels Associates Inc., U.S.
5. Dames & Moore, U.S.
6. Ekono Oy, Finland
7. HWH Architects Engineers Planners Inc., U.S.
8. Hill International Inc., U.S.
9. Smith Group, U.S.
10. WLPU Consultants, England

*Where'd you hear that?*
ENR, Top International Design Firms. Based on billings.

## Largest U.S. design firms

1. Bechtel Group Inc. (San Francisco, CA)
2. Fluor Daniel Inc. (Irvine, CA)
3. ABB Lummus Crest (Bloomfield, NJ)
4. Brown & Root Inc. (Houston, TX)
5. Parsons/Main (Pasadena, CA)
6. United Engineers & Constructions International Inc. (Philadelphia, PA)
7. Burns & Roe Enterprises Inc. (Oradell, NJ)
8. CRSS Inc. (Houston, TX)
9. Ebasco Services Inc. (New York, NY)
10. CH2M Hill Cos. Ltd. (Denver, CO)

*Where'd you hear that?*
ENR, Top 500 Design Firms. Based on 1989 billings in excess of $200 million (unspecified).

## Largest general building design firms

1. Skidmore, Owings & Merrill
2. Burns & Roe Enterprises Inc.
3. Hellmuth, Obata & Kassabaum Inc.
4. Law Cos.
5. Ellerbe Inc.
6. Gensler & Associates/Architects
7. Daniel, Mann, Johnson & Mendenhall
8. CRSS Inc.
9. Holmes & Narver Inc.
10. RTKL Associates Inc.

*Where'd you hear that?*
ENR, Top 500 Design Firms. Based on 1989 billings (unspecified).

## Largest hazardous waste design firms

1. IT Corp.
2. ENSR Corp.
3. Dames & Moore
4. ERM Group
5. ICF-Kaiser Engineers Group Inc.
6. Groundwater Technology Inc.
7. Burns & Roe Enterprises Inc.
8. CH2M Hill Cos. Ltd
9. Camp Dresser & McKee
10. Bechtel Group Inc.

*Where'd you hear that?*
ENR, Top 500 Design Firms. Based on 1989 billings (unspecified).

## Largest foreign engineering consultants in the U.S.

1. Simons International Corp., Canada
2. Lavalin Inc., Canada
3. Nethconsult, Netherlands

# GIMME SHELTER

4. Fugro-McClelland BV, Netherlands
5. Golder Associates Ltd., Canada
6. SNC Group, Canada
7. Monenco Ltd., Canada
8. Dar Al-Handasah Consultants, Egypt
9. Sandwell Swan Wooster, Canada
10. Nihon Architects, Engineers & Consultants Inc., Japan

*Where'd you hear that?*
ENR, Top International Design Firms. Based on billings.

## America's best engineering schools

1. Massachusetts Institute of Technology, with a score of 100.0
2. Stanford University, 96.7
3. University of Illinois, Urbana, 83.7
4. California Institute of Technology, 78.3
5. University of California, Berkeley, 77.4
6. Cornell University, 74.6
7. Carnegie Mellon University, 74.5
8. University of Texas, Austin, 72.4
9. University of Michigan, 71.8
10. University of Southern California, 69.8

*Where'd you hear that?*
U.S. News & World Report. Based on overall score on a survey of students selectivity, placement, graduation rates, instructional resources, and research and academic reputation.

## America's best materials and metallurgical engineering schools

1. Massachusetts Institute of Technology
2. University of Illinois, Urbana
3. University of California, Berkeley
4. Stanford University
5. Northwestern University

*Where'd you hear that?*
U.S. News & World Report. Based on results of reputational survey of engineering-school deans and academic-affairs deans.

## America's best mechanical engineering schools

1. Massachusetts Institute of Technology
2. Stanford University
3. University of California, Berkeley
4. University of Illinois, Urbana
5. Purdue University

*Where'd you hear that?*
U.S. News & World Report. Based on results of reputational survey of engineering-school deans and academic-affairs deans.

## America's best civil engineering schools

1. University of Illinois, Urbana
2. University of California, Berkeley
3. Massachusetts Institute of Technology

# GIMME SHELTER

4. Stanford University
5. Purdue University

*Where'd you hear that?*
U.S. News & World Report. Based on results of reputational survey of engineering-school deans and academic-affairs deans.

## America's best industrial engineering schools

1. Georgia Institute of Technology
2. Purdue University
3. University of Michigan
4. Stanford University
5. University of California, Berkeley

*Where'd you hear that?*
U.S. News & World Report. Based on results of reputational survey of engineering-school deans and academic-affairs deans.

## Largest foreign contractors in Africa

1. M. W. Kellogg Co. (U.S.)
2. Bouygues (France)
3. Construtora Norberto Odebrecht SA (Brazil)
4. Sezai Turkes Feyzi Akkaya Construction Co. (Turkey)
5. Fiatimpresit SpA (Italy)
6. SAE Sadelmi SpA (Italy)
7. Davy Corp. PLC (England)
8. JGC Corp. (Japan)
9. Dyckerhoff & Widmann AG (West Germany)
10. Spie Batignolles (France)

*Where'd you hear that?*
ENR, Top 250 International Contractors. Based on 1988 dollar amount of foreign contracts.

## *World's largest contractors*

1. Bechtel Group Inc. (San Francisco, CA), with $5,034.5 million
2. M. W. Kellogg Co. (Houston, TX), $4,621.4
3. Lummus Crest Inc. (Bloomfield, NJ), $4,200.0
4. Davy Corp. PLC (London, England), $3,892.3
5. Parsons Corp. (Pasadena, CA), $3,075.0
6. Nuova Cimimontubi SpA (Milan, Italy), $2,997.0
7. Foster Wheeler Corp. (Clinton, NJ), $2,739.0
8. Philipp Holzmann AG (Frankfurt/Main, West Germany), $2,622.9
9. DUMEZ (Nanterre, France), $2,587.7
10. Mitsubishi Heavy Industries Ltd. (Tokyo, Japan), $2,270.0

*Where'd you hear that?*
ENR, Top 250 International Contractors. Based on 1988 foreign contracts, in millions of dollars.

## Largest foreign contractors in the Middle East

1. Nuova Cimimontubi Spa (Italy)
2. Bechtel Group Inc. (U.S.)
3. Parsons Corp. (U.S.)
4. Mitsubishi Heavy Industries Ltd. (Japan)
5. GIE SpA (Italy)
6. M. W. Kellogg Co. (U.S.)
7. Lummus Crest Inc. (U.S.)
8. Daewoo Corp. (Korea)
9. Joannou & Paraskevaides Ltd. (Cyprus)
10. Italimpianti SpA (Italy)

# GIMME SHELTER

*Where'd you hear that?*
ENR, Top 250 International Contractors. Based on 1988 dollar amount of foreign contracts.

## Largest foreign contractors in Asia

1. Davy Corp. PLC (England)
2. Parsons Corp. (U.S.)
3. Italimpianti SpA (Italy)
4. M. W. Kellogg Co. (U.S.)
5. Lummus Crest Inc. (U.S.)
6. Mitsubishi Heavy Industries Ltd. (Japan)
7. Chiyoda Corp. (Japan)
8. Hochtief AG (West Germany)
9. Kumagai Gumi Co. Ltd. (Japan)
10. Ohbayashi Corp. (Japan)

*Where'd you hear that?*
ENR, Top 250 International Contractors. Based on 1988 dollar amount of foreign contracts.

## Largest foreign contractors in Europe

1. Foster Wheeler Corp. (U.S.)
2. Bechtel Group Inc. (U.S.)
3. Lummus Crest Inc. (U.S.)
4. M. W. Kellogg Co. (U.S.)
5. Fluor Daniel Inc. (U.S.)
6. Fiatimpresit SpA (Italy)
7. SGE Group (France)
8. Schal Associates (U.S.)
9. Lurgi GmbH (West Germany)
10. Bovis International Ltd. (England)

*Where'd you hear that?*
ENR, Top 250 International Contractors. Based on 1988 dollar amount of foreign contracts.

## Largest foreign contractors in Latin America

1. Lummus Crest Inc. (U.S.)
2. M. W. Kellogg Co. (U.S.)
3. Davy Corp. PLC (England)
4. Fluor Daniel Inc. (U.S.)
5. Fiatimpresit SpA (Italy)
6. Spie Batignolles (France)
7. SGE Group (France)
8. TECHINT Group (Italy)
9. Construtora Norberto Odebrecht SA (Brazil)
10. Ansaldo SpA (Italy)

*Where'd you hear that?*
ENR, Top 250 International Contractors. Based on 1988 dollar amount of foreign contracts.

## Largest foreign contractors in Canada

1. DUMEZ (France)
2. Bechtel Group Inc. (U.S.)
3. Davy Corp. PLC (England)
4. Lummus Crest Inc. (U.S.)
5. Guy F. Atkinson Co. (U.S.)
6. Fluor Daniel Inc. (U.S.)
7. M. W. Kellogg Co. (U.S.)
8. Bouygues (France)
9. Kiewit Construction Group Inc. (U.S.)
10. Taylor Woodrow PLC (England)

*Where'd you hear that?*
ENR, Top 250 International Contractors. Based on 1988 dollar amount of foreign contracts.

## Largest foreign contractors in the United States

1. Philipp Holzmann AG (West Germany)
2. Bovis International Ltd. (England)
3. Fletcher Construction Co. Ltd. (New Zealand)

# GIMME SHELTER

4. SAE-Societe Auxiliaire d'Entreprises (France)
5. Aoki Corp. (Japan)
6. Davy Corp. PLC (England)
7. Bilfinger & Berger Bau AG (West Germany)
8. PCL Construction Group Inc. (Canada)
9. Kajima Corp. (Japan)
10. John Brown Engineers & Constructors (England)

*Where'd you hear that?*
ENR, Top 250 International Contractors. Based on 1988 dollar amount of foreign contracts.

## Largest contractors

1. Fluor Daniel Inc., with $16,646.9 million
2. Bechtel Group Inc., $12,009.8
3. Brown & Root Inc., $10,976.7
4. Parsons Corp., $9,711.0
5. M. W. Kellogg Co., $9,394.0
6. CRSS Inc., $7,984.0
7. Rust International Corp., $5,923.0
8. ABB Lummus Crest, $5,493.0
9. Foster Wheeler Corp., $4,108.0
10. Jacobs Engineering Group Inc.,, $3,710.0

*Where'd you hear that?*
ENR, Top 400 Contractors. Based on 1988 total contracts, in millions of dollars.

## Largest general building contractors

1. Turner Corp., with $3,251.7 million
2. CRSS Inc., $3,102.8
3. Fluor Daniel Inc., $2,481.1
4. Rust International Corp., $1,842.1
5. Centex General Construction Cos., $1,824.0
6. Lehrer McGovern Bovis Inc., $1,354.6
7. Jones Group Inc., $1,204.5
8. The Clark Construction Group Inc., $1,109.2
9. Fletcher Construction (U.S.A.), Ltd., $1,032.2
10. Perini Corp., $934.4

*Where'd you hear that?*
ENR, Top 400 Contractors. Based on 1989 total contracts, in millions of dollars.

## Largest heavy contractors

1. Parsons Corp., with $1,880.4 million
2. Bechtel Group Inc.,, $1,400.7
3. Kiewit Construction Group Inc., $1,294.3
4. Granite Construction Co., $653.1
5. Fluor Daniel Inc., $560.2
6. Morrison Knudsen Corp., $552.6
7. Ebasco Services Inc., $487.3
8. J. S. Alberici Construction Co. Inc., $400.2
9. Jones Group Inc., $394.9
10. Beazer Materials & Services Inc., $381.5

*Where'd you hear that?*
ENR, Top 400 Contractors. Based on 1989 total contracts, in millions of dollars.

## Largest design-construct contractors

1. Bechtel Group Inc., with $9,248.3 million
2. M. W. Kellogg Co., $6,080.0

323

# GIMME SHELTER

3. Parsons Corp., $3,884.0
4. Foster Wheeler Corp., $3,570.0
5. Brown & Root Inc., $3,086.4
6. Fluor Daniel Inc., $3,052.6
7. Rust International Corp., $3,000.0
8. ABB Lummus Crest, $2,084.0
9. Ebasco Services Inc., $1,577.5
10. Austin Co., $1,350.0

*Where'd you hear that?*
ENR, Top 400 Contractors. Based on 1989 total contracts, in millions of dollars.

## Largest specialty contractors

1. JWP Inc. Electric Group, with $605.6 million
2. Fischbach & Moore Inc., $549.0
3. JWP Inc. Mechanical Group, $420.2
4. Natkin Group Inc., $381.0
5. MMR Inc., $305.0
6. L. K. Comstock & Co. Inc., $272.5
7. Schneider Group of Cos., $260.0
8. MMR/Wallace Group Inc., $220.0
9. Miller & Long Co. Inc., $188.6
10. Harmon Contract, $170.0

*Where'd you hear that?*
ENR, Top Specialty Contractors. Based on 1988 revenues, in millions of dollars.

## Largest electrical contractors

1. JWP Inc. Electric Group, with $605.6 million
2. Fischbach & Moore Inc., $510.6
3. MMR Inc., $305.0
4. L. K. Comstock & Co. Inc., $272.5
5. Massachusetts Electric Construction Co., $107.3
6. SASCO Group, $104.3
7. Amelco Corp., $76.1
8. Guarantee Electrical Co., $75.0
9. Steiny & Co. Inc., $74.8
10. Berg Electric Corp., $74.6

*Where'd you hear that?*
ENR, Top Specialty Contractors. Based on 1988 revenues, in millions of dollars.

## Largest mechanical contractors

1. JWP Inc. Mechanical Group, with $420.2 million
2. Natkin Group Inc., $369.6
3. MMR/Wallace Group Inc., $220.0
4. Poole & Kent Co., $130.3
5. TDIndustries, $108.2
6. Sauer Industries Inc., $104.5
7. Schneider Group of Cos., $98.8
8. Limbach Constructors Inc., $97.7
9. Midwest Mechanical Contractors Inc., $88.1
10. Wolff & Munier Inc., $72.3

*Where'd you hear that?*
ENR, Top Specialty Contractors. Based on 1988 revenues, in millions of dollars.

## Largest wall/ceiling contractors

1. Davis Cos., with $91.2 million
2. Anson Industries Inc., $57.6
3. Elliason & Knuth Cos. Inc., $48.3

# GIMME SHELTER

4. Duggan & Marcon Inc., $38.0
5. McNulty Bros. Co., $32.5
6. P & P Contractors Inc., $27.5
7. Novinger's Inc., $23.0
8. Bouma Corp., $22.3
9. R. J. C. & Associates Inc., $18.4
10. Commercial Merit Inc., $18.0

*Where'd you hear that?*
ENR, Top Specialty Contractors.
Based on 1988 revenues, in millions of dollars.

## Largest sheet metal contractors

1. Kirk & Blum Manufacturing Co., with $47.5 million
2. Limbach Constructors Inc., $41.9
3. Robert Irsay Co., $28.3
4. Brandt Engineering Co. Inc., $26.2
5. A. C. Dellovade Inc., $24.2
6. John Groce & Co. Inc., $21.4
7. Linford Air & Refrigeration Co., $20.1
8. Egan & Sons Co., $18.7
9. Hill Mechanical Construction Group, $18.0
9. Triangle Sheet Metal Works Inc., $18.0

*Where'd you hear that?*
ENR, Top Specialty Contractors.
Based on 1988 revenues, in millions of dollars.

## Largest excavation/foundation contractors

1. Malcolm Drilling Co. Inc., with $40.6 million
2. Ryan Inc. Eastern, $38.3
3. McKinney Drilling Co., $28.5
4. Urban Substructures Co. Inc., $28.3
5. Foundation Constructors Inc., $27.9
6. ICOS Corp. of America, $27.5
7. Geo-Con Inc., $24.0
8. Manafort Brothers Inc., $22.7
9. Nicholson Construction Co., $22.0
10. Griffin Dewatering Corp. & Affiliates, $21.7

*Where'd you hear that?*
ENR, Top Specialty Contractors.
Based on 1988 revenues, in millions of dollars.

## Largest steel erection contractors

1. Williams Industries Inc., with $76.6 million
2. Broad, Vogt & Conant Inc., $67.6
3. American Bridge Co., $66.8
4. Schuff Steel Co., $34.8
5. Interstate Iron Works Corp., $30.1
6. Gateway Construction Co. Inc., $23.9
7. General Steel Fabricators Inc., $22.0
8. SCI/Steelcon Inc., $21.9
9. Danny's Construction Co. Inc., $20.4
10. Bratton Corp., $19.4

*Where'd you hear that?*
ENR, Top Specialty Contractors.
Based on 1988 revenues, in millions of dollars.

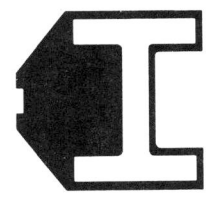

# GIMME SHELTER

### Largest roofing contractors

1. Bryant Organization Inc., with $60.0 million
2. Centimark Corp., $50.2
3. Universal Roofers Inc., $49.0
4. CEI Group, $35.2
5. Hartford Roofing Co. Inc., $29.7
6. J. P. Patti Co. Inc., $26.5
7. Schreiber Corp., $23.4
8. Campbell Cos., $21.9
9. Crown Coor Inc., $19.8
10. Baker Roofing Co., $16.6

*Where'd you hear that?*
ENR, Top Specialty Contractors. Based on 1988 revenues, in millions of dollars.

### Largest concrete contractors

1. Miller & Long Co. Inc., with $188.6 million
2. Baker Concrete Construction, $141.3
3. Conco Cement Co., $69.5
4. Cleveland Cement Contractors Inc., $25.8
5. Healy & Long Concrete Contractors, $15.2
6. Dance Brothers Inc., $14.5
7. Lawrence Construction Co., $13.5
8. SPC Concrete, $12.7
9. Dee Shoring Co., $10.2
10. Bartlett-Brainard & Eacott Inc., $10.0

*Where'd you hear that?*
ENR, Top Specialty Contractors. Based on 1988 revenues, in millions of dollars.

### Largest utilities contractors

1. Western Utility Contractors Inc., with $32.5 million
2. W. Jackson & Sons, $25.0
3. Super Excavators Inc., $24.6
4. Sturgeon Electric Co., $23.1
5. Dan's Excavating Inc., $20.4
6. Modern Continental Construction Co. Inc., $20.0
7. Bryant Electric Co. Inc., $18.5
8. Trescon Corp., $18.2
9. Cullum Construction Co. Inc., $15.0
10. Azco Group Ltd., $12.3

*Where'd you hear that?*
ENR, Top Specialty Contractors. Based on 1988 revenues, in millions of dollars.

### Largest glazing/curtain wall contractors

1. Harmon Contract, with $170.0 million
2. Cobbledick - Kibbe Inc., $45.0
3. Welling & Co. Inc., $25.3
4. Tri-States Glass Inc., $19.1
5. National Glass & Metal Co. Inc., $18.6
6. American Glass & Metals Corp., $13.1
7. Olden & Co., $12.3
8. Elward Inc., $11.0
9. Young Sales Corp., $9.0
10. N. E. B. C. Inc., $8.9

*Where'd you hear that?*
ENR, Top Specialty Contractors. Based on 1988 revenues, in millions of dollars.

# GIMME SHELTER

## Largest demolition/wrecking contractors

1. Cleveland Wrecking Co., with $56.9 million
2. Penhall International, $53.5
3. Bierlein Demolition Contractors Inc., $40.8
4. Kimmins Environmental Service Corp., $39.5
5. U.S. Dismantlement Corp., $23.6
6. Mayer Pollock Steel Corp., $23.0
7. Midwest Steel & Alloy Corp., $18.3
8. Olshan Demolishing Co., $13.4
9. O'Rourke Industries Inc., $13.0
10. Wrecking Corp. of America St. Louis Inc., $11.2

*Where'd you hear that?*
ENR, Top Specialty Contractors. Based on 1988 revenues, in millions of dollars.

## Largest painting contractors

1. M. L. McDonald Co., with $30.0 million
2. I. H. Whitehouse & Sons, $15.0
3. Swanson & Youngdale Inc., $13.0
4. Charles Shaid Co., $11.7
5. Ascher Bros. Co. Inc., $10.0
6. Ronald D. Mayhew Inc., $9.0
6. Hartman Walsh Painting, $9.0
8. Robison-Prezioso Inc., $8.2
9. Avalotis Painting Co., $8.0
10. Jeffco Painting & Contracting Inc., $7.0

*Where'd you hear that?*
ENR, Top Specialty Contractors. Based on 1988 revenues, in millions of dollars.

## Largest asbestos abatement contractors

1. Specialty Systems Inc., with $29.8 million
2. Young Sales Corp., $21.7
3. Baker Pacific Corp., $19.8
4. Ogden Allied Abatement and Decontamination Service Inc., $16.8
5. Barsotti's Inc., $13.1
6. Project Development Group Inc., $12.1
7. Kimmins Environmental Service Corp., $11.8
8. Burdco Environmental Inc., $11.4
9. Eastern Environmental Services of the Southeast Inc., $10.6
9. Anson Industries Inc., $10.6

*Where'd you hear that?*
ENR, Top Specialty Contractors. Based on 1988 revenues, in millions of dollars.

## Biggest corporations in the building materials industry

1. Owens-Illinois, with $3,692 million
2. American Standard, $3,631
3. Owens-Corning Fiber, $3,021
4. Corning, $2,469
5. Manville Corp., $2,228
6. USG, $2,201
7. Norton, $1,535
8. Lafarge, $1,497
9. Certainteed, $1,365
10. National Gypsum, $1,364

*Where'd you hear that?*
Fortune, Fortune 500 Largest U.S. Industrial Corporations. Based on 1989 sales, in millions of dollars.

# GIMME SHELTER

### Biggest corporations in the building materials industry

1. PPG Industries, with $4,530 million
2. Vulcan Materials, $1,763
3. Sherwin-Williams, $1,477
4. Lafarge, $939
5. Owens-Corning Fiberglas, $913
6. Calmat, $854
7. Tecumseh Products, $697
8. Southdown, $481
9. RMP, $440
10. Manville Corp., $408
11. Valspar, $376

*Where'd you hear that?*
Business Week, The Business Week 1000. Based on market value as of March 16, 1990, in millions of dollars.

### Most productive building materials corporations

1. Vulcan Materials, with $20.6 thousand
2. Manville Corp., $10.9
3. Owens-Corning, $9.4
4. Tyco Laboratories, $8.0
5. Armstrong World Industries, $7.3
6. Masco, $5.4

*Where'd you hear that?*
Forbes, Forbes 500s Annual Directory. Based on 1989 profits per employee, in thousands of dollars. Ranks U.S.-based corporations that were publicly traded as of March 23, 1990.

### Largest building supply companies for consumer sales

1. Home Depot, with $2,337,500,000
2. Lowe's Cos., $1,602,000,000
3. Builders Square, $1,500,000,000
4. Payless Cashways, $1,330,000,000
5. Hechinger Co., $1,178,000,000

*Where'd you hear that?*
Building Supply Home Centers, Retailer Giants. Based on 1989 sales to consumers.

### *Largest retail building supply companies*

1. Home Depot, with $2.74 billion
2. Lowe's Cos., $2.67 billion
3. Builders Square, $2 billion
4. Payless Cashways, $1.9 billion
5. Hechinger Co., $1.24 billion
6. Grossman's, $1.07 billion
7. Home Club, $1 billion
7. Wickes Lumber, $1 billion
9. 84 Lumber, $800 million
10. Wickes Cos., $675 million

*Where'd you hear that?*
Building Supply Home Centers, Retailer Giants. Based on 1989 sales volume, in billions of dollars.

### Largest building supply companies for sales to pros/contractors

1. Lowe's Cos., with $1,068,000,000
2. Wickes Lumber, $600,000,000
3. Payless Cashways, $570,000,000
4. Builders Square, $500,000,000

5. Home Depot, $412,000,000

*Where'd you hear that?*
Building Supply Home Centers, Retailer Giants. Based on 1989 sales to pros/contractors.

## Largest building supply companies for sales to commercial customers

1. Wickes Lumber, with $100,000,000
2. Scotty's, $62,700,000
3. Home Club, $60,000,000
4. Strober Organization, $49,000,000
5. Wickes Cos., $33,700,000

*Where'd you hear that?*
Building Supply Home Centers, Retailer Giants. Based on 1989 sales to commercial customers.

## Largest building supply wholesale companies

1. Georgia-Pacific Corp., with $4.68 billion
2. Weyerhaeuser Co., $2.43 billion
3. Huttig Sash & Door Co., $470.4 million
4. North Pacific Lumber, $443 million
5. MacMillan Bloedel Building Materials, $400 million
6. Universal Forest Products, $355 million
7. Morgan Distribution, $312 million
8. Furman Lumber, $291 million
9. Sequoia Supply, $285 million
10. Adam Wholesaler, $261 million

*Where'd you hear that?*
Building Supply Home Centers. Based on 1988 sales volume.

## Speciality clay consumption in the United States

1. Bentonite, with 27%
2. Attapulgite, 21%
3. Kaolin, 18%
4. Organoclay, 17%
5. Acid Activated, 7%
6. Others, total 10%

*Where'd you hear that?*
Modern Paint and Coatings. Based on percentage of total dollars of 1988 consumption. 'Others' category includes magnesium aluminum silicates, sedimentary opal clay, hectorite, sepiolite, and white bentonite.

---

### *Best selling building supply products*

1. Wood products, with 27.6%
2. Building materials, 16.7%
3. Millwork, 10.8%
4. Plumbing, 6.9%
5. Paint, 6.7%
6. Lawn & garden products, 6.6%
6. Electrical suppliers, 6.6%
8. Hardware, 5.9%
9. Tools: hand and power, 5.2%
10. Kitchen and bath products, 4.6%

*Where'd you hear that?*
Building Supply Home Centers, Retailer Giants. Based on 1989 percent of sales industry-wide.

---

# GIMME SHELTER

# GIMME SHELTER

**Largest manufactured home builders in 1989 ranked by total home production**

1. Fleetwood Enterprises, Inc. (Riverside, CA), with $520,784,000
2. Redman Homes, Inc. (Dallas, TX), $317,520,000
3. Skyline Corp. (Elkhart, IN), $268,970,000
4. Champion Enterprises, Inc. (Dryden, MI), $220,900,000
5. Fairmont Homes, Inc. (Nappanee, IN), $166,780,000
6. Clayton Homes, Inc. (Knoxville, TN), $147,725,000
7. Horton Homes, Inc. (Eatonton, GA), $106,800,000
8. Commodore Corp. (Goshen, IN), $115,476,000
9. Palm Harbor Homes, Inc. (Dallas, TX), $136,972,085
10. Schult Homes Corp. (Middlebury, IN), $132,851,000

*Where'd you hear that?*
Mobile/Manufactured Home Merchandiser, Top 25 Mobile/Manufactured Home Builders. Based on total dollar value of production.

**Largest manufacturers on non-HUD code homes in 1989**

1. Muncy Homes, Inc. (Muncy, PA), with 1,477
2. Ritz-Craft Corp. (Mifflinburg, PA), 1,350
3. Penn Lyon Homes, Inc. (Selinsgrove, PA), 796
4. Ocilla Industries, Inc. (Ocilla, GA), 639
5. Kaplan Building Systems, Inc. (Pine Grove, PA), 504
6. Fuqua Homes, Inc. (Arlington, TX), 475
7. Destiny Industries, Inc. (Moultrie, GA), 461
8. Schult Homes Corp. (Middlebury, IN), 454
9. Foremost Industries, Inc. (Greencastle, PA), 400
10. Horton Homes, Inc. (Eatonton, GA), 380

*Where'd you hear that?*
Mobile/Manufactured Home Merchandiser, Top 25 Mobile/Manufactured Home Builders. Based on number of non-HUD code homes built in 1989.

**Largest manufacturers of non-HUD code homes ranked by dollar volume**

1. Ritz-Craft Corp. (Mifflinburg, PA, with $43,000,000
2. Muncy Homes, Inc. (Muncy, PA), $42,000,000
3. Penn Lyon Homes, Inc. (Selinsgrove, PA), $34,696,068
4. Kaplan Building Systems, Inc. (Pine Grove, PA), $25,000,000
5. Foremost Industries, Inc. (Greencastle, PA), $20,000,000
6. Schult Homes Corp. (Middlebury, IN), $15,042,000
7. Poloron Homes of Pennsylvania, Inc. (Middleburg, PA), $13,464,000
8. Ocilla Industries, Inc. (Ocilla, GA), $9,720,000
9. Destiny Industries, Inc. (Moultrie, GA), $7,402,107
10. Fuqua Homes, Inc. (Arlington, TX), $6,766,000

# GIMME SHELTER

*Where'd you hear that?*
Mobile/Manufactured Home Merchandiser, Top 25 Mobile/Manufactured Home Builders. Based on dollar volume in 1989.

## Leading U.S. states for production of mobile/manufactured homes

1. Georgia, 32,956
2. Indiana, 28,716
3. North Carolina, 22,786
4. Alabama, 21,431
5. Florida, 18,412
6. Pennsylvania, 15,249
7. Tennessee, 14,389
8. California, 12,142
9. Oregon, 6,829
10. Texas, 6,510

*Where'd you hear that?*
Mobile/Manufactured Home Merchandiser. Based on number of homes produced in 1988.

## Largest owners of manufactured home communities

1. Lautrec, with 20,067
2. Clayton, Williams & Sherwood, 19,508
3. Uniprop, 14,805
4. Mobile Home Communities, 13,853
5. DeAnza Corp., 12,450
6. Aspen Enterprises, 10,734
7. Ellenburg Capital, 10,418
8. ROC Properties, 9,700
9. Planned Management Services, 9,148
10. Chateau Estates, 8,875

*Where'd you hear that?*
Manufactured Home Merchandiser. Based on number of sites owned.

## Leading U.S. states for shipments of mobile/manufactured homes

1. Florida, 23,339
2. North Carolina, 19,117
3. Georgia, 14,612
4. Alabama, 11,217
5. South Carolina, 10,978
6. California, 10,517
7. Michigan, 10,334
8. Tennessee, 8,859
9. New York, 7,937
10. Pennsylvania, 7,396

*Where'd you hear that?*
Mobile/Manufactured Home Merchandiser. Based on number of home shipped in 1988.

## America's largest apartment-rental companies

1. National Housing Partnership (Washington, DC), with 81,418
2. CRI (Rockville, MD), 73,600
3. Related (New York City), 70,146
4. Lincoln Property Co. (Dallas, TX), 63,206
5. Lefrak Organization (Rego Park, NY), 61,127
6. Balcor (Skokie, IL), 60,000
6. Southmark (Dallas, TX), 60,000
8. Cardinal Industries (Columbus, OH), 55,000
9. Winthrop Financial (Boston, MA), 50,392
10. Hall Financial Group (Dallas, TX), 49,236

*Where'd you hear that?*
Fortune. Based on number of rental units.

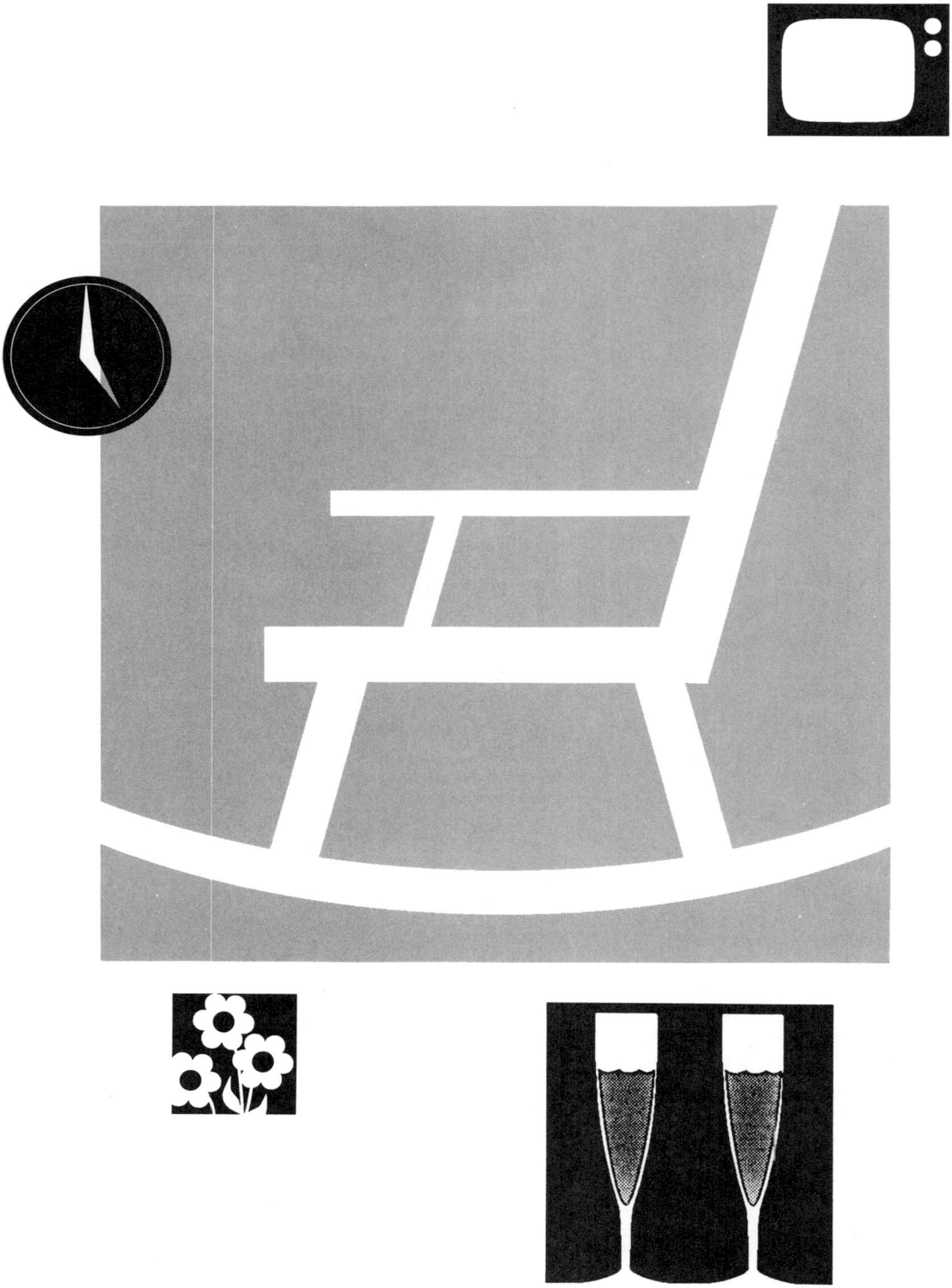

# Feathering the Nest

**Market share of gas residential furnaces**

1. United Technologies (Carrier, BDP), with 24%
2. Lennox, 15%
3. Rheem/Ruud, 14%
4. Heil-Quaker, 10%
5. American Standard (Trane), 8%
6. Ducane, 7%
7. Snyder General, 6%
7. York, 6%
9. Goodman, 4%
10. Maytag (Magic Chef), 3%

*Where'd you hear that?*
Appliance Manufacturer. Based on 1989 market share, in percent.

**Market share of oil residential furnaces**

1. Ducane, with 22%
2. Nordyne (Intertherm), 13%
3. Coleman, 12%
4. Heil-Quaker, 10%
4. Rheem/Ruud, 10%
4. Williamson, 10%
7. Maytag (Magic Chef), 7%
7. Thermo-Products, 7%
9. Lennox, 4%
10. Bard, 2%
11. Others total, 3%

*Where'd you hear that?*
Appliance Manufacturer. Based on 1989 market share, in percent.

**Market share of electric residential furnaces**

1. Rheem/Ruud, with 30%
2. Goodman, 20%
3. Lennox, 18%
4. Heil-Quaker, 13%
5. Addison, 8%
6. Nordyne (Intertherm), 6%
7. Williamson, 5%

*Where'd you hear that?*
Appliance Manufacturer. Based on 1989 market share, in percent.

# FEATHERING THE NEST

## Market share of water heaters

1. Rheem, with 24%
1. State Industries, 24%
3. Mor-Flo, 21%
4. A. O. Smith Corp., 17%
5. Bradford-White, 14%

*Where'd you hear that?*
Appliance Manufacturer. Based on 1989 market share, in percent. Figures compiled from surveys, interviews, and industry sources.

## Leading room air conditioner brands

1. Fedders, with 21.3%
2. Kenmore, 18.0%
3. WCI, 13.5%
4. General Electric, 11.0%
5. Emerson, 9.3%
6. Whirlpool, 7.0%
7. Amana, 4.7%
7. Carrier, 4.7%
9. Friedrich, 4.3%
10. Hotpoint, 4.0%

*Where'd you hear that?*
HFD, HFD Statistical Survey. Based on 1989 market share, in percent.

## Market share of duct-mounted humidifiers

1. Research Products, with 38%
2. General Filters, 12%
3. Lau Industries, 10%
4. Herrmidifier, 9%
4. Skuttle, 9%
6. Masco (Auto Flo), 7%
7. United Technologies (Carrier), 6%
8. Lennox, 4%
8. Walton Labs, 4%
10. Others, total, 1%

*Where'd you hear that?*
Appliance Manufacturer. Based on 1989 market share, in percent.

## Market share of portable humidifiers

1. Bemis Co. Inc., with 41%
2. Emerson, 32%
3. Toastmaster, 20%
4. Lasko, 7%

*Where'd you hear that?*
Appliance Manufacturer. Based on 1989 market share, in percent.

## Top hardware brands

1. Stanley, with 57%
2. Black & Decker, 55%
3. General Electric Co., 8%
4. Skil, 4%
5. Lucite, 3%
6. Rubbermaid, 2%
7. Royal, 1%
7. Bull Dog, 1%
7. Glidden, 1%
7. Great Neck, 1%

*Where'd you hear that?*
Discount Store News. Based on percentage of discount store executives surveyed naming the brand as a top performer for 1989.

## Largest paint companies

1. Sherwin-Williams, with $2,123.5 million
2. Valspar, $526.9
3. Grow Group, $412.7
4. Desoto Inc., $408.2
5. RPM Inc., $376.1
6. Standard Brands Paint, $304.4
7. Pratt & Lambert, $245.5
8. Lilly Industrial Coatings, $212.2
9. Guardsman Products, $189.7

# FEATHERING THE NEST

*Where'd you hear that?*
Chemicalweek, Chemicalweek 300. Based on 1989 sales, in millions of dollars.

## Largest retail curtain outlets

1. National Chains and Catalogs, 50%
2. Mass Merchants, 32%
3. Specialty Stores, 10%
4. Department Stores, 6%
5. Others, total, 2%

*Where'd you hear that?*
HFD, Home Textiles. Based on 1989 market share of retail sales, in percent.

## Largest retail drapery outlets

1. National Chains and Catalogs, with 51%
2. Mass Merchants, 26%
3. Specialty Stores, 13%
4. Department Stores, 8%
5. Others, total, 2%

*Where'd you hear that?*
HFD, Home Textiles. Based on 1989 market share of retail sales, in percent.

## Largest flooring companies

1. LD Brinkman & Co., with $207 million
2. Florstar Sales Inc., $111
3. Cain & Bultman Inc., $85
4. Kane Carpet, $80
4. Bayard Sales, $80
6. J. J. Haines & Co., $75
7. Lowy Enterprises Inc., $73
8. N.R.F. Distributors, $61
9. Tri-West Ltd., $60
10. Sunflooring Inc., $54

*Where'd you hear that?*
Flooring. Based on 1989 sales volume, in millions of dollars.

## Largest retail area rug outlets

1. Department stores, with 30%
1. Specialty stores, 30%
3. National chains and catalogs, 20%
4. Mass merchants, 5%
5. Others, total 15%

*Where'd you hear that?*
HFD, Home Textiles. Based on 1989 market share, in percent.

## Largest retail broadloom outlets

1. Specialty stores, with 72%
2. National chains and catalogs, 11%
3. Department stores, 5%
4. Mass merchants, 4%
5. Others, total 8%

*Where'd you hear that?*
HFD, Home Textiles. Based on 1989 market share, in percent.

## Brands of rugs rated best by department stores

1. Regal
2. Fieldcrest
3. Lacey Mills

*Where'd you hear that?*
LDB/Interior Textiles, LDB 100. Based on results of questionnaires rating suppliers.

## Brands of rugs rated best by mass merchants

1. Aladdin Mills
2. Burlington Industries
3. Antigua Mills

# FEATHERING THE NEST

*Where'd you hear that?*
LDB/Interior Textiles, LDB 100. Based on results of questionnaires rating suppliers.

## Brands of rugs rated best by specialty stores

1. Regal
2. Fieldcrest
3. Newmark Rug

*Where'd you hear that?*
LDB/Interior Textiles, LDB 100. Based on results of questionnaires rating suppliers.

## Europe's largest furniture companies

1. Ikea Einrichtungshaus GmbH Sued, with 497,245,728 ECU
2. Westofen Gesellschaft Mit Beschraenkter Haftung, 358,248,876
3. Fichet Bauche, 306,472,899
4. Bullough PLC, 305,778,766
5. Christie-Tyler PLC, 248,223,660
6. Welle Gesellschaft Mit Beschraenkter Haftung & Co. Kommanditgesellschaft, 222,635,927
7. Franke Romont Sa., 221,771,962
8. Alno-Moebelwerke GmbH & Co. Kg., 220,933,670
9. Steelcase Strafor Sa., 196,512,437
10. Hygena Ltd., 195,069,173

*Where'd you hear that?*
Dun's Europa. Based on 1989 Sales, in European Currency Units.

## Biggest corporations in the U.S. furniture industry

1. Johnson Controls, with $3,690 million
2. Interco, $3,278
3. Lear Siegler Seating Corp., $1,015
4. Leggett & Platt, $992
5. Herman Miller, $799
6. Ohio Mattress, $706
7. Hon Industries, $608
8. Kimball International, $597
9. La-Z-Boy Chair, $556

*Where'd you hear that?*
Fortune, Fortune 500 Largest U.S. Industrial Corporations. Based on 1989 sales, in millions of dollars.

## Most admired furniture corporations

1. Herman Miller, with a rating of 7.40
2. Masco, 6.88
3. Leggett & Platt, 6.73
4. Hon Industries, 6.26
5. Kimball International, 6.15
6. Ohio Mattress, 5.31
7. Mohasco, 5.22
8. Interco, 4.95

*Where'd you hear that?*
Fortune, America's Most Admired Corporations. Based on scores (0-10) derived from a survey of senior executives, outside directors, and financial analysts. Respondents ranked firms in their own industry on quality of management and products/services; innovation; long-term investment value; financial soundness; attraction and retention of talent; community and environmental responsibility; and use of assets.

# FEATHERING THE NEST

## Most productive home furnishings corporations

1. Rubbermaid, with $13.8 thousand
2. Newell Co., $8.3
3. Premark International, $3.2
4. Springs Industries, $2.8
5. Interco, -$2.2

*Where'd you hear that?*
Forbes, Forbes 500s Annual Directory. Based on 1989 profits per employee, in thousands of dollars. Ranks U.S.-based corporations that were publicly traded as of March 23, 1990.

## Most profitable home furnishings companies

1. Rubbermaid, with 21.5%
2. Leggett & Platt, 19.4%
3. Newell Co., 18.0%
4. Kimball International, 17.6%
5. La-Z-Boy Chair, 16.6%
6. Bassett Furniture Industries, 11.3%
7. Interco, 9.0%
8. Premark International, NA

*Where'd you hear that?*
Forbes, Annual Report on American Industry. Based on 10-year average return on equity. Ranks publicly held corporations only.

## Top home electronics brands

1. Emerson, with 27%
2. General Electric Co., 23%
3. Panasonic, 13%
4. Sony, 13%
5. Sharp, 13%
6. RCA, 11%
7. Magnavox, 10%
8. GoldStar, 9%
9. Nintendo, 8%
10. Soundesign, 7%

*Where'd you hear that?*
Discount Store News. Based on percentage of discount store managers surveyed naming the brand as a top performer for 1989.

## Best selling household products

1. Small electric appliances, with 20.6%
2. Cook and bakeware, 16.7%
3. Decorative accessories, 14.8%
4. Tabletop, serving products and accessories, 9.5%
5. Kitchenware and accessories, 9.1%
6. Furniture, 6.2%
7. Outdoor products and accessories, 5.1%
8. Bath, laundry closet and storage, 4.6%
9. Cleaning products, 1.9%
10. Clocks, 0.6%
11. Other, 10.9%

*Where'd you hear that?*
Non-Foods Merchandising. Based on 1988 market share, in percent.

## Most popular retail outlets for tablecloths

1. Mass merchants, with 38%
2. Department stores, 22%
3. Specialty stores, 18%
4. National chains and catalogs, 16%
5. Others, total, 6%

*Where'd you hear that?*
HFD, Home Textiles. Based on 1989 market share, in percent.

# FEATHERING THE NEST

### Largest retail bedspread outlets

1. National chains and catalogs, with 44%
2. Mass merchants, 36%
3. Department stores, 11%
4. Specialty stores, 7%
5. Others, total 2%

*Where'd you hear that?*
HFD, Home Textiles. Based on percentage of total bedspread sales in 1989.

### Largest retail comforter outlets

1. National chains and catalogs, with 31%
2. Mass merchants, 27%
3. Specialty stores, 21%
4. Department stores, 17%
5. Others, total 4%

*Where'd you hear that?*
HFD, Home Textiles. Based on percentage of total comforter sales in 1989.

### Best bedspreads sold by department stores

1. Springs Industries
2. Croscill
3. Crown Crafts

*Where'd you hear that?*
LDB/Interior Textiles, LDB 100. Based on results of questionnaires rating suppliers.

### Best bedspreads sold by specialty stores

1. Springs Industries
2. Beau Ideal
3. Dakotah

*Where'd you hear that?*
LDB/Interior Textiles, LDB 100. Based on results of questionnaires rating suppliers.

### Best bedspreads sold by mass merchants

1. Springs Industries
2. Aberdeen
3. Arley

*Where'd you hear that?*
LDB/Interior Textiles, LDB 100. Based on results of questionnaires rating suppliers.

### Market share of electric blankets

1. Fieldcrest, with 48%
1. Northern Electric, 48%
3. Belton, 4%

*Where'd you hear that?*
Appliance Manufacturer. Based on 1989 market share, in percent.

### Leading household appliance companies in Europe

1. Electrolux (Electrolux, Zanussi, Husqvarna), with 20.5%
2. Whirlpool (Philips Whirlpool, Bauknecht, Ignis, Laden), 11.5%
3. Bosch-Siemens (Bosch, Siemens, Constructa, Neff), 11.0%
4. Merloni (Merloni, Ariston, Indesit), 10.0%
5. Other, 47.0%

*Where'd you hear that?*
Fortune. Based on european market share. Original source: Salomon Bros.

# FEATHERING THE NEST

### Biggest corporations in the household appliance industry

1. Masco, with $3,929 million
2. Whirlpool, $2,313
3. Maytag, $1,861
4. Armstrong World Industries, $1,563
5. Circuit City Stores, $1,100
6. Leggett & Platt, $524
7. Kimball International, $472
8. Pier 1 Imports, $403
9. La-Z-Boy Chair, $333

*Where'd you hear that?*
Business Week, The Business Week 1000. Based on market value in millions of dollars.

### Leading household appliance companies in the U.S.

1. Whirlpool (Whirlpool, KitchenAid, Roper), with 32.7%
2. General Electric Co. (GE, Hotpoint, RCA, Monogram), 25.5%
3. Electrolux (Frigidaire, Gibson, Kelvinator, Tappan, White, Westinghouse), 18.4%
4. Maytag (Maytag, Hardwick, Jenn-Air, Magic Chef, Admiral, Norge), 14.8%
5. Other, 8.6%

*Where'd you hear that?*
Fortune. Based on U.S. market share. Original source: *Appliance Magazine.*.

### Most productive appliance corporations

1. Maytag, with $5.1 thousand
2. Whirlpool, $4.7
3. Black & Decker Corp., $-0.4

*Where'd you hear that?*
Forbes, Forbes 500s Annual Directory. Based on 1989 profits per employee, in thousands of dollars. Ranks U.S.-based corporations that were publicly traded as of March 23, 1990.

### Most profitable appliance manufacturers

1. Emerson Radio, with 18.7%
2. Whirlpool, 15.0%
3. Toro, 12.1%
4. Black & Decker Corp., 5.4%
5. Amdura, deficit
6. Allegheny International Inc., NA
7. Harman International, NA
8. Maytag, NA
9. SSMC, NA
10. Standard Shares, NA

*Where'd you hear that?*
Forbes, Annual Report on American Industry. Based on 10-year average return on equity. Ranks publicly held corporations only.

### Metropolitan areas with the highest major household appliance sales in furniture/home furnishings stores

1. Los Angeles-Long Beach, CA, with $794,183 thousand
2. New York, NY, $529,364
3. Chicago, IL, $461,267
4. Philadelphia, PA, $359,594
5. Detroit, MI, $334,572
6. Boston-Lawrence-Salem-Lowell-Brockton, MA, $328,262
7. Washington, DC, $307,897
8. Nassau-Suffolk, NY, $267,405
9. Houston, TX, $266,892
10. Tampa-St. Petersburg-Clearwater, FL, $232,143

# FEATHERING THE NEST

*Where'd you hear that?*
Sales & Marketing Management, Survey of Buying Power. Based on sales, in thousands of dollars.

## Home appliance ownership in America

1. Microwave oven, with 75%
2. Smoke alarm, 73%
3. Toaster oven, 48%
4. Food processor, 32%
5. Answering machine, 25%
6. Computer, 15%
7. Water filter, 10%

*Where'd you hear that?*
Adweek's Marketing Week. Based on percentage home ownership. Based on data from Roper Reports.

## Market share of portable electric mixers

1. Black & Decker, with 33%
2. Sunbeam, 21%
3. Hamilton Beach, 13%
4. Farberware, 9%
4. Waring, 9%
6. Rival, 8%
7. Toastmaster, 3%
8. Krups, 2%
8. Robeson, 2%

*Where'd you hear that?*
Appliance Manufacturer. Based on 1989 market share, in percent.

## Market share of can openers

1. Rival, with 28%
2. Black & Decker, 24%
3. Sunbeam, 10%
4. Oster, 7%
5. ProctorSilex, 5%
5. Waring, 5%
7. Farberware, 4%
7. Hamilton Beach, 4%
9. National Presto, 3%
9. Toastmaster, 3%
11. Robeson, 2%
12. Others, total, 5%

*Where'd you hear that?*
Appliance Manufacturer. Based on 1989 market share, in percent.

## Leading electric range companies

1. General Electric, with 23.4%
2. Kenmore, 16.0%
3. Whirlpool, 12.9%
4. Magic Chef, 7.2%
5. Caloric, 7.0%
6. Fridigaire, 6.0%
7. Hotpoint, 5.6%
8. White-Westinghouse, 5.0%
9. Tappan, 3.7%
10. Jenn-Air, 2.0%

*Where'd you hear that?*
HFD, HFD Statistical Survey. Based on 1989 percentage of market share.

## Leading gas range companies

1. Magic Chef, 17.4%
2. Caloric, 16.8%
3. General Electric, 14.1%
4. Tappan, 13.9%
5. Kenmore, 13.8%
6. Whirlpool, 4.5%
7. Montgomery Ward, 3.5%
8. Hotpoint, 2.2%
9. Roper, 2.0%
10. Maytag, 1.8%

*Where'd you hear that?*
HFD, HFD Statistical Survey. Based on 1989 percentage of market share.

## Best-selling microwave oven brands

1. Kenmore, with 13.8%
2. Sharp, 13.5%
3. General Electric, 11.2%

4. Panasonic, 6.6%
5. GoldStar, 6.3%
6. Emerson, 5.6%
7. Tappan, 5.5%
8. Amana, 4.5%
9. Samsung, 4.4%
10. Magic Chef, 4.2%

*Where'd you hear that?*
HFD, HFD Statistical Survey. Based on market share, in percent.

## Most popular brands of refrigerators

1. General Electric, with 21.8%
2. Kenmore, 19.0%
3. Whirlpool, 14.5%
4. Hotpoint, 7.0%
4. Frigidaire, 7.0%
6. Amana, 6.0%
7. Montgomery Ward, 4.8%
8. White-Westinghouse, 4.5%
9. Magic Chef, 2.4%
10. Gibson, 2.3%

*Where'd you hear that?*
HFD, HFD Statistical Survey. Based on 1989 percentage of market share.

## Market share of home freezers

1. Whirlpool, with 36%
2. Electrolux (WCI), 32%
3. Maytag (Admiral), 22%
4. Raytheon (Amana), 6%
5. Others, total 4%

*Where'd you hear that?*
Appliance Manufacturer. Based on 1989 market share, in percent.

## Market share of blenders

1. Oster, with 37%
2. Hamilton Beach, 28%
3. Braun, 17%
4. Waring, 10%
5. Black & Decker, 6%
6. Others, total, 2%

*Where'd you hear that?*
Appliance Manufacturer. Based on 1989 market share, in percent.

## Market share of food processors

1. Cuisinart, with 20%
1. Sunbeam, 20%
3. Black & Decker, 19%
4. Hamilton Beach, 16%
5. Moulinex Regal, 6%
6. Braun, 5%
6. West Bend, 5%
8. National Presto, 4%
9. Oster, 3%
10. KitchenAid, 2%

*Where'd you hear that?*
Appliance Manufacturer. Based on 1989 market share, in percent.

## Countries that exported the most tableware with silver or silverplated-handles

1. Taiwan, with $3,805,000
2. Italy, $2,728,000
3. France, $2,570,000
4. United Kingdom, $1,410,000
5. Others, total $2,918,000

*Where'd you hear that?*
Jewelers' Circular Keystone Directory. Based on 1987 value of tableware with silver or silverplated handles exported, in U.S. dollars.

## Countries that exported the most non-precious table and kitchenware to the U.S. in 1987

1. Japan, with $49,928,000
2. Taiwan, $33,565,000
3. Korea, $31,517,000

# FEATHERING THE NEST

341

# FEATHERING THE NEST

4. West Germany, $11,865,000
5. Hong Kong, $4,319,000
6. Switzerland, $4,234,000
7. Brazil, $3,468,000
8. United Kingdom, $2,787,000
9. Others, total $10,024,0000

*Where'd you hear that?*
Jewelers' Circular Keystone Directory. Based on 1987 value of non-precious table and kitchenware exported, in U.S. dollars.

### Countries that exported the most precious metal household wares to the U.S. in 1987

1. Hong Kong, with $26,501,000
2. Italy, $13,239,000
3. Korea, $10,864,000
4. United Kingdom, $8,129,000
5. Japan, $6,781,000
6. Taiwan, $2,837,000
7. France, $2,828,000
8. Portugal, $2,454,000
9. India, $2,178,000
10. Others, total $11,967,000

*Where'd you hear that?*
Jewelers' Circular Keystone Directory. Based on 1987 value of precious metal household wares exported, in U.S. dollars.

### Top countries of origin for U.S. imports of bone china

1. United Kingdom, with $41,565,000
2. Japan, $14,996,000
3. West Germany, $1,264,000
4. France, $498,000
5. Taiwan, $340,000
6. Ireland, $277,000
7. Others, total $1,017,000

*Where'd you hear that?*
Jewelers' Circular-Keystone Directory. Based on dollar value, 1988.

### Top countries of origin for U.S. imports of non-bone china

1. Taiwan, with $137,310,000
2. Japan, $122,458,000
3. China, $63,531,000
4. West Germany, $22,063,000
5. France, $19,303,000
6. United Kingdom, $14,638,000
7. Hong Kong, $12,505,000
8. Korea, $10,205,000
9. Italy, $7,735,000
10. Sri Lanka, $5,595,000

*Where'd you hear that?*
Jewelers' Circular-Keystone Directory. Based on dollar value, 1988.

### Top countries of origin for U.S. imports of earthen tableware

1. Japan, with $142,496,000
2. Korea, $50,771,000
3. Taiwan, $49,319,000
4. United Kingdom, $36,084,000
5. China, $21,980,000
6. Italy, $17,228,000
7. Brazil, $11,978,000
8. Thailand, $8,080,000
9. West Germany, $7,971,000
10. Portugal, $6,480,000

*Where'd you hear that?*
Jewelers' Circular-Keystone Directory. Based on dollar value, 1988.

### Countries receiving the most exports of U.S. earthen & ceramic ware

1. Mexico, with $5,026,000
2. United Kingdom, $4,804,000
3. Sweden, $3,008,000
4. Japan, $2,949,000
5. Canada, $2,808,000
6. South Africa, $2,226,000

7. Australia, $1,413,000
8. Belgium, $1,104,000
9. Norway, $1,045,000
10. Others, total $15,563,000

*Where'd you hear that?*
Jewelers' Circular-Keystone Directory. Based on dollar value, 1988.

## Countries exporting the most lead crystal to the U.S.

1. France, with $66,557,000
2. West Germany, $46,064,000
3. Ireland, $40,592,000
4. Yugoslavia, $16,768,000
5. Austria, $13,990,000
6. Japan, $8,428,000
7. United Kingdom, $7,961,000
8. Sweden, $7,464,000
9. Italy, $6,538,000
10. Portugal, $5,315,000

*Where'd you hear that?*
Jewelers' Circular Keystone Directory. Based on 1987 value of lead crystal exported, in U.S. dollars.

## Countries that imported the most U.S. glass tableware and stemware

1. Canada, with $17,587,000
2. Japan, $3,308,000
3. Hong Kong, $2,025,000
4. West Germany, $1,857,000
5. Australia, $1,600,000
6. United Kingdom, $1,203,000
7. Netherlands, $842,000
8. Singapore, $807,000
9. Dominican Republic, $719,000
10. Others, total $10,580,000

*Where'd you hear that?*
Jewelers' Circular Keystone Directory. Based on 1987 value of glass tableware and stemware imported, in U.S. dollars.

## Market share of electric toasters

1. ProctorSilex, with 43%
2. Toastmaster, 25%
3. Black & Decker, 18%
4. Sunbeam, 6%
5. Farberware, 2%
6. Others, total, 6%

*Where'd you hear that?*
Appliance Manufacturer. Based on 1989 market share, in percent.

## Market share of garbage disposers

1. In-Sink-Erator, with 60%
2. Electrolux (Anaheim), 30%
3. Thermador/Waste King, 5%
4. Watertown Metal Products, 2%
5. Maytag, 1%
6. Others, total 2%

*Where'd you hear that?*
Appliance Manufacturer. Based on 1989 market share, in percent.

## Market share of refuse compactors

1. Whirlpool, with 75%
2. General Electric, 14%
3. Emerson Contract, N.A.
4. Broan, 6%
5. Thermador/Waste King, 3%
6. Others, total 2%

# FEATHERING THE NEST

# FEATHERING THE NEST

*Where'd you hear that?*
Appliance Manufacturer. Based on 1989 market share, in percent.

## Market share of vacuum cleaners

1. Hoover, with 36%
2. Eureka Co., 20%
3. Ryobi (Singer), 10%
4. Whirlpool (Kenmore), 8%
5. Kirby, 6%
6. Electrolux, 5%
6. Regina, 5%
8. Matsushita (Panasonic), 3%
8. Rexaire (Rainbow), 3%
10. Bissell, 2%

*Where'd you hear that?*
Appliance Manufacturer. Based on 1989 market share, in percent.

## Best-selling brands of dishwashers

1. General Electric, with 28.0%
2. Kenmore, 20.6%
3. Whirlpool, 20.1%
4. WCI, 6.4%
5. Maytag, 6.3%
6. Hotpoint, 5.8%
7. KitchenAid, 3.5%
8. Caloric, 2.3%
8. Magic Chef, 2.3%
10. Tappan, 1.9%

*Where'd you hear that?*
HFD, HFD Statistical Survey. Based on market share of 1989 sales, in percentages.

## Top household cleaning brands

1. Tide, with 41%
2. Clorox, 27%
3. Procter & Gamble, 17%
4. Windex, 16%
5. Dow Chemical Co., 9%
6. Lever Bros., 7%
7. S. C. Johnson & Son, 6%
7. Formula 409, 6%
7. Lysol, 6%
10. Dawn, 5%

*Where'd you hear that?*
Discount Store News. Based on percentage of store managers at discount chains naming brand as a top performer.

## Most efficient advertisers among laundry detergents

1. Cheer, with $4.88
2. Tide, $7.86
3. Surf, $13.93
4. Fab, $13.95
5. All, $20.01
6. Era, $21.18
7. Wisk, $24.84

*Where'd you hear that?*
Adweek's Marketing Week, Annual Measure of Efficiency. Based on efficiency quotient (average weekly cost of television advertising divided by average number of retained impressions).

## Best-selling washing machine brands

1. Kenmore, with 33.0%
2. Whirlpool, 18.4%
3. Maytag, 13.0%
4. General Electric, 12.2%
5. Hotpoint, 4.0%
6. White-Westinghouse, 3.8%
7. Montgomery Ward, 3.2%
8. Frigidaire, 3.0%

# FEATHERING THE NEST

9. Speed Queen, 2.6%
10. Amana, 1.2%

*Where'd you hear that?*
HFD, HFD Statistical Survey. Based on market share by brand names sold in percent.

## Market share of electric dryers

1. Whirlpool, with 52%
2. General Electric, 16%
3. Maytag, 14%
4. Electrolux (WCI), 11%
5. Raytheon (Speed Queen), 3%
6. Norge, N.A.
7. Others, total 4%

*Where'd you hear that?*
Appliance Manufacturer. Based on 1989 market share, in percent.

## Market share of gas dryers

1. Whirlpool, with 52%
2. General Electric, 16%
3. Maytag, 14%
4. Electrolux (WCI), 11%
5. Raytheon (Speed Queen), 3%
6. Norge, N.A.
7. Others, total 4%

*Where'd you hear that?*
Appliance Manufacturer. Based on 1989 market share, in percent.

## Market share of electric irons

1. Black & Decker, with 49%
2. ProctorSilex, 18%
3. Sunbeam, 16%
4. North American Philips (Norelco), 6%
5. Rowenta, 5%
6. Hamilton Beach, 4%
7. West Bend, 2%

*Where'd you hear that?*
Appliance Manufacturer. Based on 1989 market share, in percent.

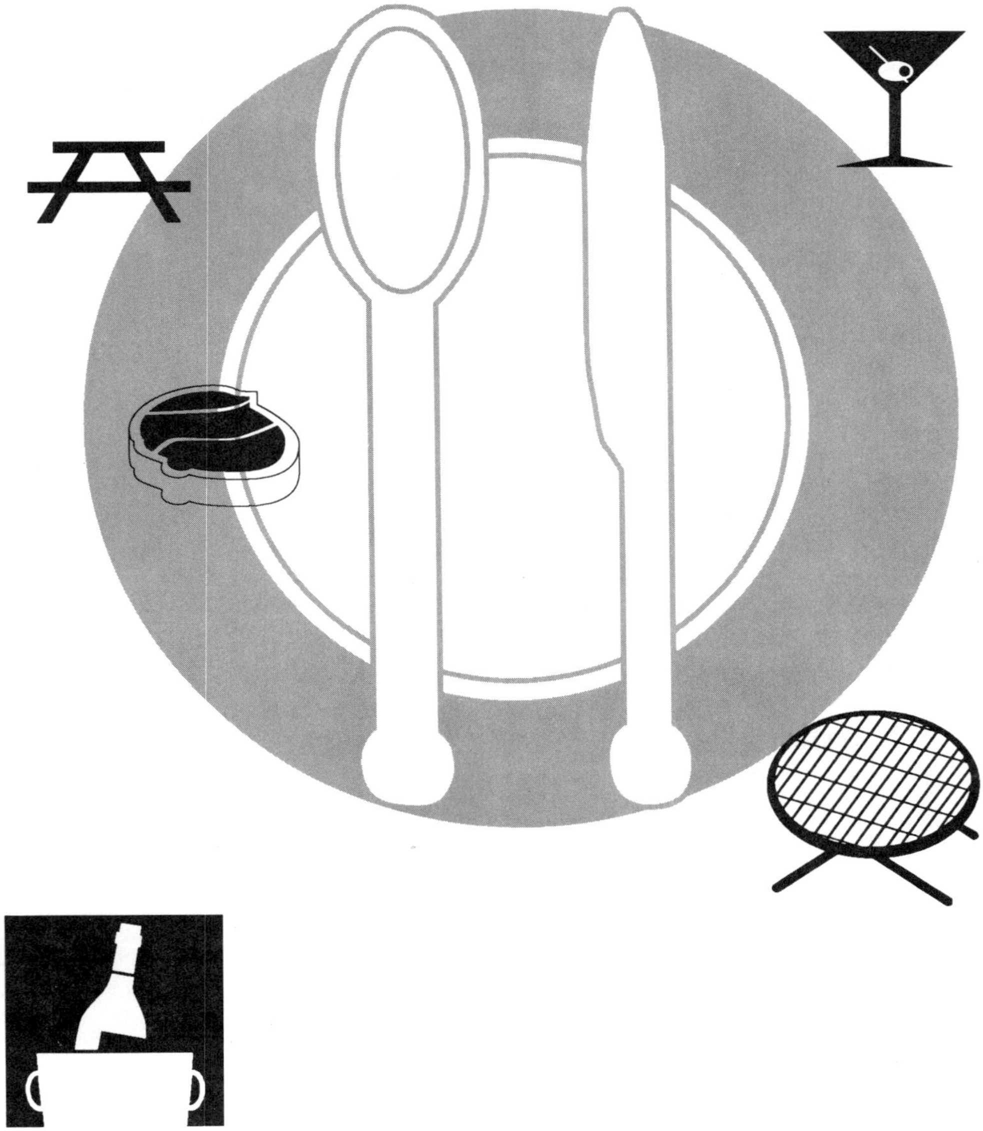

# Refreshment Stand

**Leading U.S. states in net cash income from farming**

1. California, with $6,183 million
2. Iowa, $3,941
3. Texas, $3,597
4. Illinois, $2,722
5. Minnesota, $2,703
6. Nebraska, $2,648
7. Florida, $2,639
8. Wisconsin, $2,260

*Where'd you hear that?*
Television/Radio Age. Based on 1987 net income, in millions of dollars.

**Leading farm states**

1. Rhode Island, with $6,240
2. New Jersey, $6,189
3. Connecticut, $4,914
4. Massachusetts, $3,534
5. New Hampshire, $2,037
6. Maryland, $2,014
7. Delaware, $1,895
8. Pennsylvania, $1,819

*Where'd you hear that?*
Television/Radio Age. Based on 1988 farm real estate values, in dollars per acre. Origianal source: USDA/ERS.

**Leading U.S. states in total value of farm real estate**

1. Texas, with $62,113 million
2. California, $43,701
3. Illinois, $31,850
4. Iowa, $29,803
5. Florida, $20,750
6. Kansas, $17,637
7. Missouri, $17,503
8. Nebraska, $17,280

*Where'd you hear that?*
Television/Radio Age. Based on 1988 total value, in millions of dollars.

**Largest agricultural banks in the U.S.**

1. Wells Fargo Bank, with $802.570 million
2. Security Pacific National Bank, $673.624
3. Bank of America, $669.000

347

# REFRESHMENT STAND

4. Valley National Bank of Arizona, $389.027
5. Sanwa Bank of California, $302.121
6. Seattle-First National Bank, $295.661
7. Security Pacific Bank of Washington, $287.847
8. West One Bank, Idaho, $187.950
9. Citibank, $177.000
10. First Interstate Bank of Arizona, $161.918

*Where'd you hear that?*
Agri Finance. Based on total farm loans outstanding for the quarter ended March 31, 1989, in millions of dollars.

## Largest farm and ranch management firms by total acreage

1. Farmers National Co., with 1,600,000
2. InterWest Ranch and Farm Management, 1,407,800
3. NCNB Texas National Bank, 1,355,000
4. Gillett Agricultural Management Co., 1,300,000
5. Doane-Western Co., 631,241
6. AmSouth Bank N.A., 518,627
7. Capital Agricultural Property Services, 510,208
8. Texas American Bank Fort Worth, 500,000
9. Norwest Farm Management, 495,514
10. Oppenheimer Industries Inc., 380,000

*Where'd you hear that?*
Agri Finance, Annual Report on the Farm Management Industry. Based on total acreage managed.

## Biggest corporations in the industrial and farm equipment industry

1. Tenneco, with $14,439 million
2. Caterpillar Inc., $11,126
3. Deere & Co., $7,221
4. Dresser Industries, $4,023
5. Cummins Engine Co., Inc., $3,511
6. Ingersoll-Rand, $3,447
7. Black & Decker Corp., $3,221
8. Paker Hannifin, $2,520
9. Baker Hughes, $2,328
10. Dover, $2,136

*Where'd you hear that?*
Fortune, Fortune 500 Largest U.S. Industrial Corporations. Based on 1989 sales, in millions of dollars.

## Most admired industrial and farm equipment corporations

1. Deere & Co., with a rating of 7.30
2. Caterpillar Inc., 7.25
3. Black & Decker Corp., 6.87
4. Parker-Hannifin, 6.66
5. Dover, 6.62
6. Ingersoll-Rand, 6.60
7. Cummins Engine Co., Inc., 6.47
8. Dresser Industries, 6.31
9. Baker Hughes, 6.18
10. Tenneco, 5.84

*Where'd you hear that?*
Fortune, America's Most Admired Corporations. Based on scores (0-10) derived from a survey of senior executives, outside directors, and financial analysts. Respondents ranked firms in their own industry on quality of management and products/services; innovation; long-term investment value; financial soundness; attraction and retention of talent; community and environmental responsibility; and use of assets.

**Largest farm and ranch management firms by pasture/ranch acres**

1. InterWest Ranch and Farm Management, $1,393,722
2. Gillett Agricultural Management Co., $1,235,000
3. NCNB Texas National Bank, 1,016,250
4. Doane-Western Co., 561,804
5. Texas American Bank/Fort Worth, 475,000
6. Oppenheimer Industries, 342,000
7. Farmers National Co., 320,000
8. NBC Bank-San Antonio, 280,250
9. First Interstate Bank of Oklahoma, 261,000
10. Boatmen's First National Bank of Kansas City, 149,162

*Where'd you hear that?*
Agri Finance, Annual Report on the Farm Management Industry. Based on amount of pasture and ranch acreage managed.

**Largest farm and ranch management firms ranked by crop acreage**

1. Farmers National Co., with 1,120,000
2. Capital Agricultural Property Services, 377,554
3. Norwest Farm Management, 346,860
4. Doane Farm Management, 233,680
5. NCNB Texas National Bank, 203,250
6. MFG Agricultural Services, 200,417
7. Huber Farm Management, 200,250
8. Hertz Farm Management, 144,606
9. First National Bank-Hutchinson, 126,960
10. Agri Affiliates, 114,906

*Where'd you hear that?*
Agri Finance, Annual Report on the Farm Management Industry. Based on amount of crop acreage managed.

**Largest farm and ranch management firms by number of farms**

1. Farmers National Co., with 4,230
2. NCNB Texas National Bank, 1,525
3. Norwest Farm Management, 1,041
4. MFG Agricultural Services, 979
5. Doane Farm Management Co., 950
6. Hertz Farm Management Inc., 763
7. Halderman Farm Management Service, 630
8. First National Bank–Hutchinson, 514
9. Marine Farm Management, 481
10. LeDioyt Land Co., 445

*Where'd you hear that?*
Agri Finance, Annual Report on the Farm Management Industry. Based on number of farms managed.

**Leading states in cash crops**

1. California, with $10,781 million
2. Florida, $4,125
3. Illinois, $3,913
4. Iowa, $3,510

# REFRESHMENT STAND

# REFRESHMENT STAND

5. Minnesota, $3,510
6. Texas, $3,027
7. Indiana, $2,016
8. Nebraska, $1,975

*Where'd you hear that?*
Television/Radio Age. Based on 1987 cash receipts, in millions of dollars.

## Leading U.S. states in acres planted of principal field crops

1. Iowa, with 24,692 thousand
2. Illinois, 22,949
3. Minnesota, 20,949
4. North Dakota, 19,798
5. Kansas, 19,302
6. Texas, 17,986
7. Nebraska, 17,349
8. South Dakota, 15,191

*Where'd you hear that?*
Television/Radio Age. Based on 1988 acres planted, in thousands of acres.

## Largest grain companies

1. Cargill, Inc., with 340,000,000 bushels
2. Peavey Co., 189,800,000
3. Continental Grain Co., 187,500,000
4. Union Equity Co-Operative Exchange, 166,466,000
5. Bunge Corp., 163,576,0000
6. Saskatchewan Wheat Pool, 120,521,786
7. Scoular Grain Co., 95,080,000
8. Riceland Foods, Inc., 93,776,000
9. Cargill Ltd., 64,800,000
10. Harvest States Cooperatives, 64,200,000

*Where'd you hear that?*
Grain Directory Buyer's Guide. Based on 1989 storage capacity, in bushels.

## Top 10 cold cereals by market share

1. Frosted Flakes, with 4.8%
2. Cheerios, 4.6%
3. Corn Flakes, 3.5%
3. Raisin Bran, 3.5%
3. Rice Krispies, 3.5%
6. Honey Nut Cheerios, 3.4%
7. Chex, 3.2%
8. Shredded Wheat, 3.0%
8. Cap'n Crunch, 3.0%
10. Bran Products, 2.5%

*Where'd you hear that?*
U.S. Distribution Journal. Based on 1988 market share, in percent.

## Top 10 cold cereals by share of pounds sold

1. Corn Flakes, with 5.8%
2. Frosted Flakes, 5.3%
3. Cheerios, 4.5%
4. Raisin Bran, 4.1%
5. Rice Krispies, 3.4%
6. Shredded Wheat, 3.2%
6. Chex, 3.2%
6. Cap'n Crunch, 3.2%
9. Honey Nut Cheerios, 3.1%
10. Bran products, 3.0%

*Where'd you hear that?*
Advertising Age. Based on share of market by pounds sold, in percent.

## Most efficient advertisers among breakfast cereals

1. Wheaties, with $9.00
2. Post Raisin Bran, $10.14
3. Cheerios, $12.75
4. Kellogg's Corn Flakes, $12.95
5. Quaker Oatmeal, $16.32
6. Nut & Honey, $16.58
7. Cap'n Crunch, $26.82
8. Rice Krispies, $27.97
9. Special K, $37.57

10. Frosted Flakes, $39.28

*Where'd you hear that?*
Adweek's Marketing Week, Annual Measure of Efficiency. Based on efficiency quotient (average weekly cost of television advertising divided by average number of retained impressions).

## Largest producers of pasta

1. Borden (includes Creamette and Prince), with $419.9 million
2. Hershey Foods (includes Ronzoni and San Giorgio), $364.0
3. CPC International (Mueller's), $182.0
4. Quaker Oats (Golden Grain), $39.0
5. Others, total, $295.1

*Where'd you hear that?*
New York Times. Based on estimated 1990 retail sales, in millions of dollars.

## Leading hog and pig states

1. Iowa, 13,900 thousand
2. Illinois, 5,600
3. Minnesota, 4,690
4. Indiana, 4,300
5. Nebraska, 4,050
6. Missouri, 2,850
7. North Carolina, 2,700
8. Ohio, 2,210

*Where'd you hear that?*
Television/Radio Age. Based on number of hogs and pigs, in thousands.

## Most consumed finfish and shellfish

1. Tuna (canned)
2. Shrimp
3. Cod
4. Pollock
5. Flatfish (flounder/sole)
6. Clams
7. Catfish
8. Salmon
9. Crabs
10. Scallops

*Where'd you hear that?*
Restaurant Hospitality. Based on consumption. Original source: National Fisheries Institute.

## *Largest foreign customers for U.S. agricultural commodities*

1. Japan, with $7,274 million
2. South Korea, $2,250
3. Netherlands, $2,087
4. Canada, $1,973
5. Soviet Union, $1,934
6. Mexico, $1,726
7. Taiwan, $1,577
8. West Germany, $1,306
9. Caribbean Islands, $867
10. Spain, $848

*Where'd you hear that?*
Cross Sections, Federal Reserve Bank of Richmond. Based on 1988 export value, in millions of U.S. dollars.

## Largest food trade companies in Asia

1. Kirin Brewery Co. Ltd., with $10,468,000 thousand
2. Snow Brand Milk Products Co. Ltd., $7,321,538
3. Hitachi Sales Corp., $6,509,267
4. Asahi Breweries Ltd., $5,588,964

# REFRESHMENT STAND

# REFRESHMENT STAND

5. Nippon Meat Packers Inc., $4,769,092
6. Ajinomoto Co. Inc., $4.063,251
7. Sapporo Breweries Ltd., $4,026,215
8. Nichirei Corp., $3,347,068
9. Yamazaki Baking Co. Ltd., 3,268,319
10. Meiji Milk Products Co. Ltd., $3,206,653

*Where'd you hear that?*
Asia's 7500 Largest Companies, Dun & Bradstreet. Based on 1988 sales, in thousands of U.S. dollars.

## Largest food companies in Europe

1. Nestle (Switzerland), with $14,000 million
2. Unilever (UK/Netherlands), $10,000
3. BSN (France), $4,000
4. Milk Marketing Board (UK), $3,750
5. Jacobs Suchard (Switzerland), $3,630
6. United Biscuits (UK), $3,000
7. Associated British Foods PLC (UK), $2,800
8. Ranks Hovis McDougall (UK), $2,500
9. Tate and Lyle (UK), $2,250
10. Dalgety (UK), $2,000

*Where'd you hear that?*
Marketing (U.K.). Based on turnover (sales) in food in Europe, in millions of U.S. dollars.

## Largest European food companies

1. Unilever Nv., with 26,561,999,129 ECU
2. Unilever PLC, 25,148,401,872
3. Nestle Sa., 22,900,488,005
4. Allied-Lyons PLC, 6,617,691,168
5. Bass PLC, 5,486,777,116
6. Hillsdown Holdings PLC, 5,214,223,450
7. Guinness PLC, 4,078,754,592
8. Cadbury Schweppes PLC, 3,499,265,827
9. Associated British Foods PLC, 3,338,231,424
10. George Weston Holdings Ltd., 3,260,358,948

*Where'd you hear that?*
Dun's Europa. Based on 1989 sales, in European Currency Units.

## Most popular food brands in Great Britain

1. NDC/MMB Milk, with £10,135 thousand
2. Nescafe Coffee, £9,365
3. Maxwell House, £8,253
4. Nescafe Gold Blend, £8,059
5. Weetabix, £5,851
6. Brooke Bond PG Tips Bags, £5,802
7. Kellogg's Corn Flakes, £5,766
8. Walkers Crisps, £4,796
9. Kellogg's Raisin Split, £4,649
10. Kellogg's Toppas, £4,475

*Where'd you hear that?*
Marketing, Top 500 Brands. Based on total 1989 expenditures, in thousands of British pounds sterling.

## Largest food processing companies in Canada

1. George Weston, with $150,000 thousand
2. H. J. Heinz of Canada, $39,742
3. Nabisco Brands, $26,200
4. Canada Packers, $25,211
5. Unilever Canada, $24,136
6. BC Sugar Refinery, $23,417
7. Campbell Soup Co., $21,593
8. Canada Malting, $16,664
9. Quaker Oats, $16,264
10. Robin Hood Multifoods, $14,895

*Where'd you hear that?*
Canadian Business, Canadian Business 500. Based on 1989 net income, in thousands of Canadian dollars.

## Biggest corporations in the U.S. food industry

1. Philip Morris, with $39,069 million
2. Occidental Petroleum, $20,068
3. RJR Nabisco, $15,224
4. Sara Lee, $11,738
5. ConAgra, Inc., $11,340
6. Archer Daniels Midland Co., $8,057
7. Borden, $7,593
8. Ralston Purina, $6,712
9. H. J. Heinz, $5,832
10. General Mills Inc., $5,798

*Where'd you hear that?*
Fortune, Fortune 500 Largest U.S. Industrial Corporations. Based on 1989 sales, in millions of dollars.

## Largest food companies

1. Philip Morris Cos. Inc., with $25,802.0 million
2. RJR Nabisco, Inc., $9,888.0
3. Anheuser-Busch Cos. Inc., $9,363.9
4. ConAgra, Inc., $8,590.6
5. IBP, Inc., $8,502.0
6. PepsiCo, Inc., $8,152.5
7. The Coca-Cola Co., $8,000.0
8. Archer Daniels Midland Co., $7,200.0
9. Nestle Holdings, Inc., $5,961.0
10. Campbell Soup Co., $5,700.0

*Where'd you hear that?*
Food Processing. Based on 1989 sales, in millions of dollars.

## Most admired food corporations

1. Sara Lee, with a rating of 7.51
2. General Mills Inc., 7.24
3. Quaker Oats, 7.13
4. ConAgra, Inc., 6.98
5. Ralston Purina, 6.68
6. Archer Daniels Midland Co., 6.54
7. Borden, 6.36
8. RJR Nabisco, 5.27
9. Occidental Petroleum, 5.23
10. Beatrice Cos. Inc., 4.88

# REFRESHMENT STAND

# REFRESHMENT STAND

*Where'd you hear that?*
Fortune, America's Most Admired Corporations. Based on scores (0-10) derived from a survey of senior executives, outside directors, and financial analysts. Respondents ranked firms in their own industry on quality of management and products/services; innovation; long-term investment value; financial soundness; attraction and retention of talent; community and environmental responsibility; and use of assets.

## Top food brands

1. Kellogg, with $6,600 million
2. Nabisco, $6,500
3. Kraft, $5,500
4. Campbell Soup, $2,400
5. Frito-Lay, $5,000
6. Ralston Purina, $5,600
7. Hershey, $5,000
8. Oscar Mayer, $2,941
9. Wrigley's, $2,000
10. Gerber, $825

*Where'd you hear that?*
Prepared Foods, 50 Leading Prepared Food and Beverage Processors. Based on retail category size, in millions of dollars.

## Leading food and beverage companies

1. Philip Morris, with $14,627 million
2. Kraft Inc., $12,096
3. RJR Nabisco, $9,888
4. IBP, Inc., $9,066
5. Anheuser-Busch Cos. Inc., $8,582
6. Coca-Cola Co., $8,300
7. PepsiCo, $8,152
8. ConAgra, Inc., $6,132
9. Borden, $5,385
10. H. J. Heinz, $5,244

*Where'd you hear that?*
Prepared Foods, 50 Leading Prepared Food and Beverage Processors. Based on 1988 sales, in millions of dollars.

## Largest food and beverage companies

1. Coca-Cola Co., with $1,780 million
2. Anheuser-Busch Cos. Inc., $1,223
3. RJR Nabisco, $1,215
4. PepsiCo, $1,099
5. Kraft Inc., $971
6. Kellogg Co., $794
7. H. J. Heinz, $688
8. Ralston Purina, $604
9. Philip Morris, $582
10. Borden, $479

*Where'd you hear that?*
Prepared Foods, 50 Leading Prepared Food and Beverage Processors. Based on 1988 operating income, in millions of dollars.

## Leading food packagers

1. Philip Morris Cos.
2. RJR Nabisco, Inc.
3. Kraft, Inc.
4. Campbell Soup Co.
5. Sara Lee Corp.

*Where'd you hear that?*
Packaging, Top 100 Packaging Giants. Based on 1988 consumption of packaging materials.

## Biggest corporations in the food processing industry

1. H. J. Heinz, with 7,789 million
2. Kellogg Co., $7,421
3. Sara Lee, $6,742
4. Campbell Soup Co., $6,407
5. Archer Daniels Midland Co., $5,995

6. General Mills Inc., $5,858
7. Ralston Purina, $5,220
8. CPC International, $5,037
9. Borden, $4,661
10. Quaker Oats, $3,632

*Where'd you hear that?*
Business Week, The Business Week 1000. Based on market value as of March 16, 1990, in millions of dollars.

## Largest food processing companies

1. ConAgra, Inc. with $15,500 million
2. IBP, Inc., $9,100
3. Excel Corp., $5,000
4. Sara Lee Meat Group, $2,900
5. Tyson Foods, Inc., $2,500
6. George A. Hormel & Co., $2,300
7. Oscar Mayer Foods Corp., $2,300
8. John Morrell & Co., $2,100
9. BeefAmerica, Inc., $1,600
10. Wilson Foods Corp., $1,400

*Where'd you hear that?*
National Provisioner, The Provisioner Top 100. Based on 1989-90 sales, in millions of dollars.

## Most productive food processors

1. Archer Daniels Midlands Co., $48.6 thousand
2. Kellogg Co., $24.3
3. Wm. Wrigley, Jr., $18.9
4. Pioneer Hi-Bred International, $18.1
5. McCormick & Co., $17.9
6. Hershey Foods, $14.3
7. H. J. Heinz, $12.9
8. CPC International, $10.0
9. George A. Hormel & Co., $8.9
10. Dean Foods, $8.4

*Where'd you hear that?*
Forbes, Forbes 500s Annual Directory. Based on 1989 profits per employee, in thousands of dollars. Ranks U.S.-based corporations that were publicly traded as of March 23, 1990.

## Most profitable food processing companies

1. Kellogg Co., with 38.9%
2. Ralston Purina, 33.6%
3. Tyson Foods, 27.8%
4. H. J. Heinz, 23.3%
5. Smithfield Foods, 22.9%
6. Dean Foods, 22.4%
7. ConAgra, Inc., 21.9%
8. Lance, 21.4%
9. Wm. Wrigley, Jr., 20.9%
10. CPC International, 20.9%

*Where'd you hear that?*
Forbes, Annual Report on American Industry. Based on 10-year average return on equity. Ranks publicly held corporations only.

## Biggest corporations in the food distribution industry

1. Sysco, with $2,573 million
2. Super Valu Stores, $1,931
3. Fleming Cos., Inc., $961
4. Wetterau, $583
5. International Multifoods, $365

*Where'd you hear that?*
Business Week, The Business Week 1000. Based on market value as of March 16, 1990, in millions of dollars.

# REFRESHMENT STAND

# REFRESHMENT STAND

### Most productive food distributors

1. Super Food Services, with $7.7 thousand
2. Sysco, $6.4
3. Super Valu Stores, $3.8
4. Fleming Cos., Inc., $3.4
5. Wetterau, $3.3
6. Nash Finch, $1.2
7. Marriott, $0.8
8. TW Holdings, -$0.5

*Where'd you hear that?*
Forbes, Forbes 500s Annual Directory. Based on 1989 profits per employee, in thousands of dollars. Ranks U.S.-based corporations that were publicly traded as of March 23, 1990.

### Most profitable food distributors

1. Marriott, with 23.3%
2. Super Valu Stores, 21.6%
3. Sysco, 17.9%
4. Wetterau, 16.3%
5. Super Food Services, 15.7%
6. Fleming Cos., Inc., 14.2%
7. Nash Finch, 13.4%
8. Rykoff-Sexton, 12.2%
9. Di Giorgio, 5.2%
10. Finevest Foods, NA

*Where'd you hear that?*
Forbes, Annual Report on American Industry. Based on 10-year average return on equity. Ranks publicly held corporations only.

### Biggest corporations in the food retailing industry

1. Albertson's Inc., with $3,741 million
2. Food Lion, $3,623
3. Winn-Dixie Stores, $2,390
4. American Stores Co., $2,167
5. Great Atlantic & Pacific Tea Co., $1,977
6. Giant Food Inc., $1,647
7. Weis Markets, $1,348
8. Bruno's, $1,122
9. Kroger Co., $1,071
10. Vons, $842

*Where'd you hear that?*
Business Week, The Business Week 1000. Based on market value as of March 16, 1990, in millions of dollars.

### Metropolitan areas with the largest grocery and other sales

1. New York, NY, with $9,775,604 thousand
2. Los Angeles-Long Beach, CA, $8,841,227
3. Chicago, IL, $6,538,890
4. Philadelphia, PA, $6,187,845
5. Detroit, MI, $5,454,970
6. Boston-Lawrence-Salem-Lowell-Brockton, MA, $5,042,062
7. Washington, DC, 4,678,438
8. Nassau-Suffolk, NY, $4,586,695
9. Houston, TX, $3,587,802
10. Atlanta, GA, $3,098,232

*Where'd you hear that?*
Sales & Marketing Management, Survey of Buying Power. Based on sales, in thousands of dollars.

### Largest percentage increase in grocery trade categories

1. Incontinence products, with 45.6%
2. Frozen sandwiches, 42.3%
3. Video cassette rentals, 40.6%
4. Rice and grain cakes, 35.3%
5. Aseptic packaged juices and drinks (concentrate), 35.2%
6. Antifreeze, 31.6%

7. Condoms, 28.6%
8. Instore bakery, 27.9%
9. Olive oil, 26.4%
10. Vegetable juice, 25.8%

*Where'd you hear that?*
Supermarket Business, Consumer Expenditure Study. Based on 1988 percentage increase in sales.

### Largest increase in grocery trade categories

1. Service deli, with $1,640,000 thousand
2. Instore bakery, $1,330,000
3. Cigarettes, $832,889
4. Cold cereals, $590,661
5. Beer, $589,157
6. Fresh poultry, $547,759
7. Apples, $416,752
8. Refrigerated fruit juices and drinks, $359,472
9. Fresh beef, $356,333
10. Refrigerated orange juice, $292,133

*Where'd you hear that?*
Supermarket Business, Consumer Expenditure Study. Based on 1988 volume increase in sales, in thousands of dollars.

### Largest percentage decrease in grocery trade categories

1. Other dried fruits, with -18.3%
2. Alcohol coolers, -17.1%
3. Flash bulbs and cubes, -14.6%
4. Frostings and icings, -14.0%
5. Lard, -12.3%
6. Frozen fish sticks, -12.2%
7. Paste floor wax, -11.9%
8. Pesticides (liquid non-aerosol), -11.3%
9. Fresh potatoes, -11.1%

10. Fresh citrus fruits, -10.9%

*Where'd you hear that?*
Supermarket Business, Consumer Expenditure Study. Based on 1988 percentage decrease in sales.

---

### *Most important factors in consumer selection of a grocery store*

1. Cleanliness, with 93.6
2. All prices labeled, 91.5
3. Freshness date marked on products, 91.0
4. Accurate, pleasant checkout clerks, 90.3
5. Low prices, 89.2
6. Good produce department, 88.3
7. Good meat department, 86.9
8. Convenient store location, 85.0
9. Good dairy department, 84.7
9. Good parking facilities, 84.7

*Where'd you hear that?*
Progressive Grocer, Annual Report of the Grocery Industry. Based on consumer rating, out of a maximum score of 100.

---

### Largest decrease in grocery trade categories

1. Citrus fruits, with $247,965 thousand
2. Potatoes, $220,327
3. Coffee (regular), $183,985
4. Fresh fish and other seafood, $182,456
5. Other sausage products (cooked), $180,759
6. Packaged bacon, $169,006
7. Coffee (instant), $74,166
8. Eggs, $45,723
9. Frozen pizza, $37,051
10. Butter, $25,622

# REFRESHMENT STAND

# REFRESHMENT STAND

*Where'd you hear that?*
Supermarket Business, Consumer Expenditure Study. Based on 1988 volume decrease in sales, in thousands of dollars.

## Leading food service corporations

1. McDonald's Corp., with $16,100.0 million
2. Burger King Corp., $5,400.0
3. Kentucky Fried Chicken Corp., $5,000.0
4. Pizza Hut, $3,390.0
5. Marriott Food Service Management, $3,353.4
6. U.S. Department of Agriculture Food & Nutrition Service, $3,035.8
7. Wendy's International Inc., $2,902.0
8. Hardee's Inc., $2,733.3
9. ARA Services Inc., $2,350.0
10. Domino's Pizza Inc., $2,300.0

*Where'd you hear that?*
Restaurants & Institutions, Restaurants & Institutions 400. Based on 1988 sales, in millions of dollars.

## Leading food service contract management companies

1. Marriott Food Services Management, with $3,353.4 million
2. ARA Services Inc., $1,288.8
3. Canteen Co., $1,288.8
4. Service America, $1,001
5. Morrison Custom Management, $531
6. Ogden Allied, $425
7. Dobbs International, $348
8. Greyhound Food Management Inc., $290.8
9. Sky Chefs Inc., $290.5
10. Seiler Corp., $204.8

*Where'd you hear that?*
Restaurants & Institutions, Restaurants & Institutions 400. Based on 1988 sales, in millions of dollars.

## Largest food service distributors

1. Rykoff-Sexton Inc. (Los Angeles, CA), with $407 million
2. Sysco Corp. (Houston, TX), $345
3. Edward Don & Co. (North Riverside, IL), $194
4. Kraft Foodservice Group (Glenview, IL), $92
5. Illinois Range Co. (Mt. Prospect, IL), $80
6. The Wasserstrom Cos. (Columbus, OH), $79
7. PYA/Monarch Inc. (Greenville, SC), $49.1
8. Marstan Industries, Inc. (Philadelphia, PA), $43.5
9. Superior Products Manufacturing Co. (St. Paul, MN), $41
10. Stainless Inc. (Detroit, MI), $38.5

*Where'd you hear that?*
Foodservice Equipment & Supplies Specialist, Foodservice Equipment & Supplies Specialist 100. Based on 1989 sales volume, in millions of dollars.

## Leading food service distributors

1. Sysco Corp., with $4,072,254,000
2. Kraft Foodservice Group, $2,800,000,000
3. Martin-Brower Company, $2,700,000,000
4. PYA/Monarch, Inc., $2,300,000,000
5. Rykoff-Sexton, Inc., $1,143,275,000
6. Golden State Foods Corp., $900,000,000
7. White Swan, Inc., $650,000,000
8. Mapelli Brothers Co., $635,000,000
9. Food Service of America, $618,000,000
10. MBM Corp., $605,000,000

*Where'd you hear that?*
Directory of Food Service Distributors. Based on 1988 volume.

## Largest food service consultants

1. Cini-Little International Inc., with $112 million
2. Clevenger Frable Associates, $50
3. Thomas Ricca Associates, $47.5
4. Romano/Gatland, $46
5. Perlstein, Pacifico, Brown, $43.1
6. Abrams & Tanaka, $40.5
7. Stephens Bangs Associates Inc., $32.2
8. Mulhauser/McCleary Associates Inc., $30
9. Marshall Associates, $27.5
10. H. G. Rice & Co. Inc., $27.2

*Where'd you hear that?*
Foodservice Equipment & Supplies Specialist. Based on 1989 sales volume, in millions of dollars.

## Leading military organization food services

1. U.S. Army Troop Support Agency, with $1,332.8 million
2. U.S. Navy Food Service Systems Office, $896.0
3. U.S. Army Community & Family Support Centers, $772.0
4. Army & Air Force Exchange Service, $577.9
5. U.S. Air Force Open Mess System, $337.4
6. U.S. Air Force Engineering and Services Centers, $298.8
7. Veterans Administration, $258.8
8. U.S. Marine Corps., $240.0
9. U.S. Navy Officer's and Enlisted Club System, $164.0
10. Navy Resale and Services Support Office, $117.6

*Where'd you hear that?*
Restaurants & Institutions, Restaurants & Institutions 400. Based on 1988 sales, in millions of dollars.

## Leading food service companies by percentage gain in sales

1. Subway, 120.6%
2. Everything Yogurt, 94.7%
3. Village Inn Pancake House, 90.9%

# REFRESHMENT STAND

# REFRESHMENT STAND

4. Doubletree Hotels, 87.5%
5. Stuckey's Corp., 73.3%
6. TCBY, 64.3%
7. The Registry Hotel Corp., 50.0%
8. Vie de France Bakery & Cafe, 48.0%
9. Trusthouse Forte Food Services, 45.7%
10. T. J. Cinnamon's Bakeries, 45.4%

*Where'd you hear that?*
Restaurants & Institutions, Restaurants & Institutions 400. Based on 1988 percentage sales growth.

## Leading food service companies by absolute dollar gain

1. McDonald's, with $1,769.6 million
2. Kentucky Fried Chicken Corp., $999.9
3. Burger King, $400.0
4. Subway, $328.0
5. Red Lobster, $323.0
6. Domino's Pizza Inc., $320.0
7. Sheraton Corp., $208.8
8. Little Caesars Pizza, $183.0
9. Arby's Inc., $180.0
10. International Dairy Queen, $167.0

*Where'd you hear that?*
Restaurants & Institutions, Restaurants & Institutions 400. Based on 1987-1988 sales gain, in millions of dollars.

## Top corporations in the restaurant industry

1. McDonald's, with $11,539 million
2. TCBY Enterprises, $572
3. International Dairy Queen, $506
4. Shoney's, $471
5. Luby's Cafeterias Inc., $470
6. Morrison, 442
7. Bob Evans Farms Inc., $425
8. Collins Foods International, $416
9. Wendy's International, $410
10. Jerrico, $387
11. Ryan Family Steak Houses, $386

*Where'd you hear that?*
Business Week, The Business Week 1000. Based on market value as of March 16, 1990, in millions of dollars.

## Largest independent restaurants

1. The Rainbow Room, New York, NY, with $26,700,000
2. Smith & Wollensky, New York, NY, $18,000,000
3. Phillips Harborplace, Ocean City, MD, $15,873,195
4. Spenger's Fish Grotto, Berkeley, CA, $14,050,000
5. El Charo Avitia, Carson City, NV, $14,000,000
6. Kapok Tree Restaurant, Clearwater, FL, $13,922,214
7. Zehnders, Frankenmuth, MI, $12,915,711
8. The Waterfront, Covington, KY, $12,130,000
9. Frankenmuth Bavarian Inn, Frankenmuth, MI, $11,410,000
10. Bob Chinn's Crabhouse Restaurant, Wheeling, IL, $10,810,000

*Where'd you hear that?*
Restaurant Hospitality 500. Based on 1989 total sales.

## Largest independent restaurants

1. Hilltop Steak House (Saugus, MA), with $32.130 million
2. Rainbow Room (New York, NY), $26.700
3. Tavern on the Green (New York, NY), $25.550
4. Smith & Wollensky (New York, NY), $17.500
5. Phillips Harborplace (Baltimore, MD), $15.884
6. Anthony's Pier 4 (Boston, MD), $15.096
7. The Manor (West Orange, NJ), $14.600
8. Sparks Steakhouse (New York, NY), $13.617
9. Legal Sea Foods Inc. (Boston, MA), $13.318
10. Kapok Tree Restaurants (Clearwater, FL), $12.864

*Where'd you hear that?*
Restaurants & Institutions, March 7, 1990, p. 50+. Based on 1989 sales, in millions of dollars.

## Metropolitan areas with highest restaurant sales

1. New York, NY, with $3,524,859 thousand
2. Los Angeles-Long Beach, CA, $3,454,848
3. Boston-Lawrence-Salem-Lowell-Brockton, MA, $2,094,196
4. Chicago, IL, $1,936,125
5. Washington, DC, $1,402,975
6. Philadelphia, PA, $1,371,057
7. San Francisco, CA, $1,294,559
8. Anaheim-Santa Ana, CA, $1,279,711
9. Detroit, MI, $1,252,183
10. Minneapolis-St. Paul, MN, $997,396

*Where'd you hear that?*
Restaurant Business, Annual Restaurant Growth Index. Based on 1988 sales, in thousands of dollars.

## Metropolitan areas with highest eating place sales

1. New York, NY, with $6,519,008 thousand
2. Los Angeles-Long Beach, CA, $6,450,149
3. Boston-Lawrence-Salem-Lowell-Brockton, MA, $3,964,222
4. Chicago, IL, $3,901,475
5. Washington, DC, $3,163,455
6. Philadelphia, PA, $2,971,397
7. Detroit, MI, $2,599,855
8. Anaheim-Santa Ana, CA, $2,313,829
9. Atlanta, GA, $2,254,067
10. Houston, TX, $2,176,295

*Where'd you hear that?*
Restaurant Business, Annual Restaurant Growth Index. Based on 1988 sales, in thousands of dollars.

## Markets with greatest per capita restaurant sales

1. San Francisco, CA, with $806
2. Portland, ME, $698
3. Honolulu, HI, $629
4. Santa Barbara-Santa Maria-Lompoc, CA, $608
5. Atlantic City, NJ, $566
6. Anaheim-Santa Ana, CA, $563
7. Boston-Lawrence-Salem-Lowell-Brockton, MA, $562
8. Sarasota, FL, $561
9. Burlington, VT, $538
10. Fort Lauderdale-Hollywood-Pompano Beach, FL, $537

# REFRESHMENT STAND

# REFRESHMENT STAND

*Where'd you hear that?*
Restaurant Business, Annual Restaurant Growth Index. Based on per capita sales in 1988, in dollars.

## Metropolitan areas with highest per capita eating place sales

1. San Francisco, CA, with $1,341
2. Honolulu, HI, $1,244
3. Anchorage, AK, $1,229
4. Portland, ME, $1,205
5. Boston-Lawrence-Salem-Lowell-Brockton, MA, $1,064
6. Anaheim-Santa Ana, CA, $1,018
7. Atlantic City, NJ, $1,011
8. Santa Barbara-Santa Maria-Lompoc, CA, $952
9. Fort Lauderdale-Hollywood-Pompano Beach, FL, $930
10. Burlington, VT, $924

*Where'd you hear that?*
Restaurant Business, Annual Restaurant Growth Index. Based on 1988 per capita sales, in dollars.

## Metropolitan areas with highest eating and drinking place sales

1. New York, NY, with $6,872,403 thousand
2. Los Angeles-Long Beach, CA, $6,758,662
3. Boston-Lawrence-Salem-Lowell-Brockton, MA, $4,208,691
4. Chicago, IL, $4,137,618
5. Philadelphia, PA, $3,306,048
6. Washington, DC, $3,258,324
7. Detroit, MI, $2,803,146
8. Anaheim-Santa Ana, CA, $2,397,016
9. Atlanta, GA, $2,358,039
10. Houston, TX, $2,326,480

*Where'd you hear that?*
Sales & Marketing Management, Survey of Buying Power. Based on 1988 sales, in thousands of dollars.

## Largest restaurant chains

1. McDonald's, with $11,380,212 thousand
2. Burger King Corp., $5,400,000
3. Hardee's Inc., $3,300,000
4. Wendy's, $2,901,624
5. Kentucky Fried Chicken Corp., $2,900,000
6. Pizza Hut, $2,800,000
7. Domino's Pizza Inc., $2,307,000
8. Taco Bell, $2,100,000
9. International Dairy Queen, $2,067,000
10. Denny's Inc., $1,400,000

*Where'd you hear that?*
Restaurant Hospitality, Top 100 Chains. Based on systemwide sales, fiscal year 1988/89, in thousands of dollars.

## Top 10 restaurants in total estimated media spending

1. McDonald's, with $427,589.5 million
2. Burger King, $128,474.3
3. Kentucky Fried Chicken Corp., $112,755.4
4. Wendy's, $90,534.4
5. Pizza Hut, $87,404.3
6. Domino's Pizza Inc., $62,363.3
7. Taco Bell, $59,662.4
8. Red Lobster, $56,376.5
9. Hardee's Inc., $40,664.4
10. Long John Silver's, $23,568.1

# REFRESHMENT STAND

*Where'd you hear that?*
Nation's Restaurant News. Based on 1989 total estimated media spending, in millions of dollars.

## Top restaurant chain TV advertisers

1. McDonald's, with $412,053,700
2. Burger King Corp., $161,612,900
3. Kentucky Fried Chicken Corp., $115,662,300
4. Pizza Hut, $90,658,100
5. Wendy's, $88,211,200
6. Taco Bell, $58,298,700
7. Red Lobster, $56,609,400
8. Domino's Pizza Inc., $55,613,900
9. Hardee's Inc., $38,238,700
10. Long John Silver's, $25,926,600

*Where'd you hear that?*
Restaurant Business. Based on 1989 total TV advertising expenditures.

## Most profitable restaurant chains

1. McDonald's, with 22.5%
2. Shoney's, 20.7%
3. Bob Evans Farms Inc., 19.9%
4. Collins Foods International, 16.9%
5. Morrison, 15.1%
6. Carl Karcher, 13.6%
7. Wendy's International, 12.8%
8. TGI Friday's, NA

*Where'd you hear that?*
Forbes, Annual Report on American Industry. Based on 10-year average return on equity. Ranks publicly held corporations only.

## Fastest growing restaurant chains ranked by sales growth

1. Subway, with 130%
2. El Pollo Loco, 104%
3. TCBY, 73%
4. Olive Garden, 71%
5. Orange Julius, 51%
6. Houlihan's, 45%
7. Carl's Jr., 40%
8. A & W, 34%
9. Cracker Barrel, 33%
10. Taco Bell, 31%

*Where'd you hear that?*
Restaurant Hospitality, Top 100 Chains. Based on sales growth, 1988-89, in percent.

## Fastest growing restaurant chains ranked by unit growth

1. El Pollo Loco, with 72%
2. Subway, 60%
3. Olive Garden, 45%
4. TCBY, 43%
5. Garcia's Mexican Restaurants, 31%
6. Ryan's, 28%
7. Sbarro, 26%
8. Orange Julius, 22%
9. Chili's Inc., 21%
10. Cracker Barrel, 20%

*Where'd you hear that?*
Restaurant Hospitality, Top 100 Chains. Based on unit growth, 1988-89, in percent.

## Leading dinner houses

1. Bennigan's, with $458.1 million
2. TGI Friday's Inc., $373
3. Chili's Inc., $350
4. Ground Round, $209
5. Specialty Restaurants Corp., $189

# REFRESHMENT STAND

6. Brown Derby Inc., $174
7. Ruby Tuesday, $128
8. Chart House, $111.1
9. Red Robin, $100.3
10. Benihana of Tokyo, $88

*Where'd you hear that?*
Restaurants & Institutions, Restaurants & Institutions 400. Based on sales, in millions of dollars.

## Most popular family dining restaurant chains

1. Bob Evans, with 2.56
2. Bakers Square, 2.52
3. Shoney's, 2.47
4. Perkins, 2.37
5. Swensen's, 2.35
6. Pofolks, 2.34

*Where'd you hear that?*
Restaurants & Institutions, Choice in Chains. Based on a satisfaction index based on customer surveys.

## Leading steakhouses and barbecue chains

1. Sizzler International, $850 million
2. Ponderosa Inc., $749
3. Bonanza Restaurants, $571
4. Golden Corral Corp., $456
5. Western Sizzlin' Steak House, $450
6. Quincy's Restaurants, $251
7. Ryan's Family Steak Houses, $234.0
8. Steak & Ale, $225
9. Stuart Anderson, $176.4
10. Tony Roma's, $171.2

*Where'd you hear that?*
Restaurants & Institutions, Restaurants & Institutions 400. Based on sales, in millions of dollars.

## Most popular steak restaurant chains

1. Stuart Anderson's, with 2.69
2. Steak & Ale, 2.61
3. Golden Corral Corp., 2.54
4. Sizzler, 2.52
5. Mr. Steak, 2.42
6. Bonanza Restaurants, 2.40

*Where'd you hear that?*
Restaurants & Institutions, Choice in Chains. Based on a satisfaction index based on customer surveys.

## Most popular chicken restaurant chains

1. Chick-Fil-A, with 2.44
2. Grandy's, 2.42
3. Kentucky Fried Chicken Corp., 2.33
4. Popeyes Famous Fried Chicken, 2.27
5. Bojangles', 2.25
6. Church's Fried Chicken Inc., 2.12

*Where'd you hear that?*
Restaurants & Institutions, Choice in Chains. Based on a satisfaction index based on customer surveys.

## Leading seafood companies

1. Red Lobster, with $1,300
2. Long John Silver's, $765.3
3. Captain D's, $374.3
4. Paragon Specialty Restaurants, $177
5. Skipper's Inc., $93
6. Trans/Pacific Restaurants Inc., $90
7. C. A. Muer Corp., $68
8. Rusty Pelican, $58
9. Sea Galley Stores Inc., $52
9. Legal Sea Foods Inc., $52

*Where'd you hear that?*
Restaurants & Institutions, Restaurants & Institutions 400. Based on 1988 sales, in millions of dollars.

## Largest seafood restaurant chains

1. Red Lobster, with 2.58
2. Skipper's, 2.37
3. Long John Silver's, 2.35
4. Captain D's, 2.30

*Where'd you hear that?*
Restaurants & Institutions, Choice in Chains. Based on satisfaction index (based on response to survey on chains). Those chains with less than 100 respondents were omitted from main ranking. notes strongest attribute, customers, spending level, region, and short description.

## Leading casual dining companies

1. Denny's Inc., with $1,300 million
2. Big Boy, $940
3. Shoney's, $864.1
4. Friendly Ice Cream, $564
5. Walt Disney Co., $382
6. Perkins Family Restaurants L.P., $375
7. International House of Pancakes, $315.8
8. Bob Evans Farms Inc., $290
9. Waffle House Inc., $262.1
10. Village Inn Pancake Houses, $233

*Where'd you hear that?*
Restaurants & Institutions, Restaurants & Institutions 400. Based on sales, in millions of dollars.

## Most popular casual dining restaurant chains

1. The Olive Garden, with 2.64
2. Benihana of Tokyo, 2.58
3. T.G.I. Friday's, 2.54
3. Bennigan's, 2.54
5. Houlihan's, 2.53
6. Fuddruckers, 2.48

*Where'd you hear that?*
Restaurants & Institutions, Choice in Chains. Based on a satisfaction index based on customer surveys.

## Largest cafeteria chains

1. Morrison Family Dining Division, with $323 million
2. Furr's/Bishop's Cafeterias, L.P., $27.2
3. Luby's Cafeterias Inc., $262
4. Piccadilly Cafeterias Inc., $241.7
5. Wyatt Cafeterias Inc., $189
6. Old Country Buffets, $79.8
7. International King's Table, $78
8. K & W Cafeterias, $50.2
9. MCL Cafeterias, $47
10. S & S Cafeterias, $30

*Where'd you hear that?*
Restaurants & Institutions, Restaurants & Institutions 400. Based on 1989 sales, in millions of dollars.

## Most popular cafeteria restaurant chains

1. Luby's Cafeterias Inc., with 2.58
2. Furrs, 2.46
3. Morrison's, 2.43
4. Piccadilly, 2.42

*Where'd you hear that?*
Restaurants & Institutions, Choice in Chains. Based on a satisfaction index based on customer surveys.

# REFRESHMENT STAND

# REFRESHMENT STAND

### Most popular sweets restaurant chains

1. Mrs. Fields Cookies, with 2.60
2. Baskin-Robbins Ice Cream Co., 2.59
2. TCBY, 2.59
4. T.J. Cinnamons, 2.57
5. Dunkin' Donuts, 2.36
6. International Dairy Queen, 2.35

*Where'd you hear that?*
Restaurants & Institutions, Choice in Chains. Based on a satisfaction index based on customer surveys.

### Largest restaurant franchises

1. Collins Foods International, with $1,057.4 million
2. Spartan Food Systems, $427.0
3. Riese Organization, $331.6
4. Boddie-Noell Enterprises Inc., $295.0
5. TPI Restaurants Inc., $224.0
6. Frisch's Restaurants Inc., $190.0
7. Harman Management Co., $165.0
8. National Pizza Co., $141.0
9. The Continental Cos., $140.0
10. Carrols Corp., $133.5

*Where'd you hear that?*
Restaurants & Institutions, Restaurants & Institutions 400. Based on 1989 sales, in millions of dollars.

### Largest fast-food franchisers ranked by numbers of units

1. McDonald's, with 7,907
2. Pizza Hut, 5,707
3. Burger King, 5,212
4. Kentucky Fried Chicken Corp., 4,899
5. Domino's Pizza Inc., 4,595
6. International Dairy Queen, 4,556
7. Wendy's, 3,521
8. Hardee's Inc., 3,076
9. Taco Bell, 2,878
10. Subway Sandwiches, 2,858

*Where'd you hear that?*
Wall Street Journal. Based on numbers of units in 1988.

### Largest fast-food franchisers ranked by average sales per unit

1. McDonald's, with $1,600,000
2. Burger King, $984,000
3. Hardee's Inc., $920,000
4. Wendy's, $759,000
5. Arby's Inc., $610,000
6. Kentucky Fried Chicken Corp., $597,000
7. Taco Bell, $589,000
8. Pizza Hut, $520,000
9. Domino's Pizza Inc., $485,000
10. International Dairy Queen, $408,000

*Where'd you hear that?*
Wall Street Journal. Based on average sales per unit in 1988.

### Most popular fast-food franchises

1. Subway Sandwiches, with 66.7%
2. Little Caesar's Pizza, 25.2%
3. Arby's Inc., 17.4%
4. International Dairy Queen, 16.6%
5. Domino's Pizza Inc., 16.2%
6. Pizza Hut, 12.0%
7. McDonald's, 7.6%
8. Hardee's Inc., 7.5%
9. Kentucky Fried Chicken Corp., 7.4%

10. Burger King, 3.5%

*Where'd you hear that?*
Wall Street Journal. Based on 1988 percentage growth.

## Most efficient advertisers among fast foods

1. Wendy's, with $26.51
2. Hardee's Inc., $31.03
3. Burger King Corp., $33.26
4. Arby's Inc., $41.04
5. McDonald's, $50.46
6. Taco Bell, $55.66
7. Roy Rogers, $56.40
8. Kentucky Fried Chicken Corp., $87.01
9. Long John Silver's, $93.18
10. Pizza Hut, $105.58
11. Domino's Pizza Inc., $205.45

*Where'd you hear that?*
Adweek's Marketing Week, Annual Measure of Efficiency. Based on efficiency quotient (average weekly cost of television advertising divided by average number of retained impressions).

## Largest fast-food chicken companies

1. Kentucky Fried Chicken Corp., with $5,000 million
2. Church's Fried Chicken Inc., $559.3
3. Popeye's Famous Fried Chicken, $485
4. Chick-Fil-A, $232.9
5. Grandy's, $184
6. Lee's Famous Recipe Chicken, $142.4
7. El Pollo Loco, $124
8. Brown's Chicken, $105
9. Bojangles' Corp., $102
10. Mrs. Winner's Chicken, $78.1
11. Pioneer Take Out Corp., $65
12. Sisters Chicken & Biscuits, $44

*Where'd you hear that?*
Restaurants & Institutions, Restaurants & Institutions 400. Based on 1988 sales, in millions of dollars.

## Largest sweets companies

1. International Dairy Queen, with $2,067
2. Dunkin' Donuts, $777.8
3. Baskin-Robbins Ice Cream Co., $692.7
4. Carvel, $243.8
5. Mister Donut, $226
6. TCBY, $210
7. Mrs. Fields' Cookies, $160
8. Tastee Freez, $151.2
9. Winchell's Donut House, $144
10. Braum Ice Cream and Dairy Stores, $134.9
11. Orange Julius, $125

*Where'd you hear that?*
Restaurants & Institutions, Restaurants & Institutions 400. Based on 1988 sales, in millions of dollars.

## Most popular fast foods ranked by share of sales

1. Hamburger, with 40%
2. Diverse, 20%
3. Pizza, 12%
4. Ice Cream/Doughnut, 8%
5. Chicken, 7%
6. Mexican, 6%
7. Steak, 4%
8. Fish, 3%

*Where'd you hear that?*
Restaurant Hospitality, Top 100 Chains. Based on percentage of total sales, 1988/89.

# REFRESHMENT STAND

# REFRESHMENT STAND

## Most popular fast foods ranked by share of units

1. Hamburger, with 28%
2. Pizza, 18%
2. Diverse, 18%
4. Ice Cream/Doughnut, 15%
5. Chicken, 9%
6. Mexican, 6%
7. Steak, 3%
7. Fish, 3%

*Where'd you hear that?*
Restaurant Hospitality, Top 100 Chains. Based on percentage of total units, 1988/89.

### Best burgers

1. Wendy's, with 2.34
2. Whataburger, 2.32
3. Burger King, 2.26
4. Hardee's Inc., 2.25
4. Carl's Jr., 2.25
4. Sonic Drive-Ins, 2.25

*Where'd you hear that?*
Restaurants & Institutions, Choice in Chains. Based on based on chain's satisfaction index, which is based on response to survey on chains. Those chains with less than 100 respondents were omitted from main ranking.

### Top burger restaurants

1. McDonald's, with $16,100 million
2. Burger King, $5,400
3. Wendy's International, $2,902
4. Hardee's Inc., $2,733.3
5. Jack in the Box, $755
6. Carl's Jr., $480
7. Sonic Industries, $356
8. White Castle, $282
9. Whataburger, $280
10. Krystal Co., $178

*Where'd you hear that?*
Restaurants & Institutions, Restaurants & Institutions 400. Based on 1988 sales, in millions of dollars.

### Highest rated Mexican food restaurant chains

1. Chi-Chi's Inc., with 2.52
2. El Torito, 2.51
3. Taco Bell, 2.32
4. Taco John's, 2.20
5. Del Taco, 2.15

*Where'd you hear that?*
Restaurants & Institutions, Choice in Chains. Based on satisfaction index based on response to survey on chains. Those chains with less than 100 respondents were ommitted from main ranking.

### Top Mexican food companies

1. Taco Bell, with $1,630 million
2. Chi-Chi's Inc., $422.9
3. El Torito, $390
4. Del Taco, $226.9
5. Taco John International, $116
6. El Chico Corp., $110
7. Taco Time, $85
8. Taco Villa, $80.3
9. Taco Bueno, $74
10. Garcia's Mexican Restaurants, $67

*Where'd you hear that?*
Restaurants & Institutions, Restaurants & Institutions 400. Based on 1988 sales, in millions of dollars.

## Largest pizza franchises

1. Pizza Hut, Inc., with $3.2 billion
2. Domino's Pizza Inc., $2.1 billion
3. Little Caesars Pizza, $908 million
4. Pantera's Corp., $139 million
5. Round Table Franchising Corp., $267 million
6. Godfather's Pizza Inc., $245 million
7. Shakey's Pizza Restaurants, Inc., $211 million
8. Sbarro, Inc., $271.7 million
9. Mr. Gatti's, N/A
10. Mazzio's Corp., $135 million

*Where'd you hear that?*
Pizza Today. Based on 1989 sales.

## Leading pizza/Italian food companies

1. Pizza Hut, with $3,390 million
2. Domino's Pizza Inc., $2,300
3. Little Caesars Pizza, $908
4. Pizza Inn, $325
5. Olive Garden, $300
6. Round Table Pizza, $267
7. Shakey's Pizza, $260.8
8. Godfather's Pizza Inc., $231
9. Showbiz Pizza/Chuck E. Cheese, $209.2
10. Sbarro Inc., $154

*Where'd you hear that?*
Restaurants & Institutions, Restaurants & Institutions 400. Based on 1988 sales, in millions of dollars.

## Best pizza chains

1. Pizza Hut, with 2.46
2. Little Caesar's Pizza, 2.33
2. Godfather's Pizza Inc., 2.33
4. Domino's Pizza Inc., 2.25
5. Pizza Inn, 2.24
6. Shakey's, 2.21

*Where'd you hear that?*
Restaurants & Institutions, Choice in Chains. Based on ranking based on each chain's satisfaction index, which is based on response to survey on chains. Those chains with less than 100 responses were omitted from main ranking.

## Most popular sandwich restaurant chains

1. Subway, with 2.36
2. Arby's Inc., 2.34
3. Rax, 2.32
4. A & W, 2.29
5. Roy Rogers, 2.19

*Where'd you hear that?*
Restaurants & Institutions, Choice in Chains. Based on a satisfaction index based on customer surveys.

## Largest sandwich chains

1. Arby's Inc., with $1,160 million
2. Roy Rogers, $630
3. Subway, $600
4. Rax Restaurants Inc., $366.7
5. A & W Restaurants Inc., $164.5
6. International Blimpie, $110
7. Wienerschnitzel, $107.6
8. Togo's Eatery, $55.5
9. Carousel Snack Bars of Minnesota, $52
9. Schlotzsky's Sandwhich Restaurant, $52

*Where'd you hear that?*
Restaurants & Institutions, Restaurants & Institutions 400. Based on 1988 sales, in millions of dollars.

# REFRESHMENT STAND

# REFRESHMENT STAND

### Largest school food service providers

1. New York City Board of Education, with $86.3 million
2. Los Angeles Unified School District, $64.5
3. Chicago Board of Education, $45.7
4. Puerto Rico School District, $39.7
5. Dade County (FL) School District, $20.7
6. Houston Independent School District, $20.5
7. School District of Philadelphia, $17.2
8. Hawaii Statewide Schools, $15.2
9. School Board of Hillsborough County, $14.1
10. Dallas Independent School District, $12.5

*Where'd you hear that?*
Restaurants & Institutions. Based on 1988 food and beverage purchase, in millions of dollars.

### Leaders in education food service

1. USDA Food & Nutrition Service, with $3,035.8 million
2. New York City Board of Education, $241.6
3. Los Angeles Schools, $180.6
4. Chicago Board of Education, $128.0
5. Dade County Schools, $58.1
6. Houston Independent School District, $57.4
7. School District of Philadelphia, $48.2
8. Hawaii Schools, $42.6
9. Hillsborough County School District, $39.6
10. Dallas Schools, $35.0

*Where'd you hear that?*
Restaurants & Institutions, Restaurants & Institutions 400. Based on 1988 sales, in millions of dollars.

### Largest college and university food service providers

1. Pennsylvania State University, with $10.3 million
2. Boston University, $10
3. Texas A & M University, $9
3. Michigan State University, $9
5. University of Illinois, $8.3

---

## *Top 10 salted snack categories*

1. Potato chips, with $3,598 million
2. Tortilla chips, $1,844
3. Snack nuts, $1,211
4. Microwavable popcorn, $872
5. Extruded snacks, $649
6. Corn chips, $521
7. Pretzels, $430
8. Variety pack, $269
9. Read-to-eat popcorn, $270
10. Unpopped popcorn, $238

*Where'd you hear that?*
U.S. Distribution Journal. Based on volume, in millions of dollars.

6. Rutgers University, $8
6. University of Minnesota, $8
8. Cornell University, $7.4
9. University of Notre Dame, $7.3
10. United States Air Force Academy, $7.2

*Where'd you hear that?*
Restaurants & Institutions. Based on 1988 food and beverage purchases, in millions of dollars.

## Best-selling candy bars

1. Snickers Bar, with $440 million
2. Reese's Peanut Butter Cups, $350
3. M & M's Peanut Chocolate Candies, $320
4. M & M's Plain Chocolate Candies, $310
5. Kit Kat, $160
6. Hershey's Milk Chocolate/Almonds, $155
7. Milky Way Bar, $150
8. Hershey's Milk Chocolate, $145
9. Crunch, $125
10. Butterfinger, $115

*Where'd you hear that?*
Prepared Foods. Based on estimated 1988 sales, in millions of dollars. Original source: American Consulting Corp. (Orlando, FL).

## Leading countries in world chocolate consumption

1. Switzerland, with 19.36
2. United Kingdom, 17.6
3. Norway, 17.28
4. Belgium/Luxembourg, 14.96
4. Netherlands, 14.96
4. Germany, 14.96
7. Austria, 14.74
8. Ireland, 12.54
9. Denmark, 12.32
9. Sweden, 12.32

*Where'd you hear that?*
Fancy Food. Based on pounds per capita. Original source: Chocolate Manufacturers Assoc.

## Leading beverage packagers

1. Anheuser-Busch Cos. Inc.
2. Coca-Cola Enterprises
3. Coca-Cola Co.
4. PepsiCo Inc.
5. Philip Morris Cos., Inc.

*Where'd you hear that?*
Packaging, Top 100 Packaging Giants. Based on 1988 consumption of packaging materials.

## Biggest corporations in the beverage industry

1. PepsiCo, with $15,420 million
2. Anheuser-Busch Cos. Inc., $9,481
3. Coca-Cola Co., $9,171
4. Coca-Cola Enterprises, $3,889
5. Seagold Vineyards Hldg., $3,005
6. Adolph Coors Co., $1,770
7. Brown-Forman Corp., $1,012

*Where'd you hear that?*
Fortune, Fortune 500 Largest U.S. Industrial Corporations. Based on 1989 sales, in millions of dollars.

# REFRESHMENT STAND

# REFRESHMENT STAND

## Biggest corporations in the beverage industry

1. Coca-Cola Co., with $24,686 million
2. PepsiCo, $15,855
3. Anheuser-Busch Cos. Inc., $10,153
4. Brown-Forman Corp., $2,039
5. Coca-Cola Enterprises, $2,003
6. General Cinema Corp., $1,698
7. Adolph Coors Co., $687

*Where'd you hear that?*
Business Week, The Business Week 1000. Based on market value in millions of dollars.

## Most admired beverage corporations

1. PepsiCo, with a rating of 8.16
2. Coca-Cola Co., 8.15
3. Anheuser-Busch Cos. Inc., 7.96
4. Brown-Forman Corp., 6.53
5. Joseph E. Seagram & Sons, 6.51
6. Coca-Cola Enterprises, 6.31
7. Adolph Coors Co., 6.16
8. Dr. Pepper/Seven-Up, 5.69

*Where'd you hear that?*
Fortune, America's Most Admired Corporations. Based on scores (0-10) derived from a survey of senior executives, outside directors, and financial analysts. Respondents ranked firms in their own industry on quality of management and products/services; innovation; long-term investment value; financial soundness; attraction and retention of talent; community and environmental responsibility; and use of assets.

## Largest companies in the U.S. bottled water industry

1. Perrier-owned brands, with 18.2%
2. Perrier, 5.7%
3. Anjou International, 5.2%
3. McKesson Corp., 5.2%
5. Suntory International, 4.2%
6. Clorox, 1.9%
7. Culligan, 1.8%
8. Evian, 1.7%
9. Sammons, 1.4%
10. Belmont Springs, 1.0%
11. Black Mountain, 0.8%
12. Others, 52.9%

*Where'd you hear that?*
New York Times. Based on 1988 market share, in percent.

## Leading bottled water production states

1. California, with 586,850 thousand gallons
2. Texas, 100,000
3. New Jersey, 85,550
4. Florida, 80,200
5. Pennsylvania, 77,700
6. Illinois, 67,400
7. Maine, 64,750
8. Louisiana, 52,700
9. Arizona, 52,650
10. Massachusetts, 49,650

*Where'd you hear that?*
National Beverage Marketing Directory. Based on 1988 production, in thousand of gallons.

## Largest U.S. coffee companies

1. General Foods Corp., with 33.0%
2. Procter & Gamble, 31.8%
3. Nestle, 13.0%
4. Chock Full o'Nuts, 3.4%

5. Others, total 18.8%

*Where'd you hear that?*
New York Times. Based on estimated share of the U.S. coffee market in 1988, in percent.

## Most advertised coffee, tea and cocoa brands

1. Folgers Coffee, with $64.1 million
2. Maxwell House Coffee, $44.0
3. General Foods International Coffees, $25.1
4. Sanka, $22.2
5. Taster's Choice Coffee, $18.9
6. Lipton Tea, $17.7
7. Nescafe, $8.8
8. Nestea, $7.5
9. Carnation Instant Breakfast, $7.2
10. Celestial Seasonings, $3.9

*Where'd you hear that?*
Wine Marketing Handbook. Based on 1988 advertising expenditures, in millions of dollars.

## Most efficient advertisers among coffees

1. Brim, with $2.38
2. Hills Brothers, $5.22
3. Sanka, $12.28
4. Folger's Coffee, $13.54
5. Maxwell House, $14.15
6. Taster's Choice, $17.10
7. Nescafe, $27.00

*Where'd you hear that?*
Adweek's Marketing Week, Annual Measure of Efficiency. Based on efficiency quotient (average weekly cost of television advertising divided by average number of retained impressions).

# REFRESHMENT STAND

## *Leading countries in world tea exports*

1. India, with 21.0%
2. Sri Lanka, 20.6%
3. China, 17.9%
4. Kenya, 13.9%
5. Indonesia, 9.3%
6. Others, total 17.3%

*Where'd you hear that?*
Financial Times. Based on 1987 share of world tea exports, in percent.

## Top 10 soft drink brands

1. Coca-Cola Classic, with 19.8%
2. Pepsi-Cola, 17.9%
3. diet Coke, 8.9%
4. Diet Pepsi, 5.7%
5. Dr. Pepper, 4.5%
6. Sprite, 3.7%
7. Mountain Dew, 3.6%
8. 7UP, 3.2%
9. Caffiene Free diet Coke, 2.5%
10. Caffiene Free Diet Pepsi, 1.6%

*Where'd you hear that?*
Beverage World. Based on ranked by 1989 market share, in percent.

## Most advertised soft drink brands

1. Coca-Cola Co., with $83.1 million
2. Pepsi-Cola, $66.6
3. 7Up, $27.0
4. Sprite, $22.4
5. Dr. Pepper, $14.5

# REFRESHMENT STAND

6. Slice, $12.5
7. Minute Maid, $9.3
8. Royal Crown, $6.5
9. Canada Dry, $6.4
10. Mountain Dew, $6.1

*Where'd you hear that?*
Wine Marketing Handbook. Based on 1989 advertising expenditures, in millions of dollars.

## Most advertised diet soft drink brands

1. diet Coke, with $56.5
2. Diet Pepsi, $47.2
3. Diet Dr. Pepper, $9.7
4. Diet Sprite, $7.4
5. Diet 7 UP, $7.0
6. Diet Crush, $4.3
7. Diet Minute Maid, $3.5
8. Diet Rite, $2.3
9. Diet Slice, $1.9
10. Diet A & W, $1.5

*Where'd you hear that?*
Wine Marketing Handbook. Based on 1988 advertising expenditures, in millions of dollars.

## Most efficient advertisers among soft drinks

1. Pepsi-Cola, with $8.92
2. Coca-Cola, $10.80
3. Sprite/Diet Sprite, $20.78
4. 7-Up/Diet 7-Up, $21.16
5. Diet Pepsi, $22.88
6. RC Cola/Diet RC, $24.11
7. diet Coke, $24.30
8. Dr. Pepper/Diet Dr. Pepper, $25.21
9. Slice/Diet Slice, $57.03

*Where'd you hear that?*
Adweek's Marketing Week, Annual Measure of Efficiency, March 5, 1990, p. 30. Based on efficiency quotient (average weekly cost of television advertising divided by average number of retained impressions).

## Leading non-alcoholic brews

1. Kingsbury, with 2,250 thousand
2. Moussy, 840
3. Texas Light, 765
4. Kaliber, 710
5. Birell, 645
6. Warteck, 600
7. Clausthaler, 515
8. Others, total 375

*Where'd you hear that?*
Beverage Dynamics. Based on 1988 estimated case sales, in thousands.

## Most popular lager brands in Britain

1. Carling Black Label, with 11%
2. Heineken, 8%
2. Foster's, 8%
4. Carlsberg, 6%
5. Tennents, 5%
6. Skol, 4.5%
6. Castlemaine XXXX, 4.5%
8. Harp, 3%
9. Others, total 50%

*Where'd you hear that?*
Financial Times. Based on market share.

## Largest importers of brewed beverages

1. Van Munching & Co., with 29.3%
2. Molson Breweries USA, 19.4%
3. Barton Brands, 15.4%

# REFRESHMENT STAND

4. Guinness/All Brand, 15.2%
5. Dribeck Importers, 9.1%
6. Others, total, 11.6%

*Where'd you hear that?*
Modern Brewery Age, Weekly News Edition. Based on estimated 1989 percentage of import market.

## Leading imported beer brands

1. Heineken, wtih 25.7%
2. Corona Extra, 13.6%
3. Beck's, 8.9%
4. Molson Golden, 7.8%
5. Moosehead, 5.0%
6. Labatt, 4.8%
7. Amstel Light, 3.6%
8. Tecate, 2.6%
9. St. Pauli Girl, 2.4%
9. Foster, 2.4%

*Where'd you hear that?*
Beverage Industry, Annual Beer Report. Based on 1989 estimated share, in percent.

## Top 10 U.S. brewers

1. Anheuser-Busch Cos. Inc., with 80,700,000
2. Miller Brewing, 41,900,000
3. Stroh Brewery, 18,250,000
4. Adolph Coors Co., 17,698,000
5. G. Heileman, 13,050,000
6. Pabst Brewing, 6,600,000
7. Genesee Brewing, 2,363,000
8. Falstaff Brewing, 1,362,000
9. Lotrobe Brewing, 650,000
10. Hudepohl-Schoenling, 500,000

*Where'd you hear that?*
Modern Brewery Age, MBA Statistical Study. Based on 31-barrel sales for 1989.

## Top 5 brewers

1. Anheuser-Busch Cos. Inc., with 44.0%
2. Miller, 22.8%
3. Stroh, 9.9%
4. Adolph Coors Co., 9.6%
5. G. Heileman, 7.1%
6. Others, total 6.5%

*Where'd you hear that?*
Modern Brewery Age, MBA Statistical Study. Based on market share, in percent for 1989.

## Most popular types of brewed beverages in the U.S.

1. Regular domestic, with 42%
2. 'Light' beer, 27%
3. Popular or lower-priced beer, 21%
4. Imported beers, 5%
5. Super premium beers, 3.5%
6. Malt liquor, 1.5%

*Where'd you hear that?*
D & B Reports. Based on 1988 sales percentage.

## Most efficient advertisers among beers

1. Budweiser Beer, with $17.07
2. Stroh's/Light, $18.06
3. Heineken, $18.10
4. Old Milwaukee/Light, $19.18
5. Bud Light, $20.26
6. Miller Lite, $22.69
7. Lowenbrau/Light, $31.28
8. Coors/Light/Extra Gold, $32.08
9. Miller High Life/Draft, $39.52
10. Busch/Light, $42.40
11. Michelob/Light/Dry, $60.38

# REFRESHMENT STAND

*Where'd you hear that?*
Adweek's Marketing Week, Annual Measure of Efficiency. Based on efficiency quotient (average weekly cost of television advertising divided by average number of retained impressions).

## Largest U.S. microbreweries

1. Pacific Brewing, with 11,000
2. Redhook Ale Brewery, 10,160
3. Dock Street Brewing, 7,500
4. Boulder Brewing, 7,000
5. Oldenberg Brewing, 5,800
6. Catamount Brewing, 4,950
7. Hart Brewing, 4,800
8. Massachusetts Bay Brewing, 4,431
9. Hope Brewing, 4,300
10. Firestone-Flecther Brewing, 4,300

*Where'd you hear that?*
Modern Brewery Age Blue Book. Based on 1988 sales of 31 gallon barrels.

## Top 10 wine producing countries

1. Italy, with 2,004 million gallons
2. France, 1,834
3. Spain, 1,011
4. Argentina, 687
5. USSR, 608
6. United States, 485
7. Portugal, 294
8. West Germany, 238
9. Romania, 230
10. South Africa, 182

*Where'd you hear that?*
Wine Marketing Handbook. Based on 1987 wine production, in millions of gallons.

## Countries with the highest per capita wine consumption

1. Italy, with 20.87 gallons per capita
2. France, 19.84
3. Portugal, 16.99
4. Luxembourg, 15.45
5. Argentina, 15.35
6. Spain, 14.27
7. Switzerland, 13.08
8. Chile, 9.25
9. Austria, 8.48
10. Greece, 8.40

*Where'd you hear that?*
Wine Marketing Handbook. Based on 1987 consumption per capita, in gallons.

## Leading wine exporters to the U.S.

1. Italy, with 34,949 thousand
2. France, 22,095
3. Spain, 7,036
4. West Germany, 6,063
5. Portugal, 3,490
6. Australia, 1,127
7. Japan, 1,043
8. Yugoslavia, 970
9. Chile, 760
10. Greece, 498

*Where'd you hear that?*
Wines & Vines, Wines & Vines Statistical Issue. Based on shipments into the U.S., in thousands of gallons.

## Largest wineries in the U.S.

1. E. & J. Gallo Winery, with 335,000 thousand gallons
2. Grand Metropolitan PLC, 90,945
3. Vintners International, 84,531
4. Canandaigua Wine Co., 50,000
5. The Wine Group, 50,800

6. The Beverage Source, 50,500
7. Vie-Del Company, 47,525
8. JFJ Bronco Winery, 46,800
9. Guild Wineries & Distilleries, 39,000
10. Delicato Vineyards, 38,301

*Where'd you hear that?*
Wines & Vines, Wines & Vines Statistical Issue. Based on total storage capacity, in thousands of gallons.

## Top U.S. wine marketers

1. E. & J. Gallo Winery, with 27.0%
2. Grand Metropolitan PLC, 9.9%
3. Vintners International Co., 7.5%
4. Canandaigua Wine Co., 5.1%
5. Wine Group, 3.7%

*Where'd you hear that?*
Wall Street Journal. Based on U.S. market share based on total 1988 wine shipments of 189 million cases, in percent. Figures don't include cooler, exports, and bulk wine sales to other wineries.

## Most advertised table wines

1. Gallo Wines, with $13,737.2 thousand
2. Riunite Wines, $9,930.2
3. Bolla Wines, $3,245.3
4. Inglenook Wines, $1,892.1
5. Sutter Home Wines, $1,779.5
6. Paul Masson Wines, $1,708.7
7. Taylor California Cellars, $1,488.4
8. Napa Ridge Wine, $1,333.4
9. Taylor Wine, $1,056.9
10. Folonari Wines, $1,054.9

*Where'd you hear that?*
Wine Marketing Handbook. Based on 1988 total advertising expenditures for table wines, in thousands of dollars.

## Most advertised dessert wines

1. Harvey's Bristol Cream Sherry, with $5,425.8 thousand
2. Richards Wild Irish Rose Wine, $1,104.7
3. Sandeman Founders Reserve Port, $287.4
4. Cockburns, $211.1
5. Cool Breeze, $135.3
6. Savory & James Wines, $50.1
7. Kirsberry Cherry Speciality, 34.0
8. Sandeman Character Sherry, $19.8
9. Gekkeikan Sake, $19.2

*Where'd you hear that?*
Wine Marketing Handbook. Based on 1988 total advertising expenditures for dessert wine, in thousands of dollars.

## Most advertised vermouth brands

1. Stock Vermouth, with $621.9 thousand
2. Martini & Rossi Vermouth, $10.5

*Where'd you hear that?*
Wine Marketing Handbook. Based on 1988 total advertising expenditures for vermouth, in thousands of dollars.

# REFRESHMENT STAND

# REFRESHMENT STAND

## Leading wine advertisers in magazines

1. Rioja Spain wine producers, with $407.9 thousand
2. Schieffelin & Somerset, $307.1
3. Food & Wines from France, $51.6
4. Ohio, State of, $43.4
5. Banfi Vintners, $10.6

*Where'd you hear that?*
Wine Marketing Handbook. Based on 1988 wine advertising expenditures in magazines, in thousands of dollars.

## Wine brands with the most magazine advertising

1. Korbel California Champagne, with $3,235.3 thousand
2. Bolla Wines, $1,770.1
3. Inglenook Wines, $1,490.0
4. Freixenet Spanish Wine, $1,023.0
5. Barton & Guestier Wines, $704.5
6. Mumm Champagne, $593.9
7. Perrier-Jouet Champagne, $531.0
8. Ruffino Wines, $453.2
9. Piper-Heidsieck Champagne, $442.2
10. Franzia Brothers Wine Cooler, $417.5

*Where'd you hear that?*
Wine Marketing Handbook. Based on magazine advertising expenditures, in thousands of dollars.

## Wine brands with the most newspaper advertising

1. Seagram Wine Coolers, with $386.9 thousand
2. California Cooler, $202.6
3. Cook's Champagne, $154.7
4. Ballatore Wine, $144.8
5. Krug Champagne, $139.7
6. Chateau Elan, $133.8
7. St. Regis NonAlcohol, $95.5
8. Baron Herzog, $91.1
9. Sequoia Grove Wine, $90.4
10. Marques de Riscal Wine, $85.9

*Where'd you hear that?*
Wine Marketing Handbook. Based on newspaper advertising expenditures, in thousands of dollars.

## Leading wine spot radio advertisers

1. Sutter Home Wines, with $1,779.5 thousand
2. Napa Ridge Wine, $1,333.4
3. Richards Wild Irish Rose Wine, $1,003.4
4. Beringer Wines, $909.7
5. California Cooler, $847.6
6. Monterey Vineyard Wines, $790.9
7. Stock Vermouth, $621.9
8. Freixenet Spanish Wine, $548.1
9. Tea Twister/Lemon Twister Cooler, $498.5
10. Riunite Wines, $496.3

*Where'd you hear that?*
Wine Marketing Handbook. Based on 1988 spot radio advertising expenditures, in thousands of dollars.

## Leading wine spot TV advertisers

1. Franzia Brothers Wine & Champagne
2. Ohio State Wines
3. New York State Wines
4. Domaine Chandon Winery

# REFRESHMENT STAND

*Where'd you hear that?*
Wine Marketing Handbook. Based on 1988 spot TV advertising expenditures.

## Wine brands with the most network TV advertising

1. Bartles & Jaymes Wine Cooler, with $25,824.9 thousand
2. Seagram Wine Coolers, $25,067.1
3. Gallo Wines, $10,355.6
4. Riunite Wine, $9,211.8
5. Totts Champagne, $7,188.6
6. Martini & Rossi Asti Spumanti, $4,992.0
7. Cook's Champagne, $1,820.4
8. Andre Wines, $1,460.9
9. Sun Country Classic Cooler, $1,042.9
10. Paul Masson Wines, $357.8

*Where'd you hear that?*
Wine Marketing Handbook. Based on network TV advertising expenditures, in thousands of dollars.

## Wine brands with the most spot TV advertising

1. Harvey's Bristol Cream Sherry, with $4,802.3 thousand
2. Gallo Wines, $3,155.3
3. Almaden Champagne, $2,766.1
4. Martini & Rossi Asti Spumanti, $2,647.1
5. Moet et Chandon, $1,979.8
6. Totts Champagne, $1,800.0
7. Bolla Wines, $1,475.2
8. Sun Country Classic Cooler, $1,336.7
9. Folonari Wines, $999.0
10. Paul Masson Wines, $978.9

*Where'd you hear that?*
Wine Marketing Handbook. Based on spot TV advertising expenditures, in thousands of dollars.

## Wine brands with the most cable TV advertising

1. Sun Country Classic Cooler, with $1,225.6 thousand
2. Almaden Champagne, $558.5
3. Totts Champagne, $306.8
4. Moet et Chandon, $302.1
5. California Cooler, $277.8
6. Harvey's Bristol Cream Sherry, $232.1
7. Riunite Wines, $213.8
8. Bartles & Jaymes Wine Cooler, $69.9
9. Paul Masson Wines, $46.0
10. Taylor California Cellars, $26.5

*Where'd you hear that?*
Wine Marketing Handbook. Based on cable TV advertising expenditures, in thousands of dollars.

## Leading wine consumption states

1. California, with 118,104 gallons
2. New York, 50,250
3. Florida, 32,411
4. Texas, 26,845
5. Illinois, 25,695
6. New Jersey, 24,833
7. Massachusetts, 18,846
8. Michigan, 18,274
9. Washington, 16.040
10. Ohio, 15,936

*Where'd you hear that?*
National Beverage Marketing Directory. Based on 1988 consumption, in gallons.

# REFRESHMENT STAND

**Top markets for wine**

1. California, with 46,149.7 thousand cases
2. New York, 19,601.3
3. Florida, 12,183.5
4. Texas, 11,096.0
5. Illinois, 10,444.0
6. New Jersey, 9,226.1
7. Michigan, 7,030.0
8. Massachusetts, 6,906.0
9. Ohio, 6,235.2
10. Washington, 5,658.5

*Where'd you hear that?*
Wine Marketing Handbook. Based on wine cases, in thousands.

---

## Leading wine consumption states

1. District of Columbia, with 8.21 cases
2. Nevada, 7.05
3. California, 6.07
4. Washington, 4.98
5. Vermont, 4.97
6. New Hampshire, 4.93
7. Oregon, 4.53
8. New Jersey, 4.45
9. Connecticut, 4.40
10. Alaska, 4.38

*Where'd you hear that?*
Wine Marketing Handbook. Based on 1988 wine consumption per adult, in cases.

---

**Top markets for wine**

1. District of Columbia, with 2,504.7
2. Nevada, 1,830.0
3. California, 1,638.4
4. Vermont, 1,420.0
5. New Hampshire, 1,335.0
6. Washington, 1,225.0
7. Connecticut, 1,206.7
8. New Jersey, 1,195.1
9. Massachusetts, 1,176.3
10. Oregon, 1,144.9

*Where'd you hear that?*
Wine Marketing Handbook. Based on wine cases per thousand persons.

**Top metropolitan markets for wine sales**

1. Los Angeles-Anaheim-Riverside, CA, with 23,633.2 thousand
2. New York-Northern New Jersey-Long Island, 21,265.1
3. San Francisco-Oakland-San Jose, CA, 10,823.3
4. Chicago-Gary-Lake County, IL-IN, 7,656.3
5. Boston-Lawrence-Salem, MA, 5,515.9
6. Washington, DC, 4,255.6
7. Detroit-Ann Arbor, MI, 4,154.4
8. Philadelphia-Wilmington-Trenton, 4,106.0
9. San Diego, CA, 3,677.1
10. Dallas-Fort Worth, TX, 3,656.0

*Where'd you hear that?*
Wine Marketing Handbook. Based on wine cases, in thousands.

**Top 10 markets for champagne and sparkling wines by cases sold**

1. California, with 4,017.0 thousand
2. New York, 1,545.6
3. Illinois, 1,206.3
4. Florida, 941.2
5. New Jersey, 821.6
6. Texas, 806.2
7. Michigan, 737.2
8. Massachusetts, 532.4

9. Pennsylvania, 520.1
10. Ohio, 372.5

*Where'd you hear that?*
Wine Marketing Handbook. Based on thousands of cases sold in 1988.

## Top 10 markets for champagne and sparkling wines by cases sold per thousand persons

1. Washington, DC, with 252.6
2. California, 144.5
3. Hawaii, 121.7
4. New Hampshire, 116.8
5. New Jersey, 106.4
6. Illinois, 104.5
7. Connecticut, 91.1
8. Massachusetts, 90.7
9. New York, 86.4
10. Nevada, 81.4

*Where'd you hear that?*
Wine Marketing Handbook. Based on cases per thousand persons in 1988.

## Top metropolitan areas for champagne and sparkling wines

1. Los Angeles-Anaheim-Riverside, CA, with 1,879.9 thousand
2. New York-Northern New Jersey-Long Island, 1,780.4
3. San Francisco-Oakland-San Jose, CA, 1,001.3
4. Chicago-Gary-Lake County, IL-IN, 832.4
5. Detroit-Ann Arbor, MI, 478.3
6. Boston-Lawrence-Salem, MA, 447.3
7. Philadelphia-Wilmington-Trenton, 342.3
8. San Diego, CA, 320.2
9. Dallas-Fort Worth, TX, 284.0

10. Washington, DC, 277.4

*Where'd you hear that?*
Wine Marketing Handbook. Based on thousands of cases sold in 1988.

## Leading imported champagne and sparkling wine brands

1. Freixenet Spanish Wine, with 1,175 thousand
2. Martini & Rossi Asti, 715
3. Tosti Asti, 575
4. Moet & Chandon, 460
5. Codorniu Wines, 400
6. Riunite Spumante, 285
7. Zonin Asti, 219
8. Mumm, 210
9. Gancia Asti, 195
10. Paul Cheneau, 181

*Where'd you hear that?*
Wine Marketing Handbook. Based on 1988 sales, in thousands of cases.

## Leading advertisers of champagne and sparkling wines

1. Totts Champagne, with $9,295.4 thousand
2. Martini & Rossi Asti Spumanti, $7,640.2
3. Almaden Champagne, $3,324.6
4. Korbel California Champagne, $3,235.3
5. Moet et Chandon, $2,668.8
6. Cook's Champagne, $2,518.8
7. Freixenet Spanish Wine, $1,801.1
8. Andre Wines, $1,464.5
9. Mumm Champagne, $597.1
10. Codorniu Wines, $545.9

*Where'd you hear that?*
Wine Marketing Handbook. Based on 1988 total advertising expenditures, in thousands of dollars.

# REFRESHMENT STAND

# REFRESHMENT STAND

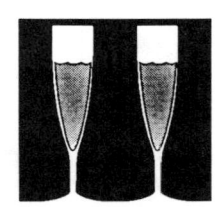

### Best-selling wine coolers

1. Seagram's, with 18.1 million cases
2. Bartles & Jaymes Wine Cooler, 16.5
3. California Cooler, 5.8
4. Sun Country, 3.5
5. White Mountain, 1.2
6. Matilda Bay, 2.4
7. Others, 3.8

*Where'd you hear that?*
Wine Marketing Handbook. Based on 1988 sales, in millions of cases.

### Leading wine coolers advertisers

1. Seagram Wine Coolers, with $26,443.5 thousand
2. Bartles & Jaymes Wine Cooler, $26,281.9
3. Sun Country Classic Cooler, $4,164.2
4. California Cooler, $1,642.6
5. Fletcher & Oakes Wine Spritzer, $674.2
6. Tea Twister/Lemon Twister Cooler, $498.5
7. Franzia Brothers Wine Cooler, $417.5
8. Marcus James Cooler, $317.5
9. Calvin Cooler, $220.4
10. Tequita Wine Coolers, $202.9

*Where'd you hear that?*
Wine Marketing Handbook. Based on total advertising expenditures for wine coolers, by brand, in thousands of dollars.

### Top markets for wine coolers

1. California, with 9,920 thousand cases
2. Texas, 4,400
3. New York, 3,514
4. Florida, 3,309
5. Illinois, 2,839
6. Michigan, 1,765
7. North Carolina, 1,550
8. Washington, 1,523
9. Ohio, 1,460
10. New Jersey, 1,336

*Where'd you hear that?*
Wine Marketing Handbook. Based on 1988 sales, in thousands of cases.

### Top markets for wine coolers

1. Vermont, with 401.1
2. Nevada, 384.6
3. Arizona, 375.9
4. California, 352.2
5. Washington, 329.8
6. District of Columbia, 307.6
7. Florida, 267.3
8. Colorado, 264.4
9. Minnesota, 262.8
10. Texas, 262.2

*Where'd you hear that?*
Wine Marketing Handbook. Based on 1988 sales, in cases per thousand persons.

### Top metropolitan areas for wine coolers

1. Los Angeles-Anaheim-Riverside, CA, with 5,085.0 thousand cases
2. New York-Northern New Jersey-Long Island, 3,674.8
3. San Francisco-Oakland-San Jose, CA, 2,168.2
4. Chicago-Gary-Lake County, IL-IN, 2,146.7

5. Dallas-Fort Worth, TX, 1,491.2
6. Houston-Galveston-Brazoria, TX, 1,291.1
7. Phoenix, AZ, 1,016.2
8. Miami-Fort Lauderdale, FL, 1,008.6
9. Detroit-Ann Arbor, MI, 1,006.7
10. Minneapolis-St. Paul, MN, 949.1

*Where'd you hear that?*
Wine Marketing Handbook. Based on 1988 sales, in thousands of cases.

## Best-selling liqueur brands

1. DeKuyper Line, with 2,550 thousand
2. Hiram Walker Line, 1,690
3. Kahlua, 1,545
4. Southern Comfort, 1,189
5. Baileys Irish Cream, 947
6. Arrow Line, 750
6. Leroux Line, 750
8. Mr. Boston Line, 497
9. Amaretto di Saronno, 388
10. Jacquin Line, 361

*Where'd you hear that?*
Jobson's Liquor Handbook. Based on 1988 estimated sales, in thousands of cases.

## Best-selling brandy and cognac brands by sales

1. E & J Brandy, with 1,854 thousand
2. Christian Brothers, 1,150
3. Hennessy, 737
4. Courvoisier, 550
5. Korbel, 335
6. Martell, 249
7. Remy Martin, 217
8. Coronet, 213

9. Paul Masson, 133
10. Old Mr. Boston, 132

*Where'd you hear that?*
Jobson's Liquor Handbook. Based on 1988 estimated sales, in thousands of cases.

## Top liquor brands

1. Bacardi (rum), with 8,000 thousand
2. Smirnoff (vodka) 6,905
3. Seagram's 7 Crown (blended), 4,145
4. Popov (vodka), 3,825
5. Seagram's Gin (gin), 3,745
6. Jim Beam (bourban), 3,715
7. Canadian Mist (Canadian), 3,650
8. Jack Daniel's (Tennessee), 3,545
9. Seagram's V.O. (Canadian), 2,555
10. DeKuyper Cordials (cordial), 2,415

*Where'd you hear that?*
Business Week, Liquor Industry Scoreboard. Based on 1989 sales, in thousands of cases.

## Leading liquor brands

1. Bacardi, with 7,345 thousand
2. Smirnoff, 6,000
3. Seagram's 7-Crown, 3,850
4. Canadian Mist, 3,415
5. Popov, 3,290
6. Jim Beam, 3,200
7. Seagram's Extra Dry, 2,800
8. Jack Daniel Black Label, 3,092
9. DeKuyper, 2,550
10. Canadian Club, 3,100

*Where'd you hear that?*
Jobson's Liquor Handbook. Based on 1988 sales, in thousands of mixed cases.

# REFRESHMENT STAND

# REFRESHMENT STAND

## Most profitable spirits brands

1. Bacardi, with $79 million
2. Jack Daniel Black Label, $77
2. Dewar's, $77
4. Smirnoff, $72
5. Kahlua, $69
6. Crown Royal, $68
7. Hennessy, $63
8. Canadian Club, $60
8. Seagram's VO, $60
10. Baileys Original Irish Cream, $57

*Where'd you hear that?*
Jobson's Liquor Handbook. Based on 1988 profit contribution, in millions of dollars.

### Best-selling spirits brands

1. Bacardi, with $369.3 million
2. Smirnoff, $309.4
3. Jack Daniel Black Label, $250.3
4. Dewar's, $228.1
5. Seagram's 7-Crown, $216.8
6. Canadian Mist, $178.9
7. Canadian Club, $178.0
8. Seagram's VO, $168.4
9. Jim Beam, $167.2
10. Seagram's Gin, $164.6

*Where'd you hear that?*
Jobson's Liquor Handbook. Based on 1988 sales, in millions of dollars.

### Leading brands of straight whiskey

1. Jim Beam, with 3,200 thousand
2. Jack Daniel Black Label, 3,083
3. Early Times, 1,151
4. Ancient Age, 962
5. Ten High, 875
6. Old Crow, 620
7. Evan Williams, 598
8. Wild Turkey, 470
9. Old Charter KY, 446
10. Old Grand-Dad, 297

*Where'd you hear that?*
Jobson's Liquor Handbook. Based on 1988 estimated sales, in thousands of cases.

### Leading brands of blended whiskey

1. Seagram's 7-Crown, with 3,840 thousand
2. Kessler, 1,085
3. Calvert Extra, 565
4. Fleischmann's Preferred, 372
5. Beams 8 Star, 330
6. Imperial, 300
7. Old Thompson, 247
8. Philadelphia, 136
9. Carstairs White Seal, 105
10. Barton Reserve, 104

*Where'd you hear that?*
Jobson's Liquor Handbook. Based on 1988 estimated sales, in thousands of cases.

### Leading brands of Canadian whiskey

1. Canadian Mist, with 3,369 thousand
2. Canadian Club, 2,350
3. Seagram's VO, 2,200
4. Windsor Supreme, 1,900
5. Black Velvet, 1,725
6. Crown Royal, 1,310
7. Lord Calvert, 1,025
8. Canadian LTD, 600
9. Canadian Hunter, 440
10. Northern Light, 380

# REFRESHMENT STAND

*Where'd you hear that?*
Jobson's Liquor Handbook. Based on 1988 estimated sales, in thousands of cases.

## Leading distilled spirits consumption states

1. California, with 48,697 thousand gallons
2. New York, 30,573
3. Florida, 25,707
4. Illinois, 18,942
5. Texas, 18,378
6. Michigan, 14,978
7. New Jersey, 14,245
8. Pennsylvania, 13,719
9. Massachusetts, 12,636
10. Ohio, 11,464

*Where'd you hear that?*
National Beverage Marketing Directory. Based on 1988 consumption, in thousands of gallons.

## Leading liquor brands in newspaper advertising

1. Johnnie Walker Black Label, with $758.7 thousand
2. Glenfiddich, $737.4
3. Johnnie Walker Red Label, $707.1
4. E & J Brandy, $606.5
5. Crown Royal, $570.4
6. Seagram's Cordials, $541.3
7. Baileys Original Irish Cream, $519.9
8. Chivas Regal, $480.1
9. Stolichnaya, $468.7
10. Seagram's 7-Crown, $404.5

*Where'd you hear that?*
Jobson's Liquor Handbook. Based on 1988 advertising expenditures, in thousands of dollars.

## Leading liquor brands in general promotion newspaper advertising

1. House of Seagram, with $565.0 thousand
2. Carillon Importers, Ltd., $41.4
3. Jim Beam Brands Co.
4. Schenley Corp.
5. Paramount Distillers, Inc.

*Where'd you hear that?*
Jobson's Liquor Handbook. Based on 1988 advertising expenditures, in thousands of dollars.

## Highest liquor-consumption states

1. Nevada, with 5.66
2. New Hampshire, 5.46
3. District of Columbia, 5.29
4. Alaska, 3.44
5. Delaware, 3.34
6. Connecticut, 2.96
7. Massachusetts, 2.93
8. Florida, 2.87
9. Maryland, 2.81
10. Rhode Island, 2.65

*Where'd you hear that?*
Jobson's Liquor Handbook. Based on 1988 adult per capita consumption.

## Leading liquor brands in magazine advertising

1. Dewar's, with $10,030.2 thousand
2. Absolut, $7,146.2
3. Chivas Regal, $6,887.1
4. Tanqueray, $6,465.6
5. Crown Royal, $6,435.3
6. Kahlua, $6,419.8
7. Bacardi, $6,059

# REFRESHMENT STAND

8. J & B, $6,021.3
9. Puerto Rican Rums, $5,498.2
10. Johnnie Walker Red Label, $5,238.4

*Where'd you hear that?*
Jobson's Liquor Handbook. Based on 1988 advertising expenditures, in thousands of dollars.

## Leading liquor brands in outdoor advertising

1. Crown Royal, with $2,532.7 thousand
2. Cutty Sark, $1,841.5
3. Bacardi, $1,481.0
4. Dewar's, $1,421.8
5. Jim Beam, $1,410.6
6. Canadian Hunter, $1,370.8
7. Kahlua, $1,366.4
8. Canadian Club, $1,099.9
9. Canadian Mist, $1,027.4
10. Stolichnaya, $999.7

*Where'd you hear that?*
Jobson's Liquor Handbook. Based on 1988 advertising expenditures, in thousands of dollars.

## Leading liquor brands in general promotion outdoor advertising

1. House of Seagram, with $714.0 thousand
2. Carillon Importers, Ltd., $710.4
3. Heublein, Inc., $115.1
4. Hiram Walker, Inc., $112.2
5. Brown-Forman Corp., $104.8
6. Maidstone Wine & Spirits, Inc., $71.3
7. Paddington Corp., $25.9
8. Jim Beam Brands Co., $4.1
9. Schieffelin & Somerset Co., $3.7
10. Glenmore Distilleries Co., $0.0

10. Potter Distillers, $0.0
10. Heaven Hill Distilleries, Inc., $0.0
10. Schenley Corp., $0.0

*Where'd you hear that?*
Jobson's Liquor Handbook. Based on 1988 advertising expenditures, in thousands of dollars.

## Most advertised liquor brands in Chicago newspapers

1. Myers's Rum, with 12.1%
1. Smirnoff, 12.1%
3. Crown Royal, 10.8%
4. Drambuie, 10.0%
5. Seagram's 7 Crown, 6.9%
6. Yukon Jack, 6.3%
7. Chivas Regal, 6.0%
8. Seagram's General Promotion, 5.9%
9. B & B, 5.4%
10. Baileys Original Irish Cream, 4.9%

*Where'd you hear that?*
Jobson's Liquor Handbook. Based on 1988 brand share, in percent.

## Most advertised liquor brands in Los Angeles newspapers

1. Crown Royal, with 19.8%
2. Seagram's General Promotion, 15.6%
3. Myers's Rum, 6.9%
4. Seagram's 7 Crown, 5.8%
5. Yukon Jack, 5.4%
6. Glenfiddich, 5.2%
6. Absolut, 5.2%
8. Bacardi, 4.3%
9. Lord Calvert, 3.4%
10. The Glenlivet, 2.9%

*Where'd you hear that?*
Jobson's Liquor Handbook. Based on 1988 brand share, in percent.

# REFRESHMENT STAND

**Most advertised liquor brands in Miami newspapers**

1. Johnnie Walker Black Label, with 17.9%
2. Johnnie Walker Red Label, 14.0%
3. Captain Morgan Spiced Rum, 9.7%
4. Baileys Original Irish Cream, 7.4%
5. Drambuie, 7.2%
6. Myer's Rum, 6.7%
7. Yukon Jack, 6.6%
8. E & J Brandy, 5.4%
9. Petite Liqueur, 4.4%
9. Tia Maria, 4.4%

*Where'd you hear that?*
Jobson's Liquor Handbook. Based on 1988 brand share, in percent.

**Most advertised liquor brands in New York newspapers**

1. Seagram's General Promotion, with 8.2%
2. Absolut, 6.7%
2. Drambuie, 6.7%
4. Johnnie Walker Red Label, 6.5%
5. Kahlua, 5.9%
6. Tanqueray, 5.3%
7. Chivas Regal, 5.2%
8. Glenfiddich, 4.5%
9. Dewar's White Label, 4.0%
10. Seagram's 7 Crown, 3.9%

*Where'd you hear that?*
Jobson's Liquor Handbook. Based on 1988 brand share, in percent.

**Most advertised liquor brands in San Francisco newspapers**

1. Crown Royal, with 26.0%
2. Famous Grouse, 8.4%
3. Seagram's General Promotion, 7.1%
4. Glenfiddich, 6.1%
5. Chivas Regal, 5.3%
6. Seagram's 7 Crown, 4.0%
7. The Glenlivet, 3.8%
8. DeKuyper Cordials, 3.7%
9. Yukon Jack, 3.6%
10. Lord Calvert, 3.0%

*Where'd you hear that?*
Jobson's Liquor Handbook. Based on 1988 brand share, in percent.

**Leading bourbon brands**

1. Jim Beam, with 3,700 thousand
2. Jack Daniels Black Label, 3,420
3. Early Times, 1,320
4. Evan Williams, 890
5. Ten High, 875
6. Ancient Age, 840
7. Old Crow, 710
8. Old Charter, 555
9. Wild Turkey, 505
10. Old Grand Dad, 480

*Where'd you hear that?*
Wall Street Journal. Based on 1988 sales, in thousands of 9-liter cases. Includes Tennessee and Kentucky whiskeys.

**Leading importers of U.S. gin**

1. Japan, with 19.5 thousand
2. Belgium, 16.7
3. Poland, 16.2
4. Canada, 10.2
5. Netherlands Antilles, 6.4
6. Others, total, 30.7

*Where'd you hear that?*
Jobson's Liquor Handbook. Based on 1988 volume, in thousands of proof gallons.

# REFRESHMENT STAND

## Leading importers of U.S. bourbon

1. Japan, with 3,587.0 thousand
2. West Germany, 1,992.9
3. Australia, 1,495.2
4. Canada, 143.4
5. France, 361.7
6. Others, total, 1,546.8

*Where'd you hear that?*
Jobson's Liquor Handbook. Based on 1988 trading volume, in thousands of proof gallons.

### Countries importing the most U.S. gin

1. United Kingdom, with 4,820 thousand
2. France, 67.3
3. West Germany, 29.6
4. Ireland, 22.4
5. Spain, 15.9
6. Others, total 30.3

*Where'd you hear that?*
Jobson's Liquor Handbook 1989. Based on thousands of proof gallons imported in 1988.

### Top gin suppliers

1. Seagram, with 30.70% market share
2. Schenley, 18.00%
3. Jim Beam, 9.70%
3. Schieffelin, 9.70%
5. Glenmore Distilleries Co., 8.30%
6. Others, total 23.60%

*Where'd you hear that?*
Jobson's Liquor Handbook. Based on 1988 market share, in percent.

### Best-selling brands of gin

1. Seagram's Extra Dry, with 3,150 thousand cases
2. Gordon's, 1,740
3. Tanqueray, 1,175
4. Gilbey's, 1,125
5. Beefeater, 930
6. Fleischmann's, 611
7. Barton, 340
8. Burnetts White Satin, 299
9. Crystal Palace, 240
10. Booths London Dry, 225

*Where'd you hear that?*
Jobson's Liquor Handbook. Based on 1988 sales, in thousands of cases.

### Most advertised gin brands

1. Tanqueray, with $7,464.5 thousand
2. Beefeater, $4,979.2
3. Seagram's Extra Dry, $4,861.9
4. Gordon's Gin, $4,692.8
5. Bombay Gin, $3,346.3
6. Gilbey's, $1,457.8
7. Bombay Sapphire, $325.4
8. Taaka, $253.5
9. Dimitri, $52.4
10. Calvert, $19.1

*Where'd you hear that?*
Jobson's Liquor Handbook. Based on 1988 advertising expenditures, in thousands of dollars.

### Most highly newspaper-advertised brands of gin

1. Tanqueray, with $325.5 thousand
2. Seagram's Extra Dry, $103.7
3. Dimitri, $52.4
4. Beefeater, $37.0
5. Gordon's, $24.0
6. Gilbey's, $8.8

7. Calvert, $5.1

*Where'd you hear that?*
Jobson's Liquor Handbook 1989. Based on advertising expenditures in newspapers, in thousands of dollars, for 1988.

## Most highly magazine-advertised brands of gin

1. Tanqueray, with $6,465.6 thousand
2. Beefeater, $4,942.2
3. Gordon's, $3,957.8
4. Seagram's Extra Dry, $3,736.0
5. Bombay, $3,325.8
6. Gilbey's, $1,107.3
7. Bombay Sapphire, $325.4
8. Virginia Gentleman, $10.5

*Where'd you hear that?*
Jobson's Liquor Handbook 1989. Based on advertising expenditures in magazines, in thousands of dollars, for 1988.

## Most highly outside-advertised brands of gin

1. Seagram's Extra Dry, with $986.3 thousand
2. Tanqueray, $589.3
3. Gordon's, $542.0
4. Taaka, $253.5
5. Gilbey's, $240.7
6. Bombay, $20.5
7. Calvert, $14.0
8. Country Club, $10.8
9. Heaven Hill, $5.6

*Where'd you hear that?*
Jobson's Liquor Handbook 1989. Based on advertising expenditures for outside advertising, in thousands of dollars, for 1988.

## Top gin markets

1. California, with 1,537.3 thousand
2. New York, 892.4
3. Florida, 845.0
4. Illinois, 658.9
5. Georgia, 627.0
6. New Jersey, 513.7
7. Pennsylvania, 474.9
8. Texas, 439.8
9. Michigan, 399.1
10. Virginia, 381.5

*Where'd you hear that?*
Jobson's Liquor Handbook 1989. Based on thousands of cases sold in 1988.

## Top gin markets by cases sold per thousand persons

1. District of Columbia, with 197.9
2. New Hampshire, 125.6
3. Georgia, 97.9
4. Delaware, 96.2
5. Nevada, 85.0
6. South Carolina, 78.9
7. Mississippi, 70.7
8. Maryland, 69.4
9. Florida, 68.3
10. Connecticut, 66.9

*Where'd you hear that?*
Jobson's Liquor Handbook 1989. Based on cases sold per thousand persons in 1988.

## Top metropolitan areas for gin consumption

1. New York-Northern New Jersey-Long Island, with 1,005.1 thousand
2. Los Angeles-Anaheim-Riverside, CA, 779.9
3. Chicago-Gary-Lake County, 537.0

# REFRESHMENT STAND

# REFRESHMENT STAND

4. San Francisco-Oakland-San Jose, CA, 431.0
5. District of Columbia, 365.0
6. Atlanta, GA, 361.4
7. Philadelphia-Wilmington-Trenton, 319.7
8. Boston-Lawrence-Salem, MA, 276.1
9. Detroit-Ann Arbor, MI, 245.4
10. Miami-Fort Lauderdale, FL, 204.2

*Where'd you hear that?*
Jobson's Liquor Handbook 1989. Based on 1988 case sales.

## *Leading importers of U.S. rum*

1. Mexico, with 189.8 thousand
2. Netherlands Antilles, 116.0
3. Netherlands, 90.4
4. United Kingdom, 58.0
5. Bahamas, 54.3
6. Others, total, 305.6

*Where'd you hear that?*
Jobson's Liquor Handbook. Based on 1988 volume, in thousands of proof gallons.

### Best-selling rum brands

1. Bacardi, with 68.30%
2. Seagram, 12.10%
3. Age International, 1.80%
4. Schenley, 1.40%
5. Charles Jacquin, 1.10%
6. Others, total, 15.30%

*Where'd you hear that?*
Jobson's Liquor Handbook. Based on 1988 market share, in percent.

### Leading rum brands

1. Bacardi, with 7,346 thousand
2. Ron Castillo, 721
3. Ronrico, 550
4. Captain Morgan, 430
5. Myers', 320
6. Don Q, 140
7. Cruzan, 117
8. Monarch, 112
9. Palo Viejo, 108
10. Mount Gay, 96

*Where'd you hear that?*
Jobson's Liquor Handbook. Based on 1988 estimated sales, in thousands of cases.

### Most advertised rum brands

1. Bacardi, with $8,368.3 thousand
2. Puerto Rican Rums, $5,498.2
3. Myers', $2,237.4
4. Bacardi Premium Black Label, $1,922.5
5. Captain Morgan Spiced Rum, $1,449.1
6. Mount Gay, $586.5
7. Don Q, $293.1
8. Ron Bacardi Gold Reserve, $170.2
9. Ronrico, $56.0
10. British Navy Pusser's, $53.0
11. Lamb's Navy, $34.7

*Where'd you hear that?*
Jobson's Liquor Handbook. Based on 1988 advertising expenditures, in thousands of dollars.

### Biggest scotch markets

1. Europe, with 35%
2. United States, 20%
3. Great Britain, 17%
4. Asia, 9%
5. Africa, 7%

6. Central and South America, 6%
7. Australia, 4%
8. Rest of world, 2%

*Where'd you hear that?*
New York Times. Based on market share of blended scotch whiskey in 1988.

## Top producers of Scotch

1. Guinness, with 36.8%
2. Allied-Lyons, 16.0%
3. Seagram, 8.4%
4. IDV (Grand Metropolitan PLC), 7.7%
5. Invergordon, 5.4%
6. Highland, 5.1%
6. American Brands (W & M), 5.1%
8. William Grant, 4.5%

*Where'd you hear that?*
Financial Times. Based on percent of production share.

## Most advertised Scotch whiskey brands

1. Dewar's, with $12,188.7 thousand
2. Chivas Regal, $7,435.1
3. J & B, $6,560.9
4. Johnnie Walker Red Label, $6,481.8
5. Cutty Sark, $3,677.7
6. Johnnie Walker Black Label, $3,411.5
7. Glenfiddich, $3,221.5
8. The Glenlivet, $2,537.0
9. Famous Grouse, $356.9
10. Johnnie Walker General Promotions, $329.9

*Where'd you hear that?*
Jobson's Liquor Handbook. Based on 1988 total advertising expenditures, in thousands of dollars.

## Best-selling brands of scotch

1. Dewar's, with 2,098 thousand
2. J & B, 1,255
3. Johnnie Walker Red Label, 1,060
4. Chivas Regal, 740
5. Cutty Sark, 730
6. Old Smuggler, 600
7. Scoresby, 598
8. Passport, 500
9. Johnnie Walker Black Label, 393
10. Usher's Green Stripe, 376

*Where'd you hear that?*
Jobson's Liquor Handbook. Based on 1988 estimated case sales, in thousands of cases.

## Best-selling single malt scotch brands

1. Glenlivet, 122,500
2. Grants Glenfiddich, 48,300
3. Macallan Glenlivet, 7,500
4. Laphroaig, 5,500
5. Glenmorangie, 4,300
6. Knockando, 3,700
7. Cardhu, 3,300
8. Claymore, 2,800
9. Glen Deveron, 2,800
10. Glen Garioch, 2,000

*Where'd you hear that?*
Jobson's Liquor Handbook. Based on 1988 case sales.

## Metropolitan areas with the most scotch whiskey sales

1. New York-Northern New Jersey-Long Island, with 2,508.7 thousand cases
2. Los Angeles-Anaheim-Riverside, CA, 1,096.4
3. San Francisco-Oakland-San Jose, CA, 742.8

# REFRESHMENT STAND

# REFRESHMENT STAND

4. Chicago-Gary-Lake County, IL-IN, 492.9
5. Washington, DC, 415.7
6. Philadelphia-Wilmington-Trenton, PA-DE-NJ,, 412.9
7. Miami-Fort Lauderdale, FL, 348.7
8. Boston-Lawrence-Salem, MA, 318.3
9. Tampa-St. Petersburg-Clearwater, FL, 218.0
10. Dallas-Fort Worth, TX, 206.6

*Where'd you hear that?*
Jobson's Liquor Handbook. Based on 1988 case sales, in thousands of cases.

## Best-selling tequila brands by market share

1. Heublein, with 46.50%
2. Domecq, 17.90%
3. Barton, 11.20%
4. Glenmore Distilleries Co., 4.80%
5. McCormick, 1.90%
6. Others, total, 17.7%

*Where'd you hear that?*
Jobson's Liquor Handbook. Based on 1988 market share, in percent.

## Leading tequila brands by sales

1. Jose Cuervo, with 1,500 thousand
2. Giro/Sauza, 607
3. Montezuma, 317
4. Juarez, 159
5. Pepe Lopez, 116
6. Arandas, 95
7. Matador, 81
8. El Toro, 78
9. Two Fingers, 64
10. Pancho Villa, 57

*Where'd you hear that?*
Jobson's Liquor Handbook. Based on 1988 estimated sales, in thousands of cases.

## Top markets for tequila case sales

1. California, with 804.9 thousand
2. Texas, 355.9
3. Florida, 170.2
4. Washington, 119.1
5. Illinois, 114.4
6. Arizona, 106.4
7. New York, 101.0
8. Michigan, 100.0
9. Colorado, 93.4
10. Georgia, 90.4

*Where'd you hear that?*
Jobson's Liquor Handbook 1989. Based on 1988 estimated sales, in thousands of cases.

## Top markets for tequila sales by cases per thousand persons

1. Nevada, with 64.7
2. Arizona, 30.7
3. New Mexico, 28.6
3. California, 28.6
5. District of Columbia, 28.5
6. Colorado, 28.4
7. Alaska, 27.9
8. Washington, 25.8
9. Hawaii, 23.0
10. Oregon, 21.5

*Where'd you hear that?*
Jobson's Liquor Handbook 1989. Based on 1988 estimated case sales per thousand persons.

# REFRESHMENT STAND

### Top metropolitan areas for tequila sales

1. Los Angeles-Anaheim-Riverside, CA, with 450.0 thousand
2. San Francisco-Oakland-San Jose, 245.1
3. New York-Northern New Jersey-Long Island, 118.7
4. Houston-Galveston-Brazoria, TX, 116.1
5. Dallas-Fort Worth, TX, 111.4
6. Chicago-Gary-Lake County, 103.5
7. Seattle-Tacoma, WA, 87.4
8. Phoenix, AZ, 79.1
9. Detroit-Ann Arbor, MI, 64.4
10. San Diego, CA, 59.3

*Where'd you hear that?*
Jobson's Liquor Handbook 1989. Based on 1988 case sales, in thousands.

### Most advertised tequila brands

1. Jose Cuervo, with $3,811.1 thousand
2. Monte Alban, $416.7
3. Sauza, NA
4. El Toro, NA
5. Puerto Vallarta, NA

*Where'd you hear that?*
Jobson's Liquor Handbook. Based on 1988 advertising expenditures, in thousands of dollars.

### Biggest magazine advertisers of tequila

1. Jose Cuervo, with $2,807.9 thousand
2. Monte Alban, $416.7

*Where'd you hear that?*
Jobson's Liquor Handbook 1989. Based on 1988 expenditures for magazine advertising, in thousands.

### Countries exporting the most vodka to the U.S.

1. Sweden, with 3,440.5 thousand
2. Soviet Union, 1,860.5
3. Finland, 468.0
4. West Germany, 118.0
5. Canada, 72.4
6. Others, total 270.3

*Where'd you hear that?*
Jobson's Liquor Handbook 1989. Based on thousands of proof gallons imported into the U.S. in 1988.

### *Largest importers of U.S. vodka*

1. Norway, with 246.4 thousand
2. Sweden, 132.7
3. Belgium, 71.2
4. Iceland, 70.3
5. Japan, 44.0
6. Others, total, 337.8

*Where'd you hear that?*
Jobson's Liquor Handbook. Based on 1988 U.S. exports, in thousands of proof gallons.

### Top 10 vodka brands

1. Smirnoff (Heublein), with 6,850 thousand cases
2. Popov (Heublein), 3,790
3. Absolut (Carillon), 2,370
4. Gordon's (Schenley), 2,140
5. Kamchatka (Jim Beam), 1,700

# REFRESHMENT STAND

6. Skol (Glenmore), 1,390
7. Gilbey's (Jim Beam), 1,310
8. Stolichnaya (Msr. Henri), 1,250
9. Wolfschmidt (Seagram), 1,010
10. Fleischmann's (Glenmore), 920

*Where'd you hear that?*
Beverage Dynamics. Based on 1989 case sales, in thousands.

### Best-selling vodka brands

1. Smirnoff (Heublein, Inc.), with 5,900 thousand
2. Popov (Heublein, Inc.), 3,250
3. Gordon's (Schenley Corp.), 1,653
4. Kamchatka (Jim Beam Brands Co.), 1,494
5. Absolut (Carillon Importers, Ltd.), 1,409
6. Skol (Glenmore Distilleries), 1,172
7. Gilbey's (Jim Beam Brands Co.), 1,160
8. Stolichnaya (Monsieur Henri Wines Ltd.), 895
9. Wolfschmidt (House of Seagram), 885
10. Fleischmann's (Glenmore Distilleries Co., 800

*Where'd you hear that?*
Jobson's Liquor Handbook. Based on 1988 estimated sales, in thousands of cases.

### Largest vodka suppliers

1. Heublein, with 33.40%
2. Jim Beam, 9.60%
2. Glenmore Distilleries Co., 9.60%
4. Schenley, 6.80%
5. Seagram, 5.90%
6. Others, total, 34.70%

*Where'd you hear that?*
Jobson's Liquor Handbook. Based on 1988 market share, in percent.

### Most highly advertised vodka brands

1. Absolut, with $7,467.9 thousand
2. Smirnoff, $6,031.5
3. Finlandia, $3,602.8
4. Stolichnaya, $3,300.3
5. Denaka, $950.3
6. Absolut Peppar Flavored, $219.0
7. Dimitri, $205.6
8. Georgi, $180.7
9. Suntory, $156.6
10. Vikin Fjord, $152.5

*Where'd you hear that?*
Jobson's Liquor Handbook 1989. Based on total 1988 advertising expenditures, in thousands.

### Most advertised vodka brands in magazines

1. Absolut, with $7,146.2 thousand
2. Smirnoff, $5,127.4
3. Finlandia, $2,883.9
4. Stolichnaya, $1,739.9
5. Denaka, $603.3
6. Absolut Peppar Flavored, $203.4
7. Elduris Iceland, $145.9
8. Vikin Fjord, $127.7
9. Romanoff, $123.8
10. Suntory, $104.7

*Where'd you hear that?*
Jobson's Liquor Handbook. Based on 1988 magazine ad spending, in thousands of dollars.

# REFRESHMENT STAND

## Most advertised vodka brands in newspapers

1. Stolichnaya, with $468.7
2. Smirnoff, $313.2
3. Dimitri, $205.6
4. Georgi, $180.7
5. Majorska, $135.7
6. Absolut, $78.1
7. Finlandia, $65.6
8. Suntory, $51.9

*Where'd you hear that?*
Jobson's Liquor Handbook. Based on 1988 newspaper ad spending in thousands of dollars.

## Most highly outdoor-advertised vodka brands

1. Stolichnaya, with $999.7 thousand
2. Finlandia, $563.7
3. Smirnoff, $561.3
4. Denaka, $311.4
5. Absolut, $243.6
6. Kamchatka, $62.6
7. Jacquin, $62.4
8. Country Club, $32.8
9. Vikin Fjord, $24.8
10. Absolut Peppar Flavored, $15.6
11. Heaven Hill, $5.7

*Where'd you hear that?*
Jobson's Liquor Handbook 1989. Based on outdoor advertising expenditures, in thousands.

## Leading metropolitan areas for vodka

1. New York-Northern New Jersey-Long Island, with 2,661.7 thousand
2. Los Angeles-Anaheim-Riverside, CA, 2,071.2
3. San Francisco-Oakland-San Jose, CA, 1,335.0
4. Chicago-Gary-Lake County, IL-IN, 1,204.5
5. Philadelphia-Wilmington-Trenton, 958.3
6. Boston-Lawrence-Salem, MA, 826.8
7. Detroit-Ann Arbor, MI, 800.4
8. Washington, DC, 757.6
9. Miami-Fort Lauderdale, FL, 544.8
10. Atlanta, GA, 511.8

*Where'd you hear that?*
Jobson's Liquor Handbook. Based on 1988 estimated sales, in thousands of cases.

## Top vodka markets by cases sold per thousand persons

1. District of Columbia, with 411.7
2. Nevada, 376.0
3. New Hampshire, 310.5
4. Connecticut, 199.6
5. South Carolina, 179.7
6. Delaware, 179.6
7. Florida, 179.2
8. Rhode Island, 169.3
9. Massachusetts, 168.6
10. Vermont, 164.6

*Where'd you hear that?*
Jobson's Liquor Handbook 1989. Based on 1988 cases sold per thousand persons.

## Top vodka markets by total cases sold

1. California, with 4,415.7 thousand
2. New York, 2,309.7
3. Florida, 2,218.5
4. Illinois, 1,396.2
5. Michigan, 1,286.0
6. New Jersey, 1,244.8
7. Texas, 1,225.3

**REFRESHMENT STAND**

8. Pennsylvania, 1,149.8
9. Massachusetts, 990.0
10. Georgia, 852.7

*Where'd you hear that?*
Jobson's Liquor Handbook. Based on total cases sold for 1988, in thousands.

# Personal Imagery

**Five largest international textile groups**

1. Kanebo (Japan), with £2.4 billion
2. Coats Viyella PLC (U.K.), £2.1
3. Armstrong (U.S.), £1.7
4. Chargeurs (France), £1.7
5. Milliken (U.S.), £1.6

*Where'd you hear that?*
Financial Times. Based on 1988 net profits, in billions of British pounds.

**World's leaders in textile exports**

1. Hong Kong, with 10.1%
1. Italy, 10.1%
3. West Germany, 9.1%
4. South Korea, 7.0%
5. China, 5.9%
6. Taiwan, 5.6%
7. France, 4.5%
8. Japan, 3.8%
9. Belgium/Luxembourg, 3.7%
10. United Kingdom, 3.3%

*Where'd you hear that?*
Financial Times. Based on 1987 share of world textile exports.

**World's leaders in textile imports**

1. United States, with 17.7%
2. West Germany, 13.6%
3. France, 6.9%
4. Hong Kong, 6.6%
5. United Kingdom, 6.3%
6. Japan, 4.7%
7. Netherlands, 4.1%
8. Italy, 3.7%
9. Soviet Union, 3.6%
10. Belgium/Luxembourg, 3.2%

*Where'd you hear that?*
Financial Times. Based on 1987 share of world textile imports.

# PERSONAL IMAGERY

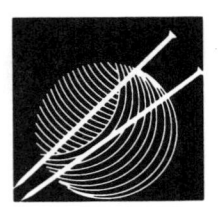

## Largest Asian textiles, clothing, and footwear companies

1. Toyobo Co. Ltd., with $4,011,307 thousand
2. Unitika Ltd., $2,643,578
3. Ssang Yong Corp., $2,141,417
4. Nisshinbo Industries Inc., $1,725,649
5. Kashiyama & Co. Ltd., $1,422,558
6. Gunze Ltd., $1,391,219
7. Nitto Boseki Co. Ltd., $1,290,622
8. Kurabo Industries Co. Ltd., $1,151,817
9. Daiwabo Co. Ltd., $1,098,351
10. Sanyo Shokai Ltd., $903,060

*Where'd you hear that?*
Asia's 7500 Largest Companies, Dun & Bradstreet. Based on 1989 sales, in thousands of dollars.

## Largest textile companies in Europe

1. Courtaulds PLC, with 3,557,449,790 ECUs
2. Coats Viyella PLC, 2,725,242,802
3. Coats Patons PLC, 1,488,392,796
4. Prouvost SA, 1,194,970,161
5. Manifatture Lane Gaetano Marzotto & Figli SPA, 971,272,000
6. Tootal Group PLC, 722,231,952
7. Boussac Saint Freres, 665,754,852
8. Forbo International SA, 657,998,537
9. John Crowther Group PLC, 525,753,818
10. Dawson International PLC, 522,058,548

*Where'd you hear that?*
Dun's Europa. Based on sales, in European currency units.

## Biggest corporations in the U.S. textile industry

1. Wickes, with $4,802 million
2. Armstrong World Industries, $2,864
3. West Point-Pepperell, $2,568
4. Burlington Holdings, $2,198
5. Springs Industries, $1,909
6. Amoskeag, $1,402
7. DWG, $1,185
8. Shaw Industries, $1,176
9. JPS Textile Group, Inc., $821
10. Cone Mills Corp., $715

*Where'd you hear that?*
Fortune, Fortune 500 Largest U.S. Industrial Corporations. Based on 1989 sales, in millions of dollars.

## Top corporations in the textile industry

1. Shaw Industries, with $911 million
2. Springs Industries, $646
3. Albany International, $428

*Where'd you hear that?*
Business Week, The Business Week 1000. Based on market value as of March 16, 1990, in millions of dollars.

## Leading textile companies

1. Burlington Industries, with $2,181,421 thousand
2. Springs Industries, $1,909,256
3. Fieldcrest Cannon, $1,362,440

4. West Point-Pepperell, $1,253,800
5. Shaw Industries, $1,175,962
6. Guilford Mills, $619,663
7. Interface Flooring Systems, $581,756
8. Dixie Yarns, $570,840
9. Delta Woodside Industries, $569,052
10. United Merchants & Manufacturers, $499,507

*Where'd you hear that?*
KSA Perspective, Textile Profile. Based on 1989 sales, in thousands of dollars.

## Largest public textile companies, by return on total equity

1. Crown Crafts, with 28.25%
2. Shaw Industries, 25.78%
3. Delta Woodside, 23.80%
4. Unifi, 21.57%
5. Texfi, 20.59%
6. Louisville Bedding, 17.04%
7. Interface, 15.63%
8. Concord Fabrics, 13.70%
9. Johnston Industries, 13.20%
10. Belding Heminway, 12.95%

*Where'd you hear that?*
KSA Perspective, Textile Profile. Based on 1989 percent of return on total equity.

## Top public textile companies by return on sales

1. Crown Crafts, with 6.98%
2. Johnston Industries, 6.75%
3. Unifi, 6.67%
4. Fab Industries, 6.38%
5. Texfi, 5.35%
6. Delta Woodside, 5.32%
7. Guilford Mills, 4.24%
8. Interface, 4.22%
9. Shaw Industries, 4.05%
10. Belding Heminway, 3.70%

*Where'd you hear that?*
KSA Perspective, Textile Profile. Based on 1989 percent of return on sales.

## *Most admired textile corporations*

1. Shaw Industries, with a rating of 7.25
2. Springs Industries, 7.09
3. Armstrong, 6.92
4. Guilford Mills, 6.72
5. Dixie Yarns, 6.55
6. Fieldcrest Cannon, 5.48
7. Burlington Holdings, 5.37
8. West Point-Pepperell, 5.18
9. DWG, 5.09
10. United Merchants & Manufacturers, 4.03

*Where'd you hear that?*
Fortune, America's Most Admired Corporations. Based on scores (0-10) derived from a survey of senior executives, outside directors, and financial analysts. Respondents ranked firms in their own industry on quality of management and products/services; innovation; long-term investment value; financial soundness; attraction and retention of talent; community and environmental responsibility; and use of assets.

## Largest textile companies in North Carolina

1. Texfi Industries, with 34.0%
2. Unifi, 21.6%
3. Wellco Enterprises, 18.8%
4. Guilford Mills, 12.7%
5. Rocky Mount Undergarment, 12.0%
6. Fieldcrest Cannon, 8.4%
7. Alba-Waldensian, 7.7%
8. Hampton Industries, 6.7%
9. B. B. Walker, 4.6%
10. Goldtex, 2.7%

# PERSONAL IMAGERY

# PERSONAL IMAGERY

*Where'd you hear that?*
Business North Carolina, Top 50 Public Companies. Based on fiscal year 1989 return on average common equity.

## Top companies in the U.S. nonwovens industry

1. Du Pont Co., with $490 million
2. Kimberly-Clark, $300
3. Veratec, $210
4. Dexter Nonwovens, $200
5. Chicopee, $160
6. Reemay, $155
7. Freudenberg, $125
7. Scott Nonwovens, $125
7. James River Corp., $125
10. Foss Manufacturing, $85

*Where'd you hear that?*
Nonwovens Industry. Based on worldwide roll goods sales, in millions of dollars.

## Best men's clothing designers

1. Don't know, with 21%
2. Calvin Klein, 13%
3. Pierre Cardin, 10%
4. Brooks Brothers, 8%
4. Hart, Schaffner & Marx, 8%

*Where'd you hear that?*
Wall Street Journal. Based on percent of respondents when asked to pick the 'finest, most elegant.'.

## Best women's clothing designers

1. Dont's know, with 17%
2. Christian Dior, 14%
3. Calvin Klein, 11%
4. Anne Klein, 8%
5. Gucci, 6%

*Where'd you hear that?*
Wall Street Journal. Based on percent of respondents when asked to pick the 'finest, most elegant.'.

## Largest apparel companies in Europe

1. Burton Group PLC, with 2.336.468.138 ECU
2. Gruppo Finanziario Tessile GFT SPA, 796.256.000
3. Benetton SPA, 778.855.268
4. Schiesser Holding AG, 751.998.328
5. William Baird PLC, 545.454.085
6. Macintosh NV, 471.411.717
7. Adler Bekleidungswerk AG & Co. KG Haibach, 421.861.536
8. Peek & Cloppenburg, 410.747.200
9. Klaus Steilmann GMBH & Co. Kommanditgesellschaft, 395.525.392
10. Groupe de la Cite, 385.206.669

*Where'd you hear that?*
Dun's Europa. Based on sales, in European currency units (ECU).

## Most productive U.S. apparel and shoe corporations

1. Reebok International, with $66.2 thousand
2. Nike, $56.4
3. Liz Claiborne, Inc., $32.0
4. Russell, $4.9
5. VF, $4.0
6. Fruit of the Loom, $2.9

*Where'd you hear that?*
Forbes, Forbes 500s Annual Directory. Based on 1989 profits per employee, in thousands of dollars. Ranks U.S.-based corporations that were publicly traded as of March 23, 1990.

## PERSONAL IMAGERY

### Biggest corporations in the apparel industry

1. Levi Strauss Assoc., with $3,628 million
2. VF, $2,540
3. Liz Claiborne, Inc., $1,411
4. Fruit of the Loom, $1,321
5. Hartmarx, $1,312
6. Crystal Brands, $857
7. Leslie Fay Cos., $786
8. Kellwood Co., $754
9. Russell, $688
10. Phillips-Van Heusen, $642

*Where'd you hear that?*
Fortune, Fortune 500 Largest U.S. Industrial Corporations. Based on 1989 sales, in millions of dollars.

### Biggest corporations in the apparel industry

1. Nike, with $2,336 million
2. Liz Claiborne, Inc., $2,105
3. Reebok International, $2,078
4. VF, $1,812
5. Russell, $1,081
6. Fruit of the Loom, $809
7. Stride Rite, $661
8. L. A. Gear Inc., $600
9. Oshkosh B'Gosh, $525
10. Gitano Group, $466
11. Brown Group, $440

*Where'd you hear that?*
Business Week, The Business Week 1000. Based on market value in millions of dollars.

### Top apparel performers

1. VF Corp., with $2,516,107
2. Sara Lee, $2,087,000
3. Liz Claiborne, Inc., $1,184,229
4. Fruit of the Loom, $1,004,700
5. Interco, $813,198
6. Kellwood Co., $698,156
7. Leslie Fay Cos., $682,690
8. Oxford Industries, $590,603
9. Hartmarx, $546,700
10. Russell Corp., $531,136

*Where'd you hear that?*
Apparel Industry Magazine. Based on sales, in thousands of dollars, for 1988.

### Most profitable apparel and shoe companies

1. Liz Claiborne, Inc., with 51.8%
2. Nike, 29.8%
3. VF, 26.3%
4. Phillips-Van Heusen, 20.3%
5. Russell, 18.3%
6. Kellwood Co., 15.3%
7. Oxford Industries, 9.6%
8. Crystal Brands, NA
9. Fruit of the Loom, NA
10. Gitano Group, NA
11. Leslie Fay Cos., NA
12. Reebok International, NA

*Where'd you hear that?*
Forbes, Annual Report on American Industry. Based on 10-year average return on equity. Ranks publicly held corporations only.

### Most admired apparel corporations

1. Liz Claiborne, Inc., with a rating of 7.87
2. VF, 7.32
3. Kellwood Co., 6.43
4. Leslie Fay Cos., 5.99

# PERSONAL IMAGERY

5. Hartmarx, 5.98
6. Phillips-Van Heusen, 5.92
7. Oxford Industries, 5.70
8. Fruit of the Loom, 5.37
9. Warnaco, 5.14

*Where'd you hear that?*
Fortune, America's Most Admired Corporations. Based on scores (0-10) derived from a survey of senior executives, outside directors, and financial analysts. Respondents ranked firms in their own industry on quality of management and products/services; innovation; long-term investment value; financial soundness; attraction and retention of talent; community and environmental responsibility; and use of assets.

## Leading manufacturers of activewear

1. Russell Corp., with $531 million
2. Tultex, $339
3. Ocean Pacific, $333
4. Bassett-Walker, $285 (est.)
5. Pannill, $248
6. Champion, $217
7. Woolrich, $180 (est.)
8. Nike, $171
9. Adidas, $164
10. Pacific Trail, $89

*Where'd you hear that?*
Sports Market Place, Market Statistics Report. Based on 1988 sales, in millions of dollars.

## Leading manufacturers of licensed apparel

1. Starter, with $60 million
2. Champion, $55 (est.)
2. Logo 7, $55 (est.)
4. Wilson, $43 (est.)
5. Chalkline, $42
6. Nutmeg Mills, $40
7. Salem Screen Printers, $20 (est.)
8. Sports Specialties, $19 (est.)
9. Artex, $15 (est.)
10. Rawlings, $12 (est.)

*Where'd you hear that?*
Sports Market Place, Market Statistics Report. Based on 1988 sales, in millions of dollars.

## Leading manufacturers of team apparel

1. Russell, with $240 million (est.)
2. Champion, $55 (est.)
3. Delong, $41 (est.)
4. Bike, $30 (est.)
5. Swingster, $21 (est.)
6. MacGregor Sand-Knit, $18 (est.)
7. Dodger, $15
8. Rawlings, $10 (est.)
8. Majestic, $10 (est.)
10. Wilson, $9

*Where'd you hear that?*
Sports Market Place, Market Statistics Report. Based on 1988 sales, in millions of dollars.

## Leading manufacturers of ski apparel

1. Head, with $33 million
2. Sport Obermeyer, $30
2. Columbia, $30
4. CB Sports, $28
5. Roffe, $24
6. White Stag, $17 (est.)
7. Skyr, $13
7. Descente, $13
9. Bogner, $11 (est.)
9. Fera International, $11
9. Slalom, $11

402

# PERSONAL IMAGERY

*Where'd you hear that?*
Sports Market Place, Market Statistics Report. Based on 1988 sales, in millions of dollars.

## Leading manufacturers of golf apparel

1. Izod, with $54.0 million (est.)
2. Aureus, $42.0
3. Pickering, $26.0 (est.)
4. La Mode, $23.0
5. Antigua, $16.2
6. SporThomson, $15.0
7. Sahara, $14.0 (est.)
8. Titleist, $12.9
9. Mark Scot, $11.0 (est.)
10. DiFini, $10.2

*Where'd you hear that?*
Sports Market Place, Market Statistics Report. Based on 1988 sales, in millions of dollars.

## Market share of sportswear sold in U.S. golf shops

1. Izod, with 14.0%
2. Aureus, 12.0%
3. Pickering, 6.5%
4. La Mode, 5.5%
5. Mark Scot, 5.0%
5. Antigua, 5.0%
7. Sahara, 4.5%
8. Titleist, 4.0%
8. PGA Tour, 4.0%
10. Tail, 3.0%

*Where'd you hear that?*
Golf Shop Operations, Annual Survey of the Golf Market. Based on 1989 market share, in percent.

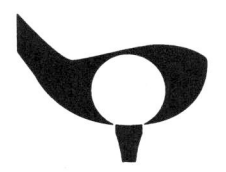

## Best leather goods

1. Gucci, with 37%
2. Don't know, 25%
3. Pierre Cardin, 8%
4. Christian Dior, 6%
5. Louis Vuitton, 5%
5. Bally, 5%

*Where'd you hear that?*
Wall Street Journal. Based on percent of respondents when asked to pick the 'finest, most elegant.'.

## Largest public shoe companies

1. F. W. Woolworth Co., with $2,574,000 thousand
2. Reebok International, $1,785,935
3. Brown Group, $1,706,565
4. Melville Corp., $1,632,346
5. Nike, $1,203,440
6. May Department Stores Co., $1,132,000
7. Edison Brothers Stores, $918,600
8. Interco, $915,447
9. Genesco, $462,766
10. Stride Rite Corp., $378,788

*Where'd you hear that?*
KSA Perspective, Footwear Profile. Based on 1988 fiscal year sales, in thousands of dollars.

## Leading manufacturers of athletic shoes worldwide

1. Adidas, with $2,350 million
2. Asics Tiger, $1,000
3. Reebok, $586
4. Puma, $423
5. Nike, $303
6. Converse, $100

403

# PERSONAL IMAGERY

7. Tretorn, $50
8. Brooks, $42 (est.)
9. New Balance, $25
10. L. A. Gear Inc., $21

*Where'd you hear that?*
Sports Market Place, Market Statistics Report. Based on 1988 sales, in millions of dollars.

## Leading manufacturers of athletic shoes

1. Reebok, with $1,155 million
2. Nike, $964
3. Converse, $232 (est.)
4. L. A. Gear Inc., $221
5. Avia, $201
6. Adidas, $168
7. Keds, $140 (est.)
8. New Balance, $98
9. British Knights, $83
10. Asics Tiger, $81

*Where'd you hear that?*
Sports Market Place, Market Statistics Report. Based on 1988 sales, in millions of dollars.

## Leading manufacturers of golf shoes

1. Foot-Joy, with $49.0 million
2. Etonic, $22.2
3. Nike, $15.0
4. Dexter, $14.0
5. Endicott Johnson, $11.2

*Where'd you hear that?*
Sports Market Place, Market Statistics Report. Based on 1988 sales, in millions of dollars.

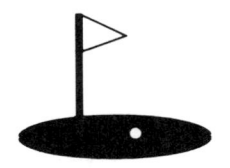

## Most productive personal products corporations

1. Clorox, with $25.8 thousand
2. Procter & Gamble, $17.8
3. Scott Paper, $13.3
4. Johnson & Johnson, $13.2
5. Colgate-Palmolive Co., $11.5
6. Kimberly-Clark, $10.9
7. Gillette Co., $9.5
8. Greyhound Dial, $3.0
9. Avon Products Inc., $1.9
10. Tambrands, $0.4

*Where'd you hear that?*
Forbes, Forbes 500s Annual Directory. Based on 1989 profits per employee, in thousands of dollars. Ranks U.S.-based corporations that were publicly traded as of March 23, 1990.

## Biggest corporations in the personal care industry

1. Procter & Gamble, with $22,929 million
2. Gillette Co., $5,036
3. Colgate-Palmolive Co., $4,049
4. International Flavors & Fragrances, $2,260
5. Clorox, $2,088
6. Avon Products Inc., $1,990
7. Tambrands, $1,626
8. Ecolab, $678
9. Alberto-Culver Co., $603
10. Block Drug, $581

*Where'd you hear that?*
Business Week, The Business Week 1000. Based on market value in millions of dollars.

## Best personal care products

1. Conair, with 46%
2. Clairol, 16%

404

# PERSONAL IMAGERY

3. Vidal Sassoon, 15%
4. Windmere, 14%
5. Remington, 13%
6. Norelco, 12%
7. Black & Decker, 9%
8. General Electric Co., 7%
9. Jerri Redding, 5%
10. Epilady, 3%

*Where'd you hear that?*
Discount Store News, Top Brands Survey. Based on 1989 percentage of discounters naming brand as best.

## Best health and beauty aids

1. Crest, with 39%
2. Colgate-Palmolive Co., 18%
3. Johnson & Johnson, 14%
4. Listerine, 13%
5. Procter & Gamble, 12%
6. Suave, 10%
7. Clairol, 7%
7. White Rain, 7%
9. Scope, 6%
9. Ivory, 6%

*Where'd you hear that?*
Discount Store News, Top Brands Survey. Based on 1989 percentage of discounters naming brand as best.

## Largest toiletries and cosmetics companies

1. Gillette Co., with $3,818.5 million
2. Avon Products Inc., $3,299.6
3. Alberto-Culver Co., $717.4
4. Helene Curtis Industries, $629.2
5. Carter-Wallace, $515.3
6. Block Drug, $409.4
7. Neutrogena, $203.2

8. MEM Co., $74.3

*Where'd you hear that?*
Chemicalweek, Chemicalweek 300. Based on 1989 sales, in millions of dollars.

## Most profitable personal products companies

1. Tambrands, with 29.1%
2. Gillette Co., 27.0%
3. Stanhome, 21.9%
4. Johnson & Johnson, 21.3%
5. Clorox, 20.1%
6. Kimberly-Clark, 17.6%
7. Block Drug, 16.9%
8. Colgate-Palmolive Co., 15.9%
9. Helene Curtis Industries, 15.2%
9. Proctor & Gamble, 15.2%

*Where'd you hear that?*
Forbes, Annual Report on American Industry. Based on 10-year average return on equity. Ranks publicly held corporations only.

## Preferred moisturizer brands

1. Oil of Olay, with 19%
2. Avon Products Inc., 11%
3. Clinique, 9%
4. Mary Kay, 5%
4. Pond's, 5%
6. Lancome, 3%
6. Estee Lauder, 3%
6. Neutrogena, 3%

*Where'd you hear that?*
Drug Store News, Gallup Poll—Women's Buying Habits. Based on percent of respondents surveyed.

# PERSONAL IMAGERY

## Biggest corporations in the soap and cosmetics industry

1. Procter & Gamble, with $21,689 million
2. Unilever U.S., $8,114
3. Colgate-Palmolive Co., $5,110
4. Avon Products Inc., $3,396
5. Revlon Group, $2,739
6. Clorox, $1,471
7. International Flavors & Fragrances, $870
8. Alberto-Culver Co., $717
9. Helene Curtis Industries, $629
10. Chemed, $594

*Where'd you hear that?*
Fortune, Fortune 500 Largest U.S. Industrial Corporations. Based on 1989 sales, in millions of dollars.

## Most admired soap and cosmetics corporations

1. Procter & Gamble, with a rating of 8.37
2. International Flavors & Fragrances, 7.45
3. Unilever U.S., 7.25
4. Noxell, 7.07
5. Clorox, 6.91
6. Colgate-Palmolive Co., 6.79
7. Alberto Culver Co., 6.03
8. Avon Products Inc., 5.04

*Where'd you hear that?*
Fortune, America's Most Admired Corporations. Based on scores (0-10) derived from a survey of senior executives, outside directors, and financial analysts. Respondents ranked firms in their own industry on quality of management and products/services; innovation; long-term investment value; financial soundness; attraction and retention of talent; community and environmental responsibility; and use of assets.

## *Leading world cosmetics companies*

1. L'Oreal, with $4.3 billion
2. Shiseido, $2.9
3. Avon Products Inc., $2.15
4. Unilever, $2.1
5. Revlon, $2.1
6. Kao Corp., $1.5
7. Procter & Gamble, $1.25
8. Estee Lauder Inc., $1.2
8. Bristol Myers Co., $1.2
10. Beiersdorf, $1.15

*Where'd you hear that?*
Financial Times. Based on 1988 estimated sales, in billions of U.S. dollars.

## Top cosmetic brands

1. Maybelline, with 74%
2. Cover Girl, 51%
3. Revlon, 35%
4. Max Factor, 11%
5. L'Oreal, 7%
6. Clarion, 3%
7. Clairol, 2%
7. Noxell, 2%
7. Maxell 2%
10. Coty, 1%

*Where'd you hear that?*
Discount Store News. Based on percentage of store managers at discount chains naming brand as a top performer.

# PERSONAL IMAGERY

## Best perfumes

1. Don't know, 18%
1. Chanel, 18%
3. Estee Lauder, 9%
3. Giorgio, 9%
5. Obsession, 6%
5. Opium, 6%

*Where'd you hear that?*
Wall Street Journal. Based on percent of respondents when asked to pick the 'finest, most elegant.'.

## Most efficient advertisers among bath soaps

1. Irish Spring, with $3.15
2. Ivory, $3.42
3. Zest, $4.82
4. Dial, $5.69
5. Coast, $6.06
6. Dove, $7.65
7. Caress, $19.71

*Where'd you hear that?*
Adweek's Marketing Week, Annual Measure of Efficiency. Based on efficiency quotient (average weekly cost of television advertising divided by average number of retained impressions).

## Leading mouthwashes

1. Warner-Lambert/Listerine, with 26.0%
2. Procter & Gamble/Scope, 23.0%
3. Pfizer/Plax, 14.5%
4. Warner-Lambert/Listermint, 6.7%
5. Merrell Dow/Cepacol, 4.5%
6. Colgate/Colgate Tartar-Control, 4.3%
7. Lever Bros./Signal, 3.4%
8. Colgate/Flourigard, 1.3%
9. Vipont/Viadent, 1.2%
10. Dep Corp./Lavoris, 1.0%

*Where'd you hear that?*
Advertising Age. Based on 1988 market share, expressed as a percentage.

## Best-selling blade razor systems

1. Gillette Co., with 32%
2. Schick, 9.2%
3. Others, total 5%

*Where'd you hear that?*
New York Times. Based on percentage of 1988 sales, out of a market total of $700 million.

## Best-selling razor systems including double-edged and injectors

1. Gillette Co., with 5.8%
2. Schick, 3.3%
3. Others, total 3.6%

*Where'd you hear that?*
New York Times. Based on percentage of 1988 sales, out of a market total of $700 million.

## Best-selling disposable razor systems

1. Gillette Co., with 24.1%
2. Bic, 8.9%
3. Schick, 4.1%
4. Others, total 4%

*Where'd you hear that?*
New York Times. Based on percentage of 1988 sales, out of a market total of $700 million.

# PERSONAL IMAGERY

### Market share of men's electric shavers

1. North American Philips (Norelco), with 49%
2. Remington, 26%
3. Braun, 16%
4. Matsushita (Panasonic), 4%
5. Ronson, 3%
6. Philips Home Products (Schick), 1%
6. Others, total, 1%

*Where'd you hear that?*
Appliance Manufacturer. Based on 1989 market share, in percent.

### Market share of women's electric shavers

1. Remington, with 62%
2. North American Philips (Norelco), 22%
3. Philips Home Products (Schick), 6%
4. Matsushita (Panasonic), 5%
5. Braun, 3%
6. Ronson, 1%
6. Others, total, 1%

*Where'd you hear that?*
Appliance Manufacturer. Based on 1989 market share, in percent.

### Leading manufacturers of hair removal products

1. Carter-Wallace, Nair, with 22%
2. Whitehall Labs, Neat, 16%
3. Inverness, One-Touch, 12%
4. Others, total, 50%

*Where'd you hear that?*
Non-Foods Merchandising. Based on market share, in percent.

### Preferred mousse brands

1. Clairol Condition, with 8%
2. Suave, 7%
2. White Rain, 7%
4. Vidal Sassoon, 4%
4. Alberto VO5, 4%
4. Salon Selectives, 4%
4. Perma Soft, 4%
8. Paul Mitchell, 3%
8. TRESemme, 3%
8. Finesse, 3%
8. Sebastian, 3%

*Where'd you hear that?*
Drug Store News, Gallup Poll—Women's Buying Habits. Based on percent of respondents surveyed.

### Preferred gel brands

1. Dep, with 9%
2. Paul Mitchell, 6%
2. Vavoom, 6%
4. L'Oreal Studio, 5%
4. Clairol, 5%
6. Dippity Do, 4%
7. Salon Selectives, 3%
7. Nexxus, 3%
9. TRESemme, 2%

*Where'd you hear that?*
Drug Store News, Gallup Poll—Women's Buying Habits. Based on percent of respondents surveyed.

### Preferred hair spray brands

1. White Rain, with 9%
2. Aqua Net, 8%
3. Final Net, 6%
4. Paul Mitchell, 5%
4. Rave, 5%
6. Salon Selectives, 3%
6. Clairol Mist, 3%
6. Finesse, 3%
6. Style, 3%

*Where'd you hear that?*
Drug Store News, Gallup Poll—Women's Buying Habits. Based on percent of respondents surveyed.

## Leading shampoos

1. Pert Plus, with 12.0%
2. Head & Shoulders, 9.5%
3. Suave, 8.5%
4. Finesse, 5.0%
5. Prell, 4.5%
5. Salon Selectives, 4.5%

*Where'd you hear that?*
U.S. Distribution Journal. Based on market share, in percent.

# PERSONAL IMAGERY

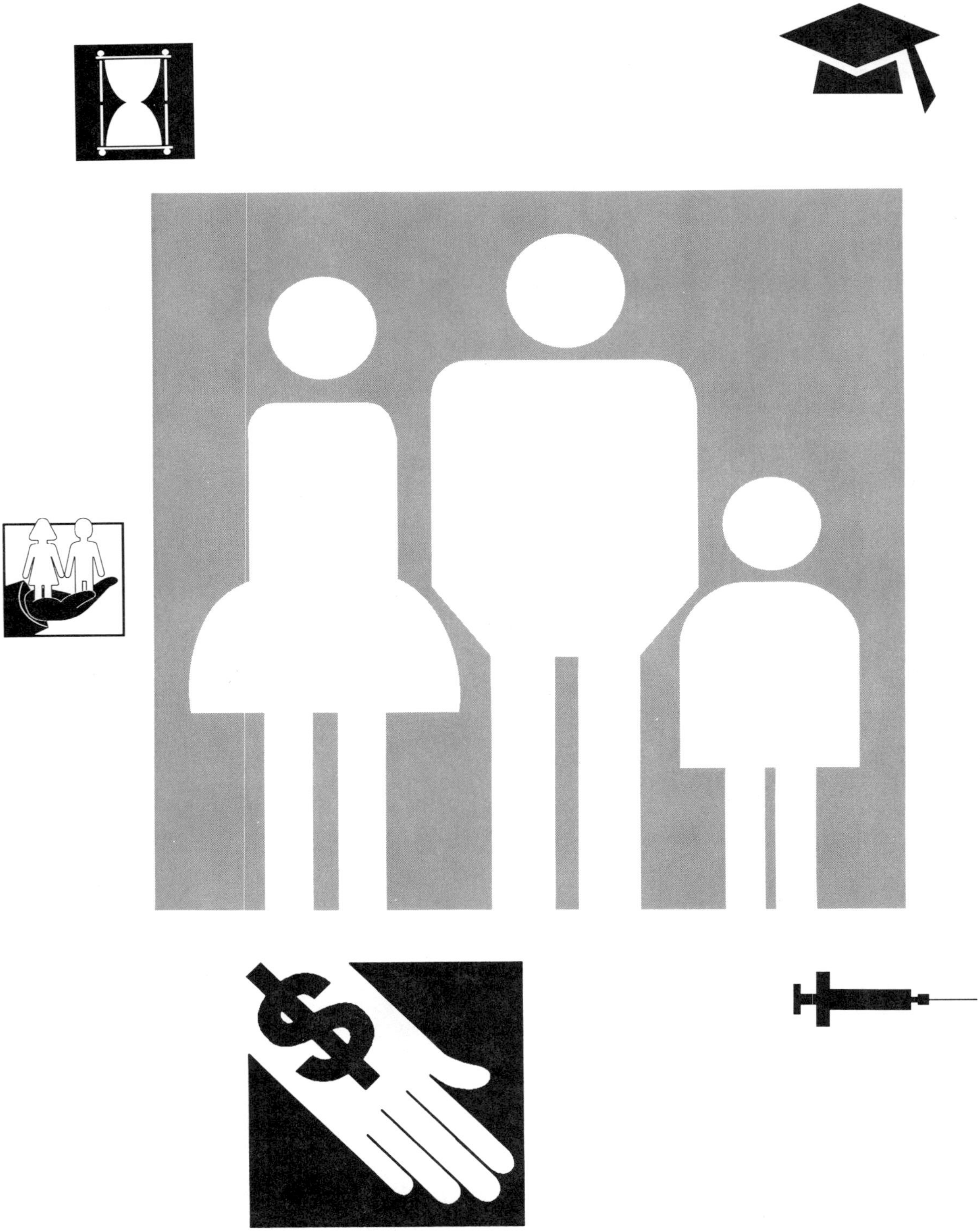

# Life Lessons

### Largest diaper manufacturers

1. Procter & Gamble, with 49%
2. Kimberly-Clark Corp., 33%
3. Weyerhaeuser Co., 10%
4. Others, total, 8%

*Where'd you hear that?*
Wall Street Journal. Based on market share, in percent.

### Best-selling disposable diapers

1. Huggies, with 32.5%
2. Pampers, 25.5%
3. Luvs, 24.5%
4. Private label diapers and others, 17.5%

*Where'd you hear that?*
Wall Street Journal. Based on market share of 1989 sales, in percent.

### Best-selling brands of disposable diapers

1. Pampers, with 50%
2. Huggies, 36%
3. Luvs, 25%
4. Store brand generic, 4%
5. Smilee/Smiles, .5%
5. Cuddles, .5%
7. Unspecified, 5%
8. Miscellaneous, 3%

*Where'd you hear that?*
Inside Print. Based on market share as reported in *American Baby*..

### Top states in primary and secondary school construction markets

1. California, with $526 million
2. Florida, $744
3. Texas, $688
4. New York, $561
5. Pennsylvania, $514
6. Georgia, $399
7. Indiana, $327
8. North Carolina, $316
9. Washington, $290
10. Virginia, $288

# LIFE LESSONS

*Where'd you hear that?*
ENR, Top 20 States in Major Construction Markets. Based on eleven-month cumulative contract awards, 1989 vs. 1988, in millions of dollars.

## Largest school districts

1. New York City Board of Education, with $6,339.0 million
2. Los Angeles Unified School District, $3,075.7
3. Chicago Public Schools, $1,887.6
4. Dade County (FL) School District, $1,593.0
5. Philadelphia School District, $1,148.5
6. Broward County (FL) School Board, $1,082.7
7. Fairfax County (VA) Public Schools, $877.8
8. Detroit Public Schools, $813.0
9. Clark County (NV) School District, $678.3
10. Hillsborough County School District (FL), $676.7

*Where'd you hear that?*
City & State. Based on fiscal year 1989 governmental funds revenue, in millions of dollars.

### States spending the most on textbooks per pupil

1. District of Columbia, with $64.71
2. South Dakota, $56.06
3. New Jersey, $50.05
4. New Mexico, $47.48
5. Arizona, $47.24

*Where'd you hear that?*
City & State, Top 50 School Districts. Based on 1987 estimates of spending per pupil.

### States spending the least on textbooks per pupil

1. Idaho, with $17.16
2. Utah, $20.04
3. Louisiana, $22.78
4. Alabama, $23.40
5. Washington, $24.58

*Where'd you hear that?*
City & State, Top 50 School Districts. Based on 1987 estimates of spending per pupil.

### States with the highest textbook sales

1. Texas, with $139.0 million
2. California, $134.2
3. New York, $125.0
4. Illinois, $87.4
5. Pennsylvania, $78.6

*Where'd you hear that?*
City & State, Top 50 School Districts. Based on 1987 textbook sales, in millions of dollars.

### States with the lowest textbook sales

1. Vermont, with $2.9 million
2. Alaska, $3.1
3. Idaho, $3.8
4. Wyoming, $4.4
5. Delaware, $5.0

*Where'd you hear that?*
City & State, Top 50 School Districts. Based on 1987 textbook sales, in millions of dollars.

# LIFE LESSONS

## Leading school and college municipal bond issuers

1. New York State Dormitory Authority, with $1,661,400 thousand
2. Florida State Board of Education, $861,100
3. Colorado Association of School Boards, $300,000
4. California Educational Facilities Authority, $286,100
5. University of California, $251,300
6. Broward County School District, FL, $210,200
7. Missouri Health & Educ. Facs. Authority, $203,000
8. Dade County (FL) School District, $200,000
9. Houston Independent School District, TX, $190,100
10. Iowa School Cash Anticipation Program, $187,700

*Where'd you hear that?*
Bond Buyer, Bond Buyer Yearbook. Based on 1989 dollar amount, in thousands.

## Leading student loan municipal bond issuers

1. South Dakota Student Loan Corp., with $396,200 thousand
2. Arizona Educ. Loan Marketing Corp., $131,100
3. Illinois Student Assistance Commission, $117,600
4. Indiana Security Market for Educ. Loans, $110,000
5. Montana Higher Education Student Assistance Corp., $105,800
6. North Dakota, $100,000
6. Braxos Higher Education Auth. Texas, $100,000
8. Illinois State Scholarship Commission, $85,100
9. Colorado Student Obl. Bond Authority, $80,000
9. Central Texas Higher Education Authority, $80,000

*Where'd you hear that?*
Bond Buyer, Bond Buyer Yearbook. Based on 1989 dollar amount, in thousands.

## Largest library automation systems

1. CLSI, with 19%
2. DYNIX, 13%
3. Innovative, 10%
4. OCLC, 9%
5. DRA, 8%
5. NOTIS, 8%
7. VTLS, 6%
7. GEAC Advanced, 6%
10. COMSTOW, 3%
10. SIRSI, 3%
10. Inlex, 3%

*Where'd you hear that?*
Library Journal. Based on percentage of U.S. market share, all years.

## Largest library automation systems

1. DYNIX, with 17%
1. Innovative, 17%
3. CLSI, 12%
3. SIRSI, 12%
5. DRA, 10%
6. INLEX, 7%
7. NOTIS, 4%
8. VTLS, 3%
8. UNISYS, 3%
10. COMSTOW, 2%
10. GEAC Advanced, 2%

# LIFE LESSONS

*Where'd you hear that?*
Library Journal. Based on percentage of U.S. market share, 1989.

## Largest gifts to education

1. New York University from Leonard N. Stern, with $30,000,000
2. Baylor College of Medicine from Albert B. Alkek, $25,000,000
2. Ohio State University from Leslie H. Wexner, $25,000 000
4. University of Texas Southwestern Medical Center from Perot Foundation, $20,000,000
4. National Academy of Sciences and the Institute of Medicine from W. K. Kellogg Foundation, $20,000,000
4. Spelman College from Bill and Camille Cosby, $20,000,000
7. Northwestern University from Joseph & Bessie Feinberg Foundation, $17,000,000
8. Massachusetts Institute of Technology from Howard Hughes Medical Institute, $15,000,000
8. Washington University from John M. Olin Foundation, $15,000,000
8. John F. Kennedy School of Government of Harvard University from A. Alfred Taubman, $15,000,000
8. Columbia University from John M. Olin Foundation, $15,000,000

*Where'd you hear that?*
Giving USA Annual Report. Based on value of gift.

## Top national universities

1. Yale University, with 100.0
2. Princeton University, 99.2
3. Harvard College and Radcliffe College, 97.6
4. California Institute of Technology, 97.2
5. Duke University, 94.3
6. Stanford University, 94.2
7. Massachusetts Institute of Technology, 90.6
8. Dartmouth College, 89.8
9. University of Chicago, 88.5
10. Rice University, 84.8

*Where'd you hear that?*
U.S. News & World Report, America's Best Colleges. Based on composite rating in five academic areas. Overall score is based on the school's percentile score when measured in the five categories. See article for details.

## Top national liberal arts colleges

1. Swarthmore College, with 100.0
2. Amherst College, 99.0
3. Williams College, 96.5
4. Pomona College, 90.7
5. Bryn Mawr College, 89.0
5. Wellesley College, 89.0
7. Smith College, 88.1
8. Wesleyan University, 87.6
9. Oberlin College, 86.8
10. Grinnell College, 85.6

*Where'd you hear that?*
U.S. News & World Report, America's Best Colleges. Based on composite rating in five academic areas. Overall score is based on the school's percentile score when measured in the five categories. See article for details.

# LIFE LESSONS

## America's best law schools

1. Yale University, with 100.0
2. University of Chicago, 91.9
3. Stanford University, 90.7
4. Columbia University, 89.2
5. Harvard University, 88.3
6. New York University, 86.0
7. University of Michigan, 85.0
8. Duke University, 84.5
9. University of Pennsylvania, 83.6
10. University of Virginia, 83.2

*Where'd you hear that?*
U.S. News & World Report. Based on overall score in *U.S. News* survey of law schools. Ranking is derived from consideration of 6 factors: student selectivity, placement, graduation rates, instructional resources, research, and academic reputation.

## Highest rated medical schools

1. Harvard University, with 100.0
2. Johns Hopkins University, 70.8
3. Duke University, 67.5
4. University of California, San Francisco, 63.9
5. Yale University, 62.4
6. Washington University, 60.5
7. Cornell University, 60.4
8. Columbia University, 59.7
9. University of Washington, 58.3
10. University of Pennsylvania, 57.8

*Where'd you hear that?*
U.S. News & World Report. Based on ranking derived from consideration of 6 factors: student selectivity, placement, graduation rates, instructional resources, and research and academic reputation. Factors are then weighted, totaled and a final ranking ach.

## Biggest lenders of student loans

1. Salle Mae, with $11,318 million
2. Citibank, $1,892
3. California Student Loan Financing, $1,314
4. Chase Manhattan Bank, $967
5. Nebraska Higher Education Loans, $837

*Where'd you hear that?*
American Banker. Based on fiscal year 1988 loans, in millions of dollars.

## World's largest arms manufacturers

1. McDonnell Douglas, with $9,726 million
2. General Dynamics Corp., $8,451
3. Lockheed Corp., $8,154
4. General Electric Co., $7,759
5. General Motors Corp., $6,858
6. British Aerospace, $5,666
7. Northrop, $5,344
8. Boeing Co., $5,125
9. Thomson-CSF, $4,693
10. Raytheon, $4,506

*Where'd you hear that?*
Financial World. Based on revenues, in millions of dollars.

# LIFE LESSONS

## Military powers with the highest military expenditures

1. Soviet Union, with $303 billion
2. United States, $296.2
3. France, $34.8
4. West Germany, $34.1
5. United Kingdom, $31.6
6. Japan, $24.3
7. China, $20.7
8. Iran, NA
9. Italy, $18.4
10. Poland, $18.0

*Where'd you hear that?*
World Military Expenditures and Arms Transfers, U.S. Arms Control and Disarmament Agency. Based on 1987 military expenditures, in billions of current dollars.

## Leading arms importers

1. Iraq
2. Saudi Arabia
3. India
4. Syria
5. Vietnam
6. Cuba
7. Egypt
8. Ethiopia
9. Turkey
10. Czechoslovakia

*Where'd you hear that?*
Aviation Week & Space Technology. Based on billions of dollars spent on arms sales, 1987. Figures originally represented by bar graph. Original soruce: ACDA.

## Most productive aerospace and defense corporations

1. GenCorp, Inc., with $13.7 thousand
2. General Electric Co., $13.4
3. Sundstrand, $8.8
4. Loral, $8.1
5. Raytheon, $6.9
6. Rockwell International, $6.5
7. Allied-Signal, $4.9
8. E-Systems, $4.8
9. Martin Marietta, $4.6
9. Textron, $4.6

*Where'd you hear that?*
Forbes, Forbes 500s Annual Directory. Based on 1989 profits per employee, in thousands of dollars. Ranks U.S.-based corporations that were publicly traded as of March 23, 1990.

## Most profitable aerospace and defense companies

1. Lockheed Corp., with 30.4%
2. Pall, 24.8%
3. General Dynamics Corp., 22.9%
4. Martin Marietta, 22.6%
5. Precision Castparts, 21.9%
6. Rockwell International, 21.4%
6. Raytheon, 21.4%
8. Sequa, 19.7%
9. Loral, 18.8%
10. E-Systems, 18.7%

*Where'd you hear that?*
Forbes, Annual Report on American Industry. Based on 10-year average return on equity. Ranks publicly held corporations only.

## Contractors receiving the largest dollar volume of military prime contract awards for RDT & E

1. McDonnell Douglas Aircraft, with $2,156,223 thousand
2. Martin Marietta Corp., $2,025,741
3. Boeing Co., $878,735
4. Grumman Aerospace Corp., $843,384
5. Raytheon Co., $840,902

# LIFE LESSONS

6. Rockwell International Corp., $737,671
7. General Electric Co., $710,174
8. McDonnell Douglas Corp., $663,984
9. TRW, Inc., $658,703
10. Lockheed Missiles & Space Co., $611,153

*Where'd you hear that?*
*500 Contractors Receiving the Largest Dollar Volume of Military Prime Contract Awards for RDT & E .* Based on fiscal year 1988 net value of Defense Department prime contract awards over $25,000 for research, development, test & evaluation (RDT & E) to business firms, in thousands of dollars.

**Largest defense contractors**

1. McDonnell Douglas, with $8,617,202 thousand
2. General Dynamics Corp., $6,899,209
3. General Electric Co., $5,771,028
4. Raytheon, $3,760,681
5. General Motors Corp., $3,691,507
6. Lockheed Corp., $3,651,547
7. United Technologies, $3,556,292
8. Martin Marietta, $3,336,555
9. Boeing Co., $2,868,416
10. Grumman Corp., $2,373,139

*Where'd you hear that?*
Defense News, Top 100 Defense Contractors. Based on 1989 award totals, in thousands of dollars.

## *Largest Japanese defense contractors*

1. Mitsubishi Heavy Industries, with 364,192 million yen
2. Kawasaki Heavy Industries, 150,253
3. Mitsubishi Electric, 100,848
4. Toshiba, 83,084
5. Ishikawajima-Harima Heavy Industries, 77,356
6. NEC, 73,583
7. Japan Steel Works, 31,117
8. Komatsu, 23,576
9. Fuji Heavy Industries, 22,139
10. Fujitsu Ltd., 16,830

*Where'd you hear that?*
Far Eastern Economic Review. Based on amount of defense contracts in 1988, in millions of Japanese yen.

**Largest defense electronics contractors**

1. General Motors Hughes Electronics, with $6.70 billion
2. Thomson-CSF, $4.64
3. Raytheon, $4.60
4. General Electric Co., $4.20
5. Lockheed Corp., $4.10
6. Martin Marietta, $3.10
7. Rockwell, $3.00
8. TRW, $2.80
9. Honeywell Inc., $2.59
10. Westinghouse, $2.45

*Where'd you hear that?*
Electronic Business. Based on 1988 worldwide sales, in billions of dollars.

417

# LIFE LESSONS

## Top Canadian life insurance companies

1. Confederation Life Insurance Co., with $3,937,633 thousand Canadian
2. Manufacturer's Life, $3,897,465
3. Great-West Life Assurance Co. of Canada, $3,470,989
4. Sun Life Assurance Co. of Canada, $3,371,331
5. Canada Life Assurance Co., $2,030,797
6. Mutual Life of Canada, $1,956,000
7. Crown Life Insurance Co., $1,946,558
8. Lonvest Corp., $1,820,796
9. London Life Insurance Co., $1,522,526
10. Metropolitan Life Insurance Co., $875,538

*Where'd you hear that?*
Financial Post 500. Based on 1989 premiums, in thousands of Canadian dollars.

## Top life and health insurance companies

1. Prudential Insurance Co. of America, with 4,722,103,171
2. Metropolitan Life Insurance Co., 2,343,051,643
3. American Family Life, Columbus, 1,806,121,047
4. Mutual of Omaha Insurance Co., 1,732,016,890
5. Connecticut General Life Insurance, 1,671,503,068
6. Health Care Service Corp., 1,614,770,441
7. Aetna Life Insurance Co., 1,604,322,490
8. Principal Mutual Life, 1,527,137,622
9. Travelers Insurance Co., 1,493,174,146
10. Continental Assurance Co., 1,333,146,276

*Where'd you hear that?*
Best's Review, Life/Health edition. Based on accident and health premiums written in 1988.

## Largest life insurance companies

1. Prudential of America, with $129,118.1 million
2. Metropolitan Life, $98,740.3
3. Equitable life Assurance, $52,511.9
4. Aetna Life, $52,022.6
5. Teachers Insurance & Annuity, $44,374.1
6. New York Life, $37,302.4
7. Connecticut General Life Insurance, $33,991.2
8. Travelers, $32,087.5
9. John Hancock Mutual Life Insurance Co., $30,924.8
10. Northwestern Mutual Life, $28,500.0

*Where'd you hear that?*
Fortune, Service 500. Based on assets as of December 31, 1989, in millions of dollars.

## Weakest life insurers

1. Tandem Insurance Group, Inc.
2. Mutual Service Life
3. Integrity Life

418

# LIFE LESSONS

4. Hartford Life & Accident Insurance Co.
5. Kemper Investors Life
6. Integrated Resources Life
7. Provident National Assurance
8. Lincoln National Pension
9. Union Labor Life
10. First Capital Life

*Where'd you hear that?*
U.S. News & World Report. Based on a combination of surplus ratio, profitability index, and investment portfolio factors.

## Strongest life insurers

1. United Insurance Company of America
2. Liberty National Life Insurance Co.
3. Jefferson-Pilot Life
4. American Family Life
5. State Farm Life
6. Associates Financial Life
7. Southern Farm Bureau Life
8. Security Life of Denver
9. United American Insurance
10. Ameritas Life Insurance

*Where'd you hear that?*
U.S. News & World Report. Based on a combination of surplus ratio, profitability index, and investment portfolio factors.

## Most productive life and health insurance corporations

1. Conseco, with $94.4 thousand
2. First Capital Holding, $70.7
3. First Executive, $50.1
4. Broad, $46.2
5. USLife, $39.0
6. UNUM, $38.2
7. Torchmark, $35.4
8. Capital Holding, $34.5
9. Jefferson-Pilot Life, $31.0
10. Provident Life & Accident, $27.9

*Where'd you hear that?*
Forbes, Forbes 500s Annual Directory. Based on 1989 profits per employee, in thousands of dollars. Ranks U.S.-based corporations that were publicly traded as of March 23, 1990.

## Most profitable life and health insurance companies

1. American Family, with 20.5%
2. Torchmark, 19.6%
3. Capital Holding, 16.5%
4. American National Insurance, 14.0%
5. Provident Life & Accident, 13.4%
6. Jefferson-Pilot Life, 11.8%
7. BMA, 11.7%
8. Monarch Capital, 11.3%
9. USLife, 10.4%
10. Liberty Corp., 9.4%

*Where'd you hear that?*
Forbes, Annual Report on American Industry. Based on 10-year average return on equity. Ranks publicly held corporations only.

## Leading life insurance companies

1. Metropolitan Life Insurance Co., with $15,504,877,797
2. Prudential Insurance Co. of America, $14,396,677,717
3. Aetna Life Insurance Co., $8,266,054,143
4. New York Life Insurance Co., $6,929,288,094
5. Principal Mutual Life, $5,078,061,328
6. Equitable Life Assurance Society, $4,934,058,984

# LIFE LESSONS

7. John Hancock Mutual Life Insurance Co., $4,865,888,636
8. Allstate Life Insurance Co., $4,298,020,124
9. Travelers Insurance Co., $4,200,875,560
10. Northwestern Mutual Life Insurance, $3,542,148,196

*Where'd you hear that?*
Best's Review, Life/Health edition. Based on 1988 premiums.

## Most admired life insurance corporations

1. Northwestern Mutual Life, with a rating of 7.30
2. Prudential of America, 6.94
3. Metropolitan Life, 6.31
4. New York Life, 6.19
5. Aetna Life, 6.05
6. Teachers Insurance & Annuity, 6.04
7. Connecticut General Life Insurance, 5.86
8. John Hancock Mutual Life Insurance Co., 5.81
9. Travelers, 5.24
10. Equitable Life Assurance, 5.16

*Where'd you hear that?*
Fortune, America's Most Admired Corporations. Based on scores (0-10) derived from a survey of senior executives, outside directors, and financial analysts. Respondents ranked firms in their own industry on quality of management and products/services; innovation; long-term investment value; financial soundness; attraction and retention of talent; community and environmental responsibility; and use of assets.

## Universal life insurance leaders by direct premiums

1. Pruco Life (AZ), with $706,437 thousand
2. Metropolitan Insurance & Annuity, $603,167
3. Transamerica Occidental, $368,622
4. New York Life & Annuity, $364,053
5. Aid Association for Lutherans, $322,826
6. State Farm Life, $260,852
7. First Capital Life, $224,759
8. Aetna Life & Annuity, $219,079
9. Lincoln National, $214,591
10. Kentucky Central, $192,899

*Where'd you hear that?*
Best's Review, Life/Health edition. Based on 1988 direct premiums, in thousands of dollars.

## Universal life insurance leaders by insurance issued

1. Metropolitan Insurance & Annuity, with $14,989,502 thousand
2. Pruco Life (AZ), $11,497,572
3. State Farm Life, $9,658,145
4. Transamerica Occidental, $5,983,784
5. Aid Association for Lutherans, $5,724,838
6. Kentucky Central, $5,079,579
7. Aetna Life & Annuity, $4,289,916
8. Farmers New World, $4,014,465
9. Ohio State Life, $3,703,447
10. Alexander Hamilton, $3,657,838

# LIFE LESSONS

*Where'd you hear that?*
Best's Review, Life/Health edition. Based on 1988 insurance issued, in thousands of dollars.

## Universal life insurance leaders by insurance in force

1. Metropolitan Ins. & Annuity, with $55,248,219 thousand
2. Pruco Life (AZ), $45,465,886
3. Aid Association for Lutherans, $41,059,033
4. New York Life & Annuity, $40,615,537
5. State Farm Life, $31,737,221
6. Transamerica Occidental, $26,257,114
7. Life of Virginia, $20,756,019
8. Aetna Life & Annuity, $20,651,203
9. SMA Life Assurance, $17,661,503
10. First Capital Life, $17,169,369

*Where'd you hear that?*
Best's Review, Life/Health edition. Based on 1988 insurance in force, in thousands of dollars.

## Best-performing variable whole life policies

1. Guardian's ValuePlus (VL), with 6.6
2. Northwestern Mutual's Variable Life, 6.2
3. Chubb Life's Ensemble II (VL), 5.6
4. Ohio National's Vari-Vest II, 4.9
4. Lincoln National's Emancipator I (VL), 4.9
6. Ameritas Life Insurance Corp's UniVar Life, 3.3

*Where'd you hear that?*
Financial Planning, Variable Life and Annuities Survey. Based on contract price index.

## Best-performing variable universal life policies

1. Safeco's Variable Universal Life, with 5.1
2. Lutheran Brotherhood's Flexible Premium Variable Life, 5.0
3. Golden American Life Insurance's Golden American (VUL), 4.7
3. Pacific Mutual's Pacific Select Exec. (VUL), 4.7
5. Manufacturers Life's Variable Universal Life, 4.1
5. Century Life's Univers-All Life 2000, 4.1
7. Northwestern National's Select Life, 3,9
8. New England's Zenith Life Plus, 3.7
9. Western Reserve Life's Equity Protector, 2.8

*Where'd you hear that?*
Financial Planning, Variable Life and Annuities Survey. Based on contract price index.

## Best-performing single-premium variable life policies

1. Northwestern Mutual's Variable Single Premium Life, with 7.9
2. Bankers Security's Dynamic Variable Life, 7.1
3. Guardian's ValuPlus (SPVL), 6.8
3. Western Reserve Life's WRL Freedom Plus, 6.8
5. Penn Mutual Life's Momentum Builder (SPVL), 6.6

# LIFE LESSONS

6. Lutheran Brotherhood's Single Premium Variable Life, 6.5
7. Mass Mutual's Variable Life Plus, 6.4
8. Ameritas Life Insurance Corp.'s Overture, 6.3
8. Lincoln National's American Legacy (VUL), 6.3
8. Pacific Mutual's Pacific Select (SPVL), 6.3

*Where'd you hear that?*
Financial Planning, Variable Life and Annuities Survey. Based on contact price index.

## Leading Canadian property and casualty insurance companies

1. Laurentian General Insurance Co., with $1,318,554 thousand Canadian
2. Allstate Insurance Co. of Canada, $748,675
3. Dominion of Canada General Insurance Co., $741,000
4. General Accident Assurance Co. of Canada, $506,095
5. Pilot Insurance Co., $484,790
6. Wawanesa Mutual Insurance Co., $426,542
7. Wellington Insurance Co., $426,350
8. Guardian Insurance Co. of Canada, $420,483
9. Co-Operators Financial Services, $394,422
10. Manitoba Public Insurance Corp., $383,563

*Where'd you hear that?*
Financial Post 500. Based on 1989 premiums, in thousands of Canadian dollars.

## Largest property and casualty insurance companies

1. State Farm Mutual Auto, with $16,872,709 thousand
2. Allstate Insurance Co., $12,896,512
3. State Farm Fire & Casualty, $5,331,663
4. Liberty Mutual Insurance Co., $5,259,319
5. Aetna Casualty & Surety, $4,616,469
6. Farmers Insurance Exchange, $4,268,664
7. Continental Casualty, $4,163,070
8. Nationwide Mutual Insurance, $4,059,449
9. United States Fidelity & Guaranty, $3,300,317
10. Travelers Indemnity Co., $3,007,927

*Where'd you hear that?*
National Underwriter, Property & Casualty edition. Based on 1989 premiums, in thousands of dollars.

## Largest property and casualty insuranace groups

1. State Farm IL, with $22,221,748 thousand
2. Allstate Insurance Group, $12,896,512
3. Aetna Life & Casualty Group, $7,564,108
4. American International Group, $7,140,432
5. Liberty Mutual Insurance Co., $6,445,195
6. Nationwide Corp., $6,000,104
7. CNA Insurance Group, $5,458,333
8. Hartford F & C Group, $4,967,431

9. Travelers Insurance Cos., $4,816,832
10. Farmers Insurance Group, $4,670,302

*Where'd you hear that?*
National Underwriter, Property & Casualty edition. Based on 1989 premiums, in thousands of dollars.

## Most productive property and casualty insurance corporations

1. Argonaut Group, with $94.3 thousand
2. 20th Century Industries, $58.5
3. Chubb Group of Insurance Cos., $42.9
4. Geico Corp. Group, $31.6
5. St. Paul Cos. $30.1
6. Hartford Steam Boiler, $22.9
7. Berkshire Hathaway, $22.4
8. Ohio Casualty, $18.3
9. Hanover Insurance, $14.3
10. Progressive, $13.1

*Where'd you hear that?*
Forbes, Forbes 500s Annual Directory. Based on 1989 profits per employee, in thousands of dollars. Ranks U.S.-based corporations that were publicly traded as of March 23, 1990.

## Most profitable property and casualty insurance companies

1. Geico Corp. Group, with 33.6%
2. Progressive, 29.9%
3. 20th Century Industries, 29.5%
4. Hartford Steam Boiler, 23.5%
5. Mercury General, 22.8%
6. Selective Insurance, 18.3%
7. First American Financial, 17.6%

8. Hanover Insurance, 17.2%
9. Berkshire Hathaway, 15.9%
10. Chubb Group of Insurance Cos., 15.2%

*Where'd you hear that?*
Forbes, Annual Report on American Industry. Based on 10-year average return on equity. Ranks publicly held corporations only.

## Largest property and casualty stock companies

1. Allstate Insurance Co., with $12,896,512 thousand
2. State Farm Fire & Casualty, $5,331,663
3. Aetna Casualty & Surety, $4,616,469
4. Continental Casualty, $4,163,070
5. United States Fidelity & Guaranty, $3,300,317
6. Travelers Indemnity Co., $3,007,927
7. St. Paul Fire & Mar, $2,536,403
8. Hartford Fire, $2,103,555
9. National Union Fire Insurance, $2,038,493
10. American Home Assurance Co., $1,957,784

*Where'd you hear that?*
National Underwriter, Property & Casualty edition. Based on 1989 premiums, in thousands of dollars.

## Largest property and casualty mutual companies

1. State Farm Mutual Auto, with $16,872,709 thousand
2. Liberty Mutual Insurance Co., $5,259,319
3. Nationwide Mutual Insurance, $4,059,449

# LIFE LESSONS

# LIFE LESSONS

4. Lumbermens Mutual Casualty, $1,987,513
5. American Family Mutual, $1,663,722
6. Auto-Owners Insurance (Mutual), $1,060,250
7. Employers Insurance of Wausau, $805,283
8. Nationwide Mutual Fire, $698,033
9. Sentry Insurance (Mutual), $672,349
10. Federated Mutual, $653,461

*Where'd you hear that?*
National Underwriter, Property & Casualty edition. Based on 1989 premiums, in thousands of dollars.

## Largest property and casualty reciprocal companies

1. Farmers Insurance Exchange, with $4,268,664 thousand
2. United Services Auto, $2,197,098
3. California State Auto, $1,345,102
4. Erie Insurance Exchange, $1,080,632
5. Inter Insurance Exchange Auto Club, $788,076
6. Auto Club Insurance Association, $757,437
7. Illinois State Medical Exchange, $145,665
8. Lumbermens Underwriter All, $135,152
9. Southern California Phys, $129,086
10. Farmers Automobile Association, $116,696

*Where'd you hear that?*
National Underwriter, Property & Casualty edition. Based on 1989 premiums, in thousands of dollars.

## Leading disability income insurers

1. Provident Life, with $268,896 thousand
2. Paul Revere Life, $191,111
3. Northwestern Mutual Life, $165,846
4. Monarch Life, $95,554
5. Equitable Life, $92,986
6. Lincoln National Life Insurance Co., $86,126
7. Massachusetts Mutual Life, $72,843
8. Connecticut Mutual Life, $69,120
9. Great-West Life, $52,911
10. Manufacturers Life, $46,798

*Where'd you hear that?*
Medical Economics. Based on 1988 income from disability premiums, in thousands of dollars.

## America's 10 least accessible transit systems for use by disabled persons

Metropolitan Transit Commission (Minneapolis, MN)
Detroit Department of Transportation (Detroit, MI)
Port Authority of Allegheny County (Pittsburgh, PA)
Mass Transit Administration of Maryland (Baltimore, MD)

# LIFE LESSONS

Greater Cleveland Regional Transit Authority (Cleveland, OH)
Indianapolis Public Transportation Corp. (Indianapolis, IN)
Via Metropolitan Transit (San Antonio, TX)
City & County of Honolulu (Honolulu, HI)
Regional Transit Authority (New Orleans, LA)
Queen City Metro (Cincinnati, OH)

*Where'd you hear that?*
Mass Transit. Criteria not stated; list is unranked.

## America's 10 most accessible transit systems for disabled persons to use

New York City Transit Authority (bus only) (New York, NY)
Southern California Rapid Transit District (Los Angeles, CA)
Golden Gate Bridge Highway & Transit District (San Rafael, CA)
Municipality of Metropolitan Seattle (Seattle, WA)
San Francisco Municipal Railway (San Francisco, CA)
Alameda Costra County Transit District (Oakland, CA)
Regional Transit District (Denver, CO)
Santa Clara County Transit District (San Jose, CA)
Cambria County Transportation Authority (Johnstown, PA)
Tri County Metropolitan Transportation (Portland, OR)

*Where'd you hear that?*
Mass Transit. Criteria not stated; list is unranked.

## Leading writers of medical malpractice insurance

1. St. Paul Group, with $735,375 thousand
2. Medical Liability Mutual New York, $298,095
3. CNA Insurance Cos., $263,115
4. Medical Protective, $203,745
5. Farmers Insurance Group, $189,877
6. American International Group, $175,318
7. Medical Malpractice Insurance, $173,033
8. Illinois State Medical Exchange, $172,592
9. Phico Insurance Co., $153,299
10. Doctors Co. Inter. Ex., $142,028

*Where'd you hear that?*
Best's Review, Property/Casualty edition. Based on 1988 direct premiums, in thousands of dollars.

## Biggest advertisers in dental publications

1. Procter & Gamble, with 3.05%
2. 3M, 2.86%
3. Warner-Lambert, 2.63%
4. Colgate-Palmolive Co., 2.23%
5. Caulk, 2.05%
6. Block Drug, 1.95%
7. Parkell, 1.94%
8. Computer products, 1.61%
9. Insurance, 1.48%
10. Burroughs-Wellcome, 1.46%

425

# LIFE LESSONS

*Where'd you hear that?*
Medical Marketing & Media, Healthcare Advertising Review. Based on percentage share of 1989 advertising expenditures.

## Products and services most heavily advertised in dental publications

1. Listerine Wash, with 1.89%
2. Computer products, 1.61%
3. Meetings, 1.52%
4. Zovirax Ointment, 1.46%
5. Courses, 1.40%
6. Lynx Handpiece, 1.26%
7. Thermafil, 1.08%
8. Sensodyne, 1.06%
9. Parkell Products, 1.03%
10. Wrigley Gum, .94%

*Where'd you hear that?*
Medical Marketing & Media, Healthcare Advertising Review. Based on percentage share of 1989 advertising expenditures.

## Leading opthalmology advertisers in opthalmology publications

1. Allergan Pharm, with 10.59%
2. Alcon Surgical, 6.35%
3. Storz Ophthalmics, 3.15%
4. Iolab Intrao, 2.81%
5. Marco, 2.12%
6. Allergan Optical, 2.09%
7. Johnson & Johnson, 2.07%
8. Alcon Labs, 2.05%
8. Bausch & Lomb, 2.05%
8. Lolab Pharm, 2.05%

*Where'd you hear that?*
Medical Marketing & Media, Healthcare Advertising Review. Based on 1989 share of total advertising expenditures.

## Leading optometry advertisers

1. Starline Opt, with 3.52%
2. Allergan Optical, 3.22%
3. Johnson & Johnson, 2.77%
4. Sola Optic, 2.68%
5. Alcon Labs, 2.66%
6. Marchon, 2.49%
7. Avant-Garde, 2.39%
8. Swank Optic, 2.34%
9. Ciba Vision, 2.24%
10. L'Amy Inc., 2.15%

*Where'd you hear that?*
Medical Marketing & Media, Healthcare Advertising Review. Based on 1989 share of total advertising expenditures.

## Biggest corporations in the medical products industry

1. Johnson & Johnson, with $19,067 million
2. Abbott Laboratories, $14,353
3. Baxter International Inc., $6,050
4. Becton, Dickinson & Co., $2,295
5. Bausch & Lomb, $1,741
6. Medtronic, $1,716
7. Sigman-Aldrich, $1,429
8. St. Jude Medical, $1,116
9. C. R. Bard, $839

*Where'd you hear that?*
Business Week, The Business Week 1000. Based on market value as of March 16, 1990, in millions of dollars.

## Leading medical/surgical advertisers

1. Merck & Co., with 6.82
2. Searle, 5.48
3. Pfizer, 5.33
4. Upjohn, 5.00
5. Marion Laboratories Inc., 4.84
6. Syntex, 3.50

7. Parke-Davis, 3.25
8. Glaxo, 3.11
9. Wyeth-Ayerst, 2.79
10. Roche, 2.72

*Where'd you hear that?*
Medical Marketing & Media, Healthcare Advertising Review. Based on 1989 share of ad dollars.

## Largest medical advertising agencies

1. Sudler & Hennessey, with $24.6 million
2. Kalliar, Philips, Ross, $21.2
3. Thomas G. Ferguson Associates Inc., $20.6
4. Lavey/Wolff/Swift, $16.1
5. William Douglas McAdams, $15.6
6. Klemtner, $15.5
7. Medicus Intercon, $14.8
8. Vicom/FCB, $13.1

*Where'd you hear that?*
Crain's New York Business. Based on 1989 gross income, in millions of dollars.

## Most heavily advertised medical/surgical products

1. Cytotec 200 Tabs (Searle), with 2.58
2. Calan SR (Searle), 2.24
3. Cardizem SR Caps (Marion), 2.22
4. Rogaine Top Solution (Upjohn), 1.67
5. Procardia (Pfizer), 1.59
6. Ansaid 100 Tabs (Upjohn), 1.40
7. Feldene 20mg Cap (Pfizer), 1.38
8. Minipress (Pfizer), 1.35
8. Cipro Tablets (Miles Labs), 1.35

10. Cardene (Syntex), 1.31

*Where'd you hear that?*
Medical Marketing & Media, Healthcare Advertising Review. Based on 1989 share of ad dollars.

## Best-selling medical/surgical product brands

1. Cardiac Preparations - Calcium Antagonist, with 9.86
2. Antiulcer Preparations, 8.55
3. Cardiac Preparations - Antihypertensive, 8.30
4. Antibiotics - BMS, 7.57
5. Antiarthritics, 6.31
6. Analgesics Non-Narcotic, 3.46
7. Cardiac Preparations - Beta Blocker, 3.26
8. Cholesterol Reducers, 3.17
9. Tranquilizers - Minor, 2.55
10. Bronchial Dilators, 2.18

*Where'd you hear that?*
Medical Marketing & Media, Healthcare Advertising Review. Based on 1989 share of ad dollars.

## Top prescription drugs—new and refill prescriptions

1. Amoxil
2. Lanoxin
3. Zantac
4. Xanax
5. Premarin
6. Cardizem
7. Ceclor
8. Synthroid
9. Seldane
10. Tenormin

# LIFE LESSONS

# LIFE LESSONS

*Where'd you hear that?*
American Druggist, Top 200 Rx Drugs. Based on new and refill prescriptions for 1989.

## Top prescription drugs—new prescriptions

1. Amoxil
2. Ceclor
3. Xanax
4. Tylenol w/Codeine
5. Seldane
6. Zantac
7. Naprosyn
8. Augmentin
9. Lanoxin
10. Monistat

*Where'd you hear that?*
American Druggist, Top 200 Rx Drugs. Based on new prescriptions for 1989.

## Top prescription drugs—refills only

1. Lanoxin
2. Zantac
3. Cardizem
4. Premarin
5. Tenormin
6. Vasotec
7. Synthroid
8. Xanax
9. Ortho-Novum 7/7/7
10. Capoten

*Where'd you hear that?*
American Druggist. Based on refill prescriptions for 1989.

## Best-selling cholesterol drugs

1. Lovastatin/Mevacor, with $520 million
2. Gemfibrozil/Lopid, $290
3. Cholestryamine/Questran, $160
4. Probucol/Lorelco, $120
5. Simvastatin/Zocor, $75
6. Colestipol/Colestid, $25
7. Others, total $160

*Where'd you hear that?*
Fortune. Based on 1989 estimated sales, in millions of dollars.

## Leading painkillers

1. Tylenol, with 27%
2. Advil, 12%
3. Bayer, 6%
4. Nuprin, 5%
5. Excedrin, 4%

*Where'd you hear that?*
Wall Street Journal. Based on 1989 market share, in percent.

## Best-selling sleeping aids at chain drug stores

1. Sominex-2, with 24.9%
2. Unisom, 23.7%
3. Benadryl, 19.5%
4. Private label/Generic, 16.0%
5. Nytol, 9.5%
6. Others, 6.4%

*Where'd you hear that?*
American Druggist. Based on 1989 market share, in percent.

## Best-selling sleeping aids at independent drug stores

1. Unisom, with 33.2%
2. Sominex-2, 20.6%
3. Benadryl, 11.4%
4. Nytol, 9.2%
5. Sleep-Eze, 3.8%
6. Private label/Generic, 3.3%
7. Sleepettes, 2.2%
7. Sleepinol, 2.2%
9. Others, 14.1%

*Where'd you hear that?*
American Druggist. Based on 1989 market share, in percent.

**Most highly recommended cold/liquid products sold by chains**

1. Dimetapp Elixer, with 18.7%
2. Nyquil, 16.3%
3. Robitussin CF, 7.8%
4. Comtrex, 7.2%
5. Naldecon Dx, 4.8%
6. Co-Tylenol, 4.2%
7. Naldecon, 3.0%
7. Triminicol, 3.0%
9. Benylin, 2.4%
9. Robitussin, 2.4%

*Where'd you hear that?*
American Druggist. Based on percentage of druggists/pharmacists naming product as best in 1989 survey.

**Most highly recommended cold/liquid products sold by independent retail**

1. Nyquil, with 16.9%
2. Dimetapp Elixer, 10.8%
3. Triaminic, 7.2%
4. Robitussin CF, 6.7%
5. Naldecon DX, 6.2%
6. Comtrex, 4.6%
6. Naldecon, 4.6%
8. Novahistine DMX, 3.6%
9. Actifed, 2.6%
9. Co-Tylenol, 2.6%

*Where'd you hear that?*
American Druggist. Based on percentage of druggist/pharmacists naming product as best in 1989 survey.

**Most highly recommended long-acting cold products sold by chains**

1. Drixoral, with 56.7%
2. Dimetapp, 15.2%
3. Contac, 5.5%
4. Sudafed, 3.7%
5. Sudafed SA, 3.0%
6. Private label Generic, 6.1%
7. Other brands, total 9.8%

*Where'd you hear that?*
American Druggist. Based on percentage of druggist/pharmacists naming product as best in 1989 survey.

**Most highly recommended long-acting cold products sold by independent retailers**

1. Drixoral, with 54.6%
2. Dimetapp, 12.8%
3. Contac, 8.7%
4. Chlor-Trimeton, 4.6%
5. Sudafed, 2.6%
5. Sudfed SA, 2.6%
5. Triaminic, 2.6%
8. Private label, Generic, 3.3%
9. Other brands, 8.2%

*Where'd you hear that?*
American Druggist. Based on percentage of druggist/pharmacists naming product as best in 1989 survey.

**Most highly recommended multi-symptom cold products sold by chains**

1. Comtrex, with 54.2%
2. Co-Tylenol, 6.0%
3. Drixoral, 4.2%
3. Triaminicin, 4.2%
5. Nyquil, 3.0%
5. Robitussin, 3.0%
7. Contac, 2.4%
7. Viromed, 2.4%
9. Private label, Generic, 4.2%
10. Other brands, total 16.4%

*Where'd you hear that?*
American Druggist. Based on percentage of druggist/pharmacists naming product as best in 1989 survey.

# LIFE LESSONS

# LIFE LESSONS

### Most highly recommended multi-sympton cold products sold by independent retailers

1. Comtrex, with 40.5%
2. Contac, 5.4%
2. Triaminicin, 5.4%
4. Drixoral, 4.9%
5. Chexit, 2.7%
6. Co-Tylenol, 2.2%
6. Nyquil, 2.2%
6. Robitussin, 2.2%
9. Private label, Generic, 11.8%
10. Other brands, total 22.7%

*Where'd you hear that?*
American Druggist. Based on percentage of druggist/pharmacists naming product as best in 1989 survey.

### Most highly recommended cold tablets sold by chains

1. Actifed, with 21.3%
2. Drixoral, 20.8%
3. Comtrex, 11.8%
4. Sudafed, 7.9%
5. Dimetapp, 7.3%
6. Co-Tylenol, 5.1%
7. Sudafed Plus, 2.8%
7. Triaminicin, 2.8%
9. Coricidin, 2.2%
10. Private label, Generic, 9.0%

*Where'd you hear that?*
American Druggist. Based on percentage of druggist/pharmacists naming product as best in 1989 survey.

### Most highly recommended cold tablets sold by independent retailers

1. Drixoral, with 28.1%
2. Actifed, 9.4%
3. Sudafed, 8.3%
4. Comtrex, 7.8%
5. Dimetapp, 5.7%
6. Ornex, 3.1%
6. Sudafed Plus, 3.1%
6. Triaminicin, 3.1%
9. Contac, 2.6%
9. Co-Tylenol, 2.6%

*Where'd you hear that?*
American Druggist. Based on percentage of druggist/pharmacists naming product as best in 1989 survey.

### Most highly recommended adult cough products sold by chains

1. Robitussin DM, with 34.7%
2. Robitussin, 34.1%
3. Delsym, 7.4%
4. Naldecon DX, 4.0%
5. Benylin, 2.8%
6. Private label, Generic, 8.5%
6. Other brands, total 8.5%

*Where'd you hear that?*
American Druggist. Based on percentage of druggist/pharmacists naming product as best in 1989 survey.

### Most highly recommended adult cough products sold by independent retailers

1. Robitussin DM, with 27.4%
2. Robitussin, 22.9%
3. Benylin, 8.0%
4. Naldecon DX, 6.5%
5. Delsym, 6.0%
6. Novahistime DMX, 4.5%
7. Naldecon, 4.0%
8. Triaminic, 2.0%
9. Private label, Generic, 8.6%
10. Other brands, total 10.1%

*Where'd you hear that?*
American Druggist. Based on percentage of druggist/pharmacists naming product as best in 1989 survey.

# LIFE LESSONS

**Best-selling sore throat liquid/sprays at independent retail outlets**

1. Chloraseptic, with 85.2%
2. Sucrets Spray/Gargle, 4.4%
3. Larylgan, 3.5%
4. Private label/generic, total 3.0%
5. Other brands, total, 12.4%

*Where'd you hear that?*
American Druggist. Based on 1989 market share, in percent.

**Best-selling sore throat lozenges at retail chains**

1. Chloraseptic, with 41.8%
2. Cepastat, 19.8%
3. Sucrets, 10.2%
4. Spec-T, 7.9%
5. Cepacol, 6.2%
6. Nice, 4.0%
7. Halls, 2.8%
8. Private label/generic, total 4.9%
9. Other brands, total, 2.4%

*Where'd you hear that?*
American Druggist. Based on 1989 market share, in percent.

**Best-selling sore throat lozenges at independent retail outlets**

1. Chloraseptic, with 38.5%
2. Cepastat, 23.0%
3. Spec-T, 8.0%
4. Cepacol, 7.5%
5. Sucrets, 7.0%
6. Mycinettes, 3.0%
7. Halls, 2.5%
8. Private label/generic, total 5.5%
9. Other brands, total 5.0%

*Where'd you hear that?*
American Druggist. Based on 1989 market share, in percent.

**Best-selling children's vitamins**

1. Private label, with 32%
2. Flinstones, 26%
3. Bugs Bunny, 10%
4. Centrum Jr., 7%
4. Sunkist, 7%
6. VI-Sol, 4%
7. Theragran Jr., 1%
8. Others, total, 13%

*Where'd you hear that?*
Advertising Age. Based on 1988 market share of sales, in percent.

*Top-selling home pregnancy tests*

1. First Response (Tambrands), with 25%
2. E.P.T. (Warner-Lambert), 22%
3. Clear Blue (Whitehall Labs), 15%
4. Fact (Ortho), 9%
5. Answer (Carter-Wallace), 8%
5. Advance (Ortho), 8%
7. Q Test (Becton Dickinson), 7%
8. Daisy (Ortho), 5%
9. Others, total, 1%

*Where'd you hear that?*
Non-Foods Merchandising. Based on 1989 market share, in percent. Original source: A. C. Nielsen.

**Best-selling multivitamins**

1. Centrum Tab 100s
2. Mult W/Min 100s
3. Mult Vit 100s
4. Thergran-M 100s
5. Mult Vit w/iron 100s
6. Geritol Tab 40

# LIFE LESSONS

7. Vit B Comp C 60s
8. B Comp C W/iron 60s
9. B Comp C w/Zinc 60s
10. Z-Bec 60s

*Where'd you hear that?*
Drug Store News, Inside Pharmacy. Based on units sold.

## States with largest Medicaid budgets

1. New York, with $9.21 billion
2. California, $5.23
3. Ohio, $2.36
4. Pennsylvania, 2.25
5. Massachusetts, 2.04
6. Texas, $1.94
7. Illinois, $1.86
8. Michigan, $1.81
9. New Jersey, $1.72
10. Florida, $1.49

*Where'd you hear that?*
City & State. Based on 1988 medicaid budget, in billions of dollars.

## Largest state medicaid programs

1. New York, with $3,288 million
2. California, $2,987
3. Pennsylvania, $1,269
4. Illinois, $1,050
5. New Jersey, $1,048
6. Ohio, $940
7. Florida, $899
8. Massachusetts, $888
9. Michigan, $732
10. Maryland, $560

*Where'd you hear that?*
Financial World. Based on total appropriated 1989 state medicaid expenditures, in millions of dollars.

## Most productive health care service corporations

1. Community Psych, with $13.8 thousand
2. Humana Inc., $5.5
3. National Medical, $2.2
4. Beverly Enterprises, -$1.0

*Where'd you hear that?*
Forbes, Forbes 500s Annual Directory. Based on 1989 profits per employee, in thousands of dollars. Ranks U.S.-based corporations that were publicly traded as of March 23, 1990.

## Most profitable health care service companies

1. Humana Inc., with 24.4%
2. Manor Care, 22.2%
3. National Medical, 15.3%
4. Universal Health, 11.8%
5. Beverly Enterprises, 7.1%
6. FHP International, NA
7. PacifiCare Health, NA
8. United HealthCare, NA
9. US Healthcare, NA

*Where'd you hear that?*
Forbes, Annual Report on American Industry. Based on 10-year average return on equity. Ranks publicly held corporations only.

## Largest health care service companies

1. Humana, with $3,906 million
2. National Medical Enterprises, $2,645
3. National Health Laboratories, $1,188

4. Community Psychiatric Centers, $954
5. Manor Care, $597
6. U.S. Healthcare, $566
7. Medical Care International, $465
8. FHP International, $452
9. American Medical International, $354

*Where'd you hear that?*
Business Week, Business Week Top 1000. Based on market value, in millions.

## Leading health care municipal bond financial advisers

1. Ponder & Co., with $1,097,700 thousand
2. Kaufman Hall & Associates Inc., $464,700
3. Bingham & Co. Capital Markets, $374,900
4. Public Financial Management Inc., $312,300
5. Cain Brothers, Shattuck & Co., $295,500
6. Price Waterhouse & Co., $246,700
7. Adams, Harkness & Hill Inc., $243,600
8. Dillon, Read & Co., $199,600
9. Smith Barney, Harris Upham & Co., $180,100
10. F. B. Garvey & Associates, $168,600

*Where'd you hear that?*
Bond Buyer, Bond Buyer Yearbook. Based on 1989 dollar amount, in thousands.

## Top designers/builders of healthcare facilities

1. Hospital Building & Equipment Co., with $459,300 thousand
2. Marshall Erdman & Associates, $135,000
3. Mitchell Associates, $93,400
4. Universal Medical Buildings, $90,000
5. Commons Development Group, $45,800
6. American Medical Buildings, $45,000
7. Carlson, $37,500
8. Simmonds, $32,450
9. Richmond Development Co., $30,700
10. Tartan Development Corp., $27,400

*Where'd you hear that?*
Modern Healthcare, Design and Construction Survey. Based on 1989 dollar volume, in thousands.

## Top healthcare facilities architectural firms

1. Henningson Durham & Richardson, with $33,000
2. Hansen Lind Meyer, $24,928
3. NBBJ, $24,640
4. Cannon, $24,200
5. HKS, $23,400
6. Ellerbe Becket, $21,955
7. Stone Marraccini & Patterson, $14,450
8. Kaplan McLaughlin Diaz, $14,400
9. URS Consultants, $14,269
10. Burt Hill Kosar Rittelmann, $13,383

*Where'd you hear that?*
Modern Healthcare, Design and Construction Survey. Based on 1989 firm fees.

# LIFE LESSONS

# LIFE LESSONS

## Top home health care companies

1. Caremark Homecare
2. Glasrock Home Health Care
3. Abbey/Foster
4. Homedco Inc.
5. Healthdyne Inc.
6. New England Critical Care
7. Lincare Inc.
8. National Medical Care
9. Primedica Home Health Centers
10. T2 Medical

*Where'd you hear that?*
Homecare, HME 50. Based on estimates based on industry activity, business creativity, and market niche.

## Largest independently owned home health care companies

1. Homedco Inc., with $185 million
2. Total Pharmaceutical Care, $22
3. Health-Mart, $20
4. Greenwood Home Care, $16.7
5. White & White Health Care, $15
6. HomeCARE, $13
7. The Bowers Companies, $12
8. National Medical Rentals, $11
9. Wasserott's, $10.5
10. Hook Superx, Inc., $10
10. Care Medical, $10
10. Kirson Medical, $10

*Where'd you hear that?*
Homecare, HME 50. Based on total sales and rental volume, in millions of dollars.

## Leading health care companies in food service

1. Beverly Enterprises, with $268.8 million
2. Hospital Corp. of America, $226.8
3. National Medical Enterprises, $226
4. Humana Inc., $88.8
5. Adventist Health System/U.S., $75.8
6. Daughters of Charity National Health System, $75
7. National Heritage, $71.4
8. Health Trust, $69.8
9. New York City Health & Hospitals Corp., $65.4
10. Manor Health Care, $56

*Where'd you hear that?*
Restaurants & Institutions, Restaurants & Institutions 400. Based on sales, in millions of dollars.

## Largest chains' foreign acute-care hospitals

1. Paracelsus Healthcare Corp., with 6,505
2. American Medical International Inc., 2,529
3. Hospital Corp. of America, 2,244
4. National Medical Enterprises, 864
5. Missionary Sisters of Sacred Heart, Western Province, 850
6. Medlantic Healthcare Group, 570
7. Humana Inc., 483
8. Mercy Health Service, 230
9. Sister of Sorrowful Mother Ministry Corp., 107
10. Shriners Hospitals for Crippled Children, 100

*Where'd you hear that?*
Modern Healthcare, Modern Healthcare 500 Multi-Unit Providers Survey. Based on 1989 total beds operated.

## Largest multihospital systems

1. Kaiser Foundation Hospitals, with $6,856.8 million
2. Humana Inc., $4,088.0
3. National Medical Enterprises, $3,962.9
4. Daughters of Charity National Health System, $2,871.2
5. American Medical International Inc., $2,750.0
6. UniHealth America, $2,000.0
7. New York City Health & Hospital Corp., $1,906.8
8. Health Trust - The Hospital Co., $1,769.0
9. Mercy Health Services, $1,288.8
10. Sisters of Providence, $1,008.1

*Where'd you hear that?*
Modern Healthcare, Modern Healthcare 500 Multi-Unit Providers Survey. Based on 1989 revenues, in millions of dollars.

## Largest multihospital systems ranked by number of hospitals

1. HCA Management Co., with 178
2. Hospital Corp. of America, 148
3. National Medical Enterprises, 140
4. Charter Medical Corp., 99
5. HealthTrust - The Hospital Co., 94
6. Humana Inc., 83
7. American Medical International Inc., 81
8. Paracelsus Healthcare Corp., 69
8. Adventist Health System/U.S., 69
10. Hospital Management Professionals, 61

*Where'd you hear that?*
Modern Healthcare, Modern Healthcare 500 Multi-Unit Providers Survey. Based on 1989 total hospitals operated worldwide.

## Largest multihospital systems ranked by number of beds

1. Hospital Corp. of America, with 27,070
2. HCA Management Co., 21,067
3. Humana Inc., 17,421
4. American Medical International Inc., 14,617
5. Daughters of Charity National Health System, 14,175
6. National Medical Enterprises, 12,800
7. HealthTrust - The Hospital Co., 12,696
8. Adventist Health System/U.S., 11,232
9. Charter Medical Corp., 9,638
10. New York City Health & Hospital Corp., 9,477

*Where'd you hear that?*
Modern Healthcare, Modern Healthcare 500 Multi-Unit Providers Survey. Based on 1989 total hospital beds operated worldwide.

## Largest centrally-managed multihospital systems

1. HCA Management Co., with 21,067
2. Hospital Corp. of America, 18,434
3. Humana Inc., 16,938
4. Daughters of Charity National Health System, 13,924

# LIFE LESSONS

# LIFE LESSONS

5. Health Trust - The Hospital Co., 12,634
6. American Medical International Inc., 11,201
7. Adventist Health System/U.S., 10,808
8. New York City Health & Hospitals Corp., 9,477
9. Hospital Management Professionals, 7,708
10. Mercy Health Services, 7,171

*Where'd you hear that?*
Modern Healthcare, Modern Healthcare 500 Multi-Unit Providers Survey. Based on 1989 number of beds in U.S. acute care hospitals.

## Largest public multihospital systems

1. New York City Health & Hospital Corp., with 9,477
2. County of Los Angeles-Dept. of Health, 4,363
3. Indian Health Service, 1,731
4. Milwaukee County Dept. of Health, 1,335
5. State of Hawaii-Dept. of Health, 1,181
6. Hillsborough County Hospital Authority, 1,000
7. Charlotte-Mecklenburg, 973
8. Metrohealth System, 831
9. Boston City Hospital, 713
10. Wake Medical Center, 656

*Where'd you hear that?*
Modern Healthcare, Modern Healthcare 500 Multi-Unit Providers Survey. Based on 1989 foreign and U.S. acute-care beds operated.

## Largest contract manager multihospital systems

1. HCA Management Co., with 21,067
2. Hospital Management Professionals, 7,708
3. Brim & Associates, 4,538
4. Catholic Health Corp., 4,536
5. SunHealth Enterprises, 2,712
6. Alliant Health System, 1,417
7. Mercy Health Services, 1,198
8. Connecticut Health System, 1,130
9. Allegheny Health Services, 878
9. Ohio Valley Health Services, 878

*Where'd you hear that?*
Modern Healthcare, Modern Healthcare 500 Multi-Unit Providers Survey. Based on 1989 foreign and U.S. acute-care beds operated.

## Largest investor-owned multihospital systems

1. HCA Management Co., with 21,067
2. Hospital Corp. of America, 20,678
3. American Medical International Inc., 13,730
4. HealthTrust - The Hospital Co., 12,634
5. Paracelsus Healthcare Corp., 8,045
6. Hospital Management Professionals, 7,708
7. National Medical Enterprises, 7,536
8. Humana Inc., 6,421
9. Brim & Associates, 4,766
10. Epic Healthcare Group, 4,399

*Where'd you hear that?*
Modern Healthcare, Modern Healthcare 500 Multi-Unit Providers Survey. Based on 1989 foreign and U.S. acute-care beds operated.

## Largest secular not-for-profit multihospital systems

1. Kaiser Foundation Hospitals, with 7,018
2. Health One Corp., 3,076
3. Lutheran Health Systems, 2,888
4. SunHealth Enterprises, 2,712
5. Intermountain Health Care, 2,685
6. Detroit Medical Center, 2,496
7. Alliant Health System, 2,391
8. Connecticut Health System, 2,260
9. UniHealth America, 2,204
10. Allegheny Health Services, 2,173

*Where'd you hear that?*
Modern Healthcare, Modern Healthcare 500 Multi-Unit Providers Survey. Based on 1989 foreign and U.S. acute-care beds operated.

## Largest Catholic multihospital systems

1. Daughters of Charity National Health System, with 13,924
2. Mercy Health Services, 7,401
3. Sisters of Charity Health Care Systems, 5,454
4. Catholic Health Corp., 4,536
5. Mercy Health Care System, 4,375
6. Eastern Mercy Health Systems, 4,179
7. Sisters of Mercy Health Systems, 4,160
8. Hospital Sisters Health System, 3,821
9. Health Care Corp. of Sisters of St. Joseph, 3,745
10. Sisters of Providence, 3,712

*Where'd you hear that?*
Modern Healthcare, Modern Healthcare 500 Multi-Unit Providers Survey. Based on 1989 foreign and U.S. acute-care beds operated.

## Largest other religious multihospital systems

1. Adventist Health System/U.S., with 10,808
2. Baptist Memorial Healthcare Development Corp., 4,281
3. U.S. Health Corp., 2,724
4. Methodist Health Systems, 2,226
5. Methodist Hospital System, 1,915
6. Evangelical Health Systems, 1,884
7. Baylor Health Care System, 1,784
8. Baptist Medical System, 1,400
9. Harris Methodist Health System, 1,392
10. Baptist Hospitals, 1,343

*Where'd you hear that?*
Modern Healthcare, Modern Healthcare 500 Multi-Unit Providers Survey. Based on 1989 foreign and U.S. acute-care beds operated. 'Other religious' in this instance means other than Catholic.

## Largest advertisers in nursing publications

1. Recruitment, with 53.80
2. Nurse Service Org., 2.78
3. Upjohn, 2.44
4. Support Systems, 1.80
5. U.S. Navy, 1.30
6. Convatec, 1.26

# LIFE LESSONS

# LIFE LESSONS

7. Hill-Romaine, .89
8. Baxter Healthcare Corp., .80
9. U.S. Army, .78
10. U.S. Air Force, .77

*Where'd you hear that?*
Medical Marketing & Media, Healthcare Advertising Review. Based on 1989 share of ad dollars.

## Highest paid health care trade executives

1. James Sammons, M.D., American Medical Assn. with $580,907
2. Gerald Mossinghoff, Pharmaceutical Manufacturers Assn., $308,337
3. John Curley, Catholic Health Assn., $304,135
4. Carl Schramm, Health Insurance Assn. of America, $298,101
5. Robert Petersdorf, M.D., Assn. of American Medical Colleges, $294,800
6. Paul Eubert, M.D., American College of Surgeons, $281,045
7. Carol McCarthy, American Hospital Assn., $254,135
8. Frank Samuel, Health Industry Manufacturers Assn., $249,687
9. Dennis O'Leary, M.D., Joint Commission on Accreditation of Healthcare Organizations, $236,636
10. Horace Deets, American Assn. of Retired Persons, $202,058

*Where'd you hear that?*
Modern Healthcare. Based on ranked by 1988 total compensation.

## Top states in nursing home and clinic construction markets

1. California, with $526 million
2. New York, $415
3. Pennsylvania, $375
4. Texas, $271
5. Florida, $188
6. Illinois, $172
7. Ohio, $161
8. North Carolina, $156
9. Maryland, $127
10. Colorado, $114

*Where'd you hear that?*
ENR, Top 20 States in Major Construction Markets. Based on eleven-month cumulative contract awards, 1989 vs. 1988, in millions of dollars.

## Largest multihospital nursing home systems

1. National Medical Enterprises Millhaven Corp., with 44,673
2. Adventist Health System/U.S., 6,740
3. Catholic Health Corp., 1,541
4. Bon Secours Health System, 1,120
5. Riverside Healthcare Assn., 1,092
6. Samaritan Foundation, 1,071
7. Wheaton Franciscan Services, 1,050
8. Benedictine Health System, 1,010
9. Sisters of Charity Health Care Systems, 930
10. North Central Health Services, 919

*Where'd you hear that?*
Modern Healthcare, Modern Healthcare 500 Multi-Unit Providers Survey. Based on number of beds in 1989.

## Largest not-for-profit nursing home systems

1. Good Samaritan Society, with 11,522
2. Eskaton, 1,954
3. Board of Social Ministry, 1,816
4. Tressler Lutheran Services, 1,373
5. Christian Homes, 1,325
6. Presbyterian Homes, 850
7. American Baptist Homes of the Midwest, 767
8. Lutheran Social Services of Illinois, 645
9. American Baptist Homes of the West, 639
10. United Church Homes, 619

*Where'd you hear that?*
Modern Healthcare, Modern Healthcare 500 Multi-Unit Providers Survey. Based on number of beds in 1989.

## Largest investor-owned nursing home systems

1. Beverly Enterprises, with 96,268
2. ARA Living Centers, 26,180
3. Manor Care, 21,637
4. Health Care & Retirement Corp., 16,799
5. United Health, 16,018
6. Life Care Centers of America, 13,612
7. National Health Corp., 8,684
8. Diversified Health Services, 7,585
9. Angell Care, 6,358
10. Meritcare, 5,923

*Where'd you hear that?*
Modern Healthcare, Modern Healthcare 500 Multi-Unit Providers Survey. Based on number of beds in 1989.

## Largest bequests

1. Estate of Daniel and Ada Rice to Art Institute of Chicago, $10,000,000
1. Estate of Louise Lenoir Locke to University of South Alabama, $10,000,000
1. Estate of Richard H. Larson to University of Nebraska, $10,000,000
4. Estate of Frank H. Ricketson, Jr. to University of Denver, $5,000,000
5. Estate of Winthrop Bushnell Palmer to Long Island University, $4,000,000
5. Estate of Edwin B. Green to University of Iowa, $4,000,000
7. Estate of Alfred L. Foulet to Princeton University, $3,800,000
8. Estate of Emert and Edna Witaschek to Illinois College, $1,250,000
9. Estate of J. Rives Childs to Randolph-Macon College, $1,200,000
10. Estate of Robert J. Gill to Western Maryland College, $1,050,000

*Where'd you hear that?*
Giving USA Annual Report. Based on value of gift.

# LIFE LESSONS

# LIFE LESSONS

## Largest individual gifts

1. Anonymous to New York Hospital-Cornell Medical Center, with $50,000,000
2. Mr. and Mrs. Harry B. Helmsley to New York Hospital-Cornell Medical Center, $33,000,000
3. Leonard N. Stern to New York University, $30,000,000
4. Albert B. Alkek to Baylor College of Medicine, $25,000,000
4. Leslie H. Wexner to Ohio State University, $25,000,000
6. Bill and Camille Cosby to Spelman College, $20,000,000
7. A. Alfred Taubman, to John F. Kennedy School of Government of Harvard University, $15,000,000
8. Herbert and Florence Irving to Columbia College, $11,000,000
9. Peter S. Kalikow to New York Hospital-Cornell Medical Center, $10,000,000
9. Paul G. Allen to University of Washington, $10,000,000
9. Henry R. Kravis to Mount Sinai Medical Center, $10,000,000
9. Bill Daniels, to University of Denver, $10,000,000

*Where'd you hear that?*
Giving USA Annual Report. Based on value of gifts given in 1988.

## Largest gifts to health

1. New York Hospital-Cornell Medical Center, from Anonymous, with $50,000,000
2. New York Hospital-Cornell Medical Center from Mr. and Mrs. Harry B. Helmsley, $33,000,000
3. Presbyterian Hospital from Milstein Family Foundation, $25,000,000
4. Mount Sinai Medical Center from Henry R. Kravis, $10,000,000
4. New York Hospital-Cornell Medical Center from Peter S. Kalikow, $10,000,000
6. To several hospitals for their strengthening Hospital Nursing Programs from Pew Charitable Trust, $8,600,000
7. New York Hospital-Cornell Medical Center from Mrs. Vincent Astor, $2,500,000
9. Children's Hospital (Medical Care) from Lucille P. Markey Charitable Trust, $2,475,000
10. National Institute of Health, from Merck & Co., $2,300,000

*Where'd you hear that?*
Giving USA Annual Report. Based on value of gifts given in 1988.

## Largest gifts to arts, culture, and humanities

1. Metropolitan Museum of Art from Laurence A. and Preston R. Tisch, with $10,000,000
1. Art Institute of Chicago from Estate of Daniel and Ada Rice, $10,000,000

3. Houston Symphony from Brown Foundation, $4,000,000
3. WGBH first PBS series on AIDS from Robert Wood Johnson Foundation, $4,000,000
5. John G. Shedd Aquarium from Estate of Daniel and Ada Rice, $3,000,000
5. Brooklyn Botanic Garden from Michael E. Steinhardt and wife, $3,000,000
7. Philadelphia Cultural Community Marketing Initiative from Pew Memorial Trust, $2,500,000
7. Greater Philadelphia Cultural Alliance from Pew Charitable Trust, $2,500,000
9. Museum of Contemporary Art from W. M. Keck Foundation, $2,200,000
10. Chicago Historical Society's Modernization Program from Estate of Daniel and Ada Rice, $2,000,000

*Where'd you hear that?*
Giving USA Annual Report. Based on value of gift.

### Largest gifts to public/society benefit

1. Police Foundation's Third Decade Fund for Improving Public Safety from Ford Foundation, with $10,000,000 (over 5 years)
2. *MacNeil/Lehrer News Hour* from John D. and Catherine T. MacArthur Foundation, $6,000,000
3. Local Initiatives Support Corporation from Ford Foundation, $4,000,000
4. Fund for Free Expression from John D. and Catherine T. MacArthur Foundation, $3,500,000
5. Enterprise Foundation from Ford Foundation, $3,000,000
6. Police Foundations Third Decade for Improving Public Safety from Ford Foundation, $2,400,000
7. Emergency Housing Assistance Program from Ford Foundation, $2,300,000
8. Mental Health Law Project from John D. and Catherine T. MacArthur Foundation, $2,000,000
9. Commission on Preservation and Access from Andrew W. Mellon Foundation, $1,500,000
9. National Public Radio from John D. and Catherine T. MacArthur Foundation, $1,500,000

*Where'd you hear that?*
Giving USA Annual Report. Based on value of gift.

### Largest gifts by foundations

1. Milstein Family Foundation to Presbyterian Hospital a gift of $25,000,000
2. The Perot Foundation to University of Texas Southwestern Medical Center, $20,000,000
2. W. K. Kellogg Foundation to National Academy of Sciences and the Institute of Medicine, $20,000,000
4. Joseph & Bessie Feinberg Foundation to Northwestern University, $17,000,000

# LIFE LESSONS

# LIFE LESSONS

5. John M. Olin Foundation to Washington University, $15,000,000
5. Howard Hughes Medical Institute to Massachusetts Institute of Technology, $15,000,000
5. John M. Olin Foundation to Columbia University, $15,000,000
8. Lucille P. Markey Charitable Trust to University of California, San Francisco, $13,7000,000
9. Lucille P. Markey Charitable Trust to Washington University School of Medicine, $12,000,000
9. Lucille P. Markey Charitable Trust to Yale University School of Medicine, $12,000,000

*Where'd you hear that?*
Giving USA Annual Report. Based on size of gift.

### Biggest charities

1. Jewish Guild for the Blind, with 118%
2. Jewish Child Care Association of New York, 102%
3. Metropolitan New York Coordinating Council on Jewish Poverty, 99%
4. AmeriCares Foundation, 98%
5. Catholic Relief Services, 97%
6. American Field Service Intercultural Programs, 96%
7. United Jewish Appeal, 95%
7. Legal Aid Society, 95%
7. National Council on the Aging, 95%
10. CARE, 94%

*Where'd you hear that?*
Money. Based on 1988 programs as a percentage of income.

### The 10 most cost-effective social service charities

1. Jewish Guild for the Blind
2. Jewish Child Care Association of New York
3. Metropolitan New York Coordinating Council on Jewish Poverty
4. Catholic Relief Services
5. United Jewish Appeal
6. Legal Aid Society
7. National Council on the Aging
8. CARE
9. Hadassah
10. International Rescue Committee

*Where'd you hear that?*
Money. Based on percentage of donations spent on good works (amounts not listed).

### The 10 most cost-effective health and medical charities

1. AmeriCares Foundation
2. New York Blood Center
3. MAP International
4. Project HOPE
5. Interchurch Medical Assistance
6. United Cerebral Palsy Associations
7. American Diabetes Association
8. City of Hope
9. National Easter Seal Society
10. Juvenile Diabetes Foundation

*Where'd you hear that?*
Money. Based on percentage of donations spent on good works (amounts not listed).

## LIFE LESSONS

**The 10 charities that watch their pennies best**

1. Metropolitan New York Coordinating Council on Jewish Poverty
2. Interchurch Medical Assistance
3. Shriners Hospitals for Crippled Children
4. AmeriCares Foundation
5. Lutheran World Relief
6. MAP International
7. Legal Aid Society
8. National Council on the Aging
9. United Jewish Appeal
10. Catholic Relief Services

*Where'd you hear that?*
Money. Based on percentage of income spent on administration and fundraising (lowest is best; amounts not given).

**Largest foundations**

1. Ford Foundation, with $216,448,295
2. John D. and Catherine T. MacArthur Foundation, $167,112,954
3. Pew Charitable Trusts, $126,270,000
4. W. K. Kellogg Foundation, $107,106,934
5. Robert Wood Johnson Foundation, $96,983,734
6. Lilly Endowment Inc., $79,231,139
7. Rockefeller Foundation, $64,465,444
8. Andrew W. Mellon Foundation, $59,794,884
9. Kresge Foundation, $52,380,000
10. Arnold and Mable Beckmann Foundation, $47,667,298

*Where'd you hear that?*
Across the Board. Based on contributions.

### Wealthiest environmental groups

1. Nature Conservancy (Arlington, VA), with $168.55 million
2. National Wildlife Federation (Washington, DC), $78.75
3. Ducks Unlimited (Long Grove, IL), $70.59
4. Sierra Club (San Francisco, CA), $37.32
5. World Wildlife Fund (Washington, DC), $35.59
6. Greenpeace (Washington, DC), $33.93
7. National Audubon Society (New York, NY), $33.60
8. Wilderness Society (Washington, DC), $14.42
9. Natural Resources Defense Council (New York, NY), $13.48
10. Environmental Defense Fund (New York, NY), $12.90

*Where'd you hear that?*
Non-Profit Times. Based on 1989 income, in millions of dollars.

**Largest wish-granting foundations**

1. Make-a-Wish Foundation of America, with $9.86 million
2. Starlight Foundation, $2.2
3. Sunshine Foundation, $1.9

*Where'd you hear that?*
Non Profit Times. Based on fiscal year 1988 revenue, in millions of dollars.

# LIFE LESSONS

## Largest non-profit institutions

1. Young Men's Christian Association, with $1,204.11 million
2. Lutheran Social Ministry Organizations, $1,027.00
3. American Red Cross, $985.18
4. Salvation Army, $865.00
5. Catholic Charities, $850.00
6. UNICEF, $709.00
7. Goodwill Industries of America, $555.00
8. Shriners Hospitals for Crippled Children, $372.6
9. Boy Scouts of America, $370.86
10. United Jewish Appeal, $361.10

*Where'd you hear that?*
Non-Profit Times, NPT 100 Supplement. Based on 1988 income, in millions of dollars.

## Fastest growing nonprofit institutions

1. Leukemia Society of America, with 160%
2. Rotary Foundation, 95%
3. Interchurch Medical Assistance, 61%
4. Lutheran World Relief, 59%
5. Father Flanagan's Boys Home, 51%
5. Covenant House, 51%
7. Mothers Against Drunk Driving, 44%
8. Cystic Fibrosis Foundation, 36%
9. Boy Scouts of America, 32%
10. Greenpeace USA, 29%

*Where'd you hear that?*
Non-Profit Times, NPT 100 Supplement. Based on percentage increase in income, 1987-1988.

## Nonprofit institutions with the biggest income declines

1. Shriners Hospitals, with a drop of 25%
2. Food for the Hungry, 23%
3. Braille Institute, 13%
4. MAP International, 12%
4. Children's Television Workshop, 12%
6. American Lebanese Syrian Assoc. Charities, 11%
7. Project Hope, 10%
8. American Institute for Cancer Research, 7.47%
9. Larry Jones International Ministries, 7.0%
10. United Jewish Appeal, 5.7%

*Where'd you hear that?*
Non-Profit Times, NPT 100 Supplement. Based on percentage decrease in income from 1987-88.

## Nonprofit institutions with the highest fundraising percentages

1. Amnesty International, with 28.70%
2. American Lung Association, 25.21%
3. Mothers Against Drunk Driving, 23.83%
4. Greenpeace USA, 23.65%
5. Christian Appalachian Project, 22.73%
6. American Institute for Cancer Research, 22.02%
7. Juvenile Diabetes Foundation, 21.25%
8. Covenant House, 19.61%
9. Holy Land Christian Mission, 19.28%
10. Foster Parents Plan, 19.12%

*Where'd you hear that?*
Non-Profit Times, NPT 100 Supplement. Based on fundraising percentage of income in 1988.

## Nonprofit institutions with the lowest fundraising percentages

1. Population Council, with 0.70%
2. Catholic Charities, 0.89%
3. AmeriCares, 1.23%
4. Catholic Relief Services, 1.50%
5. Mennonite Central Committee, 2.67%
6. American Red Cross, 2.71%
7. Girls Clubs, 2.77%
8. Hadassah, 2.83%
9. MAP International, 3.30%
10. Food for the Hungry, 3.46%

*Where'd you hear that?*
Non-Profit Times, NPT 100 Supplement. Based on fundraising percentage of income in 1988.

## Nonprofit institutions with the highest administrative costs

1. Nazareth Literary, Benevolent Inst., with 27.50%
2. Girls Clubs, 18.26%
3. United Cerebral Palsy Association, 14.67%
4. National Urban League, 14.60%
5. Evangelical Lutheran Good Samaritan Society 14.44%
6. American Friends Service Comm. 13.98%
7. Girl Scouts of the USA, 13.91%
8. Planned Parenthood Federation, 13.90%
9. Experiment in International Living, 13.04%
10. Youth for Understanding, 13.00%

*Where'd you hear that?*
Non-Profit Times, NPT 100 Supplement. Based on administrative costs percentage of income in 1988.

## Nonprofit institutions with the lowest administrative costs

1. United Jewish Appeal, with 0.72%
2. AmeriCares, 0.84%
3. Rotary Foundation, 0.92%
4. Metro New York Coordinating Council, 0.99%
5. MAP International, 1.09%
6. Joslin Diabetes Center, 1.74%
7. Shriners Hospitals, 1.99%
8. Braille Institute, 2.11%
9. CARE, 2.53%
10. City of Hope, 2.60%

*Where'd you hear that?*
Non-Profit Times, NPT 100 Supplement. Based on administrative costs percentage of income in 1988.

## Largest United Ways

1. United Way of Tri-State (NY), with $151.71 million
2. United Way Crusade of Mercy (Chicago, IL), $82.17
3. United Way Inc. (Los Angeles, CA), $79.21
4. United Foundation (Detroit, MI), $59.71
5. United Way of the National Capital Area (Washington, DC), $56.57
6. United Way of Southeast Pennsylvania (Philadelphia, PA), $55.48

# LIFE LESSONS

# LIFE LESSONS

7. United Way Services (Cleveland, OH), $47.43
8. United Way of Texas Gulf Coast (Houston, TX), $47.33
9. United Way of Massachusetts Bay (Boston, MA), $40.87
10. United Way of Metropolitan Atlanta, $38.47

*Where'd you hear that?*
Non-Profit Times, NPT 100 Supplement. Based on 1988 income, in millions of dollars.

# Diversions

## Top states in amusement, social, and recreational building construction markets

1. California, with $500 million
2. Florida, $484
3. New York, $281
4. Ohio, $274
5. Texas, $255
6. Michigan, $183
7. North Carolina, $164
8. Illinois, $147
9. Georgia, $137
10. Virginia, $122

*Where'd you hear that?*
ENR, Top 20 States in Major Construction Markets. Based on eleven-month cumulative contract awards, 1989 vs. 1988, in millions of dollars.

## Top corporations in the leisure products industry

1. Eastman Kodak Co., with $12,610 million
2. Carnival Cruise Lines, Inc., $2,795
3. Polaroid, $2,449
4. Brunswick, $1,286
5. Hasbro Inc., $1,101
6. American Greetings Corp., $1,062
7. Mattel, $977
8. Fleetwood Enterprises, Inc., $540
9. Outboard Marine, $507
10. CPI, $431

*Where'd you hear that?*
Business Week, The Business Week 1000. Based on market value as of March 16, 1990, in millions of dollars.

# DIVERSIONS

### Largest greeting card printers

1. Hallmark Cards (Kansas City, MO), with $2,300,000 thousand
2. American Greetings Corp. (Cleveland, OH), $1,275,359
3. Gibson Greetings (Cincinnati, OH), $404,000

*Where'd you hear that?*
graphic arts monthly, GAM 101. Based on 1988 sales, in thousands of dollars.

### Best stationery brands

1. Mead, with 46%
2. Bic, 27%
3. American Greetings Corp., 17%
4. Crayola, 7%
5. Papermate, 5%
6. Ambassador, 4%
6. Cambridge, 4%
6. Gibson Buzza, 4%
9. Hallmark Cards, 3%
9. Stuart Hall, 3%

*Where'd you hear that?*
Discount Store News, Top Brands Survey. Based on 1989 percentage of discounters naming brand as best.

### Most advertised cameras

1. Minolta, with $16,810.8 thousand
2. Canon, $14,883.2
3. Pentax, $7,486.0
4. Olympus, $6,778.1
5. Kodak, $6,209.3
6. Nikon, $5,778.6
7. Fuji Photo Film Co. Ltd., $1,949.8
8. Vivitar, $831.1

*Where'd you hear that?*
Marketing & Media Decisions. Based on total media expenditures in 1988, in thousands of dollars.

### Most productive photography and toy corporations

1. Polaroid, with $12.6 thousand
2. Hasbro Inc., $11.2
3. Mattel, 47.2
4. Eastman Kodak Co., $3.7
5. Brunswick, -$2.6

*Where'd you hear that?*
Forbes, Forbes 500s Annual Directory. Based on 1989 profits per employee, in thousands of dollars. Ranks U.S.-based corporations that were publicly traded as of March 23, 1990.

### Most profitable photography and toy companies

1. Fuqua Industries, with 23.6%
2. Hasbro Inc., 23.5%
3. Eastman Kodak Co., 14.3%
4. Tonka, 13.5%
5. Polaroid, 5.4%
6. Mattel, deficit

*Where'd you hear that?*
Forbes, Annual Report on American Industry. Based on 10-year average return on equity. Ranks publicly held corporations only.

### Most sought after toys

1. Nintendo Entertainment System—Nintendo
2. Barbie—Mattel
3. Teenage Ninja Turtles—Playmates
4. Teenage Mutant Turtles—Ultra
5. Micro Machines—Galoob
6. Super Mario Bros. II—Nintendo
7. Real Ghostbusters—Kenner
8. Oopsie Daisy—Tyco
9. Li'l Miss Makeup—Mattel

# DIVERSIONS

10. G.I. Joe—Hasbro

*Where'd you hear that?*
Non-Foods Merchandising. Based on unspecified criteria.

## Top toy brands at major discount chains

1. Fisher-Price, with 66%
2. Mattel, 32%
3. Playskool, 24%
4. Little Tikes, 16%
5. Milton Bradley, 11%
6. Hasbro Inc., 8%
7. Lego, 5%
7. Kenner, 5%
9. Tonka, 3%
9. Huffy, 3%

*Where'd you hear that?*
Discount Store News, Top Brands Survey. Based on percentage of managers naming brands as top performer.

## Most popular board games in Great Britain

1. Trivial Pursuit
2. Scrabble
3. Dingbats
4. Neighbours Game
5. Pictionary
6. Monopoly
7. Watergames
8. Question of Sport
9. Hungry Hippos
10. Genius

*Where'd you hear that?*
Accountancy. Based on total market value for the year ending August, 1989.

## Biggest corporations in the toy and sporting goods industry

1. Hasbro Inc., with $1,410 million
2. Mattel, $1,237

*Where'd you hear that?*
Fortune, Fortune 500 Largest U.S. Industrial Corporations. Based on 1989 sales, in millions of dollars.

## Biggest amusement attractions

1. Walt Disney World's Magic Kingdom, EPCOT Center, Disney-MGM Studios Theme Park, with 30,000,000
2. Disneyland, 14,400,000
3. Universal Studios Hollywood, 5,100,000
4. Knott's Berry Farm, 5,000,000
5. Sea World of Florida, 3,960,000
6. Sea World of California, 3,780,000
7. Busch Gardens The Dark Continent, 3,500,000
8. Kings Island, 3,169,154
9. Cedar Point, 3,150,000
10. Six Flags Magic Mountain, 3,100,000

*Where'd you hear that?*
Amusement Business, Amusement Business Annual Year-end Issue. Based on 1988 attendance.

# DIVERSIONS

### Largest waterparks

1. Wildwater Kingdom, Allentown, PA, with 778,900
2. White Water, Marietta, GA, 675,000
3. Raging Waters, San Dimas, CA, 500,000
4. Adventure Island, Tampa, FL, 482,000
5. Schilitterbahn Water Park, New Braunfels, TX, 450,000
6. Wild River, Laguna Hills, CA, 431,250
7. Atlantis, The Water Kingdom, Hollywood, FL, 365,000
8. Hyland Hills Water World, 315,000
9. Water County USA, Williamsburg, VA, 300.000
10. Oceans of Fun, Kansas City, MO, 237,415

*Where'd you hear that?*
Amusement Business, Amusement Business Annual Year-end Issue. Based on 1989 attendance.

### Top ten fairs

1. State Fair of Texas, Dallas, with 3,471,768
2. Ohio State Fair, Columbus, 3,462,310
3. Canadian National Exhibition, Toronto, Ont., 2,045,636
4. State Fair of Oklahoma, Oklahoma City, 1,815,260
5. Minnesota State Fair, St. Paul, 1,551,361
6. Los Angeles County Fair, Pomona, 1,365,873
7. Western Washington Fair, Puyallup, 1,358,752
8. Tusla (OK) State Fair, 1,280,690
9. New Mexico State Fair, Albuquerque, 1,253,277
10. Pacific National Exhibition, Vancouver, BC, 1,248,768

*Where'd you hear that?*
Amusement Business, Amusement Business Annual Year-end Issue. Based on attendance in 1988.

### Top 10 boat dealers

1. Boat World (Atlanta , GA)
2. Metz Marina (Kennewick, WA)
3. Channel Marine (Weirs Beach, NH)
4. Skipper Bud's (Milwaukee, WI)
5. Klinger Lake Marina (Sturgis, MI)
6. D & R Boats (Greenbrook, NJ)
7. Schilling Boathouse (Hilton Head, SC)
8. Action Boat Brokers (Huntington Beach, CA)
9. Perez Cove Marine (San Diego, CA)
10. Jericho Boats (Long Island, NY)

*Where'd you hear that?*
Boating Industry. Based on unspecified criteria.

### Leading inland marine insurance writers

1. American Intern Group, with $646,546 thousand
2. Home Group Insurance Cos., $253,265
3. Chubb Group of Insurance Cos., $234,591
4. State Farm Group, $221,254
5. Fireman's Fund Cos., $201,543
6. Continental Insurance Cos., $198,776

7. Cigna Group, $175,064
8. Hartford Insurance Group, $153,734
9. Aetna Life & Casualty Group, $141,665
10. American Bankers Group, $137,956

*Where'd you hear that?*
Best's Review, Property/Casualty edition. Based on 1988 direct premuims, in thousands of dollars.

## Leading foreign destinations for U.S. air travellers

1. Mexico, with 2,627,842
2. United Kingdom, 2,174,218
3. West Germany, 1,196,657
4. Bahamas, 1,002,846
5. Japan, 951,037
6. France, 698,678
7. Dominican Republic, 649,349
8. Jamaica, 588,109
9. Italy, 432,288
10. Netherlands Antilles, 417,890

*Where'd you hear that?*
Travel Industry World Yearbook: The Big Picture. Based on number of U.S. citizen air departures in 1988. Excludes Canada.

## Leading countries of embarkation for foreign tourists to the U.S.

1. Japan, with 2,759,932
2. United Kingdom, 2,153,755
3. West Germany, 1,007,002
4. Mexico, 968,633
5. France, 674,270
6. Bahamas, 415,135
7. Netherlands, 346,254
8. Italy, 294,812
9. Switzerland, 281,117
10. Brazil, 280,346

*Where'd you hear that?*
Travel Industry World Yearbook: The Big Picture. Based on number of non-U.S. citizen air arrivals from foreign countries in 1988. Excludes Canada.

## Leading countries in tourist trade with the U.S.

1. Japan, with 2,900 thousand
2. Great Britain, 1,975
3. West Germany, 1,200
4. France, 625
5. Italy, 365
5. Australia, 365
7. Switzerland, 300
8. Netherlands, 255

*Where'd you hear that?*
Wall Street Journal. Based on 1989 estimated foreign-visitor arrivals in U.S., in thousands.

## Busiest airport hotels in the U.S.

1. Red Lion Hotel, San Jose, CA, with $47,572
2. Crystal City Marriott, Arlington, VA, $47,059
3. DFW Hilton Conference Center, Grapevine, TX, $42,394
4. Radisson Plaza Hotel, Manhattan Beach, CA, $39,578
5. Days Inn, Philadelphia, PA, $39,548
6. Hyatt Regency Crystal City, Arlington, VA, $36,496
7. Embassy Suites O'Hare, Rosemont, IL, $36,177

**DIVERSIONS**

# DIVERSIONS

8. Guest Quarters Hotel-BWI Airport, Linthicum, MD, $35,944
9. Quality Inn-Airport, Philadelphia, PA, $34,088
10. Sheraton Plaza La Reina, Los Angeles, CA, $32,136

*Where'd you hear that?*
Lodging Hospitality. Based on 1988 sales per room.

## Largest hotel management companies

1. Regal-Aircoa Co., with 36,472 rooms
2. Tollman Hundley, 19,693
3. Prime Motor Inns/Prime Management Co., 19,360
4. VMS Realty Partners, 17,000
5. Omni Hotel Corp., 15,611
6. Servico, Inc., 15,267
7. Larken, Inc., 14,198
8. Continental Cos., 13,600
9. Pratt Hotel Corp., 11,838
10. Commonwealth Hospitality, Ltd., 11,437

*Where'd you hear that?*
Lodging, Hospitality, Lodgings 400 Top Performer. Based on number of rooms managed.

## Largest Asian quoted companies in hotels and restaurants for 1988

1. Skylark Co. Ltd., Japan, with $1,107,689 thousand
2. New World Development Co. Ltd., Hongkong, $678,214
3. Fujuita Tourist Enterprises Co. Ltd., Japan, $612,056
4. Restaurant Seibu Ltd., Japan, $566,598
5. Royal Co. Ltd., Japan, $552,454
6. Tokyu Hotel Chain Co. Ltd., Japan, $544,701
7. Wharf Holdings Ltd., Hongkong, $306,172
8. Genting Bhd, Malaysia, $177,371
9. The Hongkong & Shanghai Hotels Ltd., Hongkong, $146,076
10. Dai-Ichi Hotel Ltd., Japan, $124,104

*Where'd you hear that?*
Asia's 7500 Largest Companies, Dun & Bradstreet. Based on sales, in thousands of U.S. dollars.

## Top corporations in the hotel & motel industry

1. Marriott, with $2,724 million
2. Hilton Hotels Corp., $2,468
3. Circus Circus Enterprises, $1,430
4. Promus, $734
5. Caesars World, $570
6. Golden Nugget Inc., $456
7. Prime Motor Inns, $429

*Where'd you hear that?*
Business Week, The Business Week 1000. Based on market value as of March 16, 1990, in millions of dollars.

## Largest hotel and motel chains

1. Holiday Corp., with 314,900
2. Best Western International, 158,665
3. Marriott Lodging Group, 125,216
4. Quality International, 121,746
5. Ramada Hotel Group, 108,015
6. Days Inn of America Inc., 104,192
7. Hilton Hotels Corp., 94,982
8. Sheraton Corp., 89,341

# DIVERSIONS

9. Hyatt Hotels Corp., 53,539
10. Howard Johnson Franchise, 53,457

*Where'd you hear that?*
Lodging Hospitality, Lodgings 400 Top Performers. Based on number of rooms.

## Leading hotel companies in foodservice/restaurant operations

1. Sheraton Corp., with $1,600 million
2. Marriott Lodging, $1,218.3
3. Hilton Hotels Corp., $1,054
4. Hyatt Hotels Corp., $796.2
5. Holiday Inn Hotels, $751.3
6. Ramada Hotels, $547.3
7. Westin Hotels, $427.4
8. Inter-Continental Corp., $420
9. Quality Inns, $376
10. Days Inn of America Inc., $370.8

*Where'd you hear that?*
Restaurants & Institutions, Restaurants & Institutions 400. Based on sales, in millions of dollars.

## Best upscale sector hotels

1. Inter-Continental Corp., with a score of 8.17
2. Swissotels, 8.16
3. Fairmount Hotels, 8.08
4. Westin Hotels & Resorts, 8.07
5. Marriott Hotels & Resorts, 8.02
5. Hyatt Hotels Corp., 8.02
7. Wyndham, 7.89
8. Lowes Hotels, 7.87
9. Sonesta, 7.83
10. Sheraton Hotels & Resorts, 7.75

*Where'd you hear that?*
Business Travel News, U.S. Hotel Systems Survey. Based on overall composite score for 12 categories; scoring on a 10-point scale, with 10 the highest.

## World's best hotels

1. Oriental, Bangkok, with a rating of 88.9
2. Vier Jahreszeiten, Hamburg, 88.3
3. Ritz, Paris, 87.7
4. Bel-Air, Los Angeles, 87.6
5. Mandarin Oriental, Hongkong, 87.2
6. Regent, Hong Kong, 87.0
7. Peninsula, Hong Kong, 86.5
8. Shangri-La, Singapore, 86.1
9. Okura, Tokyo, 85.7
10. Le Bristol, Paris, 85.5

*Where'd you hear that?*
Institutional Investor, International edition. Based on rating in 1989.

## Best suites sector hotels

1. Point Resorts, with a score of 8.23
2. Radisson Suites, 8.03
3. Marriott Suites, 7.99
4. Park Suites, 7.77
5. Guest Quarters Suite Hotels, 7.60
6. Embassy Suites, 7.59
7. Residence Inn, 7.57
8. Pickett Suite Hotels, 7.51
9. Howard Johnson AmeriSuites, 7.44
10. Quality Suites, 7.39

# DIVERSIONS

*Where'd you hear that?*
Business Travel News, U.S. Hotel Systems Survey. Based on overall composite score for 12 categories; scoring on a 10-point scale, with 10 the highest.

## Top all-suite lodging chains

1. Embassy Suites, with 26,800
2. Residence Inn by Marriott, 20,700
3. Guest Quarters Suite Hotels, 6,200
4. Radisson Hotels International, 5,700
5. Quality Suites, 5,300
6. Comfort Suites, 4,600
7. Lexington Hotel Suites, 4,100

*Where'd you hear that?*
Hotel & Motel Management. Based on number of suites estimated to be opened by December 31, 1990.

## Best mid-priced sector hotels

1. Courtyard by Marriott, with a score of 7.69
2. Sheraton Inns, 7.52
3. Dillon Inn, 7.37
4. Clubhouse Inns of America, 7.26
5. Holiday Inn Hotels, 7.06
6. Ibis Hotels, 7.01
7. Signature Inns, 6.98
8. Ramada Inns, 6.84
9. Drury Inns, 6.74
10. Raintree Inns, 6.57

*Where'd you hear that?*
Business Travel News, U.S. Hotel Systems Survey. Based on overall composite score for 12 categories; scoring on a 10-point scale, with 10 the highest.

## Best economy sector hotels

1. Hampton Inns Inc., with a score of 6.98
2. Fairfield Inns, 6.62
3. Comfort Inns, 6.43
4. Rodeway Inns, 6.18
5. Shoney Inns, 6.08
6. Red Carpet, 6.02
7. Red Roof Inns, 5.91
8. Budgetel Inns, 5.68
9. Motel 6, 5.24
10. Econo Lodges of America, 5.23
11. Friendship Inns, 5.11

*Where'd you hear that?*
Business Travel News, U.S. Hotel Systems Survey. Based on overall composite score for 12 categories; scoring on a 10-point scale, with 10 the highest.

## Largest U.S. economy/limited service lodging chains

1. Days Inn of America Inc., with 96,900
2. Motel 6, 64,000
3. Comfort Inns, 63,000
4. Econo Lodges of America, 52,000
5. Super 8 Motels Inc., 50,300
6. Travelodge, 46,300
7. Hampton Inns Inc., 29,900
8. Hospitality International Inc., 29,500
9. La Quinta Motor Inns, 27,900
10. Red Roof Inns Inc., 23,900

*Where'd you hear that?*
Hotel & Motel Management. Based on number of rooms as of January 1, 1990.

## Top highway lodging performers

1. Madonna Inn, San Luis Obispo, CA, with $73,394
2. Hanover Inn at Dartmouth College, Hanover, NH, $49,980
3. Sheraton at Woodbridge Place, Iselin, NJ, $48,828
4. Weber's Inn, Ann Arbor, MI, $45,518
5. Sheraton Meadowlands, East Rutherford, NJ, $43,798
6. The Desmond Americana, Albany, NY, $41,667
7. Northampton Hilton Inn, Northampton, MA, $39,039
8. Holiday Inn Pyramid, Albuquerque, NM, $39,009
9. Howard Johnsons, Chelmsford, MA, $36,157
10. Best Western Grand Canyon Squire Inn, Grand Canyon, AZ, $35,933

*Where'd you hear that?*
Lodging Hospitality, Lodgings 400 Top Performers. Based on total sales per room.

## Top suburban lodging performers

1. Hilton Natick, Natick, MA, with $93,684
2. Sheraton Valley Forge Hotel, King of Prussia, PA, $88,511
3. Skipper Inn & Marina, Fairhaven, MA, $71,429
4. Oyster Point Hotel, Red Bank, NJ, $70,690
5. Scanticon Princeton Conference Center, Princeton, NJ, $65,292
6. Harrison Conference Center, Lake Bluff, IL, $59,488
7. Sheraton Smithtown, Smithtown, NY, $58,768
8. Lowes Glenpointe Hotel, Teaneck, NJ, $54,017
9. Island Inn, Westbury, NY, $49,019
10. Adam's Mark Hotel, Philadelphia, PA, $48,544

*Where'd you hear that?*
Lodging Hospitality, Lodgings 400 Top Performers. Based on total sales per room.

## Top center city hotels

1. Morgans Hotel, New York, NY, with $136,607
2. St. James's Club, West Hollywood, CA, $120,968
3. L'Ermitage Hotel, Beverly Hills, CA, $110,909
4. The Lowell Hotel, New York, NY, $101,754
5. Bel Age Hotel, West Hollywood, CA, $100,253
6. Ritz-Carlton Hotel, Chicago, IL, $95,127
7. Willard Inter-Continental Hotel, Washington, DC, $80,003
8. The Helmsley Park Lane Hotel, New York, NY, $76,923
9. The Hay-Adams Hotel, Washington, DC, $76,923
10. Fairmount Hotel, San Antonio, TX, $75,676

*Where'd you hear that?*
Lodging Hospitality, Lodgings 400 Top Performers. Based on total sales per room.

# DIVERSIONS

# DIVERSIONS

## Cities with the highest hotel costs

1. New York, NY, with $119.78
2. Boston, MA, $86.84
3. San Francisco, CA, $81.18
4. Washington, DC, $79.68
5. Honolulu, HI, $79.26
6. New Orleans, LA, $73.55
7. Chicago, IL, $73.18
8. San Diego, CA, $72.24
9. Miami/Hialeah, FL, $69.97
10. Los Angeles/Long Beach, CA, $68.23

*Where'd you hear that?*
New York Times. Based on based on monthly surveys of average room rates at 12,000 hotels in 1989.

### Top resort lodging performers

1. Holiday Isle Resort, Islamorada, FL, with $188,338
2. Caneel Bay, St. John, USVI, $136,520
3. Williamsburg Inn, Williamsburg, VA, $127,659
4. Trump Plaza Hotel & Casino, Atlantic City, NJ, $120,663
5. The Boulders Resort, Carefree, AZ, $120,083
6. Halekulani Hotel, Honolulu, HI, $114,314
7. Ventana, Big Sur, CA, $107,616
8. Longboat Key Club, Longboat Key, FL, $99,548
9. Singing Hill Country Club & Lodge, El Cajon, CA, $97,500
10. Kona Village Resort, Kailva-Kona, HI, $96,000

*Where'd you hear that?*
Lodging Hospitality, Lodgings 400 Top Performers. Based on total sales per room.

### Most profitable hotel and gaming companies

1. Hilton Hotels Corp., with 18.4%
2. Caesars World, 15.3%
3. Holiday Corp., 12.3%
4. Bally Manufacturing, 6.4%
5. Ramada, 0.4%
6. Carnival Cruise Lines, Inc., NA
7. Circus Circus Enterprises, NA

*Where'd you hear that?*
Forbes, Annual Report on American Industry. Based on 10-year average return on equity. Ranks publicly held corporations only.

### Most productive hotels and gaming corporations

1. Carnival Cruise Lines, Inc., with $15.2 thousand
2. Circus Circus Enterprises, $8.2
3. Hilton Hotels Corp., $2.9
4. Bally Manufacturing, $0.8

*Where'd you hear that?*
Forbes, Forbes 500s Annual Directory. Based on 1989 profits per employee, in thousands of dollars. Ranks U.S.-based corporations that were publicly traded as of March 23, 1990.

### Largest casinos in Atlantic City

1. Trump Plaza, with $305.7 million
2. Caesars, $303.1
3. Harrah's Marina, $293.1
4. Tropworld, $285.4
5. Bally's Park Plaza, $278.9
6. Trump Castle, $264.8

7. Showboat, $258.8
8. Resorts, $227.4
9. Sands, $219.4
10. Bally's Grand, $210.7

*Where'd you hear that?*
New York Times. Based on 1989 gaming revenues, in millions of dollars.

## Largest vacation timesharing resort companies

1. General Development Corp., Miami, Fl, with $117 million
2. Fairfield Communities, Little Rock, AR, $111
3. Marriott Ownership Resorts, Lakeland, FL, $52
4. Shell/Winners' Circle Resorts, Del Mar, CA, $40
4. Ridge Tahoe, Stateline, NV, $40
6. Orange Lake Country Club, Kissimmee, FL, $38
7. Island One, Inc., Orlando, FL, $35
7. Lawrence Welk Vacation Villas, Escondido, CA, $35
7. Westgate Vacation Villas, Orlando, FL, $35
10. Peppertree Resorts, Ltd., Asheville, NC, $34

*Where'd you hear that?*
Urban Land. Based on 1988 sales, in millions of dollars.

## Largest retail outlets for souvenirs and novelties

1. Walt Disney World/Epcot Center, with $75.5 millions
2. Pier 39, $51
3. Disneyland, $33
4. South of the Border, $31
5. Knott's Berry Farm, $16
6. Sea World of Florida, $10.5
7. Universal Studios Tour, $9.9
8. Sea World of California, $9
9. Busch Gardens, $8.8
10. Cedar Point, $7.5

*Where'd you hear that?*
Souvenirs & Novelties, Souvenirs & Novelties 500. Based on 1989 sales, in millions of dollars.

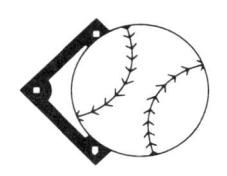

## The 10 most valuable baseball cards

1. Honus Wagner, 1910, for $95,000
2. Fred Lindstrom, 1932, $18,000
3. Napolean Lajoie, 1933, $15,000
3. Joe Doyle, 1910, $15,000
5. Eddie Plank, 1910, $9,000
6. Sherwood Magie, 1910, $8,000
7. Mickey Mantle, 1952, $6,500
8. Robin Roberts, 1951, $5,500
8. Jim Konstanty, 1951, $5,500
10. Ed Stanky, 1951, $5,500

*Where'd you hear that?*
Financial World. Based on trading value.

## Leading states in new golf course development

1. Florida, with 125
2. California, 65
3. North Carolina, 42
4. Illinois, 38
5. Georgia, 37

# DIVERSIONS

# DIVERSIONS

6. Texas, 35
7. South Carolina, 31
8. Michigan, 27
9. Ohio, 23
9. Arizona, 23

*Where'd you hear that?*
Stores. Based on number of courses under development in 1989.

## Leading manufacturers of golf clubs in the U.S.

1. Northwestern, with $84.0 million (est.)
2. Karsten, $82.0 (est.)
3. Taylor Made, $74.0
4. Spalding, $69.0
5. Wilson, $56.4 (est.)
6. Mizuno, $35.0
7. MacGregor, $30.1
8. Ram, $28.0 (est.)
9. Ben Hogan, $25.0 (est.)
10. Lynx, $22.0 (est.)

*Where'd you hear that?*
Sports Market Place, Market Statistics Report. Based on 1988 sales, in millions of dollars.

## Leading manufacturers of golf balls in the U.S.

1. Spalding, with $158.0 million
2. Titleist, $108.0
3. Dunlop, $48.0 (est.)
4. Wilson, $31.2 (est.)
5. Ram, $11.0 (est.)

*Where'd you hear that?*
Sports Market Place, Market Statistics Report. Based on 1988 sales, in millions of dollars.

## Leading manufacturers of team equipment

1. Rawlings, with $90 million (est.)
2. Wilson, $82
3. Spalding, $65 (est.)
4. Worth, $35
5. Easton, $31
6. Bike, $21 (est.)
7. MacGregor Athletic Products, $20 (est.)
7. Hillerich & Bradsby, $20 (est.)
9. Riddell, $19 (est.)
10. Dudley, $17 (est.)

*Where'd you hear that?*
Sports Market Place, Market Statistics Report. Based on 1988 sales, in millions of dollars.

## Leading manufacturers of nordic ski equipment

1. Trak, with $6 million (est.)
1. Karhu, $6
1. Salomon, $6
1. Fischer, $6
5. Alpina, $5
6. Rossignol, $4
7. Swix, $3
8. Jarvinen, $3 (est.)
9. Exel Inc., $2 (est.)

*Where'd you hear that?*
Sports Market Place, Market Statistics Report. Based on 1988 sales, in millions of dollars.

## Leading manufacturers of alpine skis

1. Rossignol, with $34 million
2. K2, $26
3. Elan, $17
4. Dynastar, $15
5. Atomic, $12 (est.)
6. Olin, $9

# DIVERSIONS

7. Head, $8
7. Kastle, $8

*Where'd you hear that?*
Sports Market Place, Market Statistics Report. Based on 1988 sales, in millions of dollars.

## Leading manufacturers of alpine ski bindings

1. Salomon, with $30 million
2. Tyrolia, $20
3. Marker, $16 (est.)
4. Geze, $6
5. Look, $3 (est.)

*Where'd you hear that?*
Sports Market Place, Market Statistics Report. Based on 1988 sales, in millions of dollars.

## Leading manufacturers of alpine ski boots

1. Nordica, with $39 million
2. Salomon, $38
3. Raichle, $19
4. Lange, $12
5. Tecnica, $10
6. Heierling, $4

*Where'd you hear that?*
Sports Market Place, Market Statistics Report. Based on 1988 sales, in millions of dollars.

## Largest manufacturers of home fitness equipment

1. Diversified Products, with $120 million
2. Weslo, $105
3. Weider, $80
4. Ajay, $60
5. Exel Inc., $58
6. Precor, $38
7. Soloflex, $32
8. Nordic Trak, $29

9. Marcy, $23
10. Voit, $21

*Where'd you hear that?*
Sports Market Place, Market Statistics Report. Based on 1988 sales, in millions of dollars.

## *Leading manufacturers of sporting goods, athletic footwear, and apparel*

1. Reebok, with $1,613 million
2. Nike, $1,135
3. Russell, $531
4. Spalding, $355
5. Tultex, $339
6. Adidas, $332
7. Coleman, $329
8. Ocean Pacific, $309
9. Wilson, $291
10. Bassett-Walker, $285

*Where'd you hear that?*
Sports Market Place, Market Statistics Report. Based on 1988 sales, in millions of dollars.

## Largest brasswinds producers

1. Selmer, with 35%
2. UMI, 25%
3. Yamaha, 20%
3. Others, total, 20%

*Where'd you hear that?*
Music Trades. Based on 1989 market share, in percent.

## Largest woodwinds producers

1. Selmer, with 35%
1. Leblanc, 35%

# DIVERSIONS

3. UMI, 20%
4. Buffet, 5%
4. Others, total, 5%

*Where'd you hear that?*
Music Trades. Based on 1989 market share, in percent.

### Largest flute producers

1. Gemeinhardt, with 40%
2. Selmer, 20%
2. UMI, 20%
4. Yamaha, 10%
4. Others, total, 10%

*Where'd you hear that?*
Music Trades. Based on 1989 market share, in percent.

### Largest string instrument producers

1. St. Louis Music, with 20%
1. Selmer, 20%
3. UMI, 15%
4. William Lewis, 10%
5. Others, total, 35%

*Where'd you hear that?*
Music Trades. Based on 1989 market share, in percent.

### Top corporations in the entertainment industry

1. Walt Disney Co., with $15,706 million
2. Paramount Communications, $5,347
3. MCA, $3,866
4. United Artists Entertainment, $1,947
5. Blockbuster Entertainment, $1,202
6. King World Productions, $1,029
7. MGM/UA Communications, $861
8. Orion Pictures, $392
9. Spelling Entertainment, $335

*Where'd you hear that?*
Business Week, The Business Week 1000. Based on market value as of March 16, 1990, in millions of dollars.

### Entertainers with the highest earnings

1. Michael Jackson, with $125 million
2. Steven Spielberg, $105
3. William H. Cosby, Jr., $95
4. Mike Tyson, $71
5. Charles M. Schulz, $60
6. Eddie Murphy, $57
7. Pink Floyd, $56
8. Rolling Stones, $55
8. Oprah Winfrey, $55
10. George Michael, $47

*Where'd you hear that?*
Forbes. Based on 1988-89 gross income, in millions of dollars.

## Top 10 promoters

1. Concert Prods. International/BCL Group, with $83,587,795
2. Metropolitan Entertainment, $25,950,020
3. Bill Graham Presents, $22,763,987
4. Avalon Attractions, $19,831,401
5. Ron Delsener Enterprises, $19,697,754
6. Cellar Door Prods., $16,587,862
7. Music Fair Prods., $14,722,765
8. Electric Factory Concerts, $14,238,157
9. Jam Prods., $13,947,656
10. Brass Ring Prods., $13,899,931

*Where'd you hear that?*
Amusement Business, Amusement Business Annual Year-end Issue. Based on total gross, December 12, 1988 - November 28, 1989.

## Biggest acts

1. The Rolling Stones, Guns N' Roses, Living Colour, Los Angeles (CA) Memorial Coliseum & Sports Arena, Oct. 18-19 & 21-22, with $9,166,937
2. The Rolling Stones Living Colour, Dou n' Dlaye Rose & Troupe, William A. Shea Stadium, Flushing, NY, Oct. 25-26 & 28-29, $7,871,842
3. The Who, Giants Stadium, East Rutherford, NJ, June 29-30 & July 2-3, $5,243,672
4. The Rolling Stones, Living Colour, Sullivan Stadium, Foxboro, MA, Sept. 29 & Oct. 1 & 3, $4,648,338
5. The Rolling Stones, Living Colour, Mar Magette, William A. Shea Stadium, Flushing, NY, Oct. 10-11, $3,735,610
6. Neil Diamond, The Great Western Forum, Inglewood, CA, June 28-30, July 2 & 5-10, $3,498,000
7. The Rolling Stones, Living Colour, Cotton Bowl Stadium, Fair Park, Dallas, TX, Nov. 10-11, $3,410,886
8. The Rolling Stones, Living Colour, Exhibition Place Canadian National Exhibition, Toronto, Ont., Sept. 3-4, $3,368,752
9. The Rolling Stones, Living Colour, Stadium Oakland-Alameda County, CA, Coliseum, Nov. 4-5, $3,347,518
10. The Rolling Stones, Living Colour, Philadelphia, PA, Veterans Stadium, Aug. 31, Sept. 1, $3,181,143

*Where'd you hear that?*
Amusement Business, Amusement Business Annual Year-end Issue. Based on gross ticket sales, December 12, 1988 - November 28, 1989.

# DIVERSIONS

# DIVERSIONS

## Biggest country music acts

1. Kenny & Christmas: Kenny Rogers, The Forester Sisters, Westbury, NY, Music Fair, Dec. 6-12, 1988, with $707,263
2. Kenny & Christmas: Kenny Rogers, The Forester Sisters, Fox Theatre, Atlanta, GA, Dec. 15-18, 1988, $508,284
3. Kenny & Christmas: Kenny Rogers, The Forester Sisters, Fox Theatre, Detroit, MI, Dec. 20-23, 1988, $489,880
4. Kenny Rogers, Lorrie Morgan, Valley Forge Music Fair, Devon, PA, Aug. 17-20, $455,196
5. Hank Williams Jr. & The Bama Band, Tanya Tucker, The Omni, Atlanta, GA, Feb. 10-11
6. George Strait, Kathy Mattea, Baillie & The Boys, Starplex Amphitheatre, Fair Park, Dallas, TX, June 15-16, $434,939
7. George Strait, Billy Joe Royal, Linda Davis, The Summit, Houston, TX, July 8-9, $434,738
8. Randy Travis, K.T. Oslin, Universal Amphitheatre, Universal City, CA, Aug. 8-10, $376,457
9. Kenny Rogers/Dolly Parton, Tacoma, WA, Dome, Dec. 31, 1988, $374,351
10. Anne Murray, The O'Keefe Centre, Toronto, ON, May 17-21, $358,494

*Where'd you hear that?*
Amusement Business, Amusement Business Annual Year-end Issue. Based on gross ticket sales, December 12, 1988 - November 28, 1989.

## Top 10 touring acts

1. The Rolling Stones, with $73,426,873
2. The Who, $34,874,576
3. Bon Jovi, $28,406,238
4. Grateful Dead, $26,159,090
5. Neil Diamond, $21,953,570
6. Metallica, $14,962,757
7. Rod Stewart, $12,674,131
8. Elton John, $9,306,778
9. Poison, $8,721,803
10. Barry Manilow, $8,190,176

*Where'd you hear that?*
Amusement Business, Amusement Business Annual Year-end Issue. Based on gross ticket sales, December 12, 1988 - November 28, 1989.

## Top 10 pay-per-view concerts

1. Rolling Stones (12/89), with 2.2%
2. Moscow Music Festival (8/89), 2.0%
3. The Who: 'Tommy' (12/89), 1.0%
3. Grateful Dead (6/89), 1.0%
5. Yes (9/89), 0.5%
5. Ultimate Event (2/89), 0.5%
5. Hank Williams, Jr. (10/89), 0.5%
8. Wayne Newton (5/89), 0.3%
8. LaToya Jackson (9/89), 0.3%
10. This Country's Rockin (7/89), 0.2%

*Where'd you hear that?*
Cable World. Based on purchase rate, in percent, for 1989.

# DIVERSIONS

## Biggest variety/specialty acts

1. The Magic of David Copperfield, Fox Theatre, Detroit, MI, March 4-6, with $756,166
2. The Magic of David Copperfield, The O'Keefe Centre, Toronto, ON, May 24-28, $676,763
3. Andrew Dice Clay, Centrum in Worcester, MA, Nov. 9-10, $545,940
4. Jackie Mason, Dennis Blair, Westbury, NY, Music Fair, May 17-21
5. Bob Hope, Toni Tennille, Fox Theatre, Detroit, MI, April 12-16, $441,928
6. Gallagher, Fox Theatre, Detroit, MI, Jan. 25-30, $416,546
7. Andrew Dice Clay, Meadowlands Arena, East Rutherford, NJ, Nov. 16, $400,000
8. George Burns/Bob Hope, Dionne Warwick, Madison Square Garden Arena, New York NY, Oct. 1, $395,032
9. Howard Stern, Nassau Veterans Memorial Coliseum, Uniondale, NY, Oct. 7, $382,500
10. The Magic of David Copperfield, Palais Des Arts, Montreal, Que. May 12-14, 70,063

*Where'd you hear that?*
Amusement Business, Amusement Business Annual Year-end Issue. Based on gross ticket sales, December 12, 1988 - November 28, 1989.

## *Top pop labels*

1. Columbia, with 10.62%
2. Atlantic, 9.33%
3. Geffen, 8.00%
4. MCA, 7.60%
5. Elektra, 6.97%
6. Warner Bros., 6.14%
7. Epic, 5.73%
8. Capitol, 5.53%
9. Mercury, 5.22%
10. Arista, 5.05%

*Where'd you hear that?*
Wall Street Journal. Based on share of Billboard's weekly top pop album list between January 7 and December 23, 1989, in percent.

## Market share of color televisions

1. Thomson (GE/RCA), with 21%
2. Zenith, 13%
3. NAP (Magnavox, Sylvania), 12%
4. Sharp, 6%
4. Sony, 6%
6. Matsushita (Panasonic, Sylvania), 5%
6. Mitsubishi, 5%
8. Emerson, 4%
8. Toshiba, 4%
10. GoldStar Co. Ltd., 2%
10. Hitachi, 2%
10. Samsung, 2%
10. Sanyo, 2%

# DIVERSIONS

*Where'd you hear that?*
Appliance Manufacturer. Based on 1989 market share, in percent.

## Market share of videocassette recorders

1. Thomson (GE/RCA), with 17%
2. Matsushita (Panasonic, Quasar), 12%
3. NAP (Magnavox, Sylvania), 9%
4. Emerson, 7%
4. Sharp, 7%
6. Zenith, 6%
7. JVC, 4%
7. Mitsubishi, 4%
7. Sony, 4%
7. Toshiba, 4%

*Where'd you hear that?*
Appliance Manufacturer. Based on 1989 market share, in percent.

## Largest motion picture distributors

1. Warner Bros., with 17.4%
2. Universal, 16.6%
3. Columbia/Tri Star, 16%
4. Buena Vista, 13.9%
5. Paramount, 13.8%
6. 20th Century Fox, 6.5%
7. MGM/UA, 6.3%
8. Orion, 4.2%
9. All Independents, 5.3%

*Where'd you hear that?*
Film Journal. Based on 1989 market share, in percent.

## Most popular movies released in the 1980s

1. *E. T. The Extra-Terrestrial*, with a U.S. box-office gross of $367.7 million
2. *Return of the Jedi*, $263.7
3. *Batman*, $251.2
4. *Raiders of the Lost Ark*, $242.4
5. *Beverly Hills Cop*, $234.8
6. *The Empire Strikes Back*, $223.2
7. *Ghostbusters*, $221.1
8. *Back to the Future*, $208.3
9. *Indiana Jones and the Last Crusade*, $195.5
10. *Indiana Jones and the Temple of Doom*, $179.9

*Where'd you hear that?*
U.S. News & World Report. Based on U.S. box-office gross, in millions of dollars.

## Biggest money losing movies released in the 1980s

1. *Inchon*, with an estimated loss of -$44.1 million
2. *Adventures of Baron Munchausen*, -$43.0
3. *Ishtar*, -$37.3
4. *Heaven's Gate*, -$34.5
5. *Cotton Club*, -$31.0
6. *Pirates*, -$30.3
7. *Rambo III*, -$30.0
8. *Santa Claus*, -$29.0
9. *Lion of the Desert*, -$28.5
10. *Once Upon a Time in America*, -$27.5

*Where'd you hear that?*
U.S. News & World Report. Based on box-office loss, in millions of dollars.

## 10 best-selling videocassettes

1. *Batman*, with 13.0 million units sold
2. *E. T. The Extra-Terrestrial*, 12.5
3. *Bambi*, 10.5
4. *Who Framed Roger Rabbit*, 8.5
5. *Cinderella*, 7.5

6. *Land Before Time*, 4.0
7. *Wizard of Oz*, 3.6
8. *Top Gun*, 3.5
9. *Lady and the Tramp*, 3.2
10. *Crocodile Dundee*, 2.5

*Where'd you hear that?*
Forbes. Based on units sold, in millions.

**Best-selling videos**

1. *E. T. The Extra-Terrestrial*, with 15.2 million
2. *Cinderella*, 7.8
3. *Lady and the Tramp*, 3.5
4. *Top Gun*, 3.2
5. *Good Morning, Vietnam*, 2.3
6. *Crocodile Dundee II*, 2.1
7. *Beverly Hills Cop (Part I)*, 1.8
7. *Star Trek IV*, 1.8
9. *Indiana Jones & The Temple of Doom*, 1.6
9. *Dirty Dancing*, 1.6

*Where'd you hear that?*
Video Store. Based on units sold, in millions.

**State lotteries spending the least to generate a government dollar**

1. Maryland, with 18.19 cents
2. New Jersey, 20.63
3. Pennsylvania, 21.78
4. Connecticut, 24.17

5. New York, 24.76
6. Illinois, 25.58
7. Delaware, 28.67
8. Massachusetts, 31.24
9. California, 34.56
10. Michigan, 34.99

*Where'd you hear that?*
Gaming & Wagering Business, Annual Study on Performance. Based on fiscal year 1988 cents spent to generate a government dollar.

## *State lotteries with the highest lottery sales*

1. Massachusetts, with 1.129%
2. District of Columbia, .915%
3. Maryland, .905%
4. Ohio, .817%
5. Michigan, .788%
6. Pennsylvania, .740%
7. Connecticut, .697%
8. New Jersey, .695%
9. Illinois, .640%
10. Delaware, .475%

*Where'd you hear that?*
Gaming & Wagering Business, Annual Study on Performance. Based on fiscal year 1988 sales as a percentage of state personal income.

**State lotteries with the highest government revenues**

1. California, with $800,473,043
2. New York, $710,390,000
3. Pennsylvania, $593,162,836
4. Ohio, $506,973,280
5. New Jersey, $502,233,173
6. Michigan, $488,436,483

**DIVERSIONS**

# DIVERSIONS

7. Illinois, $487,927,331
8. Massachusetts, $412,868,452
9. Maryland, $352,677,821
10. Florida, $230,421,815

*Where'd you hear that?*
Gaming & Wagering Business, Annual Study on Performance. Based on fiscal year 1988 government revenues.

## State lotteries with the highest ratio of revenues to sales

1. New York, with 45.37%
2. Maryland, 43.47%
3. New Jersey, 42.77%
4. Pennsylvania, 41.22%
5. Michigan, 40.67%
6. District of Columbia, 39.63%
7. Missouri, 39.31%
8. Washington, 39.08%
9. Connecticut, 39.03%
10. California, 38.00%

*Where'd you hear that?*
Gaming & Wagering Business, Annual Study on Performance. Based on fiscal year 1988 ratio of government revenues.

## State lotteries with the highest government revenues as a percentage of sales

1. Maryland, with 0.393%
2. District of Columbia, 0.363%
3. Massachusetts, 0.340%
4. Michigan, 0.320%
5. Pennsylvania, 0.305%
6. Ohio, 0.301%
7. New Jersey, 0.297%
8. Connecticut, 0.272%
9. Illinois, 0.240%
10. New York, 0.206%

*Where'd you hear that?*
Gaming & Wagering Business, Annual Study on Performance. Based on fiscal year 1988 government revenues as a percentage of state personal income.

## State lotteries spending the least to generate a sales dollar

1. Maryland, with 7.91 cents
2. New Jersey, 8.82
3. Pennsylvania, 8.98
4. Massachusetts, 9.40
5. Connecticut, 9.43
6. Illinois, 9.59
7. Delaware, 10.60
8. New York, 11.23
9. California, 13.13
10. Ohio, 13.28

*Where'd you hear that?*
Gaming & Wagering Business, Annual Study on Performance. Based on fiscal year 1988 cents spent to generate a sales dollar.

# Money Matters

## Strongest national economies

1. Japan, with 8.61
2. Switzerland, 7.96
3. West Germany, 7.73
4. Netherlands, 7.61
5. Taiwan, 7.54
6. Singapore, 7.52
7. Luxembourg, 7.50
8. Finland, 7.25
8. United States, 7.25
10. Korea, 7.24

*Where'd you hear that?*
Euromoney, World Economies. Based on overall economic performance, 1989-91, as projected by a team of economists on a scale of 1 (poor) to 10 (excellent).

## Countries with the largest gross domestic products

1. United States, with $4,864.3 billion
2. Japan, $2,858.9
3. West Germany, $1,208.3
4. France, $945.9
5. Italy, $828.8
6. Britain, $812.1
7. Canada, $486.5
8. Brazil, $384.6
9. China, $370.6
10. Spain, $342.3

*Where'd you hear that?*
Fortune. Based on 1988 GDP, in billions of U.S. dollars.

## World's largest exporters

1. West Germany, with $323,374 billion
2. United States, $321,600
3. Japan, $264.856
4. France, $167,783
5. United Kingdom, $145,166
6. Italy, $128,529
7. Canada, $116,841
8. Netherlands, $103,194
9. Belgium/Luxembourg, $92,103
10. Hong Kong, $63,163

*Where'd you hear that?*
International Development Review. Based on 1988 exports, in billions of dollars.

# MONEY MATTERS

### Leading U.S. export goods

1. Aircraft, with $20.3 billion
2. Auto parts, $13.2
3. Computer equipment and parts, $12.6
4. Computers, $11.6
5. Semiconductors, $10.4
6. Automobiles, $9.1
7. Organic chemicals, $7.8
8. Measuring instruments, $7.4
9. Rubber and plastics, $7.3
10. Jet and gas turbines, $6.2

*Where'd you hear that?*
U.S. News & World Report. Based on 1988 trade volume, in billions of dollars.

### Largest U.S. exporters

1. General Motors Corp., with $9,392.0 million
2. Ford Motor Co., $8,822.0
3. Boeing Co., $7,849.0
4. General Electric Co., $5,744.0
5. IBM, $4,951.0
6. Chrysler Corp., $4,343.9
7. E. I. du Pont de Nemours & Co., $4,196
8. McDonnell Douglas, $3,471.0
9. Caterpillar Inc., $2,930.0
10. United Technologies, $2,848.1
11. 1. Automobiles, with $47.5 billion
12. 2. Crude petroleum and products, $37.8
13. 3. Motor-vehicle parts, $14.7
14. 4. Computer equipment and parts, $11.5
15. 4. Semiconductors, $11.5
16. 6. Telecommunications equipment, $9.7
17. 7. Computers, $8.3
18. 8. Footwear, $8.0
19. 9. Paper and paperboard, $7.5
20. 9. Trucks and other vehicles, $7.5

*Where'd you hear that?*
Fortune, Top 50 Exporters. Based on 1988 export sales, in million of dollars.

### Countries that save the most

1. Japan, with 31.1%
2. Germany, 21.8%
3. Canada, 19.9%
4. Italy, 19.6%
5. France, 19.3%
6. Britain, 18.0%
7. United States, 16.9%

*Where'd you hear that?*
Wall Street Journal. Based on private and government saving percentage of gross domestic product, 1980-87.

### Metropolitan areas with the highest estimated disposable income in 1990

1. New York, NY, with $151,239,153 thousand
2. Los Angeles-Long Beach, CA, $122,635,432
3. Boston-Lawrence-Salem-Lowell-Brockton, MA, $103,706,645
4. Chicago, IL, $102,517,826
5. Washington, DC-MD-VA, $87,369,844
6. Detroit, MI, $71,819,579
7. Anaheim-Santa Ana, CA, $68,056,640
8. Philadelphia, PA-NJ, $59,892,272
9. Houston, TX, $55,971,859
10. Nassau-Suffolk, NY, $52,602,766

# MONEY MATTERS

*Where'd you hear that?*
Editor & Publisher Market Guide. Based on estimated 1990 disposable income, in thousands of dollars.

## Metropolitan areas with the highest estimated income per household in 1990

1. San Jose, CA, with $73,896
2. Vallejo-Fairfield-Napa, CA, $69,508
3. Anaheim-Santa Ana, CA, $68,274
4. Santa Barbara-Santa Maria-Lompoc, CA, $65,552
5. Santa Cruz, CA, $63,198
6. Sacramento, CA, $62,992
7. Oakland, CA, $62,417
8. San Diego, CA, $62,381
9. Oxnard-Ventura, CA, $62,359
10. Bridgeport-Stamford-Norwalk-Danbury, CT, $62,268

*Where'd you hear that?*
Editor & Publisher Market Guide. Based on estimated 1990 income per household.

## Metropolitan areas with the highest total effective buying income

1. Los Angeles-Long Beach, CA, with $129,522,222 thousand
2. New York, NY, $120,894,397
3. Chicago, IL, $87,161,650
4. Philadelphia, PA, $68,734,834
5. Washington, DC, $67,329,950
6. Boston-Lawrence-Salem-Lowell-Brockton, MA, $62,490,620
7. Detroit, MI, $56,788,300
8. Nassau-Suffolk, NY, $46,281,458
9. Houston, TX, $39,657,436
10. Anaheim-Santa Ana, CA, $38,034,417

*Where'd you hear that?*
Sales & Marketing Management, Survey of Buying Power. Based on 1988 total effective buying income, in thousands of dollars.

## Metropolitan areas with the highest suburban effective buying income

1. Los Angeles-Long Beach, CA, with $66,914,132 thousand
2. Washington, DC, $53,861,471
3. Chicago, IL, $50,346,053
4. Philadelphia, PA, $48,385,057
5. Nassau-Suffolk, NY, $46,281,458
6. Boston-Lawrence-Salem-Lowell-Brockton, MA, $44,171,737
7. Detroit, MI, $43,864,659
8. Atlanta, GA, $31,635,297
9. Anaheim-Santa Ana, CA, $31,334,947
10. Newark, NJ, $27,964,192

*Where'd you hear that?*
Sales & Marketing Management, Survey of Buying Power. Based on 1988 suburban effective buying income, in thousands of dollars.

## Metropolitan areas with the highest median household buying income

1. San Jose, CA, with $41,717
2. Nassau-Suffolk, NY, $41,534
3. Middlesex-Somerset-Hunterdon, NJ, $41,254
4. Bridgeport-Stamford-Norwalk-Danbury, CT, $40,537
5. Washington, DC, $38,489
6. Bergen-Passaic, NJ, $38,404
7. Oxnard-Ventura, CA, $37,196
8. Anaheim-Santa Ana, CA, $37,096
9. Trenton, NJ, $37,057

# MONEY MATTERS

10. Manchester-Nashua, NH, $36,437

*Where'd you hear that?*
Sales & Marketing Management, Survey of Buying Power. Based on 1988 median household effective buying income.

## Metropolitan areas with the most households with effective buying incomes over $50,000

1. Los Angeles-Long Beach, CA, with 816.9 thousand
2. New York, NY, 621.9
3. Washington, DC, 508.1
4. Chicago, IL, 493.2
5. Boston-Lawrence-Salem-Lowell-Brockton, MA, 411.3
6. Philadelphia, PA, 389.3
7. Nassau-Suffolk, NY, 337.3
8. Detroit, MI, 287.3
9. Anaheim-Santa Ana, CA, 271.5
10. Oakland, CA, 243.4

*Where'd you hear that?*
Sales & Marketing Management, Survey of Buying Power. Based on 1988 number of households with effective buying incomes of $50,000 and above, in thousands.

## Metropolitan areas with the highest buying power index

1. Los Angeles-Long Beach, CA, with 3.9019
2. New York, NY, 3.6279
3. Chicago, IL, 2.7058
4. Philadelphia, PA, 2.1747
5. Washington, DC, 1.9756
6. Boston-Lawrence-Salem-Lowell-Brockton, MA, 1.9099
7. Detroit, MI, 1.8451
8. Nassau-Suffolk, NY, 1.4180
9. Houston, TX, 1.3299
10. Atlanta, GA, 1.2487

*Where'd you hear that?*
Sales & Marketing Management, Survey of Buying Power. Based on 1988 buying power index.

## Metropolitan areas with the highest percentage of households with incomes of $50,000 or more

1. San Jose, CA, with 40.2%
1. Bridgeport-Stamford-Norwalk-Danbury, CT, 40.2%
3. Middlesex-Somerset-Hunterdon, NJ, 38.7%
4. Nassau-Suffolk, NY, 38.4%
5. Bergen-Passaic, NJ, 36.4%
6. Washington, DC, 36.3%
7. Trenton, NJ, 34.9%
8. Oxnard-Ventura, CA, 33.7%
9. Anaheim-Santa Ana, CA, 33.6%
10. Newark, NJ, 32.3%

*Where'd you hear that?*
Sales & Marketing Management, Survey of Buying Power. Based on 1988 percentage of households with effective buying incomes of $50,000 or more.

## Counties with the highest estimated income per household in 1990

1. Napa, CA, with $77,018
2. Marin, CA, $76,945
3. Fairfield, CT, $74,381
4. Santa Clara, CA, $74,062
5. Los Alamos, NM, $73,389
6. San Mateo, CA, $70,880
7. Sacramento, CA, $70,704
8. Placer, CA, $68,594
9. Orange, CA, $68,274
10. Yolo, CA, $67,842

# MONEY MATTERS

*Where'd you hear that?*
Editor & Publisher Market Guide.
Based on estimated 1990 income per household.

## Counties with the highest estimated disposable income in 1990

1. Los Angeles, CA, with $122,635,432 thousand
2. Cook, IL, $80,379,845
3. Orange, CA, $68,056,640
4. San Diego, CA, $52,398,807
5. Harris, TX, $49,475,480
6. Santa Clara, CA, $45,221,798
7. Queens, NY, $38,444,050
8. Maricopa, AZ, $37,745,350
9. Kings, NY, $33,499,485
10. Wayne, MI, $33,300,809

*Where'd you hear that?*
Editor & Publisher Market Guide.
Based on estimated 1990 disposable income, in thousands of dollars.

## Cities with the highest estimated disposable income in 1990

1. New York, NY, with $126,209,485 thousand
2. Los Angeles, CA, $39,036,888
3. Chicago, IL, $34,914,818
4. Philadelphia, PA, $22,563,259
5. Houston, TX, $20,473,804
6. San Jose, CA, $18,194,154
7. San Francisco, CA, $17,809,438
8. San Diego, CA, $17,506,767
9. Dallas, TX, $17,362,497
10. San Fernando Valley, CA, $17,297,381

*Where'd you hear that?*
Editor & Publisher Market Guide.
Based on estimated 1990 disposable income, in thousands of dollars.

## Cities with the highest estimated income per household in 1990

1. Newport Beach, CA, with $86,978
2. San Francisco, CA, $79,481
3. Palo Alto, CA, $78,152
4. Trumbull, CT, $69,632
5. Thousand Oaks, CA, $67,795
6. Pleasanton, CA, $67,377
7. Greenwich, CT, $66,740
8. Dublin, CA, $66,642
9. Wakefield, MA, $65,849
10. Dedham, MA, $65,481

*Where'd you hear that?*
Editor & Publisher Market Guide.
Based on estimated 1990 income per household.

# MONEY MATTERS

## World's largest accounting firms

1. Ernst & Young, with $4,244 million
2. KPMG, $3,900
3. Arthur Anderson & Co., $2,820
4. Coopers & Lybrand, $2,500
5. Price Waterhouse, $2,218
6. Deloitte Haskins & Sells, $1,921
7. Touche Ross, $1,840
8. BDO Binder Hamlyn, $783
9. Grant Thornton, $721
10. Horwath & Horwath, $556

*Where'd you hear that?*
Far Eastern Ecomonic Review. Based on 1988 revenues, in millions of U.S. dollars.

## Largest foreign financial companies

1. Dai-Ichi Kangyo Bank Ltd. (Japan), with $372.9 billion
2. Sumitomo (Japan), $362.4
3. Fuji Bank, Ltd. (Japan), $350.8
4. Mitsubishi (Japan), $338.5
5. Sanwa (Japan), $335.7
6. Industrial (Japan), $257.9
7. Tokai (Japan), $229.4
8. Mitsui (Japan), $198.5
9. Bank of Tokyo (Japan), $191.0
10. BNP (France), $188.3

*Where'd you hear that?*
Financial World, FW International 1000. Based on total 1988 assets, in billions of dollars.

## World's largest commercial banks

1. Dai-Ichi Kangyo Bank Ltd., with $379,322.8 million
2. Sumitomo Bank, $363,232.6
3. Fuji Bank, $360,529.8
4. Mitsubishi Bank, $348,999.0
5. Sanwa Bank, $330,705.4
6. Industrial Bank of Japan, $272,918.3
7. Norinchukin Bank, $235,944.3
8. Tokai Bank, $227,664.3
9. Mitsui Bank, $211,358.6
10. Credit Agricole, $210,566.3

*Where'd you hear that?*
Fortune, Fortune International 500. Based on 1988 assets, in millions of U.S. dollars.

## World's largest banks ranked by shareholders' equity

1. Fuji Bank Group, with $11,041.01 million
2. Dai-Ichi Kangyo Bank Ltd., $10,962.37
3. Caisse Nationale De Credit Agricole, $10,901.87
4. Sumitomo Bank, $10,736.86
5. Barclays, $10,713.48
6. Mitsubishi Bank, $10,181.88
7. Citicorp, $10,076.00
8. National Westminster Bank, $9,759.82
9. Sanwa Bank, $9,335.88
10. Industrial Bank of Japan, $9,251.62

*Where'd you hear that?*
Euromoney, Euromoney 500. Based on 1989 shareholders' equity, in millions of dollars.

## World's most leveraged banks

1. Norinchukin Bank, with 194.17
2. Bank Saderat Iran, 130.39

# MONEY MATTERS

3. Bank Melli Iran, 118.93
4. Chuo Trust & Banking Co. Ltd., 87.88
5. Svenska Handelsbanken, 84.43
6. S. E. Bank Group, 71.10
7. Banco di Napoli, 67.87
8. Deutsche Siedlungs und Landesrentenbank, 65.80
9. Bank of New England Corp., 64.04
10. Banco di Sicilia, 63.14

*Where'd you hear that?*
Euromoney, Euromoney 500. Based on 1989 leverage (liabilities/equity).

## World's largest banks ranked by net income

1. Industrial and Commercial Bank of China, with $2,838.72 million
2. Sumitomo Bank, $1,583.01
3. Dai-Ichi Kangyo Bank Ltd., $1,507.69
4. Rafidain Bank, $1,442.69
5. Fuji Bank Group, $1,399.07
6. Mitsubishi Bank, $1,315.74
7. Sanwa Bank, $1,228.66
8. Bankamerica Corp., $1,103.00
9. Bank of China, $1,071.61
10. Compagnie Financiere De Paribas, $958.63

*Where'd you hear that?*
Euromoney, Euromoney 500. Based on 1989 net income, in millions of dollars.

## World's largest financial institutions

1. I. B. J. with $85 billion
2. Sumitomo Bank, $63
3. Fuji Bank, Ltd., $59
4. D. K. B., $57
5. Mitsubishi Bank, $50
6. Sanwa Bank, $47
7. Nomura Securities, $42
8. L. T. C. B., $37
9. Tokai Bank, $35
10. Mitsui Bank, $30

*Where'd you hear that?*
Pensions & Investments. Based on market capitalization, in billions of dollars. Figures originally represented by bar graph.

## World's most profitable banks ranked by return on assets

1. Etibank, with 11.07%
2. Akbank, 4.96%
3. Gulf Bank, 2.85%
3. Gulf Investment Corp., 2.85%
5. United World Chinese Commercial Bank, 2.67%
6. Rafidain Bank, 2.64%
7. Arab Petroleum Investments Corp., 2.55%
8. International Commercial Bank of China, 2.38%
9. Bank of Communications, 2.35%
10. Singer & Friedlander Group, 2.26%

*Where'd you hear that?*
Euromoney, Euromoney 500. Based on 1989 return on assets, in percent.

# MONEY MATTERS

## World's largest banks

1. Dai-Ichi Kangyo Bank Ltd., with $405,958.9 million
2. Sumitomo Bank, $370,515.8
3. Fuji Bank, $364,888.0
4. Mitsubishi Bank, $362,256.3
5. Sanwa Bank, $355,948.1
6. Industrial Bank of Japan, $248,730.4
7. Credit Agricole, $241,983.4
8. Banque Nationale de Paris, $231,462.9
9. Citicorp, $230,643.0
10. Tokai Bank, $229,191.1

*Where'd you hear that?*
Business Week, International Bank Scoreboard. Based on 1989 assets, in millions of U.S. dollars.

## World's largest banks ranked by assets

1. Dai-Ichi Kangyo Bank Ltd., with $388.87 million
2. Sumitomo Bank, $377.21
3. Fuji Bank Group, $365.55
4. Mitsubishi Bank, $352.94
5. Sanwa Bank, $350.20
6. Industrial Bank of Japan, $268.53
7. Norinchukin Bank, $243.55
8. Caisse Nationale de Credit Agricole, $241.98
9. Banque Nationale de Paris, $231.46
10. Citicorp, $230.64

*Where'd you hear that?*
Euromoney, Euromoney 500. Based on 1989 total assets, in millions of dollars.

## World's most profitable banks ranked by return on equity

1. Svenska Handelsbanken, with 113.65%
2. S. E. Bank Group, 81.57%
3. United World Chinese Commercial Bank, 61.54%
4. Rafidain Bank, 55.35%
5. Gotabanken, 54.93%
6. Deutsche Aussenhandelsbank, 42.03%
7. Industrial and Commercial Bank of China, 32.86%
8. Akbank, 30.86%
9. International Commercial Bank of China, 30.13%
10. Nedcor, 28.85%

*Where'd you hear that?*
Euromoney, Euromoney 500. Based on 1989 return of equity, in percent.

## World's largest banks ranked by equity capital-to-assets ratios

1. Skandinaviska Enskilda Banken, with 7.19%
2. Banco do Brasil, 7.87%
3. J. P. Morgan & Co., Inc., 6.80%
4. Australia & New Zealand Banking Group Ltd., 6.53%
5. Credit Suisse, 6.15%
6. Union Bank of Switzerland Banking Group Ltd., 6.08%
7. Swiss Bank Corp, 5.99%
8. Rabobank Nederland, 5.79%
9. National Westminster Bank, 5.63%
10. Westpac Banking Corp., 5.59%

*Where'd you hear that?*
American Banker. Based on equity capital/assets ratio, December 31, 1988.

## Top banks in the world

1. Dai-Ichi Kangyo Bank Ltd., Japan, with $386,937,333,376
2. Sumitoma Bank Ltd., Japan, $376,087,770,300
3. Fuji Bank Ltd., Japan, $364,043,947,200
4. Sanwa Bank Ltd., Japan, $348,357,955,888
5. Mitsubishi Bank Ltd., Japan, $343,593,454,168
6. Industrial Bank of Japan, Ltd., Japan, $257,577,924,532
7. Norinchukin Bank, Japan, $241,947,349,684
8. Tokai Bank Ltd., Japan, $225,121,125,836
9. Mitsui Bank, Ltd., Japan, $219,666,256,008
10. Mitsubishi Trust & Banking Corp., Japan, $210,465,840,188

*Where'd you hear that?*
American Banker. Based on assets as of the end of 1988.

## World's largest banks ranked by deposits

1. Dai-Ichi Kangyo Bank Ltd., Japan, with $312,465,781,696
2. Sumitomo Bank, Ltd., Japan, $296,000,827,700
3. Fuji Bank, Ltd., Japan, $283,585,351,200
4. Mitsubishi Bank Ltd., Japan, $269,427,020,100
5. Sanwa Bank Ltd., Japan, $269,032,279,492
6. Industrial Bank of Japan, Japan, $215,397,605,132
7. Norinchukin Bank, Japan, $210,759,455,544
8. Mitsubishi Trust & Banking Corp., Japan, $185,955,516,200
9. Sumitomo Trust & Banking Co., Ltd., Japan, $177,932,182,096
10. Tokai Bank Ltd., Japan, $175,600,895,540

*Where'd you hear that?*
American Banker. Based on deposits as of December 31, 1988, in U.S. dollars.

## World's largest banks by capital

1. National Westminster, with $10,907 million
2. Barclays, $10,545
3. Citicorp, $9,864
4. Fuji Bank, $9,018
5. Credit Agricole, $8,740
6. Sumitomo Bank, $8,550
7. Dai-Ichi Kangyo Bank Ltd., $8,481
8. Mitsubishi Bank, $8,200
9. Industrial Bank of Japan, $8,155
10. Sanwa Bank, $7,567

*Where'd you hear that?*
The Banker, World Top 1000. Based on 1988 capital, in millions of dollars.

## Most productive multinational banks

1. Continental Bank, with $21.7 thousand
2. First Chicago Corp., $21.0
3. BankAmerica, $15.1
4. Citicorp, $5.5
5. Bank of Boston, $3.7
6. Chase Manhattan Bank, -$16.0
7. Manufacturers Hanover, -$27.3

# MONEY MATTERS

# MONEY MATTERS

8. Bankers Trust New York Corp., -$75.4
9. J. P. Morgan & Co., Inc., -$86.2

*Where'd you hear that?*
Forbes, Forbes 500s Annual Directory. Based on 1989 profits per employee, in thousands of dollars. Ranks U.S.-based corporations that were publicly traded as of March 23, 1990.

## Largest Latin American banks

1. Banco do Brasil, Brasilia, with $5,135 million
2. Banco Brasileiro de Descontos, Sao Paulo, $1,370
3. Banco de la Nacion, Buenos Aires, $1,325
4. Banco Itau, Sao Paulo, $1,107
5. Bancomer, Mexico, $925
6. Banco de la Rep Oriental, Montevideo, $822
7. Banco de la Prov, Buenos Aires, $764
8. Unibanco, Sao Paulo, $682
9. Banco Nacional de Mexico, $676
10. Banco do Estado de Sao Paulo, $666

*Where'd you hear that?*
The Banker, Latin America Top 100. Based on 1988 capital, in millions of U.S. dollars.

## Most profitable multinational banks and financial services

1. Bankers Trust New York Corp., with 15.4%
2. J. P. Morgan & Co., Inc., 15.2%
3. Bank of Boston, 13.9%
4. Citicorp, 11.4%
5. Chase Manhattan Bank, 10.4%
5. Chemical Banking Corp., 10.4%
7. Manufacturers Hanover, 8.8%
8. First Chicago Corp., 7.2%
9. BankAmerica, deficit
10. Continental Bank, deficit

*Where'd you hear that?*
Forbes, Annual Report on American Industry. Based on 10-year average return on equity. Ranks publicly held corporations only.

## Largest banks in Latin America

1. Banco do Brasil, with $5,063.79 million
2. Banco de la Nacion Argentina, $2,075.20
3. Banco Brasileiro de Descontos, $1,514.79
4. Banco Nacional de Mexico, $1,176.19
5. Banco Itau, $1,091.46
6. Bancomer, $925.6
7. Banco de la Republica Oriental del Uraguay, $821.99
8. Banco do Estado de Sao Paulo, $657.83
9. Banco de la Provincia de Bueuos Aires, $564.69
10. Uniao de Bancos Brasileiros, $501.82

*Where'd you hear that?*
Euromoney, Latin American 100. Based on 1988 shareholders' equity, in millions of dollars.

## Largest banks in Europe

1. National Westminster, with $10,907 million
2. Barclays, $10,545
3. Credit Agricole, $9,152
4. Union Bank of Switzerland, $6,715

5. Deutsche Bank, $6,460
6. Swiss Bank Corp., $6,055
7. Lloyds Bank, $5,867
8. Banque Nationale de Paris, $5,567
9. Midland Bank, $5,499
10. Credit Lyonnais, $5,409

*Where'd you hear that?*
The Banker, Europe Top 500. Based on 1988 capital, in millions of dollars.

## Largest Asian banks ranked by return on equity

1. Industrial and Commercial Bank of China, with 32.86%
2. International Commercial Bank of China, 26.11%
3. Norinchukin Bank, 23.98%
4. Post Office Savings Bank, 22.11%
5. Bank Ekspor Impor Indonesia, 19.95%
6. Chuo Trust & Banking Co. Ltd., 19.36%
7. Zenshinren Bank, 18.79%
8. Toyo Trust & Banking, 17.68%
9. Yasuda Trust & Banking, 17.22%
10. Bank of China, 17.15%

*Where'd you hear that?*
Euromoney, The Asian 100. Based on 1988 return on equity, in percent.

## Largest Asian banks ranked by shareholders' equity

1. Fuji Bank Group, with $8,944.42 million
2. Industrial and Commercial Bank of China, $8,638.67
3. Sumitomo Bank, $8,550.26
4. Dai-Ichi Kangyo Bank Ltd., $8,400.73
5. Mitsubishi Bank, $8,126.60

6. Sanwa Bank, $6,974.08
7. Bank of China, $6,619.57
8. Industrial Bank of Japan, $6,236.23
9. Tokai Bank, $5,087.69
10. Hongkong and Shanghai Banking Corp, $5,021.60

*Where'd you hear that?*
Euromoney, The Asian 100. Based on 1988 shareholders' equity, in millions of dollars.

## *Europe's largest banks*

1. Credit Agricole, with 181,353 million ECU
2. Banque Nationale de Paris, 169,606
3. Barclays, 157,503
4. Credit Lyonnais, 154,039
5. National Westminster Bank, 148,468
6. Deutsche Bank, 147,201
7. Societe Generale, 133,893
8. Caisse d'epargne Ecureuil, 120,060
9. Dresdner Bank, 111,362
10. Paribas, 104,730

*Where'd you hear that?*
Eurobusiness, Europe's Top 50 Banks 1988. Based on 1988 assets, in millions of European Currency Units.

## Largest Asian banks ranked by return on assets

1. Industrial and Commercial Bank of China, with 1.88%
2. Bank Ekspor Impor Indonesia, 1.73%
3. International Commercial Bank of China, 1.68%
4. Post Office Savings Bank, 1.31%
5. Overseas-Chinese Banking Corp., 1.23%

# MONEY MATTERS

# MONEY MATTERS

6. United Overseas Bank Group, 1.18%
7. Bank of China, 1.16%
8. China International Trust and Investment Corp., 1.10%
8. Shinhan Bank, 1.10%
10. Development Bank of Singapore, 1.01%

*Where'd you hear that?*
Euromoney, The Asian 100. Based on 1988 return on assets, in percent.

## Largest Asian banks ranked by total assets

1. Dai-Ichi Kangyo Bank Ltd., with $351.24 billion
2. Sumitomo Bank, $332.27
3. Fuji Bank Group, $326.28
4. Mitsubishi Bank, $316.55
5. Sanwa Bank, $298.91
6. Industrial Bank of Japan, $248.06
7. Norinchukin Bank, $231.21
8. Tokai Bank, $212.39
9. Mitsui Bank, $195.28
10. Mitsubishi Trust & Banking, $194.60

*Where'd you hear that?*
Euromoney, The Asian 100. Based on 1988 total assets, in billions of dollars.

### Largest banks in Asia

1. Bank of China, with $6,620 million
2. HongKong Bank, $5,018
3. Westpac Banking, $4,305
4. Nat Austrialia, $3,333
5. ANZ Banking, $3,063
6. Commonwealth Bkg, $2,171
7. Korea Development Bank, $1,487
8. DBS Bank, $1,282
9. Bank of Taiwan, $1,193
10. Korea Exchange Bank, $1,063

*Where'd you hear that?*
The Banker, Asian Top 200. Based on 1988 capital, in millions of dollars.

### Sub-Saharan Africa's largest banks

1. Stanbic, South Africa, with $672 million
2. First National Bank of South Africa, South Africa, $408
3. Nedcor, South Africa, $351
4. Volkskas, South Africa, $327
5. Bankorp, South Africa, $281
6. Generale de Banque, Ivory Coast, $164
7. Nigerian Ind Dev Bank, $96
8. Union Bank of Nigeria, $88
9. First Bank of Nigeria Ltd., $81
10. United Bank of Africa, Nigeria, $55

*Where'd you hear that?*
The Banker, Sub-Saharan Africa's Top 50 Banks. Based on 1988 capital, in millions of U.S. dollars.

### Sub-Saharan Africa's ten largest banks (excluding South Africa)

1. Societe Generale de Banques en Cote d'Ivoire (Ivory Coast), with $164 million
2. Nigerian Industrial Development Bank (Nigeria), $96
3. Union Bank of Nigeria (Nigeria), $88
4. First Bank of Nigeria Ltd. (Nigeria), $81
5. United Bank of Africa (Nigeria), $55

6. National Bank of Commerce (Tanzania), $54
7. Commercial Bank of Ethiopia (Ethiopia), $51
8. Kenya Commercial Bank Ltd. (Kenya), $49
9. New Nigeria Bank (Nigeria), $47
10. Banque Gabonaise (Gabon), $45

*Where'd you hear that?*
The Banker, Sub-Saharan Africa's Top 50 Banks. Based on 1988 capital, in millions of U.S. dollars.

## Largest Arab-Islamic financial institutions

1. Dar Al-Maal Al Islami, with $283 million
2. Kuwait Finance House, $166
3. Faisal Islamic Bank of Egypt, $109
4. Albaraka Islamic Investment Bank, $52
5. Faysal Islamic Bank of Bahrain, $43
6. Qatar Islamic Bank, $41
7. Albaraka International Bank, $31
8. Faisal Islamic Bank of Sudan, $30
9. Jordan Islamic Bank for Finance & Investment, $21
10. Islamic Finance House, $20

*Where'd you hear that?*
The Banker. Based on 1988 capital, in millions of U.S. dollars. An Islamic institution offers no protection for depositor nor any guarantee of a return on money as this is in conflict with 'sharia,' the Islamic doctrine.

# MONEY MATTERS

## *Canada's largest banks*

1. Royal Bank of Canada, with $114,659,558 thousand
2. Canadian Imperial Bank of Commerce, $100,212,635
3. Bank of Nova Scotia, $81,000,992
4. Bank of Montreal, $78,920,821
5. Toronto-Dominion Bank, $63,068,785
6. Trilon Financial Corp., $44,358,000
7. Royal Trustco Ltd., $39,826,000
8. Caisse de depot et placement du Quebec, $37,493,000
9. Mouvement des caisses Desjardins, $37,282,971
10. National Bank of Canada, $33,927,248

*Where'd you hear that?*
Financial Post 500. Based on 1989 assets, in thousands of Canadian dollars.

## Largest foreign banks in the U.S.

1. Bank of Tokyo Ltd., with $12,821 million
2. National Westminster Bank PLC, London, $9,595
3. Mitsubishi Bank Ltd., Tokyo, $8,357
4. Sumitomo Bank Ltd., Osaka, $7,914
5. Industrial Bank of Japan Ltd., Tokyo, $7,886
6. Sanwa Bank Ltd., Osaka, $7,859
7. Fuji Bank Ltd., Tokyo, $7,838

# MONEY MATTERS

8. Dai-Ichi Kangyo Bank Ltd., Tokyo, $6,960
9. Hongkong & Shanghai Banking Corp., Hong Kong, $6,457
10. Bank of Montreal, $5,409

*Where'd you hear that?*
American Banker. Based on business loans booked through U.S. banking offices, as of June 30, 1989, in millions of dollars.

## Largest foreign bank agencies in the U.S.

1. Industrial Bank of Japan Ltd., with $1,826.9 million
2. Long-Term Credit Bank of Japan, $1,486.9
3. Mitsui Trust & Banking Co. Ltd., $1,476.2
4. Bank of Nova Scotia, $1,322.0
5. Dai-Ichi Kangyo Bank Ltd., $956.9
6. Fuji Bank Ltd., $897.3
7. Bank of Tokyo Ltd., $834.1
8. Mitsui Bank Ltd., $822.5
9. Mitsubishi Trust & Banking Corp., $800.2
10. Yasuda Trust & Banking Co. Ltd., $751.5

*Where'd you hear that?*
American Banker. Based on commercial and industrial loans as of June 30, 1989, in millions of dollars.

## Largest foreign bank branches in the U.S.

1. Dai-Ichi Kangyo Bank Ltd., with $4,406.0 million
2. Mitsubishi Bank Ltd., $4,169.0
3. Sumitomo Bank Ltd., $3,924.0
4. Sanwa Bank Ltd., $3,789.0
5. Fuji Bank Ltd., $3,597.0
6. Bank of Tokyo Ltd., $3,475.0
7. Swiss Bank Corp., $3,137.0
8. Nippon Credit Bank, $3,056.4
9. Long-Term Credit Bank of Japan, $2,783.1
10. Banco di Napoli, $2,634.5

*Where'd you hear that?*
American Banker. Based on commercial and industrial loans as of June 30, 1989, in millions of dollars.

## Most profitable foreign bank subsidiaries in the U.S.

1. Royal Bank & Trust Co., with 14.36%
2. Canadian Imperial Bank of Commerce, 6.93%
3. Sumitomo Trust & Banking Co., 5.52%
4. Canadian Imperial Bank of Commerce, 3.87%
5. Harris Trust Co. of California, 3.80%
6. Yasuda Bank & Trust Co. USA, 3.15%
7. Harris Bank Winnetka, 2.73%
8. Harris Bank Hinsdale NA, 2.58%
9. First Omni Bank NA, 2.39%
10. LTCB Trust Co., 1.98%

*Where'd you hear that?*
American Banker. Based on return on assets for the first half of 1989, in percent.

## Cities with the most foreign bank offices in the U.S.

1. New York, NY, with 479 offices
2. Los Angeles, CA, 127
3. Chicago, IL, 89
4. Houston, TX, 75
5. San Francisco, CA, 63

6. Miami, FL, 54
7. Atlanta, GA, 27
8. Washington, DC, 14
8. Dallas, TX, 14
8. Seattle, WA, 14

*Where'd you hear that?*
American Banker. Based on total U.S. offices.

## Largest banks in the U.S.

1. Citicorp, with $9,377 million
2. J. P. Morgan & Co., Inc., $8,084
3. BankAmerica Corp., $5,626
4. Security Pacific Corp., $4,704
5. NCNB Corp., $4,682
6. Banc One Corp., 4,238
7. Chase Manhattan Corp., $3,916
8. PNC Financial Corp., $3,902
9. Wells Fargo & Co., $3,784
10. Bankers Trust New York Corp., $3,362

*Where'd you hear that?*
American Banker. Based on market capitalization as of December 31, 1989, in millions of dollars.

## Largest banks in the U.S.

1. Citicorp, with $230,643 million
2. Chase Manhattan Bank, $107,369
3. BankAmerica, $98,764
4. J. P. Morgan & Co., Inc., $88,964
5. Security Pacific, $83,943
6. Chemical Banking Corp., $71,513
7. NCNB, $66,191
8. Manufacturers Hanover, $60,479
9. First Interstate Bancorp, $59,051
10. Bankers Trust New York Corp., $55,658

*Where'd you hear that?*
Business Week, Bank Scoreboard. Based on assets as of December 31, 1989, in millions of dollars.

## Largest banks in the U.S.

1. Citicorp, with $7319 million
2. BankAmerica Corp., $4764
3. J. P. Morgan & Co., Inc., $3997
4. Chase Manhattan Corp., $3813
5. Security Pacific Corp., $3575
6. Manufacturers Hanover Corp., $2780
7. PNC Financial Corp., $2705
8. NCNB Corp., $2275
9. Chemical Banking Corp., $2199
10. Bankers Trust New York Corp., $2166

*Where'd you hear that?*
The Banker, Top 300 U.S. Banks. Based on capital in millions of dollars.

**MONEY MATTERS**

# MONEY MATTERS

## Most admired commercial banking corporations

1. J. P. Morgan & Co. Inc., with a rating of 7.54
2. Citicorp, 7.22
3. Bankers Trust New York Corp., 7.04
4. Security Pacific, 6.79
5. Bank of New York, 5.95
6. Chase Manhattan Bank, 5.60
7. BankAmerica, 5.46
8. Chemical Banking Corp., 5.34
9. First Interstate Bancorp, 4.98
10. Manufacturers Hanover, 4.55

*Where'd you hear that?*
Fortune, America's Most Admired Corporations. Based on scores (0-10) derived from a survey of senior executives, outside directors, and financial analysts. Respondents ranked firms in their own industry on quality of management and products/services; innovation; long-term investment value; financial soundness; attraction and retention of talent; community and environmental responsibility; and use of assets.

## Largest commercial banking companies

1. Citicorp, with $230,643.0 million
2. Chase Manhattan Corp., $107,369.0
3. BankAmerica Corp., $98,764.0
4. J. P. Morgan & Co., Inc., $88,964.0
5. Security Pacific Corp., $83,943.0
6. Chemical Banking Corp., $71,513.0
7. NCNB Corp., $66,190.8
8. Manufacturers Hanover Corp., $60,479.0
9. First Interstate Bancorp, $59,051.4
10. Bankers Trust New York Corp., $55,658.4

*Where'd you hear that?*
Fortune. Based on 1989 assets, in millions of dollars.

## Largest U.S. commercial banks ranked by deposits

1. Citibank NA, with $111,487,000,000
2. Bank of America NT & SA, $73,295,000,000
3. Chase Manhattan Bank NA, $61,720,245,000
4. Manufacturers Hanover Trust Co., $42,736,000,000
5. Morgan Guaranty Trust Co., $40,953,451,000
6. Security Pacific National Bank, $40,597,338,000
7. Wells Fargo Bank NA, $36,462,605,000
8. Bank of New York, $34,411,451,000
9. Chemical Bank, $32,312,000,000
10. Bankers Trust Co., $27,879,571,000

*Where'd you hear that?*
American Banker. Based on total deposits, December 31, 1989, compared with December 31, 1988.

## Largest U.S. commercial banks ranked by assets

1. Citibank NA, with $161,988,000,000
2. Bank of America NT & SA, $86,712,000,000
3. Chase Manhattan Bank NA, $83,807,666,000

# MONEY MATTERS

4. Morgan Guaranty Trust Co., $64,707,226,000
5. Manufacturers Hanover Trust Co., $54,740,000,000
6. Security Pacific National Bank, $54,313,683,000
7. Bankers Trust Co., $51,113,127,000
8. Bank of New York, $46,361,809,000
9. Wells Fargo Bank NA, $45,555,858,000
10. Chemical Bank, $45,512,000,000

*Where'd you hear that?*
American Banker. Based on total assets, December 31, 1989, compared with December 31, 1988.

## Largest Black-owned banks

1. Seaway National Bank of Chicago, with $163.840 million
2. Citizens Trust Bank, $126.486
3. Industrial Bank of Washington, $121.982
4. Freedom National Bank of New York, $120.648
5. Independence Bank of Chicago, $117.990
6. Drexel National Bank, $108.919
7. First Independence National Bank of Detroit, $100.607
8. First Texas Bank, $95.550
9. Mechanics and Farmers Bank, $92.108
10. Highland Community Bank, $74.041

*Where'd you hear that?*
Black Enterprise. Based on total assets as of December 31, 1989, in millions of dollars.

## Top U.S. community banks

1. Kentucky-Farmers Bank (Catlettsburg, KY), with 3.52
2. Pacific Heritage Bank (Torrance, CA), 3.48
3. First State Bank (Dimmitt, TX), 3.38
4. Business Bank (Vienna, VA), 3.31
5. First State Bank (Columbus, TX), 3.02
5. San Benito Bank & Trust Co. (TX), 3.02
7. Farmers Savings Bank (Spencer, OH), 2.91
7. Key Biscayne Bank & Trust Co. (FL), 2.91
9. Putnam County National Bank (Carmel, NY), 2.74
10. First Bank (Oak Park, IL), 2.64

*Where'd you hear that?*
American Banker. Based on return on average assets for 1989.

# MONEY MATTERS

## World's largest bank holding companies

1. Dai-Ichi Kangyo Bank Ltd., with $386,937 million
2. Sumitomo Bank Ltd., $376,088
3. Fuji Bank, Ltd., $364,044
4. Sanwa Bank Ltd., $348,358
5. Mitsubishi Bank Ltd., $343,593
6. Industrial Bank of Japan Ltd., $257,578
7. Norinchukin Bank, $241,947
8. Tokai Bank, Ltd., $225,121
9. Mitsui Bank, Ltd., $219,666
10. Mitsubishi Trust & Banking Corp., $210,466

*Where'd you hear that?*
American Banker. Based on assets as of December 31, 1988, in millions of dollars.

### World's largest bank holding companies by ratio of equity to assets

1. National Australia Bank Ltd., Melbourne, with 8.17
2. Banco Central, Madrid, 7.87
3. Skandinaviska Enskilda Banken, Stockholm, 7.26
4. Compagnie Financiere de Suez, Paris, 7.25
5. Westpac Banking Corp., Sydney, 7.17
6. Toronto Dominion Bank, 7.13
7. J. P. Morgan & Co. Inc., New York, 6.99
8. Australia & New Zealand Banking Group Ltd., Melbourne, 6.80
9. Banco Bilbao Vizcaya, Bilbao, 6.63
10. Bankers Trust New York Corp., 6.37

*Where'd you hear that?*
American Banker. Based on ratio of equity to assets as of December 31, 1988.

### World's fasting growing bank holding companies

1. Banco Central, with 91.16%
2. Westpac Banking Corp., 70.94%
3. National Australia Bank Ltd., 65.20%
4. Yasuda Trust & Banking Co. Ltd., 58.47%
5. Mitsubishi Trust & Banking Corp., 58.16%
6. Chuo Trust & Banking Co. Ltd., 57.88%
7. Compagnie Financiere de Paribas, 57.66%
8. Standard Chartered PLC, 55.14%
9. Banco Bilbao Vizcaya, 48.39%
10. Compagnie Financiere de Credit Ind'l et Comm'l, 45.37%

*Where'd you hear that?*
American Banker. Based on equity capital growth, December 31, 1988, in percent.

### Largest bank holding companies in assets

1. Citicorp (New York), with $230,643,000,000
2. Chase Manhattan Corp. (New York), $107,369,000,000

3. BankAmerica Corp. (San Francisco), $98,764,000,000
4. J. P. Morgan & Co. Inc. (New York), $88,963,715,000
5. Security Pacific Corp. (Los Angeles), $83,943,000,000
6. Chemical Banking Corp. (New York), $71,513,000,000
7. NCNB Corp. (Charlotte, NC), $66,190,763,000
8. Manufacturers Hanover Corp. (New York), $60,479,000,000
9. First Interstate Bancorp. (Los Angeles), $59,051,407,000
10. Bankers Trust New York Corp., $55,658,446,000

*Where'd you hear that?*
American Banker. Based on 1989 assets.

## Largest bank holding companies in primary capital

1. Citicorp (New York), with $18,109,000,000
2. J. P. Morgan & Co., Inc. (New York), $9,781,230,000
3. BankAmerica Corp. (San Francisco), $9,614,000,000
4. Chase Manhattan Corp. (New York), $8,928,000,000
5. Manufacturers Hanover Corp. (New York), $6,695,000,000
6. Chemical Banking Corp. (New York), $6,663,000,000
7. Security Pacific Corp. (Los Angeles), $6,302,000,000
8. Bankers Trust New York Corp., $5,320,575,000
9. Bank of New York Co., Inc., $4,296,296,000
10. First Chicago Corp., $4,198,000,000

*Where'd you hear that?*
American Banker. Based on 1989 primary capital.

## Largest bank holding companies by net income

1. BankAmerica Corp. (San Francisco), with $820,000,000
2. Security Pacific Corp. (Los Angeles), $740,600,000
3. Wells Fargo & Co. (San Francisco), $601,100,000
4. Citicorp (New York), $498,000,000
5. NCNB Corp. (Charlotte, NC), $447,069,000
6. PNC Financial Corp. (Pittsburgh), $377,440,000
7. Fleet/Norstar Financial Group, Inc. (Providence, RI), $371,346,000
8. Banc One Corp. (Columbus, OH), $362,868,000
9. First Chicago Corp., $358,700,000
10. Sun Trust Banks, Inc. (Atlanta), $337,318,000

*Where'd you hear that?*
American Banker. Based on 1989 net income.

## Most profitable merchant banks and finance companies in Asia

1. Paribas Asia, with 227.2%
2. BT Asia, 62.9%
3. United Merchants Finance, 49.0%
4. First Chicago HK, 47.1%
5. Citicorp International, 46.8%
6. Jardine Fleming Holdings, 46.6%

# MONEY MATTERS

# MONEY MATTERS

7. PNB International Finance, 44.0%
8. State Investment House, 40.7%
9. Indosuez Asia, 36.6%
10. Schroders Asia, 36.4%

*Where'd you hear that?*
Asian Finance, Merchant Banking. Based on return on equity, year ending December 31, 1988, in percent.

## Largest merchant banks ranked by assets

1. Senbank
2. Standard Merchant Bank
3. FirstCorp.
4. UAL Merchant Bank
5. Volkskas Merchant Bank
6. Rand Merchant Bank
7. Finansbank
8. Investec
9. Corbank

*Where'd you hear that?*
Financial Mail, Financial Mail Special Survey of Top Companies. Based on 1988 assets.

## Largest merchant banks ranked by after-tax net income

1. UAL Merchant Bank
2. Standard Merchant Bank
3. Senbank
4. Rand Merchant Bank
5. FirstCorp
6. Volkskas Merchant Bank
7. Finansbank
8. Investec
9. Corbank

*Where'd you hear that?*
Financial Mail, Financial Mail Special Survey of Top Companies. Based on 1987 after-tax net income.

## Largest U.S. savings & loan corporations

1. Great Western Financial Corp., with $2,103 million
2. H. F. Ahmanson, $1,868
3. Golden West Financial Corp., $1,835
4. Homefed, $634
5. Calfed, $476
6. Glenfed, $457

*Where'd you hear that?*
Business Week, The Business Week 1000. Based on market value as of March 16, 1990, in millions of dollars.

## Strongest savings & loan associations

1. Second Federal (Chicago, IL), with 5.65%
1. Union S & L (New Orleans, LA), 5.65%
3. Shelby-Panola Savings (Carthage, TX), 5.61%
4. Fraternity Federal (Baltimore, MD), 5.50%
4. East Side S & L (Chicago, IL), 5.50%

*Where'd you hear that?*
Money. Based on passbook rate.

## Largest Black-owned savings and loan associations

1. Independence Federal Savings Bank, with $254.269 million
2. Carver Federal Savings Bank, $238.016
3. Family Savings and Loan Association, $138.002
4. Illinois Service/Federal S & L Association of Chicago, $104.102
5. Broadway Federal Savings & Loan Association, $95.162

6. Citizens Federal Savings Bank, $68.883
7. Time Savings & Loan Association, $61.579
8. United Federal Savings & Loan Association, $53.566
9. Mutual Federal S & L Association of Atlanta, $36.946
10. Advance Federal Savings & Loan Association, $36.378

*Where'd you hear that?*
Black Enterprise. Based on assets as of December 31, 1989, in millions of dollars.

## States which are net beneficiaries of the savings and loan bailout

1. Texas, with $3,510
2. New Mexico, $3,201
3. Arkansas, $3,025
4. Arizona, $1,569
5. Alaska, $1,065
6. Kansas, $809
7. Louisiana, $741
8. Nebraska, $590
9. Minnesota, $572
10. Colorado, $548

*Where'd you hear that?*
Challenge. Based on per capita net present value of the bailout.

## Largest credit unions in the U.S.

1. Navy Federal Credit Union (Merrifield, VA), with $3,509,614,973
2. State Employees Credit Union (Raleigh, NC), $2,010,187,452
3. Pentagon Federal Credit Union (Alexandria, VA), $1,214,217,163
4. Boeing Employees Federal Credit Union (Seattle, WA), $975,365,817
5. Hughes Aircraft Employees Federal Credit Union (Manhattan Beach, CA), $880,950,263
6. Eastern Financial Federal Credit Union (Miami, FL), $854,451,802
7. Alaska USA Federal Credit Union (Anchorage, AK), $826,545,731
8. American Airlines Employees Federal Credit Union (Dallas, TX), $768,197,380
9. LMSC Federal Credit Union (Sunnyvale, CA), $646,051,638
10. Golden 1 Federal Credit Union (Sacramento, CA), $644,852,939

*Where'd you hear that?*
American Banker. Based on assets as of December 31, 1988.

## Top banks in consumer loans

1. Bank of America NT & SA, with $27,761,000 thousand
2. Citibank NA, $24,652,000
3. Wells Fargo Bank NA, $14,891,669
4. Security Pacific National Bank, $13,898,796
5. Chase Manhattan Bank, $11,041,819
6. Citibank (South Dakota) NA, $9,389,200
7. Chase Manhattan Bank, $9,294,094
8. Citibank (Nevada), $8,136,383
9. Greenwood Trust Co., $6,918,527
10. Marine Midland Bank, $6,726,582

# MONEY MATTERS

# MONEY MATTERS

*Where'd you hear that?*
American Banker. Based on total consumer loans, December 31, 1989 compared with December 31, 1988, in thousands of dollars.

## Top banks in home equity loans

1. Wells Fargo Bank NA, with $1,922 million
2. Bank of America NT & SA, $1,825
3. Citibank NA, $1,532
4. Security Pacific National Bank, $1,281
5. Connecticut National Bank, $737
6. Chase Manhattan Bank NA, $724
7. First Fidelity Bank NA, $690
8. Marine Midland Bank NA, $622
9. Connecticut Bank & Trust Co. NA, $578
10. Shawmut Bank NA, $572

*Where'd you hear that?*
American Banker. Based on home equity loans as of December 31, 1989, in millions of dollars.

## Largest home equity loan lenders

1. Wells Fargo Bank NA (CA), with $1,693,736
2. Citibank NA (NY), $1,355,000
3. Bank of America NT & SA (CA), $904,000
4. Security Pacific National Bank (CA), $669,108
5. Connecticut National Bank (CT), $573,103
6. First Fidelity Bank NA (NJ), $558,262
7. Connecticut Bank & Trust Co. NA (CT), $523,876
8. Chase Manhattan Bank NA (NY), $458,760
9. Marine Midland Bank NA (NY), $450,910
10. NCNB National Bank of North Carolina, $410,960

*Where'd you hear that?*
Mortgage Market Statistical Annual. Based on outstanding credit as of September 30, 1988.

## Top banks in mortgage loans

1. Bank of America NT & SA, with $14,822 million
2. Security Pacific National Bank, $9,866
3. Wells Fargo Bank NA, $8,434
4. Citibank NA, $7,647
5. Chase Manhattan Bank NA, $6,674
6. Boston Safe Deposit & Trust Co., $4,105
7. Chemical Bank, $2,787
8. First Union National Bank, $2,763
9. Bank of New York, $2,150
10. Connecticut National Bank, $2,148

*Where'd you hear that?*
American Banker. Based on total mortgage loans as of December 31, 1989, in millions of dollars.

## Countries with the best risk ratings

1. Japan, with 94.8
2. Switzerland, 94.6
3. West Germany, 93.8
4. United States, 90.9
5. Netherlands, 87.8
6. France, 87.2
7. United Kingdom, 87.0
8. Canada, 86.7
9. Austria, 84.6

10. Sweden, 81.3

*Where'd you hear that?*
Institutional Investor, International edition. Based on *Institutional Investor* credit rating, March, 1990.

## African countries with the best credit risk ratings

1. Algeria, with 39.4
2. Tunisia, 37.3
3. South Africa, 34.0
4. Mauritius, 33.1
5. Gabon, 29.8
6. Kenya, 29.7
7. Cameroon, 28.4
8. Zimbabwe, 27.8
9. Morocco, 26.8
10. Libya, 25.4

*Where'd you hear that?*
Institutional Investor, International edition. Based on *Institutional Investor* credit rating, March, 1990.

## Asian countries with the best credit risk ratings

1. Japan, with 94.8
2. Singapore, 77.9
3. Taiwan, 77.7
4. Australia, 71.0
5. South Korea, 69.6
6. Hong Kong, 66.6
7. New Zealand, 63.8
8. Thailand, 61.3
9. Malaysia, 59.1
10. China, 54.2

*Where'd you hear that?*
Institutional Investor, International edition. Based on *Institutional Investor* credit rating, March, 1990.

## Eastern European countries with the best credit risk ratings

1. Soviet Union, with 62.1
2. East Germany, 57.1
3. Czechoslovakia, 53.7
4. Hungary, 43.6
5. Bulgaria, 43.1
6. Romania, 33.3
7. Yugoslavia, 27.1
8. Poland, 19.0

*Where'd you hear that?*
Institutional Investor, International edition. Based on *Institutional Investor* credit rating, March, 1990.

## Western European countries with the best credit risk ratings

1. Switzerland, with 94.6
2. West Germany, 93.8
3. Netherlands, 87.8
4. France, 87.2
5. United Kingdom, 87.0
6. Austria, 84.6
7. Sweden, 81.3
8. Italy, 80.1
9. Finland, 79.7
10. Belgium, 78.9

*Where'd you hear that?*
Institutional Investor, International edition. Based on *Institutional Investor* credit rating, March, 1990.

## Middle Eastern countries with the best credit risk ratings

1. Kuwait, with 60.8
2. Saudi Arabia, 60.3
3. United Arab Emirates, 59.0
4. Qatar, 55.9
5. Bahrain, 54.5
6. Oman, 52.6
7. Cyprus, 46.1

**MONEY MATTERS**

# MONEY MATTERS

8. Israel, 36.4
9. Jordan, 28.0
10. Iran, 23.5

*Where'd you hear that?*
Institutional Investor, International edition. Based on *Institutional Investor* credit risk rating, March, 1990.

## Latin American countries with the best credit risk ratings

1. Barbados, with 38.5
2. Chile, 36.1
3. Mexico, 32.6
4. Venezuela, 31.8
4. Colombia, 31.8
6. Trinidad & Tobago, 30.4
7. Uruguay, 29.1
8. Brazil, 27.2
9. Paraguay, 25.3
10. Costa Rica, 18.8

*Where'd you hear that?*
Institutional Investor, International edition. Based on *Institutional Investor* credit risk rating, March, 1990.

## *Top collection markets*

1. Hospitals, with $83,030
2. Utilities, $40,661
3. Bad checks, $22,344
4. Physicians, $21,738
5. Bank cards, $16,398
6. Retail, $15,460
7. Commercial, $14,803
8. Health services, $14,387
9. Finance companies, $11,641
10. Cable TV, $9,827

*Where'd you hear that?*
Collector. Based on average dollar volume of gross collections.

## North American countries with the best credit risk ratings

1. United States, with 90.9
2. Canada, 86.7

*Where'd you hear that?*
Institutional Investor, International edition. Based on *Institutional Investor* credit risk rating, March, 1990.

## Top debit originators

1. Chase Manhattan Bank, with $87.5 million
2. Marine Bank of Springfield, IL, $30.3
3. Norwest Bank Minneapolis, $24.2
4. Bank of America, $13.6
5. Bank One Columbus NA, $9.6

*Where'd you hear that?*
American Banker. Based on 1989 total transactions, in millions of dollars.

## Top credit originators

1. Bank of America, with $16.6 million
2. Chase Manhattan Bank, $13.6
3. Northern Trust, $13.0
4. First National Bank of Atlanta, $11.8
5. Mellon Bank, $9.8

*Where'd you hear that?*
American Banker. Based on 1989 total transactions, in millions of dollars.

## Top orginators of automated clearinghouse payments

1. Chase Manhattan Bank NA, with 101,078,405
2. Marine Bank of Springfield, IL, 31,293,963
3. Bank of America NT & SA, San Francisco, 30,228,563

# MONEY MATTERS

4. Norwest Bank Minnesota NA, Minneapolis, 28,976,035
5. Northern Trust Co., Chicago, 19,275,848
6. Mellon Bank NA, Pittsburgh, 16,267,954
7. First National Bank of Atlanta, 14,564,745
8. Bank One Columbus NA, Ohio, 13,066,931
9. First National Bank of Boston, 10,860,483
10. NCNB Texas National Bank, Dallas, 10,101,948

*Where'd you hear that?*
American Banker. Based on 1989 total transactions.

## Largest EFT networks

1. MAC (Money Access Service), with 41,800,000
2. XPress 24, 10,605,450
3. MPACT, 9,900,000
4. NYCE (New York Switch Corp.), 9,500,000
5. Star (Star System Inc.), 8,453,720
6. Exchange/Accel, 7,000,000
7. Cash Station, 6,952,688
8. MOST, 6,430,839
9. Owl, 5,800,000
10. Pulse, 5,645,549

*Where'd you hear that?*
Card Industry Directory. Based on monthly switch volume.

## EFT networks with the most interchange transactions

1. MAC, with 41,800,000
2. XPress 24, 10,605,450
3. MPACT, 9,900,000
4. NYCE, 9,500,000
5. Star, 8,453,720
6. Exchange/Accel, 7,000,000
7. Cash Station, 6,952,688
8. MOST, 6,430,839
9. Owl, 5,800,000
10. Pulse, 5,645,549

*Where'd you hear that?*
Card Industry Directory. Based on number of monthly interchange transactions in 1989.

## EFT networks with the largest debit card bases

1. Star (Star System Inc.), with 22,585,993
2. NYCE (New York Switch Corp.), 17,300,000
3. MAC (Money Access Service), 16,300,000
4. Interlink, 12,000,000
5. Pulse, 8,000,000
6. Money Station, 7,099,939
7. MOST, 7,000,000
8. Relay, 6,500,000
9. Honor, 5,716,000
10. Network One, 5,300,000

*Where'd you hear that?*
Card Industry Directory. Based on number of debit cards.

## Largest EFT processors

1. Deluxe Data Systems, with 51,000,000
2. CoreStates Financial Corp., 41,500,000
3. Midwest Payment Systems, 25,500,000
4. Electronic Data Systems/ADP, 21,900,000
5. Bank of America, 17,940,000
6. First Interstate Bancorp, 11,000,000
7. BayBanks Systems Inc., 10,600,000
8. Wells Fargo Bank, 10,500,000

# MONEY MATTERS

9. Citicorp, 9,000,000
9. Security Pacific Bank, 9,000,000

*Where'd you hear that?*
Card Industry Directory. Based on number of transactions processed.

## Largest ATM owners

1. Citibank, with 1,600
2. Bank of America, 1,520
3. First Interstate Bancorp, 1,392
4. Wells Fargo, 1,250
5. Security Pacific National Bank, 1,229
6. Network EFT Inc., 1,055
7. Bay Banks Credit Corp., 944
8. Rocky Mountain Bank Card Systems, 840
9. Bank of New England, 628
10. Mellon Bank, 610

*Where'd you hear that?*
Card Industry Directory. Based on number of ATMs (automatic teller machines).

## Largest proprietary debit card issuers

1. First Interstate Bancorp., with 5,500,000 cards
2. Bank of America, 4,000,000
3. Security Pacific National Bank, 2,400,000
4. Wells Fargo, 2,300,000
5. Citicorp, 1,500,000
6. Marine Midland, 1,215,000
7. Rocky Mountain Bank Card Systems, 1,200,000
7. Great Western Bank, FSB, 1,200,000
9. National City Corp., 1,020,000

10. First Union National Bank, 1,000,000

*Where'd you hear that?*
Card Industry Directory. Based on number of ATM cardholders.

## Top video bankers

1. Bank of America, with 40,000
2. Citibank, 37,500
3. Chase Manhattan Bank, 9,100
4. Manufacturers Hanover, 7,200
5. Desjardins Group, 2,000
6. University Federal, 1,500
7. Hollywood Federal, 1,000

*Where'd you hear that?*
American Banker. Based on number of customers. Original sources: Jupiter Communications Co. and the American Banker.

## Largest bank card acquiring programs

1. First USA Merchant Services Inc., with 105,276
2. National Processing Co., 94,000
3. Citizens Fidelity National Bank, 80,000
4. Nabanco, 75,563
5. Security Pacific Bank, 66,000
6. Rocky Mountain Bank Card, 65,445
7. First Interstate Bancard Corp., 65,000
8. Bank of America, 60,000
8. Bank One Corp., 60,000
10. Mercantile Bank, 46,820

*Where'd you hear that?*
Card Industry Directory. Based on number of locations.

## Largest banks in credit card loans

1. Citibank South Dakota NA (Sioux Falls), with $12,107,130 thousand
2. Chase Manhattan Bank NA (Wilmington, DE), $6,732,513
3. Greenwood Trust Co. (Newcastle, DE), $5,909,337
4. Citibank (Nevada) NA, (Las Vegas), $5,765,860
5. Bank of America NT & SA (San Francisco, CA), $4,844,000
6. American Express Centurion Bank (Newark, DE) $3,818,234
7. FCC National Bank (Wilmington, DE), $2,997,421
8. Wells Fargo Bank NA (San Francisco, CA), $2,720,496
9. Bank of New York (Delaware) (Wilmington, DE), $2,666,463
10. Manufacturers Hanover Trust Co. (New York, NY), $2,117,000

*Where'd you hear that?*
American Banker. Based on credit card loans outstanding as of December 31, 1988, in thousands of dollars.

## Largest thrifts in credit card loans

1. Chevy Chase Savings Bank, FSB (MD), with $1,380,619 thousand
2. Empire of America Federal Savings Bank (Buffalo, NY), $749,416
3. Citicorp Savings of Illinois, FS & LA (Chicago), $388,681
4. California Federal Savings & Loan Association (Los Angeles), $380,611
5. Great Western Bank, FSB (Beverly Hills), $366,818
6. Glendale Federal Savings & Loan Association (CA), $352,989
7. First Nationwide Bank, FSB (San Francisco), $337,390
8. Peoples Bank (Bridgeport CT), $316,950
9. Carteret Savings Bank FA (Newark, NJ), $316,715
10. First Financial Savings Association (Stevens Point, WI), $261,720

*Where'd you hear that?*
American Banker. Based on credit card loans outstanding as of December 31, 1988, in thousands of dollars.

## Largest credit card issuers

1. Citicorp, with $21,838,890,000
2. Chase Manhattan Bank USA, $7,219,607,000
3. Bank of America, $5,994,980,000
4. Greenwood Trust Co. (Discover Card), $5,909,337,000
5. First Chicago Corp., $5,570,422,000
6. Maryland Bank, NA, 4,119,786,000
7. American Express Centurion Bank (Optima), $3,818,234,000
8. Bank of New York (Delaware), $2,726,615,000
9. Wells Fargo Bank, $2,720,496,000
10. Manufacturers Hanover Bank, $2,592,000,000

*Where'd you hear that?*
Card Industry Directory. Based on 1989 dollar receivables.

# MONEY MATTERS

# MONEY MATTERS

## Largest credit card firms

1. Citicorp, with $21,695 million
2. Chase Manhattan Corp., $7,220
3. Sears, Roebuck & Co., $6,038
4. BankAmerica Corp., $5,994
5. American Express Co., $4,035
6. First Chicago Corp., $3,470
7. Bank of New York Co., Inc., $3,138
8. Wells Fargo & Co., $2,720
9. First Interstate Bancorp., $2,366
10. Manufacturers Hanover Corp., $2,117

*Where'd you hear that?*
American Banker. Based on combined credit card loan's outstanding at commercial bank and thrift subsidiaries as of December 31, 1988, in millions of dollars.

## Largest credit card processors

1. First Data Resources Inc., with 880,000,000
2. National Data Corp., 820,000,000
3. Total System Servics Inc., 585,000,000
4. VisaNet Acquiring Services, 500,000,000
5. J. C. Penney Business Services Inc., 390,000,000
5. McDonnell Douglas Payment Systems Inc., 390,000,000
7. Southwestern States Bankcard Association, 325,000,000
8. National Processing Co., 287,000,000
9. National Bancard Corp. (Nabanco), 214,000,000
10. Bank One Corp., 194,000,000

*Where'd you hear that?*
Card Industry Directory. Based on 1989 transactions.

## Largest oil credit card programs

1. Amoco Corp., with 16,000,000
2. Mobil Oil Credit Corp., 8,800,000
3. Shell Oil Co., 8,500,000
4. Exxon Co. U.S.A, 6,900,000
5. Texaco Inc., 6,700,000
6. Chevron Co. U.S.A., 6,550,000
7. Unocal Corp., 4,400,000
8. Gulf Oil, 3,320,000
9. B P America, 3,100,000
10. Phillips Petroleum Co., 2,800,000

*Where'd you hear that?*
Card Industry Directory. Based on number of accounts.

## Highest-paid banking executives

1. Roberto G. Mendoza (J. P. Morgan & Co.), with $2,000,000
2. A. W. Clausen (BankAmerica Corp.), $1,737,500
3. John F. McGillicuddy (Manufacturers Hanover Corp. and Manufacturers Hanover Trust Co.), $1,680,323
4. Lewis T. Preston (J. P. Morgan & Co.), $1,650,000
5. John S. Reed (Citicorp), $1,545,917
6. Carl E. Reichardt (Wells Fargo & Co.), $1,522,500

7. R. J. Flamson, III (Security Pacific Corp.), $1,514,300
8. Charles S. Sanford, Jr. (Bankers Trust New York Corp.), $1,500,000
9. Barry F. Sullivan (First Chicago Corp.), $1,460,824
10. Dennis Weatherstone (J. P. Morgan & Co.), $1,450,000

*Where'd you hear that?*
American Banker. Based on financial renumeration in 1989.

## Wall Street's biggest moneymakers

1. Marvin Davis and family, with $125 million
2. Bruce Kovner, more than $110
3. Irwin Jacobs, more than $100
4. Peter Ackerman, at least $100
5. Carl Icahn, $95 to $135
6. Paul Tudor Jones II, more than $65
7. Michel David Weill and Family, at least $65
7. M. Lee Pearce, at least $65
9. George Soros, at least $60
10. Gerhard Andlinger, $60

*Where'd you hear that?*
Financial World, Wall Street 100. Based on earnings. To be eligible for list you must 'work for an investment firm, play the market or flip publicly traded companies.'.

## Most trusted sources of investment advice

1. Commercial bank, with 35%
2. Savings and loan, 24%
3. Credit union, 15%
4. Stockbroker, 11%
5. Insurance company, 5%

6. Don't know/Others, total, 10%

*Where'd you hear that?*
Wall Street Journal. Based on percentage of respondents who said they would trust most to give good advice on investing a $10,000 windfall.

## Investment banking firms with highest earnings as lead managers

1. Merrill Lynch, with $448.439 million
2. Drexel Burnham, $377.680
3. Goldman, Sachs & Co., $346.199
4. First Boston, $253.515
5. Shearson Lehman Hutton, $226.174
6. Morgan Stanley, $203.689
7. Salomon Brothers, $182.456
8. Prudential-Bache, $149.686
9. Alex. Brown & Sons Inc., $149.103
10. PaineWebber, $115.146

*Where'd you hear that?*
Investment Dealers' Digest, Investment Banks - Corporate Underwriting Rankings. Based on 1989 total gross spread, in millions of dollars.

## Largest Canadian investment managers

1. Jarislowsky & Fraser Co. Ltd., with $7,800 million
2. Sceptre Investment, $6,908
3. Gryphon Investment, $5,977
4. AMI Asset, $4,814
5. Mu-Cana Investment, $4,373
6. Confed Investment Counseling Ltd., $3,814
7. Corporate Investment, $3,614
8. Phillips Hager & North, $3,500

# MONEY MATTERS

# MONEY MATTERS

9. Knight, Bain, Seath, $2,837
10. BGH Central, $2,330

*Where'd you hear that?*
Pensions & Investments, Largest Money Managers Issue. Based on tax-exempt assets, in millions of dollars.

## Types of investments consumers feel capable of making

1. U.S. savings bonds, with 74%
2. CDs, 64%
3. Money fund, 50%
4. Shares of stock, 41%
5. T-Bills, 39%
6. Mutual fund, 38%
7. Corporate bonds, 33%
8. Tax-exempt bonds, 28%

*Where'd you hear that?*
Wall Street Journal. Based on percentage of respondents who feel that they know how to make each investment.

## Leading Canadian investment firms

1. Jarislowsky & Fraser Co., Ltd. (Montreal, PQ), with $11,000,000 thousand
2. AMI Asset Management International, Inc. (Toronto, ON), $5,686,500
3. Sceptre Investment Counsel Ltd. (Toronto, ON), $5,243,000
4. Beutel, Goodman & Company Ltd. (Toronto, ON), $5,200,000
5. Confed Investment Counseling Ltd. (Toronto, ON), $3,689,366
6. T.A.L. Investment Counsel Ltd. (Toronto, ON), $3,550,000
7. T.A.L. Investment Counsel Ltd. (Montreal, PQ), N/A
8. Toronto Investment Management Inc. (Toronto, ON), $3,272,500
9. CT Investment Counsel Inc. (Toronto, ON), $3,200,000
10. Mu-Cana Investment Counseling Ltd. (Waterloo, ON), $3,100,000

*Where'd you hear that?*
Money Market Directory of Pension Funds and Their Investment Managers. Based on 1989 tax-exempt funds under management, in thousands of dollars.

## Leading U.S. investment counsel firms

1. Wells Fargo Investment Advisors (San Francisco, CA), with $70,000,000 thousand
2. J. P. Morgan Investment Management Inc. (New York, NY), $52,964,000
3. Cigna Investments, Inc. (Hartford, CT), $33,167,364
4. Alliance Capital Management L.P. (New York, NY), $26,778,000
5. Mellon Capital Management Corp. (San Francisco, CA), $26,100,000
6. General Electric Investment Corp. (Stamford, CT), $25,002,000
7. Equitable Capital Management Corp. (New York, NY), $24,421,100
8. Boston Co., Inc. (Boston, MA), $22,891,000

9. Jennison Associates Capital Corp. (New York, NY), $22,700,000
10. Chase Investors Management Corp. (New York, NY), $22,682,271

*Where'd you hear that?*
Money Market Directory of Pension Funds and Their Investment Managers. Based on 1989 tax-exempt funds under management, in thousands of dollars.

## Largest investment management firms

1. Bankers Trust, with $79,829 million
2. Wells Fargo, $78,630
3. State Street Bank, $54,077
4. Metropolitan Life, $49,084
5. Prudential Investment, $45,351
6. Aetna Life, $44,985
7. J. P. Morgan & Co., Inc., $44,018
8. Alliance Capital, $29,190
9. General Electric Investment Corp., $27,370
10. Mellon Capital, $27,310

*Where'd you hear that?*
Pensions & Investments, Largest Money Managers Issue. Based on 1989 tax-exempt assets, in millions of dollars.

## Leading U.S. banks and trust companies

1. Bankers Trust Co. (New York, NY), with $72,443,800 thousand
2. State Street Bank & Trust Co. (Boston, MA), $43,000,000
3. The Northern Trust Co. (Chicago, IL), $18,000,000
4. Capital Guardian Trust Co. (Los Angeles, CA), $14,822,787
5. Fiduciary Trust Co. International (New York, NY), $14,791,000
6. Wilmington Trust Co. (Wilmington, DE), $12,358,892
7. Boatmen's Trust Co. (St. Louis, MO), $11,935,000
8. Manufacturers Bank (Detroit, MI), $11,671,142
9. ANB Investment Management Co. (Chicago, IL), $11,500,000
10. The Bank of New York (New York, NY), $8,800,000

*Where'd you hear that?*
Money Market Directory of Pension Funds and Their Investment Managers. Based on 1989 tax-exempt funds under management, in thousands of dollars.

## Largest banks and trust companies

1. Bankers Trust, with $79,829 million
2. Wells Fargo, $79,069
3. State Street Bank, $54,077
4. Mellon Bank, $53,634
5. J. P. Morgan & Co., Inc., $44,018
6. Capital Guardian Trust Co., $20,439
7. Chase Manhattan Bank, $16,604
8. Northern Trust, $15,287
9. Trust Co./West, $12,819
10. Boatmen's Trust, $12,535

# MONEY MATTERS

# MONEY MATTERS

*Where'd you hear that?*
Pensions & Investments, Largest Money Managers Issue. Based on 1989 tax-exempt assets, in millions of dollars.

## Institutions with highest equity holdings

1. Wells Fargo & Co., with $42,794 million
2. Bankers Trust Co., $40,858
3. American Express Co., $38,686
4. Fidelity Investments, $34,994
5. Mellon Bank Corp., $31,569
6. Capital Group, $28,382
7. Equitable Investment Corp., $26,938
8. TIAA-CREF, $25,262
9. State Street Bank, $24,070
10. J. P. Morgan & Co., Inc., $21,416

*Where'd you hear that?*
Institutional Investor, Institutional Investor 300. Based on total equities under management in 1988, in millions of dollars.

## Institutions with highest cash holdings

1. Merrill Lynch Asset Management, with $49,041 million
2. American Express Co., $38,761
3. Fidelity Investments, $34,761
4. Aetna Life & Casualty Co., $26,802
5. Bankers Trust Co., $23,452
6. Dreyfus Group, $20,437
7. Kemper Financial, $18,567
8. Prudential, $16,290
9. Sears, Roebuck Group, $15,287
10. Security Pacific Investment Group, $13,953

*Where'd you hear that?*
Institutional Investor, Institutional Investor 300. Based on total cash under management in 1988, in millions of dollars.

## Institutions with highest real estate holdings

1. Aetna Life & Casualty Co., with $26,592 million
2. Equitable Investment Corp., $24,931
3. Prudential, $24,871
4. TIAA-CREF, $19,612
5. Metropolitan Life, $19,500
6. American Express Co., $14,296
7. Travelers Corp., $11,789
8. Integrated Resources Life, $11,109
9. Cigna Asset Advisers, $10,724
10. JMB Institutional Realty Corp., $10,360

*Where'd you hear that?*
Institutional Investor, Institutional Investor 300. Based on total real estate under management in 1988, in millions of dollars.

## Leading U.S. insurance companies

1. Teachers Insurance & Annuity Association-College Retirement Equity Fund (New York, NY), with $65,000,000 thousand
2. Metropolitan Life Insurance Co. (New York, NY), $48,541,965
3. Aetna Life and Casualty Co. (Hartford, CT), $42,700,986

# MONEY MATTERS

4. The Prudential Asset Management Group (Newark, NJ), $23,705,720
5. The Travelers Insurance Co. (Hartford, CT), $21,655,282
6. John Hancock Financial Services (Boston, MA), $20,378,000
7. The Principal Financial Group (Des Moines, IA), $17,998,619
8. New York Life Insurance Co. (New York, NY), $15,716,839
9. Great West Life Assurance Co. (Englewood, CO), $11,972,950
10. Massachusetts Mutual Life Insurance Co. (Springfield, MA), $11,564,000

*Where'd you hear that?*
Money Market Directory of Pension Funds and Their Investment Managers. Based on 1989 tax-exempt funds under management in thousands of dollars.

## Largest insurance companies

1. Prudential Insurance Co., with $97,664 million
2. Equitable Insurance, $88,580
3. Metropolitan Life, $61,632
4. Aetna Life, $44,985
5. New England, $34,532
6. Travelers Insurance, $27,971
7. Pacific Financial, $27,653
8. Cigna Corp., $26,798
9. John Hancock Mutual Life, $21,377
10. Principal, $18,605

*Where'd you hear that?*
Pensions & Investments, Largest Money Managers Issue. Based on 1989 tax-exempt assets, in millions of dollars.

## Leading money managers

1. American Express Co., with $159,442 million
2. Prudential, $144,314
3. Aetna Life & Casualty, $110,413

*Where'd you hear that?*
Institutional Investor, Institutional Investor 300. Based on total amount of money managed in 1988, in millions of dollars.

## Investment management firms over $10 billion with most new international/global business

1. Wells Fargo Investment, with $2,420 million
2. State Street Bank & Trust, $1,852
3. Capital Guardian Trust Co., $850
4. Fidelity Management Trust, $827
5. Brinson Partners, $727
6. Bankers Trust, $726
7. Prudential Asset Management, $345
8. Boston Co., Inc., $229
9. General Electric Investment Corp., $125
10. INVESCO Capital, $99

*Where'd you hear that?*
Pensions & Investment Age, Scorecard for Pension Managers. Based on 1989 total of new equity and fixed-income business, in millions of dollars.

## Investment management firms, $1-$10 billion, with most new international/global business

1. Nomura Capital, with $612 million
2. Baring International, $530
3. Oechsle International, $474

# MONEY MATTERS

4. Schroder Capital, $446
5. Warburg Investment, $343
6. Rowe Price-Fleming, $307
7. County NatWest Investment, $247
8. Morgan Grenfell Investment, $184
9. BEA Associates, $183
10. TIMCO, $127

*Where'd you hear that?*
Pensions & Investment Age, Scorecard for Pension Managers. Based on 1989 total of new equity and fixed-income business, in millions of dollars.

## Top foreign owners of U.S. assets

1. United Kingdom, with $88.2 billion
2. Netherlands, $51.7
3. Japan, $48.5
4. Canada, $24.3
5. West Germany, $21.3
6. Switzerland, $15.2
7. France, $12.2
8. Others, total, $42.8

*Where'd you hear that?*
Industry Week. Based on direct investment, in billions of dollars.

## Investment management firms, $250 million-$1 billion, with most new international/global business

1. Hill Samuel Investment Advisers, with $469 million
2. Boston International Advisors, $454
3. HD International, $272
4. Marsh & Cunningham-Castegren, $212
5. SBC Portfolio Management, $185
6. Nikko Capital, $141
7. Parametric Portfolio Associates, $117
8. Julius Baer, $113
8. Dunedin Fund, $113
10. First National Bank-Omaha, $80

*Where'd you hear that?*
Pensions & Investment Age, Scorecard for Pension Managers. Based on 1989 total of new equity and fixed-income business, in millions of dollars.

## Investment management firms under $250 million with most new net international/global business

1. Wardley Investment Services, with $100 million
2. InterQuarit Capital Advisors, $80
3. Emerging Markets, $64
4. Kleinwort Benson International, $24
5. Brandes Investment, $23
6. Credit Suisse, $15
7. Oak Hall Capital Advisors, $12
8. Guild Investment, $2

*Where'd you hear that?*
Pensions & Investment Age, Scorecard for Pension Managers. Based on 1989 total of new equity and fixed-income business, in millions of dollars.

## Largest foreign investments in the U.S.

1. Seagram Co. Ltd. (Canada), with $35,938 million
2. Royal Dutch/Shell Group (Netherlands/UK), $21,070
3. British Petroleum (UK), $14,378

4. BAT Industries PLC (UK), $10,371
5. Tengelmann Group (Germany), $10,068
6. Grand Metropolitan PLC (UK), $8,891
7. Campeau Corp. (Canada), $8,062
8. Nestle SA (Switzerland), $6,589
9. Hanson PLC (UK), $6,030
10. Pechiney (France), $5,718

*Where'd you hear that?*
Forbes, Forbes Foreign Rankings 500. Based on 1988 revenues for U.S. holdings in million of dollars.

### Identified gold bar hoarding in Latin America

1. Brazil, with 88.1
2. Colombia, 4.6
3. Argentina, 0.4
3. Venezuela, 0.4
4. Peru, 0.0
5. Others, total, 0.0

*Where'd you hear that?*
Gold 1990. Based on 1989 metric tons.

### Identified gold bar hoarding in the Middle East

1. Saudi Arabia & Yemen, with 23.2
2. Turkey, 16.5
3. Arabian Gulf States, 3.4
4. Kuwait, 1.0
5. Jordan, 0.0
5. Israel, 0.0
5. Lebanon, 0.0
5. Syria, 0.0
5. Iraq, 0.0
5. Egypt, 0.0
5. Iran, 0.0

*Where'd you hear that?*
Gold 1990. Based on 1989 metric tons.

### Identified gold bar hoarding in the Indian sub-continent

1. India, with 5.0
2. Pakistan & Afghanistan, 3.0
3. Sri Lanka, 1.0

*Where'd you hear that?*
Gold 1990. Based on 1989 metric tons.

### Identified gold bar hoarding in the Far East

1. Taiwan, with 138.0
2. Japan, 119.1
3. Thailand, 46.4
4. Hong Kong, 30.0
5. Vietnam, 15.0
6. South Korea, 8.0
7. Singapore, 5.0
8. Indonesia, 4.0
9. Philippines, 2.0
9. Burma, Laos & Cambodia, 2.0

*Where'd you hear that?*
Gold 1990. Based on 1989 metric tons.

### Biggest issuers of foreign bonds

1. Credit Suisse First Boston/Credit Suisse, with $2,214.7 million
2. Union Bank of Switzerland, $1,591.5
3. Deutsche Bank, $1,174.8
4. Swiss Bank, $1,079.3
5. Nomura Securities, $952.9
6. Daiwa Securities, $577.2
7. Nikko Securities, $444.7
8. Citicorp, $424.6
9. Bankers Trust, $423.5

# MONEY MATTERS

# MONEY MATTERS

10. Barclays de Zoete Wedd, $420.8

*Where'd you hear that?*
Investment Dealers' Digest, Corporate Financing. Based on amount, in millions of dollars. Foreign bonds are defined as all non-U.S., non-European offerings outside domestic market of issuers.

## Best-performing investments

1. Coins, with 16.6%
2. Chinese ceramics, 13.3%
3. Gold, 11.5%
4. Old-master paintings, 10.9%
5. Diamonds, 10.4%
6. Stocks, 10.3%
7. Treasury bills, 8.6%
7. Bonds, 8.6%
9. Oil, 8.3%
10. Housing, 7.6%

*Where'd you hear that?*
Medical Economics. Based on compound annual rates of return over the past 20 years.

## Largest managers of international issues

1. Nomura Securities, with $37,725.5 million
2. Daiwa Securities, $19,543.8
3. Yamaichi Securities, $18,012.5
4. Credit Suisse First Boston/Credit Suisse, $17,969.2
5. Nikko Securities, $16,997.1
6. Deutsche Bank, $11,210.0
7. Merrill Lynch Capital Markets, $10,502.1
8. J. P. Morgan & Co., Inc., $8,355.2
9. Union Bank of Switzerland, $8,201.6
10. Morgan Stanley International, $7,963.4

*Where'd you hear that?*
Euromoney, Annual Financing Report. Based on 1989 amount issued, in millions of dollars.

## Leading managers of supranational Eurobond issues

1. Deutsche Bank, with $4,413.1 million
2. Salomon Brothers, $2,104.0
3. Credit Commercial de France, $653.2
4. Industrial Bank of Japan, $595.0
5. Baring Brothers, $488.9
6. Paribas Capital Markets Group, $416.6
7. Algemene Bank Nederland, $394.6
8. Swiss Bank Corporation, $386.5
9. Bankers Trust International, $385.4
10. Nomura Securities, $373.4

*Where'd you hear that?*
Euromoney, Annual Financing Report. Based on 1989 amount, in millions of U.S. dollars.

## Largest issuers of Eurobonds

1. International Bank for Reconstruction and Development, with $5,186.55 million
2. European Investment Bank, $5,063.32

3. Republic of Austria, $3,340.25
4. Republic of Italy, $3,174.42
5. Toyota Motor Corp., $2,715.96
6. General Motors Corp., $2,445.94
7. Deutsche Bank, $2,375.35
8. Marubeni Corp., $2,188.99
9. Nissan Motor Co., $2,170.00
10. IBM, $2,099.73

*Where'd you hear that?*
Euromoney, Annual Financing Report. Based on 1989 amount issued, in millions of dollars.

## Largest lead managers of Euro-yen issues

1. Nomura Securities, with 419.9 billion yen
2. Daiwa Securities, 338.0
3. Industrial Bank of Japan, 252.6
4. Long-Term Credit Bank of Japan, 155.5
5. Yamaichi Securities, 148.5
6. Nippon Credit Bank, 97.2
7. Salomon Brothers, 83.0
8. Nikko Securities, 74.0
9. Bankers Trust International, 66.0
10. Mitsui Finance International, 62.6

*Where'd you hear that?*
Euromoney, Annual Financing Report. Based on 1989 Euro-yen issues, in billions of yen.

## Most professional legal firms in the international bond market

1. Linklaters and Paines, with 34.1%
2. Allen and Overy, 24.2%
3. Clifford Chance, 19.7%
4. Slaughter and May, 10.6%
5. Freshfields, 3.8%

*Where'd you hear that?*
Euromoney, Global Financing Guide. Based on percentage of votes by borrowers polled.

## World's largest public companies

1. NTT (Japan), with $164,537 million
2. Industrial Bank of Japan, $71,239
3. IBM, $65,977
4. Sumitomo Bank (Japan), $65,738
5. Dai-Ichi Kangyo Bank Ltd. (Japan), $64,932
6. Fuji Bank (Japan), $63,364
7. Mitsubishi Bank (Japan), $57,815
8. Exxon Corp. (U.S.), $56,197
9. Royal Dutch/Shell (Netherlands, U.K.), $54,896
10. Toyota Motor (Japan), $52,572

*Where'd you hear that?*
Wall Street Journal, Annual Global Ranking. Based on market value as of June 30, 1989, in millions of dollars.

## Largest public companies by break-up value.

1. General Motors Corp.
2. Ford Motor Co.
3. Exxon Corp.
4. Mobil
5. Royal Dutch Petroleum
6. British Petroleum
7. General Electric Co.
8. Chrysler Corp.
9. Shell Transport & Trading
10. Texaco

# MONEY MATTERS

# MONEY MATTERS

*Where'd you hear that?*
Financial World. Based on break-up value.

## Most heavily traded stocks outside their domestic stock exchanges

1. Deutsche Bank, with $7762.5 million
2. Schlumberger, $4885.8
3. Reuters Holdings, $4782.5
4. Siemens, $4706.4
5. Royal Dutch/Shell, $4239.3
6. Philips, $4206.2
7. Unilever, $4136.6
8. SmithKline Beecham, $3746.4
9. British Petroleum, $3014.6
10. Canadian Pacific, $2857.7

*Where'd you hear that?*
Euromoney, International Equities. Based on 1989 turnover, in millions of U.S. dollars.

### Countries with the highest market capitalization

1. Japan, with $2,998.6 billion
2. United States, $2,069.3
3. Great Britain, $451.4
4. West Germany, $151.1
5. France, $114.8
6. Canada, $114.6
7. Switzerland, $72.9
8. Italy, $66.2
9. Netherlands, $66.1
10. Australia, $57.0

*Where'd you hear that?*
Business Week, The Global 1000. Based on composite market value of Global 1000 companies, in billions of U.S. dollars (share price on May 31, 1989 x number of shares outstanding, converted to dollars at May month-end exchange rates.

### World's best-performing stocks

1. Allgemeine Bauges, Vorzug (Austria), with 552.2%
2. Allgemeine Bauges Stamm (Austria), 533.3%
3. Universale-Bau (Austria), 515.2%
4. Wienerberger Baustoff (Austria), 463.7%
5. UMW Holdings (Mal) (Singapore), 410.8%
6. Mondadori Risp. Non. Cv. (Italy), 239.3%
7. Katakura Industries (Japan), 214.9%
8. Jaguar PLC (UK), 213.4%
9. Homestake Gold Australia (Australia), 212.5%
10. Montana (Austria), 203.9%

*Where'd you hear that?*
Wall Street Journal. Based on percent change in price over the year, 1989.

### World's worst-performing stocks

1. Chase Corp. (New Zealand), with -99.0%
2. Bond Corp. (Australia), -93.0%
3. Imperial Corp. of America (U.S.), -89.7%
4. Bell Group (Australia), -81.1%
5. Campeau Corp. (Canada), -76.6%

6. Bond Media (Australia), -75.0%
7. Northern Star Holdings (Australia), -74.6%
8. Bell Resources (Australia), -74.3%
9. Amstrad (UK), -74.0%
10. Western Union (U.S.), -70.5%

*Where'd you hear that?*
Wall Street Journal. Based on percent change in price over the year, 1989.

## Cheapest foreign stocks

1. Bond Corp. (Australia), with 1.5
2. Bell Resources (Australia), 2.7
3. Baltica Holding (Denmark), 3.4
4. Sofina (Belgium), 3.5
5. Lloyds Bank (United Kingdom), 3.9
5. Handelsbank Kjobenhavns (Denmark), 3.9
7. Alcan Aluminium (Canada), 3.8
8. Standard Chartered Group (United Kingdom), 4.0
9. Bond Corp. International (Hong Kong), 4.1
10. National Westminster Bank, 4.2
10. Privatbanken, 4.2
10. Osterr Elek, 4.2

*Where'd you hear that?*
Forbes, Forbes International 500. Based on price/earnings ratio. Ranks only stocks selling at no more than 70% of the P/E ratio of their national index, priced under the average price/book ratio for their country, and from issues with market capitalizations above $200 million.

## Industries with deepest drops in market value

1. Auto parts & Equipment, with -23%
2. Hotel & Motel, -11%
3. Banks-East, -9%
4. Instruments, -6%
4. Publishing, -6%
6. Other leisure, -5%
7. Tire & Rubber, -3%
7. Steel, -3%
7. Computers, -3%
7. Trucking & Shipping, -3%

*Where'd you hear that?*
Business Week, Business Week 1000. Based on percent change from 1989 to 1990.

## Undervalued U.S. companies

1. Doskocil, with 9.57
2. M. D. C. Holdings Inc., 9.52
3. Columbia Savings & Loan Assn., 9.41
4. Datapoint, 9.37
5. Crossland Savings, 9.33
6. S. E. Nichols, 9.26
7. Circle K Corp., 9.23
8. Northeast Savings, 8.96
9. Magma Copper Co., 8.88
10. Nortek, 8.80

*Where'd you hear that?*
Business Week, The Business Week 1000. Based on index representing ratio of market value to book value compared with other companies in their industries.

## Most popular companies for investment clubs

1. McDonald's Corp., with 2,535
2. Wal-Mart Stores Inc., 1,964
3. American Family Corp., 1,896
4. PepsiCo, Inc., 1,791
5. AT & T, 1,285

**MONEY MATTERS**

# MONEY MATTERS

6. Walt Disney Co., 1,262
7. Pfizer, Inc., 1,132
8. General Electric Co., 993
9. Abbott Laboratories, 968
10. Waste Management, Inc., 940

*Where'd you hear that?*
Better Investing. Based on number of clubs holding stocks in 1988.

## Industries with the biggest gains in market value

1. Engineering services, with 53%
2. Computer software, 48%
3. Pollution control, 46%
4. Petroleum services, 41%
5. Personal care, 37%
6. Electrical products, 32%
7. Textiles, 31%
7. Miscellaneous services, 31%
9. Gas and transmission, 30%
10. General manufacturing, 29%

*Where'd you hear that?*
Business Week, The Business Week 1000. Based on percentge change from 1989 to 1990.

## Companies with the best stock performance

1. Circuit City Stores, with 9287.0%
2. Hasbro Inc., 6606.1%
3. The Limited Inc., 6357.6%
4. Mark IV Industries Inc., 6257.1%
5. Marion Laboratories Inc., 3973.5%
6. Wal-Mart Stores, 3767.4%
7. The Gap, Inc., 3719.2%
8. Dillard Department Stores, 3705.8%
9. Shaw Industries, 3554.1%
10. Tyson Foods, 3317.0%

*Where'd you hear that?*
Forbes, Annual Report on American Industry. Based on price change over 10 years, in percent.

## Companies with the worst stock performance

1. Allegheny International Inc., with -98.5%
2. Savin, -98.0%
3. Western Union, -97.7%
4. Manville Corp., -94.9%
5. Storage Technology, -92.7%
6. Financial Corp. of Santa Barbara, -92.5%
7. Ideal Basic Industries, -91.4%
8. Navistar International, -89.8%
9. Charter, -86.4%
10. Lomas Financial, -84.5%

*Where'd you hear that?*
Forbes, Annual Report on American Industry. Based on price change over 10 years, in percent.

## Days with the largest drops in the Dow Jones Industrial Average

1. October 19, 1987, with 508.00
2. October 13, 1989, 190.58
3. October 26, 1987, 156.83
4. January 8, 1988, 140.58
5. October 16, 1987, 108.35
6. April 14, 1988, 101.46
7. October 14, 1987, 95.46
8. October 6, 1987, 91.55
9. September 11, 1986, 86.61
10. October 22, 1987, 77.42

*Where'd you hear that?*
Wall Street Journal. Based on decline.

# MONEY MATTERS

## Days with greatest percentage loss in the Dow Jones Industrial Average

1. October 19, 1987, with -22.61%
2. October 28, 1929, -12.82%
3. October 29, 1929, -11.73%
4. November 6, 1929, -9.92%
5. August 12, 1932, -8.40%
6. October 26, 1987, -8.04%
7. July 21, 1933, -7.84%
8. October 18, 1937, -7.75%
9. October 5, 1932, -7.15%
10. September 24, 1931, -7.07%

*Where'd you hear that?*
Wall Street Journal. Based on percentage decline.

## Biggest stock buy-backs

1. General Electric Co., with $10,000.00 million
2. IBM, $5,000.00
3. Du Pont, $1,927.50
4. Norfolk Southern, $1,653.75
5. Philip Morris, $1,500.00
6. Coca-Cola Co., $1,340.00
7. Polaroid, $1,125.00
8. Dow Chemical, $1,098.00
9. Time, $1,080.00
10. May Department Stores, $1,062.75

*Where'd you hear that?*
Wall Street Journal. Based on 1989 announced common stock repurchase value, in millions of dollars.

## Best performing stocks on the American Stock Exchange

1. Thermo Proc., with 299.1%
2. New World Entertainment, 273.7
3. Central Pacific, 258.3%
4. Graham Corp., 243.9%
5. Turner Broadcasting, 241.9%
6. Mission Resources, 240.0%
7. Keane Inc., 218.5%

*Where'd you hear that?*
Wall Street Journal. Based on 1989 price change, in percent.

## Best-performing stocks in the 1980s

1. Mylan Laboratories, with 6,496%
2. The Limited Inc., 6,122%
3. Mark IV Industries Inc., 4,996%
4. Marion Laboratories Inc., 3,974%
5. Wainoco Oil, 3,768%
6. The Gap, Inc., 3,722%
7. Dillard Department Stores, 3,707%
8. ServiceMaster, Ltd., 3,557%
9. Dreyfuss Corp., 3,098%
10. Hanaford Brothers, 2,723%

*Where'd you hear that?*
U.S. News & World Report. Based on price appreciation during the 1980s, in percent.

## Worst performing stocks on the American Stock Exchange

1. Seamens A, with -98.7%
2. Residential Res., -95.2%
3. Manufac. Homes, -91.0%
4. Geothermal Resources, -90.9%
5. Centrust Bank, -90.2%
6. Punta Gorda Island, -85.7%

# MONEY MATTERS

*Where'd you hear that?*
Wall Street Journal. Based on 1989 price change, in percent.

## Largest companies listed on the American Stock Exchange

1. Exxon Corp., with $79,311 million
2. IBM, $72,148
3. General Electric Co., $41,348
4. AT & T, $30,872
5. Merck & Co., $26,193
6. General Motors Corp., $26,160
7. Philip Morris, $24,411
8. Ford Motor Co., $23,356
9. E. I. du Pont de Nemours & Co., $21,125
10. RJR Nabisco, $20,884

*Where'd you hear that?*
GT Guide to World Equity Markets. Based on 1988 market value, in millions of dollars.

## Most active shares on the American Stock Exchange

1. BAT Industries PLC, with 1,736,816 hundred shares
2. Wang Labs B, 1,236,279
3. Texas Air, 1,191,205
4. Amdahl, 989,666
5. Echo Bay Mines, Inc., 844,343
6. Fruit of the Loom, 823,193
7. DWG, 644,282
8. Energy Services, 569,146
9. Diasonics Inc., 503,066
10. Bolar Pharmaceutical, 435,436

*Where'd you hear that?*
Wall Street Journal. Based on 1989 sales, in hundreds of shares.

## Top 10 AMEX leaders in share volume

1. B.A.T. Industries PLC, with 153,710 thousand
2. Texas Air Corp., 98,499
3. Wang Laboratories, Inc. (Class B), 98,132
4. Amdahl Corp., 81,988
5. Echo Bay Mines Ltd., 70,521
6. Fruit of the Loom (Class A), 66,622
7. DWG Corp., 50,478
8. Energy Service Co., Inc., 46,594
9. Diasonics, Inc., 43,007
10. Hasbro, Inc., 33,637

*Where'd you hear that?*
American Stock Exchange Fact Book. Based on 1989 AMEX share volume, in thousands.

## Top 10 AMEX leaders in price gain

1. Sierra Health Services, Inc., with 429%
2. Columbia Laboratories, Inc., 394%
3. Thermo Process Systems, Inc., 300%
4. Seitel, Inc., 269%
5. Graham Corp., 244%
6. Mission Resource Partners, L.P., 240%
7. Keane, Inc., 219%
8. Turner Broadcasting System, Inc., 202%
9. Old Spaghetti Warehouse, Inc., 198%
10. Devon Energy Corp., 184%

*Where'd you hear that?*
American Stock Exchange Fact Book. Based on 1989 percent price gain.

# MONEY MATTERS

## Top 10 AMEX leaders in market value

1. B.A.T. Industries PLC, with $20,244 million
2. Imperial Oil Ltd., $9,025
3. Washington Post Co., $3,621
4. Viacom Inc., $3,068
5. Carnival Cruise Lines, Inc., $2,676
6. Brown-Forman Corp., $2,469
7. Courtaulds, PLC, $2,398
8. Turner Broadcasting System, Inc., $2,345
9. Gulf Canada Resources Ltd., $2,104
10. New York Times Co., $2,100

*Where'd you hear that?*
American Stock Exchange Fact Book. Based on 1989 year-end market value, in millions of dollars.

## Top 10 AMEX leaders in sales

1. BAT Industries PLC, with $14,508 million
2. Ford Motor Co. of Canada Ltd., $13,367
3. Texas Air Corp., $8,573
4. Imperial Oil Ltd., $5,957
5. Courtaulds PLC, $4,398
6. Bergen Brunswig Corp., $3,923
7. Turner Corp., $3,290
8. Giant Food Inc., $2,987
9. I. C. H. Corp., $2,885
10. Wang Laboratories, Inc., $2,869

*Where'd you hear that?*
American Stock Exchange Fact Book. Based on 1989 sales, in millions of dollars.

## Top 10 AMEX leaders in shares outstanding

1. B.A.T. Industries PLC, with 1,521 million
2. Courtaulds PLC, 391
3. Wang Laboratories, Inc., 164
4. Imperial Oil Ltd., 164
5. Gulf Canada Resources Ltd., 156
6. Corona Corp., 135
6. Carnival Cruise Lines, Inc., 135
8. Amdahl Corp., 106
9. Echo Bay Mines Ltd., 99
10. International Thoroughbred Breeders, 97

*Where'd you hear that?*
American Stock Exchange Fact Book. Based on 1989 year-end shares outstanding, in millions of dollars.

## Top 10 AMEX leaders in net income

1. B.A.T Industries PLC, with $1,743 million
2. Courtaulds PLC, $432
3. Imperial Oil Ltd., $420
4. Ford Motor Co. of Canada Ltd., $226
5. Amdahl Corp., $223
6. Brascan Ltd., $220
7. Cominco Ltd., $203
8. Carnival Cruise Lines, Inc., $196
9. New York Times Co., $168
10. Tubos de Acero de Mexico, $149

*Where'd you hear that?*
American Stock Exchange Fact Book. Based on 1989 net income, in millions of dollars.

# MONEY MATTERS

### Top 10 AMEX leaders in total assets

1. B.A.T Industries PLC, with $17,910 million
2. Empire of America Federal Savings Bank, $11,281
3. CenTrust Bank, $9,764
4. I. C. H. Corp., $9,294
5. Texas Air Corp., $8,199
6. Imperial Oil Ltd., $8,112
7. American Capital Corp., $6,403
8. First Empire State Corp., $5,908
9. Citadel Holding Corp., $4,642
10. Brascan Ltd., $4,070

*Where'd you hear that?*
American Stock Exchange Fact Book. Based on 1989 total assets, in millions of dollars.

### Top 10 AMEX leaders in shareholders' equity

1. B.A.T Industries PLC, with $6,512 million
2. Imperial Oil Ltd., $4,841
3. Brascan Ltd., $1,946
4. Gulf Canada Resources Ltd., $1,918
5. Courtaulds, PLC, $1,272
6. Ford Motor Co. of Canada, Ltd., $1,188
7. Wang Laboratories, Inc., $1,131
8. Cominco Ltd., $1,023
9. Amdahl Corp., $1,011
10. Tubos de Acero de Mexico, $904

*Where'd you hear that?*
American Stock Exchange Fact Book. Based on 1989 shareholders' equity, in millions of dollars.

### Largest listed companies on the Amsterdam Stock Exchange

1. Royal Dutch, with 61,364 million florins
2. Unilever, 18,885
3. Robeco, 11,380
4. Philips Lamps, 8,820
5. Nationale-Niederlanden, 8,371
6. Rodamco, 7,152
7. AKZO, 6,193
8. Rolinco, 5,900
9. Rorento, 5,629
10. ABN-Bank, 4,844
11. AMRO-Bank, 4,251
12. Elsevier, 3,999
13. Heineken, 3,661
14. Aegon, 3,352
15. AMEV, 3,204
16. Dordtsche Petroleum, 2,329
17. KLM, 2,223
18. Volmac, 2,082
19. Wereldhave, 1,909
20. Ahold, 1,861

*Where'd you hear that?*
GT Guide to World Equity Markets. Based on 1988 market value, in millions of Dutch florins.

### Most actively traded shares on the Amsterdam Stock Exchange

1. Royal Dutch, with 22,312.5 million florins
2. Unilever, 8,712.9
3. AKZO, 7,870.0
4. Philips Lamps, 5,441.4
5. Nationale-Nederlanden, 3,907.9
6. Rodamco, 3,661.7
7. Nedlloyd Group, 3,128.8
8. ABN-Bank, 3,019.9
9. Amro-Bank, 2,784.8
10. KLM, 2,668.1

510

11. Hoogovens Groep, 2,665.9
12. Amro All-In Fund, 2,653.4
13. Elsevier, 2,475.6
14. Aegon, 2,244.3
15. Heineken, 2,210.5
16. Robeco, 2,046.6
17. Rorento, 1,848.6
18. AMEV, 1,741.5
19. KNP, 1,649.9
20. Ahold, 1,594.7

*Where'd you hear that?*
GT Guide to World Equity Markets. Based on 1988 market value, in millions of Dutch florins.

## Largest listed companies on the Athens Stock Exchange

1. National Bank of Greece, with 60,173 million drachmas
2. Finac, 50,152
3. Aluminium of Greece, 38,730
4. National Mortgage Bank, 37,908
5. Xalkis Cement, 35,100
6. Credit Bank, 29,656
7. Heracles Cement, 27,518
8. Commercial Bank, 25,792
9. Viohalco, 18,620
10. Ergo Bank, 18,288

*Where'd you hear that?*
GT Guide to World Equity Markets. Based on 1988 market value, in millions of drachmas.

## Most actively traded stocks on the Athens Stock Exchange

1. Ergo Bank, with 4,467.0 million drachmas
2. Credit Bank, 4,192.0
3. Aluminium of Greece, 3,681.1
4. National Bank of Greece, 3,271.6
5. National Mortgage Bank, 3,208.6
6. Pavlides, 2,168.4
7. Titan Cement, 1,524.3
8. Naoussa Spinning Mills, 1,522.8
9. ETMA, 1,133.1
10. Helleric Investment, 1,084.5

*Where'd you hear that?*
GT Guide to World Equity Markets. Based on 1988 trading value, in millions of drachmas.

## Most actively traded shares on the Bombay Stock Exchange

1. TISCO, with 25,380 million rupees
2. Reliance Industries, 16,930
3. ACC, 7,940
4. Bombay Dyeing, 6,990
5. Bajaj Auto, 5,800
6. Larsen & Toubro, 5,760
7. Tata Tea, 3,410
8. TELCO, 3,280
9. Great Eastern Shipping, 2,600
10. Orkay Silk Mills, 2,590

*Where'd you hear that?*
GT Guide to World Equity Markets. Based on 1988 value, in millions of rupees.

## Largest listed companies on the Brussels Stock Exchange

Petrofina, with 270.1 billion Belgian francs
Generale de Belgique, 213.3
Tractebel, 192.0
Solvay, 109.0
Intercom, 107.6
Cockerill Sambre, 88.8
Ebes, 83.3
Royale Belge-Vie, 81.7
Generale de Banque, 76.3

**MONEY MATTERS**

# MONEY MATTERS

AG Financiere, 59.4

*Where'd you hear that?*
GT Guide to World Equity Markets. 1988 market value, in billions of Belgian francs.

## Most actively traded shares on the Brussels Stock Exchange

1. Reserve Generale de Belgique, with 86,150 billion Belgian francs
2. Petrofina, 37,397
3. Tractebel, 19,545
4. Solvay, 14,048
5. Intercom, 11,853
6. GBL, 11,098
7. Delhaize, 9,803
8. GB-Inno-BM, 8,953
9. Ebes, 8,024
10. Warrant Petrofina, 7,162

*Where'd you hear that?*
GT Guide to World Equity Markets. Based on 1988 trading value, in billions of Belgian francs.

## Largest listed companies on the Buenos Aires Stock Exchange

1. Siderca, with 4,285 million australs
2. Perez Companc, 3,212
3. Indupa, 1,663
4. Aluar, 1,634
5. Cellulosa Argentina, 1,439
6. Mercado de Valores, 1,410
7. Acindar, 1,257
8. Renault Argentina, 1,090
9. Alpargatas, 1,032
10. Ledesma, 1,028

*Where'd you hear that?*
GT Guide to World Equity Markets. Based on 1988 market value, in millions of australs.

## Most actively traded shares on the Buenos Aires Stock Exchange

1. Cellulosa Argentina, with 1,044.7 million australs
2. Acindar, 669.9
3. Perez Companc, 615.7
4. Siderca, 506.3
5. Alpargatas, 355.4
6. Indupa, 343.4
7. Ledesma, 250.0
8. Ipako, 198.2
9. Renault, 173.5
10. Atanor, 160.1

*Where'd you hear that?*
GT Guide to World Equity Markets. Based on 1988 trading value, in millions of australs.

## Largest listed companies on the Caracas Stock Exchange

1. Electricidad de Caracas, with 1,880.5 million Bolivar
2. Banco de Venezuela, 1,329.7
3. Banco Provincial, 1,078.8
4. Banco Union 436.6
5. Sivensa 397.6
6. Venezolana de Cementos 175.0
7. Banco Mercantil 135.0
8. Mantex, CA 121.0
9. Banco La Guaira 106.1
10. Venepal 105.4

*Where'd you hear that?*
GT Guide to World Equity Markets. Based on 1988 trading value, in millions of Bolivar.

# MONEY MATTERS

## Largest listed companies on the Copenhagen Stock Exchange

1. D/S 1912, with 12,202,315 Danish krone
2. D/S Svendborg, 11,284,101
3. Carlsberg Ord, 10,513,732
4. Den Danske Bank, 9,179,476
5. Handelsbanken, 5,923,125
6. Novo B, 5,802,962
7. Baltica, 5,236,000
8. Codan Forsikring, 4,673,513
9. Privatbanken, 4,451,326
10. Ostasiatiske Kompagni, 4,446,643

*Where'd you hear that?*
GT Guide to World Equity Markets. Based on 1988 market value, in Danish krone.

## Most actively traded stocks on the Copenhagen Stock Exchange

1. Novo B, with 3,110,338 Danish krone
2. Ostasiatiske Kompagni, 1,813,353
3. Den Danske Bank, 1,751,898
4. Baltica Holding, 1,372,573
5. Danske Sukkerfabrikker, 1,161,749
6. Privatbanken, 1,091,730
7. Hafnia Invest, 928,714
8. Sophus Berendsen, 912,739
9. Handelsbanken, 838,358
10. Superfos ord., 762,833

*Where'd you hear that?*
GT Guide to World Equity Markets. Based on 1988 trading value, in Danish krone.

## Largest listed companies on the Dublin Stock Exchange

1. Jefferson Smurfit Corp., with 928.1 million Irish pounds
2. Allied Irish Banks, 829.0
3. Bank of Ireland, 716.2
4. CRH, 445.2
5. Waterford Glass, 408.9
6. Irish Distillers, 287.1
7. FII, 224.8
8. Woodchester, 190.7
9. Crean, 152.7
10. Independent Newspapers, 134.3

*Where'd you hear that?*
GT Guide to World Equity Markets. Based on 1988 market value, in millions of Irish pounds.

## Most actively-traded shares on the Dublin Stock Exchange

1. Jefferson Smurfit Corp.
2. Bank of Ireland
3. Allied Irish Banks
4. Waterford Glass
5. Irish Distillers
6. Kerry
7. Crean
8. CRH
9. Fitzwilton
10. FII

*Where'd you hear that?*
GT Guide to World Equity Markets. Based on 1988 trading value.

## Most actively traded stocks on the Frankfurt Stock Exchange

1. Siemens, with 25,892.2 million marks
2. Deutsche Bank, 22,029.9
3. Daimler-Benz, 19,410.1
4. Bayer, 16,236.5

513

# MONEY MATTERS

5. BASF, 14,898.7
6. Hoechst, 14,809.3
7. Volkswagen St., 14,706.7
8. VEBA, 9,475.0
9. Thyssen, 9,308.1
10. Allianz-Hold, 8,887.8

*Where'd you hear that?*
GT Guide to World Equity Markets. Based on 1988 total trading value, in millions of Deutsche marks.

## Largest companies listed on the Frankfurt Stock Exchange

1. Daimler-Benz, with 31,311.7 million marks
2. Allianz N.A., 28,095.0
3. Siemens, 25,655.5
4. Bayer, 20,502.5
5. Deutsche Bank, 19,977.6
6. Munchener Ruckversicherung, 19,078.0
7. Hoechst, 17,208.4
8. BASF, 15,984.3
9. VEBA, 10,622.5
10. Rhein-Westf. Elekrizitatsw, 10,607.4

*Where'd you hear that?*
GT Guide to World Equity Markets. Based on 1988 market value, in millions of Deutsche marks.

## Largest listed companies on the Helsinki Stock Exchange

1. Union Bank of Finland, with 11,972.0 million markka
2. Kansallis-Osake-Pankki, 8,797.5
3. Kymmene Corp., 8,388.0
4. Nokia Corp., 7,188.0
5. Pohjola Insurance Co., 6,778.0
6. Outokumpu Group, 5,523.4
7. SKOP Bank, 4,715.0
8. Enso-Gutzeit, 4,458.4
9. Rauma-Repola, 4,407.4
10. United Paper Mills, 4,181.0

*Where'd you hear that?*
GT Guide to World Equity Markets. Based on market value, in millions of Finnish markka.

## Most actively traded shares on the Helsinki Stock Exchange

1. Union Bank of Finland, with 1,543.0 thousand markka
2. Pohjola Insurance Co., 1,185.0
3. Kymmene Corp., 1,084.1
4. Rauma-Repola, 1,043.4
5. Kesko Group, 1,010.1
6. Kansallis-Osake-Pankki, 981.0
7. Nokia Corp., K, 913.2
8. United Paper Mills, K, 890.2
9. Partek Corp., 800.4
10. Pohjola Insurance Co., A Free, 780.4

*Where'd you hear that?*
GT Guide to World Equity Markets. Based on trading value, in thousands of Finnish markka.

## Largest listed companies on the Hong Kong Stock Exchange

1. Hong Kong Telecommunications, with $6,814.7 million
2. Hong Kong & Shanghai Banking Corp., $4,300.2
3. Swire Pacific, $3,639.8
4. Cathay Pacific Airways, $3,415.4
5. Hutchinson Whampoa, $3,337.1
6. Hongkong Land Co., $2,994.2
7. Hang Seng Bank, $2,539.8
8. China Light & Power, $2,410.3

9. Sun Hung Kai Properties, $2,391.1
10. Cheung Kong Holdings, $2,288.0

*Where'd you hear that?*
GT Guide to World Equity Markets. Based on 1988 market value, in millions of U.S. dollars.

## Most actively traded shares on the Hong Kong Stock Exchange

1. Cheung Kong Holdings, with $1,198.3 million
2. Hongkong Land Co., $1,148.7
3. Hongkong & Shanghai Banking Corp., $1,092.8
4. Hutchison Whampoa, $1,079.0
5. Swire Pacific 'A', $970.8
6. Sun Hung Kai Properties, $752.1
7. New World Development, $686.0
8. Cathay Pacific Airways, $531.6
9. Wharf (Holdings), $526.8
10. China Light & Power, $494.5

*Where'd you hear that?*
GT Guide to World Equity Markets. Based on 1988 trading value, in millions of U.S. dollars.

## Largest listed companies on the Indonesian Stock Exchange

1. Jakarta International Hotel, with $46.0 million
2. Unilever, $37.6
3. BAT Indonesia, $16.5
4. Multi Bintang Indonesia, $14.5
5. Sucaco, $13.1
5. Goodyear Tire & Rubber Co., $13.1

7. Panin Bank, $12.5
8. Tificorp, $12.0
9. Bayer Indonesia, $10.3
10. Semen Cibinong, $9.6

*Where'd you hear that?*
GT Guide to World Equity Markets. Based on 1988 market value, in millions of U.S. dollars.

## Most actively traded shares on the Indonesian Stock Exchange

1. Sucaco
2. Jakarta International Hotel
3. Unilever
4. BAT Indonesia
5. Goodyear Tire & Rubber Co.
6. Multi Bintang Indonesia
7. Unitex
8. Panin Bank
9. Hotel Prapatan
10. Merck Indonesia

*Where'd you hear that?*
GT Guide to World Equity Markets. Based on 1988 turnover value (unspecified).

## Largest listed companies on the Istanbul Stock Exchange

1. Eregli Demir Celik, with 207 billion Turkish lira
2. Cukurova Elektrik, 197
3. T Is Bankasi, 194
4. Brisa, 112
5. Koc Holding, 103
6. Arcelik, 90
6. Mensucat Santral, 90
8. Korosa, 79
9. Otosan, 76
10. Teletas, 70

*Where'd you hear that?*
GT Guide to World Equity Markets. Based on 1988 market value, in billions of Turkish lira.

# MONEY MATTERS

515

# MONEY MATTERS

### Most actively traded shares on the Istanbul Stock Exchange

1. Cukurova, with 16,983 million Turkish lira
2. Akcimento, 16,298
3. Goodyear Tire & Rubber Co., 13,379
4. Bagfas, 11,733
5. Kordsa, 8,376
6. Cimsa, 6,026
7. Eregli Demir Celik, 5,467
8. T. Demir Dokum, 4,519
9. Brisa, 4,057
10. T. Is Bankasi, 3,942

*Where'd you hear that?*
GT Guide to World Equity Markets. Based on 1988 turnover value, in millions of Turkish lira.

### Largest quoted companies on the Johannesburg Stock Exchange

1. Consolidated Gold Fields PLC
2. De Beers Consolidated Mines
3. Anglo American Corporation of South Africa
4. Lonrho
5. Mineral & Resources Corp.
6. Driefontein Consolidated
7. Richemont Securities
8. Rustenburg Platinum Holdings
9. General Mining Unin Corp.
10. Anglo American Gold Investment Co.

*Where'd you hear that?*
GT Guide to World Equity Markets. Based on market capitalization, end-1988.

### Most actively traded shares on the Johannesburg Stock Exchange

1. De Beers Consolidated Mines, with 745.5 million rands
2. Vaal Reefs Exploration & Mining, 398.2
3. Anglo American Corporation of South Africa, 383.0
4. Anglo American Gold Investment Co., 311.6
5. Consolidated Gold Fields PLC, 302.0
6. Barlow Rand, 244.1
7. Driefontein Consolidated, 236.8
8. Rembrandt Group, 200.7
9. Mineral & Resources Corp., 185.3
10. Sasol, 185.0

*Where'd you hear that?*
GT Guide to World Equity Markets. Based on 1988 trading value in millions of rands.

### Largest listed companies on the Korea Stock Exchange

1. POSCO, with 3,466.6 million won
2. Han Il Bank, 1,631.0
3. Korea First Bank, 1,597.0
4. Bank of Seoul, 1,584.6
5. Commercial Bank of Korea, 1,549.0
5. Cho Heung Bank, 1,549.0
7. Dawewoo, 1,328.5
8. Hyundai Engineering & Construction Co., 1,287.9
9. Daewoo Securities, 1,233.4
10. GoldStar Co. Ltd., 1,206.0

*Where'd you hear that?*
GT Guide to World Equity Markets. Based on 1988 value, in millions of won.

## Most actively traded shares on the Korea Stock Exchange

1. Commercial Bank of Korea, with 2,325,927 million won
2. Daewoo Corp., 1,954,414
3. Cho Heung Bank, 1,913,862
4. Bank of Seoul, 1,859,316
5. Hyundai Engineering & Construction Co., 1,738,711
6. Korea First Bank, 1,707,846
7. Han Il Bank, 1,575,255
8. Daewoo Electronics, 1,155,454
9. GoldStar Co. Ltd., 1,007,733
10. Chung Buk Bank, 902,054

*Where'd you hear that?*
GT Guide to World Equity Markets. Based on 1988 trading volume.

## Largest listed companies on the Kuala Lumpur Stock Exchange

1. Overseas-Chinese Banking Corp., with M$6,208.8 million
2. Development Bank of Singapore, M$4,438.8
3. Sime Darby Bhd., M$4,433.3
4. Malaysian International Shipping Corp., M$3,475.0
5. United Overseas Bank, M$3,045.6
6. HMPB, M$2,834.0
7. Malaysian Airline System Bhd., M$2,327.5
8. Malaysian Breweries, M$2,265.8
9. Kuala Lumpur Kepong Bhd., M$2,139.7
10. Malayan Banking Bhd., M$1,920.8

*Where'd you hear that?*
GT Guide to World Equity Markets. Based on 1988 market value, in millions of Malaysian dollars.

## Most actively traded shares on the Kuala Lumpur Stock Exchange

1. Malaysian International Shipping Corp., with M$341.1 thousand
2. Malaysian Airline System Bhd., M$308.7
3. Sime Darby Bhd., M$271.1
4. Innovest, M$132.2
5. Promet, M$127.9
6. Malaysian United Industries Bhd., M$127.9
7. MMC, M$119.7
8. Antah Holdings, M$102.0
9. Public Bank, M$99.7
10. Raleigh Bhd., M$79.4

*Where'd you hear that?*
GT Guide to World Equity Markets. Based on 1988 share turnover, in thousands of Malaysian dollars.

## Largest listed companies on the Lisbon Stock Exchange

1. Sociedad Portuguesa de Celulose, with 166.25 million escudo
2. Banco Comercial Portugues, 78.78
3. Companhia Portuguesa Radio Marconi, 69.71
4. Industria e Investimentos, 56.50
5. Banco Portugues de Investimento, 49.35
6. Companhia de Celulose do Caima, 41.58
7. Banco Manufacturers Hanover (Portugal), 39.71
8. Companhia de Investimentos e Servicos Financeiros, 22.30
9. Banco de Comericio e Industria, 22.14
10. Salvador Caetano, 19.84

# MONEY MATTERS

517

# MONEY MATTERS

*Where'd you hear that?*
GT Guide to World Equity Markets. Based on 1988 market value, in millions of Portuguese escudo.

## Largest listed companies on the London Stock Exchange

1. British Telecom, with £15,469.2 million
2. British Petroleum, £15,183.2
3. Shell Transport & Trading, £11,566.0
4. Glaxo Holdings, £7,922.1
5. ICI, £6,885.8
6. BAT Industries PLC, £6,882.6
7. British Gas PLC, £6,668.9
8. Hanson PLC, £5,923.6
9. GEC, £5,042.9
10. BTR, £5,030.3

*Where'd you hear that?*
GT Guide to World Equity Markets. Based on 1988 market value, in millions of British pounds.

## Most actively traded shares on the Lisbon Stock Exchange

1. Companhia de Celulose do Caima, with 11,447,791 million escudo
2. Banco Comercial Portugues, 8,469,136
3. Companhia Portuguesa Radio Marconi, 7,531,763
4. Banco Portugues de Investimento, 6,880,804
5. Companhia de Investimentos e Servicos Financeiros, 4,983,959
6. Industria e Investimentos, 4,621,340
7. Betao Liz, 4,200,836
8. Empresa Fabril Maquinas Electricas, 2,677,712
9. Investimentos, Participacoes e Gestao, 2,670,231
10. Sociedade Portuguesa de Locacao Financeira, 2,398,866

*Where'd you hear that?*
GT Guide to World Equity Markets. Based on 1988 trading value, in millions of Portuguese escudo.

## Largest listed companies on the Luxembourg Stock Exchange

1. Royal Dutch, with 1,147,211 million Luxembourg francs
2. Deutsche Bank, 415,547
3. Bayer, 397,101
4. Unilever, 352,091
5. Hoechst, 329,260
6. Chrysler Corp., 240,737
7. Elf Aquitaine, 225,711
8. Robeco, 203,479
9. Volkswagen, 176,160
10. Dresdner Bank, 172,896

*Where'd you hear that?*
GT Guide to World Equity Markets. Based on 1988 market value, in millions of Luxembourg francs.

## Most actively traded shares on the Luxembourg Stock Exchange

1. J. P. Morgan French Franc Bond Fund, with 3,582.0 million Luxembourg francs
2. J. P. Morgan French Franc Liquid Fund, 1,643.8
3. Banque Generale du Luxembourg, 857.0
4. Banque Internationale a Luxembourg, 462.9
5. ARBED, 290.5

6. IMMAG, 258.2
7. Espirito Santo Financial Holding, 238.0
8. Transpacific Fund, 221.1
9. Belgo-Mineira (ordinary shares), 206.6
10. Royal Dutch, 190.4

*Where'd you hear that?*
GT Guide to World Equity Markets. Based on 1988 turnover value, in millions of Luxembourg francs.

### Largest companies listed on the Madrid Stock Exchange

1. Banco Bilbao Vizcaya, with 905.5 million pesetas
2. Telefonica, 765.4
3. Banco de Santander, 722.7
4. Banco Central, 418.6
5. Endesa, 413.9
6. Banesto, 365.3
7. Banco Hispano, 322.9
8. Banco Popular, 257.2
9. Hidroelectrica Ibercia, 252.0
10. Hidroelectrica Espanola, 185.8

*Where'd you hear that?*
GT Guide to World Equity Markets. Based on 1988 market value, in millions of pesetas.

### Most actively traded shares on the Madrid Stock Exchange

1. Cia Telefonica National de Espana, with 117,897 million pesetas
2. Banco Santander, 107,661
3. Banesto, 74,094
4. Banco Hispano, 68,401
5. Banco Popular, 66,689
6. Cia Espanola de Petroleos, 65,126
7. Asland, 56,776
8. Hidroelectrica Ibercia, 54,420
9. Banco Bilbao, 47,692
10. Energias, 47,592

*Where'd you hear that?*
GT Guide to World Equity Markets. Based on 1988 trading value, in millions of pesetas.

### Largest issues listed on the Manila Stock Exchange

1. San Miguel A, with 14,513 million pesos
2. Philippine Long Distance Telephone, 10,246
3. San Miguel B, 9,674
4. Ayala A, 8,025
5. Philex Mining A, 3,925
6. Bank of the Philippine Islands, 3,040
7. Philex Mining B, 2,684
8. Philippine Commercial International Bank, 1,864
9. Atlas Consolidated A, 1,829
10. Lepanto Consolidated A, 1,664

*Where'd you hear that?*
GT Guide to World Equity Markets. Based on 1988 market value, in millions of pesos.

### Most actively traded shares on the Manila Stock Exchange

1. Atlas Consolidated A, with 1,227 million pesos
2. Philippine Long Distance Telephone, 978
3. San Miguel A, 651
4. San Miguel B, 594
5. Lepanto Consolidated A, 480
6. Oriental Petroleum A, 434
7. Philex Mining A, 422
8. Philex Mining B, 413
9. Philippine Overseas Drilling A, 336
10. Lepanto Consolidated B, 272

**MONEY MATTERS**

# MONEY MATTERS

*Where'd you hear that?*
GT Guide to World Equity Markets. Based on 1988 turnover value, in millions of pesos.

## Largest companies listed on the Mexico Stock Exchange

1. Vitro, with 1,785.0 million pesos
2. Cementos Mexicanos, 1,099.5
3. Grupo Cermoc, 1,475.3
4. Cia Minera de Canannea, 1.259.8
5. Telefonos de Mexico, 1,169.3
6. Grupo Industrial Minera Mexico, 1,024.7
7. Valores Industriales, 1,016.5
8. Grupo Industrial Alfa, 945.9
9. Industrias Penoles, 927.9
10. Kimberly-Clark de Mexico, 860.2

*Where'd you hear that?*
GT Guide to World Equity Markets. Based on 1988 market value, in millions of pesos.

## Most actively traded shares on the Mexico Stock Exchange

1. Vitro, with 1,132,388.9 million pesos
2. Industrias Penoles, 1,044,084.2
3. Telefonos de Mexico, 722,596.6
4. Cifra, 597,243.8
5. Cemex, N/A
6. Industrias Nacobre, 471,972.5
7. Desc Sociedad de Fomento Industrial, 445,695.6
8. Corporacion Industrial San Luis, 437,513.9
9. Cydsa, 388,917.0
10. Celanese Mexicano, 361,699.1

*Where'd you hear that?*
GT Guide to World Equity Markets. Based on 1988 trading value, in millions of pesos.

## Largest companies on the Milan Stock Exchange

1. Assicurazioni Generali, with 13.02%
2. Fiat SpA(ordinary), 7.77%
3. La Fondiaria, 2.89%
4. Stet, 2.72%
5. RAS, 2.67%
6. Montedison, 2.48%
7. Mediobanca, 2.30%
8. Olivetti, 2.27%
9. Fiat (preferred), 2.17%
10. Ferfin, 1.94%

*Where'd you hear that?*
GT Guide to World Equity Markets. Based on 1988 percentage of exchange.

## Most actively traded shares on the Milan Stock Exchange

1. Fiat SpA(ordinary), with 4,844 billion lire
2. Assicurazioni Generali, 3,548
3. Olivetti, 2,539
4. Montedison, 2,436
5. Fiat (preferred), 1,700
6. CIR, 1,416
7. RAS, 925
8. Mediobanca, 908
9. SME, 812
10. Gemina Ordinaria, 782

*Where'd you hear that?*
GT Guide to World Equity Markets. Based on 1988 turnover value, in billions of lira.

520

# MONEY MATTERS

## Most actively traded shares on the Montreal Exchange

1. Alcan Aluminium, with $852.7 million Canadian
2. BCE, $845.9
3. Inco, $788.6
4. Canadian Pacific, $510.2
5. Royal Bank of Canada, $437.2
6. Bank of Montreal, $394.0
7. Nova Corporation of Alberta, $373.6
8. Laidlaw Transportation Limited Class B, $373.6
9. Falconbridge, $324.1
10. Canadian Imperial Bank of Commerce, $302.9

*Where'd you hear that?*
GT Guide to World Equity Markets. Based on 1988 trading value, in millions of Canadian dollars.

## Largest companies listed on the Montreal Exchange

1. IBM, with $86,517 million
2. General Motors Corp., $31,291
3. Ford Motor Co., $27,049
4. BCE, $10,794
5. USX Corp., $8,879
6. Imperial Oil Ltd., $8,161
7. Chrysler Corp., $7,768
8. Seagram, $7,219
9. Canadian Pacific, $6,969
10. Alcan Aluminium, $6,204

*Where'd you hear that?*
GT Guide to World Equity Markets. Based on 1988 market value, in millions of Canadian dollars.

## Largest companies listed on the New York Stock Exchange

1. Exxon Corp., with $79,311 million
2. IBM, $72,148
3. General Electric, $41,348
4. AT & T, $30,872
5. Merck & Co., $26,193
6. General Motors Corp., $26,160
7. Philip Morris, $24,411
8. Ford Motor Co., $23,356
9. E. I. du Pont de Nemours, $21,125
10. RJR Nabisco, $20,884

*Where'd you hear that?*
GT Guide to World Equity Markets. Based on 1988 market value, in millions of dollars.

## Most actively traded shares on the New York Stock Exchange

1. AT & T, with 4,620,651 hundred
2. IBM, 4,023,326
3. General Electric Co., 3,576,287
4. Exxon Corp., 3,361,985
5. Union Carbide, 3,168,541
6. Texaco, 2,972,602
7. USX, 2,866,437
8. Eastman Kodak Co., 2,818,632
9. Philip Morris, 2,803,425
10. Ford Motor Co., 2,638,824

*Where'd you hear that?*
Wall Street Journal. Based on 1989 sales, in hundreds of shares.

## Top 10 performing stocks on the New York Stock Exchange

1. Spain Fund, with 198.8%
2. L. A. Gear Inc., 184.6%
3. Claire's Stores, 179.5%
4. Asia Pacific Fund, 178.4%
5. Thai Fund Inc., 174.5%
6. Mylan Labs, 173.2%
7. Holiday Corp., 165.7%

# MONEY MATTERS

8. Shaw Industries, 163.8%
9. Tyler Corp., 163.6%
10. Germany Fund, 156.7%

*Where'd you hear that?*
Wall Street Journal. Based on percent increase, 1989.

## Largest foreign equities on the New York Stock Exchange

1. Royal Dutch, with $8313.2 million
2. Schlumberger, $4664.0
3. SmithKline Beecham, $3745.6
4. Alcan Aluminium, $3476.1
5. British Petroleum, $2879.6
6. Racal Telecom, $2716.6
7. Inco, $2576.9
8. Unilever, $2344.2
9. Seagram, $2317.7

*Where'd you hear that?*
Euromoney, International Equities. Based on 1989 turnover, in millions of U.S. dollars.

## Best stocks on the New York Stock Exchange by return to investors

1. L. A. Gear Inc., with 185%
2. Mylan Labs, 176%
3. Shaw Industries, 169%
4. Holiday Corp., 166%
5. Conseco, 145%
6. Enterra, 140%
7. Apache, 139%
8. Crawford & Co., 133%
9. Sea Containers Ltd., 129%
10. WorldCorp, 126%

*Where'd you hear that?*
Fortune, Best and Worst Stocks of 1989 on the New York Stock Exchange. Based on 1989 total return to investors, in percent.

## Worst performing stocks on the New York Stock Exchange by price change

1. Integrated Resources Life, with -98.7%
2. Western S & L, -94.7%
3. Lomas Financial, -92.1%
4. Bay Financial, -91.4%
5. Commonwealth Mtg. Co. of Am., -90.6%
6. Imperial Corp. of America, -89.7%
7. Continental Informations Systems, -89.7%
8. NBI Inc., -86.9%
9. Home Owners Savings Bank, -86.6%
10. Thortec International, -85.0%

*Where'd you hear that?*
Wall Street Journal. Based on 1989 price change, in percent.

## Worst stocks on the New York Stock Exchange by return to investors

1. Integrated Resources Life, with -99%
2. Lomas Financial, -92%
3. Bay Financial, -91%
4. Imperial Corp. of America, -90%
5. Home Owners Savings Bank, -87%
6. Crossland Savings, -79%
7. Rexene, -75%
8. National Education, -70%
8. Circle K Corp., -70%
10. MAI Basic Four, -66%

*Where'd you hear that?*
Fortune, Best and Worst Stocks of 1989 on the New York Stock Exchange. Based on 1989 total return to investors, in percent.

## Largest listed companies on the New Zealand Stock Exchange

1. Fletcher Challenge, with NZ$4,619.1 million
2. Brierley Investments, NZ$2,199.8
3. Elders Resources NZFP, NZ$2,194.5
4. Bank of New Zealand, NZ$1,158.1
5. Magnum Corp., NZ$1,027.2
6. Lion Nathan Group, NZ$1,017.5
7. Carter Holt Harvey, NZ$944.8
8. Feltrax International, NZ$914.7
9. Robert Jones Investments, NZ$590.2
10. NZI Corporation, NZ$527.0

*Where'd you hear that?*
GT Guide to World Equity Markets. Based on 1988 market value, in millions of New Zealand dollars.

## Most actively traded shares on the New Zealand Stock Exchange

1. Brierley Investments, with NZ$254.7 million
2. Fletcher Challenge, NZ$244.3
3. Goodman Fielder Wattie, NZ$110.9
4. NZI Corp., NZ$92.6
5. Chase Corp., NZ$74.0
6. Feltrax International, NZ$67.4
7. Robert Jones Investments, NZ$66.5
8. Industrial Equity Pacific, NZ$51.8
9. Elders Resources NZFP, NZ$47.7
10. Carter Holt Harvey, NZ$46.3

*Where'd you hear that?*
GT Guide to World Equity Markets. Based on 1988 trading value, in millions of New Zealand dollars.

## Largest listed companies on the Oslo Stock Exchange

1. Norsk Hydro, with 16,431 million krone
2. Hafslund, 8,682
3. Bergesen, 7,453
4. Vard, 4,216
5. Orkla-Borregaard, 3,868
6. Kvaerner Industrier, 2,916
7. Saga, 2,904
8. Elkem, 2,570
9. Aker, 2,438
10. DnC, 2,189

*Where'd you hear that?*
GT Guide to World Equity Markets. Based on 1988 market value, in millions of Norwegian krone.

## Most actively traded shares on the Oslo Stock Exchange

1. Norsk Hydro, with 3,449.4 million krone
2. Elkem, 2,084.2
3. Hafslund Nycomed A-aksjer, 1,740.4
4. Kvaerner Industrier, 1,485.9
5. Orkla-Borregaard, 1,277.4
6. Bergesen D.Y. A-aksjer, 1,128.8
7. Bergesen D.Y. B-aksjer, 946.7
8. Kosmos, 828.5
9. Saga Petroleum, 825.2
10. Vard, 808.5

# MONEY MATTERS

# MONEY MATTERS

*Where'd you hear that?*
GT Guide to World Equity Markets. Based on 1988 trading value, in millions of Norwegian krone.

## Largest listed companies on the Paris Stock Exchange

1. Cie du Midi, with 39.1 billion French francs
2. Elf-Aquitaine, 38.7
3. LVMH, 37.7
4. Peugeot, 34.3
5. Saint Gobain, 34.0
6. BSN, 33.3
7. Societe Generale, 30.2
8. Cie Generale des Eaux, 28.3
9. Banque Paribas, 27.6
10. Suez, 27.5

*Where'd you hear that?*
GT Guide to World Equity Markets. Based on 1988 market value, in billions of French francs.

## Most actively traded shares on the Paris Stock Exchange

1. LVMH, with 76.79 billion French francs
2. Cie du Midi, 73.90
3. Societe Generale, 65.66
4. Peugeot, 59.12
5. Cie Generale des Eaux, 47.38
6. Suez, 38.92
7. Saint Gobain, 37.74
8. Michelin, 35.25
9. Banque Paribas, 33.13
10. BSN, 31.72

*Where'd you hear that?*
GT Guide to World Equity Markets. Based on 1988 average daily volume, in billions of French francs.

## Largest listed companies on the Santiago Stock Exchange

1. Copec, with $809.78 million
2. Cartones, $590.61
3. Endesa, $446.17
4. Telefonos, $359.51
5. Cap, $264.80
6. Soquimich, $229.80
7. CCT, $219.46
8. Entel, $161.12
9. Minera, $159.28
10. Indo, $157.83

*Where'd you hear that?*
GT Guide to World Equity Markets. Based on 1988 market value, in millions of U.S. dollars.

## Most actively traded shares on the Santiago Stock Exchange

1. Endesa, with $24,518.9 thousand
2. Cap, $16,944.1
3. Copec, $14,721.5
4. Soquimich, $14,715.3
5. Iansa, $10,254.8
6. Telefonos A, $10,169.8
7. Entel, $9,885.7
8. Cartones, $6,434.2
9. Chilgener, $5,826.8
10. Enersis, $3,731.9

*Where'd you hear that?*
GT Guide to World Equity Markets. Based on 1988 trading value, in thousands of U.S. dollars.

## Largest listed companies on the Sao Paulo Stock Exchange

1. Petrobras, with $2,767,813 thousand
2. Nemofeffer, $1,662,811
3. Banco do Brasil, $1,572,523
4. Copene, $1,237,001

5. Electrobras, $1,101,609
6. Vale R Doce, $963,146
7. Bradesco, $945,003
8. Aracruz, $929,140
9. Itausa, $792,392
10. Souza Cruz, $650,533

*Where'd you hear that?*
GT Guide to World Equity Markets. Based on 1988 market value, in thousands of U.S. dollars.

## Most actively traded shares on the Sao Paulo Stock Exchange

1. Petrobras
2. Paranapanema
3. Copene
4. Banco do Brasil
5. Papel Simao
6. Itausa
7. Bradesco
8. Polipropileno
9. Suzano
10. Sharp

*Where'd you hear that?*
GT Guide to World Equity Markets. Based on 1988 trading value.

## Largest listed companies on the Singapore Stock Exchange

1. Hongkong Land Co., with 11,639.1 million Singapore dollars
2. Singapore Airlines, 7,808.0
3. Overseas-Chinese Banking Corp., 4,502.8
4. Algemene Bank Nederland, 4,320.3
5. Sime Darby, 3,211.0
6. Development Bank of Singapore, 3,182.7
7. United Overseas Bank, 2,185.6
8. Harrisons Malaysian Plantations, 2,047.3
9. Singapore Press Holdings, 1,848.7
10. K. L. Kepong, 1,533.8

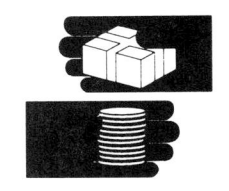

*Where'd you hear that?*
GT Guide to World Equity Markets. Based on 1988 market value, in millions of Singapore dollars.

## Most actively traded shares on the Singapore Stock Exchange

1. DBS Land, with 223,889 thousand
2. Sime Darby, 214,997
3. Promet, 194,571
4. NOL, 188,552
5. Tan Chong Motor Holdings, 169,952
6. City Developments, 150,192
7. United Industrial Corp., 129,507
8. Keppel Investment Warrants 1991, 128,527
9. NOL Transferable Subscription Rights 1993, 126,733
10. United Pulp & Paper Co., 122,886

*Where'd you hear that?*
GT Guide to World Equity Markets. Based on 1988 trading volume, in thousands of units.

## Largest listed companies on the Stockholm Stock Exchange

1. Volvo, with 30.79 billion krona
2. Skanska, 24.77
3. ASEA, 23.75
4. SE-Banken, 22.25
5. Electrolux, 21.68
6. SCA, 20.89
7. STORA, 19.81

# MONEY MATTERS

# MONEY MATTERS

8. Astra, 16.40
9. Sandvik, 16.06
10. Svenska HandelsBanken, 16.03

*Where'd you hear that?*
GT Guide to World Equity Markets. Based on 1988 market value, in billions of krona.

## Most actively traded shares on the Stockholm Stock Exchange

1. Volvo, with 7.34 billion krona
2. Electrolux, 4.87
3. Holmens Bruk, 4.47
4. Trelleborg, 4.17
5. Astra, 3.82
6. L. M. Ericsson, 3.76
7. Skandia International Holding, 3.47
8. SKF, 3.22
9. Stora Kopparberg, 3.07
10. Pharmacia, 2.76

*Where'd you hear that?*
GT Guide to World Equity Markets. Based on 1988 trading volume, in billions of krona.

## Largest listed companies on the Sydney Stock Exchange

1. Broken Hill Proprietary Co., with $9,263 million Australian dollars.
2. Elders IXL Ltd., $6,553
3. Westpac Banking Corp., $5,251
4. National Australian Bank, $4,839
5. Australia and New Zealand Banking Group Ltd., $4,821
6. Coles Myer Ltd., $4,686
7. BTR Nylex, $4,644
8. CRA, Ltd., $4,531
9. Western Mining Corp. Holdings, $4,207
10. News Corp., $3,591

*Where'd you hear that?*
GT Guide to World Equity Markets. Based on 1988 market value, in millions of Australian dollars.

## Most actively traded shares on the Sydney Stock Exchange

1. Broken Hill Proprietary Co., with $2,022 million Australian dollars
2. Western Mining Corp. Holdings, $1,300
3. National Australia Bank, $1,025
4. Elders IXL Ltd., $1,024
5. Australia and New Zealand Banking Group Ltd., $856
6. CPA, $833
7. MIM Holdings, $743
8. Westpac Banking Corp., $712
9. CSR, $639
10. Coles Myer Ltd., $471

*Where'd you hear that?*
GT Guide to World Equity Markets. Based on 1988 turnover, in millions of Australian dollars.

## Most actively traded shares on the Taiwan Stock Exchange

1. Chung Shing Textile, with 4,352 million
2. China Rebar, 3,877
3. Hualon-Teijran, 3,758
4. Tatung, 3,439
5. Nan Ya Plastic, 2,499
6. Taiwan Synthetic Rubber, 2,492
7. Yue Loong Motor, 2,126
8. Taiwan Paper, 2,118

9. Formosa Chemicals & Fibre Corp., 2,029
10. Formosa Plastics Corp., 1,994

*Where'd you hear that?*
GT Guide to World Equity Markets. Based on 1988 trading volume, in millions of shares.

## Largest listed companies on the Tel Aviv Stock Exchange

1. Dead-Sea Works, with $557 million
2. IDB Development Corp., $179
3. Teva Pharmaceutical Industries, $165
4. Israel Corp., $126
5. Clal (Israel), $121
6. Discount Investment Corp., $99
6. Clal Industries, $99
8. Super-Sol, $96
9. First International Bank of Israel, $89
10. Industrial Development Bank of Israel, $84

*Where'd you hear that?*
GT Guide to World Equity Markets. Based on 1988 market value, in millions of U.S. dollars.

## Most actively traded shares on the Tel Aviv Stock Exchange

1. Dead-Sea Works, with $58.2 thousand
2. IDB Development Corp., $47.8
3. Teva Pharmaceutical Industries, $46.6
4. Discount Investment Corp., $46.4
5. Clal (Israel), $40.4
6. Israel Corp., $31.9
7. Delek, The Israel Fuel Corp., $32.3
8. IDB Development Corp., $31.7
9. FIBI, $29.1
10. First International Bank of Israel, $26.7

*Where'd you hear that?*
GT Guide to World Equity Markets. Based on 1988 turnover value, in thousands of U.S. dollars.

## Largest listed companies on the Securities Exchange of Thailand

1. Siam Cement, with 35,052.00 million baht
2. Bangkok Bank, 16,380.00
3. Siam City Cement, 13,264.53
4. Thai Farmers Bank, 10,530.00
5. Siam Commercial Bank, 7,056.00
6. Siam Pulp & Paper, 5,782.00
7. Padaeng Industry, 5,408.00
8. Thai Plastic & Chemical, 4,160.00
9. Thai Military Bank, 3,840.00
10. First Bangkok City Bank, 3,512.40

*Where'd you hear that?*
GT Guide to World Equity Markets. Based on 1988 market value, in millions of Baht.

## Most actively traded shares on the Securities Exchange of Thailand

1. National Finance & Securities
2. Padaeng Industry
3. Siam Cement
4. Bangkok Bank
5. Saha-Union
6. Chareon Pokphand Feedmill
7. Union Asia Finance
8. Asia Fiber
9. Bank of Ayudhya

# MONEY MATTERS

# MONEY MATTERS

10. Bangkok Produce Merchandising Co. Ltd.

*Where'd you hear that?*
GT Guide to World Equity Markets. Based on 1988 trading volume (unspecified).

### Largest listed companies on the Tokyo Stock Exchange

1. Industrial Bank of Japan, with 10,229 billion yen
2. Sumitomo Bank, 9,989
3. NTT, 9,774
4. Fuji Bank, 9,397
5. Tokyo Electric Power, 9,257
6. Dai-Ichi Kangyo Bank Ltd., 9,090
7. Mitsubishi Bank, 8,924
8. Sanwa Bank, 7,536
9. Toyota, 7,185
10. Nomura Securities, 7,147

*Where'd you hear that?*
GT Guide to World Equity Markets. Based on 1988 market value, in billions of yen.

### Largest foreign equities on the Tokyo Stock Exchange

1. Deutsche Bank, with $2057.3 million
2. IBM, $1717.1
3. Philip Morris, $1289.6
4. General Electric Co., $1128.9
5. E. I. du Pont de Nemours & Co., $1109.0
6. Waste Management, $1048.3
7. Walt Disney Co., $1022.5
8. AT & T, $696.7
9. Bank of America, $616.7
10. Dow Chemical, $572.1

*Where'd you hear that?*
Euromoney, International Equities. Based on 1989 turnover, in millions of U.S. dollars.

### Most actively traded shares on the Tokyo Stock Exchange

1. Nipon Steel, with 13,669 billion yen
2. Kawasaki Steel Corp., 9,707
3. Mitsubishi Heavy Industries, 8,164
4. Nippon Kokan, 7,979
5. Toshiba, 6,386
6. Sumitomo Metal Industries, 5,124
7. Ishikawajima-Harima Heavy Industries, 4,913
8. Hitachi Ltd., 4,391
9. Kobe Steel Ltd., 4,326
10. Mitsubishi Electric Industrial, 3,869

*Where'd you hear that?*
GT Guide to World Equity Markets. Based on 1988 trading value, in billions of yen.

### Most actively traded shares on the Toronto Stock Exchange

1. INCO, with $4,998 million Canadian
2. Alcan Aluminium, $3,178
3. Falconbridge, $2,524
4. Canadian Pacific, $2,312
5. Polysar Energy, $2,284
6. Laidlaw Transportation Class B NV, 1,890
7. Nova Corporation of Alberta A, $1,826
8. Royal Bank of Canada, 1,518
9. BCE, $1,415

10. Noranda, $1,250

*Where'd you hear that?*
GT Guide to World Equity Markets. Based on 1988 trading value, in millions of Canadian dollars.

## Largest companies listed on the Toronto Stock Exchange

1. IBM, with $86,962 million Canadian
2. British Petroleum, $32,295
3. General Motors Corp., $31,969
4. Ford Motor Co., $27,477
5. Mobil, $23,525
6. Amoco Corp., $23,086
7. Dow Chemical, $22,759
8. British Telecom, $17,238
9. American Express, $14,307
10. British Gas PLC, $14,112

*Where'd you hear that?*
GT Guide to World Equity Markets. Based on 1988 market value, in millions of Canadian dollars.

## Most actively traded shares on the Vienna Stock Exchange

1. Leykam-Muerzta, with 1,767 million schillings
2. CA-BV Vorzug, 1,084
3. Constantia Industriehold, 997
4. Strabag Oester, 845
5. Montana, 811
6. Lenzing, 721
7. Radex-Heraklit, 695
8. Laakirchen, 625
9. LB Vorzug, 586
10. Erste Allgemeine (common shares), 478

*Where'd you hear that?*
GT Guide to World Equity Markets. Based on 1988 trading value, in millions of Austrian schillings.

## Largest listed companies on the Vienna Stock Exchange

1. Erste Allgemeine, with 8.845 million
2. OMV, 8,550
3. Osterreichische Landerbank, 7,304
4. Creditanstalt-Bankverein, 6,827
5. Leykam-Murztaler, 4,597
6. Veitscher Magnesitwerke, 4,190
7. Wiener Allianz, 4,032
8. Constantia Industriehold, 3,995
9. Austrian Airlines, 3,906
10. Steirmarkische Elektriziotat, 3,200

*Where'd you hear that?*
GT Guide to World Equity Markets. Based on 1988 market value, in millions of Austrian schillings.

## Largest listed companies on the Zurich Stock Exchange

1. Nestle, with 24,173.7 million francs
2. Schweiz, Bankgesellschaft, 15,329.7
3. Schweiz, Bankverein, 12,150.4
4. Ciba-Geigy Corp., 11,848.0
5. Sondoz, 11,380.7
6. Schweiz, Kreditanstalt, 10,023.2
7. Zurich Versicherungen, 7,294.5
8. Jacobs Suchard, 5,054.4
9. Winterhur Versicherungen, 4,978.4
10. Schweiz, Ruckvers.-Ges., 4,684.7

# MONEY MATTERS

# MONEY MATTERS

*Where'd you hear that?*
GT Guide to World Equity Markets. Based on 1988 market value, in millions of Swiss francs.

## Most actively traded shares on the Zurich Stock Exchange

1. Nestle, with 24,173.7 million francs
2. Schweiz Bankgesellschaft, 15,329.7
3. Schweiz Bankverein, 12,150.4
4. Ciba-Geigy Corp., 11,848.0
5. Sandoz, 11,380.7
6. Schweiz Kreditanstalt, 10,023.2
7. Zurich Versicherungen, 7,294.5
8. Jacobs Suchard, 5,054.4
9. Winterhur Versicherungen, 4,978.4
10. Schweiz Ruckvers.-Ges., 4,684.7

*Where'd you hear that?*
GT Guide to World Equity Markets. Based on 1988 trading value, in millions of Swiss francs.

## Most actively traded over-the-counter stocks

1. MCI Communication, with 4,853,772 hundred
2. Apple Computer Inc., 4,545,602
3. Intel Corp., 3,843,374
4. Sun Microsystems, 2,958,495
5. Seagate Tech, 1,992,470
6. Jaguar PLC, 1,966,783
7. Coral Cos., 1,955,445
8. TeleComm A, 1,849,148
9. Oracle Systems, 1,822,017
10. First Executive, 1,679,654

*Where'd you hear that?*
Wall Street Journal. Based on 1989 sales volume, in hundreds.

## Top over-the-counter stocks

1. MCI Communications, with $9,625.0 million
2. Tele-Communications, $6,024.8
3. Apple Computer Inc., $5,642.7
4. Intel Corp., $5,538.5
5. McCaw Cellular Communications, $5,528.5
6. American Television & Communications Corp., $5,011.8
7. Lin Broadcasting Inc., $4,881.8
8. Food Lion, $3,653.8
9. Microsoft, $3,051.8
10. Nordstrom, $2,751.4

*Where'd you hear that?*
OTC Review, OTC Review 1,000. Based on market value, in millions of dollars.

## Best performing stocks on over-the-counter markets

1. American Travellers, with 318.4%
2. Pacificare Health, 316.3%
3. Oceaneering, 300.1%
4. Adaptec Inc., 283.8%
5. Vivigen Inc., 266.7%
6. Offshore Logistics, 248.1%

*Where'd you hear that?*
Wall Street Journal. Based on 1989 price change, in percent.

## Largest companies listed on North American Securities Dealers Automated Quotations

1. MCI Communications, with $5,465.3 million
2. Apple Computer Inc., $4,951.6

530

3. Intel Corp., $4,282.7
4. Tele-Communications, $3,921.8
5. LIN Broadcasting Inc., $3,664.5
6. Microsoft, $2,869.7
7. Nordstrom, $2,463.2
8. Laidlaw Transportation, $2,056.9
9. St. Paul Cos., $2,016.1
10. Wheelabrator Group, $1,864.9

*Where'd you hear that?*
GT Guide to World Equity Markets. Based on 1988 market value, in millions of dollars.

## Most actively traded shares according to North American Securities Dealers Automated Quotations

1. MCI Communications Corp., with 473.044 thousand
2. Intel Corp., 457,724
3. Apple Computer Inc., 369,807
4. Seagate Technology, 236,043
5. Lotus Development Corp., 194,181
6. Sun Microsystems, 193,855
7. Micron Technology, 185,356
8. Tele-Communications, 179,321
9. Liz Claiborne, Inc., 167,554
10. MiniScribe Corp., 131,533

*Where'd you hear that?*
GT Guide to World Equity Markets. Based on 1988 trading volume, in thousands of shares.

## Best foreign brokerage companies

1. Morgan Stanley
2. Goldman, Sachs & Co.
3. First Boston/Credit Suisse
4. Nikko
5. Nomura

*Where'd you hear that?*
Financial World, Financial World Annual Survey of Money Managers. Based on points in survey of institutions.

## Largest U.S. brokerage firms

1. Merrill Lynch & Co., with $10,048.4 million
2. Shearson Lehman Hutton, $8,966.0
3. Salomon Brothers Holding Co., $5,757.0
4. Goldman, Sachs & Co., $4,018.0
5. Morgan Stanley & Co., $2,648.0
6. Prudential-Bache Securities, $1,840.4
7. First Boston Corp., $1,783.0
8. PaineWebber Group, $1,523.1
9. Bear, Stearns & Co., $1,444.0
10. Dean Witter Reynolds Inc., $1,429.0

*Where'd you hear that?*
Institutional Investor. Based on 1989 consolidated capital, in millions of dollars.

## Most productive brokerage and commodity corporations

1. Morgan Stanley, with $67.9 thousand
2. Salomon, $54.3
3. Bear, Stearns & Co., $23.3
4. Charles Schwab, $7.5
5. PaineWebber Group, $4.0
6. Merrill Lynch, -$5.1

*Where'd you hear that?*
Forbes, Forbes 500s Annual Directory. Based on 1989 profits per employee, in thousands of dollars. Ranks U.S.-based corporations that were publicly traded as of March 23, 1990.

**MONEY MATTERS**

# MONEY MATTERS

### Brokers providing the best service in underwriting high-yield debt

1. Merrill Lynch
2. Drexel Burnham Lambert Inc.
3. Salomon Brothers
4. First Boston
5. Goldman, Sachs & Co.

*Where'd you hear that?*
Financial World, Financial World Annual Survey of Money Managers. Based on points in survey of chief financial officers.

### *World's largest securities brokers*

1. Nomura Securities (Japan), with $12,416 million
2. Salomon (U.S.), $10,330
3. Merrill Lynch (U.S.), $9,768
4. Daiwa Securities (Japan), $8,448
5. Shearson Lehman Hutton (U.S.), $8,157
6. Nikko Securities (Japan), $7,191
7. Yamaichi Securities (Japan), $7,054
8. Dean Witter (U.S.), $5,370
9. Goldman, Sachs & Co. (U.S.), $2,771
10. Morgan Stanley (U.S.), $2,414

*Where'd you hear that?*
Wall Street Journal, Annual Global Ranking. Based on fiscal year 1988 capital, in millions of dollars.

### Brokers providing the best service in underwriting investment-grade debt

1. Salomon Brothers
2. Goldman, Sachs & Co.
3. Merrill, lynch
4. First Boston
5. Morgan Stanley

*Where'd you hear that?*
Financial World, Financial World Annual Survey of Money Managers. Based on points in survey of chief financial officers.

### Brokers providing the best service in equity underwriting

1. Merrill Lynch
2. Goldman, Sachs & Co.
3. Morgan Stanley
4. Salomon Brothers
5. First Boston

*Where'd you hear that?*
Financial World, Financial World Annual Survey of Money Managers. Based on points in survey of chief financial officers.

### Brokerage firms with most employees

1. Merrill Lynch & Co., with 41,000
2. Shearson Lehman Hutton, 38,000
3. Prudential-Bache Securities, 19,000
4. Dean Witter Reynolds Inc., 17,470
5. PaineWebber Group, 12,943
6. Smith Barney, Harris Upham & Co., 7,553
7. A. G. Edwards & Sons Inc., 7,258
8. Morgan Stanley & Co., 6,747
9. Salomon Brothers Holding Co., 6,612
10. Goldman, Sachs & Co., 6,400

*Where'd you hear that?*
Institutional Investor. Based on number of employees in 1989.

# MONEY MATTERS

## Brokers providing the best service in mergers and acquisitions

1. Goldman, Sachs & Co.
2. First Boston
3. Merrill Lynch
4. Morgan Stanley
5. Shearson Lehman Hutton
6. Morgan Stanley

*Where'd you hear that?*
Financial World, Financial World Annual Survey of Money Managers. Based on points in survey of chief financial officers.

## Ten largest employee stock ownership plans

1. Health Trust, with $1.8 billion
2. Avis, $1.75 billion
3. Procter & Gamble, $1 billion
3. Bell Atlantic Corp., $1 billion
5. Epic Healthcare Group, $866 million
6. J. C. Penney Co. Inc., $700 million
6. Ameritech, $700 million
6. ITT Corp., $700 million
9. Parsons, $560 million
10. Minnesota Mining & Manufacturing, $550 million

*Where'd you hear that?*
Modern Healthcare. Based on total value.

## Largest privatizing deals, 1979-89

1. RJR Nabisco Inc., for $24,561.6 million
2. Beatrice Cos. Inc., $5,361.6
3. Safeway Stores Inc., $4,198.4

4. Borg-Warner Corp., $3,798.6
5. Southland Corp., $3,723.3
6. Owens-Illinois Inc., $3,631.9
7. Hospital Corp. of America, $3,602.1
8. Fort Howard Paper Co., $3,574.2
9. NWA Inc., $3,524.5
10. R. H. Macy & Co. Inc., $3,484.7

*Where'd you hear that?*
Mergerstat Review. Based on purchase price, in millions of dollars.

## Most successful annual dividend achievers

1. Sherwin-Williams Co., with 43.6%
2. Golden Enterprises, Inc., 31.7%
2. Progressive Corp. (Ohio), 31.7%
4. Ennis Business Forms, Inc., 27.8%
5. Service Corp. International, 27.4%
6. Syntex Corp., 27.0%
7. Waste Management Inc., 26.9%
8. ServiceMaster L.P., 23.7%
8. Shared Medical Systems Corp., 23.7%
10. John H. Harland Co., 23.4%

*Where'd you hear that?*
Moody's Handbook of Common Stocks. Based on dividend growth-rate percentage over a period of at least 10 years.

## Largest privatizing deals ever

1. Kohlberg Kravis Roberts & Co. (buyer), RJR Nabisco (seller), for $24,561.6 million
2. Kohlberg Kravis Roberts & Co. (buyer), Beatrice Cos Inc. (seller), $5,361.6

# MONEY MATTERS

3. SSI Holdings Corp. (buyer), Safeway Stores Inc. (seller), $4,198.4
4. Private group led by Merrill Lynch Capital Partners (buyer), Borg-Warner Corp. (seller), $3,798.6
5. Private group led by John & Jere Thompson (buyer), Southland Corp. (seller), $3,723.3

*Where'd you hear that?*
Mergerstat Review. Based on purchase price, in millions of dollars.

## Wealthiest international billionaires

1. Sultan Hassanal Bolkiah (Bandar Seri, Begawan Brunei), with $25.0 billion
2. King Fahd Bin Abdul Aziz Al Saud (Riyadh, Saudi Arabia), $18.0
3. Forrest E. Mars, Sr. (Las Vegas, NV); Forrest E. Mars, Jr. (McLean, VA); John F. Mars (Arlington, VA); Jacqueline Mars Vogel (Bedminister, NJ), $12.5
4. Queen Elizabeth II (London, England), $10.9
5. Samuel I. Newhouse, Jr. (New York, NY), Donald E. Newhouse (New York, NY), $10.0
6. Tsai Wan-Lin (Taipei, Taiwan), $9.0
7. Sam Moore Walton (Bentonville, AR), $8.9
8. Albert Reichmann, Paul Reichmann, Ralph Reichmann (Toronto, ON), $8.4
9. Gerald Grosvenor (London, England), $6.9
9. Kenneth Roy Thomson (Toronto, ON), $6.9

*Where'd you hear that?*
Fortune. Based on assets, in billions of U.S. dollars.

## Top foreign billionaires

Taikichiro Mori, Japan, over $10 billion
Yoshiaki Tsutsumi, Japan, over $10 billion
Brenninkmeyer family, Holland, over $5 billion
Eitaro Itoyama, Japan, over $5 billion
Hans and Gad Rausing, Sweden, over $5 billion
Paul, Albert and Ralph Reichmann, Canada, over $5 billion
Shin Kyuk-ho, Korea, over $5 billion
Hirotomo Takei, Japan, over $5 billion
Kenneth Roy Thomson, Canada, over $5 billion
Haruhiko Yoshimoto with family, Japan, over $5 billion

*Where'd you hear that?*
Forbes, World's Billionaires. Above persons are listed, not ranked, by categories of estimated net worth.

## MONEY MATTERS

**Richest people in America**

1. John Werner Kluge
2. Warren Edward Buffett
3. Sumner Murray Redstone
4. Ted Arison
5. Ronald Owen Perelman
6. Samuel Irving Newhouse, Jr., Donald Edward Newhouse
7. Barbara Cox Anthony, Anne Cox Chambers
8. Henry Ross Perot
9. Jay Arthur Pritzker, Robert Alan Pritzker
10. A. Alfred Taubman

*Where'd you hear that?*
Forbes, The 400 Richest People in America. Based on personal wealth.